Rethinking Cyber Warfare

Rethinking Cyber Warfare

The International Relations of Digital Disruption

R. DAVID EDELMAN

OXFORD
UNIVERSITY PRESS

Oxford University Press is a department of the University of Oxford.
It furthers the University's objective of excellence in research, scholarship,
and education by publishing worldwide. Oxford is a registered trade mark of
Oxford University Press in the UK and in certain other countries.

Published in the United States of America by Oxford University Press
198 Madison Avenue, New York, NY 10016, United States of America.

© R. David Edelman 2024

All rights reserved. No part of this publication may be reproduced, stored in a retrieval system,
or transmitted, in any form or by any means, without the prior permission in writing of Oxford
University Press, or as expressly permitted by law, by license or under terms agreed with the
appropriate reprographics rights organization. Inquiries concerning reproduction outside the
scope of the above should be sent to the Rights Department, Oxford University Press, at the
address above. You must not circulate this work in any other form and you must impose this same
condition on any acquirer

Library of Congress Cataloging-in-Publication Data
Names: Edelman, R. David author.
Title: Rethinking cyber warfare : the international relations of digital
disruption / Dr. R. David Edelman.
Description: New York : Oxford University Press, 2024. |
Includes bibliographical references and index. |
Identifiers: LCCN 2023050061 | ISBN 9780197509685 (hardback) |
ISBN 9780197509708 (epub) | ISBN 9780197509692 (updf) | ISBN 9780197509715 (online)
Subjects: LCSH: Cyberspace operations (International law) | Information
warfare (International law) | Aggression (International law) |
Self-defense (International law) | Humanitarian law.
Classification: LCC KZ6718 .E34 2024 | DDC 341.6/3—dc23/eng/20231025
LC record available at https://lccn.loc.gov/2023050061

DOI: 10.1093/9780197509715.001.0001

Printed by Integrated Books International, United States of America

Note to Readers
This publication is designed to provide accurate and authoritative information in regard to the
subject matter covered. It is based upon sources believed to be accurate and reliable and is intended
to be current as of the time it was written. It is sold with the understanding that the publisher is not
engaged in rendering legal, accounting, or other professional services. If legal advice or other expert
assistance is required, the services of a competent professional person should be sought. Also, to
confirm that the information has not been affected or changed by recent developments, traditional
legal research techniques should be used, including checking primary sources where appropriate.

*(Based on the Declaration of Principles jointly adopted by a Committee of the
American Bar Association and a Committee of Publishers and Associations.)*

You may order this or any other Oxford University Press publication
by visiting the Oxford University Press website at www.oup.com.

Contents

Preface vii
Acknowledgments ix

Introduction 1

PART I CYBERATTACKS AND RESTRAINT

1. Defining and Studying Cyberattacks 11
   1.1 Estonia Was a Rehearsal 11
   1.2 Topic and Scope 14
   1.3 Defining Cyberattacks 19
   1.4 Assumptions and Present Realities 40

2. Defining and Studying Restraint 53
   2.1 Framing the Analysis 54
   2.2 Concepts and Methodologies 55
   2.3 Evolution of the Literature 66
   2.4 Critiquing Restraint 78
   2.5 Overview of Book 84

PART II DETERRENCE

3. Evaluating Deterrence 87
   3.1 Defining Rationalist Deterrence 90
   3.2 Cyberattack Capabilities as a Deterrent 102
   3.3 Alternative Deterrence Frames 121
   3.4 Moving Beyond Cyber-Deterrence 125

4. Constructing Deterrence 127
   4.1 Defining Structural Deterrence 128
   4.2 Evidence of Structural Deterrence 133
   4.3 Whose Deterrence Succeeds? 150
   Conclusions 152

PART III INTERNATIONAL LAW
AND THE USE OF FORCE

5. Limiting the Use of Force 157
   5.1 Locating Relevant Law 159
   5.2 Cyberattacks as an Article 2(4) Use of Force 167
   5.3 Cyberattacks as Violations of Integrity, Independence,
       or Purposes 182
   Conclusions 197

6. Constructing Self-Defense 200
   6.1 Applying the Remedial *Jus ad Bellum* 202
   6.2 Cyberattacks and the Remedial *Jus Ad Bellum* 209
   6.3 Structural Remediation 227
   Conclusions 236

PART IV HUMANITARIAN PROTECTIONS

7. Humanitarian Protections 239
   7.1 Approaching Humanitarian Protections 242
   7.2 Indiscriminateness 253
   7.3 Injury to Protected Classes 266
   7.4 Disproportionality 281
   Conclusions 286

8. Constructing a Prohibition 289
   8.1 Moving Beyond Cyber Arms Control 291
   8.2 Structural Prohibition 294
   8.3 Understanding Prohibitive Norms 301
   8.4 Cyberattack Norm Construction 306
   8.5 Cyberattack Norm Evolution 322
   Conclusions 333

Conclusion 335

Bibliography 343
Index 387

Preface

When I began work on this topic in the early 2000s, the idea of a state-on-state cyberattack was hypothetical and a physical conflict precipitated by one was far-fetched. "There's nothing new under the sun in warfare," one eminent military historian warned me a few years later, "so take your talents and apply them to something more practical." As my graduate students often remind me, it is sometimes best to ignore one's elders—or at least seek out competing counsel. I was lucky that another professor, who would later become a mentor and dear friend, was equally curious about my off-the-wall question: "What if one country shut down another's internet?"

Then times changed around this topic, and continue to, seemingly daily. As I wrapped up my first analysis of what we now call cyberattacks, the world witnessed (and during, largely sat idly by as) Kremlin-directed hackers knocked digitally dependent Estonia offline. As my second study was heading to the printer several years later, news emerged alleging a US and Israeli attack on Iran's illicit nuclear apparatus—entirely absent, of course, from its pages. One can only imagine what new developments will take place in the months between now and the ink drying on this bound edition (though artificial intelligence's sudden explosion into public use is an appropriately "disruptive" start).

So one must begin every work on this topic with a preemptive apology for omitting some new development and begging indulgence for any evolution in thinking that might result. That disclaimer aside, though, perhaps most remarkable to me is how certain arguments about state behavior in cyberspace have remained not just true, but now demonstrable. With over fifteen years of practice and an explosion of literature to draw from, the time is right to revisit these ideas.

I witnessed the elaboration of the record of cyber conflict first as a researcher, then for many years as a practitioner in the US government, only to return now to the role of commentator. Given that interregnum, complete objectivity is probably impossible. Though official sources and information used herein are exclusively public and unclassified, the views expressed are strictly my own, and some frames of reference are at least in part informed by my time in government. Even those policies on which I was fortunate to work, none were mine alone—they embodied the diverse perspectives and insights of first a few dozen, and later hundreds of dedicated policy officials who were trying to make sense of and navigate this novel phenomenon in international relations. Enriched by that collective expertise, it is my hope that this work provides the academy with a fresh outlook on those questions, offering new ways to engage the evidence, evaluate its comparative importance for state practice, and think about the interface between commentary and on the conduct of international relations.

The pages that follow are international relations scholarship, but their insights may extend beyond academia. At a minimum, they will hopefully make sense of the more puzzling aspects of states' approach to cyberattacks. They may also, for some states, call into question the durability of now deeply ingrained policies. Enough time has passed to provide a fresh assessment of that era, since even in areas of high technology, there is no guide like the past. Perhaps that eminent military historian was onto something after all.

Acknowledgments

I am humbled to benefit from so many exceptional minds who shared their time and insights to bring this work to life.

Within academia Rosemary Foot, Yuen Foong Khong, and Robert Johnson all provided guidance at key moments to connect disparate parts to the whole and situate this study within the field. A special debt of gratitude is owed to Sarah Percy, whose initial and unequivocal encouragement to pursue the topic set me not only on the studies that preceded this one, but the courage to draw together thoughts before, during, and after government service into a greater whole. Ngaire Woods's guidance in helping to steer this project in its early stages was invaluable as it was generous.

Dapo Akande and Jennifer Welch provided crucial feedback as this project began to delve deeper into international law and normative theory, and their insights on the book's structure, as well as how to think about evolutions in the law of war, were guiding lights throughout. Jonathan Zittrain and Neil MacFarlane offered insights from their own learned frames of reference, ensuring that the project remained not only true to the discipline of international relations, but also relevant to those thinking about domestic governance of technology.

While not a work of public policy, my time as a practitioner enriched it immeasurably. All I have learned during that time was due to selfless and supportive mentors—Tony Blinken, Jim Steinberg, John Merrill, Randy Fort, John Dinger, Judith Strotz, Michele Markoff, Howard Schmidt, John Brennan, Jason Furman, Gene Sperling, Jeff Zients, Denis McDonough, John Podesta, Todd Park, Megan Smith, and Bill Webster—and the scores more patient colleagues in and outside government. To those I have forgotten to name: you know who you are, and yes, I owe you a drink.

The MIT Internet Policy Research Initiative, under the leadership of its founding director Danny Weitzner, was an exceptionally welcoming intellectual home that allowed me to incubate this project after government. I am indebted to Danny, Hal Abelson, David Clark, Taylor Reynolds, and the whole IPRI team for their support. I have also been fortunate to have some amazing students; through their insights in 6.805 and graduate advising, they helped keep this work both grounded and up to date.

At the MIT Center for International Studies, Dick Samuels, Barry Posen, and Taylor Fravel were kind to include me in their exceptional community of scholars and former practitioners, without which this project would have also never progressed. Indeed, when this project entered the dreaded first-draft form, Ken Oye provided deeply thoughtful and detailed commentary drawing on his own rich history at the intersection of novel technology and national security, for which I am deeply grateful. Elsewhere in Boston, Cameron Kerry at the Media Lab helped me contend with matters of data policy just as he had for all the years prior in government, and Susan Landau's inclusion in Tufts workshops helped refine this work considerably. Ben Buchanan and Tim Maurer also took time out of their own important book projects to help inform this one, a profound gesture not soon forgotten.

In pivoting to publication, Alex Flach at Oxford University Press deserves appreciation for first encouragement, kudos for exceptional guidance in revision, and a gold medal for patience. In the final stages of writing and the depths of a global pandemic, the work of three exceptional research assistants—Zhanna Malekos Smith, Elisabeth Siegel, and Jennie Kim—improved the work immensely with their dedication. And as we began to see light at the end of the tunnel, Christopher Fonzone showed exceptional generosity with his trenchant insights on applied international law, as did Avril Haines before being called back to government service as well.

In the finest tradition of the book's subject, I have no choice but to blame most errors and omissions on hostile cyber actors' interception of this manuscript and intentional introduction thereof.

The rest are, I regret, mine and mine alone.

Introduction

Questions in the Corridors

"Will they know it was us?"
"Is the precedent clear?"
"What will this mean for our allies?"
"Do they have a right to defend themselves?"
"Does it open us up to retribution?"
"Have we mapped out all the effects?"
"Is the law on our side here?"

From London's Whitehall to Beijing's People's Liberation Army HQ, and from Paris's Hotel de Brienne to "The Tank" buried deep inside Washington's Pentagon, these questions are familiar to military planners and the political leaders that command them. Over the course of six years at the White House, I heard them time and again. In most national security contexts, they would be pro forma: an unremarkable checklist for the diligent planner or policy hand to ensure nothing unusual would transpire. In the sort of meetings that I was part of, though, they were all genuine questions, each more urgent than the last. And on some matters of international cybersecurity, the were as open questions in my last meeting in the Situation Room as in my very first.

Criticizing the pace of policy development is usually hackneyed and wrong-headed, and often the product of a competing agenda for a preferred rebalancing of priorities. It is hard to know whether cyber matters are any exception. By the end of 2016, we were a decade into an era in which cyberattacks—as a distinct phenomenon from spying, stealing, or propagandizing—were widely known and openly discussed instruments of interstate coercion. But it would also be fair to argue that more had changed and then stayed the same over those interceding years—from the comparative dependence on technology, to the changing capabilities of states, to the frequency of targets, and even fundamental questions about attribution and nonstate involvement in attacks.

If in 2007 states even knew they were engaged in a new game of international security, whatever rules they might have written then almost certainly needed changing by now. But these are not unspoken phenomena, neither in the policy literature nor in our various corners of the Academy. My first bibliography of scholarly work on international cyberattacks could fit on a single page; indeed, the number of theses written on the topic was at or near zero. This volume alone cites roughly 1,200 primary documents and secondary studies of interest. In an important respect, then, neither the United States' nor other countries' activities—policymaking and policy planning, defense planning and military operations, diplomacy and multilateral deal-making—were happening in the dark either.

And yet such questions persisted. It is their persistence that motivates this work. How could it be, with all of the cumulative insights of the past decade and a half, that so much of state policy appears to be furtive, unpredictable, and disconnected from the lessons of the past? What is missing about the way we as scholars are thinking about the international relations of cybersecurity?

Nowhere is this more salient than when it comes to one of the cyber world's most significant instruments: cyberattacks. Untold hours and millions of flight miles have been logged in the pursuit of cyber diplomacy. Billions of dollars have been spent to establish military cyber units and billions more poured into defense against them. Presidents and prime ministers have been drawn and coaxed into national projects building and resisting dozens of norms of behavior. Are we any closer, today, to the confidence that these tools will not be used to bring ways of life to a halt, infrastructures to meltdown, or militaries to an early surrender?

If not, perhaps states—and the academy—need to be rethinking cyber warfare.

The Restraint Imperative

As a former practitioner, I cannot shake the feeling of whiplash. The contrast between hesitation and exuberance on the part of certain strategically significant powers suggests that the most common and intertwined sources of restraint in the international system—deterrence, international law, and humanitarian concerns—are at a minimum unevenly restraining, and they are perhaps even failing to operate in cyberspace altogether.

As a scholar, the potential failure of these systems suggests there is something significant playing out in international relations, perhaps with profound lessons for how we think about coercion and cooperation in the midst of new technologies.

As a citizen, though, I am perhaps most concerned about the growing and potentially unchecked risk to civilian populations—of escalation, of economic harm, and of social upheaval—should broad-based cyberattacks become generally acceptable instruments of coercion.

From all these perspectives, this topic of restraint from cyberattacks demands dedicated attention. Looking comprehensively at *restraint*—specifically, its sources and effects on decision-making—is a crucial way to understand state behavior in this first decade and a half of cyberattacks' availability, and perhaps even more importantly, how cyberattacks' use might be shaped in the decades to come.

Underlying many important questions in international cybersecurity is a rarely spoken of and far more fundamental issue, one that perhaps only researchers can approach: states may well deem it in their interest to know how to prevent cyberattacks; yet today, many simply lack much understanding of how. Why is this question approached in policy circles only in hushed tones? For one, to admit interest in restraint could show weakness to a domestic constituency, to be accused of foreclosing as yet unrealized strategic advantage in the indeterminate long term. Easier, instead, for states to dismiss restraint behind their inability to predict adversaries' intentions. Or perhaps achieving durable restraint is unthinkable within the political lifespans of those making nearer-term, operational decisions. Thus, the notion of truly restraining adversaries' cyberattack designs would best be left to another generation of practitioners, once a more thorough record of action and inaction has been established. This sense of resignation or even fatalism, when faced with destructive capability with complex technological origins, may be familiar to scholars of arms control and disarmament, who need no reminder that three dozen instances of first use were not required to understand the dynamics of nuclear restraint.

With that context in mind, that question of restraint becomes not just imperative, but also answerable.

The wisdom of one particular country's strategy is a question for policymakers and think-tank commentators—and not the focus of this volume. Whether effective strategies can even exist, and what they tell us about how conflicts will play out on the international stage, are questions suitable for scholarly analysis.

Motivating Observations

This book concerns state-on-state cyberattacks disabling broad swathes of information infrastructure—not the only kind of digital disruption, and indeed not the only activity others have given that label—but one of early and enduring concern to national governments. It begins with three foundational observations that motivate its methodology and conceptual underpinnings: (1) that state cyberattack capabilities are significant, and that maintaining peace and security will require restraint on their use; (2) that the forces that have traditionally restrained states in possession of novel weaponry demand rigorous examination of how they shape state decision-making on cyberattacks; and (3) that the present moment is an opportune inflection point to engage these questions due to both maturation of the relevant technology and literature.

Despite an impressive volume of scholarship, the study of these kinds of cyberattacks in international relations runs the risk of getting "stuck." The preliminary observations of state practice, confirmed by my own experience in the field, suggests two related causes. The first is that disciplines have, as disciplines do, largely pursued questions of cyberattacks from their own methodological silos. Fields of international law, strategic studies, and normative theory may each land glancing blows against the other's frames, but rare is the study in the field that seeks to genuinely engage them all. State decision-making can and should be engaging all three overlapping sets of considerations, but leaving them in silos leaves perhaps too much to their selective synthesis and could produce outcomes learning the lessons of none. The reason this is problematic is the second concern: even some of the most impressive projects in the space are penned with little reference to whether and how states will operationalize their conclusions. This is different from saying the scholarship is "inadequately policy-oriented" or "not readily actionable"; it need not be. Rather, it is a question about the overall purpose of and value to which these considerable insights are put. On this matter, studies are not normatively unmoored so much as normatively absent, leaving to the practitioners the "balancing of equities." This combination runs the risk of driving international cybersecurity studies into a sort of analytical purgatory reminiscent of nuclear security studies in the early 1950s: marked by impressive and increasingly authoritative commentary on the abstract concepts of deterrence and law, but with an inadequate record against which to test these propositions or conduct intricate process-tracing of state decisions. That period emerged without a nuclear catastrophe, but just barely.[1]

So, are we resigned to simply accept the status quo for another decade or two? This study argues no: that even in the absence of a longer record of outright attacks, there is much we can learn by looking deeply at contemporary history. Many scholars have been studying the question of cyberattack use literally—can cyberattacks deter or be deterred; are they presumptively illegal uses of force; do they cross humanitarian boundaries—while states have by and large regarded those questions as unanswerable and begun to compete at a higher level of abstraction.[2] It is here that an underdocumented but central form of proto-competition is playing out among states. This is a process to construct the contexts in which their cyber doctrine and ultimately, operations, are considered. Within this process we can actually observe not just what *ought* to occur based on our understanding of the international system's history, but what is most likely to actually hold back cyberattacks in practice.

Overview and Structure of Argument

This argument informs the structure of the study. Each part covers a source of restraint: classical deterrence, the law governing recourse to force, and international humanitarian concerns.[3] Within each part are two chapters. The first argues how the nature of cyberattacks frustrate either the operation

---

[1] See, for example Graham Allison and Philip Zelikow, *Essence of Decision: Explaining the Cuban Missile Crisis*, 2nd ed. (New York: Pearson, 1999 [originally published 1971]); Tony Long, "Sept. 26, 1983: The Man Who Saved the World by Doing . . . Nothing," *Wired*, September 26, 2007; Robert F. Kennedy and Arthur Meier Schlesinger, *Thirteen Days: A Memoir of the Cuban Missile Crisis* (New York: Norton, 1999). As Nye reminds in *Nuclear Ethics*, while we "have more than two decades' additional experience of deterrence without war . . . the moral dilemmas persist"—and, in the case of cyberattacks, so too do the practical ones. Joseph S. Nye, *Nuclear Ethics* (New York: Simon & Schuster, 1988), 3.

[2] This is not to say that state doctrine lacks views on these questions entirely (many do); rather, as a practical matter, their actions or inactions reveal their "answers" to be "nonanswers"—pinning so much on context-specificity as to render them functionally useless for planning and signaling.

[3] These logics are presented not to suggest any operates in a vacuum from another, but to engage with the largely distinct literatures emerging about them. Chapter 2 will explain further how such logics were selected, for those unfamiliar with this common frame within international security studies.

of that logic or the regime designed to enforce it, engaging with the extensive recent literature thereupon. The second pushes that analysis further, documenting and exploring the implications of the *structural competition* in which states are significantly engaged to determine whether and how that logic operates on cyberattacks.

Part II explains how deterrence would function in the case of cyberattacks but does not, due to certain underlying characteristics of the technology and significant ambiguities in understanding adversary behavior. Recognizing that uncomfortable state of affairs, it argues that states are instead engaged in a process of *structural deterrence* centered around defining which noncyber forces might be reasonably levied as a means to develop the otherwise lacking strategic vocabulary of mutual deterrence.

Part III applies similar analysis to the law governing the use of force, validating and concurring with the thesis that cyberattacks are presumptively illegal, but questioning the explanatory power of that conclusion, absent enforcement mechanisms. Arguing that cyberattacks frustrate the remedial *jus ad bellum* in practice, it uses the behavior of non-Western states such as North Korea, Russia, and China to demonstrate that a competitive dynamic called *structural remediation* is presently underway and challenging the utility of the present *jus ad bellum* in meaningfully restraining cyberattacks.

Part IV posits that absent the foregoing, humanitarian concerns may well be the most promising vector for restraining cyberattacks. After demonstrating that cyberattacks may indeed be particularly "unusable" under the law of armed conflict (the *jus in bello*), it questions whether such concerns might be reframed not as matters of legal compliance, but rather as a normative taboo. Reconceptualizing this humanitarian imperative within the active competition over *structural prohibition*—to define the institutions and terms of debate over banning their use—it finds surprising commensurability in key state motivations, signaling the potential for alignment and eventually, a durable, prohibitive norm even without breaking the political logjam over "cyber arms control."

Value and Significance

Understanding restraint in the use of cyberattacks serves three crucial purposes: an explanatory tool of the seemingly puzzling contradictions of state doctrine to date, a predictive tool to help project future dynamics in international security, and a guide for future scholarly and policy efforts to identify avenues of particular impact.

Roughly fifteen years into the era of interstate coercion in cyberspace, this study offers an opportunity for critical assessment and synthesis, both states' initial forays into this space and scholars' assessments of them. Given the novelty of the space, a number of presumptions motivated the way states architected their public cyber doctrine. In a few cases, significant assumptions were incorrect. Others proved more durable. This proved similarly true for initial literature seeking to predict the then largely hypothetical manner of state conduct in the space. Thus, the moment is opportune to draw together and enrich abstract observations with even the short volume of case studies now available. The result is an opportunity for informed critical analysis that aims to make more sense of state conduct in this space, explaining some apparent contradictions, and dispelling some stubborn myths.

While prediction is rarely more dangerous than in areas of technology—except perhaps in international affairs—this volume intends to offer a clearer lens through which to understand the likely (if not always rational) direction of certain state behavior in the years to come. This work is decidedly not an attempt at a predictive model. It seeks to understand the prospects for restraint of cyberattacks over a longer time frame than any one conflict and wider than any competing dyad. It argues that understanding both the theoretical dynamics of how cyberattacks fall within certain state logics of restraint, enriched by the key case studies and clearer views of interstate dynamics, sheds light on one possible (and indeed significant) direction states may head in contemplating their doctrine going forward. Its conclusions, perhaps surprising to some both in the scholarly and policy communities, suggest a new approach to realizing restraint that may not have been seriously considered. Whether some states abandon their current choices in lieu of the approach outlined here, however, is beyond this volume's capacity to predict.

Suggesting a new and potentially open pathway to realize an attractive state goal is not without perils to the underlying analysis. Potential policy impact in its conclusions may in some ways distinguish the study, but as its purpose is not to direct policy, it takes two measures to avoid that potential misreading.

First, it aims to be explicit about its ethical orientation and normative priors. This is a book about how cyber-restraint might be possible, but as such, it necessarily acknowledges the *need* for restraint. As the next chapter will explain in greater depth, its approach begins by recognizing a very real—if contestable—ethical and political value in the cessation of a particular state practice (broad-based cyberattacks on public–private critical information infrastructure). In short, this study begins with the assumption that cyberattacks create various forms of harm that the international community at a minimum would do well to understand *how* to prevent, should states or peoples be convinced by the wisdom of prevention.

Second, it aims to avoid policy prescription. Readers who wish to take my word for it on the prospects for deterrence and the operation of international law can advance to Chapter 8 and read what this study concludes to be the next fertile ground for international relations of cybersecurity. However, readers who aim to engage with the full argumentation will find Parts II (Deterrence), Part III (Recourse to Force), and Part IV (Humanitarian Protections) devoid of explicit policy recommendations that might sap objectivity of the scholarly analysis.

This volume is not a template for "cyber arms control." It aims, instead, to be a more nuanced guide to which forces might motivate what it regards as much-needed restraint and which have less promise. As the next part will show, the answer is of profound and increasing interest to states, their governments, and their militaries; to economies and the companies within them; and to communities—not just the 5.3 billion people using the internet daily, but the 8 billion and counting who rely on basic but increasingly internet-connected infrastructure, from electricity, to dams, to drinking water.[4]

---

[4] International Telecommunications Union, "Two-Thirds of the World's Population Uses the Internet, But 2.7 Billion People Remain Offline" (Geneva: United Nations, 2022).

PART I
CYBERATTACKS AND RESTRAINT

1
Defining and Studying Cyberattacks

1.1 Estonia Was a Rehearsal

A new era in international security began, unnoticed to much of the world, in the small Baltic republic of Estonia.

It is difficult to overstate the Estonian dependence on digital technology for governance and business. In the mid-2000s Estonians were already voting digitally, carrying a digital identity card, filing taxes via the internet, and consuming the majority of their news online.[1] Digital transformation also swept across the Estonian economy, which had by necessity rebooted in the post–Soviet era to be squarely postindustrial.[2] What Bangalore was to outsourced call centers, Tallinn—Estonia's capital—was to outsourced code.

But on April 27, 2007, Estonian government officials and private citizens alike awoke to discover that their country—the most wired in Europe—was suffering from a massive computer network outage.[3] The minister of defence was unable to access web pages or check his military email. On the streets, ATM terminals stopped functioning and bank transactions would not clear. Online, access to domestic and foreign media outlets was blocked, and information from Europe's leader in "e-Government" was unavailable.

The computer-based attacks that caused this mass disruption commenced only a few days after the relocation of a Soviet-era memorial from a central square in Estonia's capital of Tallinn, a move that occasioned great protest by Russian nationalists and Kremlin officials.[4] Machines used in the attack were traced to Russian internet addresses, and claims that the attack was of Russian origin and had government coordination appeared throughout online chat

---

[1] PBS NewsHour, "How Estonia Built a Digital First Government," April 29, 2018.
[2] Nathan Heller, "Estonia, The Digital Republic," *The New Yorker*, December 11, 2017: "Its government presents this digitization as a cost-saving efficiency and an equalizing force. Digitizing processes reportedly saves the state two percent of its G.D.P. a year in salaries and expenses."
[3] Joshua Davis, "Hackers Take Down the Most Wired Country in Europe," *Wired*, August 21, 2007.
[4] BBC News, "Estonia Hit by 'Moscow Cyber War,'" May 17, 2007. Gadi Evron, "Battling Botnets and Online Mobs: Estonia's Defense Efforts During the Internet Wars," *Georgetown Journal of International Affairs* 9, no. 1 (2008).

rooms and message boards.[5] The volume of the attack suggested that a state played a role, as did the common knowledge among internet experts that law enforcement within Russia was notoriously (and perhaps intentionally) lax at prosecuting the online criminals capable of facilitating such an attack.[6]

The intentional disruption of Estonia's networks was unprecedented in its coordination and effectiveness, but far more troubling for policymakers and defense officials were its implications.[7] With so much circumstantial evidence pointing to Russian responsibility, Estonian officials began asking the difficult question: Were the events of April 27 tantamount to an armed attack by Russia? If so, how should the government respond? Would the international community even recognize the attack as a prohibited use of force, and could Estonia legitimately consider a reprisal, armed or otherwise? Even more complicated was the question of whether or not its main military alliance, the North Atlantic Treaty Organization (better known as NATO) had an obligation to interpret the episode as an "attack against them all," thus activating member states' treaty obligations to respond militarily.[8] Ene Ergma, then-Speaker of the Estonian Parliament and a nuclear physics expert, argued after her country came under a small-scale cyberattack, "when I look at a nuclear explosion and the explosion that happened in our country, I see the same thing . . . like nuclear radiation, cyberwar doesn't make you bleed, but it can destroy everything."[9] Estonian officials like Ergma brought the issue to NATO's attention, securing a special "break-out" session on the agenda of the 2008 NATO summit in Bucharest.[10] When that review was inconclusive, the Alliance went about setting up a research center—a sort of doctrinal consolation prize to the invocation of the mutual defense pact—in central Tallinn.[11]

---

[5] Iain Thompson, "Russia 'Hired Botnets' for Estonia Cyber-War: Russian Authorities Accused of Collusion with Botnet Owners," Computing.co.uk, May 31, 2007.

[6] Trevor McDougal, "Establishing Russia's Responsibility for Cyber-Crime Based on Its Hacker Culture," *International Law and Management Review* 11 (2015): 58, 178; Tim Maurer, "Why the Russian Government Turns a Blind Eye to Cybercriminals," *Slate*, Februrary 2, 2018.

[7] Eneken Tikk and Kadri Kaska, "Legal Cooperation to Investigate Cyber Incidents: Estonian Case Study and Lessons," in *Proceedings of the 9th European Conference on Information Warfare and Security, Thessaloniki, Greece, 1-2 July 2010*, (Reading, UK: Academic Publishing Limited, 2010).

[8] North Atlantic Treaty, April 4, 1949, 63 Stat. 2241, 34 U.N.T.S. 243, Art. 5.

[9] Davis, "Hackers Take Down the Most Wired Country in Europe."

[10] *Sydney Morning Herald*, "Estonia Urges Firm EU, NATO Response to New Form of Warfare: Cyber Attacks," May 16, 2007.

[11] The NATO Cooperative Cyber Defence Centre for Excellence (CCDCOE), established in 2008, bills itself as a "multinational and interdisciplinary hub of cyber defence expertise," publishing several important manuals on international law and cybersecurity.

The challenge for both Estonia and NATO in defining the event began with the sheer incommensurability of a flooded computer network and traditional notions of state-based military action. The effects lasted only days, but that was hardly known to the victim government in planning its initial response. It held a large percentage of the Estonian economy, government, and aspects of its military hostage. There appeared no ready way to identify with any certainty the individual(s) manipulating the thousands of machines used. Moreover, this was no traditional "smash-and-grab" operation aimed at stealing sensitive state information (thus relegating it to the sphere of espionage); instead it targeted computer network infrastructure shared by both the civilian and military sectors. Response in kind was impossible for a number of reasons, yet a military response would be unprecedented. Ultimately, the matter ended in a state of uneasy inaction and hushed debate over the inapplicability of defense plans to this new threat.

NATO's lack of a clear response revealed uncertainty about how to assess what Estonia had just sustained, as well as serious concerns about the legality of mounting a response. This trepidation was not entirely new. Some NATO members had already attempted to grapple with these same international legal issues during the 1999 action in Kosovo. After that intervention, unnamed senior defense officials in the US government were quoted admitting that plans to use computer-based attacks against Serbian technology infrastructure existed, but were scuttled after Defense Department lawyers suggested that such tactics might be considered "war crimes."[12] Similar concerns held back cyberattacks that the United States reportedly contemplated against Saddam Hussein's interests during the Second Gulf War as well.[13] What was abandoned then as legally tenuous was brought to the fore in Estonia, with apparently few guiding precedents developed in the intervening years. Such questions persisted as Estonian networks went offline in 2007—in a country whose level of digitalization was perhaps a decade ahead of most. Now, over a fifteen years on, Estonia appears a harbinger of essential—and despite their growing significance, still unsettled—matters of international security.

---

[12] Bradley Graham, "Military Grappling with Guidelines for Cyberwar," *Washington Post*, November 8, 1999.

[13] Committee on Armed Services, United States Senate, *Hearing to Consider the Nomination of Lt. Gen. Keith B. Alexander to Commander, U.S. CYBERCOMMAND*, April 15, 2010; John Markoff and Thom Shanker, "Halted '03 Iraq Plan Illustrates U.S. Fear of Cyberwar Risk," *New York Times*, August 1, 2009.

New methods of conflict can usher in tectonic shifts in the international system, reconfiguring power, institutions, and norms of state behavior. Like the longbow, the warship, the bomber, and the ballistic missile, cyberattacks are a new innovation providing states with a novel way to coerce one another into changing behavior, and perhaps even into submission. Cyberattacks are the newest—and perhaps equally consequential—entry into that field. And restraining them, this study argues, requires a reconceptualization of how security competition is playing out among states today and in the future.

1.2 Topic and Scope

This study explores interstate conflict involving cyberattacks and how current dynamics, regimes, institutions, and customs of international relations could limit it. It seeks to answer the question:

> Which, if any, forces in the international system might restrain state use of cyberattacks, despite the strategic advantage they confer?

The answer has profound implications on two levels. First, it can help articulate the likely impact of cyberattacks on international security dynamics moving forward, as more countries become dependent on digital technologies. Second, it offers a critical referendum on these forces of restraint, since, if those forces and the regimes built around them are robust, they should apply with equal strength to new weapons as well as old. If they do not, the discussion must turn to why, and how must we reorient discussions not just about cyber warfare but the maintenance of peace more broadly.

These are questions increasingly central to the future of international security. In the words of former US Homeland Security Advisor John Brennan, "those of us who are involved with international, national, and homeland security policies as well as with the future of the global economy and human rights and freedom must pay attention to cyber issues and be actively engaged in cyber policy formulation."[14] Yet at the present time, states appear to be relying on generic deterrence statements, far from universal understandings of applicable law, and few applicable norms in their defense

---

[14] John O. Brennan, "Remarks at the Launch of the U.S. International Strategy for Cyberspace" (Washington, DC: The White House, 2011).

planning vis-à-vis cyberattacks. This uneasy state seems similar to the period of cautiousness and doctrinal head-scratching that accompanied other advances in weaponry, from the strategic and tactical debates over the use of nuclear weapons, to the legal and normative debates accompanying the development of chemical weapons. Such parallels form both a context and historical basis for this analysis.

International peace and security depend on restraining cyberattacks; therefore, there is an urgency in determining which frameworks and regimes of international relations will influence states' decisions not to use them. Ene Ergma's sentiment is not without parallel elsewhere. Numerous experts in the United States, Europe, and beyond continue to cite a "dire" threat in cyberspace.[15] For instance, in President Obama's address at the National Cybersecurity Communications Integration Center in 2015, he noted that "cyber threats pose an enormous challenge for our country. It's one of the most serious economic and national security challenges we face as a nation."[16] Finnish Justice Minister Antii Hakkanen expressed concern that "we are only beginning to learn how to cope with these new challenges. The risk is we are constantly one step behind."[17] The Australian Cyber Security Centre's Signals Directorate has taken a similar stance in its threat assessment reports, noting that the "cyber threat to Australian organisations is undeniable, unrelenting, and continues to grow. If an organisation is connected to the internet, it is vulnerable. The incidents in the public eye are just the tip of the iceberg."[18] Similar sentiments can be heard in the corridors of defense and foreign ministries throughout the world.

Then-US Vice President Joe Biden famously remarked: "Show me your budget, and I'll tell you what you value," and by that metric, policymakers are showing real concern for the integrity of their digital systems. In 2008, the Obama administration asked Congress for $7.2 billion to support its cyber-defense initiatives. In 2009, a comprehensive American policy study on the "digital threat" determined that "the loss of information has inflicted unacceptable damage to U.S. national and economic security," and that the

---

[15] National Cyber Security Centre, "The Cyber Threat to UK Business," Government Communications Headquarters (GCHQ), 2017–2018.
[16] The White House, "Remarks by the President at the National Cybersecurity Communications Integration Center" (Washington, DC: Government Printing Office, 2015).
[17] Kim Sengupta, "'We Are Constantly One Step Behind': Finland Worries About Cyber Warfare in Shadow of Russia," *The Independent*, October 1, 2018.
[18] Government of Australia, *The Australian Cyber Security Centre Threat Report 2015* (Canberra: Australian Signals Directorate, 2015).

nation's response would have to be "comprehensive . . . using all the tools of U.S. power in a coordinated fashion."[19] By 2015, that budget request had almost doubled its request to $14 billion and by 2020, topped $17.4 billion.[20] In the UK, cyber-defense spending was one of the only budget lines that not only escaped massive spending cuts in 2010 but received an increase to £650 million over four years.[21] Just six years later, Downing Street nearly tripled that request, to £1.9 billion.[22] In 2016, Israel increased its budget to reach ILS 2.5 billion ($714 million USD) by 2021.[23] Singapore announced its decision to invest SG$1 billion ($704 million USD) over 2020–2022 to build up the Government's cyber and data security capabilities.[24] France's cyber-defense budget is estimated to reach €1.6 billion between 2019 and 2025.[25]

Clearly, some states have concluded that one of the best means to counter offense is investing in defense. But is it? Despite these investments and policy shifts, as recently as 2018 US Director of National Intelligence Dan Coats likened the risk of cyberattack to critical infrastructure—and lack of effective measures to limit it—to the days before the 9/11 terrorist attacks: "In the months prior to September 2001 . . . the system was blinking red. And here we are nearly two decades later, and I'm here to say the warning lights are blinking red again."[26] What is preventing states from a sense of confidence that these systems will not be brought down by an adversary?

---

[19] Commission on Cybersecurity for the 44th Presidency, "Securing Cyberspace for the 44th Presidency" (Washington, DC: Center for Strategic and International Studies, 2008). See also White House Council of Economic Advisors, "The Cost of Malicious Cyber Activity to the U.S. Economy" (Washington, DC: Executive Office of the US President, 2018), ""which estimates "malicious cyber activity cost the U.S. economy between $57 billion and $109 billion in 2016."

[20] Davis, "Hackers Take Down the Most Wired Country in Europe"; Andrea Shalal and Alina Selyukh, "Obama Seeks $14 Billion to Boost U.S. Cybersecurity Defenses," *Reuters*, February 2, 2015; Symantec Corporation, "Here Comes the CNCI, and the Era of Proactive IT Security," Symantec News Forum, 2008; "Obama Seeks $14 Billion to Boost U.S. Cybersecurity Defenses"; The White House, "Administration Presents President Trump's Fiscal Year 2020 Budget Request," 2019.

[21] UK Cabinet Office, *Keeping the UK Safe in Cyberspace* (London: The Stationary Office, Her Majesty's Government, 2013).

[22] Philip Hammond, "Chancellor Speech: Launching the National Cyber Security Strategy" (London: Cabinet Office of Cybersecurity, 2016).

[23] James Andrew Lewis, "Advanced Experiences in Cybersecurity Policies and Practices: An Overview of Estonia, Israel, South Korea, and the United States" (Washington, DC: Inter-American Development Bank, 2016).

[24] Zhang Lim Min, "Singapore Budget 2020: $1b Over Next 3 Years to Shore Up Cyber and Data Security Capabilities," *The Straits Times*, February 18, 2020.

[25] Marie Baezner, "Study on the Use of Reserve Forces in Military Cybersecurity: A Comparative Study of Selected Countries" (Zurich: Center for Security Studies, ETH Zurich, 2020).

[26] Daniel R. Coats, "Transcript: Dan Coats Warns The Lights Are 'Blinking Red' On Russian Cyberattacks" (Washington, DC: Hudson Institute, July 13, 2018). See also Ashish Kumar Sen, "U.S. Sen. Mark Warner and Adm. Michael Rogers Make the Case for Cyber Security" (paper presented at the Atlantic Council's Annual Forum, Washington, DC, December 14, 2018).

Reliable restraint, this study contends, may be the missing ingredient to achieving greater stability in international cybersecurity. It considers three so-called logics of restraint, overarching influences on government decision-making that lead to states rethinking their use of a particular tool or tactic. Each part of this study is devoted to one of three such logics—categories that will be familiar to scholars of international relations but not yet systematically applied to cyberattacks—and asks which, if any, are likely to lead states to reconsider their use. They include the rationalist mode of deterrence; the regulative mode of the *jus ad bellum*, or international law regulating recourse to force and self-defense; and the more constitutive mode of norms limiting particular means and methods of warfare.

The recurring argument throughout this work is that to locate sources of restraint, we must evaluate cyberattacks from both *within* and *without* a given logic: understanding first whether a given logic operates on cyberattacks in the abstract, and when terminal ambiguities exist, consider second how states are competing to shape others' understanding of that outcome. That first stage is a process of contextualization, then evaluation. It involves placing cyberattacks within a given logic, such as deterrence; identifying how it operates; and considering whether cyberattacks fit neatly there within or have features that frustrate their "mainstreaming" within existing security dynamics. In short, it asks whether and how cyberattacks fit within a logic. The second process, then, seeks to understand whether that fit is adequate to guide states' cyberattack decisions. When it is not, it assesses how states are "filling in the gaps" of their collective understanding of how cyberattack security dynamics operate—competing to shape the outcome. This is a process referred to throughout as "structuring" of a particular restraint: deterrence, retribution, or humanitarian prohibition.

Given the abundance of state policies and postures on cyberattacks, this study focuses on nation-states rather than nonstate actors. As a later section in this chapter will explore, this position was once controversial, but it has been proven out over the years to be a more enduring and significant focus for a project such as this.[27] As a framing matter, a key reason to concentrate on states is that as perpetrators and principal planners of response, they are,

---

[27] This choice in scope echoes Nye's observation about state cyber primacy in the context of international power: "Although a hacker and a government can both create information and exploit the Internet, it matters for many purposes that large governments can deploy tens of thousands of trained people and have vast computing power." Joseph Nye, *The Future of Power* (New York: PublicAffairs, 2011), 117.

have been, and for the foreseeable future will remain the locus of cyberattacks that threaten national and international security significantly enough for this study's framing. National policy documents such as the US *International Strategy for Cyberspace* further confirm this orientation as most fix their focus primarily on state-based actors for these reasons—as later chapters will explore in greater depth.[28] Even more importantly, the persistently disruptive capabilities of nonstate actors alone (excluding when co-opted or sponsored by a state), are simply not commensurate with those of nation-states, are ill-suited to this kind of analysis—at least not as independent phenomena.[29] Individually, nonstate actors are more likely to pose a nuisance rather than a comprehensive threat to a state's national security, as a part of a coordinated, well-funded cyberattack.[30] Their potential involvement complicates but does not undermine questions raised herein. Even if low barriers to entry could allow nonstate actors to develop coercive tools; these actors typically do not identify with, find themselves bound by, or behave in accordance with the customs, regimes, and norms relevant to this study.

The explicitly ethical concerns that cyberattacks raise are not the focus of this study; however, this study does engage them indirectly with reference to certain regimes with strong ethical character, such as the *jus in bello*. This study does not lose sight of that broader context, but it is neither a work of comparative ethics nor strict international normative theory. As a matter of normative framing, this study merely presupposes that cyberattacks can and will have negative impacts on the "peaceful" interaction of states, their economies, and their people. As with any instrument capable of causing human suffering, there is arguably ethical value in restraining its use. This is not to say that this study regards cyberattacks as ethically inferior (or superior, as some literature does), to traditional conflict.[31] Rather, this study shares a narrower normative orientation that seeks peaceful international relations

---

[28] The White House, *The United States' International Strategy for Cyberspace* (Washington, DC: US Government Printing Office, 2011). See in particular 14. The *International Strategy* was, from 2011 to 2017, the primary US document explaining its positions on foreign policy issues related to cyberspace and cybersecurity.

[29] "Cyber-terrorism," once frequently used to describe terrorist use of cyberattack tools, has all but fallen out of the international lexicon, as will be explored in more depth later in the chapter.

[30] James A. Lewis, "Cognitive Effect and State Conflict in Cyberspace" (Washington, DC: Center for Strategic and International Studies, 2018).

[31] See, for example George R. Lucas, "Permissible Preventive Cyberwar: Restricting Cyber Conflict to Justified Military Targets," in *The Ethics of Information Warfare*, edited by Luciano Floridi and Mariarosaria Taddeo (New York: Springer, 2014), 73; Neil C. Rowe, "Towards Reversible Cyberattacks," in *Leading Issues in Information Warfare and Security Research*, edited by Julie Ryan (Reading, UK: Academic Conferences Limited, 2011). On the ethics of retaliatory cyberattacks,

generally and regards unrestricted employment of cyberattacks as inconsistent therewith.[32]

Having now outlined the topic and scope of the study, the rest of this introduction will define cyberattacks and illustrate their potential with recent cases, summarize the relevant literature, and outline the methodology and argument of subsequent chapters.

1.3 Defining Cyberattacks

This section begins with the technological context that explains cyberattacks' operation and significance, and then offers a formal definition that distinguishes them from other "lesser" phenomena of cybercrime and cyber-espionage. It concludes by making that definition concrete, outlining the early, small-scale example that played out in Estonia in 2007; citing several more examples from history; and clarifying what sorts of activities are excluded from this analysis.

Context: Ubiquitous and Vulnerable Digital Systems

Cyberattacks pose a significant and growing threat to modern economies and societies for two principal reasons: increasing economic, social, and governing dependence on "networked information infrastructure" and the vulnerabilities inherent in those systems.

It is difficult not to notice that in the developed world, these electronic systems enable, facilitate, and regulate innumerable aspects of daily life.[33] From computers to automobiles, mobile phones to traffic signals, advanced avionics to banking, these systems—and the information stored and

---

see Randall R. Dipert, "The Ethics of Cyberwarfare," *Journal of Military Ethics* 9, no. 4 (2010). On building in features that could lead to more ethical outcomes in a future in which cyberattacks are normalized, see Rowe, "Towards Reversible Cyberattacks."

[32] Chapter 2 engages with some possible critiques of this orientation.
[33] Technological dependence, and the risks associated with it, has become a cause célèbre of many states' national defense and security strategies for over a decade. For some of the earliest examples, see, e.g., The White House, *The National Strategy to Secure Cyberspace* (Washington, DC: US Government Printing Office, 2009); Government of Australia, *E-Security Review*, 2008. Further, the international community has recognized this dependence in the social and economic spheres at the United Nations in A/RES/64/211 and other resolutions focused on "building a global culture of cyber-security."

transmitted in their operation—all employ digital signals. As early as 2011, then-US Secretary of Homeland Security Janet Napolitano consistently cited cybersecurity as the agency's top priority alongside counterterrorism, "our economies, our healthcare systems, and our transportation networks all depend on secure and resilient cyber networks."[34] Her counterparts in the Governments of Germany, France, and New Zealand came to similar conclusions, and by and large continue to do so.[35]

This technological ubiquity and dependence are shared by civilian and defense sectors. As one senior US intelligence official put it, "close to 98 percent of the nation's most important information is housed on [sites] ending in .com," the vast majority of which share the same underlying protocols.[36] Equally dual-use are the most important cables and switches transmitting both private commercial and highly sensitive government data.[37] Increasingly, public utilities control the flow of water and electricity remotely, via computers connected to the public internet.[38] Some military experts have even noted that major armed forces' ability to mobilize would be fundamentally jeopardized by the disruption of shared, public, and unclassified fiber-optic networks used by their logistics command.[39] As summarized by a 2010 United Nations Group of Governmental Experts (GGE), the second

---

[34] Janet Napolitano, *Remarks at the Launch of the U.S. International Strategy for Cyberspace* (Washington, DC: The White House, 2011); Amber Corrin, "Cyber Executive Order Close, Napolitano says," *Federal Computer Weekly*, September 28, 2012; Janet Napolitano, *Appointment of New Deputy Under Secretary for Cybersecurity* (Washington, DC: Department of Homeland Security, 2013).

[35] See, e.g., Silvia Amaro and Hadley Gamble, "Cyberattacks Are the Single Greatest Threat to Global Stability, German Defense Minister Says," CNBC.com, 2018; Patrick Howell O'Neill, "Germany Launches New Cybersecurity Research Agency Modeled After DARPA," *Cyberscoop*, 2018; Government of France, "Déclaration de Madame Florence Parly, ministre des armées, sur la stratégie cyber des armées" (Paris: Ministre des Armées, 2019); Government of New Zealand, *New Zealand Strategic Defense Policy Statement* (Wellington, 2018); Gerard O'Dwyer, "Finland's Top National Security Risk? Cyber," *Fifth Domain*, March 26, 2018.

[36] Donald M. Kerr, "Remarks by the Principal Deputy Director of National Intelligence at the Association for Intelligence Officers (AFIO) Annual Intelligence Symposium" (McLean, VA: Office of the Director of National Intelligence, 2008).

[37] Peter Svensson, "Finger-Thin Undersea Cables Tie World Together," *The Associated Press*, January 31, 2008. The United States Congressional Research Service (CRS) has warned for almost 20 years that the US military "relies significantly on the civilian information infrastructure." US Congressional Research Service, "Computer Attack and Cyber Terrorism: Vulnerabilities and Policy Issues for Congress" (Washington, DC: US Congress, 2003).

[38] "Emerging Cyber Threat Reports, 2011" (Atlanta, GA: Georgia Tech Information Security Center, 2011); John Markoff, David Sanger, and Thom Shanker, "In Digital Combat, U.S. Finds No Easy Deterrent," *New York Times*, January 25, 2010.

[39] Daniel T. Kuehl, "China and Cybersecurity" (paper presented at the National Security Seminar, Heritage Foundation, April 28, 2010).

such body tasked to develop consensus statements about the status of information technology in the context of information security: "Because they are inherently dual-use in nature, the same [technologies] that support robust e-commerce can also be used to threaten international peace and national security."[40]

There are countless components, operating across numerous media, that come together to make these technologies function. While they utilize the electromagnetic spectrum, they often do so by means of man-made appliances that exist in real space. They transmit data in the form of signals, over networks that exist both digitally—in terms of the communication among appliances to exchange those signals—and physically, via cables and switches. Hence, components of the "electronic" world may not appear to be, at first glance, particularly electronic at all.

Underlying the operation of all these electronics is a category of technology called "information infrastructure," hardware and software ubiquitous and increasingly fundamental to modern economies, societies, and militaries.[41] Information infrastructure can be thought of as the physical infrastructure that enables a computer's operation, or the electronic processes that keep computer networks functioning as digital signals pass from machine to machine to transmit data. In sum, information infrastructure is the shared hardware and software that enables devices to communicate with one another, and thus underlies most day-to-day interaction with technology.

The same attributes that make information infrastructure so versatile—allowing a network router to be as useful to a military planner as it is to an online retailer—also make those networks inherently vulnerable. The internet was designed with versatility and accessibility in mind—but not necessarily security.[42] Many of the core internet technologies are trust-based systems; they are designed and continue to operate under principles

---

[40] United Nations Group of Governmental Experts (2008-9), *Report Group of Governmental Experts on Developments in the Field of Information and Telecommunications in the Context of International Security (2008-9)* (Geneva: United Nations Institute for Disarmament Research, 2010), 6 (hereafter "*GGE 2010*").

[41] US Office of Technology Assessment, "Information Security and Privacy in Network Environments" (Washington, DC: Government Printing Office, 1994). This is also the definition favored by noted military/cybersecurity commentator Greg Rattray in his early and influential work on the subject. See Greg Rattray, *Strategic Warfare in Cyberspace* (Cambridge, MA: MIT Press, 2001).

[42] Fritz E. Froehlich and Allen Kent, *Froehlich/Kent Encyclopedia of Telecommunications*, vol. 15 (New York: Marcel Dekker, 1997), 233; US Government Accounting Office, *Computer Security: Hackers Penetrate DOD Computer Systems* (Washington, DC: GAO, 1991).

that maximize interoperability between diverse systems and innovation in their use.[43] This is why, for instance, an intentional misconfiguration allowed the Government of Pakistan to briefly interrupt the entire world's access to YouTube.[44] In order to be maximally compatible, these networks are designed to accept signals from a range of machines, thus depending on "open" standards and protocols that pass and accept malicious data often as easily as legitimate data. This "openness" and "interoperability" is therefore responsible for both the pace of innovation and the infrastructure's inherent insecurity. That vulnerability is compounded by the fact that not only are the same types of infrastructures vital to the functioning of modern economies and militaries, but often the very same devices are shared by them in the form of switches, satellite connections, and fiber optic cables.

Physical information infrastructure can be disabled, with similar effect, by a kinetic (i.e., physical) or nonkinetic (i.e., digital) attack as part of effects-based cyber operations; critical components can be blown up and network cables severed, or they can be flooded with damaging information and viruses. Fiber optic cables, microwave dishes, routers and hubs that connect that infrastructure are physical, often fragile, and susceptible to destruction. Most internet traffic routed overseas, for instance, travels through one of only a few hundred commercially owned fiber-optic cable bundles running across the ocean.[45] Several contemporary episodes of these lines being accidentally severed (by ships' anchors or earthquakes), and the deployment of navies to protect them from pirate attack off the Somali coast, demonstrate the fragility of the system.[46] In 2009 near San Francisco, phone and internet access

---

[43] For example, the fundamental Border Gateway Protocol (BGP) used to help route internet requests is subject to frequent hijacking by users misleading other machines as to their proximity to a particular site. For technical approaches to tracking those exploiting this technique, see Cecilia Testart et al., *Profiling BGP Serial Hijackers: Capturing Persistent Misbehavior in the Global Routing Table*, Proceedings of the Internet Measurement Conference (Amsterdam: Association for Computing Machinery, 2019).

[44] Ryan Singel, "Pakistan's Accidental YouTube Re-Routing Exposes Trust Flaw in Net," *Wired*, February 26, 2008.

[45] Svensson, "Finger-Thin Undersea Cables Tie World Together."

[46] In 2006, four major fiber optic lines were severely damaged following a major earthquake in Taiwan; subsequent underwater mudslides damaged nine cables laid in the Luzon Strait south of Taiwan, destroying all eastward data routes from Southeast Asia. It took forty-nine days for crews on eleven giant cable-laying ships to fix all of the twenty-one damage points. International Cable Protection Committee, "Subsea Landslide is Likely Cause of SE Asian Communications Failure," News release, March 21, 2007. https://www.iscpc.org/documents/?id=9; Tahani Karrar, "Third Undersea Cable Reportedly Cut Between Sri Lanka, Suez," *Dow Jones Newswire*, February 1, 2008; Lily Hay Newman, "Cut Undersea Cable Plunges Yemen Into Days-Long Internet Outage," *Wired*, January 13, 2020; Tom Westbrook, "Severed Cable Sends Tonga 'Back to Beginning of the Internet,'" *Reuters*, January 24, 2019.

was disabled through broad swathes of the world's largest technical hub—California's Silicon Valley—when what is presumed to have been a single disgruntled maintenance technician, armed only with a pair of wire clippers and knowledge of the system, severed some of the region's fiber-optic lines.[47] A similar incident near Phoenix, Arizona, in 2015 disrupted ATM, emergency response, and financial transactions for fifteen hours in most of the city.[48]

If coordinated by a state deploying several highly trained operatives, the impact could be much greater—a prospect given voice by senior national security officials including Former US Secretary of Defense Leon Panetta.[49] Blunter kinetic approaches would also be effective. Several central locations throughout the United States, and only a few throughout the United Kingdom, serve as hubs for routing internet traffic; the simultaneous destruction of two or more could cause considerable damage to the system. The destruction of a handful of communications satellites would also substantially disrupt information flows—explaining Western concern over China's 2007 and Russia's 2016 anti-satellite weapon tests.[50]

The lagging security of vast swaths of critical infrastructure—the utilities and other systems helping mediate modern society and the economy—also makes it increasingly easy to attack with severity and from afar. Much of this infrastructure is, far more often than appreciated, remotely operated and dependent on internet-accessible networks. Such Supervisory Control and Data Acquisition (SCADA) systems are responsible for the operation of countless functions like water treatment and distribution, electric power generation (including nuclear power), pipelines, chemical plants, and other industrial processes for manufacturing and production.[51] Similar to

---

[47] Marguerite Reardon, "Vandals Blamed for Phone and Internet Outage," *CNet News*, April 10, 2009.

[48] Felicia Fonseca, "Vandalism in Arizona Shows the Internet's Vulnerability," *Associated Press*, February 26, 2015.

[49] Leon Panetta, *Remarks on Defending the Nation from Cyber Attack (11 October)* (Washington, DC: Department of Defense, 2012).

[50] Carin Zissis, "Backgrounder: China's Anti-Satellite Test" (New York: Council on Foreign Relations, 2007); Westin Williams, "Russia Launches Anti-Satellite Weapon: A New Warfront in Space?," *Christian Science Monitor*, December 22, 2016.

[51] The US Congressional Research Service defines SCADA as referring to "the function of those systems, which are often used to control processes in industrial facilities and to log information about status and conditions. They often communicate electronically with central computer systems that are connected to the Internet." US Congressional Research Service, "Creating a National Framework for Cybersecurity: An Analysis of Issues and Options" (Washington, DC: United States Congress, 2005).

many other technological systems, as SCADA systems have become more networked and designed for remote use, they have become less secure.[52]

The most dramatic—and from an international security standpoint, significant—effects of such an attack would not be confined to networks.[53] In 2008, the Hatch Nuclear Power Plant in the United States reportedly underwent an emergency shutdown as a result of a software update to its business systems. Subsequent investigation found that those business networks were directly linked to (and able to access) critical SCADA systems responsible for functions such as cooling at the plant.[54] Similarly, the Browns Ferry nuclear facility in the United States shut down in 2006 when a network traffic overload locked up pump controls.[55] In 2013, the SCADA command-and-control systems of Bowman Avenue dam in Rye Brooke, New York, were repeatedly compromised via a wireless internet connection.[56] A targeted virus, such as the one researchers allege sabotaged the Iranian nuclear program, represents a small-scale and targeted version of such an attack vector.[57] Just as with that worm, the consequences of a cyber-enabled SCADA disruption may well be physical, to include widespread blackouts, shutdown, or ignition of energy production or transport facilities such as oil and natural gas pipelines.[58] These were clearly among the concerns when the US Justice Department brought criminal charges against four Russians accused of hacking this

---

[52] Ross Anderson, *Security Engineering: A Guide to Building Dependable Distributed Systems*, 2nd ed. (Indianapolis: Wiley & Sons, 2008), 389–414.

[53] Senate Select Committee on Intelligence, *Statement for the Record on the Worldwide Threat Assessment of the US Intelligence Community* (Washington, DC: US Senate, January 29, 2014): "Critical infrastructure, particularly the Industrial Control Systems (ICS) and Supervisory Control and Data Acquisition (SCADA) systems used in water management, oil and gas pipelines, electrical power distribution, and mass transit, provides an enticing target to malicious actors."

[54] United States Department of Homeland Security, *Alert: Increasing Threat to Industrial Control Systems*, ed. Industrial Control Systems Cyber Emergency Response Team (Washington, DC: Department of Homeland Security, 2012).

[55] For actions being taken to close such SCADA security gaps, see Jacob Goodwin, "FERC Seeks to Close Any Cyber-Security 'Gaps' at Nuclear Plants," *Government Security News*, March 25, 2009.

[56] The US Department of Justice charged a hacker in 2016 who was allegedly backed by the Islamic Revolutionary Guard Corps of Iran for the cyber intrusions. US Attorney's Office (Southern District of New York), *Manhattan U.S. Attorney Announces Charges Against Seven Iranians For Conducting Coordinated Campaign Of Cyber Attacks Against U.S. Financial Sector On Behalf Of Islamic Revolutionary Guard Corps-Sponsored Entities* (Washington, DC: Department of Justice, 2016).

[57] John Markoff, "A Silent Attack, but not a Subtle One," *New York Times*, September 26, 2010; Robert McMillan, "Siemens: Stuxnet Worm Hit Industrial Systems," *Computerworld*, September 14, 2010.

[58] Joel Brenner, *Glass Houses: Privacy, Secrecy, and Cyber Insecurity in a Transparent World*, reprint ed. (New York: Penguin, 2013), 99.

sort of infrastructure—including, most notably, the Wolf Creek Nuclear Operating Corporation.[59]

This vulnerability has not been lost on countries like the United States and United Kingdom, who see a substantial risk, but also potential advantage.[60] Over twenty years ago, US military officials claimed that "as infrastructure becomes modernized and networked in most nations throughout the world, reaching system SCADA . . . is quickly becoming a milestone in any military operation."[61] Today, some of the United States' potential adversaries appear to possess those such capabilities as well. In March 2018, the US Department of Homeland Security (DHS) and Federal Bureau of Investigation (FBI) issued a joint technical alert about the Russian government's "multi-stage intrusion campaign" targeting US Industrial Control Systems (ICS) since 2016.[62] Apart from Russian actors, nonstate actors such as the Iranian hacker group dubbed "APT 33" have also targeted the producers and manufacturers of control systems.[63] According to the security firm that first identified it publicly, APT 33's targeting of ICS "could be a means to conduct a disruptive or destructive attack, or it could be an easy way to get into lots of energy companies, because energy companies rely on those technologies."[64]

These attacks could be further exacerbated by the stealth installation of digital "kill-switches." Often undetectable in complex systems once installed, this kind of malicious software is designed to cause disruption, with no more than an activation signal, at any time after its installation.[65] Intelligence and defense officials have specifically noted the likelihood of such an attack. According to a 2009 report, British intelligence chiefs warned that China may have gained the capability to effectively cripple the UK's telecommunications through digital sabotage, which could in turn be used to halt critical

[59] "U.S. Accuses 4 Russians of Hacking Infrastructure, Including Nuclear Plant," *New York Times*, March 24.
[60] UK Centre for the Protection of National Infrastructure, "Process Control and SCADA Security" (London: CPNI, 2008).
[61] UK Centre for the Protection of National Infrastructure, "Process Control and SCADA Security"; Bruce A. Wright, "Remarks before the Defense Colloquium on Information" Operations (quoted in William Church, "Information Operations Violates Protocol I," 1999, http://www.ase.md/~osa/publ/en/puben06.html).
[62] US Department of Homeland Security, *Alert (TA18–074A) Russian Government Cyber Activity Targeting Energy and Other Critical Infrastructure Sectors* (Washington, DC: Department of Homeland Security, 2018).
[63] Andy Greenberg, "A Notorious Iranian Hacking Crew Is Targeting Industrial Control Systems," *Wired*, November 20, 2019.
[64] Ibid.
[65] David Fulghum, "Israel Used Electronic Attack in Air Strike Against Syrian Mystery Target," *Aviation Week*, October 8, 2007; Sally Adee, "The Hunt for the Kill Switch," *IEEE Spectrum* May 2008.

services such as power or water supplies.[66] Cyberattacks on the Ukrainian power grid in 2015 and 2016—predating the full-scale invasion in 2022—caused US officials to reportedly grow increasingly concerned that Russia possesses the capabilities to do the same with the US power grid.[67]

A final, salient point for the international context is that a cyberattack's effects likely multiply exponentially with the overall level of the victim state's digitization or reliance on information infrastructure.[68] An economy or society with a very low level of reliance on networked systems would suffer minimal effect from even a sophisticated cyberattack, as was largely the case when Russia launched a digital offensive on computers in Georgia on the eve of its 2008 invasion.[69] In technology dependent states though—including most Western democracies, Japan, South Korea, and others—a profound and exponential feedback effect exists among large information economies, advanced militaries, and the corresponding levels of daily technology use. The principle of interconnectedness is not terribly new: studies of globalization and trade often examine how technological and human networks grow and become increasingly beholden to the smooth functioning of the larger system.[70] The same is true with digital systems that underlie the economies, societies, and military of modern states. Not just any disruption of these systems would constitute a national security event, yet given some countries' high levels of dependence on information infrastructure and the increasing interconnection between those systems, new avenues are available for a sophisticated state actor to effect a large-scale, cascading failure. It is this general concept of interconnection and vulnerability that helps frame what a cyberattack means in international relations.

---

[66] Kim Zetter, "Inside the Cunning, Unprecedented Hack of Ukraine's Power Grid," *Wired*, March 3, 2016.

[67] Ellen Nakashima, "Russia Has Developed a Cyberweapon That Can Disrupt Power Grids, According to New Research," *Washington Post*, November 6, 2017; Senate Select Committee on Intelligence, *Statement for the Record on the Worldwide Threat Assessment of the US Intelligence Community*, February 13, 2018.

[68] These effects could be thought of as the digital equivalent of a bombing-induced "firestorm," where an attack of sufficient intensity renders itself broader and more destructive by exploiting feedback the initial damage creates.

[69] Alex Kingsbury, "In Georgia, a Parallel War Rages Online," *U.S. News & World Report*, August 13, 2008. Incidentally, the global dimension of these feedback effects—at least with regard to economic externalities (such as disruptions to trade flow)—suggest that less developed, less technology-dependent states would be more likely to conduct a cyber assault against a more developed enemy, seeking to maximize the asymmetry inherent therein.

[70] See, e.g., John Baylis, Steve Smith, and Patricia Owens, eds., *The Globalization of World Politics*, 6th ed. (New York: Oxford University Press, 2014), 16.

Formal Definition

One can see how this shared infrastructure creates a highly appealing target for the would-be attacker seeking to disable or otherwise disrupt a technology-dependent state or subdivision thereof. In essence, the following definition of a cyberattack constitutes a subset of the previously described effects-based cyber operations. Using this capability to significant national security effect is the subject of this study:

> A cyberattack is an act of coercion or sabotage that exploits the security vulnerabilities of networked systems, disrupting or destroying information infrastructure or the critical infrastructure dependent on it, to significant national security effect.

"An act of coercion or sabotage." First, the act in question must be an intentionally *coercive act*, which is to say designed by an aggressor state to achieve a particular change in behavior from the victim state (ranging from new policy choices to outright surrender) or diminishes their overall ability to compete, for instance economically or militarily.[71] This characteristic distinguishes cyberattacks from cybercrime, which is traditionally thought of as financial in motivation and carried out by individuals on their own or their syndicate's behalf.[72] It also distinguishes cyberattacks from cyber-espionage, which is, by contrast, seeking to amass information but not to harm it, in order to inform decision-making or gain strategic advantage.[73] In the cases of cyber-crime and cyber-espionage, cyberspace offers only a new venue in which to undertake well-known activities.[74] Digital systems may make these actions easier or possible on a greater scale, but beyond that potential intensification

---

[71] Throughout, in describing cyberattacks generically, this study favors the use of the phrase "coercion" to other characterizations (such as "aggression"), wherever possible for the purposes of clarity. Other phrases would, potentially, presuppose or otherwise prejudice the analysis of later chapters examining whether those legal designations apply. It also uses "coercion" as shorthand for "coercion or sabotage," for efficiency and recognizing the former is a somewhat intellectually richer focus.

[72] See Susan W. Brenner, *Cybercrime and the Law: Challenges, Issues, and Outcomes* (Boston: Northeastern University Press, 2012).

[73] Some governments refer to this category of "hacking" as computer network exploitation (CNE), which, along with a few other specialized operations, generally comprises the kind of data exfiltration characteristic of digital espionage.

[74] So-called cyber-terrorism is also excluded from this definition; because of the fundamentally contested (and potentially applicable) nature of concepts of a terrorist act, part of Section 6.2 briefly explores the applicability of this tactical concept.

there is little deeply novel from the standpoint of international relations.[75] By contrast, and as the balance of this study will argue, states are engaged in significant competition over the applicability and practical effect of even basic tenets of law.

"Disrupting or destroying information infrastructure." What sets cyberattacks apart is the likelihood that they will exploit critical information infrastructure. This is a technologically complex task, and studies of the technical tools of disruption in cyberspace are consistent in the view that states retain preeminence in developing these most sophisticated and effective tools—in other words, those capable of widespread disruption on a national scale.[76] As such, in the strategic cyber-defense literature, there exists a compelling consensus that as *primary* actors, state actors will maintain enduring relevance due to particular resource and organizational advantages.[77] Because states have at their disposal intelligence services, long-term military planning, and vast economic resources, they are most capable of making devastating cyberattacks that target and disrupt critical infrastructure, including information infrastructure.

This is not to say that cybercrime tools or actors could not be used, in aggregate, by states seeking to orchestrate a less attributable cyberattack. Talented rogue actors may develop one-off tools capable of significant damage. Hackers for hire, often affiliated with organized crime, offer unsophisticated cyberattack tools at prices within reach of even moderately resourced militaries. Indeed, some organized crime elements are known to have developed cyberattack tools and may have even amassed the kind of rudimentary capability that disabled Estonian information infrastructure.[78] Therefore the

---

[75] Russian interference in the 2016 US presidential election and the Brexit votes comes closest to raising an exception to this claim; later sections will address it, given governments' belated classification of election infrastructure as critical infrastructure and international law's longstanding recognition of threats to political independence.

[76] See Jason Andress and Steve Winterfeld, *Cyber Warfare: Techniques, Tactics, and Tools for Security Practitioners* (Oxford: Syngress, 2011), 71; McAfee Labs and Good Harbor Consulting, "Virtual Criminology Report 2009" (San Jose, CA: McAfee Laba, 2009); Dennis C. Blair, *Annual Threat Assessment of the US Intelligence Community for the Senate Select Committee on Intelligence* (Washington, DC: Congressional Record, US Government Printing Office, 2010) 2; *Statement for the Record on the Worldwide Threat Assessment of the US Intelligence Community*; Senate Select Committee on Intelligence, *Statement for the Record on the Worldwide Threat Assessment of the US Intelligence Community*, January 29, 2019: "China has the ability to launch cyber attacks that cause localized, temporary disruptive effects on critical infrastructure—such as disruption of a natural gas pipeline for days to weeks—in the United States."

[77] See US Air Force, "Air Force Doctrine Document 2-11: Cyberspace Operations" (Washington, DC: LeMay Center for Doctrine Development and Education, 2008); Gary D. Solis, "Cyber Warfare," *Military Law Review* 219 (2014); Michael Schmitt, "Classification of Cyber Conflict," *International Law Studies* 89 (2013).

[78] Thompson, "Russia 'Hired Botnets' for Estonia Cyber-War."

technological sophistication of a country may not correspond to its ability to obtain or deploy cyberattack tools. Consider that North Korea has per capita internet penetration roughly equivalent to the Democratic Republic of the Congo, yet is also believed to have reportedly orchestrated a number of disruptive digital incidents from 2008 to the present, ranging from financial theft (stealing over $80 million USD from the Bank of Bangladesh) to large-scale commercial disruption (including the hack of Sony Pictures and dissemination of the WannaCry ransomware that infected several hundred thousand machines).[79] An attacker need not create all cyberattack tools domestically; military-scale spending can narrow some military asymmetries, as can a willingness to transact with criminal actors. The proliferation of machine learning-based tools like large language models, often shorthanded as artificial intelligence (AI), may supercharge this proliferation of capability, as automation of the search for narrow software exploits and the honing of code replace previously labor-intensive deployment of offensive cyber tools.[80] While their emergence in general use is a new phenomenon, later parts of the study briefly consider the impact on a range of cyberattack dynamics.

This definition diverges in one important way from how similar phrases may appear in official state doctrine and the media. Several reports suggest that US doctrine drew its crucial distinctions not in the targeting of infrastructure per se, but in whether cyber activities (sometimes called "weapons") had certain kinds of "effects" on computer or physical systems.[81] While all cyberattacks described here would fall under such a category, not all cyber operations are cyberattacks—instead, to qualify, an operation's effects must be felt specifically by the information infrastructure and/or other infrastructure dependent thereupon. This caveat creates critical exclusions defined in more depth shortly and are of particular significance in later chapters looking at international law.

---

[79] International Telecommunications Union, "ICT Indicators Database 2010" (Geneva: ITU, 2010); *BBC News*, "South Korea Blames North for Bank and TV Cyber-Attacks," April 10, 2013; David Sanger, Nicole Perlroth, and David D. Kirkpatrick, "The World Once Laughed at North Korean Cyberpower. No More," *New York Times*, October 15, 2017; Elias Groll, "NSA Official Suggests North Korea Was Culprit in Bangladesh Bank Heist," *Foreign Policy*, March 21, 2017; International Telecommunications Union, "ICT Indicators Database 2010" (Geneva: ITU, 2010); *BBC News*, "Ransomware Cyberattack Threat Escalating—Europol," May 14, 2017.

[80] Elias Groll, "ChatGPT Shows Promise of Using AI to Write Malware," *CyberScoop*, December 6, 2022; Davide Castelvecchi, "Are ChatGPT and AlphaCode Going to Replace Programmers?," *Nature*, December 8, 2022.

[81] Herbert S. Lin, "Reflections on the New Department of Defense Cyber Strategy: What It Says, What It Doesn't Say," *Georgetown Journal of International Affairs* 17, no. 3 (2016).

"Or the critical infrastructure dependent on it." Cyberattacks of national consequence would target the shared critical infrastructure outlined in the prior section. That infrastructure can take two forms: the information infrastructure itself, which permits digital systems to operate, or a disruption that degrades the functioning of more traditional infrastructure reliant upon it, such as electrical grids. Although cyberattacks would in most instances be executed from afar and via electronic signals, they could conceivably include targeted disruption of physical infrastructure. The referent object of this definition is the infrastructure itself, not the method of its disruption. A nonkinetic "digital" attack uses computer signals carried over a network to cause effects either to other digital systems, or perhaps as a second-order consequence to the physical assets they control (such as an electrical grid, as Russia is widely believed to have done to the Ukraine in 2015).[82] Even surgically precise disruption can lead to profound military effects, as Syria learned when an Israeli cyberattack reportedly disabled some of Damascus' radar systems before an airstrike on a covert nuclear facility.[83] Western defense officials have also made public their specific preparations for such an attack.[84]

---

[82] What the US government refers to as computer network operations (CNO) falls generally within this area. CNO is a blanket term that includes computer network exploitation (CNE), namely reconnaissance and espionage; and computer network attack (CNA), namely sabotage and remote system disablement. Cyberattacks thus include CNA, but not solely CNE (as will be discussed shortly). *Note on operative US doctrine*: In 2012, US President Barack Obama signed Presidential Policy Directive 20 (PPD-20), which articulated the administration's legal and policy vision for responding to hostile cyber acts. According to the Obama administration's unclassified fact sheet on PPD-20, this policy sought to establish "principles and processes for the use of cyber operations so that cyber tools are integrated with the full array of national security tools we have at our disposal." See The White House, "Fact Sheet on Presidential Policy Directive 20" (Washington, DC: January 2013). In August 2018, however, US President Donald Trump rescinded PPD-20, citing reasons such as easing restrictions on offensive cyber operations. PPD-20 was therefore replaced with National Security Presidential Memoranda (NSPM) 13 on Offensive Cyber Operations, which remains classified. NSPM 13 is reportedly more focused on changing the mechanism for the approval of military cyber operations, as well as the definitions of the types of operations themselves: see Dakota S. Rudesill, "Trump's Secret Order on Pulling the Cyber Trigger," *Lawfare*, August 29, 2018; The White House, "National Security Presidential Memoranda [NSPMs] Donald J. Trump Administration" (Washington, DC: US Government Printing Office, 2017); Erica D. Borghard, "What Do the Trump Administration's Changes to PPD-20 Mean for U.S. Offensive Cyber Operations?" (New York: Council on Foreign Relations, September 10, 2018); Eric Geller, "Trump Scraps Obama Rules on Cyberattacks, Giving Military Freer Hand," *Politico*, August 16, 2018.

[83] Kingsbury, "In Georgia, a Parallel War Rages Online"; Fulghum, "Israel Used Electronic Attack in Air Strike Against Syrian Mystery Target."

[84] For example, the US military encountered just such a case in the "Buckshot Yankee" episode. See William J. Lynn III, "Defending a New Domain: The Pentagon's Cyberstrategy," *Foreign Affairs* September/October (2010). See also Julian E. Barnes, "Cyber-Attack on Defense Department Computers Raises Concerns," *Los Angeles Times*, November 28, 2008; *Agence France-Presse*, "Growing Threat from Cyber Attacks: US General," April 7, 2009.

"*To significant national security effect.*" Finally, the act in question must possess a quality of severity in the context of national and international security. This point cannot be overemphasized, given the pattern of hyperbole that tends to accompany contemporaneous accounts of disruptive events in cyberspace. To be sure, unsuccessful and minor attempts by a rogue regime or individual to disrupt information infrastructure of a less favored state does not truly constitute a cyberattack as examined in this study. Those types of "attacks" are common—so common, in fact, that the top US general tasked with cyberspace defense numbers them in the millions annually.[85]

The issue then is the severity of effect—an attribute impossible to quantify, but the permutations of which will be explored throughout.[86] For the purposes of definition, however, such an incident must *cause severe disruption, degradation or destruction of critical systems*—or, put another way, must be of sufficient effect as to be judged by the victim to constitute a real threat to national and economic security and/or social stability. These concepts were echoed in various pieces of doctrine relating to cyberspace activities, such as the US Defense Department's (DOD) 2015 Cyberspace Strategy, which aims to deter acts "of significant consequence on the US homeland and against US interests, including loss of life, significant destruction of property, or significant impact on US foreign and economic policy interests."[87] Similarly, US cyber-focused sanctions from 2016 set their threshold at a "significant threat to the national security, foreign policy, or economic health, or financial stability of the United States."[88]

Despite attempts by some policy-focused literature to quantify these threats, this is a qualitative judgment of effect, rather than a quantitative threshold (such as declaring a cyberattack any computer-based event that, for instance, disrupts power to ten million or more homes).[89] Some doctrine has attempted to define more precisely this concept of severity. Bilateral and plurilateral defense arrangements, as later sections will explore, have

---

[85] *BBC News*, "US Cyber War Defences 'Very Thin', Pentagon Warns," March 16, 2011.
[86] The perception of severity is in the eye of the beholder; for analytical purposes, preemptively assigning a quantitative or even overly precise threshold to the gravity of an event to qualify as a cyberattack would be counterproductive. Later chapters will explore different approaches to evaluating this concept.
[87] US Department of Defense, *The Department of Defense Cyber Strategy* (Washington, DC, 2015).
[88] The White House, Executive Order 13694, 2016; US Department of Defense, *The Department of Defense Cyber Strategy* (Washington, DC: Department of Defense, 2015).
[89] See, by contrast, the metrics developed by US Cyber Consequences Unit. Scott Borg, "The Cyber Defense Revolution: A Synthesis (Presentation of the U.S. Cyber Consequences Unit)" (Tallinn: NATO CCD-COE, 2009).

sought to apply equivalent standards between what would invoke those arrangements in the kinetic space and actions with a cyber predicate.[90] The problem with those statements, however, is that they retain the uncertainty bound up in those alliance's operations—which, in the case of NATO, becomes reflexive.[91] In other words, the benefit of NATO's New Strategic Concept clarifying that cyberspace actions may trigger collective defense obligations in fact says far less than NATO's prior inaction during the 2007 Estonia attacks.

By way of preliminary analogy, it may be true that any itinerant bullet whizzing over national borders could be judged an attack. It may further be true that if an identified soldier fired that shot, it too could register as such. Were a civilian struck and killed by that bullet, it may indeed be an attack of some consequence. The ultimate determinant, however, is one of context. If that gunshot were fired today across the Canada–US border, neither Washington nor Ottawa would deem it *casus belli*. It would not be a national security incident of consequence. If, however, that gunshot crossed the 38th parallel that separates North and South Korea, striking a guard, the atmosphere of tensions would have an altogether more explosive effect. As a study within international relations, and prior to engagement with the relevant international law that explores the particular significance of that term, the notion of an attack is often shorthand—excluding events of minor import and

---

[90] At the September 2011 AUSMIN Summit, the US and Australia reaffirmed that the ANZUS treaty would include responses to a cyberattack; "We endorsed a Joint Statement on Cyber declaring that cyber attacks could be invoked under the ANZUS Treaty, demonstrating the adaptability of our Alliance." See Australia Department of Foreign Affairs and Trade, *AUSMIN 2011: Transcript of joint press conference with Defence Minister Stephen Smith, U.S. Secretary of State Hillary Clinton and U.S. Secretary of Defense Leon Panetta (15 September)* (Canberra: Government of Australia, 2011).

[91] For NATO's New Strategic Concept history: in 2010 the UN Secretary-General appointed a group of twelve experts, led by Madeleine K. Albright, to develop NATO's New Strategic Concept. The expert's report recommended that NATO respond to the dangers of cyberattacks. North Atlantic Treaty Organization, *Active Engagement, Modern Defence: Strategic Concept for the Defence and Security of the Members of the North Atlantic Treaty Organization* (Lisbon: NATO, 2010), 16–17: "Attacks involving weapons of mass destruction, terrorist strikes, and efforts to harm society *through cyber assaults* or the unlawful disruption of critical supply lines. To guard against these threats, which may or may not reach the level of an Article 5 attack, NATO must update its approach to the defence of Alliance territory while also enhancing its ability to prevail in military operations and broader security missions beyond its borders." This recommendation was incorporated into the 2010 New Strategic Concept: noting the alliance intends "to prevent, detect, *defend against and recover from cyberattacks*, including by using the NATO planning process to enhance and coordinate national cyber-defence capabilities, bringing all NATO bodies under centralized cyber protection, and better integrating NATO cyber awareness." NATO formally adopted the Strategic Concept during its Lisbon Summit in November 2010. North Atlantic Treaty Organization, *Lisbon Summit Declaration Issued by the Heads of State and Government participating in the meeting of the North Atlantic Council in Lisbon* (Lisbon: NATO, 2010).

drawing attention to those of national and international consequence. So too does this study, in the case of cyberattacks.

Cyberattacks are thus a distinct form of interstate coercion, and one that because of its novelties, eludes comprehensive analogy. The point was well summarized by the 2010 United Nations GGE, a consensus-driven but nonbinding group that has produced multiple reports over the years, which concluded that networked technologies:

> Have unique attributes that make it difficult to address threats that States and other users may face . . . are ubiquitous and widely available . . . are neither inherently civil nor military in nature, and the purpose to which they are put depends mainly on the motives of the user. Networks in many cases are owned and operated by the private sector or individuals. Malicious use . . . can easily be concealed. The origin of a disruption, the identity of the perpetrator or the motivation can be difficult to ascertain. Often, the perpetrators of such activities can only be inferred from the target, the effect or other circumstantial evidence . . . these attributes facilitate [their] use for disruptive activities.[92]

The DOD, in a 2018 update to its foundational policy document on cyberspace operations, also includes many similar factors in considering distinctly cyber operations that "create various direct denial effects in cyberspace (i.e., degradation, disruption, or destruction) and manipulation that leads to denial that is hidden or that manifests in the physical domains."[93] Included in this DOD definition are physical effects. Excluded are, for instance, acts of espionage and cyber theft. Yet this is still a broad definition, lacking (as this study proposes) a severity of effects limitation. The DOD's choice likely reflects a policy consideration—operational flexibility—rather than an intent to treat any miniscule degradation to their communications as distinctive within military doctrine.[94]

Other governments' official definitions of "cyberattack" or its next closest term, particularly in translation, can be quite wide-ranging. Germany's government, for instance, specifies that cyberattacks are aimed at "damaging IT security" or compromising IT "security, confidentiality,

---

[92] *GGE 2010*, 3.
[93] US Department of Defense, "Joint Publication 3-12: Cyberspace Operations" (Washington, DC: Joint Chiefs of Staff, 2018).
[94] Section 6.3 offers a potential explanation of and further context for the US DOD's approach.

integrity, and availability," while Japan's government uses yet a broader definition, regarding cyberattacks as a "cyberactivity" that "cause[s] or may cause significant damage to the citizen's life, body, property, or national land."[95] Canada, on the other hand, defines a cyberattack as any cyberactivity that "include[s] the unintentional or unauthorized access, use, manipulation, interruption or destruction (via electronic means) of electronic information and/or the electronic and physical infrastructure used to process, communicate and/or store that information." Such definitions are too broad to be the focus of this study and, as later chapters will explore, their diversity is creating nontrivial barriers to harmonization of positions.[96]

With this in mind, and given how rife the field is with competing definitions of various levels of inclusiveness, it is worth engaging with some of the examples in the historical record to help situate the concept under discussion here.

Cyberattacks Post-Estonia

The years subsequent to 2007 have provided an extensive catalogue of potentially unfriendly cyberspace incidents with a state nexus. Many of the most spectacular, such as Stuxnet and NotPetya, have received monographs by leading journalists documenting their origins, spread, and implications.[97] Add to that scores of contemporary articles written about each new cybersecurity incident—over 150 of which can be found in the bibliography, and the potential for confusion abounds.[98] Putting into practice the definition above, a few incidents come to the fore as bone fide cyberattacks

---

[95] Government of Germany, *German National Cyber Security Strategy* (Athens: European Union Agency for Cybersecurity, 2016), 14; Government of Japan, *Common Standards for Information Security Measures for Government Agencies and Related Agencies (FY2018)* (Tokyo: National Center of Incident Readiness and Strategy, 2018).

[96] Government of Canada, *Canada's Cyber Security Strategy: For a Stronger and More Prosperous Canada* (Ottawa, 2010), 3.

[97] Kim Zetter, *Countdown to Zero Day: Stuxnet and the Launch of the World's First Digital Weapon* (New York: Broadway Books, 2014); Andy Greenberg, *Sandworm: A New Era of Cyberwar and the Hunt for the Kremlin's Most Dangerous Hackers* (New York: Doubleday, 2019).

[98] For a useful database of individual cyber incidents and reporting associated with them, see Council on Foreign Relations, "Cyber Operations Tracker," https://www.cfr.org/interactive/cyber-operations.

under this definition and will serve as some of the most important examples explored later in this volume. They include, inter alia:[99]

- The 2007 Estonia incident (albeit on a small scale, but as later sections will explore, most notable for the threat actor in question and its effect on military and government operation).
- The 2010 Stuxnet incident in which malware was reportedly intentionally inserted into computers at Iranian nuclear facilities to disrupt the uranium enrichment process.[100]
- The 2012 Shamoon data deletion attacks on over 30,000 computers belonging to Saudi Arabia's state-owned oil company Saudi Aramco.[101]
- The 2015 attacks on power grids in Ukraine, which reportedly left more than 230,000 residents without power.[102]
- The 2017 attempts that reportedly disrupted North Korean nuclear program elements (alleged but unverified).[103]
- The 2021 broad-based attacks on Albania, over which it severed diplomatic ties with Iran.[104]
- The 2022 Russian attacks on Ukrainian power, broadband, broadcast systems.[105]

Also notable are the events that might have met these criteria had they achieved their desired effect, but for a variety of reasons, failed to do so. Thus, they fail to satisfy the third prong of national security effect. Such potentially significant but failed cyberattacks include:

---

[99] When assessing against datasets like Council on Foreign Relation's (CFR), all of the incidents noted in the example would fall under sabotage, data deletion, or denial of service, but not—as the next section will illuminate—defacement, doxing, or espionage.
[100] Zetter, *Countdown to Zero Day*.
[101] Nicole Perlroth, "In Cyberattack on Saudi Firm, U.S. Sees Iran Firing Back," *New York Times*, October 23, 2012.
[102] Michael J. Assante, "Confirmation of a Coordinated Attack on the Ukrainian Power Grid" (Rockville, MD: SANS Institute, 2016); Zetter, "Inside the Cunning, Unprecedented Hack of Ukraine's Power Grid"; SANS Institute, "Analysis of the Cyber Attack on the Ukrainian Power Grid" (Rockville, MD: SANS Institute & Electricity Information Sharing & Analysis Center (E-ISAC), 2016).
[103] David Sanger and William Broad, "Trump Inherits a Secret Cyberwar Against North Korean Missiles," *New York Times*, March 4, 2017.
[104] Tom Starks, "Albania is the First Known Country to Sever Diplomatic Ties Over a Cyberattack," *The Cybersecurity 202*, September 8, 2022.
[105] Microsoft Digital Security Unit, "An Overview of Russia's Cyberattack Activity in Ukraine" (Redmond, WA: Microsoft Corporation, 2022).

- The 2009 Fourth of July and 2011 Ten Days of Rain denial-of-service incidents against US and South Korean targets, presumed to be North Korean in origin—but unsuccessful in bringing about major disruption of government or media functions.[106]
- Iran's 2012–2013 attacks on retail banking, later the subject of US indictments.[107]
- The 2017 WannaCry ransomware attacks in multiple countries, including the UK National Health System, attributed to North Korea and resulting in a US indictment.[108]

Other Cybersecurity Incidents

Not all cybersecurity incidents are cyberattacks, and such distinctions become particularly critical as we examine a question like restraint, where different forces may operate differently or not at all depending on the action's precise objective or tactic employed.[109] While vital subjects for study, and indeed of most immediate concern for policymakers, these other cybersecurity incidents are not the subject of this study, including:

Exploitation. As described previously in this chapter, actions taken with the principal purpose of gathering intelligence on an adversary, its capabilities, or the means to exploit its networks, are acts of espionage, not attack. True espionage (instead of reconnaissance) falls in a distinct category within international security notable for its lack of formal regulation, which later sections will address more fully. While certain bilateral or multilateral dynamics have developed between allies and adversaries pertaining to its collection, these rarely take the form of other international security agreements such as treaties.[110] Even states have developed their own vocabularies distinct

---

[106] Matthew Shaer, "North Korean Hackers Blamed for Sweeping Cyber Attack on US Networks," *Christian Science Monitor*, July 8, 2009.

[107] US Attorney's Office (Southern District of New York), "Manhattan U.S. Attorney Announces Charges Against Seven Iranians For Conducting Coordinated Campaign Of Cyber Attacks Against U.S. Financial Sector On Behalf Of Islamic Revolutionary Guard Corps-Sponsored Entities" (Washington, DC: Department of Justice, 2016).

[108] *United States of America v. Park Jin Hyok (Criminal Complaint)*, Washington, DC, 2018; Ellen Nakashima, "The NSA Has Linked the WannaCry Computer Worm to North Korea," *Washington Post*, June 14, 2017; "South Korea Blames North for Bank and TV Cyber-Attacks."

[109] Ben Buchanan, *The Cybersecurity Dilemma: Hacking, Trust, and Fear Between Nations* (Oxford: Oxford University Press, 2016), 102.

[110] For a rare, formalized example, see US Office of the Director of National Intelligence, "Five Eyes Intelligence Oversight and Review Council (FIORC)." (The Five Eyes partnership is an intelligence alliance between the United States, the United Kingdom, New Zealand, Canada, and Australia.)

to the practice of intelligence on when such actions are acknowledged or otherwise. This is not to say that the capabilities that digital systems provide to the practice of espionage are insignificant; in fact, some policy officials have opined that the volume of espionage—made possible by low human risk and remote operations—have shifted the dynamic to permit states to act, possibly forcefully, in self-defense.[111] Such an assertion is best regarded as a political statement (intended to influence, in this case, Chinese behavior) than an assertion of legal analysis; nonetheless, it suggests that the lines dividing certain types of cybersecurity incidents are more easily drawn in the abstract, with perfect information about an aggressor's intentions and tactics, than in reality. Buchanan best elucidates this point, noting that the classical "security dilemma" in international relations—that one state's actions taken in defense may well be indistinguishable, and thus misperceived, by an adversary as preparations to coerce—is even more acute in many cybersecurity incidents.[112] Thus while this study generally excludes acts of espionage and reconnaissance in its definition of cyberattack, the fact that states suffer from imperfect information in their assessments of cybersecurity incidents may well lead to the perception that one constitutes the other, prompting action.

Influence Operations. Fifteen years ago, one could have dispensed with political influence operations as excluded from this analysis in a single line; after the 2016 US election and the UK's Brexit vote, however, a few further words are necessary. Prior to those events, the notion of internet content-based political influence as a means for coercion was not unknown. As later sections will explore in-depth, Russian, Chinese, and Cuban efforts to establish sovereign zones of influence over the internet their citizens use created an imperative of regarding so-called destabilizing political content as "information weapons."[113] These positions have origins that predate the internet

[111] Armed Services Committee, *Cyber Deterrence Statement by Dr. Craig Fields Chairman, Defense Science Board and Dr. Jim Miller Member, Defense Science Board Former Under Secretary of Defense (Policy) before the Armed Services Committee, United States Senate*, March 2, 2017: "Third, a range of state and non-state actors have the capacity for persistent cyber attacks and costly cyber intrusions against the United States, which individually may be inconsequential (or be only one element of a broader campaign) but which cumulatively subject the Nation to a 'death by 1,000 hacks.'" See also Joseph Marks, "That Muscular Response Strategy May Sow Confusion and Risk Escalation," *NextGov*, September 5, 2018: "In an address at George Washington University, Homeland Security Secretary Kirstjen Nielsen stated 'By the time a country is attacking civilian networks, civilian assets . . . it's not a fair fight,' Nielsen said when asked about U.S. efforts to deter adversary nations' cyber meddling. 'That's not how the international world has created norms and standards and I don't think [our response] should be commensurate, I think it should be more.'"
[112] Buchanan, *Cybersecurity Dilemma*.
[113] Sean Kanuck, "Sovereign Discourse on Cyber Conflict under International Law Symposium: Law at the Intersection of National Security, Privacy, and Technology: II. Cybersecurity and Network Operations," *Texas Law Review*, no. 7 (2009): 1574.

itself; Cuba, for instance, has routinely sought to classify US transmissions of from its government-funded Spanish-language radio network, Radio Martí, as a form of illegal aggression or, at a minimum, violation of sovereignty.[114] Unsurprisingly, such views were assiduously rebuffed by the United States and its allies, who, in multilateral fora, have consistently excised content-based issues from the definition of international cybersecurity matters of concern.[115] In short, prior to 2016, this was an existent but unremarkable dividing line in the global cybersecurity and internet regulation debate.[116]

Russian interference in the 2016 US election, however, again illustrates the chasm between elegant abstract distinctions and the on-the-ground realities for nations facing novel digital threats.[117] Some of the most notable and potentially influential aspects of Russia's election interference bore no hallmarks of "cybersecurity" incidents at all. Those actions leveraged memes, not man-in-the-middle attacks; they achieved virality without even using a virus. They were, ironically, the precise sorts of "information attacks" that Russia obliquely urged the members of various organizations to fret about in years prior.[118] Of course, some Russian activities did cross into the territory

---

[114] See, e.g., emblematic statements of the Cuban Permanent Representative to the United Nations: "Cuba is again obliged to denounce before this forum the radio and television aggression that the U.S. Government continues to wage against our country. This radio-electric aggression openly infringes the principles of International Law that regulate the relations between States . . . These illegal radio and television broadcasts seek to promote the Cuban people's unease with and questioning of its Revolution, contempt of the country's constitutional order, confrontation of its authorities, and illegal emigration putting their lives at risk—through false statements, distorted information and misleading propaganda." UN 29th Session, *Statement by H.E. Mr. Rodrigo Malmierca Díaz, Permanent Representative of Cuba to the United Nations*, May 1, 2007. Howard H. Frederick, "Cuban-American Radio Wars: Ideology in International Telecommunications," *Foreign Affairs* 15, no 2 (1986).

[115] Kanuck, "Sovereign Discourse on Cyber Conflict under International Law Symposium," 1574.

[116] See, e.g., Internet Governance Forum, "Chair's Summary, Connecting Continents for Enhanced Multistakeholder Internet Governance" (Paris, IGF, 2014). *Cf.* Internet Governance Forum, "WS #304 Responsible Behaviour in Cyberspace" (paper presented at the Internet Governance Forum, Paris, 2018). Noting a shift in focus to expressly examine how "the growing use of ICT by State and non-State actors for malicious purposes—threatening not only peace and security but also the entire digital society and economy—is of significant concern to the international community. Promoting the responsible behaviour of all actors is key to ensuring a peaceful, secure and stable cyberspace. To date, most efforts have focused predominantly on identifying norms of responsible State behaviour (for instance, the work of the UN General Assembly First Committee's Groups of Governmental Experts").

[117] See, e.g., David E. Sanger and Catie Edmondson, "Russia Targeted Election Systems in All 50 States, Report Finds," New York Times, July 25, 2019; US Office of the Director of National Intelligence, "Background to 'Assessing Russian Activities and Intentions in Recent US Elections': The Analytic Process and Cyber Incident Attribution" (Washington, DC, 2017); Robert S. Mueller III, *Report on the Investigation into Russian Interference in the 2016 Presidential Election* (Washington, DC: Department of Justice, 2019); Report of the Select Committee on Intelligence, the U.S. Senate on Russian Active Measures Campaigns and Interference in the 2016 Election (Washington, DC: Government Printing Office, 2019).

[118] Kanuck, "Sovereign Discourse on Cyber Conflict under International Law Symposium," 1575.

of cybersecurity incident—using social engineering and other techniques to "dox" senior Clinton campaign officials, releasing their emails in an attempt to embarrass and damage them politically.[119] On their face, however, none of these incidents crossed the line of attacking a nation's critical information infrastructure—nor, presumably, did the United States' reported November 2018 targeted actions jamming servers of Russian-linked forces.[120] Later sections will evaluate how the US federal government's 2017 amendments deeming election systems as "critical infrastructure" in 2017 may influence the terms of debate over events of this sort, but as an edge case to test the reach of that mechanisms of restraint.

Is This the Right Distinction?

There are legitimate objections to the value of drawing these sorts of distinctions—particularly if they result in excluding significant events in recent history from analysis. One, as noted, is that an analyst's ability to draw them in retrospect greatly exceeds a country's ability to perceive them in the moment, creating a potential division between the ideal conditions of scholarly analysis and the practical actions of states. This critique is, however, not unique to cybersecurity or even international security issues; indeed, they are on some level endemic to any policy-adjacent social science. This study seeks to correct for this issue in two ways; first, through the careful selection of the best-documented case studies and fact patterns that provide the strongest insights into states' past and thus potential future actions. Second, it aims to give careful consideration to edge cases, at times hypothetical, that blur these lines in the way that future as yet unobserved cyberattacks may as well.

---

[119] For an authoritative review of Russian tactics and techniques, see *Report on the Investigation into Russian Interference in the 2016 Presidential Election*, 4. The most famous Russian doxing effort was against Campaign Chairman John Podesta: "In March 2016, the GRU began hacking the email accounts of Clinton Campaign volunteers and employees, including Campaign Chairman John Podesta. In April 2016, the GRU hacked into the computer networks of the Democratic Congressional Campaign Committee (DCCC) and the Democratic National Committee (DNC). The GRU stole hundreds of thousands of documents from the compromised email accounts and networks. Around the time that the DNC announced in mid-June 2016 the Russian government's role in hacking its network, the GRU began disseminating stolen materials through the fictitious online personas DCLeaks and Guccifer 2.0. The GRU later released additional materials through the organization WikiLeaks."

[120] Dustin Volz, "White House Expands Use of Cyber Weapons but Stays Secretive on Policies," *Wall Street Journal*, December 30, 2019.

Another critique, perhaps more significant, is that many notable cybersecurity incidents of the last fifteen years elude such neat distinctions. Most would rightly consider Russian election interference as having "significant national security effect," perhaps given the changes in US–Russia relations in the years that followed, and even tectonic significance to international security. In drawing these distinctions, the goal here is not to suggest these incidents are unimportant. Rather, it is to recognize that seeking restraint from these sorts of actions almost certainly invoke an entirely different set of forces and institutions—with far less by way of legal and institutional development than restrictions on the recourse to and conduct of war. In this respect, this study seeks not to contribute, in the cyber field, the critique Kiras levels at irregular warfare studies, that "authors are inclined to lump everything together under a concept to the point where a term describes everything and explains nothing."[121] To meaningfully understand their restraint, a definition of cyberattacks cannot be so ecumenical.

1.4 Assumptions and Present Realities

It is also time to reconsider the core assumptions that animated early international cyber policy. In the early days of scholarship on the topic, some governments and commentators sought to establish certain baselines for the development of cyber doctrine and analysis. As this section will outline, the march of technology and state practice has indeed passed some very important assumptions by, and in turn, demand rethinking some of the core assumptions about how states might operate in the midst of cyberattack capabilities.

States, Not Terrorists

The first, easiest to debunk myth of the early cyber era was the waning relevance of nation-states in international cybersecurity. The disintermediating influence of the internet may have been the case for news and information, it has in very few senses of the word been truly *democratizing*—least of all

---

[121] James Kiras, "Irregular Warfare," in *Understanding Modern Warfare*, ed. David Jordan (Cambridge: Cambridge University Press, 2008), 229.

for nonstate actors seeking to challenge state counterparts. Early literature in this space speculated otherwise; the last fifteen years have proven those fears largely overblown.

The principal nonstate actors in international security this century—organized terrorist groups such as Al-Qaida, Al-Shabaab, and ISIS/ISIL—reportedly aspired to cyberattack capabilities, but never amassed them.[122] To be clear, links were drawn between terrorist and cybersecurity risks by numerous senior officials in the US government post-9/11.[123] Those fears were never borne out in publicly available evidence, confirmed by the mostly empty record of so-called cyber-terrorism.[124] It is notable, appropriate, and telling that at least the "cyber-terrorism" neologism has largely fallen from the lexicon and the field of primary study.[125] The recognition that terrorist use of the internet and recruitment represents significant but distinct threats from cyberattacks has also gained general consensus, even if the US drone strike on ISIL hacking led by Junaid Hussain was a first-of-its-kind operation against an enemy combatant for his digital (propagandizing) skills.[126]

Analysts once predicted that the absence of a state monopoly on cyberattack tools, in contrast to nuclear weapons, for example, has the potential to upend the security paradigm.[127] The reality has been decidedly less

---

[122] See, e.g., Richard A. Clarke, "Vulnerability—What are Al Qaeda's Capabilities?," *Frontline*, March 18, 2003: "Some day we may see Al Qaeda, if it's still alive and operating, use cyberspace as a vehicle for attacking infrastructure, not with bombs but with bytes."

[123] "Wyden Questions DNI Director Blair About Cyber Terrorism Threats," in *Senate Intelligence Committee Hearing* (2009); John M. McConnell, "The Cyber War Threat Has Been Grossly Exaggerated" (paper presented at the Intelligence Squared Debate, June 8, 2010). (McConnell argued squarely in the negative at this public debate, in part based on the cyber-terror threats.)

[124] Such claims, when made by officials or those to whom they listened, may have served a more instrumental role: bridging the funding gap between readily available counterterrorism funding and the comparatively paltry sums available at that time for a future risk those officials saw as growing and underresourced. As additional documentary evidence of early budget lines for cybersecurity activities are stood up, scholars may be able to prove this or other anomalies in the record, or simply conclude that those officials were slightly overbroad in their concerns.

[125] Amidst works that overemphasized the terrorist threat, Lewis's 2002 review provided an early counterpoint, which would presage a decade's worth of subsequent work to maintain this definitional accuracy and commitment to disaggregating and contextualizing threats. See James A. Lewis, *Assessing the Risks of Cyber Terrorism, Cyber War and Other Cyber Threats* (Washington, DC: Center for Strategic and International Studies, 2002).

[126] Kimiko de Freytas-Tamura, "Junaid Hussain, ISIS Recruiter, Reported Killed in Airstrike," *New York Times*, August 27, 2015.

[127] Laurie R. Blank, "International Law and Cyber Threats from Non-State Actors," *International Law Studies* 89 (2013): 416–17 (discussing how cyber threats or attacks by nonstate actors "poses perhaps unique challenges because of the ability to dissemble and present an attack as coming from one or more different States or locations, or simply because an attack passes through or can be traced back to multiple—even over a hundred—States. For this reason, the victim State must tread carefully and seek as much clarity regarding the source of the attack as possible to avoid launching a self-defense response in the wrong direction. This challenge is particularly acute with regard to responding to attacks by non-State actors unaffiliated with a State because there may well be fewer accountability

revolutionary. Hackers-for-hire and organized criminal actors have played some role in the evolving security dynamic, but due in part to changes in attribution described below, their role has not been seen as significant as many imagined. The case of Estonia may have been partly responsible for scholarship's overindexing for this concern. There, the patriotic hackers responsible for the denial-of-service attacks were seeming instrumentalities of Russian foreign policy objectives, but not necessarily under the kind of explicit direction now widely acknowledged as the case. This novel (though hardly unprecedented) employment of shadowy nonstate actors to pursue state aims via cyberattack seemed neoteric, and as long as attribution remained elusive, paradigmatic. Yet more recent significant cyber incidents have tended to reflect states either acting directly and with concern (Stuxnet, Shamoon, Ukraine), or through thinly veiled cutouts purporting to be nonstate actors for (im)plausible deniability (North Korea's use of the "Guardians of Peace" in the Sony hack, for instance, or Russian military intelligence's use of "Guccifer 2.0" and "DCLeaks" in their 2016 US election interference).[128]

Companies as Supporting Cast

The most interesting, novel, and potentially significant nonstate actors in this space may in fact be companies, who routinely feature into cyber scenarios as important supporting castmembers. While the topic merits a separate study, it is worth noting that private companies are playing at least four roles in state-on-state cyber operations of interest, at least three of them reasonably novel.

Most typical are companies as "providers of materiel," in essence, the defense contractors and arms dealers of modern cyber operations. Rather than fighter jets or missile systems, a new breed of contractors are providing some of the "zero-day exploits"—previously unknown vulnerabilities in code that can be exploited to cause software to malfunction—as well as actual attack tools upon which programs can be built. The notoriety of these players lies

---

trails to follow or venues for attributing responsibility"). See also James Jay Carafano, "Fighting on the Cyber Battlefield: Weak States and Nonstate Actors Pose Threats," *Washington Examiner,* November 8, 2013.

[128] David Sanger, Jim Rutenberg, and Eric Lipton, "Tracing Guccifer 2.0's Many Tentacles in the 2016 Election," *New York Times,* July 15, 2018.

not in their sale to nonstate groups, but in their help to states with low or middling capabilities in developing more sophisticated cyber programs, usually for espionage (or, with identical tools, domestic surveillance).[129] Some states have even sought to curtail the proliferation of these tools by sanctioning brokers or adding particular tools to export control or munitions lists—however these efforts have been patchwork, and at times, abortive.[130]

Second and more novel is the role that private companies play as defenders of government systems. Part of this condition is evolutionary; as owners and operators of most shared information infrastructure, companies have always been on the front lines of threats to those systems, and as such, shared commercial imperative in their protection. Some cybersecurity firms, however, have both visibility into and ability to act on threats to government networks that governments themselves do not. Takedowns of significant botnets, for instance, as well as defensive measures against malware used by state-based offensive cyber actors, have both been made possible because private security firms like Palo Alto Networks, CrowdStrike, Fortinet, and Google were able to serve as a form of early warning, detection, intervention, and even inoculation against attack.[131] The integration of companies in the defense sector is not new, of course. President Dwight Eisenhower observed with alarm the political significance of this growing "political-military complex," and far more recently, American commentators have sounded warnings about Chinese concepts of "civil-military fusion," indicating a subsuming of

---

[129] Ronen Bergman and Mark Mazzetti, "The Battle for the World's Most Powerful Cyberweapon," *New York Times Magazine*, January 28, 2022; Paul Mozur, Jonah M. Kessel, and Melissa Chan, "Made in China, Exported to the World: The Surveillance State," *New York Times*, April 24, 2019.

[130] Tom Cross, "New Changes to Wassenaar Arrangement Export Controls Will Benefit Cybersecurity," *Forbes*, January 16, 2018; The White House, Executive Order 13694. (EO 13694 "authorize[s] the imposition of sanctions on individuals and entities determined to be responsible for or complicit in malicious cyber-enabled activities that result in enumerated harms that are reasonably likely to result in, or have materially contributed to, a significant threat to the national security, foreign policy, or economic health or financial stability of the United States." The White House, Executive Order 13757, 2015: "amends EO 13694. E.O. 13757 focuses on specific harms caused by significant malicious cyber-enabled activities, and directs the Secretary of the Treasury, in consultation with the Attorney General and the Secretary of State, to impose sanctions on those persons he determines to be responsible for or complicit in activities leading to such harms." "Wassenaar Arrangement on Export Controls for Conventional Arms and Dual-Use Goods and Technologies," (The Hague: December 19, 1995).

[131] On industry-led takedowns of botnets—an important tool in various cyber operations—see Kim Zetter, "Microsoft Seizes ZeuS Servers in Anti-Botnet Rampage," *Wired*, March 26, 2012. On private-sector warnings to governments of various state-based attempts at intrusions, see, e.g., Swapnil Patil, "Government Sector in Central Asia Targeted With New HAWKBALL Backdoor Delivered via Microsoft Office Vulnerabilities," *Trellix Insights*, June 6, 2019; Matt Bromiley, "Hard Pass: Declining APT34's Invite to Join Their Professional Network," *Mandiant Threat Research*, July 18, 2019.

the purported private sector by military aims.[132] What is novel is that these companies are often positioned to provide *strategic* warning to the government in their *private* capacity. Defense contractors are paid to perform this service; some cybersecurity firms simply find themselves with such a reality.

Third and yet more distinctly, private companies are increasingly finding themselves as the *victims* of disruptive cyber operations planned and executed by nation-states. During the Cold War, any number of third countries played host to horrors of proxy warfare and strategic competition for spheres of influence, but that rivalry rarely played out in attacks on domestic company operations. The Soviet Union may well have had a distaste for press outlets, producers of films portraying Russia in an unflattering light and financial systems that conferred to their rival a certain geostrategic sway, yet neither were direct targets of overt military disruption. It seems outlandish to imagine Soviet paratroopers landing on the roof of the Coca-Cola Company, smashing computers, rummaging through records, and bundling up blackmail on executives to dump days later—yet it could describe, in digital form, North Korea's attacks on Sony Pictures prior to the release of the comedy film *The Interview*.[133] So, too, did Iranian military actors attack on the financial markets not by razing a major stock exchange, but by attacking the web portals that consumers rely on to access their bank balances and services, aimed at shaking stability in the US financial systems.[134] When their ire turned to their neighbors, they unleashed a computer-wiping virus on the oil company Saudi Aramco described in the media as the "worst hack in world history."[135] These are not attacks on defense contractors, nor are they commercially motivated attempts to steal intellectual property—though both have also become endemic to modern geopolitics. Instead, these are significant attempts at international coercion, some potentially rising to the level of cyberattacks as defined here, but with private companies as the targets for disruption. The uptick in these sorts of incidents, combined with the enduring reality that the private sector remains the principal owner and operator of critical information infrastructure, suggests an important and notable

---

[132] Dwight D. Eisenhower, "Farewell Address by President Dwight D. Eisenhower, January 17, 1961" (Washington: National Archives and Records Administration, 1961); Audrey Fritz, "China's Evolving Conception of Civil-Military Collaboration," in China Innovation Policy Series (Washington, DC: Center for Strategic and International Studies, 2019).
[133] Sanger, Perlroth, and Kirkpatrick, "The World Once Laughed at North Korean Cyberpower. No More."
[134] US Attorney's Office (Southern District of New York), "Manhattan U.S. Attorney Announces Charges."
[135] Jose Pagliery, "The Inside Story of the Biggest Hack in History," *CNN*, August 5, 2015.

trend in projecting the future shape of cyberattacks and shaping the case for their restraint.

Fourth and most unprecedented is the extent to which some private-sector actors now play the role of attributors of major cyber incidents—sometimes as part of their regular course of business, and sometimes as matters of circumstance and complex corporate strategy. In the latter category is Google, a company that today provides communications infrastructure (in the form of email) to about 1.2 billion people globally, or 20 percent of the global email market.[136] In 2009–2010 when the company found several security and email services compromised by what it concluded with little doubt to be Chinese intelligence actors, the company was faced with a decision typically reserved for states: stay quiet and possibly invite further attacks, or publicize the incident in an attempt to deter and suffer whatever diplomatic consequences may come as a result.[137] In choosing the latter, perhaps made easier by the company's lack of official operation in the People's Republic of China, it resigned itself to that status quo for the foreseeable future.[138] Then-Secretary of State Hillary Clinton's decision to weigh in on the matter came only after Google's public announcement.[139] This episode was a microcosm of what would play out time and again, under slightly varying circumstances, to companies around the world.[140] For most, the question revolves around reporting to national law enforcement or publicly shaming the perpetrator country for network intrusions. In more disruptive or business-destructive cases, fiduciary duties to inform investors and the public markets may play a significant factor—particularly where securities regulations mandate a certain level of

---

[136] Google, "1.5 Billion Users and Counting. Thank You," @Gmail, Twitter, October 26, 2018.

[137] Kim Zetter, "Google Hack Attack Was Ultra Sophisticated, New Details Show," *Wired*, January 14, 2010. Google to Google Official Blog, January 12, 2010. Andrew Jacobs and Miguel Helft, "Google, Citing Attack, Threatens to Exit China," *New York Times*, January 12, 2010.

[138] It would be eight years until Google was revealed to be planning an internally controversial attempt at re-entering the Chinese market. For more on this controversy, see Ryan Gallagher, "Google China Prototype Links Searches to Phone Numbers," *The Intercept*, September 14, 2018; Natasha Tiku, "A Top Google Exec Pushed the Company to Commit to Human Rights. Then Google Pushed Him Out, He Says," *Washington Post*, January 2, 2020.

[139] Alexander Burns, "Clinton Weighs in on Google-China Clash," *Politico*, January 14, 2010.

[140] "Designed to wipe data, Shamoon destroyed more than 35,000 workstations on the network of Saudi Aramco, Saudi Arabia's national oil company, bringing the company to its knees for weeks. It was reported at the time that Saudi Aramco purchased most of the hard drives in the world in its effort to replace its destroyed PC fleet, driving HDD prices up for months after, while vendors struggled to keep up with demand." Andy Greenberg, "The Untold Story of NotPetya, the Most Devastating Cyberattack in History," *Wired*, August 22, 2018; Zetter, "Google Hack Attack Was Ultra Sophisticated, New Details Show"; Catalin Cimpanu, "A Decade of Hacking: The Most Notable Cyber-Security Events of the 2010s," *ZDNet*, December 11, 2019.

public reporting of cybersecurity risks and incidents.[141] Of course an unknown number choose to stay silent, meaning those in the public record are likely only a small fraction of the overall affected population.[142]

Within the role of companies as attributors, most notable in the long term may be the role that *cybersecurity* firms themselves play in this ecosystem: as third parties, neither attacker nor agent of national government, but with implications no less significant. Firms take varying approaches to "naming and shaming" state-sponsored cyber activities—which, as Lin convincingly argues, can mean identifying "a machine, a specific perpetrator initiating that activity, [and/or] an adversary that is deemed ultimately responsible" for the activity.[143] Most cybersecurity firms take a middle ground, pointing not to individuals nor responsible governments per se, but rather the common tools, techniques, and practices (TTPs) that they regularly employ in their operations. The naming of certain advanced persistent threats (APTs) follows certain company conventions. The cybersecurity firm CrowdStrike, for instance, chooses to obfuscate only slightly, giving public codenames to state actors' tools such as PANDA for China, BEAR to Russia, KITTENS to Iran, and TIGERS to India.[144] Others, such as Cisco Talos and Dell Secureworks, use common but less evocative nouns.[145] Some do not attribute in the way at all, likely as a means to operate more feely within countries who would bristle

---

[141] See, for example, the US Securities and Exchange Commission's rule on cybersecurity risk disclosure requirements for public companies: "Commission Statement and Guidance on Public Company Cybersecurity Disclosures," in *17 CFR Parts 229 and 249* (Washington, DC: The Securities and Exchange Commission, 2018).

[142] Attempting to quantify this aggregate reported and unreported loss in the United States alone, the White House Council of Economic Advisors put the cost of malicious cyber operations in 2016 at between $57 billion and $109 billion, further noting that "cyberattacks and cyber theft impose externalities that may lead to rational underinvestment in cybersecurity by the private sector relative to the socially optimal level of investment." White House Council of Economic Advisors, "The Cost of Malicious Cyber Activity to the U.S. Economy," 1.

[143] Herbert Lin, "Attribution of Malicious Cyber Incidents : From Soup to Nuts," *Journal of International Affairs* 70, no. 1 (2016). See also Sasha Romanosky and Benjamin Boudreaux, "Private Sector Attribution of Cyber Incidents: Benefits and Risks to the U.S. Government" (Santa Monica, CA: RAND Corporation, 2019). For earlier analysis that helped inform the field's early development, see also David D. Clark and Susan Landau, "Untangling Attribution," in *Proceedings of a Workshop on Deterring Cyberattacks*, ed. Herbert Lin (Washington, DC: National Academies Press, 2010).

[144] Adam Meyers, "Meet The Threat Actors: List of APTs and Adversary Groups," *CrowdStrike Blog*, Februrary 24, 2019.

[145] Danny Adamitis, David Maynor, and Kendall McKay, "It's Alive: Threat Actors Cobble Together Open-Source Pieces Into Monstrous Frankenstein Campaign" (San Jose, CA: Cisco Talos, 2019). (Cisco Talos uses such colorful nouns as Frankenstein, which "refers to the actors' ability to piece together several unrelated components—leveraged four different open-source techniques to build the tools used during the campaign.") Dell SecureWorks, "LYCEUM Takes Center Stage in Middle East Campaign," August 27, 2019. (Dell SecureWorks uses the term "Lyceum" to describe a threat group that target organizations of "strategic national importance.")

at their operational infrastructure being analyzed in the open. The cumulative effect is that states no longer possess three key monopolies: over whether to attribute incidents at all, the granularity of detail provided, and the timing such information is released. This dynamic may be shifting as states ret to reclaim this prerogative, with the United States and United Kingdom actively pursuing agendas of rapid and collective attribution bilaterally, and with broader groups of allies and partners.[146] Regardless, the addition of private sector actors in a range of attribution scenarios will continue to have implications for escalation control and ultimately restraint, as later chapters will explore.

Attribution Is Possible, Yet Delayed and Fallible

Commentators have long noted that whether for defense or the operation of law, attribution can cause challenges—there may be less here than meets the eye.[147] As Kello points out in his approach to a broader category of offensive cyber tools he deems "the virtual weapon," "the greater the sophistication of a cyberattack"—undoubtedly including the sort under discussion here—"the lesser the difficulty of authenticating its source," given the "lengthy planning and enormous resources" involved.[148]

In fact, the recent history of the most significant cyber incidents suggests that for matters of profound national security significance, attribution is, in the context of sophisticated and rudimentary nation-state cyber programs

---

[146] See, inter alia, The White House, "The United States, Joined by Allies and Partners, Attributes Malicious Cyber Activity and Irresponsible State Behavior to the People's Republic of China," news release, Washington, DC: July 19, 2021, https://www.whitehouse.gov/briefing-room/statements-releases/2021/07/19/the-united-states-joined-by-allies-and-partners-attributes-malicious-cyber-activity-and-irresponsible-state-behavior-to-the-peoples-republic-of-china.

[147] On attribution challenges in deterrence, see Thomas Rid and Ben Buchanan, "Attributing Cyber Attacks," *Journal of Strategic Studies* 38, no. 1–2 (2015); Herbert S. Lin, "Attribution of Malicious Cyber Incidents: From Soup to Nuts," *Journal of International Affairs* 70, no. 1 (2016); Jacquelyn Schneider, "Deterrence In and Through Cyberspace," in *Cross-Domain Deterrence*, ed. Jon R. Lindsay and Erik Gartzke (Oxford: Oxford University Press, 2019), 106–08. On attribution challenges in the operation of international law and the use of force, see Scott J Shackelford, "From Nuclear War to Net War: Analogizing Cyber Attacks in International Law," *Berkeley Journal of International Law* 27 (2009); James D. Morrow, "International Law and the Common Knowledge Requirements of Cross-Domain Deterrence," in *Cross-Domain Deterrence: Strategy in an Era of Complexity* (New York: Oxford University Press, 2019), 191–201; Henning Lahmann, *Unilateral Remedies to Cyber Operations: Self-Defence, Countermeasures, Necessity, and the Question of Attribution* (Cambridge: Cambridge University Press, 2020), 65–107.

[148] Lucas Kello, *The Virtual Weapon and International Order* (New Haven, CT: Yale University Press, 2017), 5.

alike, surprisingly possible. This is the third myth to explode: that despite the warnings of last decade, the partially anonymizing features of the internet have not stopped wholesale the attribution of incidents—least of all significant ones.[149]

Rather, the combination over the last twenty or so years of increased investment by key states in surveilling potential threat actors, the far more open environment of public discussion of cybersecurity incidents, and the presence of both nonstate victims and attributors all create an environment in which many significant incidents are quickly attributed, at least (as Rid and Buchanan aptly note) to a level of confidence sufficient to the political imperative.[150] This question of "adequacy" in attribution objectivity has prompted several proposals to "adjudicate" attribution—three focused on a kind of court, as proposed in 2012 by Jason Healey, then at the Atlantic Council; Charney et al. in 2016, then at Microsoft; and a group of MIT scholars in 2019 focused on uniting technical research firms for a similar purpose.[151] The significance of these proposals is their starting premise: that technical attribution to levels of adequate certainty for decision-making in international security is indeed possible. It is rather politics, and the potential for it to cloud the veracity of those pronouncements, that complicates their utility.

In the international relations of cyberattacks, it is easy to overstate the significance of urgency. While in-the-moment attribution may create its own challenges of accuracy and objectivity, the circumstances of several significant cyber events to date have afforded the victim some time for assembly of evidence, review, and third-party confirmation of state's assignments of responsibility, to significant geopolitical effect. To use just one example, some cybersecurity researchers initially questioned the United States' attribution of North Korea in the Sony attacks, skeptical of the country's capacity for such

---

[149] See, e.g., Kim Zetter, "Experts Are Still Divided on Whether North Korea Is Behind Sony Attack," *Wired*, December 23, 2014; Pauline C. Reich and Eduardo Gelbstein, *Law, Policy, and Technology: Cyberterrorism, Information Warfare, and Internet Immobilization* (Hershey, PA: IGI Global, 2012) (explaining that according to Professor Martin Libicki at RAND Graduate School, the "problem of attribution made it impossible for NATO to undertake a response on behalf of Estonia").
[150] Rid and Buchanan, "Attributing Cyber Attacks."
[151] Jason Healey et al., "Confidence-Building Measures in Cyberspace: A Multistakeholder Approach for Stability and Security" (Washington, DC: Atlantic Council, Brent Scowcroft Center on International Security, 2014); Scott Charney, Erin English, Aaron Kleiner, Nemanja Malisevic, Angela McKay, Jan Neutze, and Paul Nicholas, "From Articulation to Implementation: Enabling Progress on Cybersecurity Norms" (Redmond, WA: Microsoft Corporation, 2016); Adelaide Oh, Daria Osipova, Ryan Ramseyer, and Nick Stathas, "The Roles of Companies in Cybersecurity: A Case for Private Sector Involvement in Cyberspace Governance," Department of Electrical Engineering & Computer Science (Cambridge, MA: MIT, 2019).

DEFINING AND STUDYING CYBERATTACKS 49

a sophisticated operation and unconvinced by the meager evidence publicly available.[152] As time progressed, however, a novel dance of cross-verification took place between US authorities, namely the FBI, and the cybersecurity research community, ultimately yielding far more public evidence (including a public indictment) and general consensus that the reclusive country was indeed behind an attack previously seen as beyond its means.[153]

The most interesting cases of advanced cyberattack capabilities have states seeking not to hide behind nonstate cutouts but borrowing widely available tell-tales of other governments' programs and sprinkling them throughout the code used in cyber operations. The reputedly Russian malware responsible for disrupting the opening ceremonies of the 2018 Winter Olympics in Pyongchang, South Korea, for example, reportedly contained as many as five other states' signatures in order to fool malware researchers.[154] Most remarkable about Russia's efforts to throw researchers off the scent is that those efforts were largely unsuccessful. Even in this complex case, attribution satisfying some of the needs of foreign policy decision-making was achieved, eventually.

As later sections will explore, the ability to conduct even imperfect attribution or delayed attribution can have significant implications for restraint of cyberattacks. Most importantly, it means that the most relevant actors in the space are ones that have historically been subject to several logics of restraint: deterrence, positive international law, and more explicitly, normative prohibitions. States have better-developed patterns of habituation of cause and effect, as well as better-developed vocabularies for communicating consequences, leaving greater potential for negotiated restraint than might otherwise have been possible. It provides a set of potentially uniform approaches to evaluate the potential efficacy of those logics which, for instance, carry a far different calculus for organized criminal actors or terrorist groups. Finally, it imposes some interesting complications specific to state decision-making, as the time requirements of doing so may well shape the character of not just *what* manner of restraint may operate, but also *when* it is likely to do so.

---

[152] Zetter, "Experts Are Still Divided on Whether North Korea Is Behind Sony Attack."
[153] US Department of Justice, "North Korean Regime-Backed Programmer Charged With Conspiracy to Conduct Multiple Cyber Attacks and Intrusions," news release, September 6, 2018; Sanger, Perlroth, and Kirkpatrick, "The World Once Laughed at North Korean Cyberpower."
[154] Andy Greenberg, "Inside Olympic Destroyer: The Most Deceptive Hack in History," *Wired*, October 17, 2019.

An Important corollary to this new paradigm of attribution is that the pace of decision-making in this space turns out to be at human, not light speed. For nearly a decade, one of the most repeated assumptions of emerging international cybersecurity was that because network signals travelled at light speed, there could be no time for meaningful deliberation. In this view, largely espoused by military operators in the burgeoning US cyber-defense apparatus, decisions needed to be preprogrammed and delegated; responses needed to occur "at network speed."[155] Some of the nation's highest-ranking officials gave testimony, sought changes to legislation, stood up new billion-dollar programs, and decried legal and policy impediments to the ability to respond to the sorts of incursions they were witnessing on government networks.[156] Over time, as incidents posing the very questions that began this book mounted, two factors appear to crystallized in the minds of at least some operators. First, with the relatively poor state of signaling in the space, policy officials concluded that the risks of inadvertent escalation due to automated responses were significant and required greater oversight.[157] Second, when combined with the realities and timeline of technical attribution, that deciding from the range of possible response options available necessarily demanded time—especially when they crossed domains or legal authorities, such as responding with criminal referrals or economic sanctions. While motivations no doubt differed by individual and administration, and complaints about the pace of response never truly subsided, the reality to which US officials appear to have become habituated is that response planning need not be instantaneous.[158] The consequences of this revision are significant; enabling a greater range of responses, the potential for more iterative learning, and deeper legal consideration—but also for attackers to retain some measure of control if the event is accompanied by surprise, and

---

[155] US House Armed Services Committee, Subcommittee on Terrorism, Unconventional Threats, and Capabilities Subcommittee, *Statement for the Record by Lieutenant General Keith Alexander Commander Joint Functional Component Command for Network Warfare*, May 5, 2009; US House of Representatives, Committee on Armed Services, Subcommittee on Intelligence, Emerging Threats and Capabilities, *Information Technology and Cyber Operations: Modernization and Policy Issues to Support the Future Force*, March 14, 2013, 9, 14.

[156] Jason Bamford, "NSA Snooping Was Only the Beginning. Meet the Spy Chief Leading Us Into Cyberwar," *Wired*, June 12, 2013.

[157] Nearly every US diplomatic effort in this space has featured some attention to confidence-building measures that would reduce this risk of an incident spiraling out of control; the fifteen-year progression of the UN Groups of Governmental Experts being an illustrative example. See Chapter 5, note 18.

[158] Dustin Volz, "Trump, Seeking to Relax Rules on U.S. Cyberattacks, Reverses Obama Directive," *Wall Street Journal*, August 15, 2018.

for responses to be misunderstood if the state "time and place of [a state's] choosing" is not properly communicated to the other side.[159]

Independent Cyberwar Is Elusive

The last assumption needing correction may well be the one most responsible for public attention to the topic of cybersecurity: the beguiling but ultimately misguided concept of cyberwar. As compelling as the phrase is in drawing attention, it is, for a study like this, conceptually fraught, problematically imprecise, and at worst, misleading. The cyberwar idea is built upon one of two premises: either that a new form of warfare has emerged among great powers in the form of more aggressive espionage and with the potential for sabotage; or that future conflicts will be primarily waged in cyberspace by cyber means. Uniting both is the concept that cyberwar is distinct from physical (also known as "kinetic") conflict.

The record of cyber operations has not borne these assertions out. Certainly, the capacity for lower-risk intelligence activities do create novel national security challenges, but no states have yet declared those activities predicate for or justification of armed conflict—rather, trade sanctions and indictments have emerged as the preferred means of punishing and potentially deterring those activities. The notion of tit-for-tat, "cyber-on-cyber" may someday obtain, but it has not to date. As later chapters will explore, most unstable state dyads of the last fifteen years have featured clear military asymmetries (US–North Korea, US–Iran, Russia–Georgia, Israel–Syria, etc.), creating a higher premium on cyberattacks for one party, but a far less significant value on them for the other. Add to that the reality that cyber capabilities have been integrated into many militaries, feature significantly into their military exercises, and have been used to accompany incursions, and it becomes clear that the motivations to use of cyberattacks *in and around the context of war* is perhaps more significant than their use *distinct from war*.[160] As Chapter 5 will expand upon, the fact that cyberattacks so-defined almost certainly invoke the legal frameworks governing recourse to force and just conduct in war mean that even if a state were seeking to create a condition

---

[159] President Barack Obama, "Statement by the President on Actions in Response to Russian Malicious Cyber Activity and Harassment," December 29, 2016.
[160] See, e.g., US Department of Defense, "DOD Announces Start of Exercise Ulchi Freedom Guardian," 2017.

of cyberwar distinct from armed conflict itself, it should be met with significant practical and conceptual resistance. Thus, rejecting this distinct notion of cyberwar, as Rid has convincingly argued, leads to a more fruitful consideration of how states reconsider this otherwise attractive means of coercion.[161] Recognizing that there are indeed novel dynamics that cyberattacks' technical nature and record present, the fact that they exist within, and not distinct from, the laws and norms governing interstate conflict provides a solid basis for considering the practical effect these rules will have on their cyberattack decisions.

The record of cybersecurity incidents since 2007 provides some clear assumptions, grounded in reality, that motivate the chapters that follow: (1) that states remain the principal cyberattack actors, though companies will complicate their conduct of international relations thereupon; (2) that once-elusive attribution is indeed possible, but perhaps not on convenient timelines; and (3) that cyberattacks are not distinct from war, but potentially inextricable from it going forward. Brief though the record may be, these truths appear to have endured over fifteen years' scrutiny.[162] For these reasons, and their significance to the topic at hand, they will help shape the analysis that follows.

---

[161] Thomas Rid, "Cyber War Will Not Take Place," *Journal of Strategic Studies* 35, no. 1 (2012); Thomas Rid, *Cyber War Will Not Take Place* (London: C Hurst & Co. Publishers, Ltd., 2013).

[162] R. David Edelman, "Cyberattacks in International Relations," D.Phil. diss., University of Oxford, 2009.

2
Defining and Studying Restraint

Clausewitz taught us that conflict "is simply the continuation of policy by other means."[1] Cyberspace operations are a popular means to extend both politics—and, potentially war—by yet new means, and in new theaters. In possession of these new capabilities, countless states have used them as instruments of espionage, and (depending on measures) over a dozen have used them to coerce or sabotage a rival.[2] Achieving stability will require a change in behavior, incentives, or both.

The question motivating the following chapters is whether any of the forces that have traditionally restrained the coercive tendencies of threatened or aggrandizing states can meaningfully apply to their use of cyberattacks—and if not, how to make them operate better. This brief chapter explains *why* restraint is the focus of such a study, and *how* it will go about considering restraint's role in state decision-making and ultimately international politics. As broad as the concept is, it is certainly not the only force shaping contemporary international relations; nor are cyberattacks the only tool borne of computing that merit restraint. But, as the subsequent chapters will continue to argue, it is the most important force we may have to bring about the most important change to the status quo.

---

[1] Carl von Clausewitz, *On War*, trans. Howard Michael and Paret Peter, reprint ed. (Princeton, NJ: Princeton University Press, 2008 [originally published 1832]), 642.

[2] See Council on Foreign Relations, "Cyber Operations Tracker." According to the Council of Foreign Relations' Cyber Operations Tracker timeline, from 2007 to 2019 there were approximately forty-five state-sponsored cyberspace operations involving such acts of data destruction (10), denial of service (17), and sabotage (18), with some overlap in multiple categories. The methodology employed in the cyber operations tracker "categorizes all instances of publicly known state-sponsored cyber activity since 2005. The tracker only contains data in which the perpetrator, also known as the threat actor, is suspected to be affiliated with a nation-state. The tracker focuses on state-sponsored actors because its purpose is to identify when states and their proxies conduct cyber operations in pursuit of their foreign policy interests. Furthermore, state-sponsored incidents generally have the most accurate and comprehensive reporting. Reporting on nonstate actors, such as hacktivist groups, tends to be murkier and makes for less reliable data."

The sections that follow will argue why it is important to focus on restraint; define what is meant here by the concept and its manifestations; explain how abstract notions of restraint shape actual state decision-making; and provide some insights into its operation. The chapter will conclude by connecting this discussion to the oft-cited discourse on "cyber norms," and addressing several important critiques, before previewing the rest of the book's arguments in-depth.

2.1 Framing the Analysis

This book focuses on restraint because its presence—or absence—will determine whether or not cyberattacks will fundamentally disrupt conditions of peace and, perhaps more fundamentally, the status quo of international security. As the short historical record has shown, the capacity to inflict harm via cyberattacks is present and growing. States looking to bring about changes in one another's behavior—through coercion—may well find these tools both available and efficacious. The same holds true of countries trying to slow another's progress toward certain economic or military gains. The combination of availability and efficacy produce attractiveness, which, combined with uncertainty, produces novel opportunities to coerce or sabotage. Absent forces of restraint that make this particular means of coercion unattractive, there is no reason to believe it will not be used, and the more it is effectively used, the greater chance it becomes commonplace.[3]

If cyberattacks become commonplace means of coercion or competition, then the effects would be substantial. Individuals will experience substantial risk to anything that depends on the operations of critical information infrastructure—the cellular networks we use to communicate, the navigation systems that guide us home, the electronic markets that store our retirement savings, and beyond. Nations will experience an uptick in interstate conflict of various forms, as this novel means to coerce provides the opportunity to "relitigate" previously settled disputes and resettle arrangements of power on the basis of cyberattack capabilities. The global system, too, will see the status quo of international security change, with previously peaceful states incented to coerce or sabotage, or previously weak states gaining the means to secure new capacities.

---

[3] Chapter 8 considers this thesis in greater depth.

If there is a force (or series of forces) that reduce the incentive to coerce or sabotage in this manner, to dampen the attractiveness of this tool, or even to limit the real or perceived availability or efficacy thereof, it would prevent fundamental alteration of the security environment. Restraint—with its varying origins—may be that force.

2.2 Concepts and Methodologies

What is meant by "restraint" in the international system, and how does the concept play out in the choices that states make? These two questions are fundamental to the study and by no means unique to cyberattacks. This section provides a grounding in the way previous scholars have, from a range of perspectives, interpreted forces of restraint on state decision-making, and then considers which approaches might be most applicable here.

Defining Restraint

The definition of "restraint" for the purposes of this inquiry are rather simple: restraint is rethinking; declining to take an otherwise advantageous act either due to reconsideration or preemptive rejection of the act. In short, it is bridled ambition, or a declination to act in a particular way despite available opportunities. As a matter of logic, it is the dispositive element in deciding to act. As a matter of state practice, it is the evidence, intuition, or argumentation that leads decision-makers to choose another path in achieving a particular aim—or not even realistically considering it in the first place.

Of course, this is but one way to approach the concept of restraint. Scholars of international security have ably catalogued the conceptions used in evaluating different phenomena. Among the examples, in international security, Reiss explores the concept of restraint through quantity, considering why countries would *constrain* their nuclear capabilities.[4] Rublee looks at the same weapon from the vantage of countries who have held back on

---

[4] Mitchell Reiss, *Bridled Ambition: Why Countries Constrain Their Nuclear Capabilities* (Washington, DC: Woodrow Wilson Center Press, 1995), 5.

their development in the first place such as Japan, Egypt, Libya, Sweden, and Germany.[5] Some works have also tried to develop more general theses of the concept of restraint, such as Adler in the context of the effect of security communities.[6] Brent J. Steele chooses another context—freedom and heteronomy—fixing in part on the idea that "the limitations on our autonomy created by the limited autonomy of others."[7]

In international law, the concept of normative restraint serves to inhibit states from waging war against one another; for instance, the Kellogg-Briand Pact, Nuremberg Judgment, and Charter of the United Nations "formalized the renunciation of non-defensive claims to use force to resolve international disputes with other governments."[8] According to Falk, the "decline in normative restraint can be partly understood as an inevitable outgrowth of these earlier legal efforts to limit use of force to self-defense. The generality of these legal prohibitions left gray areas, especially the failure to delineate boundaries upon the concept of self-defense."[9]

In the literature on international norms, Ikenberry writes that strategic restraint serves as a type of institutionalized assurance to weaker secondary states: "Cooperative order is built around a basic bargain: the hegemonic state obtains commitments from secondary states to participate within the postwar order, and in return the hegemon places limits on the exercise of its power. The weaker states do not fear domination or abandonment—reducing the incentives to balance—and the leading state does not need to use its power assets to enforce order and compliance."[10]

The concept of restraint approached herein is intentionally broad.[11] This ecumenicism is borne out of methodological necessity: it is necessary to

---

[5] Maria Rost Rublee, *Nonproliferation Norms: Why States Choose Nuclear Restraint* (Athens: University of Georgia Press, 2009), 53–200.

[6] Emanuel Adler, "The Spread of Security Communities: Communities of Practice, Self-Restraint, and NATO's Post—Cold War Transformation," *European Journal of International Relations* 14, no. 2 (2008).

[7] Brent J. Steele, *Restraint in International Politics* (Cambridge: Cambridge University Press, 2019), 25. "From knights and courtiers currying favor with the King through the display of self-controlled emotions and manners, through increased power of the state to centralize taxes and monopolize force, such changes led to a transformation in manners for everyday individuals and subjects. The external constraints of the state led to the internalization of self-restraint."

[8] Richard Falk, "The Decline of Normative Restraint in International Relations," *Yale Journal of International Law*, no. 2 (1984): 263.

[9] Ibid.

[10] G. John Ikenberry, "Institutions, Strategic Restraint, and the Persistence of American Postwar Order," *International Security* 23, no. 3 (1998–1999): 45.

[11] Steele argues the value of conceptualizing restraint broadly as a spectrum for it "provides a common situated analytical space for diverse thinkers. Put another way, the spectrum provides a number of productive of avenues for both theoretical and empirical work not only on restraint but other international social phenomena." Steele, *Restraint in International Politics*, 26.

engage with, compare, and critically evaluate three distinct *logics of restraint*—or underlying motivations that animate restraint as a force in state decision-making. Each has, embedded within it, certain understandings about the organization and operation of the international system. All are worthy of engagement—and in this study perhaps for the first time—because what unites their distinct underpinnings is a sense that restraint is possible, only through a range of specific vocabularies. These are the premises tested in the sections that follow, but first, it is worth reviewing these logics of restraint and their distinct theories about why such forces operate.

Logics of Restraint and Their Origins

Whether from a pragmatist's perspective on interstate conduct, a pessimist's view of human nature, or a logician's view of the historical record—in any telling, the threat or reality of interstate conflict is never far. Arguments about the waning of major power war are encouraging, but at a general level, history shows that new technologies have an uncanny way of allowing the vanquished to revisit historical grievances under potentially changed odds. The asymmetries of cyberattacks offer such an opportunity.[12] Other arguments for optimism about the improvements in the human condition have one major blind spot—their gains are fragile if human life and society depend on infrastructure so easily targeted and disrupted for political or strategic gain.[13] If cyberattacks were presently and effectively circumscribed as a means of coercion, there would be no need for a study such as this.

---

[12] See, e.g., John Mueller, *Retreat from Doomsday: The Obsolescence of Major War* (New York: Basic Books, 1989). Of course its conclusions are challenged by others who see Thucydides's trap as inevitable, particularly in the context of Sino–US relations. See, e.g., Graham Allison, *Destined for War: Can America and China Escape Thucydides's Trap?* (New York: Houghton Mifflin Harcourt, 2017), 29. (Allison describing the Thucydides trap as "the severe structural stress caused when a rising power threatens to upend a ruling one. In such conditions, not just extraordinary, unexpected events, but even ordinary flashpoints of foreign affairs, can trigger large-scale conflict.") This structural observation about balancing is complemented by the historical record on new military innovations. For instance, consider Afghanistan's history of anti-aircraft weapons, the Man-portable Air Defense Systems (MANPADS), most notably the American Stinger missile, "which played a decisive role in the US-funded insurgency that ended nine brutal years of Soviet occupation in the 1980s. Prior to the arrival of the Stinger, none of the weapons procured and distributed to the Afghan rebels by their three main benefactors—the United States, Pakistan, and Saudi Arabia—had proven effective against Soviet aircraft, which bombed villages, attacked rebel strongholds, and strafed supply caravans with impunity." Matthew Schroeder, "Stop Panicking About the Stingers," *Foreign Policy*, July 28, 2010.

[13] Steven Pinker, *The Better Angels of Our Nature: Why Violence Has Declined* (New York: Penguin, 2011), 479.

Because they are not, preserving the trajectories Mueller and Pinker describe may well depend on whether the recourse to cyberattacks is, by some force, limited.

The three main parts of this book orient themselves around this notion of restraint, manifested in three distinct forms or "logics": (1) a rationalist logic that manifests itself in deterrence; (2) a regulative logic that manifests itself in positive international law; and (3) a more normative, constitutive logic found in humanitarian protections. To introduce these concepts and their underpinnings, consider the various international relations theories under which the conditions of peace come to pass. Between two competitive states in a resource-scarce environment, peace, and its sibling "stability," could be imposed, regulated, or constructed.

Rationalist: Imposed Peace. Most obviously, when one state's military dramatically outstrips the other such that the latter would invite certain ruin by provoking the former into conflict, this is a form of "imposed" peace. Also, if two states are roughly militarily matched but are aware that triggering military conflict would be locally ruinous, such a peace could also be considered imposed. Both of these are rationalist calculations of gain and loss. As a theory driving international relations, they find their theoretical home in international relations as Morgenthau's *realism* or Waltz's *neorealism*.[14] They accept a zero-sum framing fixed around state acquisition of military (and to some, economic) power: interactions between them are fundamentally defined by competition.[15] In such a telling, the means to achieve peace is through *imposed stability*, a rationalist logic aiming to change the calculus of loss to supersede the expected gain of risking conflict. This *rationalist logic of restraint* animates the concept of "deterrence," the subject of Part I of the study.

Neoliberal: Agreed Peace. In another telling, these two competitive states find conditions of peace due to institutions they have created between them, for instance, a regional security agreement following a long-past conflict or a productive and deep trade relationship. Even if the two states were not

---

[14] Hans J. Morgenthau, *Politics Among Nations: The Struggle for Power and Peace*, 5th ed. (New York: Knopf, 1973); Kenneth N. Waltz, *Theory of International Politics*, Reprint ed. (New York: Waveland, 2010 [first published 1979]).

[15] Realist theorist Robert G. Gilpin regarded state power broadly to include economic power: according to Helen Milner, "for Gilpin, realism meant that the state was the primary actor in world politics and economics, that power and the use of force were the ultimate instruments of statecraft, that war was the major mechanism of change in international affairs." Helen V. Milner, "The Enduring Legacy of Robert Gilpin: How He Predicted Today's Great Power Rivalry" (2018).

bound by such explicit regulation precluding a particular conflict, they may discover that more aggressive means of achieving gain would unwind the international commitments they have made to third parties. Such institutional commitments may even be direct, as when countries are bound to one another's mutual defense by treaty—creating a kind of reflexive prohibition on war-waging with one another. These are regulative strictures mediating state decisions. As a frame through which to view international relations, *neoliberal institutionalists* highlight these sorts of arrangements, which in turn regard state interests and gains as absolute rather than relative, and thus advantageously shaped—and implicitly circumscribed—by the institutions of which it is a part.[16] Put differently, the argument is that states are incentivized to follow international law, not out of a position of fear from sanctions or other coercive measures, but from a desire to adhere to the treaty based on dynamic, multilateral influences.[17] International legal instruments like treaties play an outsize role here, creating the positive obligations and enforcement mechanisms that animate this kind of *regulated stability*. This *regulative logic of restraint* animates much of international law, and in particular, the law governing the recourse to force or *jus ad bellum*—the subject of Part II of this study.

Constructivist: Constructed Peace. Of course, a third approach to achieving peace and stability emerges among two states who simply regard the prospect of conflict with one another as unthinkable or uncivilized. Such a framing could be an endogenous evolution of culture or political mandate, exogenous reflection of a broader political environment that precludes triggering conflict, or more likely, the two combined into something more powerful: a shared identity. At one further level of abstraction, this frame helps explain why, for example, two neighboring countries such as the United States and Canada are not destined for proximate war despite the competitive value in securing extractive rights to the Arctic Circle. It is simply not *conceivable* to either nation's leaders, in today's configuration of international politics, that competition would be permitted to lead to war. In an immediate conception of stability, it also helps explain why otherwise advantageous weaponry is left off the battlefield, even if the prospect of an

---

[16] Joseph S. Nye, "Power and Interdependence," *Survival* 15, no. 4 (1973). See also Robert O. Keohane, *After Hegemony: Cooperation and Discord in the World Political Economy* (Princeton, NJ: Princeton University Press, 1984).

[17] Abram and Antonia Chayes refer to this, in the context of treaty regimes, as a "managerial model" of compliance. Abram Chayes and Antonia Handler Chayes, *The New Sovereignty Compliance with International Regulatory Agreements* (Cambridge, MA: Harvard University Press, 2009).

adversary's in-kind retribution is minimal—the United States' nonuse of robust nuclear earth penetrators, for instance, in the second Gulf War, or poison gas in its wars in Afghanistan.[18] Both these weapons face a certain normative opprobrium—that they are "not usable." Key scholars tracing the phenomena of restraint in nuclear first-use and chemical weapons deem their use a "taboo," varyingly enshrined in positive international law, but invoking a restraining custom with a deeper basis—a phenomenon Part IV will consider in greater depth.[19] In international relations, this approach finds its theoretical home in *constructivist* thinking by the likes of Wendt, Ruggie, Finnemore, and Kratochwil.[20] This is a normative, *constitutive logic of restraint*: that states' identities as "part of a rules-based order" or "humanitarian" give form to other norms that in turn preemptively narrow their option space and shape core decisions that might otherwise be in defiance of rationalist logic and not strictly defined by regulative institutions. As a distinctive source of restraint, in the context of restraints on the conduct of war, it is the subject of Part III of this study.

While the logics motivating them differ, the key behavior states are exhibiting in the maintenance of peace and stability is *restraint*. In fact, the act of restraining what pressures or indictments would otherwise lead them to engage in conflict is the clearest dividing line between peace and the alternative.

Rethinking the current strategic environment, from assumptions and early doctrine through present-day state practice, permits this study to make a unique contribution to the literate: engaging with all three of these logics of restraint under a single cover and doing so both on their own terms and at their intersections. In fact, while much of the literature hews to a single logic for reasons of disciplinarity, it is at those intersections that many of the

---

[18] While the United States did not use chemical weapons in its wars in Afghanistan and ratified the 1925 Geneva Protocol prohibiting the use of chemical weapons in 1975, the Soviet Union, did use chemical weapons in its Afghanistan War. See US Central Intelligence Agency, *Soviet Motivations for the Use of Chemical Weapons in Afghanistan and Southeast Asia: An Intelligence Assessment*, CIA Historical Review Program Released As Sanitized 1999, 1983.

[19] Richard M. Price, *The Chemical Weapons Taboo* (Ithaca, NY: Cornell University Press, 1997); Nina Tannenwald, *The Nuclear Taboo: The United States and the Non-Use of Nuclear Weapons Since 1945* (Cambridge: Cambridge University Press, 2007); Richard Price and Nina Tannenwald, "Norms and Deterrence: The Nuclear and Chemical Weapons Taboos," in *The Culture of National Security*, ed. Peter Katzenstein (New York: Columbia University Press, 1996).

[20] Alexander Wendt, *Social Theory of International Politics* (Cambridge: Cambridge University Press, 1999); John Gerard Ruggie, "What Makes the World Hang Together? Neo-Utilitarianism and the Social Constructivist Challenge," *International Organization* 52, no. 4 (1998); Martha Finnemore, *National Interests in International Society* (Ithaca, NY: Cornell University Press, 1996); Friedrich V. Kratochwil, *Rules, Norms, and Decisions* (Cambridge: Cambridge University Press, 1989).

most interesting and potentially powerful observations about state behavior lie with respect to cyberattacks. The field of international relations offers an opportunity sometimes denied to other fields by engaging with multiple influences on decision-making, which in turn fit beneath varying methodological schema. This book also reframes questions raised within those disciplines with a distinctive pragmatic aim and in a synthetic style that reflects the discipline of international relations broadly. The result is an inquiry that compares and contrasts these three potential logics; interrogates how they might serve as sources of restraint alone and in concert; and probes how states are contending with their operation vis-à-vis cyberattacks—or lack thereof.

Restraint in Practice

Distinctions among these three logics of restraint are elegant in theory but muddied in practice. While the appeal of preemptively aligning a study with a single unifying theory of international relations is attractive, here it is infeasible and unduly limiting. In the abstractions above, it is easy to imagine how a regulated stability could emerge from or evolve into a shared identity—military alliances or intentionally porous borders being common examples. Constructed stability could emerge from even an imposed condition, as comingling of stronger and weaker powers' populations leads to conditions making strife between them first proscribed, then unpalatable, and ultimately unthinkable. That is why these three forces must be examined together, evaluated individually for coherence but contrasted to one another in terms of their efficacy in actually bringing about restraint. Accepting the intermingling of influences, the question then turns to: *Influencing what?* How does an appealing *logic* of restraint actually result in the *practice* of restraint?

In practice, the generic operation of restraint is straightforward, even if no two decision-paths are identical. When faced with a potentially advantageous course of action, the national-level decision-maker concludes—or is more often advised—that such a course of action lacks its otherwise apparent appeal. This is an abstraction but not hard to concretize using a fictitious example: Asgard stands to benefit economically and militarily from the massive disruption of Babel's infrastructure, but its prime minister chooses not to launch such an attack. Inquiring as to the courses of action, she is presented by her advisors with a range of considerations. Her defense minister notes that Babel might convince its allies the attack was unprovoked action that merits an overwhelming military response against which Asgard could not defend. The foreign minister adds that the attack would be a clear violation of international law, and according to the justice minister, could even risk individual criminality for violations of human rights. Regional ambassadors note the unilateral and unprovoked attack of a neighbor is an unacceptable course of action that threatens to delegitimize its international standing and reputation for promoting international peace. Armed with this varying input, the prime minister concludes that the reasons against such an attack outweigh the reasons to proceed—she provides no answer, though, as to which was dispositive to her thinking (if she herself could even articulate as much). Unsatisfying though it may be to the analyst, this is restraint in practice.

So, too, would be a subtler situation: one where despite the potential objective value of such an attack, it is never offered to the prime minister as an option, nor brought by her to advisors for consideration. While perhaps less observable, this situation is no less an example of restraint in practice. It too, like the more actively considered example above, is a case of forces acting to shape, and specifically limit, the recourse to potentially advantageous activities. In our scenario above, one sees multiple logics of restraint in play simultaneously: rationalist calculation, regulative adherence to structure, and constitutive notions of identity. In this situation, one could argue that the key forces are almost exclusively constitutive, if despite the strategic gain the prospect of attack is so outside of the socially constructed universe of plausibility that it is not as a practical matter available to the prime minister. Constructivists argue that this is a uniquely powerful force in international relations, and indeed, one sees how it can be—provided, of course, that such notions of identity and permissible conduct have time to cohere.

While these logics of restraint are perhaps not truly separable from one another in practice, one can nonetheless identify certain conditions—of time, of existing relations between two states, or of particular contexts of their interaction—where one force may be more or less likely to be dispositive than the others. This is the subtlety that the chapters that follow will also aim to identify: whether that logic of restraint is not just plausible, but also likely to hold sway over state practice.

Evaluating Restraint: In Theory and Practice

As these examples suggest, the theory of change motivating this study aims to marry the scholar's anatomizing of sources of restraint with the practitioner's appreciation for the elusiveness of the provably dispositive factor. It argues that states have incentives to engage in cyberattacks, but that three key potential logics—rationalist, regulative, and constitutive—might lead to restraint. They do not operate in equal measure, and while neither do they operate in isolation, it is possible to critically evaluate first the soundness of the logic itself, and second, its potential or observed effect. This involves a layered, critical process.

Layer one is analytical: informed by analogy (a methodology discussed shortly), do the salient features of cyberattacks lead to a coherent case compelling to the leadership of states, given certain baseline assumptions about incentives and behavior? If this case is indeed coherent given precedent that states recognize, that logic of restraint has the *potential* to serve as a meaningful restraint. If not, the inquiry shifts to what activities states instead are pursuing, if any, to impose, negotiate, or construct such a logic of restraint if it suits their interests.

With this outcome in mind, the second layer of analysis asks the practical question of whether and how this logic of restraint exists in practice; in other words, what evidence (if any) is there that it will weigh significantly on state decision-making? What are we observing with respect to states' actual conduct, and do those provide us with indications regarding that logic's capacity for success; presage its failure; or call for new ways of considering the logic itself and the nature of its influence?

Methodological Parallels

Cyberattacks are a reasonably new phenomenon in international relations, lacking any thorough international regimes devoted to them and few explicit customs governing their use. Methodologically, the subject of this study is a phenomenon novel enough it presents two challenges: limits to applicable precedent that preclude a narrow focus on case studies, and rapid technological changes that could render analysis quickly obsolete. Moreover, with little authoritative public material available on how states are arriving at even preliminary decisions regarding cyberattacks and cyber-defense, a process-tracing or genealogical approach would be analytically unsatisfying.[21] Other explicitly predictive approaches run the obvious risk of speculation. They are also ill-suited to a study that, despite its potential implications for future state practice, probes the applicability of *existing* regimes and practices of restraint to a new phenomenon.

Given these considerations, this study begins by pursuing a methodology based on systematic analogy, then engages critically with the recent literature examining those concepts. It elucidates a novel phenomenon by reference to the methods of restraint already in operation in international relations and informed by prior examples of those means of coercion (especially weapons) toward which states do presently show restraint. Specifically, each chapter represents a different line of inquiry into how the forces that restrain state behavior might operate on cyberattacks. To do so, it begins by defining both the essential features on which that force acts and the conditions necessary for it to obtain and effectively constrain state behavior. It then examines both the essential qualities of a cyberattack, and where relevant, other weapons or tactics throughout history on which the force has had effect. In doing so, it follows in a robust tradition of analogical reasoning across the physical and social sciences, as well as philosophy and political theory. The adoption of this approach by the physical sciences with respect to novel phenomena offers a detailed and relevant methodology. Hesse's groundbreaking 1963 work on models and analogies in science recognized that novel phenomena often elude existing explanatory theory—or, more specifically, a "model" in which to situate them. In these instances, Hesse argues for an explicitly analogical approach with two phases: first, developing a list of observable qualities or "predicates" of a phenomenon; and second, of the causal relations they instantiate.[22] By bridging essential qualities of old and new, an analogical approach contextualizes novel phenomena and tests the durability of existing models and systems.[23] The approach here, examining the relationship between certain emblematic qualities of a phenomenon and the system in which it exists, approximates Hesse's predicate-relational effect.

---

[21] See Stephen Van Evera, *Guide to Methods for Students of Political Science* (Ithaca, NY: Cornell University Press, 1997), 64.

[22] Mary B. Hesse, *Models and Analogies in Science* (London: Sheed & Ward, 1963), Chapter 2.

[23] Max Black further emphasized this interface, noting the ability of this kind of associative reasoning to lend conditions of meaning otherwise impossible by the two subjects independently. See Max Black, "More About Metaphor," in *Metaphor and Thought*, ed. Andrew Ortony (Cambridge: Cambridge University Press, 1979), 28. See, more generally: Max Black, *Models and Metaphors* (Ithaca, NY: Cornell University Press, 1962).

Elsewhere in international relations, practical philosophers have also adopted variants of this approach, though primarily as a means to evaluate a philosophical system, rather than to evaluate the fit between the action and various systems. A notable example in the discipline is Walzer's *Just and Unjust Wars*, which in a manner highly recognizable within this study, illustrates the boundaries of a given philosophical system through historical example.[24] On the question of how historical analogies shape the policy decision-making process, works by Neustadt and May, as well as Khong, demonstrate how illuminating such an approach can be.[25] For the purposes herein, the term "analogical reasoning" is preferable to "historical illustrations" due to the dynamism of some of the norms under discussion and to avoid the presumption this study was fixed around certain historical cyberattacks.

The methodology is not without challenges—many of which are described well by other scholars who frame their works exclusively around analogies of cyber conflict.[26] Analogical reasoning's focus on similarities between two phenomena can run the risk of obscuring more profound distinctions; as Levite and Percovich put it, analogies' "educational value stems in no small part from identifying where, when, and how an analogies does not work well."[27] Here, concerns about overextension of an analogy are partly attenuated by drawing comparison not just between similar qualities of a proscribed act and a cyberattack, but also between the *effects* of that force of proscription on both. The study also endeavors to pay regular attention to qualities of cyberattacks that are truly unique or are even dispositive to the effect of a restraining regime itself, as exists in a few important cases.

A second challenge comes in the temptation to implicitly tie the fit of an analogy to causation in decision-making, unduly jettisoning context from the complex set of decisions that influenced particular outcomes, suggesting single-factor causation in a multivariate environment.[28] It is for that reason that this study does not rely on any single analogy nor orient itself by

---

[24] Michael Walzer, *Just and Unjust Wars*, 4th ed. (New York: Basic Books, 1977).
[25] Richard E. Neustadt and Ernest R. May, *Thinking in Time: The Uses of History for Decision-Makers* (New York: Free Press, 1986); Yuen Foong Khong, *Analogies at War: Korea, Munich, Dien Bien Phu, and the Vietnam Decisions of 1965* (Princeton, NJ: Princeton University Press, 1992).
[26] See generally George Perkovich and Ariel E. Levite, eds., *Understanding Cyber Conflict: 14 Analogies* (Washington, DC: Georgetown University Press, 2017), 2; Emily O. Goldman and John Arquilla, eds., *Cyber Analogies* (Monterey, CA: Naval Postgraduate School, 2014), 5.
[27] Perkovich and Levite, *Understanding Cyber Conflict*, 2.
[28] Here, Khong's work on the abuses of historical analogy in public defenses of foreign policy decisions is particularly apt. See Khong, *Analogies at War*.

extended parallel to any single interstate act (say, privateering, or nuclear weapons, other interesting works have sought to), but rather it offers a range of examples across different tactics, technologies, and time frames.[29] Finally, the predicate need of an analogical approach to define essential qualities of a technological act also creates exposure to obsolescence. This risk is inevitable with any work dealing with high technology, but this work accepts it as preferable to fixation on particular and imperfect case studies, which would only exacerbate this and the prior two concerns.

2.3 Evolution of the Literature

With respect to formal sourcing, the primary material for this study is, in all instances, drawn from publicly available documents. The first category of sources pertains to recent state activities in cyberspace. Given their contemporary nature, the principal historical record comes from newspaper and technical press accounts, which are referenced to provide some factual basis for certain key historical events. Supplementing these accounts, the best in-depth data on cyberattack incidents and capabilities come from the reports of technical cybersecurity firms, many of which have invested hundreds of millions of dollars in observing malicious activity online. While some such firms are noted for lacking objectivity, those reports referenced herein are generally regarded among technical and cybersecurity experts as neutral in their presentation.[30]

In recent years, traditionally tight-lipped states are occasionally commenting directly (via their foreign ministries or leaders) or indirectly (as press sources) on individual cyberspace incidents. Recent years have also offered numerous opportunities to observe more abstract positions: in the United Nations context, they include the construction of annual General Assembly (UNGA) resolutions and the state views they solicit, in negotiations of Groups of Governmental Experts (GGEs) from key players in international security, and in statements of senior officials during UN-sponsored events such as the Internet Governance Forum. The G20 communiqués in

---

[29] Florian Eglof, "Cybersecurirty and the Age of Privateering," in *Understanding Cyber Conflict: 14 Analogies*, ed. George Perkovich and Ariel E. Levite (Washington, DC: Georgetown University Press, 2017); Steven E. Miller, "Cyber Threats, Nuclear Analogies? Divergent Trajectories in Adapting to New Dual-Use Technologies," in *Understanding Cyber Conflict*.

[30] Greg Myre, "Tech Companies Take a Leading Role In Warning Of Foreign Cyber Threats," *National Public Radio: All Things Considered*, January 23, 2020.

2015 also paved a way for the group's further attention to these issues. Third-party venues, some with thinly veiled state sponsorship, also offer important venues for states to articulate their positions on the issue of cyberattacks. The London Conference on Cyberspace in 2011 and its successor events in Budapest, Seoul, and The Hague, as well as the annual cybersecurity forum in Garmisch-Partenkirchen, are but a few.

Some governments with histories of advocacy in this space have also issued comprehensive documents that provide core documentary evidence of their views. The United States, Australia, United Kingdom, and Russia have likely produced the largest number of these documents in the form of military whitepapers and doctrine statements, foreign ministry proclamations, and whole-of-government (White House/Kremlin) cyberspace policies. Dozens of other states have also developed versions of these national strategies, though many focus primarily on domestic vulnerability and governance, and only a few contain sections devoted to international relations.[31] Finally, public bilateral and multilateral agreements between key powers and their allies also provide an important documentary basis for their evolving views.

Each chapter also has a literature specific to its line of inquiry. The examination of rationalist deterrence in Chapters 3 and 4 is the most straightforward. Absent any governing document, the chapters draws on the rich academic and historical debate about the origin and function of deterrence before, during, and after the Cold War—including the more recent and hotly

---

[31] Particularly useful for a separate, comparative analysis of domestic policies outside the scope of this study, key examples include The United States: The White House, "National Cyber Strategy of the United States of America" (Washington, DC, 2018); US Department of Defense, "The Department of Defense Cyber Strategy"; US Department of Defense, "Summary of the Department of Defense Cyber Strategy" (Washington, DC, 2018); US Department of State, "Department of State International Cyberspace Policy Strategy" (Washington, DC, 2016). Other governments: Government of Australia, "Cyber Security Strategy," Canberra, 2009; Government of Canada, "Canada's Cyber Security Strategy: For a Stronger and More Prosperous Canada"; Republic of Austria, "Austrian Cyber Security Strategy," Vienna, 2013; Federal Republic of Germany, "Cyber Security Strategy for Germany," Berlin, 2011; Government of Finland, "Finland's Cyber Security Strategy," Helsinki, 2013; Government of France, "Information Systems Defence and Security: France's Strategy," Paris, 2011; Government of Japan, "Information Security Strategy for Protecting the Nation," Tokyo, 2010; Government of New Zealand, "New Zealand's Cyber Security Strategy," Wellington, 2011; Government of Norway, "Cyber Security Strategy for Norway," Oslo, 2012; Government of the Kingdom of the Netherlands, "National Cyber Security Strategy 2: From Awareness to Capability," The Hague, 2013; Government of Switzerland, "National Strategy for the Protection of Switzerland Against Cyber Risks," Bern, 2012; Government of Poland, "Cyberspace Protection Policy of the Republic of Poland," Warsaw, 2013; Government of Turkey, "National Cyber Security Strategy and 2013–2014 Action Plan," Ankara, 2013; Government of Israel, "Decision No. 3611 of the 32nd Government: Promoting National Cyber Capabilities," 2011; Government of the United Kingdom, "The National Cyber Security Strategy 2016 to 2021" (London: Her Majesty's Government, 2017).

contested practical and critical debate over concepts of cyber deterrence. Chapters 5 and 6, which focus on restraints on the use of force within international law, use the UN Charter as their cornerstone and develop their analysis through key rulings of the International Court of Justice (ICJ) and related scholarship. Chapters 7 and 8 examine the numerous documents that comprise the *jus in bello* canon of law, including the Hague and Geneva canons of law, in particular including their Protocols Additional (especially the Geneva Convention's Additional Protocol I), laying their development against the historical record on how, when, and to what end various means and methods of war were deemed unusable. As examples, these chapters draw upon the legal literature on the formation of specific legal regimes against chemical weapons, land mines, cluster munitions, and other weapons of war inviting particular humanitarian considerations. These chapters also rely upon specialized literature within international relations tracing the processes of norm formation to consider the pathways by which a "cyberattack taboo" might form.

As a practical matter, the era of cyberattacks in international relations began in earnest in 2007; as a doctrinal and academic matter, however, many had seen the precursors of such a development years and even decades prior. Since the balance of this study will focus on the restraining effects that determine state doctrine, law or use of force, and humanitarian norms have on the decision to use cyberattacks, all of which is informed by the doctrine scholarship on these topics, it is worth situating and briefly critically analyzing its impact.

Early Literature on Information Warfare

The first direct contribution to the study of cyberattacks can be traced back to military theory and doctrine from the late 1970s through early 1990s. These studies are often neglected but important in explaining the intellectual origins of present-day state policies regarding cyberattacks.

Such works were products of their historical era in seeking to understand, for the first time, the wartime effects of increased computing power and the reliance on information systems. As a function of that framing, terminology differed, and many works sought to extend well-known concepts of "information operations" to "information warfare." In what was probably the earliest modern use of the term in this context, a researcher for the US

DEFINING AND STUDYING RESTRAINT   69

Office of Net Assessment used the term "information warfare" in the 1970s to describe the competition between competing "cybernetics" or control systems.[32] Absent any examples of a state using purely attacks advantage to achieve military aims, the earliest works sought to apply precepts of military theory to a hypothetical environment where information, rather than conventional firepower, provides a state with superior resources to fight and win a war.[33] Most notable in this literature is the notion of digital capabilities as a discrete concept contributing to military power. This theme, while underdeveloped in the military-focused doctrine of the era, was prescient in considering cyberattacks as a force influencing states' perceptions of power in their international relations.[34]

Bridging this early work and the present topic, consideration of which began in earnest in the mid-1990s and early 2000s, were three key volumes—all by affiliates of the RAND Corporation. These books, for the first time, analyzed in the international context the role of a discrete attack originating from computer networks. While still relying upon earlier terminology, Daniel and Julie Ryan paved new ground in defining a concept very much akin to the subject of this study, situating their work around the notion that "information warfare is, first and foremost, warfare. It is not information terrorism, computer crime, hacking, or commercial or state-sponsored espionage using networks for access to desirable information."[35] Likewise, Khalilzad and White's edited volume represents the most expansive and topical of these works, supplemented by Arquilla and Ronfeldt's volume considering the full range of cyberattack possibilities.[36] While not fully durable in today's analysis, and carrying outdated terminology, both volumes remain

---

[32] David Tubbs, Perry G. Luzwick, and Walter Gary Sharp, "Technology and Law: The Evolution of Digital Warfare," in *Computer Network Attack and International Law*, ed. Michael Schmitt and Brian O'Donnell (Newport, RI: Naval War College, 2002), 36. This concept is distinct from the sort of "information advantage" in warfare present in doctrine from Sun Tzu to Clausewitz; rather than competing for the most information, the present-day form of "information warfare" envisaged competition of systems for controlling information, what today we would regard as computing power and networking speed.

[33] See, e.g., Davis Alberts and Richard Hayes, *Power to the Edge: Command . . . Control . . . in the Information Age* (Washington, DC: DOD Command and Control Research Program, 2005).

[34] These contributions presaged works such as Nye's 2011 chapter-long meditation on "cyberpower." See Nye, *The Future of Power*, Chapter 5.

[35] Daniel J. Ryan and Julie C. H. Ryan, "Protecting the National Information Infrastruture Against InfoWar," in *Information Warfare: Chaos on the Electronic Superhighway*, ed. Winn Schwartau (New York: Thunder's Mouth Press, 1994), 672.

[36] John Arquilla and David Ronfeldt, *Networks and Netwars: The Future of Terror, Crime, and Militancy* (Santa Monica, CA: RAND Corporation, 2001); Zalmay Khalilzad and John P. White, eds., *Strategic Appraisal: The Changing Role of Information in Warfare* (Santa Monica, CA: RAND Corporation, 1999).

markedly forward-looking in considering the full range of disruptive actions falling short of the cyberattacks considered herein, such as early "hacktivist" website defacements and terrorist use of the internet.[37]

All three of these works stand out for their relevant focus, while much of the rest of related literature in the 1990s, by scholars such as Stein, Alger, and Denning, had difficulty articulating and forming a discrete program of study, in part due to an approach deeming "information warfare" nearly every coercive act utilizing information of any sort.[38] These problems of definition are not unique to the cyber field; in discussions of irregular warfare, Kiras has pointed out, "authors are inclined to lump everything together under a concept to the point where a term describes everything and explains nothing."[39] In this respect, history appears to repeat itself: there are meaningful parallels to the overexpansion of the "information warfare" concept in the 1990s to the cyberwar that kicked off a second wave of literature on the topic.

Threat-Based Literature

A second category of literature, focused on documenting and sounding the alarm on cybersecurity risks to national security, is made up primarily of popular monographs, think-tank studies, and some scholarly articles. These works occupied the vast majority of attention during the period from 2008 to 2012, a proliferation in part attributable to a massive increase in spending by the US government on cyber-defense since 2004, and even more so following the attacks in Estonia. Emblematic of these works are Clarke and Knake's 2009 volume *Cyber War*, a popular monograph that vividly illustrates the potential threats of state-based cyberattack, but which suffers from many of the same definitional challenges of early work on "information warfare."[40]

---

[37] John Arquilla and David Ronfeldt, "Emergence and Influence of the Zapatista Social Netwar," in *Networks and Netwars*, ed. John Arquilla and David Ronfeldt (Santa Monica, CA: RAND Corporation, 2001).

[38] George J. Stein, "Information Warfare and Neutrality," *Airpower Journal* 9, no. 1 (1995); John Alger, "Introduction to Information Warfare," in *Information Warfare: Chaos on the Electronic Superhighway*, ed. Winn Schwartau (New York: Thunder's Mouth Press, 1994); Dorothy Denning, *Information Warfare and Security* (Reading, MA: Addison-Wesley, 1999).

[39] Kiras, "Irregular Warfare," 229.

[40] Richard A. Clarke and Robert K. Knake, *Cyber War: The Next Threat to National Security and What to Do About It* (New York: HarperCollins, 2010). Farwell and Rohozinski's 2012 article is emblematic of academic journals also playing accessory to this blurring of concepts and acceptance of policy focus. See James P. Farwell and Rafal Rohozinski, "The New Reality of Cyber War," *Survival* 54, no. 4 (2012).

Brenner's *America the Vulnerable* is a slightly more recent and notable contribution in the same canon.[41] Works like *Cyber War* amplified a tendency in the press and, to some extent, academia to abuse terms of art like "warfare" and "attack" to describe any unfriendly cyber activity, including well-understood acts like espionage, when conducted via the internet. This terminological confusion persists—with a few notable exceptions, also largely in the policy and think-tank literature, seeking to refute Clarke's prediction of the outbreak of general cyberwar.[42]

Several other notable works of long-form journalism warrant mention for providing insights into specific cybersecurity incidents the details of which would otherwise be unavailable to researchers. Among them, books by journalists Kim Zetter, Shane Harris, and Andy Greenberg cover some of the seminal cybersecurity incidents of the last several years, with an understandable emphasis on their purportedly secretive nature.[43] They are valuable as windows into the technical and political details and effects of these incidents, more than cybersecurity incidents and some first-hand accounts of their effects, as sweeping statements of how cyberattacks fit into the broader context of international security, geopolitics, or law. Of course, there is danger in overreliance on these sources, particularly when they cover matters on which official government records have not yet been released. For this reason, this study's analysis does not hinge on the specifics of individual incidents—for instance what and when particular states knew about particular incidents—preferring instead insights that are broadly applicable regardless of time frame and fact pattern.

Other influential works focus squarely on influencing policymaking, including early think-tank reports by experts such as James Lewis, and later several special commissions appointed to examine the threat.[44] Following

---

[41] Joel Brenner, *America the Vulnerable: Inside the New Threat Matrix of Digital Espionage, Crime, and Warfare* (New York: Penguin, 2011). Emblematically, the book heralds itself as: "An urgent wake-up call that identifies our foes; unveils their methods; and charts the dire consequences for government, business, and individuals."

[42] James A. Lewis. "The Cyber War Has Not Begun" (Washington, DC: Center for Strategic and International Studies, 2010); Rid, "Cyber War Will Not Take Place"; Rid, *Cyber War Will Not Take Place*.

[43] Zetter, *Countdown to Zero Day*; Fred Kaplan, *Dark Territory: The Secret History of Cyber War* (New York: Simon & Schuster, 2017); Shane Harris, *@War: The Rise of the Military-Internet Complex* (New York: Mariner Books, 2014); Greenberg, *Sandworm*.

[44] James A. Lewis, ed. *Cyber Security: Turning National Solutions into International Cooperation* (Washington, DC: Center for Strategic and International Studies, 2003). Commission on Cybersecurity for the 44th Presidency, "Securing Cyberspace for the 44th Presidency." See also more recent entry such as James A. Lewis, "A Cybersecurity Agenda for the 45th President" (Washington, DC: Center for Strategic and International Studies, 2017); Thomas E. Donilon and Samuel J. Palmisano, "Commission on Enhancing National Cybersecurity" (Washington, DC: National

those earlier works, dozens of similar documents have proliferated, primarily seeking to contextualize for policymakers the publicly available evidence of states' use of cyberspace (for spying and potentially attacking). The most significant of these policy-focused volumes—works edited by Kristin Lord, David Bentz, Franklin Kramer, and Herb Lin—use the domestic vulnerability as a starting point to examine the implications for foreign policy and national security.[45] Follow-up works by Lewis and later, a White House–appointed Commission, had similar orientations but did reflect the state of contemporary thinking on the intersection of homeland security and cyber foreign policy.[46]

Generally missing from many popular works, of course, is terminological consistency and methodological grounding, particularly in the history and theory of international relations. The vast majority of this literature is directed not at understanding the impact of cyberattacks on the relations of states, but on one or more nation's immediate national security policy. Such works tend to be oriented around how a single state should invest and organize given these changes in security practice—but in so doing, tend to orient observations and argument on the nation whose policymakers they seek to influence. These studies offer recommendations worth pursuit and further study—such as Finnemore's extended recommendations on promulgating norms of responsible behavior in cyberspace, Libicki's on cyberdeterrence, or Nye's on "deterrence and dissuasion in cyberspace"—but missing is a comprehensive understanding of how such an approach might bring stability to the space, and upon what precedent such an effort might rely.[47] Ben Buchanan's carefully argued case for the security dilemma's

---

Institute of Standards and Technology, 2016); *U.S. Cyberspace Solarium Commission Report*, (Washington, DC: US Cyberspace Solarium Commission, 2020).

[45] Some of the most significant efforts relevant to international relations include Kristin Lord and Travis Sharp, eds., *America's Cyber Future: Security and Prosperity in the Information Age* (Washington, DC: Center for New American Security, 2011); David J. Betz and Timothy C. Stevens, eds., *Cyberspace and the State: Towards a Strategy for Cyberpower (Adelphi series)* (London: Routledge, 2012); Franklin D. Kramer, Stuart H. Starr, and Larry K. Wentz, eds., *Cyberpower and National Security* (Washington, DC: Potomac Books, Inc., 2009); US National Research Council, "Technology, Policy, Law, and Ethics Regarding U.S. Acquisition and Use of Cyberattack Capabilities" (Washington, DC: US National Research Council, 2009).

[46] "A Cybersecurity Agenda for the 45th President"; "Commission on Enhancing National Cybersecurity."

[47] Martha Finnemore, "Cultivating International Cyber Norms," in *America's Cyber Future: Security and Prosperity in the Information Age*, ed. Kristin and Travis Sharp Lord (Washington, DC: Center for New American Security, 2012); Marin C. Libicki, *Cyberdeterrence and Cyberwar* (Santa Monica, CA: RAND Corporation, 2009); Marin C. Libicki, *Cyberspace in Peace & War* (Annapolis, MD: Naval

applicability to cyberspace may be an exception, and does the field a service through its precise terminology and more comprehensive approach to the issue.[48]

Legal Literature

A third category of literature is aimed at understanding the appropriate framework to situate cyberattacks in domestic and international law.

The earliest examples of this literature can be found in the early 2000s, when as previously mentioned, military literature began to regard technology not just as an enabler of future military operations, but also as a potential venue for them. Perhaps the most important, but often ignored, epoch for the emergence of cyberattack literature was following the Gulf War and NATO intervention in Kosovo, when the first studies considering "computer network attack" in the context of international law took shape. The latter milestone may have been particularly significant in explaining the legal establishment's early and short-lived interest in the field, as media outlets began reporting that the United States considered using cyberattack tools against the Hussein regime or Serbian targets' financial accounts during the Kosovo intervention.[49] These early works included contributions in international law from those who were first and foremost technical security experts, such as Steve Lukasik and Sy Goodman.[50] Similarly, individual studies by legal scholars such as Walker helped bridge the gap between analysis of "information warfare" fixated on military doctrine and the international law it implicated.[51]

The capstone of this early period in the literature was a comprehensive volume that brought together a range of noted international law scholars, including Yoram Dinstein, Anthony D'Amato, and Daniel Silver, to produce

---

Institute Press, 2016); Joseph Nye, "Deterrence and Dissuasion in Cyberspace," *International Security* 41, no. 3 (2016–2017).

[48] Buchanan, *The Cybersecurity Dilemma*.
[49] Elizabeth Becker, "Pentagon Sets Up New Center for Waging Cyberwarfare," *New York Times*, October 8, 1999: A16; John Markoff, "Military Breaks the Rules of Military Engagement," *New York Times*, October 17, 1999: L5.
[50] Gregory D. Grove, Seymour Goodman, and Stephen Lukasik, "Cyber-Attacks and International Law," *Survival* 42, no. 3 (2000).
[51] George K. Walker, "Information Warfare and Neutrality," *Vanderbilt Journal of Transnational Law* 33, no. 5 (2000).

a single comprehensive study of the legal status of the hypothetical threat of computer network attacks.[52] This volume, edited by Michael Schmitt and Brian O'Donnell, remains exceptionally relevant, broaching many of the topics challenging lawyers examining cyberattacks today.[53] It did, however, engage with issues in the context of that day's technology, but with a limited sense of the scale of possible disruption, an overemphasis on the novelty of terrorist use of the internet, and without any concrete examples (like Estonia) against which to evaluate its theories.[54] Perhaps given this drought of precedent, no comparable contributions to this field of the literature emerged in the years immediately following Schmitt and O'Donnell's work.

Entries in the legal literature have become far more numerous in the last several years, particularly following the growth of policy-focused literature last decade. Some of the most useful examples include Schmitt's return to the topic, and the entry of other, established scholars of international law such as Oona Hathaway into these reinvigorated debates.[55] These more recent works are notable for overcoming some of the technological aging and topical meandering of works from the early 2000s, though they rely on largely the same cast of scholars and baseline international law as the prior period. What even these present-day legal works often lack, however, are conclusions about how their findings should or might be applied in the present environment. This focus either on defining areas for legal consideration or offering recommendations on how states might conduct "legal" cyberattacks is entirely understandable—those were the questions practitioners were asking with the most urgency. Indeed, one of the most consistent criticisms of this subfield was that the absence of clear legal consensus rendered the policy process impractically plodding and inadequately decisive. As Baker and Dunlap put it:

---

[52] See Yoram Dinstein, "Computer Network Attacks and Self-Defense," in *Computer Network Attack and International Law*, ed. Michael Schmitt and Brian O'Donnell (Newport, RI: Naval War College, 2002); Anthony D'Amato, "International Law, Cybernetics, and Cyberspace," in *Computer Network Attack and International Law*; Daniel B. Silver, "Computer Network Attack as a Use of Force under Article 2(4) of the United Nations Charter," in *Computer Network Attack and International Law*.

[53] Michael Schmitt and Brian O'Donnell, eds., *Computer Network Attack and International Law* (Newport, RI: Naval War College, 2002).

[54] See, e.g., Charles J. Dunlap Jr., "Meeting the Challenge of Cyberterrorism," in *Computer Network Attack and International Law*, ed. Michael Schmitt and Brian O'Donnell (Newport, RI: Naval War College, 2002).

[55] Michael Schmitt, "Cyber Operations and the Jus in Bello: Key Issues," *Naval War College International Law Studies* (2011); Oona Hathaway and Rebecca Croontof, "The Law of Cyber-Attack," *California Law Review*, no. 817 (2012); Herbert S. Lin, "Cyber Conflict and International Humanitarian Law," *International Review of the Red Cross* 94, no. 886 (2013).

Military lawyers are tying themselves in knots trying to articulate when a cyberattack can be classed as an armed attack that permits the use of force in response. State Department and National Security Council lawyers are implementing an international cyberwar strategy that relies on international law "norms" to restrict cyberwar. CIA lawyers are invoking the strict laws that govern covert action to prevent the Pentagon from launching cyberattacks. Justice Department lawyers are telling our military that it violates the law of war to do what every cybercriminal has learned to do— cover their tracks by routing attacks through computers located in other countries. And the Air Force recently surrendered to its own lawyers, allowing them to order that all cyberweapons be reviewed for "legality under [the law of armed conflict], domestic law and international law" before cyberwar capabilities are even acquired.[56]

Yet this criticism should not always be taken at face value, particularly outside of its moment in time. After all, the seminal 2013 *Tallinn Manual* (*Tallinn 1.0*) and 2017 *Tallinn Manual 2.0* projects will be central reference points for Chapters 5, 6, and 7 precisely because they provide ample guidance on how abstract matters of international law should apply to operations and the conduct of war in this context—even identifying the areas where consensus among Western experts was elusive.[57] In this respect, under Schmitt's enduring leadership, *Tallinn* offers an important contribution to the overall effort to bring cyberattacks under some international regulation and a frequent reference point for its overlapping subject matter, despite beginning its analysis from the premise that cyberattacks will be unrestrained but for specific recommendations of law.

---

[56] Stewart A. Baker and Charles J. Dunlap Jr., "What Is the Role of Lawyers in Cyberwarfare?," *American Bar Association Journal* (2012).

[57] Michael Schmitt, ed., *Tallinn Manual on the International Law Applicable to Cyber Warfare: Prepared by the International Group of Experts at the Invitation of the NATO Cooperative Cyber Defence Centre of Excellence* (Cambridge: Cambridge University Press, 2013); Michael Schmitt, ed., *Tallinn Manual 2.0 on the International Law Applicable to Cyber Operations: Prepared by the International Group of Experts at the Invitation of the NATO Cooperative Cyber Defense Centre of Excellence.*, 2nd ed. (Cambridge: Cambridge University Press, 2017).

Early Histories

Finally, some notable works have also sought to provide a certain near-term historical context for the recent period of international relations in cyberspace. The earliest such works stem from the immediate aftermath of the Estonia incident, as the NATO-sponsored Cybersecurity Center for Defense Center of Excellence (CCD-COE) prepared as part of its initial legal assessment of law some relevant precedents that might inform subsequent analysis.[58] Among the most useful early reference works in this space is Jason Healey's history through 2012, commendable for its breadth in considering relevant precedent and citing technical details, is Jason Healey's history through 2012.[59] More recently, works by Fred Kaplan and David Sanger have sought to provide more sweeping, journalistic yet narrative accounts of the evolution of the space.[60] John Carlin's account provides a unique vantage within an underdiscussed but important perspective of cybersecurity issues at the intersection of foreign policy and law enforcement.[61] Adam Segal's work provides particular insights on how some of the key cyber episodes in Iran, Russia, and China map onto—and in many cases disrupt—traditions of statecraft, diplomatic and military.[62] Alex Klimberg makes a similar contribution.[63] Without the same narrative arc but with while including details exceptionally useful to researchers is the Cyber Operations Tracker developed by the Council on Foreign Relations (under Segal's leadership), provides for easier comparison between incidents.[64] Cognizant that many of the details of these events remain classified and with documentary evidence that may take decades to reveal, these sources' overlapping coverage of many of the key events provide invaluable sources for the scholar seeking to understand and contextualize the key episodes in the history of cyberattacks in international relations.

---

[58] Eneken Tikk, ed., *Frameworks for International Cyber Security: Legal and Policy Instruments*, 6 vols., vol. 1 (Tallinn: Cooperative Cyber Defence Centre of Excellence [CCD-COE Publications], 2010).

[59] Jason Healey, *A Fierce Domain: Conflict in Cyberspace, 1986 to 2012* (Washington, DC: Cyber Conflict Studies Association, 2013).

[60] Kaplan, *Dark Territory*; David Sanger, *The Perfect Weapon: War, Sabotage, and Fear in the Cyber Age* (New York: Crown, 2018).

[61] John P. Carlin and Garraett M. Graff, *Dawn of the Code War: America's Battle Against Russia, China, and the Rising Global Cyber Threat* (New York: Hachette, 2018).

[62] Adam Segal, *The Hacked World Order: How Nations Fight, Trade, Maneuver, and Manipulate in the Digital Age*, reprint ed. (New York: PublicAffairs, 2017).

[63] Alexander Klimberg, *The Darkening Web: The War for Cyberspace* (New York: Penguin, 2017).

[64] Council on Foreign Relations, "Cyber Operations Tracker."

Relationship to Cyber Norms

To bridge both concepts and literature, it is important to acknowledge how this study differs from the framing applied by many Western states in their pursuit of more predictable international relations in cyberspace—sometimes called "cyber norms."

The avowed policies of the United States and many of its allies have been remarkably voluminous and discursive on the topic of norms in cyberspace. Since at least 2009, senior US officials have called ad nauseam for clearer norms of state behavior—in policy strategies, at ministerial meetings, in unilateral statements, bilateral dialogues, and multilateral venues.[65] It might appear that the US government regarded the norm-building process as a kind of ritual incantation—that, said enough, would make them take hold. As a conceptual matter that may not be far off: after all, as Part III will explore, the process of building durable norms (particularly in international security) demands some clear understanding of action and reaction, habituated over time. This may partly be because the claims embedded within those norms reflected widely embraced international custom enshrined elsewhere: concepts of state responsibility to minimize criminality, respect for intellectual property, and advisability of mechanisms for crisis communications.[66]

That said, some (most notably the Trump administration) have critiqued the prior US approach as favoring rhetoric over results and as talking about expectations of behavior but not enforcing outcomes when those preferred

---

[65] See, of just a small subset, The White House, "The United States' International Strategy for Cyberspace," 8; The White House, "National Cyber Strategy of the United States of America," 20; John Kerry, "An Open and Secure Internet: We Must Have Both" (Washington, DC: Department of State, 2015); Tom Donilon, "Remarks By Tom Donilon, National Security Advisor to the President: 'The United States and the Asia-Pacific in 2013'" (Washington, DC, 2013); Hillary Clinton, "Remarks on Internet Freedom" (Washington, DC, 2010); US Department of State, "Department of State International Cyberspace Policy Strategy"; Michele Markoff, "Advancing Norms of Responsible State Behavior in Cyberspace," *DIPNOTE: US Department of State Official Blog*, July 9, 2015; US Department of State, "The Third U.S.-France Cyber Dialogue" (US Department of State, Global Public Affairs, 2020); Christopher Painter, "G20: Growing International Consensus on Stability in Cyberspace," *DIPNOTE: US Department of State Official Blog*, 2015.

[66] Under the direction of EO13800, "Strengthening the Cybersecurity of Federal Networks and Critical Infrastructure," in May 2018, the US State Department prepared a report "on the Nation's strategic options for deterring adversaries and better protecting the American people from cyber threats." The report offered four key recommendations: "With respect to activities below the threshold of the use of force, the United States should, work with likeminded partners when possible, adopt an approach of imposing swift, costly, and transparent consequences on foreign governments responsible for significant malicious cyber activities aimed at harming US national interests." US Department of State, "Recommendations to the President on Deterring Adversaries and Better Protecting the American People from Cyber Threats," 2018.

outcomes are unobserved.[67] It seems reasonable to conclude that while not jettisoning the diplomatic emphasis on norms, the Trump administration deployed a new public stance on "persistent engagement" and "defending forward" as a kind of supplementary remedial mechanism to the great "norms debate."

While taking official statements of national policy at face value, this study does not (except in conclusory material) intend to engage with the principally *policy-focused* aspects of the debate over the efficacy of specifically the United States' pursuit of those specific norms over the last few years. Those debates, engaged with by Grigsby and Rosenzsweig, among others, continue to play out in real time on commentary pages, at think-tank panels, and beyond.[68] Instead, this work will engage with these questions as ones of the prospects of norm formation, informed by precedent and theory, in the sorts of analyses pursued by Schmitt and Vihul, Fennimore and Hollis, Tikk-Ringas, and Maurer.[69] In short, this work is not focused on giving this pillar of US cyber policy a report card; however, its conclusions may well have much to say about the value of framing a policy of restraint around them.

2.4 Critiquing Restraint

The concept of restraint as a focus for study is not without its critics. It is worth acknowledging and addressing some of these key critiques: namely, that restraint obtaining is improbable, that it is inadvisable, that it is already

---

[67] Ellen Nakashima, "White House Authorizes 'Offensive Cyber Operations' to Deter Foreign Adversaries," *Washington Post*, September 20, 2018. Following the Trump administration's debut of its new national cyber strategy, then-national security adviser John Bolton, praised the White House for authorizing "offensive cyber operations" and lessening the restrictions to leverage cyberspace to protect the US' national security interests and deter adversaries: "Our hands are not tied as they were in the Obama administration." The *Washington Post* reported that Bolton touted the new strategy for "creat[ing] structures of deterrence that will demonstrate to adversaries that the cost of their engaging in operations against us is higher than they want to bear."

[68] Alex Grigsby, "The End of Cyber Norms," *Survival* 59, no. 6 (2017); Paul Rosenzweig, Steve Bucci, and David Inserra, "A Congressional Guide: Seven Steps to U.S. Security, Prosperity, and Freedom in Cyberspace" (Washington, DC: The Heritage Foundation, 2013).

[69] Michael Schmitt and Liis Vihul, "The Nature of International Law Cyber Norms," *NATO Cooperative Cyber Defence Centre of Excellence Tallinn Papers*, no. 5 (2014); Martha Finnemore and Duncan B Hollis, "Constructing Norms for Global Cybersecurity," *American Journal of International Law* 110, no. 3 (2016); Finnemore, "Cultivating International Cyber Norms"; Eneken Tikk-Ringas, "International Cyber Norms Dialogue as an Exercise of Normative Power," *Georgetown Journal of International Affairs* 17, no. 3 (2016); Tim Maurer, "Cyber Norm Emergence at the United Nations," *An Analysis of the UN's Activities Regarding Cyber-security* (Cambridge, MA: Belfer Center for Science and International Affairs, 2011).

in operation, that it is inadequate, and that it is inhumane. The first two are in fact policy objections that are best revisited subsequent to this analysis; the latter three merit some further engagement as a framing matter.

Improbable

One line of reasoning would contend that a study aiming to find the most plausible pathway to restraint in cyberspace is a doomed exercise, since cyberattacks are at once so appealing and so novel that any efforts to bring them to heel is bound to fail. On its surface, this is a policy objection—and one that is not unreasonable. After all, as the next section will document in-depth, numerous states have pinned years of policy on the premise that cyberattacks create novelty that fundamentally frustrates the conduct of international relations. In this respect, it is reasonable to wonder whether states should invest their efforts in pursuing restraint at all (instead of accumulating an offensive advantage). More deeply, however, this critique is expressing skepticism about the ability of any logic, particularly one that is not imposed, to be a substantial force of restraint from a valuable tool.

The short response to this critique is: "We'll see." This study aims to critically examine that assumption with a variety of approaches: reframing some of these discussions to, for example, recognize that seeking offensive advantage *is* seeking a form of restraint (via deterrence); that incommensurability with existing law does not inherently weaken the regime, but tests its operation; and that certain proposals about how cyberattacks might be stigmatized may not be so far-fetched as once imagined under a now-vintage set of technological assumptions. By the end of this analysis, it may still be that there is no plausible pathway for restraint of cyberattacks to obtain—but that will be in the eyes of the reader, presented with the full evidence of both principle and practice.

Inadvisable

The second policy-inspired critique would be that any efforts directed at restraint might provide a template for depriving a "well-intentioned" power the advantage that helps it maintain stability. After all, the United States has long purported to enjoy preeminence in its offensive cyber capabilities, and efforts to restrain those capabilities are inherent calls for containment of the projection of US power abroad. As a framing matter, the bulk of this study aims to be framed not around US capabilities and power, but to study the phenomenon of cyberattacks from several international vantages.

Yet aside from that particular objection rooted in national strategy, it is worth raising some fundamental questions about the durability of its underlying claims. While there is no reason to reject the view that the United States enjoys significant, if not singular, technical advantage, that position may be eroding by the day, and regardless, it says little about the broader sustainability of the security environment for any state so positioned.[70] For instance, it says nothing about the relative (and variable) level of risk that states run based on their economic dependence on digital infrastructure, or critical infrastructure's capacity for disruption. It also disregards the potential that such advantage—particularly if disproportionate—erodes broader security dynamics outside cyberspace, as a convincing source of instability or potential miscalculation. In short, in order to assess the advisability of any policy of restraint, we must first consider all the ways in which *unrestrained* cyberattacks create far more inadvisable outcomes. This is a question for policymakers, but one that must be informed by whether or not prospects for restraint are even plausible—the task of the chapters that follow.

In Operation

Another critique of this study's framing is that it may be asking a question that has already been answered: some states already possess the capability to conduct major cyberattacks against one another, and have chosen not to, suggesting that restraint is already in effect. Some scholars have, in certain contexts, already posited this theory, for instance, Maness and Valeriano, as

---

[70] See International Institute of Strategic Studies, "Cyber Capabilities and National Power: A Net Assessment" (London: IISS, 2021). See also Jennifer Valentino-DeVries and Danny Yadron, "Cataloging the World's Cyberforces" (2015). The *Wall Street Journal* conducted a survey of more than sixty countries to catalogue which countries possessed the best offensive cyber capabilities and found that the US' capabilities "surpass anything known in terms of complexity and sophistication of techniques." See also Andrew Weiss's remarks at the Aspen Institute's Idea Festival in 2018 that the "United States has the sharpest rocks in cyberspace—to borrow the line from one of our former cyberoperators—but it lives in the glassiest house." Andrew Weiss, "Russia the World's Outlaw State," in *Aspen Ideas* (Washington, DC: Aspen Institute, 2018).

well as Goodman, in the context of deterrence, for instance.[71] Despite substantial work by Schmitt, the *Tallinn Manual* process, Roscini, and others to clarify how existing international law applies to cyber operations, and while participants and observers alike remain hopeful that it will, few have yet demonstrated that these particular understandings are currently having significant practical restraining effect—particularly without reference to other, longstanding prohibitions.[72] The analytical record that both critically evaluates various means of restraint and evaluates it in the context of present and potential state conduct is surprisingly thin—and nonexistent when considering works bridging all three logics of restraint. All this calls for a fresh look at the issue on these terms, engaging with those prior conclusions about deterrence, for instance, but pushing the analysis further to determine which if any logics of restraint may plausibly obtain.

Inadequate

Another important critique centers around whether cyberattacks, as defined herein, are the right focus for a study with an explicit goal of improving the international security environment. Indeed, some of the most interesting work in cybersecurity examines precisely this grey zone between stability and war.[73] Kello refers to this conduct as "unpeace," a "new form of midspectrum harm and international rivalry that is neither fatal nor physically destructive . . . nor desirable or even tolerable like conventional forms of peaceful rivalry."[74] In a similar vein, Buchanan devotes much of his second study to studying this "grey zone"—though notable disagreement exists between whether such actions are more or less concerning and problematic than the sort of cyberattack contemplated herein.[75] Both authors, by focusing on conduct short of war, implicitly argue that large-scale cyberattacks

---

[71] Ryan C. Maness and Brandon Valeriano, *Cyber War versus Cyber Realities: Cyber Conflict in the International System* (Oxford: Oxford University Press, 2015); Will Goodman, "Cyber Deterrence: Tougher in Theory than in Practice?," *Strategic Studies Quarterly* Fall (2010).

[72] Schmitt, "Cyber Operations and the Jus in Bello"; *Tallinn 1.0*; *Tallinn 2.0*; Marco Roscini, "Threats of Armed Force and Contemporary International Law," *Netherlands Law Review* 54 (2007).

[73] Ben Buchanan, *The Hacker and the State* (Cambridge, MA: Harvard University Press, 2020).

[74] Kello, *The Virtual Weapon and International Order*, 249.

[75] Buchanan, *The Hacker and the State*. Notably, Buchanan's second volume is framed around the idea that significant cyberattacks of the sort examined in this study are elusive, and that the concept should be extended to include nearly all disruptive cyber operations. I agree that those events are both more numerous and worthy of study; however, we part ways on whether that prevalence is license to downplay the lower-probability and higher-impact event.

are at best less interesting (since they are simply supplementary features of conventional conflict) and at worst irrelevant (since they are not as commonplace as other coercive acts). It is also important to distinguish this concern from the critique of the field Rid raises, for instance, in claiming that "cyber war will not take place."[76] That issue concerns whether or not offensive cyber operations are likely to take place in a manner unique and distinct from overarching armed conflict, in a perpetual state of bloodless but disruptive cyberwar. On that issue, this study agrees.

Certainly, instances of cyber-related acts of unpeace are of great interest to international security, particularly given the way in which digital technologies have been used to create instability in democratic campaigns and elections; to suppress critical journalism, academic studies, and other forms of free expression; and to steal unprecedented quantities of private information for commercial and intelligence gain.[77] This is a natural progression: as more of our political, economic, and private lives are mediated by technology, new means to subvert our patterns of behavior are created, and potentially exploitable. Thus, all those questions are worthy of review and disciplined study.

That does not make the case, however, that the expansion of states' coercive arsenals is reason to ignore perhaps the most significant disruptive tools at their disposal. Just as the field of nuclear security studies did not wither in the absence of nuclear weapons used in war, the study of cyberattacks and their restraint merits pursuit as a similarly high-impact, lower-frequency event. The potential implications of a single, major cyberattack would be orders of magnitude more significant than the subconflict coercion that has become commonplace in recent years—creating a growing attractiveness to do so, absent restraint. This closer look will also help confront an emerging question in the field: whether the full range of offensive cyber activities follow similar trajectories and are shaped by identical forces and in similarly predictable ways, or whether those at a higher level of disruption (like the cyberattacks discussed here) require a different frame of analysis. This work

---

[76] Rid, *Cyber War Will Not Take Place*.

[77] See, e.g., Mueller, "Report on the Investigation into Russian Interference in the 2016 Presidential Election"; David D. Kirkpatrick, "Signs of Russian Meddling in Brexit Referendum," *New York Times*, November 15, 2017; Ninon Bulckaert, "How France Successfully Countered Russian Interference During the Presidential Election," *Euractiv*, July 17, 2018; Zaid Shoorbajee, "Chinese Hackers Tried to Spy on U.S. Think Tanks to Steal Military Strategy Documents, CrowdStrike Says," *CyberScoop*, December 21, 2017; BBC News, " 'China Hackers' Attack NY Times," January 31, 2013.

hypothesizes the latter; the chapters that follow, read in concert with the works cited above, offer a first test for that supposition.

Inhumane

The final critique emerges from the ethical orientation of the book itself: that underlying its pragmatic goal of "improving the international security environment" must lie a commitment to reducing human suffering. As the previous chapter explored, there is great potential for cyberattacks to increase human suffering, but might there be an argument that they, perversely, reduce suffering in comparison to the alternative? If cyberattacks offer states an opportunity to attempt to coerce or change competitive dynamics, and these actions replace alternatives that would result in human suffering or loss of life (such as kidnapping civilians, destroying civilian cargo vessels, etc.), one could argue the existence of cyberattacks offers an ethically preferable alternative. History suggests this consideration is not so far-fetched; the Iranian attempts against both Saudi Aramco and the US financial infrastructure in 2011–2012—in retribution for perceived acts of aggression against the Islamic Republic—may well have played out more violently had cyber options not been available.[78]

This argument is rightly of concern to both practitioners and ethicists evaluating the acceptability of the emerging status quo of cyber operations.[79] There are no ready answers to it. Certainly, the presence of particularly low-level offensive cyber operations—not necessarily meeting the bar of a cyberattack—may result in fewer casualties than actions states would otherwise take. Absent an authoritative record demonstrating how states came to such conclusions, though, it is difficult to assert that to be the case. Moreover, as Part III will explore, secondary effects of cyberattacks in the near term are presently difficult to assess; the aggregate harm from them on institutions

---

[78] For more on these incidents, see Perlroth, "In Cyberattack on Saudi Firm, U.S. Sees Iran Firing Back"; US Department of Justice, "Seven Iranians Working for Islamic Revolutionary Guard Corps-Affiliated Entities Charged for Conducting Coordinated Campaign of Cyber Attacks Against U.S. Financial Sector," March 24, 2016.

[79] Denning and Strawser, for example, advocate for the use of cyber weapons versus kinetic weapons because "cyber weapons could cause considerably less harm than the kinetic weapons they replace, while still accomplishing a justified military objective equally as effectively. Thus, there are two morally compelling reasons to use cyber weapons in place of physical weapons where possible: they can reduce both the risk to one's own (presumably just) military forces and they can reduce the harm incurred to the adversary and others." Dorothy Denning and B. J. Strawser, "Moral Cyber Weapons," in *The Ethics of Information Warfare*, ed. Luciano Floridi and Mariarosaria Taddeo (Cham, Switzerland: Springer, 2014), 5.

of trust, social cohesion, economic productivity, and other material factors toward long-term life and prosperity are near impossible to quantify. While this study is sympathetic to the idea that effectively restraining cyberattacks might lead to an increase in the use of other tools and in turn lead to ethically inferior outcomes, this is a matter that can effectively be dealt with in applying its conclusions. The public policies influenced by its conclusions about the prospects for restraint can and should weigh them against the full range of potential outcomes—including this one.

2.5 Overview of Book

With the framing of the study set and those critiques considered, the next three parts of the book will follow the logics of restraint articulated in this chapter, considering both the abstract and applied case for it having practical effect. The overview of the arguments of each part are as follows:

Part II will demonstrate how cyberattacks are poorly suited for classical deterrence models (Chapter 3), arguing that given the low-information environment in which states find themselves, current behavior is both more explainable—and potentially more eligible for restraint—through *structural deterrence*, a sort of proto-competition to define the context in which cyberattacks may be used (Chapter 4).

Part III will critically examine the growing consensus about how cyberattacks are treated under the *jus ad bellum* (Chapter 5), but given the absence of a functioning remedial regime or custom, it will push further by arguing that better indicia of restraint may be the current competition over *structural remediation*—whereby states engage in or eschew retribution to situate cyberattacks in the frame that reflects their preferred function of the law (Chapter 6).

Part IV will present the evidence and critically evaluate the scholarship on whether humanitarian concerns preclude use of cyberattacks, first considering the *jus in bello* (Chapter 7), then considering an active process of *structural prohibition* underway to determine modalities of restraint—rooted in a shared vision to regulate cyberattacks but requiring reconceptualization as a prohibitive norm to realize its full potential (Chapter 8).

Finally, the conclusion offers thoughts on a new direction for international cybersecurity scholarship—one combining the practical interface of rationalist, regulative, and normative considerations to both explain *and* shape state decision-making—and proposes several directions for future research along these lines.

PART II
DETERRENCE

3

Evaluating Deterrence

States may seek to acquire certain capabilities as much for their value in keeping the peace as their value in war, reflecting a quality of those capabilities commonly referred to as "deterrent value." States may also acquire and demonstrate capabilities with the hopes of preventing an adversary from acquiring or using a particular military capability against it. If successful, the first state is said to have "deterred" its adversary. Because it holds the potential on the positive side to shape behavior without overt conflict, and perhaps even stabilize tumultuous interstate relationships, deterrence is one of the more powerful forces in international relations.

Given cyberattacks' attractiveness in affording asymmetrical power, is it inevitable that more states will seek to acquire them? Does the potential for a destructive cyberattack make developing those capabilities a strong deterrent (and thus desirable to states seeking to maximize security)? Might it be impossible to deter a state from developing a capability that can be amassed so covertly, thus increasing further the incentives to acquire? In this framing, cyberattacks might proliferate unchecked.

Setting aside the hype related to cyberattacks, one might contrarily ask: Do cyberattacks provide real value to the average state seeking to improve its lot in international security? Or are they "niche" weapons that only a handful will find worth the effort? Is their utility limited to a single attack, and one that is largely unrepeatable? And might cyberattacks be kept in check by other states possessing similar capabilities, similar to the mutual deterrence that characterized the Cold War superpowers? Here, then, and perhaps counterintuitively, cyberattacks might not be crucial to the vast majority of states, or might even play a role in keeping the peace.

Likewise, if they are of little use, they would be relatively straightforward to restrain—after all, why would states go to the trouble and expense if the tools ultimately do little for their national security? Surely the rush to acquire these tools suggests states regard them as valuable for *something*, but for what, precisely, is less than clear. Perhaps they will become a necessary complement to traditional kinetic forces, as air power was ultimately internalized into ground and sea-focused militaries. Perhaps they will offer the potential to shift the balance of a military conflict by according asymmetric power. Or might they, even more intriguingly, serve a purpose like nuclear weapons after 1945: a means to deter, but not necessarily to be used in battle?

This part of the book asks whether cyberattack capabilities, as tools of deterrence, might play a role in keeping the peace, even without featuring into war. The answers rest on two fundamental questions that undergird the chapter: whether or not cyberattacks are effective at deterring attacks, and whether they, in turn, can be meaningfully deterred.[1] Respectively, these questions define the "pull toward" and "push against" acquiring cyberattack capabilities. Understanding whether cyberattack capabilities have deterrent value, and whether states can be deterred from acquiring and using them, provides a rationalist means to explain their uptake among states or restraint therefrom. If their deterrent value is high, the likelihood that more states will actively seek and acquire them is as well. However, if their deterrent value is low, the reward that accompanies having the capability is substantially depreciated. Likewise, if a state can be easily deterred from acquiring or using them, their value might decline—but, alternatively, if the best way to counter a cyberattack is with another, those capabilities may proliferate even further. This Part II of the study seeks to answer these questions, and in turn, inform whether cyberattacks might be restrained under a rationalist logic of restraint.

Chapter 3 begins by defining deterrence and situating it within the rationalist logic of restraint. It then navigates the various frames of conventional and nuclear deterrence to find one well-suited to the particularities of state cyberattack decision-making. It then explores whether and how cyberattacks might be useful as deterrents generally, and then the extent to which states might be deterred from using them—either by other cyberattacks, or otherwise. It then considers whether states are even able to form the calculations

---

[1] When they appear in Part II, characterizations of "aggressive" acts, "aggressors," or "attacks" are meant generically and descriptively; they do not in this context imply any particular legal or customary status (e.g., as with "acts of aggression" or "armed attacks"). Part III engages those terms as matters of law.

necessary for deterrence to function—or if such an approach may be necessary.

Chapter 4 then outlines just such an approach: a new approach to conceiving of the competition that states are engaged in to shape the outcome of interstate deterrence. It explains why this "structural deterrence" concept is particularly useful for cyberattacks based on both the thin customary record and their novel features, and then explores the various strategies states are pursuing individually and collectively to shape how threats are perceived by adversaries.

Outline of Argument

This chapter examines the role of deterrence in restraining state use of cyberattacks, both as a general matter and in light of state practice. It is oriented around three key questions. In seeking to restrain state use of cyberattacks, will states: self-restrain if cyberattacks are of limited deterrent value; be deterred from acquiring or using cyberattack capabilities by other states doing the same; and deterred from acquiring or using them by other states' more traditional (noncyber) capabilities?

As Chapter 1 outlined, cyberattacks can be recognizably destructive but also possess unique characteristics that distinguish them from other unfriendly acts. So how does a state deter something that cannot be observed with the naked eye, traditional surveillance, or reconnaissance, and whose effects vary dramatically based on the level of technology in a victim state?

In answering these questions, this chapter argues that cyberattacks deprive states of the ability to make meaningful rationalist calculations, rendering cyber capabilities both poor deterrents and difficult to deter. Consequently, restraining cyberattacks requires more than amassing greater, similar capabilities in the manner of most conventional and nuclear deterrence. Instead, it argues, that a different and novel strategy is necessary—and already in use: a strategy of *structural deterrence*, shaping the international environment through alliances and law to favor their strengths within an overall deterrence relationship. In exhausting the explanatory power of conventional deterrence concepts, it previews the contention of the next chapter: that we are presently observing a form of "cyber-deterrence," but not of the sort upon which military science literature narrowly focuses. Rather, the contest in which states are presently engaged to restrain one another's use of cyberattacks is one of rationalist dissuasion through neoliberal means.

In detail, the chapter's argument is as follows. An introductory section defines the notion of deterrence and situates it within the theories of international relations into which it features prominently. The chapter then argues four key points to address these questions. First, it outlines the general criteria required for states to make rational deterrence calculations. Second, laid against those criteria, it argues that cyberattack capabilities meet very few of them given the complex aspects of observing and attributing them, making them poor instruments of deterrence. Third, it argues that there are substantial difficulties in deterring cyberattacks with other cyberattack capabilities (in-kind deterrence), but that—like any other unfriendly acts—states can be effectively deterred from using them in other ways (most obviously threat of military reprisal). The credibility of that threat of military reprisal is, however, presently contested, leaving states unable to amass the information necessary to make full, rationalist deterrence calculations. Those engaged in the project of restraint thus find little to practically bind states—but also a paradox in explaining their present behavior accumulating cyberattack capabilities. This enigma demands, and the next chapter argues for, a reconceptualization of how deterrence activities are taking place with respect to cyberattacks.

3.1 Defining Rationalist Deterrence

The most accessible, intuitive logic of restraint in interstate conduct is that of *rationalist deterrence*—which this section explores in concept and theory, before narrowing to discuss the kind of calculations that might be most directly relevant to states' cyberattack decision-making.[2]

---

[2] As a broad concept in today's literature, rationalist deterrence incorporates two means of affecting adversary choices: the *deterrent* influence of expected retaliation, and the *dissuasive* influence of limited impact/inexpensive recovery. If an attacker were dissuaded from an attack based on an adversary's rapid and inexpensive reconstitution from it (so-called deterrence by denial), it would not have "significant national security effect," and would not be of much relevance to this analysis. Therefore, this concept is largely excluded from the argumentation here.

Situating Deterrence: Concept and Theory

Rationalism, or rational choice theory, is a straightforward way of explaining state choices: simply, that states' decisions are based fundamentally on expectations of gain and loss. Formally, a rationalist calculation for a given state action is straightforward: expected gain minus expected loss provides a positive or negative sum. If positive, the action is undertaken, if negative, it is not. This concept is made complex (and meaningful in international relations) by problematizing the "currency" of gain and loss—the premise upon which the principal theories of the discipline diverge, and which will be discussed shortly. In the interim, however, it is most important to keep in mind this basic rationalist calculation of gain and loss informing decisions to act.

As it was generally understood before and throughout its intellectual heyday during the Cold War, deterrence is—at its core—a rationalist concept. From the standpoint of a would-be aggressor, it explains behavior of restraint when the expected loss of a coercive act outweighs the expected gain, due to certain anticipated actions or known attributes of the intended victim. In contrast a state that carries out an act of coercion is by definition undeterred, implying that its perceptions of relative loss were outstripped by perceptions of gain. Such was the case, for instance, in the United States' decision to enter the region and repel Iraq during the 1990–1991 Gulf War (the United States was, correctly, undeterred by Saddam Hussein's military's ability to repel an attack).[3] Likewise, in its far more legally complex strike on a Syrian nuclear reactor in 2007, Israel was undeterred by the likelihood of Syrian air defenses (dissuasion) or counterattack (deterrence).[4] By contrast, a state is effectively deterred when it refuses to take a coercive action that might otherwise bring it immediate or precedential gain: for instance, both Hussein's Iraq and Assad's Syria were deterred from waging a direct counterattack on their opponents' territory. Both India and Pakistan, despite persistent small-scale hostilities running across their borders, have mutually deterred one another from both broader outbreak of conflict and the use of nuclear weapons they

---

[3] This example is not to be confused with the more comprehensive point about a shift in US foreign policy that Lawrence Freedman aptly observes regarding the American invasion of Iraq in 2003, where the paradigm of that country's strategy markedly shifted away from deterrence and toward a pre-emptive doctrine. See Lawrence Freedman, *Deterrence* (Cambridge: Polity, 2004), 4, 96–105.

[4] See Erich Follath and Holger Stark, "The Story of 'Operation Orchard': How Israel Destroyed Syria's Al Kibar Nuclear Reactor," *Spiegel Online International*, November 2, 2009. For a more technical discussion, see Fulghum, "Israel Used Electronic Attack in Air Strike Against Syrian Mystery Target." That this attack may have been aided by a cyber operation against Syria's radar systems is orthogonal.

both possess. Deterrence can describe such monumental security choices as going to war or more limited ones such as selection of a response to a diplomatic or political slight. However, the concept is at its clearest in decisions for and against coercive or disruptive actions that could reasonably lead to the general outbreak of hostilities, a category into which cyberattacks clearly fall.

From the standpoint of more system-level international relations theory, this notion of rational choice is also the basis for *realist* explanatory theories of state action, such as the one popularized by Hans Morgenthau.[5] In this orientation arrangement, as Morgenthau puts it, "politics, like society in general, is governed by objective laws that have their roots in human nature," and that the "main signpost that helps political realism to find its way through the landscape of international politics is the concept of interest defined in terms of power."[6] In these general theories of international relations, the referent object of "gain" or "loss" is dynamic while traditionally conceived of in international security as military power: it might in an only slightly more expansive reading be territory, natural resources, valuable populations, or military hardware. But if those qualities of gain and loss are calculated in an abstract zero-sum concept of interstate "power," that concept is fixed around international security choices such as whether and when to attack one another, and more contemporary international relations theorists systematize those state choices as "neorealism."[7]

Both of these schools take states as the primary actor in the international system, and in turn accept two fundamental attributes about them: (1) that they are rational egoists (i.e., interest maximizers in the utilitarian sense); and (2) that that they are prone to conflict (most readings of Waltz suggest almost a Hobbesian state of nature or *"bellum omnium contra omnes"*).[8] In reviewing various logics of restraint, then, from the rationalist vantage of international relations, deterrence has substantial explanatory value, as it shapes state decision-making through the finite and limited capacity for gain from those conflicts. In a rationalist mode, the most meaningful check on states using every means of coercion at their disposal is the potential for relative loss—unless they are, in other words, deterred.

---

[5] Morgenthau, *Politics Among Nations*.
[6] Ibid., 4–5.
[7] See, most famously, Waltz, *Theory of International Politics*.
[8] Variously translated as a "war of all against all," or "of every man versus every man." Thomas Hobbes, *Leviathan (with selected variants from the Latin edition of 1668)*, ed. Edwin Curley (Indianapolis: Hackett, 1994 [1668]), 76.

Deterrence is also an important *practical* force in the realist mode of international relations; it is, in many ways, a particularly resource-efficient way to project power. Consider that to directly coerce an opponent, a state must first incur the material cost of acquiring that weapon, then material and reputational costs of using it, then the costs of any retributive consequence such as a counterattack. If, however, the mere investment in that capability carried with it the ability to avert attack *and* coerce by threat, the cost of deterring by acquisition is far less than the cost of also using. Therefore as a strategy, deterring has its appeal to both potential aggressor (because it is cheaper) and defender (because it reduces the chances of being victimized).[9]

Mutual deterrence should not, however, be confused with stability. A kind of post–Cold War celebratory amnesia seems to have gripped contemporary accounts of how the two superpowers averted conflict, but in so doing, it obscured that mutual deterrence is not a harmonious condition. While the United States and the Soviet Union deterred one another and successfully avoided outright full-scale conflict during the Cold War, those decades were hugely expensive, the peace was fragile, and the outbreak of humanitarianly disastrous "side" conflicts was numerous. In fact, histories are now revealing how individuals like Soviet Lt. Col. Stanislav Petrov, by ignoring the policy guidance—the careful tuning of which was once credited with creating stability—actually prevented nuclear Armageddon.[10] Nonetheless, deterrent effects quite indisputably played an important role in restraining the use of (at the very least) nuclear weapons throughout the Cold War, and for similar reasons, those effects are worth studying in the context of cyberattacks as well.[11]

Deterrence can be undeniably effective at restraining a state's use of particular capabilities and may offer a resource-efficient way to do so. Given that potential, the balance of this section more carefully defines what conditions are necessary for deterrence to take shape, and lays the foundation for the

---

[9] Dustin Volz, "U.S. Lacks Key Abilities to Avert Cyberattacks, Commission Says," *Wall Street Journal*, March 10, 2020.
[10] Long, "Sept. 26, 1983: The Man Who Saved the World by Doing... Nothing."
[11] Tannenwald makes a compelling case, examined in Chapter 8, that the formation of a "taboo" normative played an equally and perhaps even more important role in the decisions not to use nuclear weapons in particular during the mid- to late Cold War, and on the American side, in earlier spats like the Quemoy-Matsu crisis and Korean War. Nonetheless, her examination is limited to American calculations (not Soviet decision-making), and arguments are strongest when they relate to the later period in which the norm she defines has taken stronger root. See Tannenwald, *Nuclear Taboo*.

next section's analysis of how cyberattacks fit within (and in some cases challenge) that basic dynamic.

Narrowing the Concept of Deterrence

Before examining the compatibility of deterrence to cyberattacks, it is important to note that deterrence describes not a unitary concept, but rather a plurality of concepts once hotly debated, though somewhat less so with the waning of the Cold War.[12] Most systemic views on interstate deterrence share an orientation around the state and a basic understanding of rational egoism. For the time being, this chapter's analysis accepts that framing as well. Beyond that, however, there are multiple definitions of deterrence at varying levels of political and temporal specificity. This section narrows the field to the specific type of deterrence relevant to this study and outlines its recognizable features.

With respect to the political scope or kind of activity being restrained, perhaps the broadest condition would be George and Smoke's description of deterrence as "persuasion of one's opponent that the costs and/or risks of a given course of action he might take outweigh its benefits."[13] Mearsheimer offers a similar view, regarding deterrence "in its broadest sense" to be "persuading an opponent not to initiate a specific action because the perceived benefits do not justify the estimated costs and risks."[14] Mueller marginally narrows the reference sphere of influence to the military space, but implies

---

[12] Central works shaping in this debate include Bernard Brodie, *Strategy in the Missile Age* (Princeton, NJ: Princeton University Press, 1959); Thomas C. Schelling, *The Strategy of Conflict* (Cambridge, MA: Harvard University Press, 1960); Glynn Snyder, *Deterrence and Defense: Towards a Theory of National Security* (Princeton, NJ: Princeton University Press, 1961); Thomas C. Schelling, *Arms and Influence* (New Haven, CT: Yale University Press, 1966); George Questor, *Deterrence Before Hiroshima* (New York: John Wiley, 1966); Stephen Maxwell, *Rationality in Deterrence*, vol. 50, Adelphi Papers (London: International Institute of Strategic Studies, 1968); Alexander George and Richard Smoke, *Deterrence in American Foreign Policy: Theory and Practice* (New York: Columbia University Press, 1974); Robert Jervis, *Perception and Misperception in International Politics* (Princeton, NJ: Princeton University Press, 1976); Robert Jervis, "Deterrence Theory Reconsidered," *World Politics* 39 (1979); Lawrence Freedman, *The Evolution of Nuclear Strategy* (New York: St. Martin's Press, 1981); George Questor, *The Future of Nuclear Deterrence* (Lexington, MA: Lexington Books, 1986); Richard Ned Lebow and Janice Gross Stein, "Rational Deterrence Theory: I Think, Therefore I Deter," *World Politics* 41, no. 2 (1989); Robert Powell, *Nuclear Deterrence Theory: The earch for Credibility* (Cambridge: Cambridge University Press, 1990); Patrick Morgan, *Deterrence Now* (Cambridge: Cambridge University Press, 2003); Freedman, *Deterrence*; Colin Gray, *The Future of Strategy* (Cambridge: Polity, 2015); Colin Gray, *Theory of Strategy*, (Oxford University Press, 2018)
[13] George and Smoke, *Deterrence in American Foreign Policy*, 11.
[14] John J. Mearsheimer, *Conventional Deterrence* (Ithaca, NY: Cornell University Press, 1983), 14.

an almost Hobbesian realism, noting that given "the absence of war between two countries . . . it is reasonable to conclude that each is currently being deterred from attacking the other."[15] In Mueller's definition, any nonwar condition is a function of deterrence—defensible but, as Morgan notes, also "not rewarding analytically" for purposes such as this study of a specific kind of disruptive and potentially destructive attack.[16]

Early Cold War literature offers a more precise concept related to military coercion, and one that seems more properly tailored to the purposes here. Snyder's seminal work, for instance, defines deterrence as "discouraging the enemy from taking military action by posing for him the prospect of cost and risk outweighing the prospective gain."[17] Such a definition, favored by contemporary deterrence theorists like Morgan, also seems to have the best durability in the practical literature.[18] Thus, the DOD's Dictionary defines deterrence as "the prevention from action by fear of the consequences. Deterrence is a state of mind brought about by the existence of a credible threat of unacceptable counteraction."[19]

Having limited the kind of deterrence under discussion to activity known to be coercive, if not overtly military in character, it is also worth defining the timescale of deterrence under discussion. If deterrence informs a would-be attacker's decision space and, when successful, results in forbearance, one can envision this force acting across two general timescales. In the first, relations between a dyad of states are such that "at least one would consider attacking if a suitable occasion arose," and in which "the other maintains forces and offers warnings" such that "the first party never goes beyond preliminary consideration of attacking because of the threat from the second party."[20] This is deterrence played out on a long timescale, a concept that Huth and Russett note is "among the most important and least systematically studied phenomena of international politics."[21] This is *general deterrence*, a particular

---

[15] Mueller, *Retreat from Doomsday*, 70.
[16] Morgan, *Deterrence Now*, 2.
[17] Snyder, *Deterrence and Defense*, 35.
[18] Yet another, "compellence," focuses on the use of threat to get another party to engage in positive activity it otherwise would not. Morgan refers to deterrence and compellence in concert as "coercive diplomacy"—a compelling concept, but one that conceptually strays beyond the direct focus of this study. For a comparison, see Morgan, *Deterrence Now*, 3. For an in-depth treatment, see Lawrence Freedman, ed. *Strategic Coercion: Concepts and Cases* (Oxford: Oxford University Press, 1998).
[19] United States Joint Chiefs of Staff, *JP1-02: Department of Defense Dictionary of Military and Associated Terms* (Washington, DC: Department of Defense, 2001).
[20] Morgan, *Deterrence Now*, 80.
[21] Paul Huth and Bruce Russett, "General Deterrence Between Enduring Rivals: Testing Three Competing Models," *American Political Science Review* 87, no. 1 (1993). See also Morgan, *Deterrence: A Conceptual Analysis*.

interstate condition of conflict or nonconflict, rather than the use of a particular opportunity. It is a kind of overarching deterrence *theory*, having "to do with anticipating possible or potential threats, often hypothetical and from an unspecified attacker, and adopting a posture designed to deter other actors from ever beginning to think about launching an attack"—of any kind.[22] It is not necessarily tied to a specific challenge, to a single assessment of capabilities, and is thus far more prone to include considerations broader than simply retributive capability.[23]

Focus on a longer timescale is important to avoiding the practical shortcomings, and concomitant criticism leveled against the subfield of general deterrence. General deterrence's utility, at least in the form that dominated international relations analyses in the 1970s and 1980s, has come under criticism for disconnection from the practice of states.[24] As Kissinger laments, "the nuclear age turned strategy into deterrence and deterrence into an esoteric intellectual exercise"; in other words, the study of war's potential outbreak seemed almost detached from the geopolitical realities and even a broader security context.[25] This is where more recent accounts of cyber-specific deterrence concepts, such as Kello's "punctuated deterrence" and Tor's "restrictive cumulative cyber deterrence" have sought to bring these discussions back into the realm of practicality.[26] And while they do provide meaningful insights, they do so in explaining different circumstances than those under discussion here: namely, multiplicity of events and evolution of response over time. Useful though they may be in the context of international relations, they concern different subject matter than cyberattacks as defined here—cases that, by their significance, are higher impact, lower frequency, and thus far less suitable to routine tit-for-tat learning between fractious states. Instead, unlike the broad concept of all "cyber acts of aggression"

---

[22] Morgan, *Deterrence Now*, xvi.

[23] Nye's concept of "deterrence by entanglement," where "governments may find themselves sufficiently entangled in interdependent relationships that a major attack would be counterproductive" is for these purposes best considered a common feature of successful general deterrence—however it can also be relevant to an immediate deterrence decision when a it is a dispositive factor. Nye, *The Future of Power*, 146–47.

[24] Freedman takes perhaps less umbrage with the prior era's analytical approach, but challenges the same orthodoxy by demonstrating a coherent norms-based approach to understanding of deterrence. Sharing those concerns about the limitations of a purely interest-based approach to explain the present environment, the next chapter will carry Freedman's observation forward in attempting to develop a more norms-focused consideration of the deterrent dynamic. Freedman, *Deterrence*.

[25] Henry Kissinger, *Diplomacy* (New York: Simon & Schuster, 1994), 208.

[26] Kello, *The Virtual Weapon and International Order*, 205, 09-10; Uri Tor, "'Cumulative Deterrence' as a New Paradigm for Cyber Deterrence," *Journal of Strategic Studies* 40, no. 1–2 (2017).

occupying Tor's attention, this study rejects the notion that *this* manner of cyberattack is functionally unpreventable.[27] In studying one particular coercive act, as this study does, a tighter focus on single-point security decisions rather than the entire bilateral security dynamic in a relational context aims to be more conclusive.

The notion of *immediate deterrence* is therefore more relevant to a study focused on the use/nonuse of a particular method of coercion.[28] Best defined retrospectively but helpfully by Morgan in his review of the discipline's many strains, immediate deterrence relates to the circumstances of preparation for and reaction to *impending* attack by a known adversary—"linked to specific military capabilities and the threats built on them," rather than "overall military posture and the broad image it conveys."[29] When describing the relationship between potential adversaries, the immediate deterrent relationship focuses primarily on preconditioned markers of behavior and known prospects of retaliation. The difference could also be framed thusly: the mutual success of immediate deterrence is more a matter of survival, whereas the success of general deterrence could result in a state thriving.[30]

For these purposes, immediate deterrence refers to the particular use and nonuse choices to engage in particular kinds of coercion; likewise, it refers to a particular decision set. Distinctly, in this study general deterrence refers to the establishment of regularized deterrent situations across numerous immediate events, resulting in a more robust equilibrium. It can also be said, and is worth noting for future study, that general deterrence is the broader construct of habituated, predictable immediate deterrence episodes. The closest relevant frame is the vision of deterrence as "restrictive" (for which Tor argues), rather than "absolute," as he observes most American conceptions of the topic do as an inheritance of their nuclear history.[31] These concepts are, however, most useful for cases not rising to the significant national security

---

[27] Tor, "'Cumulative Deterrence' as a New Paradigm for Cyber Deterrence," 95.

[28] Patrick Morgan, *Deterrence: A Conceptual Analysis* (Thousand Oaks, CA: SAGE Publications, 1997), 28. This is not to be confused with Herman Kahn's concept of immediate deterrence, in contrast to extended, which focuses not on time frame but on to whom a threat is directed: the entity to be deterred or a third party.

[29] Morgan, *Deterrence Now*, 81–85.

[30] In between punctuated and cumulative deterrence, aiming to explain strategies of delayed deterrent action to ambivalence-creating events—and in that scope, forcing us to set them aside for now.

[31] Tor, "'Cumulative Deterrence' as a New Paradigm for Cyber Deterrence," 93. Tor notes that by contrast to this American perspective, Israeli deterrence concepts tolerate "a specific failure . . . resulting in a short burst of violence . . . is an inherent part of the 'learning process' between the parties." Ibid., 94. See also Thomas Rid, "Deterrence Beyond the State: the Israeli Experience," *Comparative Security Policy* 33, no. 1 (2012).

effect, and thus far more repeatable, than those under discussion here. For these reasons, a stricter examination of immediate deterrence is most appropriate given the lack of habituation of states' use and nonuse decisions vis-à-vis cyberattacks. Moreover, such an approach lends itself to more durable study and may perhaps serve as a useful starting point to other analyses of general cyber-deterrence when the phenomenon has more evidence in state practice and more documentation of state decision-making is available.

General Features of Immediate Deterrence

Immediate deterrence, regardless of the particular coercive tactic in question, requires certain general requirements to obtain. This section traces those general features, setting the stage for their application to cyberattacks.

Considering the dynamic between two states, would-be aggressor Asgard and defender Babel, Babel successfully deterring Asgard requires a number of factors be known to both parties. These are *preconditions* of immediate deterrence, since without any one of which it would be impossible for one to successfully exert deterrent influence over the other.

The first preconditions, worth mentioning only briefly, are strictly relational. In a bilateral dynamic, Babel must believe or know that Asgard, or a similarly positioned actor, poses a threat to it—in essence, a reason to pursue a strategy of deterrence. If that threat is imagined but not real, Babel might pursue such a strategy, but any success the former attributes to it would be irrelevant and misleading to precedent. Thus, this chapter takes as basic premises that Asgard and Babel are geopolitical foes in which the former perceives material gain from an attack on the latter, and that Babel recognizes the potential for Asgard to do it harm. Actions and reactions in immediate deterrence are based thereupon, rather than grounded in misperception or utter anomaly.[32]

With those basic premises in mind, the most analytically important preconditions are *recognition* (of a weapon) and *attribution* (of its owner/controller).

---

[32] Misperception can in some security contexts be worthy of analysis for its spiraling of bilateral/multilateral deterrent relationships, but principally in the mode of general rather than immediate deterrence, and thus not appropriate for these purposes. A template for that separate study might begin with:

Recognition. In assessing the decision to attack, Asgard must first be able to *recognize* the material (presumably military) forces that Babel would bring against it in the event of coercion. Recognition, in turn, has two constituent factors: *instrument recognition* and *effect recognition*. The first is an act of identification: literally, knowing upon observation the weaponry that may be deployed in retaliation to an attack. The second is an act of contextualization: knowing how the deployment of those retaliatory forces would adversely impact the attacking state.

Instrument recognition has taken many forms throughout the years, usually via what we now call reconnaissance. It has been aided by factors like night vision, thermal imaging, and satellite observation. It has been obscured by covert development, as well as by deception tactics as simple as canopies over inactive fighters, or as sophisticated as the hundred-mile network of underground tunnels connecting various fortified installations underneath Pyongyang.[33] In each case, though, forces were in some way (either directly, or via the plans leading to their manufacture) *observable* to the would-be aggressor. Were they not, they would serve only coercive, rather than deterrent effect, and thus would be of utility only during the outbreak of conflict.

Effect recognition, by contrast, is an understanding of the likely damage that deployment of the aforementioned instrument(s) would incur. The two are related but distinct. A landlocked country is less likely to be deterred by its adversary's massive naval fleet. Instrument informs, but does not dictate, effect. Even with more complex examples, it would be tempting but incorrect to assume that many categories of weaponry render this distinction between instrument and effect meaningless. A nuclear blast is a devastating occurrence, but not in all circumstances a state-terminating one.[34] As strategic literature developed during the Cold War pointed out, even the deployment of a half-dozen nuclear weapons was viewed as a differently "survivable" situation for the Eastern seaboard of the United States and Western half of the Soviet Union—particularly given different population densities between the two.[35]

---

[33] Bradley K. Martin, *Under the Loving Care of the Fatherly Leader: North Korea and the Kim Dynasty* (New York: St. Martin's Griffin, 2004), 85, 563.
[34] This is not to say that nuclear weapons did not take on the reputation for such a consequence in the popular and military consciousness—an issue Part IV will explore.
[35] See, for example, the deterrence posture enshrined on the United States' Single Integrated Operations Plan (SIOP) developed in the early 1960s. McGeorge Bundy, *Danger and Survival: Choices about the Bomb in the First Fifty Years* (New York: Random House, 1988), 322.

So a crucial precursor to Babel deterring Asgard from an attack would be the latter's recognition of the weaponry the former might bring to bear, and its specific destructive effect should it do so.

Attribution. All of this is reasonably straightforward, so long as Babel's flag is neatly painted on the outside of every missile, rifle, and ship it possesses, and visible for Asgard to see. Particularly in a world of global power projection, where military capabilities might reside within the borders of allies, in international waters, or outer space, the matter of attribution is crucial.

A would-be aggressor must be able to *attribute* material forces that might be brought to bear against it; in other words, Asgard must believe certain capabilities belong to Babel and not, say, Camelot. Knowing "whose guns are whose" is essential to assessing the loss likely to be incurred in any attack and is rapidly made complex by global alliances and defense relations both overt and otherwise.

One or more of three methods can yield positive attribution: knowing identity, conducting a process of elimination, and ascertaining monopoly. These are deductive qualities to knowing the possessor of a particular capability or perpetrator of a particular act. Identity answers the question of "who did." Elimination focuses on "who, *therefore, did not.*" Monopoly strives at "who *else* could." Conclusive evidence of the first renders the latter two moot; but for many capabilities, the calculation is not so simple. This section will describe each in turn, given the relevance of all three in confronting a cyberattack.

Identity attribution can, even in international politics, take the form of a "smoking gun," such as a country's uniformed soldiers, visible from their home territory in the direction of another's. Likewise, a squadron of fighter jets on the tarmac at a known state airfield would, if visible from a satellite, provide relatively simple attribution in the form of identity.

Elimination can play an important role when identity is not readily ascertainable. The presence of a few grounded fighters in a contested region such as Kashmir yields more conclusive knowledge of their attribution. Absent distinct markings (required under the *jus in bello* but not always visible) on the planes and knowledge of which country favors a particular landing site, identity may not be immediately clear.[36] However, perhaps a particular class of sophisticated fighter jet is only used by one of the three claimants to the

---

[36] See Chapter 4 for an extended discussion of these *jus in bello* requirements and their potential effect on cyberattacks.

disputed region. As a logical matter, knowing, for instance, China possesses a kind of jet that its neighbors Pakistan and India do not, could provide convincing attribution via elimination.

Monopoly helps further inform attribution in deterrence by answering whether a particular capability can be developed or deployed by additional actors beyond a classic deterrent dyad of two states. With respect to development, knowing whether a particular capability's production, acquisition, and possession remains sufficiently complex, expansive, or risky as to remain the sole provenance of states can eliminate an entire layer of complexity in a deterrent relationship. Many of the most powerful, highly sophisticated military capabilities fall in this category: aircraft carriers, advanced jets, modern tanks, and (to date, thankfully and in all but the most marginal predeployment cases), the tools for nuclear and large-scale chemical weapon delivery.[37] Other capabilities, however, have proliferated substantially to nonstate actors, including terrorists and organized crime—these include, inter alia, small arms, rocket-propelled grenades, and small submarines. Knowing that states maintain a development and/or deployment monopoly on a particular capability can help positively identify it as belonging to a would-be attacker or defender.[38]

These three general methods of attribution are important to some of the most complex and important conditions of immediate deterrence. Consider, for example, the question of attribution vis-à-vis an intercontinental ballistic missile (ICBM). Today, its in-flight attribution has become knowable thanks to sophisticated telemetry. It was not always so.[39] ICBMs offer a helpful illustration of both distinction and monopoly. Given that only two states possessed the weapons early in their advent, the Soviet Union could generally know that an incoming missile was not their own; therefore, by elimination attribution, any inbound ordnance of that sort was of American origin.[40]

---

[37] With very limited exceptions, individuals have played only an intermediary brokering role in states' acquisition of these capabilities, lacking the capability to deploy them directly. The A. Q. Khan network represents perhaps the most famous of this former category. Perhaps the most notable exception in the case of chemical weapons was the Aum Shinrikyo cult's possession and use of chemical weapons in their 1995 Tokyo subway attack—though to reinforce the point, the group lacked any sophisticated deployment system for those weapons.

[38] Less salient for this study, but worth noting parenthetically, is the question of whether a capability is available to third parties; i.e., if a weapon developed and deployed by Asgard, aimed at Babel, might be used by Camelot without the others' express permission. Such a capability might then be considered *available* to Camelot and Asgard, enhancing the deterrent posture of both.

[39] Bundy, *Danger and Survival*, 471.

[40] Of course, the stationing of ICBMs in third-party allies offers precisely the kind of complexity that this chapter explores later in the context of cyberattacks.

Likewise, there was little to no risk that such a weapon came from a nonstate source because states maintained a monopoly over the ICBM's development and deployment.[41] Before the tracking of ICBM capabilities and regular testing became a feature of the nuclear era, these two features—elimination and monopoly—were more salient mechanisms for assessing and acting upon the origin of a potential ICBM attack than identity attribution itself.[42] The same logic applies for deterrence purposes to the possession and deployment of ICBMs; elimination narrows the field of potential actors (including third-party allies that maintain deployments of others' weapons, such as in Europe), producing a dynamic of immediate deterrence even absent discernable identity of a capability.[43]

To recap: for the purposes of this analysis, the most helpful framing of the question is immediate deterrence or the information and choices leading to a single decision to execute or hold back from an attack. However, for Babel to deter Asgard from attacking it, Babel's weapons need to be recognizable (both observable and with known effect) and must be reliably attributable to it and/or available for its use. Together, recognizable and attributable capabilities provide the two necessary inputs for the rational calculations of immediate deterrence between two states.

3.2 Cyberattack Capabilities as a Deterrent

For the state considering its defensive options, is developing cyberattack capabilities a safe bet in seeking to deter other cyberattacks, or attacks more generally? More specifically, can cyberattack capabilities effectively deter would-be attackers engaging in rationalist calculations? This section uses the methodology just outlined to examine whether cyberattacks are a powerful (and thus attractive) tool for deterring an adversary across domains. It argues that despite attention to them in recent years, cyberattacks are an almost uniquely poor deterrent, due to particular qualities that deeply frustrate

---

[41] The recent advent of a robust commercial space launch industry, bringing the capabilities to launch if not deliver complex payloads not dissimilar from warheads, may portend a change in this state of affairs over the decades.

[42] For example, the 1955 US defense report *Meeting the Threat of Surprise Attack*, which Bundy regards as "one of the most influential in the history of American nuclear policy," was straightforward about these assumptions. Science Advisory Committee Technological Capabilities Panel, United States, *Meeting the Threat of Surprise Attack*: The White House, 1955. See also Bundy, *Danger and Survival*, 325–28.

[43] See Nuclear Threat Initiative, "Nuclear Disarmament—NATO," 2019.

traditional rationalist deterrence models. Futuristic prospects of a wholesale military shift to cyber capabilities or a kind of mutual cyber-deterrence are largely dashed.[44] Therein lies, this section argues, some cause for optimism for the restraint project: once their novelty wears off, when states making zero-sum investments in coercive capabilities might not find the deterrent value sufficient to merit the investment.

The prior section outlined the details of how rationalist deterrence operates as a generic theory of state behavior given a particular security threat. Its maxims, in that respect, function regardless of the weapon used; otherwise, the theory would be of little explanatory value, calling into question why it is the subject of so many fine studies. Indeed, the prior analysis confirms much of that account: principles of deterrence work well in forming state behavior relative to both traditional coercive means such as troop movements, and more recently invented ones such as ICBMs.

Yet cyberattacks pose some significant challenges to rationalist deterrence, and approaches that would make rationalist deterrence usefully explanatory in international relations falter in explaining state choices to develop or use cyberattack capabilities. The reason, as this section argues, is that these capabilities themselves offer little as a reliable deterrent.

Disaggregating Cyberattack Capabilities

Deterrence is an information-dependent phenomenon; a state must know enough about the capabilities of its adversary to make a rational choice. As this section argues, a would-be attacker's knowledge of specific components of an opponent's capability—whether gleaned covertly or advertised by the defender—can have vastly different effects on deterrence calculations. This calculus of international politics, Jervis reasons, flows from states' fear of anarchy:

> If another's behavior seems innocuous, they will look for a hidden and menacing significance. They see not only plans, but sinister ones. Within society this perspective characterizes the paranoid. But since threats and

---

[44] See generally Libicki, *Cyberdeterrence and Cyberwar*.

plots are common in international relations, the perception that others are Machiavellian cannot be easily labeled pathological.[45]

Bohrghard and Lonegran observe that because of the historic secrecy associated with cyber operations generally—including cyberattack preparations—and makes it difficult for adversaries to asses one another's capabilities.[46] While generally true from the standpoint of the thin record of state demonstrations of cyberattack capabilities, what more can be said about *why* these dynamics are presently significant, and whether they are functions of state preference for secrecy, or more durable conditions of the capabilities themselves? For this reason, this section disaggregates cyberattack capabilities into the constituent technologies that are needed to develop, deploy, and use them against another state. Some early rationalist studies sought to consider the elements of a cyberattack as a single capability, for example a Distributed Denial of Service Attack, but at considerable analytical peril.[47] Reducing cyberattacks to a single capability, for the purposes of studying a deterrent effect so deeply tied to another state's specific knowledge of that capability, would be equivalent to regarding all airborne forces as equal in makeup and deterrent implications. Just as now the status of an air force's readiness and models of their airplanes matter tremendously for deterrence, so too does knowing the specific status of a cyberattack capability. An aggressor might have insights into only one of these data points, substantially changing its deterrent value: just as finding a large airfield is not proof positive of a substantial air force, but seeing a squadron of mobilizing bombers yields more reliable information. Therefore, this section embarks on a more detailed analysis that is essential to evaluate whether and how those discrete capabilities—individually or combined—provide meaningful deterrent value to their possessor.

Cyberattack capabilities, then, for the purposes of informing deterrence, can be thought of as three distinct elements: *development infrastructure*; *deployment network(s)*; and *execution tool(s)*.[48] Recalling that for effective

---

[45] Jervis, *Perception and Misperception in International Politics*, 320 and Part III: Common Misperceptions.

[46] Erica D Borghard and Shawn W Lonergan, "The Logic of Coercion in Cyberspace," *Security Studies* 26, no. 3 (2017): 465.

[47] For example, Libicki's military-focused volume on "cyber-deterrence" at times takes this monolithic approach, except to distinguish cyberattacks from certain kinds of spying activity, further positing that distributed denial-of-service attacks, like the one waged against Estonia in 2007, constitute "a worst, a minor nuisance to organizations (e.g., the military, electric power producers) that can run without interacting with the public at large." Libicki, *Cyberdeterrence and Cyberwar*, xiv.

[48] Excepting, for the moment, the simpler case of physical attacks on digital infrastructure.

immediate deterrence, the would-be attacker first needs to have recognition (of instrument and effect), second, a means of attribution (either direct identity attribution, or via ancillary deductive means like actor elimination and status of a force monopoly) of the target state's retributive force. Given those inputs, this section now considers the development, deployment, and execution components of a cyberattack to critically examine their deterrent value—specifically, to determine whether states are likely to receive the necessary inputs to make deterrent calculations.[49]

Development Environment. Cyberattack capabilities' development environment is composed of, essentially, the hardware and software tools needed to create (but neither deploy nor execute) its "ordnance"—typically malicious software.[50] Developing the malicious software (often called "malware") is, from the vantage of traditional military reconnaissance tools, a rather mundane affair, difficult to detect or observe. Therein lies the first manner in which it frustrates deterrence models.

Development of the malware itself—the first stage in the lifecycle and well before its deployment or use—can take place by an individual or a team working on one or multiple general-purpose computers. Unlike the specialized manufacturing facilities for aeronautics, or enrichment equipment required for certain nuclear weapons, the computers used to develop malware require few if any special characteristics.[51] Development can take place on most any off-the-shelf, dual-use computer, while even testing of sophisticated attack capabilities against esoteric infrastructure (like a certain kind of electrical transformer or water pump) would require little more than a single example of such a victim device. So when considering what constitutes a cyberattack capability, it is essential to bear in mind that those capabilities commonly begin on commercial technology distinguishable only by contents and use, not design.

---

[49] Again, this section does not explore the question of *dissuasion*, since the likelihood of an attack's success is largely case-specific and more significant for general deterrence relationships.

[50] The most common cyberattack capabilities are, as discussed in Chapter 1, software-based. They function by disrupting the normal operation of software (code) on computers upon which an increasingly large fraction of daily lives in developed countries and their economies rely. This analysis holds, however, when considering a hardware-enabled cyberattack (say, one in which the destructive feature is incipient within the computers/devices put into place by the victim state). The demonstrated case of malicious software is however more widely known, and therefore a more accessible use case.

[51] For example, none of the attacks described in Anderson's comprehensive work on security engineering necessarily require military-grade technologies. See Anderson, *Security Engineering*, 633–52.

Is either part of this development environment, either the infrastructure or code itself, helpful in assessing a state's cyberattack capabilities, and in turn, its deterrent value? Here the general criteria of instrument recognition, effect recognition, and attribution offer clues.

The infrastructure that constitutes the development environment, at its most generic, provides no meaningful instrument or effect recognition to an adversary. Substantial computing centers filled with servers generating significant heat and connected to thick fiber-optic lines are one kind of infrastructure often associated with cyberattack capabilities. In reality, however, they only indicate a state's level of investment in digital technology. Thus, a state's development of new data centers or dedication of computing facilities to the military—touted by the American, Korean, and Russian militaries as evidence of their cybersecurity prowess—is not tantamount to specific cyberattack capabilities.[52] With respect to attribution, it is plausible that large-scale computing centers would be positively identified as belonging to an adversary, but offer little aid in assessing capability, for the reasons above. This sort of ancillary infrastructure is not a reliable metric of attack capability and is even less useful in the assessment of those tools' effects.

The other feature of the development environment—the malicious code itself—does offer some more valuable information in making deterrence calculations. Locating such code while in development can reveal clues as to a would-be attacker's designs and sophistication, providing rough instrument recognition to a very sophisticated observer, certain common design procedures would offer clues on authorship, but such a situation is hardly predictable. However, the majority of malicious software targets general vulnerabilities shared by hundreds of thousands or even millions of machines—the Windows operating system, for instance. Rarer, though not unheard of, is the piece of malware that is designed to infect a single machine. For example, malicious software that is designed to disrupt only the most specific infrastructure (such as a particular brand of power transformer), or the rare piece of software with its targets "hard-coded" into it (akin to finding a missile's targets displayed on its exterior when aerially photographed) could without

---

[52] Henry Kenyon, "Work Commences on $1B NSA 'Spy' Center," *Defense Systems*, January 7, 2011; Markoff, "A Silent Attack, But Not a Subtle One"; David Talbot, "Russia's Cyber Security Plans: As Washington Airs Plans for a New 'Cyber Command,' A Top Russian Official Discusses the Threat of Cyberweapons," *MIT Technology Review*, April 16, 2010; Vasudevan Sridharan, "Russia Setting up Cyber Warfare Unit Under Military," *International Business Times*, 2013.

much difficulty remain largely enigmatic until it is deployed on networks.[53] In other words, observing even the software in development might not reveal its target, and thus, without observing deployment, a state could glean little about its likely effects.

Compounding this recognition challenge is another practical obstacle: the fundamental need for secrecy combined with the difficulty of witnessing code in development. Consider first that unlike explosives or other capabilities routinely exercised by the military, software-based tools that make up an effective cyberattack are often single-use because they exploit vulnerabilities that can be directly mitigated, if known.[54] As this chapter will explore in-depth in later sections, maintaining secrecy in development is not just preferable but essential for an effective capability. Here, efficacy and deterrent value can be in direct opposition—a feature the implications of which are discussed in-depth in subsequent pages. In order to maintain secrecy, the development infrastructure could be disconnected from the public internet until work was complete and the code was ready for deployment. The result would be a development environment that is necessarily obfuscated and produces tools that are perennially novel—at least in their method of operation. Thus, the investment required to find the particular machine on which development of malicious code is taking place often represents a considerable—and sometimes insurmountable—intelligence and surveillance challenge.[55]

---

[53] Stuxnet was reportedly a rare example of such malware, apparently specifically designed to activate only in the presence of a single type of infrastructure believed to be associated with the Iranian nuclear program. As the next paragraph outlines, this case illustrates the tension between credible (i.e., demonstrable) deterrent effect and efficacy of the attack itself.

[54] Max Smeets, "A Matter of Time: On the Transitory Nature of Cyberweapons," *Journal of Strategic Studies* 41, no. 1-2 (2018): 12. Smeets reasons that "cyberweapons are exceptional in that they belong to the group which is the most transitory as its ability and effectiveness to cause harm declines relatively quickly. Cyberweapons from this perspective are merely unique in that there is the potential of a quick adaptation of defence measures in cyberspace rendering the specific weapon ineffective."

[55] In some instances, the combination of world-class intelligence capabilities and disciplined attention on the part of the attributor, as well as the sloppiness of the attributed party, has yielded sufficient information to provide attribution of certain offensive activities at the individual (and organizational) level. While few in number and focused on repeated activities that may be easier to track than many large-scale cyberattacks under consideration here, indictments brought against Chinese and Iranian hackers offer important clues of future directions for the topic. China: US Department of Justice, "Two Chinese Nationals Charged with Laundering Over $100 Million in Cryptocurrency From Exchange Hack," March 2, 2020; US Department of Justice, "Chinese Military Personnel Charged with Computer Fraud, Economic Espionage and Wire Fraud for Hacking into Credit Reporting Agency Equifax," February 10, 2020; US Department of Justice, "Two Chinese Hackers Associated With the Ministry of State Security Charged with Global Computer Intrusion Campaigns Targeting Intellectual Property and Confidential Business Information," December 20, 2018; US Department of Justice, "U.S. Charges Five Chinese Military Hackers for Cyber Espionage Against U.S. Corporations and a Labor Organization for Commercial Advantage," May 19, 2014. North Korea: US Department of Justice, "North Korean Regime-Backed Programmer Charged With Conspiracy to Conduct Multiple Cyber Attacks and Intrusions," September 6, 2018. Iran: US

Attribution of malicious code in development is notably difficult for three reasons: the likely lack of state identity, the imprecision of elimination, and the typical absence of monopoly. While not excepting that states have engaged in this activity, to date no state has publicly and positively claimed credit for a piece of malicious software in development, and only a handful of massively disruptive viruses have had their author unmasked.[56] Even after the fact, states have not attributed to themselves disruptive cyberattacks widely considered their handiwork—a crucial fact explored throughout, and especially in Chapter 5.[57]

Barring public acknowledgment, elimination can be helpful in refining the sophistication of an actor responsible for malicious code, but little else.[58] Security researchers have generally been effective in distinguishing "run of the mill" viruses from sophisticated tools intended for deployment against another state's national security, though the line between the tools of organized crime and sophisticated nation-states remains blurry.[59] Dedicated state actions to obfuscate the authorship of their malware, such as creating Frankenstein-like malware that is a patchwork of other states' leaked offensive cyber tools and reflecting their techniques, further complicate this picture—though not universally.[60] Regardless, that information would be of little comfort to any state with two or more technologically sophisticated adversaries. Moreover, it is difficult to eliminate the potential that even

---

Department of Justice, "Nine Iranians Charge With Conducting Massive Cyber Theft Campaign On Behalf Of The Islamic Revolutionary Guard Corps," March 23, 2018; US Department of Justice, "Seven Iranians Working for Islamic Revolutionary Guard Corps-Affiliated Entities Charged for Conducting Coordinated Campaign of Cyber Attacks Against U.S. Financial Sector," March 24, 2016. The conclusion explores how state-of-the-art machine learning-driven (AI) tools may frustrate this capability.

[56] See, e.g., Phil Stewart, "Old Worm Won't Die After 2008 Attack on Military," *Reuters*, June 16, 2011. As of this writing, even physical attacks on digital infrastructure, such as the event that disabled much of San Francisco's internet connectivity for a period of several hours, remains unsolved.

[57] See, e.g., previously cited coverage of the Russia-Georgia attacks, Operation Orchard, and Stuxnet.

[58] Were a state able to locate the precise machine(s) on which malicious code development was taking place, identity attribution would be possible; however, for the reasons mentioned above, it would be unrealistic to rely upon that capability to inform immediate deterrence calculations.

[59] For specific cases noting this blurring, see McAfee, *Protecting Your Critical Assets: Lessons Learned from "Operation Aurora"* (San Jose, CA: McAfee Labs, 2010); McAfee, *Global Energy Cyberattacks: "Night Dragon"* (San Jose, CA: McAfee Labs, 2011); Kaspersky Lab, *Kaspersky Lab Identifies Operation "Red October," an Advanced Cyber-Espionage Campaign Targeting Diplomatic and Government Institutions Worldwide* (Moscow: Kaspersky Lab, 2013); SecDev Group, "Tracking GhostNet: Investigating a Cyber Espionage Network," *Information Warfare Monitor*, March 29, 2009.

[60] See, e.g., Greenberg, "Inside Olympic Destroyer: The Most Deceptive Hack in History" *Wired*, November 2019; Brian Barrett, "The Mysterious Return of Years-Old APT1 Malware," *Wired*, October 18, 2018.

Table 3.1 How Development Environment Informs Deterrence Calculations

	Recognition		Attribution		
	Instrument	Effect	Identity	Elimination	Monopoly
Development Infrastructure	?	☒	✓	✓	✓
Code in Development	✓	?	☒	?	☒

✓ = *Meaningful contribution*   ? = *Indeterminate*   ☒ = *No contribution*

carefully protected, state-developed tools might leak out and be reused or repurposed—as the North Koreans reportedly did in 2019.[61] Transferring code from one developer to another is as simple as sending an attachment to an email or physically handing off a thumbnail-sized flash drive. Therefore, elimination may be sporadically informative, but given the increasing list of states deemed "capable" in this space, is far from conclusive.

The same frustrations apply to monopoly, perhaps the least-informative criteria with respect to malicious code development. Generally speaking, the development infrastructure for most cyberattack tools is generic. Destructive code can be written (i.e., developed) as easily on a home laptop as on a government-issued performance computer—and without monopoly, the universe of attribution is vast. Cyberattack development thus stands in stark contrast to most sophisticated weapons, which require dedicated facilities, equipment, and supply chains.

The result is that easily observed cyberattack infrastructure yields little knowledge about specific cyberattack capabilities and while the exceptionally difficult-to-observe code development may yield some information, it is incomplete for a state interested in making a rational choice calculation. Even together, knowing the details of an adversary's development environment is not enough for a state's cyberattack capabilities to render effective deterrent value to a would-be adversary, as Table 3.1 summarizes.

Deployment Network. The second phase of cyberattack capabilities is the deployment network, or networks to deliver malicious software. These are

---

[61] Lily Hay Newman, "North Korea Is Recycling Mac Malware. That's Not the Worst Part," *Wired*, February 25, 2020.

more easily recognizable than code development, but far more challenging to attribute.

A deployment network is, for this simple case, the network of machines and/or communications pathways that deliver the "payload" of malicious software to their target computers. For example, in the kind of disruption Estonia experienced, the victim could theoretically have known about the existence of a disruptive network of computers awaiting orders prior to the event. This would, in the particular technical circumstances of that attack, have provided more visibility into the potential for an attack—though not necessarily its nature. Technical surveys of the size of various "botnets" or certain other deployment networks for cyberattack capabilities are possible and precise, to a point.[62] Thus a state may be able to roughly scale the nature of the threat that could be brought to bear against it—should the evolution of technology useful in cyberattacks continue to evolve along those lines.

Nonetheless, deployment is not the same as use, and not always indicative of the probable effect of an attack. Therefore, absent an execution order with final instructions on the networks to attack, it may not be possible to know much about the scale of capabilities. Even less would be known about the effects, which are already highly variable, given that no state possesses full knowledge of how system outages will cascade and cause damage across the victim state's economy, military, and society, and highly salient for comportment with the law of armed conflict, as Chapters 7 and 8 explore.

In this scenario, since cyberattack development infrastructure would be distributed across civilian and government, public and private networks, it nearly defines the absence of identity, inability to eliminate, and loss of force monopoly. Moreover, cyberattack deployment networks invoke the other complicating aspect of force monopoly—third-party availability. For example, the network of machines that attacked Estonia, infected with a virus to take over its operation and mobilize against the Baltic nation's critical infrastructure, was later reported to be available for hire to the highest bidder.[63] In fact, many small-scale disruptive networks featuring in a cyberattack are

---

[62] Amit Kumar Tiyagi and G. Aghila, "A Wide Scale Survey on Botnet," *International Journal of Computer Applications* 34, no. 9 (2011); Hossein Rouhani Zeidanloo, Farhoud Hosseinpour, and Farhood Farid Etemad, "New Approach for Detection of IRC and P2P Botnets," *International Journal of Computer and Electrical Engineering* 2, no. 6 (2010).

[63] John Markoff and Mark Lander, "Digital Fears Emerge After Data Siege in Estonia," *New York Times*, May 29, 2007.

Table 3.2 How Deployment Network Informs Deterrence Calculations

	Recognition		Attribution		
	Instrument	Effect	Identity	Elimination	Monopoly
Deployment Network	✓	?	☒	?	☒

✓ = *Meaningful contribution*   ? = *Indeterminate*   ☒ = *No contribution*

available for hire for as little as a few hundred dollars—and have been for many years.[64]

With respect to attribution, one might roughly analogize the deployment network to a squadron of incoming aircraft over international waters—visible on radar, but only in their direction, formation, rough size, and quantity. Such networks offer a better sense of the scale of an imminent cyberattack but still frustrate meaningful assessment by denying any meaningful and direct information about attribution. As such, these indicators of cyberattack capabilities offer far less information than would be necessary for them to provide their controlling state with a strong and recognizable deterrent when discovered by an adversary. Table 3.2 summarizes these conclusions.

Execution Tools. A third category of cyberattack capability, the *execution tool(s)*, is the most imminent and forward-deployed component of an attack—and, of the three, it constitutes the most promising candidate to inform immediate deterrence.

Execution tools can be thought of as the command-and-control infrastructure for hardware- or software-based cyberattack. They represent the

---

[64] Trend Micro, "Russian Underground 101" (Cupertino, CA: Trend Micro, 2012), 3,6. In 2018, Europol shut down the website, webstresser.org, which offered paying customers a distributed denial of service attack service. "The site reportedly had 136,000 registered users, and was behind as many as six million DDoS strikes. Packages cost as little as $19 per month, and members could summon attacks as strong as 350 Gbps." Elena Lacey, "The Biggest DDoS for Hire Site Goes Down," *Wired*, April 28, 2018. Adam Goldman, "Takeaways From The Times's Investigation Into Hackers for Hire," 2019. "A New York Times investigation detailed this new era of digital warfare and the multibillion-dollar industry behind it. Two firms—NSO, an Israeli company, and DarkMatter, based in the United Arab Emirates—have hired former government hackers to help their government clients not only hack criminal elements like terrorist groups and drug cartels but in some cases to also act on darker impulses, targeting activists and journalists." Ken Dunham and Jim Melnick, *Malicious Bots: An Inside Look Into the Cyber-Criminal Underground of the Internet* (Boca Raton, FL: CRC Press, 2008), 60–61. Describing how bots can be leveraged for rent or for hire with a case study from June 2007 involving the Russian hacker, "Lyric." On the Portal for Russian Hackers (Xakepy.ru), Lyric posted that "the price for a "quality" DDoS attack would vary, depending on the complexity of the attack ordered, but that the "average price was around 100 WMZ (WebMoney equivalent of USD $100)."

final phase in the lifecycle of planning a cyberattack, well after development on the attacker's own networks/machines and deployment that would normally transit third-party networks. Execution tools, by contrast, would be found in two places: either on the victim's networks (such as a power grid network or other critical infrastructure) awaiting the command to execute, or on an attacker's networks, waiting to issue that command. Thus, with respect to recognition and attribution, locating execution tools could provide much of the requisite information for a state to assess the nature of a potential attack—though doing so would indeed prove highly difficult.

In the case of tools known to be on a victim's network, instrument recognition seems highly probable (by their very presence), as would be the effect (by examining their intended purpose on that machine). This potentially powerful message is blunted by two facts. The first, already outlined, is that knowledge of the presence of these tools on a victim's networks invites their rapid inoculation—making cyberattack capabilities difficult to "exercise." Second, attribution of such tools located on a victim's network may well be only briefly possible. An attacker seeking deniability (as all appear to have to date) would take measures to obscure the identity of the responsible machine.[65] Looking ahead, this condition seems likely to persist. As a general matter, failure to execute the desired cyberattack would jeopardize the credibility of the deterrent. Moreover, discovery of a capability may unduly escalate tensions at a time different from the would-be attacker's preferred moment. Therefore, deniability remains an important asset for cyberattack capabilities, and "self-advertising" seems unlikely. Frustrating attribution appears practically important but also deeply undermines cyberattacks' value as a credible deterrent.

Were the means of execution discovered on a would-be attacker's networks—including, for example, if the tools needed to activate malware already installed on the victim network—the input to a deterrence calculation would be perhaps most significant. Here, attribution speaks for itself: in this simplified example, the location of that execution tool is known to be an

---

[65] Were the attack both sophisticated and on the scale under principal discussion in this study, opportunities for attribution by elimination would present themselves by narrowing the field to those with sufficient capability and reasonable intent. Still, a state with two such adversaries would potentially be left with crucial uncertainty. Moreover, a modicum of certainty on force monopoly in the case of the final execution tools (reserved for a single actor to execute and sophisticated enough to be of national security concern to a state) offer some additional potential in providing attribution.

Table 3.3 How Execution Tools (at Various Locations) Inform Deterrence Calculations

	Recognition		Attribution		
	Instrument	Effect	Identity	Elimination	Monopoly
Execution Tools (Victim's network)	✓	✓	☒	?	?
Execution Tools (Attacker's network)	✓	☒	✓	✓	✓
Combined	✓	✓	✓	✓	✓

✓ = Meaningful contribution   ? = Indeterminate   ☒ = No contribution

attacker's machine.[66] Recognition is also possible at least by half-measure; one can easily connect execution tools' controlling mechanisms to the tools they manage, but it is less likely that the full scale (effect) of the tool would be identified in this way.

As Table 3.3 illustrates, a combination of the two (linking execution tools on both the attacker's networks and victim's networks) would provide all necessary inputs to inform immediate deterrence.

Therefore, in the abstract, a state could rely on others' knowledge of its cyberattack execution tools—their location, likely effect, and attribution—to meaningfully inform its adversaries' deterrence calculations. This deterrence information should not, however, be confused with full attribution of the sort necessary for criminal prosecution or assessment of individual responsibility.

This latter point has, perhaps unduly, frustrated the literature on the international response to cyberattacks. In the rationalist framing, states' first preoccupation postattack is unlikely to be an assessment of the *individual* responsible. By analogy, the identity of who flipped the switch in launching the missile, who flew the airplane, or even who in the military chain of command issued the order is for the most part militarily, diplomatically, and politically irrelevant. The salient question is only whether those individuals were part of the organized defense forces, or directly controlled by them. On the scale of

---

[66] While simplified this scenario is not far-fetched; the attacker-side execution tool is likely to remain on computers owned and operated by the state in question for the same reasons of trust that launch codes and the most sensitive radar systems remain in capitals and not on allies' territory.

attacks under discussion in this study, that kind of broad-brush attribution is eminently possible.[67] With the right inputs, it is conceivable that states might be able to form deterrence calculations—but, as the following sections will discuss, exceedingly difficult in practice.

The Specificity Paradox

One further technical reality sets cyberattacks apart and deeply frustrates their use as a credible deterrent: the uniquely strong relationship between knowledge of an attack vector's specifics and defense against it. Many of the tools of cyberattacks (as mentioned earlier) are ephemerally efficacious; they exploit previously unknown vulnerabilities in the millions of lines of code that make up modern digital systems.[68] Once their method of attack is known, it can in most cases be readily "patched"—in essence, correcting the flaws in the system that were vulnerable to exploitation. Such patches are often distributed, like inoculations, across the entire population of machines, rendering the attacking virus inert.[69] This is what might be called the *specificity paradox*, which has substantial implications for cyberattack capabilities' deterrent value.

While more information released about a given state's cyberattack capabilities may provide it additional deterrence value, that value is not positive and linear. Once a certain level of specificity is known, defense against it becomes possible, and its deterrence value falls to almost zero.[70] Consider, by contrast, nuclear weapons: detailed knowledge of how a weapon works does not provide meaningful defense against its destructive power. Likewise, with advanced missiles, artillery, or submarines, knowledge of their technical

---

[67] See the US indictments of individual Russian, Chinese, and Iranian hackers, above.
[68] See Chapter 2, note 55.
[69] Such "patching" happens, in the case of a consumer personal computer, weekly if not more—sometimes with several hundred or more "inoculations" per cycle. Governments also play a role in the content of those patches, to the extent they are aware of critical vulnerabilities. See, for example, Cybersecurity and Infrastructure Security Agency, "Mozilla Patches Critical Vulnerability" (Arlington, VA: CISA, January 10, 2020).
[70] This feature may be one of the present moment and the present current state of technology, and as with all such things difficult to consider fixed. Some alternative scenarios are conceivable, where a truly ubiquitous technology has a significant vulnerability that is near impossible to fix in a timely manner, and is exploited. See, e.g., Gilad Maayan, "Five Years Later, Heartbleed Vulnerability Still Unpatched," *MalwareBytes*, September 16, 2019; Tom Warren, "A Major New Intel Processor Flaw Could Defeat Encryption and DRM Protections," *The Verge*, March 6, 2020; Nael Abu-Ghazaleh, Dmitry Ponomarev, and Dmitry Evtyushkin, "How the Spectre and Meltdown Hacks Really Worked," *IEEE Spectrum* (2019).

workings would at best provide means of sabotage, but not direct defense against their offensive capabilities.

When cyberattacks are introduced into an international security environment, so too is a kind of heterogeneity in the potential threats, and in turn, a pervasive opacity as to the kind of deterrent those capabilities provide. If a state's threats of cyberattack are specific enough to be credible to their adversary, they may consequently be simultaneously self-defeating.[71]

The Dangerous Middle

Another paradox adds additional texture. The ease of attribution in any of the contexts listed above takes place on a cosine curve: easier at the lowest and highest ends of sophistication, but increasingly challenging in the dangerous middle, where many state capabilities now cluster. On one end of the curve, unsophisticated actors make operational errors that for capable states, make tracing their signals or patterns of behavior trivial compared to more sophisticated ones. But on the other end, certain extremely sophisticated actors' operations are also comparatively simple to attribute by elimination, particularly if they employ cutting-edge techniques like accessing computers physically disconnected from another network (so-called airgap-hopping).[72] Increasingly, though, states of moderate capability are using and reusing one another's tactics, techniques, and procedures and coopting one another's infrastructure, and doing so sometimes without the distinctive tradecraft of more sophisticated actors.[73] Add to that the willingness of certain commercial and even state actors to provide generic offensive services for hire, and this part of the attribution picture becomes quickly more complex—and context-dependent.[74] As a practical matter, it may be that it is the midrange

---

[71] This same phenomenon explains why general (instead of immediate) deterrence against cyberattacks is less than promising: since attacks are so inherently "perishable," it would be difficult for much habituation of action and reaction, or understanding of escalation thresholds, to be obtained.

[72] Kello, *The Virtual Weapon and International Order*, 200.

[73] See, e.g., China Chopper, a malicious code developed by Chinese hackers. According to Cisco's Talos: "This web shell is widely available, so almost any threat actor can use. This also means it's nearly impossible to attribute attacks to a particular group using only presence of China Chopper as an indicator," Talos researchers write. "Because it is so easy to use, it's impossible to confidently connect it to any particular actor or group." Shannon Vavra, "'China Chopper' Web Shell Makes a Comeback in Lebanon, Other Asian Countries," *CyberScoop*, August 27, 2019.

[74] Anne An, "Chinese Cybercriminals Develop Lucrative Hacking Services" (San Jose, CA: McAfee Labs, 2018); Bergman and Mazzetti, "The Battle for the World's Most Powerful Cyberweapon."

actors that represent some of the most challenging cases for restraint given the surprising difficulty of attributing them.

Conclusions and Implications for Cyberattack Capabilities' Proliferation

There exist a number of seeming paradoxes in studying deterrence of cyberattacks. In the abstract, deterrence might obtain, but demonstrating how has often yielded some of Kissinger's "esoteric intellectual exercises," due to their disconnection from present state practice. A study with more practical implications for international politics must necessarily accept imperfect and incomplete information. As just argued, though, certain types of information are essential to a state making any approximation of a rational choice on that basis. Within the lifecycle of cyberattack capabilities' development, deployment, and final use, knowledge of the latter—and the fortuitous triangulation of attacker and victim network—is the most (perhaps only) promising candidate to consistently provide the necessary information to meaningfully deter an adversary.

In short, states will favor cyberattack tools for offense over defense, and for use over threatening use. Cyberattack tools are difficult to observe and hard to locate while in development, easy to obfuscate during deployment, and generally single-use. As Maness and Valeriano put it: "How would one know that a threat hurts unless a demonstration of capability is made? The paradox is that once a demonstration of capability is made, the cyber weapon is then put out into the wild for all to dissect."[75] A would-be attacker is unlikely to be deterred by a state's cyberattack capabilities alone. Presume again that Asgard and Babel are two countries with similar vulnerability to a generic cyberattack. Babel's development, deployment, and preparations to execute all but the sloppiest or most disposable cyberattacks would not meaningfully inform Asgard's rational choice to attack. Moreover, if Asgard's information about Babel's cyberattack capabilities is credibly specific, the former's ability to defend against a counterattack increases substantially. It seems implausible that cyberattack capabilities represent a sound investment for Babel if it is strictly seeking to deter its aggressor. Table 3.4 summarizes the conclusions

---

[75] Maness and Valeriano, *Cyber War versus Cyber Realities*, 56.

Table 3.4 Overview: How Cyberattack Capabilities Inform Deterrence Calculations

	Recognition		Attribution		
	Instrument	Effect	Identity	Elimination	Monopoly
Development Infrastructure	?	☒	✓	✓	✓
Code in Development	✓	?	☒	?	☒
Deployment Network	✓	?	☒	☒	☒
Execution Tools (Victim)	✓	✓	☒	?	?
Execution Tools (Attacker)	✓	☒	✓	✓	✓

✓ = Meaningful contribution   ? = Indeterminate   ☒ = No contribution

of the prior sections and provides a comprehensive overview of the information states would use to inform their deterrence calculations against cyberattack capabilities.

There are a few exceptions to this general conclusion. A state with only one plausible, capable adversary and exceptional reconnaissance might be informed of the threat and origin and find itself deterred generally. A state with exceptional attribution capabilities, for instance by virtue of persistent presence on global telecommunications networks would also have greater insights—a long-term fear animating a significant amount of US commercial diplomacy in the Trump administration.[76] Another case would find Asgard highly dependent on technology and Babel not, in which the former's discovery of the latter's sophisticated cyberattack program may more effectively deter than may otherwise be the case.[77] Beyond these narrow cases, however, cyberattack capabilities appear to offer little direct deterrent value in a rationalist decision-making space.

While one might counter that the ability to demonstrate an offensive activity provides far more information than the sort of forensic, preattack,

---

[76] See, for example US Department of State, "Press Briefing with Deputy Assistant Secretary Robert Strayer," October 15, 2019; Mark Landler and Ana Swanson, "About That Much Vaunted U.S.–U.K. Trade Deal? Maybe Not Now," *New York Times*, March 2, 2020.

[77] Another might be a state's sloppy preparation or public demonstration of cyberattack capabilities; however, doing so would likely lower the efficacy of that attack to the point of insignificance.

in situ observations just explored, even with repeated opportunities, cyberattacks offer little to envy as a direct deterrent. Aforementioned, such demonstrations are expressions of general capability but suffer from the specificity paradox. The most sophisticated actors demonstrating the most sophisticated capabilities—who may in this case not want to obfuscate—also run the risk that those capabilities are copied by those in the dangerous middle, removing over time the distinctiveness of the deterrent. This is where general critiques of credibility in cyberattack threats are at their strongest.[78] Combined, these two factors suggest a short half-life for even those cyberattack capabilities that advanced states might hope would deter an adversary.

Those states publicly known to have a significant cyberattack capability have not seen the peacetime balance of power swing tectonically in their favor as a result. Nor, for that matter, have any states comprehensively realigned their military posture or drawn down traditional forces in preference of cyberattack capabilities (as was occasionally proposed for states possessing nuclear weapons).[79] The former is particularly notable if it remains true that states with reportedly strong cyberattack capabilities, like Israel and Australia, fail to gain visible concessions from adversaries seeking to avoid becoming victims of those tools. As states develop a greater understanding of the tactic, even as their susceptibility to it may increase with their technological dependence, from this analysis it seems unlikely that cyberattack capabilities will form the core of a state's deterrent posture. Both of these conclusions suggest a limited role for cyberattacks in deterring generally, given their inherent attributes. In this respect, the drive to acquire cyberattack capabilities may be self-limiting.

Limited Deterrent Value: A Plausible But Weak Restraint

As information about their real capabilities and limitations grows, the long-term pull to acquire cyberattack capabilities may be weaker than journalism and popular literature suggests, to the extent acquisition decisions

---

[78] Maness and Valeriano, *Cyber War versus Cyber Realities: Cyber Conflict in the International System*, 60.
[79] Jennifer Bradley, "Increasing Uncertainty: The Dangers of Relying on Conventional Forces for Nuclear Deterrence," *Air & Space Power Journal* 29, no. 4 (2015): 72. For several other examples of tectonic shifts in technology shifting reliance on previously preponderant forces, see Stephen Biddle, *Military Power: Explaining Victory and Defeat in Modern Battle* (Princeton, NJ: Princeton University Press, 2004), 77.

are made for purposes of deterrence as well as use. Cyberattacks are not, from the standpoint of rationalist deterrence, a sound investment for a state seeking a significant peacetime deterrent in the way that, for instance, many scholars have long regarded nuclear arms to be.[80] In the rationalist mode, states make investments in their security on the basis of perceived threat and perceived vulnerability weighed against the value of the strategic investment. Vulnerability and threat may both be high, but the deterrent value of investing in such difficult-to-demonstrate cyberattack capabilities render them a less attractive investment than more conventional, credible attack vectors. Therefore, though cyberattacks possess a substantial and growing disruptive threat to states, they are not the sine qua non of maintaining international security in that state's favor. They are not, as some have labelled them, "the perfect weapon"—at least not in the abstract.[81] From the standpoint of restraint, this is an encouraging, if preliminary, sign.

Yet that conclusion appears to be at odds with present state practice. After all, if these tools provide little deterrent value, why are so many states clamoring to acquire them? It is important not to lose sight of the fact that limited deterrent value does not equate to limited offensive value. Indeed, for states pondering full-scale conflict against an adversary, a cyberattack might for the reasons outlined in Chapter 1 shift the balance of a conflict. The fact also remains that while information about cyberattacks may be limited for strictly rationalist calculations, apprehension of them (and hyperbole about their destructive power) is currently quite high. Thus, when top Russian officials warn of "the huge potential [for] information-computer technologies [to] be used to ensure military-political domination, the use of force and blackmail to open doors to new trends of arms race," and American officials worry that "the next Pearl Harbor we confront could very well be a cyberattack that cripples our power systems, our grid, our security systems, our financial systems, our governmental systems," the result may be a (potentially irrational)

---

[80] See James J. Wirtz, "How Does Nuclear Deterrence Differ from Conventional Deterrence?," *Strategic Studies Quarterly* 12, no. 4 (2018): 58; Robert Peters, Justin Anderson, and Harrison Menke, "Deterrence in the 21st Century: Integrating Nuclear and Conventional Force," *Strategic Studies Quarterly* 12, no. 4 (2018): 15; James Wood Forsyth, "Nuclear Weapons and Political Behavior," *Strategic Studies Quarterly* 11, no. 3 (2017): 115. It is not, however, a settled matter. Other scholars argue that nuclear weapons' peacetime deterrent value is in fact quite limited; see, e.g., Tom Sauer, "A Second Nuclear Revolution: From Nuclear Primacy to Post-Existential Deterrence," *Journal of Strategic Studies* 32, no. 5 (2009): 745; Matthew Kroenig, "The History of Proliferation Optimism: Does It Have a Future?," *Journal of Strategic Studies* 38, no. 1–2 (2015): 98; Christopher J. Fettweis, "Pessimism and Nostalgia in the Second Nuclear Age," *Strategic Studies Quarterly* 13, no. 1 (2019).

[81] Sanger, *The Perfect Weapon*.

pull on policymakers.[82] This pull, while defying the cold calculations upon which most deterrence theories are based, is both meaningful and instructive at this particular historical moment. Chapter 8 considers its potential effects more broadly.

Some states may be acquiring those capabilities for deterrent potential more than proven deterrent value. Consider, for instance, that the United States, Germany, Russia, the United Kingdom, South Korea, Iran, and North Korea all publicly claim to be developing some sort of cyberattack or cyber warfare capability—and this is only a partial list.[83] One might assume that states are clearly *claiming* development of cyberattack capabilities, and that in so doing they are attempting a sort of in-kind deterrence (examined momentarily). As a political matter, which is to say one of national reputation, there may indeed be signaling value in broadcasting such developments. As a rational deterrence matter, however, there is little to be gleaned from such a claim. Far more salient is the fact that even among those with "declared" dedicated cyberattack capabilities, none claimed responsibility for an event approximating a successful cyberattack—and only a few have successfully demonstrated those capabilities for would-be aggressors to see and assess. Assumptions may be the currency of deterrence in the absence of solid intelligence, however, as of this writing no countries have publicized a successful thwarting of a cyberattack, save for one Israeli case that has not been independently verified.[84] In the context of this analysis those states may also be disappointed as the short-term decisions of policymakers run up against the underlying realities of immediate deterrence. States may come to such a realization over the course of trial and error, but whether for reasons of

---

[82] Andrey Krutskikh, "Information Challenges to Security (1999)," in *International Information Security: The Diplomacy of Peace*, ed. Sergei Komov (Moscow: Russian Federation Official Publications, 2009), 7; Armed Services Committee, United States Senate, *Hearing to Consider the Nomination of Hon. Leon E. Panetta to be Secretary of Defense*, June 9, 2011.

[83] *Information Technology and Cyber Operations: Modernization and Policy Issues to Support the Future Force*; Federal Republic of Germany, *Cyber Security Strategy for German*; Talbot, "Russia's Cyber Security Plans"; *BBC News*, "Interview with Prime Minister Gordon Brown: 'We Must Not Be Victims,'" June 25, 2009; Sang-ho Song, "Military eyes 'proactive cyberactivities,'" *Korea Herald*, October 8, 2014; *Chosun Ilbo*, "N. Korea 'Confident' in Cyber Warfare Capabilities," April 8, 2013; and Paul Bucala and Caitlin S. Pendleton, "Iranian Cyber Strategy: A View from the Iranian Military," November 24, 2015. Citing a translated news report on Iran's military leadership as reported by the Mehr News Agency on November 7, 2015, "Cyberspace requires a comprehensive strategy." For an overview of Iran's Cyber Organization, see US Congressional Research Service. "Iranian Offensive Cyber Attack Capabilities" (Washington, DC: U.S. Congress, 2020).

[84] See Israeli Defense Force (IDF), "We thwarted an attempted Hamas cyber offensive against Israeli targets. Following our successful cyber defensive operation, we targeted a building where the Hamas cyber operatives work. HamasCyberHQ.exe has been removed.," @IDF (Twitter, May 5, 2019).

optimistic experimentation, self-delusion, or inadequate consideration, they do not appear to be substantially motivated at present. While cyberattacks' failures as a deterrent may dampen enthusiasm, it is best to mute expectations about that reality being decisive in near-term restraint.

3.3 Alternative Deterrence Frames

There are other ways that rationalist calculations can create meaningful restraint: for instance, if states were particularly concerned about a boomerang effect of a cyberattack they use coming back to harm themselves, or if cyberattacks capabilities were narrowly but particularly effective at deterring in kind. This section considers both these possibilities.

Self-Deterrence

A specialized source of rationalist restraint posited by scholars—"self-deterrence"—does little to move these conclusions. The concept here, posited by Farwell and Rohozinski as well as Valeriano and Maness, is that states might eschew offensive cyber operations entirely for fear that the same attack vector they employ would be turned rapidly back upon them (what the latter call "cyber straitjacketing").[85] Several years ago this theory seemed promising, and indeed appealing to those who aimed to prove that cyberattack tools are far less attractive than they might appear.[86] Unfortunately, the passage of time has offered little to support this theory and new developments in the frequency and scale of disruptive cyber incidents suggest even dimmer prospects—even as cumulative, mutual dependence on digital infrastructure grows.

The leakage of offensive cyber tools is a non-novel technical reality; their reuse has been a feature of hacking since its inception, and was discussed previously. It has apparently not caused any of the nations and their militaries previously mentioned to stand down from such developments. In fact, the repurposing of tactics, techniques, and procedures from one country

---

[85] Nye, *The Future of Power*; James P. Farwell and Rafal Rohozinski, "Stuxnet and the Future of Cyber War," *Survival* 53, no. 1 (2011); Maness and Valeriano, *Cyber War versus Cyber Realities*.

[86] Maness and Valeriano, *Cyber War versus Cyber Realities*, 62.

to obfuscate one's own have become common tradecraft, suggesting an environment that is more promiscuous than wary.[87] Chinese tools, for example, have reportedly become a popular choice, given the prolific nature of Beijing's hacking apparatus.[88] So, too, were purported NSA tools used by the DPRK, Russia, and China in subsequent attacks—according to some reports, including those holding the municipal government networks of Baltimore, Maryland hostage for ransom.[89] The dynamic nature of the security environment—that no country can expect its tool to be instantaneously used back on them, and that no tool remains equally potent over a long time frame—combined with occasional arrogance on the part of those using the tools, likely prevents this concern from preempting first use.[90]

A broader trend may also be responsible for the failure of self-deterrence: for reasons inside and outside of states' intentional erosion and occasional dramatic decloaking of the secrecy surrounding offensive cyber tools in recent years. While a few slapped-together high-grade scripts do not a world-class cyber-offense make, public knowledge of capabilities also has the effect of creating rapid inoculation against some of them, accelerating the pace of that dynamic security environment just noted, and reducing the potential costs of retributive use of the same techniques. The emergence of vulnerability equities processes (VEPs) are perhaps the nail in the coffin of self-deterrence, given that they offer sophisticated states a means to consider and control these reflexive effects.[91] In the US case, officials claim that one of the key criteria in slating a newly discovered vulnerability for public release and patching (rather than offensive use) is the potential for use against the government's own networks to significant national security effect.[92] While imperfect, the implication is twofold: countries with such programs regard their ability to ascertain reflexive risk as substantial, and the tools they select for operational use are selected partly for minimization of that risk. Even this last resort of functional deterrence on its own terms seemingly leaves

---

[87] See notes 61 and 62.

[88] Barrett, "The Mysterious Return of Years-Old APT1 Malware"; Vavra, "'China Chopper' Web Shell Makes a Comeback in Lebanon, Other Asian Countries."

[89] Nicole Perlroth and Shane Scott, "In Baltimore and Beyond, a Stolen N.S.A. Tool Wreaks Havoc," *New York Times*, May 25, 2019.

[90] Yuna Huh Wong, et al. "Deterrence in the Age of Thinking Machines" (Santa Monica, CA: RAND Corporation, 2020).

[91] Michael Daniel, "Heartbleed: Understanding When We Disclose Cyber Vulnerabilities" (Washington, DC: The White House, 2014).

[92] Ari Schwartz and Robert Knake, "The Government's Role in Vulnerability Disclosure" (Cambridge, MA: Harvard Kennedy School, 2016).

few options—not adding value to acquiring cyberattack tools, but also not making doing so any riskier.

In-Kind Deterrence

Can states effectively fight fire with fire, deterring the threat of cyberattack with similar in-kind capabilities? Because they are poor general and immediate deterrents and offer little defensive value against similar capabilities, any state seeking to deter a cyberattack would do well to look beyond developing the same capabilities to respond in kind. The principal reason, the difficulty of signaling and assessing in order to make a meaningful deterrent calculation, does not require recapitulation. However, some distinct strategic characteristics of cyberattacks explain why one should not expect in-kind capabilities to meaningfully deter an attack.

As previously noted, cyber-defense and cyber-offense are largely incommensurate. Most offensive cyberattack tools do not, by their nature, have inherent defensive value, in the way for instance fighter jets, tanks, destroyers, or aircraft carriers do. Most tools outlined in the previous section are purpose-built to disrupt, but (at least today) are not immediately adaptable, as deployed, to defend.[93]

The one exception to this claim would be the potential for pre-emptive or retaliatory disarmament of their attacker: using cyberattack tools to cripple a would-be aggressor's own capabilities in a kind of "counterforce" attack, to borrow from the nuclear lexicon. In this scenario, one could envision such malware being deployed to disable either the delivery network or execution tools of an adversary. "Defend forward" efforts US authorities report they have undertaken to disrupt forthcoming digital influence operations provide small-scale, targeted examples of this kind of activity.[94] At the scale of broad-based cyberattacks, however, relevant technologies are on the near-term horizon at best. Machine learning-driven (AI) tools may enable to the production and execution of such counterforce capabilities at

---

[93] Depending on the technical depth or generality at which one is considering cyberattack tools, there are exceptions to this claim. For instance, tools such as password crackers and vulnerability identification suites both can also aid system defenders by demonstrating where technical investment is needed to reduce risk. It is the next step—whether to patch a hole or drop a malicious payload—that differentiates defense from offense.

[94] See, inter alia, "Pentagon Launches First Cyber Operation to Deter Russian Interference in Midterm Elections," *Washington Post*, October 23; US Department of Defense, "DOD Has Enduring Role in Election Defense" (Washington, DC: February 10, 2020).

the scale and with the diversity necessary to thwart such an attack, however this remains to be seen. (This rapidly changing state of the art, is explored in greater depth in the conclusion.) For now, reliance on this sort of technique would be at present impractical due to the overwhelming reconnaissance needs and potential for significant collateral effects.[95] Moreover, non–software-based cyberattacks, including destroying information infrastructure or disabling other critical hardware, again have no meaningful defensive use. Today's cyberattack capabilities, in other words, have little counterforce value.

The result is that in deterring cyberattacks, those same cyberattack capabilities have at best "countervalue" utility—which is of course still limited by the difficulty signaling it, as outlined in the prior section. Nonetheless, if analogies are to be drawn, cyberattacks in this context bear closer resemblance to intercontinental ballistic missiles, artillery, and other tools useful for offense both initial and retaliatory, but not immediate defense itself. Put differently, cyberattack capabilities in and of themselves do little to *dissuade* or provide deterrence by denial, which is to dampen or nullify the success of an incoming attack.[96] Given this technical nature, the likely outcome of a dyad of states each developing cyberattack capabilities for use is *not* mutual restraint to limit potential damage, but build-up. In this respect as well, strategic planning for the use of a cyberattack bears some resemblance to the dynamic of nuclear stockpiling and ballistic missile rivalry during the Cold War, absent the controls ultimately developed to try to contain them.[97] There is some evidence that this sort of stockpiling is taking place, albeit in a considered way—a fact that in refuting the *volume* of such stockpiling, White House cybersecurity officials publicly described as early as 2014.[98]

---

[95] See Chapter 1, note 155 on revisions to the once-popular concept of defense at "network speed."

[96] Notably, some national cyber-defense strategies appear to recognize this distinction and specifically note it, including both the US *International Strategy* and *Defense Strategy for Operating in Cyberspace*.

[97] Such an inquiry would fall outside the scope of this study and without much history behind it, may be better suited to military science than international relations. It may however be fruitful for subsequent scholars to examine in-depth in such a context.

[98] Daniel, "Heartbleed."

3.4 Moving Beyond Cyber-Deterrence

From the preceding sections it appears that cyberattacks may be attractive, but as tools for use, not to deter generally, nor even in the narrow context of deterring other cyberattacks. Combined with scant evidence of self-deterrence, this is not encouraging for those seeking a rationalist regime capable of imposing restraint. Cyberattack acquisition may not have the rationalist appeal of decisive weaponry such as nuclear weapons, but their proliferation also lacks the natural check of a functioning deterrence regime. This chapter explained why, as a general matter, cyberattack capabilities are poor investments for deterrence. As states develop these capabilities, meaningful in-kind deterrence is unlikely to limit them; if anything, the perceived threat of cyberattack by an adversary would more likely result in a build-up, rather than drawdown of those capabilities.

The conclusion here is that attempts to define and rely upon a discrete and self-contained notion of cyber-deterrence—which is to say, deterrence defined solely by the contribution of cyberattack capabilities—are misguided. A cyberattack cannot be meaningfully deterred by another cyberattack. Instead, the only realistic prospects for deterring it appear to be through the full scope of state powers that would be brought to bear to deter any other unfriendly state action, whether diplomatic, economic, or military. Former UK Defence Minister Nick Harvey has echoed this conclusion arguing in 2011 that "cyberspace adds a new dimension, but its use in warfare should be subject to the same strategic and tactical thought as existing means."[99]

If deterring a cyberattack is not well done via a defender's own similar capabilities, is then the natural solution to deter via traditional (i.e., noncyber) means? Certainly, a state with an overwhelming traditional military presence would hope so. And indeed, were cyberattacks simply another addition to any conventional military arsenal, the answer would almost certainly be "yes." After all, while in some cases similar capabilities may dissuade (such as warships), other types of coercion are best deterred by different compelling capabilities (say, a nuclear deterrent to conventional invasion). The latter is particularly true of weapons that favor offense, like cyberattacks.

Large-scale cyberattacks will likely play a limited role in the maintenance of peacetime international security and prospects for a specialized self- or

---

[99] Nick Harvey, *Armed Forces Minister—Responding to Cyber War*, ed. UK Ministry of Defence (London: The Stationary Office, Her Majesty's Government, 2011).

in-kind cyber-deterrence seem dim. These findings produce a number of conclusions. First, it is an underacknowledged reality that like other coercive actions, cyberattacks may be most reliably deterred by an adversary's overwhelming military arsenal or other capabilities. Second, a state with cyberattack capabilities must principally rely on those other strengths and capabilities to deter adversaries, and as a result, restraining cyberattacks will depend how closely cyberattacks are tied to those other tools.[100] Third, the adversary's perception of the threat of a cyberattack is more likely to result in a build-up of these capabilities, versus a drawdown.[101]

There is only one concern, trivial to military planning but vital to the international relations of cyberattacks: these kinds of capabilities are not universally regarded as weaponry in the traditional sense. A cyberattack is not necessarily considered, by all states at the present time, an incident that invokes the same kind of comparative military force analysis that defines the prototypical immediate deterrence calculation. Therefore, in weighing the gains and losses of a cyberattack, it is decidedly unclear whether or not military retaliation is on the table. Knowing so would be of fundamental importance to deterring a cyberattack—and, in turn, to restraining them generally. After all, if states were to universally acknowledge that their conventional forces are off limits in retaliation, it would dramatically skew a would-be attacker's calculations about undertaking one, particularly against a well-armed adversary. Or, perversely, the absence of likely armed retaliation may incentivize the use of cyberattacks relative to other forms of interstate coercion. So today, as an empirical matter, cyberattacks occupy a kind of purgatory where states are unable to make rationalist decisions about them other debates are resolved.

The next chapter argues that this very debate, with fundamental implications for whether and how cyberattacks can be deterred, is presently playing out on the world stage. Underlying it is the reality that cyberattacks' status within customary practice (of states and their militaries) is unsettled. For this and the reasons articulated, it is impossible for states to undertake purely rationalist deterrence calculations. Consequently, states are in the midst of deploying variants of a similar strategy to deter one another from using cyberattacks by linking them to, or decoupling them from, conventional military arsenals.

---

[100] Erik Gartzke, Jon Lindsay, and Michael Nacht, "Cross-Domain Deterrence: Strategy in an Era of Complexity" (paper presented at the International Studies Association Annual Meeting, Toronto, 2014).
[101] See Tables 3.1–3.4; see also Buchanan, *Cybersecurity Dilemma*.

4
Constructing Deterrence

Most discussions of deterrence take as a given the universe of potential responses available to an attacker or defender—yet in the case of cyberattacks, as we have seen, it is difficult if not impossible for a state to rationally assess gain and loss. Deterrence is of little practical significance if states lack the information to form the cost-and-benefit calculations needed to make an informed, rational decision. If that is the case, then there would be no way for a state to *predictably* deter cyberattacks by another, and prospects for international stability among states possessing cyberattack capabilities might be fleeting. Purely rationalist analysis, if it takes state response options as determined and static, would relegate the question to a policy matter, and await definitive documentary evidence of when states have been effectively restrained from an overwhelming interest in executing a cyberattack. In short, it would provide little insight to the present-day scholar—and even less hope for the restraint project.

So must we give up on deterrence until a later date with a richer customary record and clearer accounts of state decision-making? This chapter argues no: states are in fact presently trying to escape this "deterrence purgatory" by short-circuiting their opponents' deterrence calculations, specifically revolving around whether acceptable responses to cyberattacks are military in nature. This is the missing link in rationalist restraint, and if solved for, would make deterrence matter as a potential source thereof. The argument here is not abstract; states are aware of this crucial ambiguity and are seeking, in a novel realm of interstate competition, to set the parameters for future deterrence of cyberattacks.

Outline of Argument

This chapter calls for a more nuanced notion of rationalist deterrence necessary to explain both conceptually how deterrence involving cyberattacks might operate and how states are presently seeking to do so. It starts from the basic premise that the only way to meaningfully deter cyberattacks is by tying them to a conventional arsenal that is, itself, viewed as overwhelmingly deterrent and available for use in response. This method of deterrence is premised not directly on amassing one capability or the other but primarily on shaping the customary environment for its use to swing rationalist deterrent calculations to one's own advantage, which is deemed here "structural deterrence." It first defines the notion of structural deterrence and provides some rough historical parallels and related concepts in recent commentary. Next, it argues that states are already making use of this strategy vis-à-vis cyberattacks and documents some of the most important examples. Finally, it concludes by asking which side of this particular structural deterrence debate is likely to succeed: those who would link cyberattacks to their traditional military deterrent, or those who would assert that cyberattacks ought not be countered by conventional military means.

4.1 Defining Structural Deterrence

Structural deterrence adds a third dimension to the conventional rationalist calculation by recognizing that states must shape the acceptable universe of "inputs" that others use in calculating the advantage of using novel capabilities. This more textured composition of deterrence is one in which states strive to achieve outcomes in a rationalist environment through neoliberal means.

Structural deterrence exists in the same analytical framework of rationalism, which takes state interests as given and sees actions that reflect normative and institutional preferences as in service of that abiding interest. However, it does not treat the context of cyberattacks' use as static.

Freedman, in his 2004 book, provides the genesis for this general premise of normatively informed rationalist calculations; however, the concept of structural deterrence here is not an organically normative one.[1] Here, norms are instrumental to informing a rationalist calculation in favor of the party seeking to deter. Later chapters will consider in-depth the merits of scholars such as Stevens who claim that effective deterrence involves "the exercise of many elements of foreign policy, rather than the use of threatened use of

---

[1] Freedman, *Deterrence*.

military force alone."[2] This section argues that it is precisely that question of threatened use of military force that is the starting point for understanding how states are positioning their acquisition of cyberattack capabilities.

Structural deterrence, when necessary, precedes immediate deterrence. It is obviated by states' ability to conduct reliable rationalist calculations about a given coercive act. Thus, for well-established means of attack, such as moving ground troops to occupy a territory or dispatching of fighters to enter airspace on a bombing sortie, structural deterrence is hardly necessary. An attacker using such conventional means could easily calculate the range of potential retaliatory actions from their target—at least until the calculation begins to consider cyberattack capabilities. In this emerging arena, however, the calculation may break down thanks to the difficulty of assessing the ramifications of a counterattack. It is even harder to assess if the primary tool is a cyberattack.

Structural deterrence becomes necessary to a rationalist calculation when three preconditions are met.

First, that method of coercion must not be a state-ending capability, such as nuclear weapons (which most populations rightly equate to regime destruction and military defeat, the margins of Cold War planning aside).[3] For example, a novel and undetectable delivery system for nuclear weapons or a catastrophic biological weapon would immediately invoke the full strength of a would-be defender's available arsenal. Conversely, a new method for seizing government officials' assets would under no reasonable circumstances put all such options into play. Cyberattacks, for the general reasons outlined in the prior chapter and the paucity of state custom regarding their use, fall between the two.

Second, it must be one that, either by its nature or the evolution of present technology, eludes direct assessment of likely threat. Such circumstances come to pass when the disruptive consequences are principally second-order and third-order, and highly complex—such as a disruption to a crucial part of a global supply chain, food supply, or general-use information

---

[2] Timothy C. Stevens, "A Cyberwar of Ideas? Deterrence and Norms in Cyberspace," *Contemporary Security Policy* 33, no. 1 (2012).

[3] For an excellent overview of the differences between both theories, the distinction between them in the nuclear and conventional contexts, see Robert A. Pape Jr., "Coercion and Military Strategy: Why Denial Works and Punishment Doesn't," *Journal of Strategic Studies* 15, no. 4 (1992). For a more in-depth presentation of the punishment strategy in the nuclear context, see Robert Powell, "Nuclear Deterrence and the Strategy of Limited Retaliation," *American Political Science Review* 83, no. 2 (1989).

network—and/or if the capability itself is presently difficult or impossible to detect, as cyberattack capabilities indeed are.

Third and most importantly, it must not be able to be deterred in-kind as described previously, thus requiring exogenous capabilities to effectively deter another state's use thereof. Combined, these three conditions create the circumstances under which traditional rationalist deterrence is not meaningfully possible, and where a strategy of structural deterrence is the only means for states to develop and, ideally, shape the rationalist calculations of others. Such is the case, as this chapter will briefly examine, with cyberattacks.

Parallels in History and Commentary

Cyberattacks are not alone in blurring the line between civilian and military coercion and as the next chapter will explore as a legal matter, peacetime and wartime coercion. In their seminal 1974 study of deterrence in the context of American foreign policy, George and Smoke remark on the underdeveloped study of those "deterrence or threats of conflict below limited war on the spectrum of violence."[4] Such events, they argue, constitute "a range of phenomena" where violence may be "covert, low-level, or not yet visible."[5] Even their study, however, draws a dividing line between situations like "counterinsurgency, and guerrilla warfare, espionage . . . and 'black' operations," which might be not deterred through explicitly military or diplomatic means.[6] Furthermore, their study avoids exploration of actions that themselves occupy a customary interstitial space between them—where their status is neither definitively below nor equivalent to limited war from the standpoint of custom. Yet cyberattacks presently exist in that sort of limbo, and such, merit more careful examination than general deterrence theories outlined above.

Structural deterrence is better suited to explain potential pathways for a strategic relationship than a retrospective interpretation of how individual decisions contributed to a particular outcome. In other words, it is normative-prescriptive rather than historical-explanatory, recognizing that some historical parallels are relevant, though imperfect.[7] For example,

---

[4] George and Smoke, *Deterrence in American Foreign Policy: Theory and Practice*.
[5] Ibid.
[6] Ibid., 44.
[7] George and Smoke make similar provisos about deterrence of limited war. Ibid., 61.

peacetime blockades have long been a questionable act in international relations, falling at the intersection of economic coercion (by effect) and military coercion (by method).[8] The legal dynamics are discussed in Chapter 5, which examines questions of cyberattacks as uses of force and their potential for invoking rights of self-defense under international law. As a matter of rationalist deterrence, it is worth noting that peacetime blockades have invoked a similar kind of retributive ambiguity: consider, for example, the 1827 French, Russian, and British blockade in support of Greek rebels against Turkey; the British blockade of the Republic of New Grenada in 1837; the partial 1962 American quarantine of Cuba during that year's Missile Crisis; and the blockade of the Gaza Strip by Israel and Egypt that began in 2007. In such cases, it was not entirely clear to the aggressor whether or not the full measure of traditional military force could be, or would be, brought to bear to terminate the action. It was difficult to assess the likely threat given their second-order consequences. And while the instrument (traditionally warships) could certainly be deterred in-kind (with a strong navy), the tactic of blockade itself did not lend itself to in-kind retribution. The result is a still-simmering, century-old practical question about whether a blockade actually and reliably results in military response.[9]

A similar historical parallel to modern cyberattacks might be considered in the case of unilateral peacetime economic sanctions. States executing such sanctions absent international mandate, particularly when the nature of

---

[8] Blockades have long been a feature of declared war since their earliest record, from the Athenian blockade of the island of Aegina during the First Peloponnesian War (458–57 BC), to the Fatimid Caliphate's naval blockade of the Kingdom of Jerusalem in 1102, to the 1991 blockade of the Croatian coast by the Serbian navy during the Bosnian Crisis (Croatian War of Independence).

[9] See Michael Fraunces, "The International Law of Blockade: New Guiding Principles in Contemporary State Practice," *Yale Law Journal* 101 (1999): 909. As an act of war in the *jus in bello*, a blockade is primarily governed under the 1856 Paris Declaration Respecting Maritime Law and 1909 London Declaration Concerning the Laws of Naval War. "A substantial risk of strong negative responses by neutrals with powerful navies may cause decisionmakers to reduce blockade size or even to forgo conducting a blockade altogether. Nevertheless, where the need to realize blockade objectives exceeds the expected ramifications of neutral responses, decisionmakers choose the blockade form and size necessary to meet their objectives." See also Yoram Dinstein, *The Conduct of Hostilities under the Law of International Armed Conflict* (Cambridge: Cambridge University Press, 2004), 259. Dinstein explains that although the starvation of civilians as a method of warfare is illegal, "Article 54 of AP/I does not render blockade unlawful as a method of warfare." Further noting that the San Remo Manual prohibits blockades under the following circumstances: "Either (i) if it has the 'sole purpose of starving the civilian population or denying it other objects essential for its survival'; or (ii) the expected injury to the civilian population in the wake of a blockade is 'excessive' in relation to the military advantage anticipated from the blockade." See also Gary D. Solis, *The Law of Armed Conflict: International Humanitarian Law in War* (Cambridge: Cambridge University Press, 2016), 701.

such sanctions are novel—such as those against Iranian petroleum interests or targeting telecommunications—may do so without full knowledge of whether or not they will trigger any kind of traditionally understood military response by the other side. Economic sanctions may be punitive, but they can also be a defeat strategy, as in the case of a fragile regime depending on a single commodity like oil.[10] Finally, while deep economic interdependency between two states might render an in-kind response to economic sanctions an effective deterrent, as a practical matter, the condition would also hold for noninterdependent would-be belligerents.[11] Thus, nations subject to economic sanctions invoking the threat and use of traditional military force against their instigators, while the nations enforcing those sanctions (which are preferable to military conflict) deny such outright confrontation as a result.[12]

The concept of cross-domain deterrence is reasonably novel as a subject of dedicated focus, but offers some opportunities to connect concepts. As Lindsay and Gartzke's edited volume on the topic explores, several new technology environments, with cyber and space included among them, create a range of logistical, practical, and legal challenges to formation of traditional deterrence dynamics.[13] Recognizing the differentiating contours of these domains can help liberate state responses from the kind of narrow in-kind dilemmas just surfaced with cyberattacks. This is an position that states may indeed be coming to, perhaps in part due to individual or collective realization of the bankruptcy of the cyber-deterrence project, or concern that, as Schneider notes, "the vast majority of current policy progress on cyber deterrence [has focused] on a much more rudimentary (and unmilitarized) level" than large-scale cyberattacks.[14] Whatever the reason, the result has been a series of experiments in new punishment strategies that seek to isolate cyber activity they find distasteful, while "mainstreaming" the activities they seek

[10] The law is clearer on this matter for economic sanctions generally, less so for cyberattacks. See Chapter 5.
[11] This exception is, however, significant—for instance, one might argue that such conditions presently exist between the United States and People's Republic of China, with the former far less willing to coerce over human rights and other abuses in the same way it does with a nation upon which it is far less dependent, e.g., Iran. This is a side effect of Nye's "deterrence by entanglement." See note 23.
[12] It is also for this reason that a number of scholars and advocacy organizations examine the questions both within the framework of international legality and existential humanitarian concerns—rather than strictly in the context of the *jus in bello*. See, e.g., Anna Segall, "Economic Sanctions: Legal and Policy Constraints," *International Review of the Red Cross*, no. 836 (1999).
[13] Erik Gartzke and Jon R. Lindsay, eds., *Cross-Domain Deterrence* (Oxford: Oxford University Press, 2019), 16–17.
[14] Schneider, "Deterrence In and Through Cyberspace," 103.

to pursue. The former are a series of early adventures in this "cross-domain deterrence," seeking mechanisms like criminal indictments and sanctions for activities in cyberspace (like economic espionage) but where in-kind punishment is a poor fit. But what about those activities that are of even greater concern either because states want to engage in them with impunity, or prevent their normalization—in cyberspace, but with implications beyond it? As Schneider points out, what has made cyber activity unusual to date "is the lack of perceived risk. Without the deterrence of physical risk that is prominent in any manned physical attack, actors are more likely to operate in the virtual domain than they may be in other physical warfighting domains."[15] It is here, in this particular space, where states are pursuing their structural deterrence strategies—aiming to port over the information their adversaries have about their kinetic capabilities and intentions, and building the institutional and customary basis to validate their choices globally.

A glimpse at these cases offers a preview of the overwhelming evidence that states are engaging in structural deterrence. It is to this evidence that the study now turns.

4.2 Evidence of Structural Deterrence

As discussed previously, other than measures to defang inbound intelligence or disruptive operations (including by so-called defending forward) there are few to no truly useful cases of states demonstrating *and* decisively claiming credit for the deployment or use of cyberattack capabilities—frustrating their ability to deter using accumulated cyberattacks capabilities.[16] However, states do still actively engage in efforts to deter one another's cyberattacks. As this section will argue, states are actively exercising strategies of structural deterrence, with the prospect of traditional military defense at the fulcrum.

States seeking to deter cyberattacks against them are doing so via two strategies of structural deterrence. One, typified by the Unites States, United Kingdom, and their allies, would shape the international environment such that a would-be attacker pondering a cyberattack would have to factor the

---

[15] Ibid., 108. (Junaid Hussein notwithstanding, and presumably a signal from the United States and UK that the status quo is temporary.)
[16] With the potential, narrow exception aforementioned Israeli case; see "We thwarted an attempted Hamas cyber offensive against Israeli targets."

likelihood of a traditional military retribution into its rationalist calculations. The other, bolstered by Russia and China, seeks the opposite outcome: that cyberattacks would evade traditional military response, and thus, the rationalist calculations of responding to them would be limited to other diplomatic and economic means.

Inclusive Strategy: Cyberattacks as Unremarkable Weapons

In cases of structural deterrence, states seek to shape others' expectations about acceptable reaction to a practice via their individual and collective posturing, particularly true in the case of the United States, the UK, and Australia. There is evidence that states are individually and, more powerfully, collectively advancing a complex strategy of structural deterrence that seeks to link traditional military force and well-known military alliances to the rational calculations of a state pondering a cyberattack against them.

These states are promoting what can be deemed the "inclusive view" of cyberattacks in a deterrent calculation, which would normalize cyberattacks—and most importantly their consequences—with kinetic military force against them.[17]

States pursuing this "inclusive strategy" do so by asserting three specific claims about cyberattacks within international relations: first, a *negative* assertion that cyberspace is not a distinct international space for the maintenance of international security; second, a *positive* assertion about willingness to invoke rights of self-defense when faced with a cyberattack; and third, a *collective* assertion of applicable treaty obligations—all aimed at shaping international custom and the development of international law. This section will document those claims, using the United States as a focal point and expanding analysis to its close and second-tier alliances, before presenting the counterpoint pursued by this group's historical adversaries in the space.

The United States' *International Strategy for Cyberspace* represents the synthesis of years of private deliberations and consultations with allies on the issue of international cybersecurity.[18] It is also rare in being a comprehensive,

---

[17] The two chapters that follow explore the legal veracity of claiming such actions constitute uses or force or armed attacks. While not leaving aside that important and related series of questions under international law, for the purposes of this chapter, that distinction is less relevant than the rationalist calculation states make in deciding how or if to respond to such an act.

[18] Brennan, *Remarks at the Launch of the U.S. International Strategy for Cyberspace*.

dedicated official policy statement on international relations and cyberspace, making it the strongest basis for understanding that state's foundational strategy for deterring others from using cyberattacks.[19] The Trump administration's 2018 *National Cyber Strategy* is largely consistent, though elaborating on this policy in a few key areas, namely concerning the balance of offensive action to international engagement and norm-building.[20]

Early in the International Strategy, the United States refutes the idea that cyberspace is somehow exceptional in international security, and might portend new expectations of action and reaction to attack:

> Cyberspace does not require a reinvention of customary international law, nor does it render existing international norms obsolete. Long-standing international norms guiding state behavior—in times of peace and conflict—also apply in cyberspace.[21]

For those not as well versed in international relations or law, the characterization here can be understood as an implicit refutation of the inclusive view espoused by the United States' prime adversaries in cyberspace (explained in depth below). More importantly, it grounds US cyber-defense policy in the existing *jus ad bellum*,[22] *jus in bello*,[23] conventions on human rights,[24] and other relevant obligations the United States views as applicable under international law. President Barack Obama's foreword to the document reinforces this idea, stating "the digital world is no longer a lawless frontier, it is a place

---

[19] Thus, this document is a more important barometer of the state's policy than, for instance, its Defense Department's *Strategy for Operating in Cyberspace*. It is also more relevant in the context of the national-level decision-making that would go into an armed response to a cyberattack, since in the American system, final military command and decisions to use force rest in the White House with the president in his role as military commander-in-chief.

[20] The White House, *National Cyber Strategy of the United States of America*. The continuity is helpful from an analytical standpoint, as the document is too new to effectively gauge its impact on other states' responsive positioning.

[21] Brennan, *Remarks at the Launch of the U.S. International Strategy for Cyberspace*, 9.

[22] Ibid., 9–10.

[23] Ibid., 14.

[24] Ibid., 9. While beyond the scope of this chapter, it is worth noting the pursuit of a parallel and consistent policy by the United States, supported most vocally by Switzerland, Sweden, France, and the Council of Europe, in extending existing human rights law to this space. In particular, references to the applicability of the Universal Declaration of Human Rights (esp. Art. 19), the International Covenant on Civil and Political Rights, and Council of Europe protections on freedoms of expression, privacy, and civil liberties have all been employed to considerable effect internationally. Further evidence of the formation of this norm—particularly as it relates to Egypt's domestic internet shutdown—as an exemplar for security-focused cyber norms, is taken up in the final part of this study.

where norms of responsible, just and peaceful conduct have begun to take hold."[25]

If this statement forms the basis for the negation of cyberspace as demanding *lex specialis*, the assertion that it is no less willing to respond to substantial cyberattacks as with any coercion of similar consequence is similarly unequivocal: "We reserve the right to use all necessary means—diplomatic, informational, military, and economic—as appropriate and consistent with applicable international law, in order to defend our Nation, our allies, our partners, and our interests."[26] The United States is making two related claims: first, its willingness, and second, its right to armed self-defense when faced with a cyberattack of sufficient gravity.

The former is more clearly a statement designed to inform rationalist deterrence calculations and is the foundation of the United States' structural deterrence strategy. Perhaps less subtly, a senior US military official was quoted in the *Wall Street Journal* asserting, "if you shut down our power grid [with a cyberattack], maybe we will put a missile down one of your smokestacks"—taken abroad as a signal of a new, bellicose posture relative to cyber incidents.[27] This aspect of the structural deterrence posture is over a decade old; to quote retired US Air Force Major General Charles Dunlap Jr., "a cyber attack is governed by basically the same rules as any other kind of attack *if the effects of it are essentially the same*."[28]

But this structural deterrence posture is incomplete with the second claim relative to legitimacy. Especially when used by states that doctrinally proscribe or freely authorize certain uses of force based upon their understanding of legitimacy under international law, statements like these reinforce the credibility of the purely deterrent statement.[29] The caveats that the White House unilaterally applies to its use of force in this context of structural deterrence echo its prior National Security and National Military strategies: "In so doing, we will exhaust all options before military force whenever we can; will carefully weigh the costs and risks of action against the costs of inaction; and will act in a way that reflects our values and strengthens our

---

[25] Ibid., Preface.
[26] Ibid., 6, emphasis added.
[27] Siobahn Gorman and Julian E. Barnes, "Cyber Combat: Act of War," *Wall Street Journal*, May 30, 2011.
[28] Ibid. (emphasis added).
[29] Thus, the section's appeal to inherent right of self-defense, and therein, that the language in the US president's assertion mirrors that of the UN Charter's Chapter VII, Article 51. The next chapter evaluates the durability of this claim, as well as the potential limitations on such a response.

legitimacy, seeking broad international support whenever possible."[30] These policy statements also squarely ground the United States' self-defensive posture in the UN Charter, which is important for the legal analysis in the chapters that follow. By drawing a connection to the international legal framework that would legitimize the act, the United States is seeking to construct the deterrence space to favor its preferred balance, in which a would-be cyberattacker would face the prospect of the United States' overwhelming military capabilities.

This credibility of the deterrent is buttressed by its third claim: that it is collective, and that military alliances will interpret cyberattacks in a similarly inclusive manner. The US strategy articulates a basis for what Washington describes as a "regional and international consensus of states" on core security norms in cyberspace (including self-defense), and in a critical but less-cited passage, the US strategy adds, "certain hostile acts conducted through cyberspace could compel actions under the commitments we have with our military treaty partners"—a clear invitation for other treaty partners to share this view.[31]

This view both reflects, and presages invocation of Article 31, paragraph 4(b) of the Vienna Convention on the Law of Treaties, which asserts that a treaty interpretation may also take account of "any subsequent practice in the application of the treaty which establishes the agreement of the parties regarding its interpretation."[32] Many of the United States' defensive treaty commitments stem from either party recognizing and activating rights of self-defense, and so it seems natural that the United States would seek to first establish its own basis for action, and reinforce that basis through treaties premised on the collective exercise of that same right.

Next, this study turns to two strong and early examples of nations seeking to elaborate this structural deterrent, particularly in the context of their defensive treaty commitments: Australia and the UK, two of the United States' closest military allies

Australia has joined the United States in asserting, in recent years, a clear willingness to respond with traditional military force to a cyberattack—focusing in particular on its grounding in collective defense treaties. Australia

---

[30] Brennan, *Remarks at the Launch of the U.S. International Strategy for Cyberspace*, 14. See also United States Joint Chiefs of Staff, *National Military Strategy* (Washington, DC: Department of Defense, 2008).
[31] Brennan, *Remarks at the Launch of the U.S. International Strategy for Cyberspace*, 18, 14.
[32] United Nations, "Vienna Convention on the Law of Treaties," 1969.

has, in Joint Statements with the United States, routinely highlighted the inclusive view of cyberattacks within international custom, most clearly at the 2011 AUSMIN Summit between the Australian and US Defense and Foreign Secretaries, which focused in large part on the question of cyberattacks in the context of the Australia, New Zealand, and United States (ANZUS) Treaty. That communiqué read, in part, "our Governments share the view that, in the event of a cyber attack that threatens the territorial integrity, political independence or security of either of our nations, Australia and the United States would consult together and determine appropriate options to address the threat."[33] Ten years on, joint statements continue to affirm similar concepts.[34]

The Australian defence minister emphasized at the summit that a "substantial cyber attack" on either country would trigger the ANZUS treaty; reflecting alignment with Chapter 1's definitions that "we're talking here at a level that is much higher than, for example, people using the internet, using cyber space to steal commercial or state secrets. We're talking about a significant attack upon the communications fabric of a nation"—precisely the kind of attack in discussion here.[35]

As with the United States, Australia has brought top leadership to shape the discourse on this particular topic. Kevin Rudd (who has served as both foreign and prime minister) reinforced his government's thinking, noting "one cyber attack can cripple an economy for hours and days on end. Let there be no doubt, cyber attacks are not only attacks on governments. They can cripple private businesses, and Australian businesses are not immune . . . that is why it is critical that this become a formal part of our alliance deliberations."[36] Thus, beyond asserting that Australia might invoke its military capabilities in response to a substantial cyberattack, Australia simultaneously commits allied capabilities to its defense in this respect as well. The combined effect is a powerful strategy of structural deterrence, publicly linking those overwhelming capabilities in the hope that they will factor into Australia's adversaries' calculus in considering a cyberattack.

---

[33] Australia Department of Foreign Affairs and Trade, "AUSMIN 2011: Transcript of joint press conference with Defence Minister Stephen Smith, US Secretary of State Hillary Clinton and US Secretary of Defense Leon Panetta (15 September)" (Canberra: Government of Australia, 2011).
[34] US Department of State, "Joint Statement on Australia–U.S. Ministerial Consultations (AUSMIN) 2021" (Washington, DC: September 16, 2021).
[35] Simon Mann, "Cyber War Added to ANZUS Pact," *Sydney Morning Herald*, September 16, 2011.
[36] Australia Department of Foreign Affairs and Trade, *AUSMIN 2011*.

Like Australia, the UK has also asserted its willingness and right to mobilize conventional forces in response to cyberattack—both individually and in concert with its American ally.

From a matter of defense policy and with similar deterrent implications, the UK government was an early adopter of doctrine tying cyberattack and defense capabilities to traditional military force. The UK 2010 Strategic Defence and Security Review notes, in somewhat less specificity than its American counterpart, that "future conflict will see cyber operations conducted in parallel with more conventional actions in the maritime, land and air environments," and vows to "bring together existing expertise from across Defence, including the Armed Forces . . . in a way that integrates our activities in both cyber and physical space."[37] Specific statements by senior officials mirror written doctrine. Foreign Minister William Hague said in a widely publicized interview, "we will defend ourselves in every way we can, not only to deflect but to prevent attacks that we know are taking place," adding in a separate interview, "the need for governments to act proportionately in cyberspace . . . and in accordance with national and international law."[38] Defence Minister Nick Harvey pointed out from a doctrinal standpoint that "cyberspace adds a new dimension, but its use in warfare should be subject to the same strategic and tactical thought as existing means."[39] In 2017, in response to the breach of British Parliament's IT facilities and the WannaCry ransomware attack that compromised its National Health Service systems, Defence Minister Michael Fallon strengthened the country's cyber-deterrence posture by saying that by increasing its military budget, the government is "signaling to potential cyber strikers that the price of an online attack could invite a response from any domain, air, land, sea, or cyber space."[40]

---

[37] David Cameron, *Securing Britain in an Age of Uncertainty: The Strategic Defence and Security Review*, ed. Cabinet Office (London: The Stationary Office, Her Majesty's Government, 2010), 27.

[38] Murray Wardrop, "William Hague: 'Britain Faces Growing Cyberspace Arms Race,'" *The Telegraph*, October 18, 2011. William Hague, *Foreign Secretary's closing remarks at the London Conference on Cyberspace*, ed. Foreign & Commonwealth Office (London: The Stationary Office, Her Majesty's Government, 2011).

[39] Harvey, *Armed Forces Minister—Responding to Cyber War*; Government of the United Kingdom, *National Security Strategy and Strategic Defence and Security Review 2015: A Secure and Prosperous United Kingdom* (London: Her Majesty's Government, 2015), 24, noting "we will treat a cyber attack on the UK as seriously as we would do an equivalent conventional attack, and we will defend ourselves as necessary." See also Government of the United Kingdom, *National Security Strategy and Strategic Defence and Security Review 2015: Third Annual Report* (London: Her Majesty's Government, 2019).

[40] Michael Fallon, "Defence Secretary's speech at Cyber 2017 Chatham House Conference" (London: Ministry of Defence, Her Majesty's Government, 2017).

Clearly, the strategy of structural deterrence is shared between more than a single alliance; the UK, for its part, has reserved some of its more specific statements about international security and cyberspace to joint statements with its American ally. For example, during their May 25, 2011, meeting, the UK prime minister and US president asserted, "the same kinds of 'rules of the road' that help maintain peace [and] security ... internationally must equally apply in cyberspace."[41] Cameron noted a desire to expand consensus about these state rights referred to previously, citing an aspiration to "continue to build our cyber security alliances, including through the already strong relationship with the United States and the establishment of new relationships with like-minded nations."[42] This approach has animated subsequent, similar joint statements by US and UK leadership.[43]

This collective enthusiasm for shared, structural deterrence does have limits, demonstrating the utility and potential peril of this inclusive strategy of structural deterrence. The United States, United Kingdom, and New Zealand appear committed to ensuring the credibility of their structural deterrence project is not undermined by alliances calling for but failing to execute a response. In its alliance with North Atlantic Treaty Organization (NATO) members, and its separate security pact with South Korea, the United States appears to be exercising greater cautiousness, resulting in a careful balance between exerting deterrent influence and overexertion that might result in strategic entanglement. If the US–UK and ANZUS alliances show the full measure of a strategy to shape the international environment and bring collective military defense to deter cyberattacks, then the NATO and US–South Korea alliances demonstrate its limits.

Under the competing influences, the thirty-member NATO alliance has moved more slowly, advancing a cautious posture that acknowledges, but does not truly echo, member states' assertions of a collective right of self-defense to cyberattack.[44] NATO claims in public documents to have been

---

[41] The White House, "Joint Fact Sheet: U.S. and UK Cooperation on Cyberspace" (Washington, DC: 2011).

[42] Cameron, *Securing Britain in an Age of Uncertainty*, 48.

[43] See, inter alia, The White House, "Fact Sheet: U.S.–United Kingdom Cybersecurity Cooperation" (Washington, DC: 2015); The White House, "Joint Statement on the Visit to the United Kingdom of the Honorable Joseph R. Biden, Jr., President of the United States of America at the Invitation of the Rt. Hon. Boris Johnson, M.P., the Prime Minister of the United Kingdom of Great Britain and Northern Ireland" (Washington, DC: June 10, 2021).

[44] For further background on NATO's strategic challenges and role in cybersecurity issues, see R. David Edelman, "NATO's Cyber Decade?," in *NATO: From Regional to Global Security Provider*, ed. Yonah Alexander and Richard Prosen (New York: Lexington Books, 2015).

considering aspects of cybersecurity since at least 2002.[45] However, the focus was strictly on cyber-defense and force readiness—in essence, the protection of NATO and host countries' digital systems—and not on the potential activation over the treaty's Articles 4 and 5 on the basis of a cyberattack.[46] As previously noted, an arduous process led to a more public posture in the 2010 New Strategic Concept.[47] It was not until 2014—a full seven years after the Estonia incident, that NATO government leaders assembled in Newport, Wales and pledged their support for the Wales Summit Declaration. This declaration aligned NATO with two broad cyber-related positions: first, that "international law, including international humanitarian law and the UN Charter, applies in cyberspace," second, that cyberattacks "can reach a threshold that threatens national and Euro-Atlantic prosperity, security, and stability. Their impact could be as harmful to modern societies as a conventional attack."[48] The Alliance's decision to affirm cyber-defense as part of NATO's core task of collective defense was notable yet still restrained; the declaration further stipulated that any decision "as to when a cyber attack would lead to the invocation of Article 5 would be taken by the North Atlantic Council on a case-by-case basis."[49]

So why the caution, and what does it tell us about the inclusive strategy of structural deterrence generally? The answers rest on questions of priorities and credibility. There remains a significant and longstanding tension within the alliance over the proper role cyber-defense should play: whether the specter of cyberattack should be dealt with as a tactical and strictly defensive or strategic and deterrent matter. The former view would devote limited Alliance resources to defending NATO and host country military networks against cyber-threats implicating planning and force readiness. Countries holding this view, chiefly France and the UK, see NATO's extremely limited cybersecurity capacity on its own networks as indication that the institution

---

[45] NATO's own public-facing introduction to the topic highlights, "Although NATO has always been protecting its communication and information systems, the *2002 Prague Summit* first placed cyber defense on the Alliance's political agenda." North Atlantic Treaty Organization, "Cyber Defense: Background & History," last updated September 14, 2023.

[46] NATO's reasons for approaching the problem thusly stem in large part from recent experience: in 1999, anonymous hackers attempted to overload the Alliance's messaging system in advance of Operation Allied Force. See North Atlantic Treaty Organization, "Wales Summit Declaration." 2014.

[47] See Chapter 1, note 91.

[48] North Atlantic Treaty Organization, "Wales Summit Declaration" (Brussels: NATO, July 5, 2014).

[49] Ibid.

is ill-prepared to deal with the strategic implications of a cyberattack, and that such issues are best left to member states defining their own rights, such as in a bilateral context. These countries hereto enjoyed preeminence in the articulation of NATO's defensive posture—characterizing the cyber-threat as a principally technical defensive matter, rather than, say, regulated or deterred—and their view is reinforced by the 2010 New Strategic Concept, 2010 Lisbon Summit Declaration, and subsequent statements by the NATO Secretary-General.[50] A vocal dissenting community, however, views the issue as core to the Alliance's continued relevance, and believes it must be comprehensively built into NATO's doctrine and planning, including in the context of Articles 4 and 5.[51]

A contrasting view might argue that key Member States in the Alliance have not yet consolidated their views, and that this lack of clarity within NATO simply functions as a developing and highly imperfect consensus about the rights of self-defense. Yet that argument ignores the political dynamics of NATO's policy formulation. The United States and UK are exceptionally influential in the formulation of NATO alliance policy; it seems unlikely that a concerted effort to use NATO as a mouthpiece for their structural deterrence strategy.[52] Certainly, countries like Estonia were seeking similar commitments from the Alliance. Pursuing a similar agenda to build like-minded consensus at NATO would allow them to widen the base of their structural deterrent strategy. Indeed, the United States, the UK, and Australia have practiced no such evangelical restraint in multilateral forums like the UN General Assembly, UN Groups of Governmental Experts on the issue, or the Organization for Security and Cooperation in Europe (OSCE).[53] This

---

[50] North Atlantic Treaty Organization, *Active Engagement, Modern Defence: Strategic Concept for the Defence and Security of the Members of the North Atlantic Treaty Organization*, 11–12, 16–17 (Lisbon: NATO, 2010); North Atlantic Treaty Organization, *Lisbon Summit Declaration Issued by the Heads of State and Government Participating in the Meeting of the North Atlantic Council in Lisbon* (Lisbon: NATO, 2010); North Atlantic Treaty Organization, "Press Conference by NATO Secretary General Anders Fogh Rasmussen Following the NATO Defence Ministers Meeting on 4 June 2013," news release, June 4, 2013.

[51] Note the relatively restrained language in NATO's 2010 *New Strategic Concept* in contrast to the pointed statements, in NATO's own publications, by alliance member heads of state such as Estonia's Toomas Hendrik Ilves. See Chris Riley, "Interview with Toomas Hendrik Ilves: Cyber attacks, NATO—and Angry Birds," *NATO Review Magazine*, June 13, 2013.

[52] Julie Garey, *The US Role in NATO's Survival After the Cold War* (London: Palgrave Macmillan, 2020), 10.

[53] See, for example, any of those states' submissions to the 2010 UN GGE or to annual resolutions found at Chapter 5, note 9, such as United Nations Secretary-General, "Developments in the field of information and telecommunications in the context of international security: Report of the Secretary-General" (New York: United Nations, 2011), Australian Submission (18–23, esp. 22). For OSCE, see Organization for Security and Co-Operation in Europe (OSCE), "Remarks of the

restraint is therefore less explainable as a glaring omission, and far more so as an intentional practice.

What emerges is a distinct sense of uncertainty not on the wisdom of tying conventional arms to cyberattacks in the abstract, but on who is to be entrusted with their implications—in other words, a conscious effort to ensure the inclusive strategy of structural deterrent remains *credible*. There is little question that the events in Estonia served to motivate both internal deliberations and public deterrent statements by NATO members and others.[54] If these statements were indeed many years in the making and largely deliberate, it suggests that such claims develop in direct proportion to states' trust of one another if empowered with such a mandate. Specifically, the United States and other NATO states remain conflicted about asserting a full-fledged Article 4/5 response to cyberattacks, fearing *overexpansion* of self-defense rights in ways that could undermine credibility by excessively lowering the threshold of response. Recent steps to create a "virtual rapid response cyber capability" is sufficiently modest as to underline just how limited the scope of present cooperation is relative to the broader threat.[55] That said, certain Allies appear to be making this choice consciously: as cited previously, NATO member Estonia's political leadership first responded to the attack by likening it to nuclear war.

This anxiety appears to manifest at least in the US–South Korea relationship's present lack of collective deterrent statements similar to the US–UK or ANZUS ones cited above.[56] This may stand to reason: South Korea has, as of this writing, suffered several national-scale cybersecurity incidents—though none reaching the level of a cyberattack, due to their minimal effects.[57] Yet South Korea's official statements in response have often

Coordinator for Cyber Issues, U.S. Department of State" (paper presented at the OSCE Conference on a Comprehensive Approach to Cyber Security: Exploring the Future OSCE Rule, Vienna, May 9–10, 2011.

[54] Eneken Tikk, Kadri Kaska, and Liis Vihul, *International Cyber Incidents: Legal Considerations*, ed. Eneken Tikk, vol. 1 (Tallinn: NATO Cooperative Cyber Defence-Centre of Excellence, 2010), Preface, 8.
[55] Thie White House, "Fact Sheet: The 2022 NATO Summit in Madrid" (Washinton, DC: June 29, 2022).
[56] Thus far, United States–South Korea leader-level statements on the matter have committed only to "deepen cooperation" in "domains . . . including cyber . . . to ensure an effective joint response against emerging threats." Thie White House, *U.S.-ROK Leaders' Joint Statement (May 21, 2021)* (Washington, DC: Government Printing Office, 2021).
[57] *BBC News*, "New 'Cyber Attacks' Hit S Korea," July 9, 2009; Council on Foreign Relations, "Cyber Operations Tracker"; Greenberg, "Inside Olympic Destroyer: The Most Deceptive Hack in History," 2019 The Fourth of July (2009, 2010) incidents involved a "series of denial of service incidents affecting at least thirty-five government and commercial websites in South Korea and the United States." The suspected state sponsor of the attack is the DPRK.

drawn broad conclusions about what occurred, citing "attack," "invasion," and not just a right, but necessity to respond both in-kind and with force.[58] South Korea has thus responded to such incidents with fiery rhetoric that if given the full weight of American defensive treaty commitments, could commit the latter to a wholly unwanted response.

Exclusive Strategy: Cyberattacks as Novel and Unregulated

> The Parties shall cooperate and act in the international information space within the framework of this Agreement . . . including the principles of peaceful settlement of disputes and conflicts [and the] non-use of force.[59]

Naturally, the practice of structural deterrence is competitive. One nation's or group of states' interest in shaping the deterrence calculation in their favor will surely find opposition from potential adversaries. Just as the United States, United Kingdom, and Australia have sought to exploit a preponderant conventional military advantage, a second bloc of states led by Russia and China are practicing a similar but inverse strategy, this one seeking to *deny* those states the availability of force in the event of a cyberattack. This second group of states does so with full and public knowledge that, in the words of Russia's top expert on cybersecurity issues, cyberattacks "are a powerful tool for enhancing military potential."[60] This "exclusive strategy" is far simpler to document but no less important in the broader context of self-defense's customary development in international law.

This group premises its exclusive strategy of structural deterrence on two claims: first, cyberspace has circumstances materially different from

---

[58] See, e.g., interview with South Korean National Assembly member HA Tae-Kyoung, summarizing the government's position and response of the Blue House and President Park Geun-hye. Jong Ik Cho, "Ha Tae Kyoung Interview on the Growing Cyber-Terrorism Threat from North Korea and the South's Response," *NK Vision*, May 15, 2013.

[59] Shanghai Cooperation Organisation, *Agreement between the Governments of the Member States of the Shanghai Cooperation Organisation on Cooperation in the Field of International Information Security* (Beijing: SCO, 2009). In Sergei Komov, ed. *International Information Security: The Diplomacy of Peace* (Moscow: Russian Federation Official Publications, 2009), 202–13.

[60] Andrey Krutskikh, "Advancement of Russian Initiative to Ensure International Information Security (Chronicles of the Decade)," in *International Information Security: The Diplomacy of Peace*, ed. by Sergei Komov (Moscow: Russian Federation Official Publications, 2009), 126. Here, Krutskikh is referring specifically to the United States.

traditional international security space as to merit exceptional consideration under international law; and second, that states have an obligation to settle disputes pacifically in all circumstances that arise from cyberspace—implicitly excepting them from the *jus ad bellum* and by extension any need for the *jus in bello*. These claims combine into a thesis that would deny would-be victims legitimacy in responding with military force to a cyberattack, thus preserving the opportunity to use this asymmetric tool against a better-armed adversary with a more favorable deterrence calculation.

A rich canon of Russian strategic literature and official doctrine has sought to advance that nation's structural deterrence strategy for more than fifteen years.[61] Writings from top Russian security officials responsible for new and emerging threats as early as 1999 observed "no international laws . . . regulate the use of information weapons, to limit them as is done under treaties with other weapon types and military activities."[62] Citing this gap, the same official heighted "objective needs to legally regulate the world-wide processes . . . of information security."[63] Subsequent doctrine, notably the *Russian Federation Military Policy for Provision of International Information Security*, repeatedly calls for definition of "allowable methods" of cyberattack, noting that "there is no doubt that in order to implement the Russian Federation's military policy in the international information security areas, it is necessary to improve . . . existing international law."[64] At the international level, too, Moscow sought to build international consensus on its frame, with successive Russian-sponsored UN resolutions repeatedly identifying "information security" risks as a distinct phenomenon in international security, and calling—in their procedural aims—for new elaborations of international law.[65]

It is worth noting the evolution of this position at least insofar as it relates to the Russian Federation—it is in its later formations not a complete rejection of international law's applicability to cyberspace, but implicitly and as borne out in the strategy's pursuit, a denial of the law governing the use of force. Prior to the 2008–2009 Group of Governmental Experts (GGE), Moscow

---

[61] See, e.g., S. G. Chekinov and S. A. Bogdanov, "Strategic Deterrence and Russia's National Security Today," *Voennaya Mysl (Military Thought)* 21, no. 3 (March 2012)."
[62] Krutskikh, "Information Challenges to Security (1999)," 12.
[63] Ibid., 13.
[64] Ibid., 32; Sergei Komov, "Russian Federation Military Policy in the Area of International Information Security: Regional Aspect," in *International Information Security: The Diplomacy of Peace*, ed. Sergei Komov (Moscow: Russian Federation Official Publications, 2007), 43.
[65] See Chapter 5, note 8.

routinely asserted the insufficiency, and regularly the *outright inapplicability*, of international law (meaning, in context, the *jus ad bellum* and *jus in bello*) to cyberspace.[66] One emblematic conclusion, included by the Kremlin as reference points to Russian official doctrine on the matter, concluded, "current national and international legal frameworks are insufficient... to address the scope and complexity of the subject of cybercrime, cyberterrorism and cyber warfare."[67] Joining with consensus in the 2011–2012 GGE, however, Russia signaled for the first time a shift in position, acknowledging that such international law *applied* to this space, but continuing to insinuate that it remains generally insufficient—a strategy that remains apparently paramount in its institutional pursuits at the UN.[68] This pursuit of a UN-negotiated cyberspace treaty—initially scoped to cybercrime but unlikely to be so narrowly circumscribed if it gains momentum—demonstrates an extension of the strategy.[69] By relegating significant offensive cyber activity to subforce context of crime, Russia and its like-minded partners could ultimately use this vehicle to negate US claims to military response to cyberattacks.

A notable part of the Russian effort has long been the replacement of the Budapest Convention on Cybercrime, which was developed by the Council of Europe, and leaves to other instruments of law national security incidents like cyberattacks.[70] It is this division that the Russian strategy of structural deterrence would seek to collapse, as it would relegate all such incidents to the "lesser" status of cybercrime. After fifteen years of failure to build momentum for such a proposal, US withdrawal from this and other United Nations debates in 2019 permitted, for the first time, the formation of a group to establish such a replacement treaty, under Russian-designed auspices.[71] It

---

[66] Anatoly A. Streltsov, "International Information Security: Description and Legal Aspects," in *International Information Security: The Diplomacy of Peace*, ed. Sergei Komov (Moscow: Russian Federation Official Publications, 2008).

[67] World Federation of Scientists Permanent Monitoring Panel on Information Security, *Toward a Universal Order of Cyberspace: Managing Threats from Cybercrime to Cyberwar*, ed. Henning Wegener (Geneva: World Federation of Scientists, 2003).

[68] United Nations Group of Governmental Experts (2011–12), *Report of the Group of Governmental Experts on Developments in the Field of Information and Telecommunications in the Context of International Security (2011–12)* (Geneva: United Nations Institute for Disarmament Research, 2013) (hereafter *"GGE 2012"*).

[69] Deborah Brown, "Cybercrime is Dangerous, But a New UN Treaty Could Be Worse for Rights," *Human Rights Watch*, August 13, 2021.

[70] Council of Europe, "Convention on Cybercrime" (Strasbourg: Council of Europe, 2004).

[71] For the Resolution adopted by the General Assembly, paving the way for the new treaty, see United Nations General Assembly (Third Committee), "Countering the Use of Information and Communications Technologies for Criminal Purposes" (New York: UN, 2019). See also Allison Peters, "Russia and China Are Trying to Set the U.N.'s Rules on Cybercrime," *Foreign Policy*, September

would be reasonable to assume that leveraging this momentum, Moscow will enlist its allies in the near future to seek a similar "dedicated instrument" for "information security" threats to "international security." As one European official put it, Russian intentions on this matter are not unknown: "This is not about cybercrime . . . this is about who controls the Internet."[72]

The apparent goals of the Chinese government are different, but Beijing's strategy is generally aligned with the Russian Federation on how to leverage structural deterrence to achieve a favorable deterrence arrangement vis-à-vis cyberattacks. Consider, for instance, China's position during those same 2008–2009 GGE negotiations, in which China actually strengthened its attachment to the position excluding cyberattacks from operative international law. A review of that session's negotiating history indicates that at its penultimate session, the Chinese delegate removed any reference to the Law of Armed Conflict applying to cyberspace.[73] Instead, that language was replaced with a general assertion of the applicability of the UN Charter, making special reference to noninterference in sovereign matters. The subsequent Draft Code of Conduct circulated in September 2011 by Russia, China, Tajikistan, and Uzbekistan also went to great pains to avoid reference to "self-defense," while noting the desire to prevent the use of cyberspace to "carry out hostile activities or acts of aggression, pose threats to international peace and security or proliferate information weapons or related technologies."[74]

Structural deterrence is competitive; Russian documents repeatedly lament how the process of consolidating their positions internationally has been "extremely slow on account of counterproductive attitudes displayed by the United States" and other nations with opposing views on the specific matter.[75] Indeed, an early (2004–2005) UN GGE was unable to produce a consensus report due to, according to Russian officials, "the question of whether international humanitarian law and international law sufficiently

---

16, 2019; Ellen Nakashima, "U.N. Votes to Advance Russian-led Resolution on a Cybercrime Treaty," *Washington Post*, November 19, 2019.

[72] Ellen Nakashima, "The U.S. Is Urging a No Vote on a Russian-Led U.N. Resolution Calling for a Global Cybercrime Treaty," *Washington Post*, November 16, 2019; Nakashima, "U.N. Votes to Advance Russian-Led Resolution on a Cybercrime Treaty."
[73] Compare, for instance, the United States Expert's submission to China's, and in turn, the final product. *GGE 2010*. On file with Texas Law Review.
[74] See Russian Federation et al., "Letter to the Secretary-General on a Draft International Code of Conduct for Information Security" (New York: United Nations, 2011).
[75] Komov, "Russian Federation Military Policy in the Area of International Information Security," 34.

regulate the security aspects of international relations in cases of 'hostile' use of ICTs for politico-military purposes."[76] In other words, the United States and its allies Australia and the UK argued for the inclusive view; the Russians, Cubans, and Belarusians for the exclusive position—producing deadlock on the most important question for deterrence from cyberattacks.

It is simple to see how this position's second core claim—that armed self-defense should not be extended to cyberattacks for fear of inviting the creep of larger military forces into cyberspace—formed. For over a year prior to the release of the US Department of Defense's *Defense Strategy for Operating in Cyberspace* (DSOC), the US military and others engaged in what can be described as purely rhetorical deterrence by punishment.[77] In 2011, General James Cartwright was quoted as saying "if your approach to the business is purely defensive in nature, that's the Maginot line approach."[78] The incoming General of US Cybercommand made clear that "under the right circumstances," his command "would have the authority to use offensive cyber weapons against military command and control networks, weapons, power grids, transportation-related networks, national telecommunications networks, and even enemies' financial institutions."[79] In response, round criticism followed from Kremlin- and Beijing-backed think tanks and press outlets, accusing the United States of stoking a "new cyber arms race," and seeking to exploit "technological superiority" to wage "new forms of aggression" abroad.[80] Subsequent statements, for instance, by then-US Secretary of Defense Leon Panetta claiming "we are all going to have to work very hard not only to defend against cyberattacks but to be aggressive with regards to cyberattacks as well" only served to stoke this perception with the United States' adversaries.[81]

The result is that in practicing its own form of structural deterrence, Russia in particular has pursued a strategy that would both emphasize the illegitimacy of armed reprisal to a cyberattack and deemphasize the

---

[76] See, for example "Contribution by Russian Federation Expert" to the 2010 GGE; SCO Agreement.
[77] US Department of Defense, "Department of Defense Strategy for Operating in Cyberspace" (Washington, DC: DOD, 2011).
[78] David Alexander, "Pentagon to Treat Cyberspace as 'Operational Domain,'" *Reuters*, July 14, 2011.
[79] US Senate Committee on Armed Services, *Hearing to Consider the Nomination of Lt. Gen. Keith B. Alexander to Commander, U.S. CYBERCOMMAND*, Washington, DC, April 15, 2010
[80] Xinhua News Agency, "U.S. Cyber Strategy Dangerous: Chinese Experts," *China Daily USA* 2011; Igor Panarin, "Supremacy in Cyberspace: Obama's 'Star Wars'?," *RT*, January 11, 2012.
[81] Mann, "Cyber War Added to ANZUS Pact."

invocation of any rights of self-defense. Nearly every bilateral or multilateral agreement or statement submitted by the Russian Federation on the issue of cyberattacks contains binding provisions calling for the pacific settlement of disputes arising from cyberspace.[82] None refer to recourse to armed force, or any of the self-defense rights of the UN Charter or mutual defense treaties, contrasting markedly with states pursuing an inclusive strategy. In fact, in its first six successive UN First Committee resolutions on "International Information Security," Russia made no mention of the potential for state use of cyberattacks at all.[83] Even in that period, challenges to the legitimacy of military use of and response to a cyberattack were clear, with an initial draft of the resolution noting its purpose was to "prevent military applications [of cyberattacks] that may be compared to the use of weapons of mass destruction."[84]

Russia and China's likely motivations, though difficult to authoritatively document, stand to reason: both seek to prevent escalation of a cyberattack emanating from their territory into a kinetic military conflict in which their adversaries have decisive traditional military advantage. Moreover, if press accounts and public testimony are to be believed, the volume of malicious activity (cyber-enabled espionage, industrial theft, and low-level attack) emanating from China is substantial and perhaps greater than any other state. Given that, the potential for armed reprisal to any of China's real or perceived cyberspace activities, individually or in aggregate, might be particularly acute; denying victims of that activity the legitimate use of their strongest deterrent would help create more favorable conditions for preserving an advantageous status quo.

By definition, a successful structural deterrence posture must enjoy reasonable consensus of states, or preponderance of power, to affect the inputs of states' deterrence calculations generally. Russia and China have sought

---

[82] See, e.g., Shanghai Cooperation Organisation, *Agreement between the Governments of the Member States of the Shanghai Cooperation Organisation*; Russian Federation et al., "Letter to the Secretary-General on a Draft International Code of Conduct for Information Security"; Association of Southeast Asian Nations (ASEAN) Regional Forum, "Statement by the Ministers of Foreign Affairs of the ASEAN Regional Forum Participating States on Cooperation in Ensuring International Information Security" (Bandar Seri Begawan, Brunei: ASEAN, 2010).

[83] See, inter alia, G.A. Res. 58/32, U.N. Doc. A/RES/58/32 (December 8, 2003); G.A. Res. 57/53, U.N. Doc. A/RES/57/53 (November 22, 2002); G.A. Res. 56/19, U.N. Doc. A/RES/56/19 (November 29, 2001); G.A. Res. 55/28, U.N. Doc. A/RES/55/28 (November 20, 2000); G.A. Res. 54/49, U.N. Doc. A/RES/54/49 (December 1, 1999); G.A. Res. 53/70, U.N. Doc. A/RES/53/70 (December 4, 1998).

[84] "Letter Dated 23 September 1998 from the Permanent Representative of the Russian Federation to the United Nations Addressed to the Secretary-General" (New York: United Nations, 1998); Tikk, Kaska, and Vihul, *International Cyber Incidents: Legal Considerations*, 1, 3.

to export these views in a manner consistent with the one previously documented in the context of the US–UK and ANZUS alliances. The key venue for doing so has been the Shanghai Cooperation Organisation (SCO).[85] SCO members jointly promoted a baseline Agreement that seems designed to form an initial *lex specialis* for cyberattacks in the context of international security.[86] It enjoys some formal status, having been cited among others by Russian President Medvedev in his 2011 SCO Heads of State meeting.[87] This effort was followed up at the United Nations by a similar text—submitted by most SCO countries but failing to include support from Kazakhstan and Turkmenistan—which the Chinese Foreign Ministry hailed as "the first relatively comprehensive and systematic document in the world ... to formulate international rules to standardize information and cyberspace behavior."[88]

By seeking an opposing consensus to the Western bloc, the Russian-aligned group has sought to create conditions whereby the legitimacy of using conventional arms in response to cyber incidents would be unsupported—by law or custom. Were this approach to succeed in narrowing states' conceptions of available response options to a cyberattack, the result would deprive them of the ability to use traditional military capabilities to deter a cyberattack. This normative enterprise would have profound effects on the rationalist calculations of states in assessing whether to carry out a cyberattack.

4.3 Whose Deterrence Succeeds?

To date, neither the inclusive position championed by the United States, Australia, and the UK nor the exclusive approach led by Russia and China enjoys preeminence. With so few examples of substantial cyberattacks within or outside a traditional military conflict, test cases are limited. Nonetheless, it is worth briefly probing the prospects for success of these dueling positions, particularly in the context of the specifically rationalist calculations they seek to inform.

---

[85] *Agreement on Cooperation in Ensuring International Information Security between the Member States of the Shanghai Cooperation Organisation,* (Yekaterinbourg: Shanghai Cooperation Organisation, June 16, 2009). SCO member states include China, Kazakhstan, Kyrgyzstan, Russia, Tajikistan, and Uzbekistan.
[86] See Section 5.1 for more in its legal significance.
[87] Russian Federation et al., "Letter to the Secretary-General on a Draft International Code of Conduct for Information Security."
[88] Ibid.

In the narrowest realist mode, one could note that as a matter of sheer resources, the members of the Shanghai Cooperation Organisation combined barely constitute half of the defense spending of the United States alone (to say nothing of its treaty allies).[89] Even adding to the former group swing states like India and Brazil (hardly staunch supporters of the exclusive position), their aggregate military spending again does not come close to eclipsing that of the United States'. For structural deterrence positions to succeed, they require the clear support of not just large and powerful states, but those with the military backstop to impose those conditions on others.

Likewise, in a neoliberal mode, one could point to the importance of broad institutional coalitions, driving consensus among a plurality of smaller states' views. In this strategy, a state would remain (as Russia has) committed to leveraging international institutions whose designs seek to level the playing field—like votes at the United Nations General Assembly. But even there, as evidenced by limited institutional progress toward a new and distinct international law of cyber, those states with the greatest self-interest in the exclusive view have yet to win enough friends, or demonstrate enough suasion in political-military affairs, to create a culture where their version of self-interest overcomes those of the inclusive view.

Neither of these indications are, however, necessarily predictive. After all, accepting them as such would be to presuppose that national power, or the current configuration of geopolitics, will inform the outcome of this particular debate, which is possible but intellectually unsatisfying. Left out would be the third dimension that structural deterrence introduces: the merits of each particular argument for or against opening the aperture of legitimate responses. That debate's battle lines may be geopolitical, yet another series of inputs—its substantive, legal basis—may inform if not dictate which frame succeeds.

The unsettled nature of this debate creates an opportunity for critical analysis that neither party has yet fully seized: to evaluate the veracity and durability of states' numerous arguments about the status of cyberattacks within international law. Such a survey of regulative restraint of cyberattacks will be valuable in its own right—as states continue to apply their approach to influencing international law and custom—but, for the reasons just articulated, will also shape the prospects for rationalist restraint of cyberattacks. If

---

[89] Peter G. Peterson Foundation, "U.S. Defense Spending Compared to Other Countries" (New York: Peter G. Peterson Foundation, 2020).

international law deems cyberattacks an illegal use of force permitting armed reprisal with traditional weapons, the prospects that rationalist deterrence might restrain their use go up exponentially. This is the study that the book's next part undertakes.

Conclusions

This chapter explained the imperfect fit between cyberattacks prevailing mechanisms of restraint in rationalist international security. As a general matter, any deterrent dynamic requires state recognition of both potential coercion and its likely effect, as well as some reliable sense of its nation of origin. While those general criteria hold for a number of well-known means of coercion, the development, deployment, and execution tools of a cyberattack could only form a credible deterrent under narrow circumstances. The result is that cyberattack capabilities may be powerful instruments of war but notably weak in projecting power in peacetime.

Just as it is difficult to leverage cyberattack capabilities as deterrents, it is also challenging to deter a state from developing or using those capabilities. In-kind deterrents would leave neither defender nor attacker with any greater ability to defend. That condition would more readily lead to an arms race than it would mutual restraint, on purely rationalist grounds. Consequently, hopes for a discrete notion of cyber-deterrence are misplaced; deterring cyberattacks can only be meaningful in the broader context of international security, where the full measure of diplomatic, economic, and military tools can be brought to bear.

Marshaling traditional state power—especially military power—against a would-be cyberattacker is not straightforward. States do not agree on whether or not a traditional military response would be appropriate to a cyberattack. With little custom upon which to base their behavior, even the scope of potential responses to an attack is unclear. Again, the basic inputs of informed, rational deterrence are unavailable, making it not just impossible to assess whether a state will be deterred, but far more practically, making it difficult for states themselves to determine how to respond to cyber-threats. One is left either giving up on this logic of restraint as presently meaningful or moving beyond rigid strictures that were in most instances architected for a different, bipolar (and explicitly nuclear) era in international relations.

Rationalist deterrence will be impossible until states reach customary consensus over whether or not militaries can lawfully repel cyberattacks; indeed, states are already seeking to influence that outcome. That process, called structural deterrence, seeks to shape the rationalist outcome through neoliberal means, in which states vie to build legal, bilateral, and institutional consensus for what measures can be used to deter that kind of attack. States are doing so, this chapter argued, with profoundly rationalist motivations: whether in the case of the US-allied bloc in seeking to deter cyberattacks by tying their response to overwhelming military force, or the Russian-allied bloc seeking to deny that ability to limit prospects for undesired escalation. Both camps are seeking to leverage their various institutional arrangements to further their position, though none presently enjoys consensus.

Most notably, all of these states are staking the outcome of their deterrence postures on legal claims that may not vindicate their desired responses to an attack. Whether rationalist deterrence meaningfully restricts state use of cyberattacks hinges on the "victor" of this structural project; the outcome is also deeply tied to whether the victor can credibly claim international law is also in its favor. The balance of this study conducts such a critical analysis: first, whether there is any merit and practical restraining effect to state claims that cyberattacks constitute an illegal use of force invoking a right of self-defense (Chapters 5 and 6); and second, whether restraint might be found in the prohibition of cyberattacks under the law governing just conduct in war (Chapters 7 and 8). While each represents a distinct regime shaping state action, this chapter has demonstrated that the interconnections between them are equally impossible to ignore.

PART III

INTERNATIONAL LAW AND THE USE OF FORCE

5
Limiting the Use of Force

Part II explained why the rationalist logic of restraint is unlikely to curtail state use of cyberattacks, given the key information on state deterrence calculations lack outlined in Chapter 3, and the unsettled state of the competition that Chapter 4 explained there are currently engaged in to fill in the gaps.

Part III begins to look then at the regulative logic of restraint: how and whether the formal strictures of positive international law will have a direct or indirect restraining function on state decisions to use cyberattacks. It does so through the lens of the *jus ad bellum*, the canon of law limiting states' recourse to force, (Chapter 5) and defining permissible acts of self-defense (Chapter 6).

As we have seen, states are staking deterrence strategies in large part on the (un)-usability of conventional arms in reprisal. Yet in order to establish such a durable international custom, they would almost certainly need to ground that decision in robust and mutually understood interpretations of international law. Such interpretations will no doubt play a role in the success of the structural deterrence project just outlined, but is international law doing more than allowing states to rationalize their preferred deterrence projects?

Numerous cybersecurity and defense doctrines invoke the language of the UN Charter as evidence of cyberattacks' illegality and states' "inherent" right to defend against them. Do those claims have any basis in international law? Does the *jus ad bellum* durably apply to cyberattacks, and can it in turn play a significant role restraining states contemplating cyberattack—either directly as effective *opinion juris* or by empowering victims to respond with force? The next two chapters address those questions, which are important in their own right, and essential to the outcome of both the structural deterrence process outlined in Chapter 4 and the relevance of the *jus in bello* that Chapters 7 and 8 will discuss.

Chapter 5 presents the law and engages with the key debates in scholarship that might inform whether and how the *jus ad bellum*'s prohibitions on the use of force apply to cyberattacks. The chapter then reframes this analysis by considering whether this presumptive illegality is sufficient to create restraining effect—and if not, what it will take for this regulative logic of restraint to operate effectively.

Chapter 6 then seeks out the contours of what would make this regime functional: some form of enforcement for violations. It grounds state rights of self-defense from cyberattacks in the longstanding debates over that topic generally, considering whether enough distinguishes cyberattacks to create reliability in the operation of so-called remedial j*us ad bellum*. It then considers recent evidence suggesting states see this regime as inadequate, and are instead engaged in a competitive, dynamic reshaping of the rules of the game—a process called *structural remediation*.

Outline of Argument

This chapter begins by orienting the reader to the *jus ad bellum* and arguing that based on its bedrock status within international law and absent more specialized regimes covering cyberattacks, the UN Charter regime is the right starting point in considering international law's potential for restraint.

The next section explores the contours and present debates over what defines prohibited "uses of force." Only if cyberattacks are recognized as meeting this threshold can the legal framework (and the customary practice) fashioned around it be activated, providing a potential for regulative restraint. It argues that in trying to define whether cyberattacks would qualify as prohibited "uses of force," some of the early scholarship situating cyberattacks within Article 2(4) was unnecessarily limited by an overemphasis on two features of cyberattacks: their potential for economic disruption alone, and the nonobvious military character of the tools themselves. Engaging with the evolving literature on these questions both generally and in the context of cyberattacks, it offers several ways through this analytical thicket that clarify how cyberattacks are, indeed, prohibited uses of force.

It then argues that though this conclusion has growing support within the literature, states are still left with a key gap in their cyberattack decision-making: the consequences for a violation of this debatable limit. This, it argues, is the most significant remaining question in evaluating regulative restraint of cyberattacks, and predictably, the most contested among states. It concludes that the practical ambiguities here are likely to overwhelm even Article 2(4)'s universally recognized status. The need is to understand how states might bridge the gap between illegality and corrective action; in essence, whether the remedial *jus ad bellum* will durably activate to restrain states' adversaries or themselves—as Chapter 6 then considers.

5.1 Locating Relevant Law

This section considers briefly various sources of positive international law potentially restraining state use of cyberattacks and why, ultimately the UN Charter framework is the appropriate starting point for analysis. It considers the possibility for cyberattack-specific *lex specialis* governing the space, but finding none, instead turns to the *lex generalis* applicable to a range of state activities, into which states and scholars are attempting to fit cyberattacks.[1]

Sorting Through Sources

The sources of positive international law applying specifically to restraining cyberattacks are something of a dry well but are worthy of brief mention to frame the documents, how states have engaged with them, and in turn why the UN Charter framework endures in its appeal here. For the purposes of distinction, sources of law might fall into four categories depending on how two criteria apply: their specificity and their germaneness (to cyberattacks and, more specifically, to state's use of them to coerce or sabotage). Unspecific and irrelevant sources merit no further discussion, but the others will be considered in turn.

Specific, Peripheral. Some examples of specific but, for these purposes, only peripherally relevant treaty law, do exist and have at times featured into broader debates about how to limit cyberattacks. The probable preeminent feature of an international *lex specialis* as it pertains to cybersecurity is the Council of Europe's Budapest Convention on Cybercrime.[2] This treaty-level instrument, which has over sixty-five signatories, establishes certain

---

[1] For more on this distinction and its general use within international law, see Antonio Cassese, *International Law*, 2nd ed. (Oxford: Oxford University Press, 2005), 154.
[2] Council of Europe, "Convention on Cybercrime."

baselines for criminalization of domestic digital malfeasance, and atop that foundation, establishes certain mechanisms of cooperation to combat cross-border investigations.[3] Important as a manifestation of how states can confront the changes that technology poses to existing governance regimes, its topic is cybercrime: an individual activity in contravention of domestic laws, the enforcement of which is conducted by the state. This context is distinct from matters of international peace and security, in which states, not individuals, are the relevant subjects of jurisdiction.[4] The Russian-led project for a new UN-brokered cybercrime convention may well seek to be more applicable—but only if successfully completed.

Some commentators have also suggested that the International Telecommunications Union's Constitution and Convention—the UN body's treaty-level governing document approved by all of its Member States—serves a relevant function.[5] Article 42 of the treaty does, prima facie, proscribe states from "harmful interference their administration might cause to the radio services of other Member States."[6] This clause was cited, for instance, by the *Tallinn Manual Group of Experts* as a legal basis for Estonia's subforce act of retorsion suspending some services to Russian internet addresses during the 2007 incident.[7] Besides problems of ascribing such intentionality to a nearly 150-year-old series of articles, that section governs not Member State behavior writ large, but rather the maintenance of Special Arrangements concluded between them in the service of global telegraph (now telecommunications) networks. Such arguments might in the future play a role in managing cyberattacks, but at present, do not feature significantly. Thus, in both cases, such treaty law is specific as to subject matter, but not particularly relevant to this inquiry.

Specific, Germane. Treaty instruments that speak specifically to state-on-state cyberattacks in one form or another are rare but do exist in some narrow contexts. As Chapter 8 will explore, establishing one has been an abiding aim of Russia for over twenty-five years. By some accounts, creating the institutional predicate for such an instrument also motivated its annual UN

---

[3] Council of Europe, "Details of Treaty No.185," 2020; Amalie M. Weber, "The Council of Europe's Convention on Cybercrime," *Berkeley Technology Law Journal* 18, no. 1 (2003).
[4] Later chapters will raise cases in which this line is blurred, particularly for exceptional transgressions of international humanitarian law.
[5] Richard Hill, "WCIT: Failure or Success, Impasse or Way Forward?," *International Journal of Law and Information Technology* 21, no. 3 (2013): 8.
[6] "Constitution of the International Telecommunications Union," in *Constitution and Convention of the International Telecommunications Union*, S. Treaty Doc. No. 104-34 (2010), Article 42.
[7] Tallinn 1.0, 40–41.

General Assembly Resolutions[8] on, and annual appeals seeking state commentary related to, these matters. Returning to the role of such resolutions and responses shortly, Russia ultimately established one treaty-level agreement on these matters with its close allies in the Shanghai Cooperation Organisation (SCO), mentioned in the last chapter.[9] While relevant for disputes among those states, and providing a source of law upon which subsequent judicial opinions and commentary might draw, the number of states bound by it remains quite small. Such is the case for multilateral, not truly international, treaties. They may represent "accumulated wisdom," as Baxter puts it, but are not necessarily reflective of genuine shared custom.[10] To that end, subsequent efforts to establish a treaty instrument with broader recognition received a cool reception at the United Nations, and though accession processes were reported to have begun for India and Pakistan (a significant development if true), no significant action appears to have been taken since.[11] No other, parallel instruments exist—though Chapter 8 will discuss the significance of various attempts to motivate them. Consequently, and for the purposes of understanding cyberattacks as a general phenomenon within international law, the SCO treaty is not an ideal focus for analysis.

If there existed such a relevant, specific, well-developed, and widely applicable *lex specialis* pertaining to state-on-state use of cyberattacks, it would be

---

[8] G.A. Res. 77/36 U.N. Doc. A/RES/77/36 (December 7, 2022); G.A. Res. 76/19 U.N. Doc. A/RES/76/19 (December 6, 2021); G.A. Res. 75/240 U.N. Doc. A/RES/75/240 (December 31, 2020); G.A. Res. 74/29 U.N. Doc. A/RES/74/29 (December 12, 2019); G.A. Res. 73/27 U.N. Doc. A/RES/73/27 (December 5, 2018); [No 2017 Resolution]; G.A. Res. 71/28 U.N. Doc. A/RES/71/28 (December 5, 2016); G.A. Res. 70/237 U.N. Doc. A/RES/70/237 (December 23, 2015); G.A. Res. 69/28 U.N. Doc. A/RES/69/28 (December 2, 2014); G.A. Res. 68/243 U.N. Doc. A/RES/68/243 (December 27, 2013); G.A. Res. 67/27 U.N. Doc. A/67/27 (December 3, 2012); G.A. Res. 66/24, U.N. Doc. A/RES/66/24 (December 2, 2011); G.A. Res. 65/41, U.N. Doc. A/RES/65/41 (December 6, 2010); G.A. Res. 64/25, U.N. Doc. A/RES/64/25 (December 12, 2009); G.A. Res. 63/37, U.N. Doc. A/RES/63/37 (December 2, 2008); G.A. Res. 62/17. U.N. Doc. A/RES/62/17 (December 5, 2007); G.A. Res. 61/54, U.N. Doc. A/RES/61/54 (December 6, 2006); G.A. Res. 60/45, U.N. Doc. A/RES/60/45 (December 8, 2005); G.A. Res. 59/61, U.N. Doc. A/RES/59/61 (December 3, 2004); G.A. Res. 58/32, U.N. Doc. A/RES/58/32 (December 8, 2003); G.A. Res. 57/53, U.N. Doc. A/RES/57/53 (November 22, 2002); G.A. Res. 56/19, U.N. Doc. A/RES/56/19 (November 29, 2001); G.A. Res. 55/28, U.N. Doc. A/RES/55/28 (November 20, 2000); G.A. Res. 54/49, U.N. Doc. A/RES/54/49 (December 1, 1999); G.A. Res. 53/70, U.N. Doc. A/RES/53/70 (December 4, 1998).

[9] *Agreement on Cooperation in Ensuring International Information Security between the Member States of the Shanghai Cooperation Organisation,* (Yekaterinbourg: Shanghai Cooperation Organisation, June 16, 2009). See also Section 4.2.

[10] Richard R. Baxter, "Multilateral Treaties as Evidence of Customary International Law," *British Yearbook of International Law* 41 (1965): 275. Russian-led efforts to author a new cybercrime treaty notwithstanding; though these two projects may well intersect in the Kremlin's strategy, there has yet to be significant uptake on the SCO agreement to give it direct momentum in the UN context.

[11] Russian Federation et al., "Letter to the Secretary-General on a Draft International Code of Conduct for Information Security"; *Radio Free Europe*, "After BRICS, Putin Hosts Shanghai Cooperation Organization Summit in Ufa," July 10, 2015.

especially powerful in shaping state decision-making, particularly restraint. Regrettably, it does not.

General, Germane. Any number of treaties *could* be applicable to the circumstances of cyberattacks; however, only some are of adequate significance as to merit deliberation in these contexts. A preliminary filter are those treaties concerning matters of international security. There within, some important sources have already been noted in Chapter 4: a range of bilateral and multilateral defense treaties that—without mentioning cyberattacks—oblige states to one another's defense.[12] The North Atlantic Treaty that created NATO is one such example, as would the United States' mutual defense treaties with Japan, South Korea, Australia, and New Zealand, to the extent they have language committing to national defense.[13] Under this approach, a significant number of documents provide some general relevance to these questions—but only as a general matter. Table 5.1 summarizes these potential sources of law and the nature of their relevance.

What does stand out upon review of each, however, is repeated reference to the UN Charter. In fact, in all of the aforementioned US security and defense treaties refer to it both directly as a source of authority ("undertake, as set forth in the Charter of the United Nations"), and indirectly through incorporating its key concepts into language ("including the *use of armed force*").[14] They suggest that the correct and perhaps most powerful starting place for such an inquiry is the UN Charter itself. After a brief discussion of other relevant sources, the next section argues this case.

Additional Sources. As noted, none of these generally applicable documents speak specifically to the role cyberattacks would play. Instead, governments are through their statements seeking to elaborate, and signal, their interpretations of these general treaty obligations as they apply to cyberattacks. It is worth a brief mention of these additional sources of customary international law that elaborate upon, illuminate behavior relative to, and in turn inform subsequent treaty law.

The International Court of Justice's (ICJ) Statute, Article 38.1, explains that in addition to Treaties ("international conventions ... establishing rules

---

[12] See, e.g., Section 4.3.
[13] North Atlantic Treaty; Mutual Defense Treaty Between the United States and the Republic of Korea; Treaty of Mutual Cooperation and Security Between Japan and the United States of America; Security Treaty Between the United States, Australia, and New Zealand (ANZUS).
[14] North Atlantic Treaty, Art. 1, Art. 3.

Table 5.1 Examples of Treaty Law in the Context of State-on-State Cyberattacks

	Germane	Peripheral
Specific	SCO Agreement	ITU C&C (e.g., Art. 42) Budapest Convention
General	North Atlantic Treaty (NATO) US/ROK Mutual Defense Treaty *Foundational: UN Charter*	[Not significant to this analysis]

expressly realized"), the other sources of law relevant for consideration include "international custom . . . the general principles of law as recognized by civilized nations; and judicial decisions and other teachings of the most highly qualified publicists of the various nations."[15] This study does not intend to reproduce the many debates concerning the status and contours of each, but rather to identify the rough categories that will inform in various measures the analysis that follows.

Easiest first are judicial decisions, which can be dispensed with most immediately. As of this writing, no ICJ or other equally eminent judicial opinions of international law relating specifically to cyberattacks—or for that matter, cyberspace. Parts III and IV of this study will, however, identify some key questions upon which judicial elaboration may be particularly useful to firming up their respective logics of restraint.

Bilateral or multilateral executive agreements not forming treaties—in vogue whenever national legislatures face gridlock or do not require implementation in domestic law—represent another source insofar as they read on actual questions of law or behavior governed by it.[16] The SCO agreement falls, nominally, in this category. Many of these in the cyber context fall under the more concrete end of the "norms" project. While the potential for norms generally will be the subject of Chapter 8, for preliminary purposes, it suffices to note that most explicit norm projects that have shown results do not specifically fix their focus on cyberattacks as defined herein, but range in scope: some seeking to engage with all unfriendly cyber acts, some pursuing specific operational measures seeking to prevent the outbreak of conflict due

---

[15] United Nations, *Statute of the International Court of Justice* (1946), Chapter II: "Competence of the Court," Article 38.
[16] On the relative status of such executive agreements relative to treaties, see "Agora: The End of Treaties?," *AJIL Unbound* 108 (2014).

to misperception, and others aiming at the cessation of certain espionage activities.

International forums and records created under the auspices of the United Nations provide states an opportunity to opine when it suits them, giving insights into their thinking by providing commentators the opportunity to identify trends and impasses. At the intersection of cyber matters and international security, the annual *Developments in the Field of Information Security* resolution has created one such record.[17] More significant for these purposes, however, are the series of GGEs, also chartered by those resolutions, which provided states a non–treaty-based vehicle to discuss matters of international cybersecurity—including cyberattacks.[18] While technically only a reflection of the views of experts present, and operating on a consensus model, the GGEs are widely understood to reflect official doctrine of its participants. Particularly because of its formal negotiating model, as well as the broad cross-section of participating states (including UN Security Council Permanent Members), it offers a particularly useful stream of perspectives on how states regard the evolution of customary international law. The Open-Ended Working Group (OEWG), formed as a counterpoint to Russian-led efforts to negotiate a novel cybercrime treaty, provides another important lens into the evolution of state views, particularly in consensus reports (of which one has been released to date).[19]

Expressions of how states individually recognize their obligations under treaty law include, for instance, political declarations by national leaders

---

[17] See note 8.
[18] Four of the five GGEs on this topic produced final reports; one (2017) ended in impasse. See United Nations Group of Governmental Experts (2008–9), "Report of the Group of Governmental Experts on Developments in the Field of Information and Telecommunications in the Context of International Security (2008–9)" (Geneva: United Nations Institute for Disarmament Research, 2010); Stewart, "Old Worm Won't Die After 2008 Attack on Military"; United Nations Group of Governmental Experts (2014–15), "Report of the Group of Governmental Experts on Developments in the Field of Information and Telecommunications in the Context of International Security" (Geneva: United Nations Institute for Disarmament Research, 2015); Michele Markoff, "Explanation of Position at the Conclusion of the 2016–2017 UN Group of Governmental Experts (GGE) on Developments in the Field of Information and Telecommunications in the Context of International Security," June 23, 2017; United Nations Group of Governmental Experts (2019–21), "Report of the Group of Governmental Experts on Developments in the Field of Information and Telecommunications in the Context of International Security" (Geneva: United Nations Institute for Disarmament Research).
[19] United Nations Open-Ended Working Group on Information and Communication Technologies, "Report of the Open-Ended Working Group on Security of and in the Use of Information and Communications Technologies 2021–2025" (Geneva: United Nations Institute for Disarmament Research, 2021).

about how their defense obligations might be invoked by cyberattacks.[20] Such unilateral statements by governments—from the national cybersecurity and foreign policy strategies aforementioned, to the military manuals and legal interpretations that will feature into later analysis, particularly in Chapter 7.[21] To the extent they begin to form a mosaic of consistent state practice, or are explicitly used to substantially inform state action at the margins of law, these statements may be important indices of the direction of international custom. The same is true, to a different degree, of multilateral political statements on related topics, including at times the economic and political dimensions of cyberattacks.[22]

Among the "teachings of the most highly qualified publicists," in the project of the international law of cyber activities, the *Tallinn Manual* project led by Schmitt is worthy of special mention. Its outputs, the 2013 *Tallinn Manual 1.0* and 2017 *Tallinn Manual 2.0*, represent the work of a large panel of eminent experts on the *jus ad bellum* and *jus in bello*.[23] It aims to offer guidance that is authoritatively comprehensive, including and in particular for its explicitness about where consensus was not reached and debate among experts was significant. Like any source aiming to comment on and inform law, it has its limits. *Tallinn*'s scholars hailed from only a handful of (mostly Western) countries; governments observed but were not formal authors; and some practitioners regard a handful of its most important conclusions as out of step with state custom.[24] Nonetheless, where its experts reached consensus, and where that consensus was in a similar context to the discussions herein, it features significantly into this work.

---

[20] See, e.g., NATO, "Bucharest Summit Declaration," April 3, 2008; "Wales Summit Declaration"; The White House, "Joint Fact Sheet: The United States-Republic of Korea Alliance: Shared Values, New Frontiers" (Washington, DC: 2015); Steven Smith, "Minister for Defence—Australia-United States Ministerial Consultations (AUSMIN)," September 16, 2011.

[21] Theodor Meron, "The Continuing Role of Custom in the Formation of International Humanitarian Law," *American Journal of International Law* 90, no. 2 (1996).

[22] See, for example, the then- Group of 8 (G8), *Deauville Declaration: Internet (Final Declaration of the G8 Leaders at the Deauville Summit)*, Deauville, France, 2011; Organisation for Economic Cooperation and Development, "Principles for Internet Policymaking" (Paris: OECD, 2014); The White House, "Fact Sheet: The 2016 G-20 Summit in Hangzhou, China" (Washington, DC: 2016).

[23] *Tallinn 1.0*; *Tallinn 2.0*.

[24] See, e.g., Dieter Fleck, "Searching for International Rules Applicable to Cyber Warfare— A Critical First Assessment of the New Tallinn Manual," *Journal of Conflict and Security Law* 18, no. 2 (2013); Dan Efrony and Yuval Shany, "A Rule Book on the Shelf? Tallinn Manual 2.0 on Cyberoperations and Subsequent State Practice," *American Journal of International Law* 112, no. 4 (2018); Oliver Kessler and Wouter Werner, "Expertise, Uncertainty, and International Law: A Study of the Tallinn Manual on Cyberwarfare," *Leiden Journal of International Law* 26, no. 4 (2013).

Combined, these sources help illuminate the law as it might apply to cyberattacks, particularly their relationship to the UN Charter—which is a starting point both for many of the sources above and the sections that follow.

The UN Charter and the *Jus Ad Bellum*

The UN Charter is a natural starting point in situating cyberattacks within interstate conflict in the *jus ad bellum*. As a legal document, the key objectives of the UN Charter are to recognize acts of illegal coercion and set out the mechanisms to limit them. Analytically, the United Nations Charter, and in particular Article 2(4), offers the most robust evaluative framework judging the legality of coercion in international politics. Specifically, it serves as the bedrock for the present-day *jus ad bellum*, "the first expression of the basic rules [regulating the use of force] in their modern form."[25] The Charter's terminology has even become the basic vocabulary for identifying and evaluating such illegality—"uses of force"—in the international system.

This is not to say that Article 2(4) is without challenge, but rather that it is without peer in terms of a codified and recognized *jus ad bellum* regime.[26] The precise contours of its operation may be imperfect, but the capacity of the international system to recognize, if not fully adapt to new conceptions of its core tenets, is rarely in question. To the former, Melzer points out and as later sections will pursue in-depth, "certain aspects of that law, such as the precise modalities governing the use of force in a case of self-defence, for instance, are not regulated in the UN Charter and must be derived from customary law as reflected in state practice and *opinio juris* and identified in international jurisprudence."[27] Of course, the UN Charter as drafted did not expressly contemplate technology such as cyberattacks. However, law can—and many commentators observe, must—be adapted to new problems.

---

[25] Christine D. Gray, *International Law and the Use of Force*, 3rd ed. (Oxford: Oxford University Press, 2008), 4.

[26] Certainly, following the US invasion of Iraq, substantive challenges regarding intervention and pre-emptive self-defense led even the UN's own Secretary-General to deem the international community at a "fork in the road" regarding use of force "no less decisive than 1945 itself, when the U.N. was founded." Kofi Annan, *Address of the Secretary-General to the General Assembly (23 September)* (New York: United Nations, 2003).

[27] Nils Melzer, "Cyberwarfare and International Law" (Geneva: United Nations Institute for Disarmament Research, 2011). "In the absence of a treaty definition, the concept of "force" must be interpreted in good faith in accordance with the ordinary meaning to be given to the term in its context and in the light of the Charter's object and purpose."

A diverse cross-section of states seem to support in doctrine this sort of "interpretive reorientation"—one that scholars like Randelzhofer have long argued for generally, and that contemporary scholars such as Waxman and Roscini further advance in the context of cyber operations.[28] And though problematized later in this study, the high-level conclusion of the 2011-12 UN GGE on international cybersecurity matters was able to agree that "international law, and in particular the Charter of the United Nations, is applicable and is essential to maintaining peace and stability."[29] Other states articulate as much in their doctrine both before and after that landmark report.[30] It is no accident that the UN Charter system remains the reference point of the *jus ad bellum,* case law, and scholarship—and is thus the appropriate starting place for this analysis. With the procedural matter of the UN Charter's applicability and suitability established, the next section turns to the substantive questions of precisely *how* its provisions apply to cyberattacks—and to what end?

5.2 Cyberattacks as an Article 2(4) Use of Force

This section analyzes the basis for considering cyberattacks a use of force, the behavior perhaps most straightforwardly prohibited by the UN Charter. Article 2(4) of the Charter states: "All Members shall refrain in their international relations from the threat or use of force against the territorial integrity or political independence of any state, or in any other manner

---

[28] Albrecht Randelzhofer, "Article 51," in *The Charter of the United Nations: A Commentary,* ed. Bruno Simma (Munich: C. H. Beck, 1995), 1400; Matthew C. Waxman, "Cyber-Attacks and the Use of Force: Back to the Future of Article 2(4)," *Yale Journal of International Law* 36 (2011): 437. Examples of state doctrine explicitly emphasizing the applicability of the *jus ad bellum* and/or *jus in bello* to this context includes The White House, *The United States' International Strategy for Cyberspace*; Harold Hongju Koh, "Remarks as Prepared for Delivery to the USCYBERCOM Inter-Agency Legal Conference" (paper presented at the USCYBERCOM Inter-Agency Legal Conference, September 18, 2012); United Nations General Assembly, "Developments in the Field of Information and Telecommunications in the Context of International Security" (New York: UN, 2011), 6; United Nations General Assembly, "Developments in the Field of Information and Telecommunications in the Context of International Security" (New York: UN, 2002), 3; European Union, Cybersecurity Strategy of the European Union: An Open, Safe, and Secure Cyberspace (Brussels: EU, 2013), 15–16. Russian Federation, Conceptual Views on the Activities of the Armed Forces of the Russian Federation in the Information Space (Moscow, 2000).

[29] *GGE 2012.*

[30] See, for example The White House, *The United States' International Strategy for Cyberspace,* 10; Government of France, *France Defence and National Security Strategic Review* (Paris: Ministre des Armées, 2017), 61.

inconsistent with the Purposes of the United Nations."[31] According to Gray, "states and commentators generally agree that the prohibition is not only a treaty obligation but also customary law and even *jus cogens*"—meaning that it is "peremptory and may not be derogated from by any treaty (or by ordinary customary practices)."[32] The article's basic proscription on the use of force outside of the narrow provisions permitted for self-defense (per Article 51) or pursuant to Security Council action (per Chapter VII), has been reaffirmed in its basic content numerous times, in General Assembly Resolutions, Security Council Debates, and by the International Court of Justice.[33] It has been operationalized, inter alia, in the form of Article 4 of the NATO alliance, which declares, "the Parties will consult together whenever, in the opinion of any of them, the territorial integrity, political independence or security of any of the Parties is threatened."[34]

However, while the prohibition itself has exceptional agreement within international law, its scope is a matter of substantial debate—which cyberattacks both accentuate and further complicate.[35] Assessing the provision's relevance to cyberattacks, two questions leap to the fore: First, is a cyberattack recognizable as a use of force by nature or its effects; and second, how does a cyberattack threaten a state's territorial integrity, political independence, or run afoul of the UN's purposes? These questions immediately confront some of the most important of the debates over Article 2(4)'s scope and application, which this section will consider. The two most significant debates pertain to how international law judges edge cases that may or may not meet the threshold of a use of force. The first is the extent to which, in order to maintain its broader aim of preserving peace and security, the Charter excludes "lesser acts" of political or economic force. The second, related question, is what salient features help identify an act as a use of force, particularly if it has some of those qualities of lesser acts. Both

---

[31] Charter of the United Nations, Article 2, para 4. The "threat of force" falls outside the scope of this study, but further resources in this regard can be found generally in Nikolas Stürchler, *The Threat of Force in International Law* (Cambridge: Cambridge University Press, 2007). Specific to cyberattacks, see Herbert S. Lin, "Offensive Cyber Operations and the Use of Force Cybersecurity Symposium: National Leadership, Individual Responsibility," *Journal of National Security Law & Policy* 4, no. 1 (2010): 76; Roscini, "Threats of Armed Force and Contemporary International Law," 229; Gray, *International Law and the Use of Force*, 8.

[32] Cassese, *International Law*, 199; Gray, *International Law and the Use of Force*, 30.

[33] See Declaration on the Inadmissibility of Intervention in the Domestic Affairs of States, G.A. Res. 2131 (XX) (1965); Declaration of the Principles of International Law, G.A. Res. 2625 (XXV) (1970); *Definition of Aggression*, G.A. Res. 3314 (XXIX) (1974).

[34] North Atlantic Treaty, Article 4.

[35] Gray, *International Law and the Use of Force*, 30.

are covered, at some point, in the cyberattack scholarship—and, in both cases, were stumbling blocks in its early development. The sections that follow address each in turn, proposing that balances definitional discipline with evaluative dynamism permits a thorough and appropriate consideration of cyberattacks as uses of force.

Lesser Uses of Force?

Much of the early scholarship considering the international law of cyberattacks hinged on the extent to which these events might have more in common with an economic sanction than the kind of attack as traditionally conceived. To preface this discussion, it is important to locate the origins of the conclusion that held back much of the earlier scholarship—primarily, the dismissing of economic and political means of coercion as "lesser" uses of force.[36] The concern is well founded; the majority of scholarly opinion appears to favor this view that regardless of the method of analysis, *strictly* economic and political coercive measures do fall short of the use of force standard.[37] Many point to the *travaux préparatoires* of the Charter, and that the San Francisco Conference failed to adopt a proposal to extend the use of force to economic sanctions, implying their exclusion a lesser category.[38] After all, the premise of the Charter was not to ban every possible form of coercion, but to "save succeeding generations from the scourge of war."[39] Here, the elaboration process of the term "use of force" is quite relevant, particularly the *Nicaragua* case at the ICJ, which lifted up the 1974 *Definition of Aggression* and the 1970 *Declaration on Friendly Relations* to identify customary law on the issue. Proponents of the restrictive view on the use of force therefore note that economic and political instruments are never codified as "functional" uses of force and are explicitly separated from the supplemental

---

[36] Melzer, "Cyberwarfare and International Law," 7.
[37] See also Jack Plano, Lawrence Ziring, and Roy Olton, *International Relations: A Political Dictionary* (Santa Barbara, CA: ABC-CLIO, 1995), 358; Marco Roscini, "World Wide Warfare—Jus Ad Bellum and the Use of Cyber Force," *Max Planck Yearbook of United Nations Law* 14 (2010): 105.
[38] For further context, see Edward Gordon, "Article 2(4) in Historical Context," *Yale Journal of International Law* 10 (1985). With regard to computer network attack, see Silver, "Computer Network Attack as a Use of Force under Article 2(4) of the United Nations Charter," 80–82; Michael Schmitt, "Computer Network Attack and the Use of Force in International Law: Thoughts on a Normative Framework," *Columbia Journal of Transnational Law* 37 (1999).
[39] *Charter of the United Nations*, Preamble; Marco Roscini, *Cyber Operations and the Use of Force in International Law* (Oxford: Oxford University Press, 2014), 45.

view offered by the 1987 *Declaration on the Non-Use of Force*.[40] As a defense of the logic of Article 2(4), this restrictive approach is coherent: as Silver notes, scholars have primarily rejected a more liberal interpretation out of fears of a "slippery slope" that permitting nonmilitary physical force to qualify would have "similarly devastating effects."[41]

On its own, this majority, restrictive definition of "force" is impossible to ignore, which is the starting point from which many scholars early in the debate over cyberattacks took. In one his earliest works on the topic, Libicki held that "a cyberspace attack on a nation's infrastructure is likely to be a pale subset of full-scale economic warfare (e.g., an enforced embargo), which, in turn, is slower and less violent than strategic bombardment, whose efficacy, in turn, is still being debated."[42] Several other early volumes featured variants of this critique—itself largely fixed in what was technologically cognizable in that era.[43] Had it remained dominant, cyberattacks would be relegated to "lesser" status, not covered by a strict reading of Article 2(4). Yet as other scholars would later point out, this reading was both too simplistic, and no longer appropriate to the scale of possible damage. Kilovaty, for instance, noted this fork in the road: "What contemporary definitions of cyberattacks fail to mention or address is that cyberattacks can also cause economic effects which are as severe as kinetic effects."[44] The 2022 GGE report started to recognize complete this as well, noting the "fundamental importance" of information infrastructure in this context, calling it the "backbone of society's vital functions, services, and activities" and crucially noting that "significantly impaired or damaged, the human costs as well as impact on the State's economy, development, political, and social functioning, and national security could be substantial."[45] It is on this basis that scholars turned to a more textured debate in the *jus ad bellum*, focused not on exclusions, but on

---

[40] United Nations General Assembly, "Declaration on the Enhancement of the Effectiveness of the Principle of Refraining from the Threat or Use of Force in International Relations," 1987.

[41] Silver, "Computer Network Attack as a Use of Force under Article 2(4) of the United Nations Charter," 83.

[42] See, e.g., Marin C. Libicki, "Information War, Information Peace," *Journal of International Affairs* 51, no. 2 (1998): 417.

[43] *Computer Network Attack and International Law*; Silver, "Computer Network Attack as a Use of Force under Article 2(4) of the United Nations Charter."

[44] Ido Kilovaty, "Rethinking the Prohibition on the Use of Force in the Light of Economic Cyber Warfare: Towards a Broader Scope of Article 2(4) of the UN Charter," *Journal of Law & Cyber Warfare* 4, no. 3 (2015): 224.

[45] United Nations Group of Governmental Experts (2019–21), *Report of the Group of Governmental Experts on Developments in the Field of Information and Telecommunications in the Context of International Security* (Geneva: United Nations Institute for Disarmament Research, 2021), para 42 (hereafter *GGE 2021*).

key criteria to evaluate incidents, on the premise those criteria might produce more holistically considerate outcomes.

Evaluating a Use of Force: Target, Instrument, or Effect?

Intuitively, determining whether an act rises to the level of a use of force could invoke a number of considerations: what was the target, real or intended; what was the tool or instrument used to cause the damage in question; and what as the scale of the effects caused? The evolution of the scholarship on this question, both generally and as it might apply to cyberattacks, helps inform how to best evaluate them in the present context.

Target. Some scholars propose looking, in such edge cases, to the target of the event. One approach to determining the nature of a use of armed force target-based theory suggests, for instance, that by virtue of targeting infrastructure, any cyber operation would constitute armed force.[46] This is an approach that in some of the influential early works in the field, scholars took this view—perhaps due in part to uncertainty over the broader effects possible (which at that time were difficult to visualize).[47] As time has progressed, others have raised significant challenges to using target as a principal criterion. First, critics argue its breadth renders it not particularly useful.[48] Second, it may be too permissive, allowing events that "only cause minor inconvenience or merely aim to collect information" to be qualified as a use of force—ultimately causing the prohibitions to be self-defeating.[49] For the purposes herein; one of these objections can be dispensed with; discipline in defining cyberattacks to necessarily have a gravity requirement eliminates both minor inconveniences and acts of espionage from being unduly swept under the definition.[50] The other, however, is more notable—simply selecting any category (even including military targets, as the next chapter considers in the context of an "armed attack"), seems artificial. Therefore, the question turns not to whether looking in a more nuanced way at effects might be more satisfying and supported by scholarship.

---

[46] Roscini, *Cyber Operations and the Use of Force in International Law*, 47.
[47] Walter Gary Sharp, *The Use of Force in CyberSpace* (Falls Church, VA: Aegis Research Corporation, 1999), 129–31; Christopher C. Joyner and Catherine Lotrionte, "Information Warfare as International Coercion: Elements of a Legal Framework," *European Journal of International Law* 12, no. 5 (2001): 855.
[48] Roscini, *Cyber Operations and the Use of Force in International Law*, 47.
[49] Ibid.
[50] See Section 1.3.

Effects. An alternative approach cited by some considering the issue focuses on effects, comparing in particular the *kinetic* effects of cyberattack to if the same action were rendered by noncyber means. The approach here draws on the ICJ's holding in *Nicaragua*, which pointed first to the "scale and effects" of an event to distinguish it from a "mere frontier incident."[51] It echoes, as well, the formula excluding "acts and consequences not of sufficient gravity" highlighted in the *Definition of Aggression*.[52] This "kinetic equivalence doctrine," however, is rightly controversial. Cyberattacks may well do real harm without causing physical damage recognizable to military historians—and that harm is no less significant by mere absence of a "boom factor."[53] Melzer rightly points out that it is "unsatisfactory . . . to interpret the 'scale and effects' criterion exclusively in terms of effects equivalent to physical destruction," which will "end up being too restrictive [or, though less convincingly, overinclusive]."[54] Tsagourias likewise paints a vivid and compelling picture of the risks of overrestriction.[55]

Instrument. A third and intuitively appealing approach other scholars have taken focuses not on the target or effects, but the *instrument* in question. This argument long predates the discussion of cyberattacks, and to its proponents, is a clear-cut means of distinguishing the act from other, lesser acts of coercion—which, by and large, tend to be evaluated on the basis of their effects.[56] In the simplest cases, it appears to suffice. Causing a crisis within a state's military through economic sanctions on arms transfers is not a use of force; using aerial bombardment to destroy a state's stock exchanges would be. This also avoids some other practical pitfalls associated with the doctrine of kinetic equivalence. However it, too, has limits. Some read the ICJ's *Nuclear Weapons* opinion to undercut this approach in its holding

---

[51] *Military and Paramilitary Activities in and against Nicaragua (Nicaragua v. United States of America), Merits, Judgment*, ICJ Reports 14, para 195 (1986). The Court was opining here on whether the event should be classified as an "armed attack"; however, as Chapter 6 will clarify, events fitting that criteria would inherently be uses of force.

[52] United Nations General Assembly, *Definition of Aggression (A/RES/3314 [XXIX])* (1974), Art. 2.

[53] Kilovaty, "Rethinking the Prohibition on the Use of Force in the Light of Economic Cyber Warfare," 224.

[54] Melzer, "Cyberwarfare and International Law," 14. The concern of overinclusion, however, is more significant under Melzer's subject than the one of this study, as "large-scale denial of service attack[s] . . . against non-essential, purely civil service providers such as, for example, online shopping services" would not qualify here.

[55] Nicholas Tsagourias, "Cyber Attacks, Self-Defence and the Problem of Attribution," *Journal of Conflict & Security Law* 17 (2012): 231.

[56] See Silver, "Computer Network Attack as a Use of Force under Article 2(4) of the United Nations Charter," 87, in particular his critique of Sharp's "destructive effect" standard.

that Article 2(4) "applies to any use of force, regardless of the weapon employed."[57] To do so, however, is to accept a circular logic in the part of the Court. A more considered read of the passage sees its intent as preventing the undue exclusion of a use of force solely by virtue of the weapon used, not to undermine the use of an instrument-based analysis whatsoever. Rather, the challenge comes with edge cases like cyberattacks, which operate based on computer code, and the capabilities of which are far more difficult to distinguish than traditional military hardware.

Alternatives. However, cyberattacks do not naturally lend themselves to instrument-based analysis, hence this complex rationale for what is ultimately a standard evaluation. There may, however, be a third path—identifying a particular kind of instrument beyond such a rigid taxonomy. More useful then is the notion that this instrument-based classification is meant as a "prescriptive shorthand" to what is at its core an exhaustive consequence-based rationale within the overall context of the UN Charter.[58] Schmitt argues that in order to make assessments within the existing international framework, instrument-based analysis cannot simply be ignored in preference of effects, as it is in works such as Silver's. They are, in his words, "an acknowledgement of the ambiguity resident in the use of force norm" but advance "some of the key extralegal influences on that complex process."[59] Such an approach is based on the idea that "because the results of applying economic and political instruments generally constitute lesser threats to shared community values, the use of force standard serves as a logical breaking point in categorizing the asperity of particular coercive agents."[60]

This view is largely compelling; it accommodates both differences between an unfriendly state's acts and outright uses of force, and the need for more nuance and complexity in judging borderline candidate actions. Schmitt advances a consequence-based approach to examining cyberattacks that relies upon six input factors to assess whether the cyberattack is tantamount to an armed attack; these factors will in part help inform the analysis of the section that follows.[61] This is the evaluative mechanism that Schmitt first proposed in his most comprehensive early study of Article 2(4) and cyberattack

---

[57] *Legality of the Threat or Use of Nuclear Weapons, Advisory Opinion*, ICJ Reports 226, para. 39 (1996).
[58] Schmitt, "Computer Network Attack and the Use of Force in International Law," 917.
[59] Ibid., 317.
[60] Schmitt, "Computer Network Attack and the Use of Force in International Law," 912.
[61] Schmitt notes that those proposed criteria "are merely factors that influence States making use of force assessments; they are not formal legal criteria." *Tallinn 1.0*, 47.

concepts. Although in the case of cyberattacks as defined herein, it may end up in the same place, these criteria are also more enduringly satisfying than Roscini's proposal to rely knowledge of the primary target for this confirmatory process.[62]

Therefore, the subsections that follow ask longstanding questions in a new context: Must "force" be "military" force; how to determine uses of force when that criterion is uncertain; and what do these frameworks tell us about the inherent legality of cyberattacks as a use of force?

Must Force Be Military?

No overwhelming consensus exists on whether Article 2(4)'s scope is limited to use of "armed" force in the sense of it being military in nature or execution. The UN Charter evinces a particular if historically fixed preoccupation with military activities. Recognizing that, the *Tallinn* experts concluded that a "nexus between the cyber operations . . . and military operations heightens the likelihood of characterization as a use of force."[63] But what about the general proposition? Does the fact that the use of force has traditionally been understood to imply force employed by the military or other armed forces also mean that must be true for *any* recognized use of force?

Within this debate, Randelzhofer regards the use of force described in Article 2(4) as something of an anomaly, claiming that in the context of paragraph 7 of the Preamble, as well as Article 44, the term "force" in 2(4) "clearly means armed force."[64] He further claims that the subsequent *Friendly Relations Act* adopted by the General Assembly in 1970 clarifies the term in that it "deals solely with *military* force."[65] Yet that Act is hardly a sufficient interpretation of the Charter to be satisfying in the given context. As Dinstein points out, the "the expression of 'force' is not preceded by the adjective 'armed,' whereas the phrase 'armed force' appears elsewhere in the charter."[66] There is something of a paradox here, as Dinstein further claims "the term 'force' in Article 2(4) must denote . . . military force."[67] The "armed attack"

---

[62] Roscini, *Cyber Operations and the Use of Force in International Law*, 62.
[63] *Tallinn 1.0*, 50.
[64] Randelzhofer, "Article 2(4)," 112.
[65] Ibid.
[66] Yoram Dinstein, *War, Aggression and Self-Defence*, 4th ed. (Cambridge: Cambridge University Press, 2005), 85–86.
[67] Ibid.

standard that is routinely used in the remedial context in the UN Charter is not the same as the more nuanced, expansive use of force broadly asserted in Article 2(4)'s prohibitive context. "Armed attack" is far more explicit and evocative of kinetic and military attack than simply "force"—but is also not the standard of the Article 2(4), which a majority of commentators regard as lesser threshold than "armed attack" found elsewhere in the Charter.[68]

A balance must be struck then between a generic notion of force in the Charter's prohibitive text, and the explicit requirement of armed attack in its remedial sections to which we will shortly turn. That middle ground, and indeed the most straightforward, accepts that force would in most cases be implicitly military—but also accepting that the concept of military force can be a dynamic one since, as Silver points out, "as the techniques of warfare evolve, so too does the general understanding of what constitutes 'military' force."[69] This accords with the view of the *Tallinn* experts, who note that "the use of force is traditionally understood to imply force by the military or other armed forces," but might be recognizable instead by targeting militaries, and "need not necessarily be undertaken by a state's armed forces" per se.[70]

The corollary to this approach is that we must exclude *strictly* political and economic instruments of coercion from the definition of illegal force. This is the critical litmus test of activities that might fall in the grey zone between use of force and otherwise. The rest of this chapter will therefore focus on what (in the prescriptive shorthand approach) other features might single out cyberattacks as uses of force under Article 2(4).

Beyond Rigid Instrument Analysis: The Dual-Use Counterpoint

The preceding section has offered one way that cyberattacks can be reliably (if provisionally) deemed military instruments. But upon what grounds did some of the earliest scholars in the field dismiss them as largely excluded nonforce? Is it not somewhat artificial, in the context of a cyberattack, to ignore effects entirely? Indeed, the shared nature of information infrastructure might appropriately lead one to question the durability of Article 2(4) analyses relying exclusively on the nature of an instrument.

---

[68] See Section 6.2.
[69] Silver, "Computer Network Attack as a Use of Force under Article 2(4) of the United Nations Charter," 84.
[70] *Tallinn 1.0*, 50–51, 43.

This section proposes an important role for an effects-based analysis, in the case of cyberattacks, and potentially for other use of force analyses moving forward. It argues that in cases where the line between economic and military effects might be blurry, targets and consequences do have some confirmatory value; they can be used as a secondary test to verify the military character of the instrument. Owing to today's reliance on that shared infrastructure, this approach is particularly relevant to cyberattacks and provides a secondary basis for recognizing the act as an illegal force under international law.

Part of what frustrated previous scholars' attempts at excising the economic and political components of cyberattacks was the lack of a meaningful distinction in the nature of the technological instrument itself. There is no fundamental difference between a computer intended for military operations and one used for civilian purposes. Computing architecture is, by its very design, inherently capable of executing any function that code dictates to its processor. It is for this reason that computers arrive "out of the box" with little more than an operating system but are capable of being customized with any number of applications of the user's preference. Computers utilized by governments, including ministries of defense, are, in all but the rarest cases, commercial off-the-shelf products of the same type available to the general public.[71]

Dual-use technologies exist across every domain. On land, a Humvee is an example of a dual-use technology—it can haul playground construction equipment or can just as easily have affixed to it a machine gun to render it a weapon. On the high seas, cargo ships designed for commerce can conceal weapons, as the history of naval interdictions during the First and Second World Wars demonstrates.[72] In the air, some warplanes might appear quite distinctive from commercial jets, but history shows how even that civilian

---

[71] David Tubbs, Perry G. Luzwick, and Walter Gary Sharp, "Technology and Law: The Evolution of Digital Warfare," in *Computer Network Attack and International Law*, ed. Michael Schmitt and Brian O'Donnell (Newport, RI: Naval War College, 2002), 11. Whilst some security experts find this state of affairs outrageous, this preference is quite justifiable on three grounds. First, governments avoid having to be responsible for the development of such technology. Second, using commercial off-the-shelf products takes advantage of the private sector's short lifecycle for technology products, permitting upgrades to better (and more secure) technology on a more regular basis. Third, it provides the security advantage of a heterogeneous environment, as the use of diverse commercial products reduces the likelihood that any single vulnerability creates risk across an entire ecosystem.

[72] Lance Davis and Stanley Engerman, *Naval Blockades in Peace and War* (New York: Cambridge University Press, 2006), 239–45.

platform can be instantly weaponized. Instrument-based analyses cannot be sidetracked by the regular, or indeed the predominant, use of a platform for economic purposes. What matters in the context of 2(4) is the character of the contents and purpose, not the carrier.

To this end, perhaps one of the most profound developments of the past thirty years has been the endurance of the "open" or fully interoperable network architecture, lack of robust security, and the utilization of shared information infrastructure for the vast majority of private *and public* computer networking.[73] Much of this was unanticipated by early literature on cyberattacks, when a greater distinction existed between public and private, military and civilian information infrastructure. Cyberattacks, which exploit or attack this infrastructure, therefore have much greater potential on the whole to do damage across many more critical sectors than was true in the late 1990s and early 2000s. As this chapter's introduction explained, the most serious large-scale cyberattacks disrupt data of all sorts, thus (by some interpretations) blurring the line of economic, political, and military instruments of coercion. So what may have seemed a largely economic instrument to previous analysts is at the very least multidimensional given today's system. Even if one were to reject the analysis from the previous section, cyberattacks are simply irreconcilable with rigid (and largely artificial) distinctions between coercive and noncoercive instruments. Noting that, the only serious alternative then is to sacrifice the primacy of the instrument-based distinction and seek a standard that draws upon the effects of an attack as a nonideal ancillary test. In this case as well, cyberattacks meet the standard of use of force.

If instrument-based distinctions are not fully satisfying, and cyberattacks at their most complex combine economic, political, and military coercion, the feature of reference for this *jus ad bellum* analysis is its military component. Recall that in evaluating an armed attack (a higher standard addressed in the next chapter), the ICJ ruled in *Nicaragua* that a key criteria were "if such an operation, because of its *scale and effects*, would have been classified as an armed attack rather than as a mere frontier incident, *had it been carried out by regular armed forces*."[74] When (because an instrument-based evaluation is incomplete) effects are used to verify a use of force, the mere presence of economic and political externalities cannot exempt a cyberattack from

---

[73] Jonathan Zittrain, *The Future of the Internet—and How to Stop It* (New Haven, CT: Yale University Press, 2008), 43–52.

[74] *Military and Paramilitary Activities in and against Nicaragua*, 1986 (emphasis added).

meeting the threshold. This more modern analysis of cyberattacks in their most complex form—causing mass disruption across multiple sectors—further suggests they can indeed be assessed within the use of force framework of Article 2(4), simply with appropriate caveats. All this does not render the preceding scholarship on cyberattacks and international law useless; rather it makes usable the broadly affirmed tools of Article 2(4) by recognizing, on even restrictive grounds, that cyberattacks bear a functional similarity to acknowledged use of force instruments.

It is therefore clear that various aspects of cyberattacks, primarily as instrument and confirmed by its effects, render them strong candidates for recognition as a use of force under Article 2(4).

Evaluating Other Criteria

In addition to the perhaps most significant question of military involvement, several other aspects help distinguish a use of force under Article 2(4) from their "lesser" for instance economic and political, counterparts. The *Tallinn Manual* offers these for general consideration, noting they are not legal factors per se; for these purposes, several are also not relevant to the narrower subject of examination.[75] However, those that offer both a useful methodology to consider how a cyberattack as defined herein might fare, when it is not readily identifiable as a military instrument or having clear military effect, as well as an opportunity to identify where reconsideration of the criteria themselves may be needed.

These most relevant criteria for this assessment, briefly, are the *immediacy* of an attack (rather than those that take time to have an effect, like sanctions); its *directness* (with consequences directly tied to the coercive act, rather than requiring contributory factors to operate); *invasiveness* (occurring physically in the victim state, violating sovereign rights); the *measurability of effects* (quantifiable if not observable); and its *presumptive legality* (not falling into categories of known "lesser" activities such as propaganda).[76]

---

[75] These are selected from the so-called Schmitt Criteria (see note 60) but pared down for this different and narrower context. Those criteria already covered are the *severity* of an attack and *state involvement* (included in this definition of cyberattack), as well as its *military character* (see Section 5.2).

[76] *Tallinn 2.0*, 336–37.

Consider, first, an emblematic case that would fall squarely within these criteria. Here, the attacker directed its military's offensive cyber unit to target and destroy the transformers at an electricity-generating facility on an adversary's offshore island used mostly for staging air combat. The result of the attack shorted out the transformers causing an explosion, fire, and loss of power to the military base and surrounding town. By severity alone, by causing physical harm to individual or property, many hold this event would be automatically a use of force.[77] Buttressing that view, under the criteria in question, such an attack was *immediate*; the code that executed it traveled at the speed of light to reach its destination, but more importantly, its effect were felt more or less contemporaneously with the attack. It was *direct* in its connection between digital signal and explosion, explosion and fire, and ultimately loss of power to the military facility. It was *invasive* in penetrating not just networks known to be inside the victim state, but those selected for their proximity to critical assets of the state. Its effects were measurable in the sense that they were both qualitatively observable and quantitatively significant (dollar value and number of damaged systems, time without power, etc.). Finally, only the most extreme viewpoints of economic target exclusion would hold this action out as presumptively legal—even the debunked doctrine of kinetic equivalence should regard this action as presumptive use of force. In short, for cases like these, such criteria are illuminating guides as to why states may regard such a case as an unlawful use of force.

Consider that same scenario, however, if it targeted a water facility. In this case, the cyberattack delivered its payload immediately, causing a change in the sensor systems and permitting some amount of toxic fluids into the drinking water used by the base and surrounding town. The change was caught by a backup sensor, but resulted in the water no longer being potable for months; hundreds of troops were forced to move off-base; several maintenance cycles for military equipment were delayed; and the town had to be quarantined until the source was identified. Here, the analysis is more difficult.

This case suggests that the distinctness of immediacy, directness, and measurability may require another look. Here the attack was immediate in the delivery of its payload—such signals travel at roughly the speed of light regardless, but despite some scholars' use of it as a synonym for immediacy,

---

[77] See ibid., 334(a).

it is in fact insignificant as a practical matter.[78] More relevant is the immediacy of the effect. But is the effect here the change in the sensor systems, or the change in water composition? The change could have been caused by any number of digital factors: some immediate (a virus simply shutting down the sensor), some slower (causing interference that slowed the frequency of system self-diagnostics to facilitate such an oversight), and some unknowable (removing protocols to fail-over to a backup system whenever a breakdown occurs). It becomes clear that the line between immediacy and directness is necessarily blurred. Digital signals travel at the pace they travel, and they effectuate change at the speed at which code is run—neither are particularly useful at differentiating edge cases on their own. Moreover, that they effectuate their actions with a time delay, or even over a period of time, is not as significant as when they become apparent (measurability). In this example the number of gallons of tainted water, grounded aircraft, and dislocated people are measurable factors—but all are salient at a time of recognition, and at best two are literally visible. What if rather than mix with generically toxic chemicals, the manipulated sensor resulted in a slow drip of certain heavy metals into the water. Effects on the maintenance of aircraft, or even later rare cancer clusters in residents, might only appear months or years later. If the origins of this phenomenon were traced back to the attack on a water system, would the immediacy be of significance on its own? Would directness, if delayed over such a long time? If the sensor were (as many are) not physically located near that military base, but in another region entirely—or, perhaps, overseas—would the attack no longer be *invasive* since the computers in question did not sit on the victim state's soil? These are the sorts of threshold questions that states will confront and, in the context of restraint, test.

Finally, consider a similar scenario but rather than target electric transformers at a generation facility, it targeted the manufacturer of smart meters known to be used in the victim country, and distinguished by particular municipal compliance code found on them. In this scenario, the attacker modifies a planned patch to the firmware (permanent software programmed into read-only memory) that, pushed intermittently over months, would be in operation at homes and military facilities around the island. When run, at unpredictable intervals, the code would cause the meters to short out. Fires

---

[78] See, e.g., Matthew Miller, Jon Brickey, and Gregory Conti, "Why Your Intuition About Cyber Warfare is Probably Wrong," *Small Wars Journal* (November 29, 2012).

caused by electricity shorts were *post facto* observed to increase by five percent, but barely outside statistical significance and complicated by environmental factors like climate change. Most simply experienced interrupted power, causing a host of other complications, but none carefully catalogued since the malicious nature of the event would not be known for weeks. Here, the severity or measurability are blurred, and indeed, might not be conclusively known to victim or attacker. Directness is weakened by the multiple steps between interference and effect. Invasiveness may in the first instance be nonexistent, if the manufacturer were in a third country altogether—or even within the attacker's own borders. And in this latter potentiality, might the event be presumptively legal as an exercise of its own national security laws?

Thus scenarios like these, admittedly fixed to the moment but representing some salient cyberattack scenarios of concern, raise questions about this framework in brightening the line of the use of force. In Schmitt and the *Tallinn* experts' defense, they are not intended to be legal tests.[79] However, states may well be drawn to them in advancing a political argument about usability, which in turn, is of great significance to the restraint project.

One way forward would be to propose a revised set of criteria, ones that would help minimize the potential for states to exploit gaps in contravention of the spirit of the laws of war. Such a revision could serve the purposes of other scholarly projects or policy deliberations. If so, it would be advisable to generally find ways first to provide an indication of hierarchy or weights for evaluation of inputs when combined. More specifically, such an approach should find ways to (1) de-emphasize invasiveness (to better reflect the realities of remote computing and storage); or (2) refine invasiveness it so as to be less tied to geography (since effect in multiple countries should not weigh against classification) and classes of defensive security (which may only be relevant for cases already obviously uses of force by other criteria); as well as (3) find ways to express the inherent relationship between immediacy directness, and measurability (to recognize the fuzziness of "decisive points" in a cyberattack and, as Healey rightly points out, that "strategically meaningful cyber conflicts rarely occur at the 'speed of light' or at 'network speed' ").[80]

---

[79] Schmitt, "Computer Network Attack and the Use of Force in International Law," 420, 422; *Tallinn 2.0*, 333.
[80] Jason Healey, "Claiming the Lost Cyber Heritage," *Strategic Studies Quarterly* 6, no. 3 (2012): 14.

For these purposes, however, it is sufficient to recognize that such edge cases do exist, and that the sorts of cyberattacks defined in this study would typically not fall into this grey zone. In such cases, presumptive illegality is less clear under either instrument or effects analysis, and when the question turns therefore to *recognized* presumptive illegality, cyberattacks that are not military in character or target may fall through the cracks. The next section explores what other elements of the UN Charter may cover those sorts of events more effectively, as well as provide a confirmatory backstop for those that the law would already recognize as unlawful under Article 2(4).

5.3 Cyberattacks as Violations of Integrity, Independence, or Purposes

On the question of legality, the final remaining issue is whether a use of force specifically imperils rights of "territorial integrity" or "political independence" stated in the Charter or whether it is otherwise consistent with the "purposes of the United Nations." This section argues how, given both broad and narrow interpretations of these clauses, cyberattacks clearly violate these provisions as well—and thus are, in the damaging form under analysis herein, presumptively illegal under the *jus ad bellum*.

Violations of the Purposes of the United Nations

As a general matter, the Charter broadly recognizes uses of force "inconsistent with the Purposes of the United Nations" to be illegal. Somewhat reflexively, it considers such threats or uses of force beyond its strict authorization to be inconsistent with its purposes. Many scholars see this provision as a functional catchall, understood to extend coverage to any use of force not otherwise authorized by the Charter.[81] This position, that "this 'other manner' language extends coverage to virtually any use of force not authorized within the Charter," is generally regarded as a mainstream position among international legal experts.[82]

---

[81] Dinstein, *War, Aggression and Self-Defence*, 86; Randelzhofer, "Article 2(4)," 106, 17–18.
[82] Schmitt, "Use of Force," 901–04.

Given this expansive and mainstream reading of the "Purposes" clause, cyberattacks are self-evidently illegal. If the Charter's aims are to "maintain international peace and security," and promote "international cooperation" and the "economic and social advancement of all people," disrupting the information infrastructure of another state would seem to threaten the peace, create insecurity, run afoul of one of the better manifestations of global cooperation, and largely retard economic and social progress.[83] Yet this self-evidence of illegality is not without its controversy, and for the purposes of applying the broadest swathe of the relevant international law, not necessarily sufficient as an evaluative tool for this study.

A more intriguing question is whether a cyberattack targeting shared infrastructure during a time of particular dependence thereupon would be a better reference-point for a violation of the Charter's "Purposes." In 2020, the coronavirus pandemic and fears of COVID-19 forced a sizable number of primary, secondary, and higher learning in the United States to online-only instruction.[84] Professional service businesses, municipal meetings, and other, previously in-person interactions were similarly moved into virtual form.[85] The majority of meetings within Joe Biden's presidential transition, and later his early White House, were also virtual—as were UK cabinet meetings, reportedly leveraging commercial communications platforms.[86] The result was a profound magnification of the vulnerability explained in Chapter 1; critical information infrastructure became not just dual-use, but

---

[83] Charter of the United Nations, *Preamble*, Article 1(1), Article 1(3).

[84] *Education Week*, "Map: Coronavirus and School Closures," April 17, 2020. In terms of the impact on K-12 public and private schooling in the United States, as of April 17, 2020, *Education Week* reported that "30 states, three U.S. territories, and the District of Columbia . . . ordered or recommended school building closures for the rest of the academic year, affecting approximately 33.2 million public school students. School closures due to coronavirus . . . impacted at least 124,000 U.S. public and private schools and affected at least 55.1 million students."

[85] The US state of Utah's legislature was among the first states to conduct business remotely: "In the final days of this year's legislative session, as the COVID-19 outbreak spread to Utah, state leaders approved legislation allowing them to meet digitally in times of emergency—though they will still be required to comply with open meeting laws by making meetings available to the public." Bethany Rodgers and Taylor Stevens, "Utah Legislature Calls Historic Special Session to Address Coronavirus Impacts," *Salt Lake Tribune*, April 13, 2020. Federally, the US House Democrats proposed amending the rules to allow remote voting during COVID-19. "If approved by the House, the switch to proxy voting would be the first time in the history of Congress that lawmakers could cast votes other than in person." Sheryl Gay Stolberg, "House Democrats Back Changing Rules to Allow Remote Voting During Pandemic," 2020.

[86] Colum Lynch and Jack Detsch, "The Virtual Transition," *Foreign Policy*, December 8, 2020; Josh Rogin, "The White House's Use of Zoom for Meetings Raises China-related Security Concerns," *Washington Post*, March 3, 2021; BBC News, "UK Government Defends PM's Use of Zoom," April 1, 2020.

omnipresent, existential, and to some equally as vital as the physical infrastructure (e.g., roads) that governments maintain. A broad-based cyberattack against this infrastructure—or, perhaps, even narrower, of just a few dominant videoconferencing providers (e.g., Zoom, Skype, and Google)—would certainly be at odds with the Charter's "Purposes" *and* potentially missing from the other means of identifying illegal force identified prior.

It may be, however, that diplomatic competition may frustrate agreement on Article 2(4)'s applicability to even that basic use case. In sum, for those taking the less mainstream view that the "Purposes" provision weakens the Charter's practical application or that new recognition of uses of force would benefit from additional support, the analysis that follows evaluates how a cyberattack runs afoul of the more clearly enumerated guarantees.

Article 2(4)'s Specific Provisions

Article 2(4)'s more specific provisions, recognizing outright uses of force against the territorial integrity or political independence of a state, offer an additional and compelling case for the illegality of a cyberattack—particularly for those unconvinced by a broad interpretation of 2(4)'s "Purposes" clause. Apart from being customary law, Article 2(4) also is "considered a jus cogens norm, that is, one from which no deviation is permitted."[87] These specific clauses can be read two ways, first as a narrow proscription on occupation or annexation, or as a more expansive opprobrium on interstate coercion that highlights those extreme cases. While a few scholars have favored the former interpretation, a close reading of the Article's history seems to demonstrate original intent of the latter.[88] In the Dumbarton Oaks preparatory conference draft, Article 2(4) initially left out those two illustrative clauses of territorial integrity and political independence, reading: "All members of this Organization shall refrain in their international relations from the threat or use of force in any manner inconsistent with the purposes of this Organization."[89] Only later, in San Francisco, did states insist on specific

---

[87] Michael Schmitt and Andru E. Wall, "The International Law of Unconventional Statecraft," *Harvard National Security Journal* 5 (2015): 357.

[88] Ian Brownlie, *International Law and the Use of Force by States* (Oxford: Oxford University Press, 1963), 265–68, 69, 78–79.

[89] United Nations Conference on International Organization, Dumbarton Oaks Proposals, Doc 1, G1, 3. As quoted in Thomas M. Franck, *Recourse to Force: State Action Against Threats and Armed Attacks* (Cambridge: Cambridge University Press, 2002), 12.

provisions on the duty to respect the territorial integrity and political independence of states—which, as a product of its historical moment, was an unremarkable emphasis.[90]

Thus the mainstream interpretation on this clause, that it was intended not to create exceptions for so-called minor or temporary incursions but to emphasize particular concerns of Member States, seems quite reasonable. Michael Wood similarly concludes, "it is clear from the negotiating history" that the territorial integrity and political independence clauses "were inserted to strengthen the Principle, not to create a loophole."[91] Franck also emphasizes "the Charter's absolute prohibition on states' unilateral recourse to force, Article 2(4), is deliberately located in Chapter I, titled 'Purposes and Principles.' The drafters considered these enumerated principles of transcendent importance, elucidating all other provisions of the Charter."[92] Assuming that the intention of this additional clause was to water down the provisions of the 2(4) would be "utterly incongruent . . . with the evident intent of the sponsors" of the amendment itself.[93]

This is not to suggest that those two clauses are simply anachronistic throwaways; they do guide recognition of the use of force. Uses of force that jeopardize the territorial integrity or political independence of a state would serve as the most obvious cases of recognized force; those that do not may well be recognized, simply less obviously. While the following sections do not intend to assert that these two general provisions are somehow uniquely applicable to cyberattacks, they do offer an even more exhaustive study of how cyberattacks might most obviously run afoul of even a restrictive view of the law.

Cyberattacks as a Threat to Territorial Integrity

In looking to the first clause of Article 2(4) and its concern for territorial integrity, it is hard to find grounds upon which cyberattacks threaten a state's territorial integrity in a conventional sense, and yet it is essential to examine this consideration. As Ago notes, "any assault whatsoever on the

---

[90] Ibid.
[91] Michael Wood, "International Law: Lecture 3," in *Hersch Lauterpacht Memorial Lectures* (Cambridge: Cambridge University Press, 2006), 7.
[92] Franck, *Recourse to Force: State Action Against Threats and Armed Attacks*, 11.
[93] Ibid., 12.

territorial sovereignty of another state, irrespective of its magnitude, duration, or purposes" is accorded recognition as force in interpretations of Article 2(4).[94] There is also surprisingly thin treatment of evolving conceptions of sovereignty in the *Tallinn Manual 1.0*, despite the concept of sovereignty being essential to the framing of Article 2(4)'s prohibitions and numerous large states' emphasis on its preeminence in their own considerations of the space.[95] All this suggests room for more nuanced consideration.

Superficially, in the most straightforward scenarios, the direct consequence of a cyberattack is unlikely to be the loss of a sovereign state's territory to the attacking power. Attacks on a nation's digital infrastructure may *violate* its sovereignty by affecting physical machines within its borders, but this violation is not tantamount in any literal sense to the severance or occupation of a state's land. From this vantage, a cyberattack may be threatening but does not meet the criterion.

But what about scenarios at the margins? What if in Estonia, where both information and economic flows are particularly digitally mediated, a Russian cyberattack persistently rendered Estonian internet providers inoperative to border regions, while leaving unharmed (and inviting use of) a Russian wireless alternative? If that internet service blocked access to any Estonian state information, government services, and the like, but permitted all the same activities available to Russian citizens, how confident could all be that the territorial integrity of Estonia had not been violated? What if it supplemented that blockage-and-service regime with additional state-like services from an allied substate group, in an arrangement similar to that of Hamas in Gaza—again, can we truly say there is no threat to territory? After all, the archetypical incursions the Charter envisages concern the dislocation of people from their provider of state services, and ultimately, identity as much as the dirt the flag flies above. These are the sort of textured concerns

---

[94] Robert Ago, "Addendum—Eighth Report on State Responsibility by Mr. Roberto Ago, Special Rapporteur—the Internationally Wrongful Act of the State, Source of International Responsibility (Part 1)," *Yearbook of the International Law Commission* II(1) (1980): 41. Ago goes on to argue that "there can now no longer be the possibility of considering that there exists . . . an actual 'right of intervention' in foreign territory," however this section does not intend to take a position on that particularly fraught debate.

[95] In this space, nearly every consensus document that includes China or Russia as signatories reiterates its grounding in respect for sovereignty. See, e.g., United Nations Group of Governmental Experts (2014–15), *Report of the Group of Governmental Experts on Developments in the Field of Information and Telecommunications in the Context of International Security* (Geneva: United Nations Institute for Disarmament Research, 2015), 3; *GGE 2021*, 6, 13, 17.

about sovereignty that arguably are embodied in the Charter's notion of territorial integrity but are cast in new light by new technologies.

This study accepts the mainstream view that the Charter's proscriptions are general and adaptable. Scholars such as Reisman object to such an approach, arguing that the Charter cannot be read or interpreted separately from the historical context of its authorship nor from the basic and outdated assumptions that it makes about state practice.[96] Such originalist views are, however, insufficiently vindicated by current practice of enduring state recognition of—if not always fidelity to—the UN regime. Nonetheless, Reisman's argument is compelling in one respect: it acknowledges that cyberattacks pose a dilemma for the international peace and security regime *if it lacks the ability to recognize them*. Cyberattacks may indeed challenge the utility of the "contiguous land" and "borders-in" view of protected sovereignty.

With this frame in mind, there are two ways in which, through an expanded view of the notion of "territorial integrity," a cyberattack would satisfy the conditions of Article 2(4).

Threat to Integrity. Expanding the notion of "territorial integrity" offers a novel view of how cyberattacks might be recognized under Article 2(4). To be sure, territorial integrity was in original construction a straightforward proposal, a sign of the psychological wounds of Czechoslovakia and indeed all of German-occupied Europe. The state practice intentionally circumscribed by the UN Charter was the forceful annexation of the territory of sovereign states, or the forceful breakup of a weak state to its more powerful neighbors. But is that all territorial integrity can connote?

If one looks beyond the original context of the term, the phrase "territorial integrity" can easily incorporate what it signifies today. "Integrity" means, quite literally, the condition of being unified. Clearly, this cannot imply contiguity; after all, the present-day United States is a noncontiguous union of territories some of which lie over 5,000 miles from one another, as were the remnants of the British Empire in 1945. Russia would hastily point to its own noncontiguous territory in Kaliningrad. The meaning must imply that the integrity of a state is a political or social condition; in full meaning, states are prohibited from functionally dislodging territories from their capitals, or the other constituent parts of their state.

---

[96] Michael Reisman, "Coercion and Self-Determination: Construing Charter Article 2(4)," *American Journal of International Law*, no. 78 (1984): 642.

An attack of sufficient gravity on information infrastructure might well have the effect of threatening unification by upending the means of connection between noncontiguous areas and the rest of their nation. It is easier by the year to visualize the technical means and sociopolitical impact of such a widespread disruption, as criminal gangs have demonstrated small-scale capabilities holding cities like Baltimore, Maryland and Atlanta, Georgia.[97] During the 2020 COVID-19 pandemic, for instance, numerous organs of government met strictly by digital means—including the UK Cabinet.[98] Imagine the further economic disruption if the US Centers for Disease Control and Prevention (CDC) were unable to communicate public health and safety advisory notices to the public or if the Internal Revenue Service were wholly unable to send direct-cash stimulus payments to millions of Americans as part of the federal government's actions to help financially struggling business and families during acute economic crises.[99] Such dislocation was presumably an intention of the Estonia attack, and quite plainly of Iran's cyberattack on Albania, over which diplomatic relations were severed and Washington rallied allies and partners for broad condemnation of the affair.[100] In the latter case, Albanian Prime Minister Edi Rama noted the attack "threatened to paralyze public services, delete systems, and steal state data, steal electronic communications within the government system and fuel insecurity and chaos in the country."[101] In an era of digital governance, this sort of connectivity goes beyond the exercise of rights to freely seek and impart information; it is core to the exercise of political control (and thus, political integrity). Thus it is worth recalling the physical realities that undergird cyberspace and as such, the means of cutting off a territory from contact is not terribly difficult to envision.

---

[97] Emily Stewart, "Hackers Have Been Holding the City of Baltimore's Computers Hostage for 2 Weeks," *Vox News*, May 21, 2019; Alan Blinder and Nicole Perlroth, "A Cyberattack Hobbles Atlanta, and Security Experts Shudder," *New York Times*, March 27, 2018.

[98] Andrew Woodcock, "Coronavirus: UK's First Digital Cabinet Meeting Takes Place as Three Ministers Self-Isolate," *The Independent*, March 31, 2020.

[99] Katie Lobosco, "When Will You Get Your Stimulus Cash, and How?," *CNN*, April 2, 2020. In the wake of the COVID-19 pandemic, "Federal circuit, district, and bankruptcy courts are utilizing multiple audio and video conferencing technologies to host oral arguments, initial appearances, preliminary hearings, arraignments, misdemeanor sentencings, and other procedures remotely." Administrative Office of the US Courts, "Courts Deliver Justice Virtually Amid Coronavirus Outbreak," April 8, 2020.

[100] The White House, "Fact Sheet: Biden-Harris Administration Delivers on Strengthening America's Cybersecurity" (Washington, DC: October 11, 2022).

[101] Starks, "Albania Is the First Known Country to Sever Diplomatic Ties Over a Cyberattack."

Two very different vectors exist if one seeks to attack information infrastructure to "cut off" a territory—both of which could be combined for a particularly severe disruption to a territory's connections to the outside world.[102] Cyberspace may be a nonphysical concept, but the actual fiber optic cables, microwave dishes, routers, and hubs that serve it are indeed physical, and often reside within national borders. The effects of a major cyberattack against a far-flung territory, if well-coordinated and planned, could be the near-complete severance of a territory's military, economic, and private-sector communication to the rest of the state.[103] One can think specifically about the effect that severing one major fiber-optic cable, and disrupting a handful of satellite downlinks, would have on a remote territory such as the US state of Hawaii—or even, in the case of the aforementioned attack on telecommunications providers, severing governments' means of communication with its officials and citizens during the COVID-19 pandemic. The practical reality of such an attack may, in this view, amount to a direct threat to the unity of that territory with the rest of its nation, particularly if an ethnic or political group promoted factionalism within the affected area. In this respect, then—with little ability to communicate, govern directly, or transact commerce—there may be substantial basis to see a cyberattack as a threat to the territorial integrity of the overall victim state.

Three Conceptions of Cyberspace Territory. But to what extent does that perspective depend on how states' views about sovereignty over cyberspace evolve? A cyberattack could threaten territorial integrity in a more diffuse sense as well, if one accepts the view that a nation's networks constitute its sovereign "territory." This subsection examines the competing views on that issue, arguing that both the view holding sovereignty impossible, and the view holding it fully applicable to "cyberspace," are neither fully correct. Rather, it makes the case for a conception of cyberspace sovereignty that focuses on the physical assets that enable it—while accepting that the technology poses unique challenges to a bordered conception of the state. Of course, territorial integrity is hardly the only object of focus of Article

---

[102] A third possibility, the deployment of an electro-magnetic pulse, could potentially disrupt many electronic components in a wide area, most significantly by detonating a nuclear device just above the upper atmosphere. While technically a kind of cyberattack, it is so far at the margins of this discussion, and so massive in its consequence, that there is little question its use would classify as prohibited force in the international context.
[103] Because of an increasing convergence of such data traveling over shared information infrastructure, the cascading effects of such an attack are immense, and exponentially proportionate to the level of technology dependence in that territory.

2(4); many scholars hold that its reference is illustrative and emphatic, not restrictive. However, given the dynamism of the debate over how sovereignty and cyberspace intersect, and the potential for customary law to be shaped accordingly, these subclauses of Article 2(4) may merit another look.

Cyberspace is made of physical infrastructure, but that infrastructure routes data without regard to geography. This architecture is both physical and conceptual, militarily useful but largely commercial, and inextricable from its global linkage. For all these reasons, cyberattacks pose a conceptual challenge to the relevance of state borders in judging acts of hostility. Internationally, three principal perspectives exist on the relation of cyberspace to sovereign borders. Each of these three perspectives can yield dramatically different outcomes as to whether or not forceful violations of that space might be prohibited by international law.

Cyberspace as Post-Westphalian. Historically, the first dominant (and somewhat utopian) view of global networks was articulated by the internet's first engineers and user-evangelists through the 1980s and 1990s. In that view, articulated most evocatively in activist John Parry Barlow's *Declaration of the Independence of Cyberspace*, global networks represented a self-governing and inviolable commons not subject to the jurisdiction or regulation of sovereign "national" states.[104] In a view that came to define a central pillar of early internet policy, Barlow contended that states "have no sovereignty" in cyberspace and "legal concepts of property, expression, identity, movement, and context do not apply."[105] Equally popular during this period was the more causal view, that the information revolution would render sovereignty irrelevant, and economic success largely a function of connectivity.[106] This utopian view is, for the purposes of this study, largely a *postnational* vision of the relationship between cyberspace and sovereign territory. In its original version, it accords to internet users a post-Westphalian identity bounded only by technology. Though it may seem quaint, as recently as twenty years ago, it was a serious intellectual proposition not out of step with other attempts to envisage a post–Cold War world order.[107] As such, it merits some

---

[104] John Perry Barlow, "A Cyberspace Independence Declaration," *Electronic Frontier Foundation*, February 8, 1996.
[105] Ibid.
[106] See, e.g., Walter Wriston, *The Twilight of Sovereignty: How the Information Revolution Is Transforming Our World* (New York: Scribner Books, 1992). Wriston argued that even manufactured products (so-called hard goods) would have increasing information content, decoupling geography and production and reducing the relevance of national borders.
[107] See, e.g., Francis Fukuyama, "The End of History?," *The National Interest*, no. 16 (1989).

consideration, even if that future did not come to pass, and online identities have not supplanted national identities—indeed, if anything, nationalism has even become a powerful force for conflict and disruption enabled in part by the internet.[108]

This postnational vision suffers from its radical incompatibility with today's international environment, which remains largely dominant. The view seizes too much upon the challenges of applying law and policy to a conceptual space, and ignores the physical, territorial realities of the technology. More a product of futurism and ideology, the simple fact that state regulations *can* be placed on human behavior online, in accordance with the state claiming jurisdiction over that individual or corporation, seems to disprove its core assertions. The fact remains that while *cyberspace* cannot be regulated, the behaviors of the humans and firms that interact thereupon, and to some extent the states conducting their affairs there as well, are subject to enticement and dissuasion in the form of law or custom. It is little wonder then that attempts to recognize this kind of postnational vision of cyberspace, and of its critical resources, failed to take root at the United Nations both at the World Summit on the Information Society, and in subsequent General Assembly debate.[109]

Cyberspace as National Territory. By contrast, at various times over the last fifteen years Russia, Cuba, and China have claimed the applicability of sovereign boundaries to cyberspace—listing "trans-border" flows of "destabilizing information" as tantamount to a physical incursion.[110] This view of sovereign and bordered cyberspace, distinctly in the minority but nonetheless asserted publicly, was also expressed strongly in a 2009 Shanghai Cooperation Organisation *Agreement on Information Security*, binding Russia, China, Kazakhstan, Kyrgyzstan, Tajikistan, and Uzbekistan to definitions that consider "the information space" national territory.[111] This is a "territorial extension" view of cyberspace: that it can somehow be meaningfully nationalized, and is therefore subject to the same claims of noninterference as physical territory.

---

[108] See, e.g., Xu Wu, *Chinese Cyber Nationalism* (New York: Lexington Books, 2007).
[109] World Summit on the Information Society (WSIS), *Tunis Agenda for the Information Society*, (Geneva: United Nations Press, 2005). See especially para 30. See also U.N. A/RES/65/141.
[110] See Chapter 1, note 110.
[111] Shanghai Cooperation Organisation, *Agreement between the Governments of the Member States of the Shanghai Cooperation Organisation on Cooperation in the Field of International Information Security*.

This territorial extension view offers little in the way of evidence for how, precisely, the nationalization of conceptual cyberspace will be realized, except for declarations against noninterference in the "political, moral or spiritual systems of other states."[112] This theory does not ground its analysis in the material reality of cyberspace—that its switches and fiber exist in real space. Moreover, despite extensive literature asserting sovereign rights to the space, these views fail to account for the transnational *reality* of much of what transpires online.[113] Data can traverse dozens of countries en route to its destination, irrespective of origin or destination. Individual "packets" of data are not tagged by national origin, nor sorted in accordance with their contents' suitability to the host country's social mores. The technology that undergirds cyberspace is functionally neutral in this regard, and thus claims of sovereignty (and the calls for strict or intermediary liability for states or internet service providers via whom data is emanating or transmitted) have little beyond political desire that reinforces them. The absence of legal or customary justification for this view render such a view rhetorically useful but unsatisfying. It also, ironically, shows serious incongruence with the Russian Federation's other positions; it would seem to suggest applicability of international legal principles, simply extended to cyberspace. It thus stands in contrast to the earlier-cited statements about the insufficiency of international law in dealing with the potential for "information weapons."

From a practical standpoint, states' attempts to assert the same kinds of claims over cyberspace that customarily apply to physical territory are equally unconvincing. After all, for most of the internet's existence, users sign up for social networking sites, or purchase online goods, without much attention to that website's place of incorporation or legal regime. While recent advances in national privacy regimes such as the European General Data Privacy Regulation (GDPR) may upset that dynamic, it remains generally true that average users interact with states online only in the case of interference to their access or prosecution of their conduct. Leaving aside mercantilist or political impositions to hold data resident within geographic borders, the infrastructure itself does not distinguish between nationalities.

---

[112] *Diplomacy of Peace*, 594.

[113] See Tim Wu, "Cyberspace Sovereignty—The Internet and the International System," *Harvard Journal of Law and Technology* 10 (1996); Henry H. Perritt Jr, "Cyberspace and State Sovereignty," *Journal of International Legal Studies* 3 (1997); David J. Betz and Tim Stevens, "Chapter Two: Cyberspace and Sovereignty," *Adelphi Series* 51, no. 424 (2011); Eric Talbot Jensen, "Cyber Sovereignty: The Way Ahead," *Texas International Law Journal* 50, no. 2 (2015): 296–301; Michael N Schmitt and Liis Vihul, "Respect for Sovereignty in Cyberspace," *Texas Law Review* 95 (2016).

While the previous examination found grounds upon which the *act* of a cyberattack would *result* in a threat to territorial integrity so construed, few conclusions can be drawn *ex ante* as to the applicability of the same rights to cyberspace.

Cyberspace as Global; Infrastructure as Sovereign. A final, more moderate view neither accepts nor rejects the notion of cyberspace as a place where sovereignty can be asserted but focuses those claims (and legal jurisdiction) where they can be most readily exercised: over individuals and physical infrastructure residing within the borders of a state. Legal scholar Jack Goldsmith brought this view to prominence in 1998, and in his subsequent volume with Tim Wu asserted that the digital networks on which individuals rely are built upon physical machines and human transactions—and applying law and regulation to this realm is not *ex ante* impossible.[114] While this argument is most often applied to the applicability of legal regimes and regulatory measures, it has important defenders in the context of international security. As cited previously, in 2009, US President Obama asserted that his country's "*digital infrastructure*—the networks and computers we depend on every day—will be treated as they should be: as a strategic national asset. Protecting this infrastructure will be a national security priority."[115] Notable is not just its elevation of this technology to the level of a strategic asset (one that quite plainly "will be defended"), but its emphasis on the *infrastructure*. To borrow a phrase from securitization theory, the "referent object" of security is the physical infrastructure that enables networks to form and transactions to take place, not "cyberspace" per se.[116]

This is the position that the *Tallinn Manual* appears to accept as its middle ground as well, noting "a State may exercise control over cyber infrastructure and activities within its sovereign territory."[117] The *Tallinn* experts concluded that if States hold sovereignty over cyber infrastructure within their territory, the effect is twofold: "First, that cyber infrastructure is subject to legal

---

[114] Jack Goldsmith, "Against Cyberanarchy," *University of Chicago Law Review* 65 (1998); Jack Goldsmith and Tim Wu, *Who Control the Internet?: Illusions of a Borderless World* (Oxford: Oxford University Press, 2006). For more on the increasingly bordered reality of the internet, see Michael Geist, "Cyberlaw 2.0," *Boston College Law Review* 44 (2003).

[115] Barack Obama, "Remarks by the President on Securing Our Nation's Cyber Infrastructure" Washington, DC: The White House, May 29, 2009). Emphasis added.

[116] For more on securitization theory, from which this terminology draws, see Barry Buzan, Ole Waever, and Jaap de Wilde, eds., *Security: A New Framework for Analysis* (Boulder, CO: Lynne Rienner Publishers, 1998), 23–25.

[117] *Tallinn 1.0*, 15. Despite this general consensus around the precepts of this rule, the *Tallinn* experts could not reach a consensus on whether employing malware "that causes no physical damage" constitutes a violation of sovereignty. Ibid., 16.

and regulatory control by the State. Second, the State's territorial sovereignty protects such cyber infrastructure. It does not matter whether it belongs to the government or to private entities or individuals, nor to the purposes matter."[118] This is the in fact the premise from which Lindsay and Gartzke begin when they contend that cyberspace "is best considered a domain in the functional sense rather than the geographic sense," since it is "a heterogeneous assemblage of technical and institutional components . . . physically located on land, under water, in the air, and in orbit."[119]

States may obviously claim reasonable sovereignty over the physical information *infrastructure* that resides on their shores, and the commercial activity that their citizens and corporations conduct online. But even if a state's "networks and computers" are considered "strategic national assets," does that render the data upon them tantamount to digital territory?[120] Radziwill maintains that Westphalian order begins to break under the tension of fitting traditional notions of sovereignty into cyberspace and that "sovereignty over infrastructure does not mean that it extends into the virtual world itself, but the Russian and a number of SCO states' governments stand for 'national control of all internet resources' that lie within state borders."[121] A state defends the operation of storefronts on a Main Street—with police and, if necessary to repel foreign invasion, the military. Are the online storefronts— the websites—of Amazon.com or Baidu.com assured freedom from disruption by virtue of being an extension of a state's territory? And how are states lacking their own substantial digital infrastructure, whose economic actors choose instead the common path of renting from global providers like Amazon Web Services (AWS) or Google, to regard their citizens' use of foreign infrastructure? These questions also reveal a certain amount of ambivalence in US policies on these issues, with domestic law enforcement favoring territorial and even extraterritorial view of US sovereign jurisdiction enabled by cyberspace, whereas most diplomatic and administration-level strategies frequently reject the construction that the logical aspect of cyberspace (in place of its infrastructure) and the content thereupon exists

---

[118] Ibid.
[119] Erik Gartzke and Jon Lindsay, "Cross-Domain Deterrence, From Practice to Theory," in *Cross-Domain Deterrence: Strategy in an Era of Complexity*, ed. Erik Gartzke and Jon Lindsay (Oxford: Oxford University Press, 2019), 4.
[120] The *Tallinn* experts explain that "although no State may claim sovereignty over cyberspace per se, States may exercise sovereign prerogatives over any cyber infrastructure located on their territory, as well as activities associated with that cyber infrastructure." *Tallinn 1.0*, 16.
[121] Yaroslav Radziwill, *Cyber-Attacks and the Exploitable Imperfections of International Law* (Leiden: Brill Nijhoff, 2015), 101.

on an extension of sovereign territory.[122] This is not a novel complexity for the United States; indeed, a bedrock of international human rights law, the Universal Declaration of Human Rights, simultaneously recognizes the right "to seek, receive and impart information and ideas through any media and regardless of frontiers" subject to abridgement as the "just requirements of morality and public order" require.[123]

Herein lie the limitations of relying on the present, majority view of what constitutes a state's most critical assets in the context of interstate coercion. States' comments on the disruption accompanying cyberattacks have not yet been placed in terms of a violation of its territorial integrity. It seems, however, that grounds may exist and that such a practice is possible, as states do engage in a process asserting sovereign jurisdiction over the infrastructure that cyberattacks disrupt.[124] The next section considers the second clause of Article 2(4), which is a somewhat more straightforward basis for cyberattacks' illegality.

Cyberattacks as a Threat to Political Independence

There are indeed grounds upon which a cyberattack might threaten a state's "political independence." While the next chapter will consider this concept in the context of state rights of self-defense against its violation, political independence may be regarded along a spectrum from strict interpretation, focusing on the absence of occupation of a foreign force in a nation, to a broader one that would encompass both the legal authority of a state and the ability of that structure to perform the functions of government and provide basic services.[125]

The latter, more expansive definition comports with the customarily understood meaning of political independence, grounded in the UN Charter

---

[122] Gary P. Corn and Robert Taylor, "Sovereignty in the Age of Cyber," *AJIL Unbound* 111 (2017): 209.

[123] "Universal Declaration of Human Rights" (1948), Art. 19, 29.

[124] The law of state responsibility—most notably in the context of holding third-party actors operating on one's territory accountable—has occupied a considerable portion of the literature in this context. In keeping with the scope, however, this section will not engage with it in-depth.

[125] Also engaging with this premise of "political independence" is the extensive commentary on humanitarian intervention, self-determination, and other significant debates challenging the scope and content of existing prohibitions on force when that force has generally accepted benefits to an oppressed party. While these debates center on some of the same issues, it is impossible to do them justice in this context and drawing extended connections between them and this study would likely leave both too speculative at the present moment.

and further custom and international law reaffirming the independence of governments to act by their own accord—or to use more common terminology, affirming the "non-intervention" of foreign powers in domestic governance.[126] Just as the ICJ ruled in *Nicaragua* that the Charter, strictly interpreted, "by no means covers the whole area of the regulation of the use of force in international relations," so too has the customary interpretation of political independence expanded somewhat since 1945.[127] Even then, its meaning was less clearly less a function of its historical moment than "territorial integrity."

While armed occupation is obviously at the core of this provision's concerns, it represents the violation of political independence at its most extreme. Elsewhere, of course, the Charter makes consistent reference to "sovereign equality"—Article 2(1)—and holds as a core tenet a defense of the doctrine of noninterference. Scholars such as Randelzhofer argue that any nonmilitary coercion is covered not by Article 2(4) but by the general principle of noninterference.[128] While the simplicity of this view is attractive, subsequent interpretation does not support that clear a distinction. At least, Article 2(4)'s guarantees of political independence and the principle of noninterference are consistent, and in the expansive view, interwoven.

Focusing not on the physical condition then (which cyberattacks do not realistically threaten outright), but the essence of the operation of political independence—decision-making and maintenance of order—there are several important and related ways in which cyberattacks can threaten political independence. The first and more obvious way a cyberattack might threaten political independence would be the breakdown of civic order, particularly by exploiting the feedback of dependencies between information infrastructure and the constituent elements of high-tech societies. In short, jeopardizing a government's ability to maintain law, order, and communication with its citizenry renders it unable to perform the basic functions of a politically independent state. Secondly, there are a number of ways in which modern, developed societies' political independence has become reliant on the functioning of various global commons, including global trade flows and international information infrastructure (which largely regulates logistics

---

[126] See Cassese, *International Law*, 53–56; Brownlie, *International Law and the Use of Force by States*, 312; L. Oppenheim, *International Law, A Treatise*, vol. 2 (London: Longmans, Green and Co., 1912), 406.

[127] Oscar Schachter, "In Defense of International Rules on the Use of Force," *University of Chicago Law Review* 53 (1986): 14 at Para. 176.

[128] Randelzhofer, "Article 2(4)," 113.

of the former). In this respect, the interruption of shared resources would bring about a similarly damaging effect on civic order and restrict political decision-making even if the event itself is outside a nation's borders.

Political independence is also directly related to military preparedness. Any action that appears to be (or is actually) seriously disadvantaging a state in an impending military conflict could be judged as threatening its political independence. As noted earlier, it is difficult as a practical matter to separate civilian and military information infrastructure; as such, a disruption of the former may well disrupt military command and control, and—by extension—to a state's political independence of a more basic form.

It is important to reiterate that only a major cyberattack, and one targeting a highly technologically dependent nation that has placed considerable functions of governance online, appears an obvious candidate for outright recognition under this clause. By analogy, physically destroying electricity grids across a broad region would cause not simply the loss of power, but economic losses, compounding civic unrest and stressing law enforcement, which would itself be crippled by the loss of telecommunications that facilitate first responders. Major cyberattacks replicate this feedback across many more critical sectors. Therefore, this conclusion, coupled with the very real grounds upon which cyberattacks can be considered generally as uses of force, suggest compelling additional grounds for recognizing their illegality under Article 2(4).

Conclusions

This chapter has identified several grounds upon which cyberattacks can be recognized as generally and specifically prohibited by Article 2(4) of the UN Charter. Broadly, it developed the arguments that suggest international law would recognize cyberattacks as uses of force under the *jus ad bellum*, sharing both meaningful qualities and significant effects with those activities recognized in the kinetic space as "force."

However, state practice does not start where the law ends. As Schmitt notes:

> Adding to the uncertainty regarding the precise legal parameters of cyber warfare is the fact that public international law is by nature a dynamic creature ... its content, interpretation, and application evolve over time in response to transformation of the security environment in which it applies.

Such ambiguity makes it inconceivable that the extant law of cyber warfare, which responds to cyber operations that are still in their relative technological infancy, will survive intact. This reality begs the question, quo vadis the law of cyber warfare? It is a question that the International Group of Experts consciously avoided, but which was always the unspoken elephant in the room.[129]

This analysis goes beyond the methodological challenges that frustrated analysis by Schmitt and others a decade ago, as the method and impact of what are understood today as cyberattacks are clearer to those conducting both legal analysis of the present moment, permitting more forward-looking considerations of where it may be headed next. To complete that assessment, it also demonstrated how those uses of force so-recognized fell within a range of criteria set forth by Article 2(4): as inconsistent with the UN's purposes, as threats to political independence, and in some limited cases—with an expansive reading—even territorial integrity. In all these circumstances, and regardless of the breadth of one's reading of Article 2(4), cyberattacks with the consequences discussed herein appear prohibited as a matter of international law.

The most conclusive analysis possible, within the spirit and letter of the *jus ad bellum*, merely acknowledges that such attacks are *presumptively* illegal—and that this position may well be used by a state articulating the policy decision to respond on the basis of that illegality. Estonian Ministry of Defence and NATO legal expert Eneken Tikk-Ringas, when asked what precise conditions would constitute a use of force, summarized that "even the NATO defence board examining the issue [of cyberattacks] agreed . . . we should not worry about threshold. That is a policy question. The real question is what happens next."[130] While that view may overindex toward the decisiveness of policymakers and underaccount for the impact of lawyers in the room, it points to a fundamental truth: that such events are happening, in real time, and even certainty on the status of international law is not certainty over the status of restraining effect.

As we have seen, Article 2(4) serves as a kind of last resort in the international community—a blanket and aspirational prohibition on force that can

---

[129] *Tallinn 1.0*; Michael Schmitt, "The Law of Cyber Warfare: Quo Vadis?," *Stanford Law and Policy Review* 25 (2014): 271.

[130] Eneken Tikk, ed., *Frameworks for International Cyber Security: Legal and Policy Instruments*, vol. 1 (Tallinn: NATO Cooperative Cyber Defence Centre of Excellence, 2010).

be construed both narrowly and broadly. But law alone is not what restrains state behavior. This is a crucial distinction between a treaty and its operation, between law and regime. To have a durable effect on state behavior, the UN regime hinges in practice upon its remedial mechanisms and the framework of lawful self-defense that accompanies them.

The next chapter evaluates how this illegality could serve as the foundation for justifying a response, in self-defense. Illegality under Article 2(4) is a necessary precondition to the activation of rights of self-defense under the Charter's remedial framework. It is necessary but insufficient. Different standards and customs, themselves subject to interpretation, permit action by a victim state in response to such an act. Determining how the UN Charter framework not only condemns but might also function to *limit* the use of cyberattacks by justifying a forceful response in self-defense is the question to which this study now turns.

6
Constructing Self-Defense

If cyberattacks are presumptively unlawful under international law, and are by many accounts illegal uses of force, what is to prevent their use? And how influential can this viewpoint really be when its main proponents are Western, like-minded states? What assurances do states have that international law would not only recognize illegality, but that it would create adequate disincentives to those who would otherwise transgress?

This particular dilemma is not a new one to policy or law, nor is it specific to cyberattacks: in fact, it was recognized at the San Francisco Conference that first chartered the United Nations itself in 1945. There, delegates recognized that regulations this important, and on such existential matters, require mechanisms to enforce their operation. The result was the creation, within the UN Charter, of provisions for not just keeping the peace but enforcing it. This law covers a great deal: the rights that states have to their own self-defense; the procedures they should undertake to resolve instances of illegal force; and even the conditions permitting them to take forceful measures to repel an incoming attack. The last eighty years have witnessed this interlocking regime—the so-called remedial *jus ad bellum*—be subject to both evolution and profound challenge. Key aspects of the UN system's operation have not gone according to the San Francisco Convention's plan, and states have routinely acted in contravention of its diktats on matters of the use of force. Yet despite all those challenges, it remains a bedrock of the international system; a recurring reference point for state action; and the best lens through which to approach even novel uses of force—particularly cyberattacks.

So does the remedial *jus ad bellum* reliably permit states to deploy force in their own self-defense against cyberattacks, and under what circumstances? These are the questions that occupy this chapter. The sections that follow will introduce the law, engage with key rulings and scholarly debates and inform how the system would regard self-defense from a cyberattack, and then question whether these amount to enough to render the *jus ad bellum* as a whole a reliable source of restraint. Where lacunae exist, it considers what actions states are taking—within and outside of interpretation of the law—to shape the contours of the regime and their positions within it.

Outline of Argument

This chapter begins with the question of whether and how cyberattacks would invoke the "remedial *jus ad bellum*," and specifically, the lawful rights of self-defense under the UN Charter. If they are available to defending states, the combination of presumptive illegality *and* lawful repellent force would provide a powerful disincentive for a would-be attacker. If instead a would-be attacker is bound to suffer little beyond reproach by the legal community—knowing the victim had no substantial and lawful means to repel—cyberattacks may be even more attractive than other means of coercion.

Following this general argument, the next section will orient readers to the remedial *jus ad bellum* and its present operation, then argue that two key debates—over the scope of its applicability and the threshold at which it is triggered—are central to understanding cyberattacks' position there within. To meet what it argues is a necessarily heightened standard (of an "armed attack," a more stringent category than the "use of force" analysis that occupied the last chapter) it considers cyberattacks within four commonly recognized criteria—first their scale and effects in identifying them, and second the attribution and intent that ensure properly directed response.

After making this case, it evaluates whether they are adequate, both from the standpoint of law and states' ability to activate that regime. It finds that as with deterrence, major gaps remain, and argues that states are seizing upon these gaps and racing to fill them through a process called "structural remediation"—a kind of "operational preparation of the environment" (OPE) for the legal battlefield—that aims to create the customary conditions for their preferred outcome of law.

The balance of the chapter documents this "structural remediation" dynamic, where in the absence of certainty about the law's operation, states are at once testing whether the international legal environment will sustain more robust acts of "self-defense" against legally dubious uses of force or armed attacks, as well as creating a customary record of reaction that would habituate other states to a sizable response. It argues that given divergent strategies state are pursuing, the outcome of this competition is unlikely to deliver reliable restraint but will substantially shape the environment of international law and security of cyberattacks regardless.

6.1 Applying the Remedial *Jus ad Bellum*

Presumptive illegality, however important for the long-term contours of international politics, does not guarantee restraint. The authors of the UN Charter recognized this reality, as well as the radical departure from state practice the Charter would constitute if it denied parties all recourse to their inherent right of self-defense. The remedial regime that emerged to enforce Article 2(4)—leveraging the Security Council under Article 39 and a specific right of self-defense under Article 51—was designed to marry idealism with pragmatism. Its operation is essential to the relevance of the modern *jus ad bellum*, especially its prospects for restraining state recourse to cyberattacks.

Framing the Law

Under Chapter VII of the UN Charter, states falling victim to an illegal use of force—including, as we have seen, a cyberattack—are potentially entitled to two remedies. They may petition the Security Council under Article 39 for a third-party authorization of force or other corrective action.[1] They may also, without third-party authorization, employ forceful self-defense outlined in Article 51—but only if the use of force constitutes what some argue is a higher standard: armed attack.[2] The former is uncontroversial but also unsatisfying; the latter, far from automatic, is potentially more powerful but also places this discussion at the center of several longstanding debates in international law that this section will address.

The successful operation of this regime is a matter of perennial controversy, and this chapter does not seek to sidestep that reality. The sheer number of armed conflicts after 1945 might lead one to question whether the Charter's provisions motivate any meaningful restraint. To paraphrase US

---

[1] U.N. Charter, Art. 39.
[2] Ibid., Art. 51.

Secretary of State Madeleine Albright, while states often take action outside of the Charter, "despite such violations, the standards in the Charter remain relevant, just as laws against murder remain relevant even though murders are still committed."[3] (Whether they might restrain as a practical matter is the subject of this chapter's later sections.)

It is also true, and perhaps a reflection of its enduring significance, that "never in history has there been such widespread and well-founded recognition of the costs and horrors of war."[4] Commentators such as Schachter have repeatedly and effectively rebutted the notion of the *jus ad bellum*'s bankruptcy by outlining states' understanding of costs associated with noncompliance, and with clear evidence of states adapting to their perceptions of the regulations it imposes.[5] Moreover, as Grey aptly points out, states' repeated reference to the regime in justifying their actions and recriminating adversaries is more than just the "ritual incantation of a magic formula"; it reflects a need to counter awareness with third-party legitimacy for forceful action.[6] It is notable that states feel a need to advance legal arguments to defend such security decisions.[7] While disagreements persist—particularly in the scope of self-defense, and issues tangential to this study such as humanitarian intervention and interference in civil conflict—the core substantive law is largely coherent and not "so vague and fragmentary as to allow ... unlimited latitude to use force."[8] This chapter does not presuppose that activation of the remedial regime necessarily means the *jus ad bellum* regime will function to restrain every cyberattack, or even some. Instead, this chapter begins such an inquiry by testing if the regime with its existing strengths and shortcomings can even operate on this new technology. Recognition under the remedial regime is essential to presumptive illegality being more than the weakest of restraints, inviting that cynical "ritual incantation" after obvious violation.

---

[3] Madeleine K. Albright, *The Mighty & The Almighty: Reflections on America, God, and World Affairs* (New York: Harper Collins, 2006), 59.
[4] Oscar Schachter, "The Right of States to Use Armed Force," *Michigan Law Review* 82, no. 5/6 (1984): 1620.
[5] Schachter, "In Defense of International Rules on the Use of Force," 114.
[6] Gray, *International Law and the Use of Force*, 119.
[7] Schachter, "In Defense of International Rules on the Use of Force," 123.
[8] Schachter, "The Right of States to Use Armed Force," 1645.

Article 39 and the UN Security Council

An aggrieved state may seek guidance from the Security Council under Article 35 of the UN Charter.[9] In turn, under Article 36, the Security Council may advise on the methods appropriate to resolve the issue at hand.[10] Chapter V of the UN Charter grants the Security Council "primary, but not exclusive responsibility for the maintenance of peace and security," a role reaffirmed by the ICJ in its consideration of how UN expenses are disbursed.[11] Specifically for these purposes, Article 39 directs the Security Council to "determine the existence of any threat to the peace, breach of the peace, or act of aggression, and ... make recommendations, or decide what measures shall be taken ... to maintain or restore international peace and security."[12] The result is a particularly broad remit to render judgment on the acceptability of cyberattacks—broader, in fact, than the criteria of Article 2(4) just discussed.

The Security Council could take on the issue of cyberattacks, which the prior analysis has shown would more than qualify within one of Section 39's criteria, and its assessment would depend on the circumstances before it.[13] One would presume that eventually the Security Council will render judgment on such an act, given its primary responsibility for the maintenance of peace and security and the clear prospects for cyberattack capabilities to affect those responsibilities adversely.

In such a case, the Council would call upon the parties in question to comply with "provisional measures" to prevent aggregation of the crisis (Article 40), decide what measures short of force might be applied (Article 41). Included among those measures is an intriguing possibility: calling upon Member States to effectuate "complete or partial interruption of economic relations and of rail, sea, air, postal, *telegraphic, radio, and other means of communication*, and the severance of diplomatic relations."[14] Clearly, "telegraph, radio, and other means of communication" would provide basis for in-kind or associated mechanisms to interfere with a country's ongoing execution of a cyberattacks. Economic sanctions also offer an implied and potential

---

[9] U.N. Charter, Art. 35. States that are not members of the UN may also bring matters before the Security Council or General Assembly "if it accepts in advance, for the purposes of the dispute, the obligations of pacific settlement provided in the present Charter" based on Article 35.
[10] Ibid., Article 36, para 1.
[11] Vaughn Lowe et al., eds., *The United Nations Security Council and War* (Oxford: Oxford University Press, 2010), 5.
[12] U.N. Charter, Art. 39; Sharp, *The Use of Force in CyberSpace*, 68.
[13] Roscini, "World Wide Warfare—Jus Ad Bellum and the Use of Cyber Force," 110.
[14] U.N. Charter, Art. 41. Emphasis added.

avenue.[15] This analysis will not speculate as to the most likely modalities of such actions, except to point to some intriguing starting points for discussion of their multilateral potential: multistate law enforcement operations to stop botnets, or state-level sanctions against particular cyber operators or their institutions, for instance.[16] As of this writing, though, no state has successfully brought cyberattack activity before the Security Council.[17]

Lacking any precedent, scholars' ability to examine any deeper the interface between the Security Council and cyberattacks is limited. Such an examination would also be methodologically perilous, given the approach of this study. Analysis under the letter of the law or drawing analogy to well-known means and methods of war is generally possible, with principal risks of over- and underinclusion. Analogizing between prior Security Council decisions to propose future choices would be to compare conclusions that are on all sides context-dependent. It is not a judicial body, which affords it a certain dynamism, but also means that its decisions inescapably reflect political circumstances as well.[18] For these purposes, examining the "automatic" operation of the Charter's remedial provisions—those permitting a state to exercise its rights to self-defense enshrined in Article 51—is likely to bear more fruit.[19]

---

[15] Roscini posits that the Security Council could explore "impos[ing] a cyber blockade on that state responsible of the cyber attack in order to prevent its continuation or repetition." Roscini, "World Wide Warfare—Jus Ad Bellum and the Use of Cyber Force," 111.

[16] See, e.g., a 2020 botnet takedown in which Microsoft reported to be "working with ISPs, domain registries, government CERTs and law enforcement in Mexico, Colombia, Taiwan, India, Japan, France, Spain, Poland and Romania, among others." Tim Burt, "New Action to Disrupt World's Largest Online Criminal Network" Microsoft blog (Redmond, WA: Microsoft Corporation, March 10, 2020). On Sanctions, see Council of the European Union, "Cyber-Attacks: Council Is Now Able to Impose Sanctions. European Council," news release, May 17, 2019; The White House, Executive Order 13757; Peter Harrell, "The Right Way to Sanction Cyber Threats," *The National Interest* (2015).

[17] While no Member State has formally brought a cyberattack event to the Security Council for action, in May 2017, US Senators sent a letter to the UN Security Council urging them to take action on North Korea's nuclear program and to address its malicious cyber behavior. See Rebecca Kheel, "GOP Senators Urge UN Security Council Action on North Korea," *The Hill*, May 16, 2017.

[18] The institution's dynamism when faced with new security issues is well captured in several chapters of Lowe, Roberts, Welsh, and Zaum's edited volume on the Security Council, including those by Cortright, et al., Greenstock, Welsh, and Boulden. See *The United Nations Security Council and War*, Chapters 8, 10, 24, and 27. On political dynamics, see Schachter, "In Defense of International Rules on the Use of Force," 122.

[19] The Charter endows the UN as an institution with other functions that may well be relevant to cyberattacks, such as Articles 33-8 on pacific settlement of disputes, and Article 26 on arms control plans. Though outside the scope of this study, they could form a fruitful basis for further inquiry. For a comprehensive overview, see Lowe et al., *The United Nations Security Council and War*, 2–10.

Article 51 and the Inherent Right to Self-Defense

"Nothing in the present Charter shall impair the inherent right of individual or collective self-defense"—so begins Chapter VII, Article 51, which many scholars regard as the cornerstone of the UN Charter's remedial landscape for states confronted with an illegal use of force.[20] The content of the article—that states retain a right to individual and collective self-defense even in the presence of the Charter's ban on force—is generally intuitive. Its scope, by contrast, is a subject of considerable debate. How far this right extends, and in response to what actions, is one of the most important debates in international law and international security more generally. After noting the connection between this and Article 39, this section frames the basic contours of the debate between "restrictive" and "expansive" interpretations of Article 51 and suggests a framework for analysis of cyberattacks.

Though the balance of this section will examine the debates and applicability of Article 51, it should be noted that the operation of Articles 51 and 39 are inescapably linked, and conclusions about one may ultimately inform the other. The Charter-guaranteed right of self-defense is designed only as a temporary and stopgap measure "until the Security Council has taken measures necessary to maintain international peace and security."[21] Many overlook this provision, regarding it as stillborn—at least, as originally conceived.[22] For this reason, and out of the desire to avoid speculation or prognostication, this chapter will focus on what action would be deemed justified *prior* to potential intervention by the Security Council, or perhaps more plausibly, in its absence.

The Contested Scope of Article 51

The debate over the scope of Article 51 is fundamental to this study because it informs whether there is a meaningful distinction between what makes a cyberattack an illegal use of force, and what renders it lawful to respond to *with* force. While the approach favored by this study does recognize a heightened

---

[20] U.N. Charter, Article 51.
[21] Ibid.
[22] See Paul Kennedy, *The Parliament of Man: The Past, Present, and Future of the United Nations* (New York: Random House, 2006), 51–52.

standard for the deployment of force, it is worth outlining the divided scholarship on the issue and reasons for making this choice.

This longstanding academic debate hinges on divergent views of the origins and meaning of "inherent right," and as a consequence, on the significance of armed attack—the phrase Article 51 uses to describe when that right is actionably implicated.[23] The more expansive of the two viewpoints regards the legal "right" asserted in the Charter as a codification of a fundamental state right to survival, which has its origins in the "primitive" legal concept of self-help.[24] Self-defense is also rooted in many domestic legal systems, where it is often sanctified. Further, a carve-out for self-defense was deeply relevant in 1945, when unrestrained warfare was dwindling but not yet obsolete.[25] Proponents of this view either consider the notion of armed attack functionally identical to other explanations of illegal force appearing elsewhere in the Charter, or affirm that the Charter has no intention of restricting the scope of a right independent of the document.[26] While the ICJ has taken great strides not to weigh in on this matter,[27] some dissenting opinions have lent this debate some credence arguing the issue on fundamentally pragmatic grounds (most famously, Judge Schwebel's dissenting opinion in the *Nicaragua* case).[28] This view has a handful of outspoken adherents in the legal academic

---

[23] See E. Jiménez de Aréchaga, "International Law in the Past Third of a Century," *Recueil des Cours de l'Academie de Droit International (RCADI)* 59, no. 1 (1978): 94–96; Brownlie, *International Law and the Use of Force by States*, 270–75; Dinstein, *War, Aggression and Self-Defence*, 175–82; Gray, *International Law and the Use of Force*, 117–21. For the distinction between "right" and "inherent right"—important but not germane to the argument of this section—see Dinstein, *War, Aggression and Self-Defence*, 178–79.

[24] International Court of Justice, *Legality of the Threat or Use of Nuclear Weapons, Advisory Opinion*, ICT Reports 136 (2004) (hereafter, *Nuclear Weapons Advisory Opinion*), 226, 63. See also Yoram Dinstein, "International Law as a Primitive Legal System," *NYU Journal of International Law and Policy* 19, no. 1 (1986–1987): 12. For origins of this argument, see Hans Kelsen, *General Theory of International Law and State* (Cambridge, MA: Harvard University Press, 1945), 339.

[25] On the waning of this right in the historical context, see Georg Schwarzenberger, "The Fundamental Principles of International Law," *Recueil des Cours de l'Academie de Droit International (RCADI)* 87 (1955). For a novel and compelling expansion of that argument in the modern context, see Mueller, *Retreat from Doomsday*.

[26] Aréchaga, "International Law in the Past Third of a Century," 95.

[27] Christine D. Gray, "The Charter Limitations on the Use of Force: Theory and Practice," in *The United Nations Security Council and War*, ed. Vaughn Lowe, Adam Roberts, Jennifer Welsh, and Dominik Zaum (Oxford: Oxford University Press, 2010), esp. 95 note 31.

[28] International Court of Justice, *Military and Paramilitary Activities in and against Nicaragua (Nicaragua v. United States of America), Merits, Judgment*. ICJ Reports 14 (1986) (hereafter, *Nicaragua*), 558–637. Schwebel does not however contend that the ICJ (or UN organs broadly) lack competence or authority to adjudicate or define matters invoking rights of self-defense—only that the origin of the right lies beyond the restrictive view that ascribing intentionality to the phrase "armed attack" necessitates. See Stephen Schwebel, "Aggression, Intervention and Self-Defense in Modern International Law," in *Justice in International Law: Selected Writings of Judge Stephen M. Schwebel*, ed. Stephen Schwebel (1994).

community, including those commenting specifically on cyberattacks—though in the *Tallinn Manual* process, represented a minority.[29]

By contrast, experts such as Dinstein and Gray regard the expansive reading "counter-textual, counter-factual, and counter-logical," and argue that it is "at variance with the mass of state practice and has to discount the views of the vast majority of states."[30] Instead, they argue for a more restrictive reading of Article 51 that centers on the phraseology at the time of authorship and the broader Charter context. Specifically, proponents of this view note the special status that the UN Charter's authors clearly intended for the construction of armed attack used in Article 51, instead of other constructions like use of force or "aggression." It is impossible to discount the precise insertion of the armed attack concept, the absence of which is notable in Articles 2(4), 39, and elsewhere throughout the Charter. By inference, the concept of an armed attack is a specific form of the use of force which, "because of its seriousness, creates a '*periculum in morta*' entailing the right to use force in legitimate defense, rather than waiting for measures of protection by the United Nations."[31] The result is that Article 51 considerably restricted the scope of permitted self-defense from the "vague customary right [of] self-preservation," yet left it intact to preserve the maintenance of the *jus ad bellum* regime.[32] This view comports largely with UN practice;[33] with evidence of their origins in the text,[34] and the range of subsequent legal analysis that makes clear Article 51 carefully enumerates limited exceptions to the blanket prohibition on the use of force, and does not introduce a distinct reference extra-textual natural law.[35] Aréchaga goes so far as to claim

---

[29] For example: D. W. Bowett, *Self-Defence in International Law* (New York: Praeger, 1958), 184–85; Stephen Schwebel, "Aggression, Intervention and Self-Defense in Modern International Law," in *Justice in International Law: Selected Writings of Judge Stephen M. Schwebel*, ed. Stephen Schwebel (1994); Julius Stone, *Aggression and World Order: A Critique of United Nations Theories of Aggression* (Clark, NJ: The Lawbook Exchange, Ltd., 1958), 44; Schachter, "The Right of States to Use Armed Force," 1634; *Tallinn 2.0*, 333.

[30] Dinstein, *War, Aggression and Self-Defence*, 183; Gray, *International Law and the Use of Force*, 118.

[31] Aréchaga, "International Law in the Past Third of a Century," 95. See also Dinstein, *War, Aggression and Self-Defence*, 184–86.

[32] Brownlie, *International Law and the Use of Force by States*, 274. See also Norman M. Feder, "Reading the U.N. Charter Connotatively: Toward a New Definition of Armed Attack," *NYU Journal of International Law and Policy* 19 (1986–1987): 405.

[33] For example, see cases outlined in Rosalyn Higgins, *The Development of International Law through the Political Organs of the United Nations* (Oxford: Oxford University Press, 1963), 200–01.

[34] Aréchaga notes that the alternative viewpoint is neither "convincing nor in accordance with the canons of treaty interpretation agreed at the Vienna Conference on the Law of Treaties." Aréchaga, "International Law in the Past Third of a Century," 96.

[35] Randelzhofer, "Article 2(4)," 603. Randelzhofer refers to this as the "dominant view," and is further supported by Kelsen, Oppenheim, Skubiszewski, Lamberti, and Zanardi. For support of this

that while "the political and moral justification for [a distinct armed attack] requirement in the Charter is so obvious in the world of today that it would seem unnecessary to have to justify it from a legal point of view."[36] That said, the scholars and states favoring the more restrictive reading are more numerous and, it seems, generally more convincing.[37] The International Law Commission, in its comprehensive survey and analysis, also favors such a restrictive view.[38]

In line with those scholars, this study regards this "majority view" favoring a restrictive interpretation of Article 51 as generally more compelling as well as in line with the preceding interpretation of Article 2(4). It provides a more useful and circumscribed analytical framework in which to understand whether cyberattacks invoke self-defensive rights, because it focuses on armed attacks, rather than some general natural law right of self-defense that may have only a speculative connection to modern cyber threats. The narrower interpretation is also the kind of useful analytical framework to explore Article 51's scope and relevance to a cyberattack.[39]

6.2 Cyberattacks and the Remedial *Jus Ad Bellum*

This section considers what special criteria beyond presumptive illegality a cyberattack would need to meet in order to reach the armed attack criteria, then considers the separate but related question of what conditions must be met for forceful self-defense to be permissible under international law.

Approaching Armed Attack

The 1987 *Declaration on the Non-Use of Force* states that "states have the inherent right of individual or collective self-defence if an armed attack occurs,

---

view within UN practice, see Higgins, *The Development of International Law Through the Political Organs of the United Nations*, 200–01.

[36] Aréchaga, "International Law in the Past Third of a Century," 95–96.
[37] See Higgins, *The Development of International Law through the Political Organs of the United Nations*, esp. 167–230.
[38] International Law Commission, *Report of the International Law Commission to the General Assembly* (1980).
[39] Feder, "Reading the U.N. Charter Connotatively," esp. 410–12.

as set forth in the Charter," but as the ICJ stipulated in *Nicaragua*, "whether self-defence be individual or collective, it can only be exercised in response to an 'armed attack.'"[40] While there is no meaningful dispute as to *whether* an armed attack permits self-defensive action, the central debate revolves around what constitutes an armed attack.

The emblematic case envisaged by the Charter's authors is clear-cut: one nation's army marching on another's territory, using military instruments (an army) in an illegal use of force that could threaten a state's existence with political overthrow and territorial occupation. However, the history of state and nonstate use of force since 1945 complicates this straightforward approach. As Franck noted as early as 1970, in many instances, of modern warfare "has inconveniently bypassed" these practices.[41]

This makes the absence of a definition in the Charter not just historically curious, but persistently problematic. Even in the context of the Charter's initial development, advances in air power had threatened traditional concepts of military movement and targeting, and nuclear weapons were challenging conventional notions of military deterrence. Yet the *travaux préparatoires* makes clear that delegates in San Francisco never seriously entertained defining the term armed attack.[42]

States have rushed into that lacuna, loath to apply a formal definition, but eager to push its boundaries.[43] The results are illuminating case law on the boundaries of armed attack and these rights of self-defense, including the legality of logistical support paramilitary groups (*Nicaragua*), of cross-border incursions (*Congo*), and of armed response to attacks on nonmilitary targets (*Oil Platforms*).[44] Like the ICJ, neither has the Security Council produced

[40] "U.N. Declaration on Threat or Use of Force in International Relations, A/RES/42/22"; *Nicaragua*, para 187–201. 1986

[41] Thomas M. Franck, "Who Killed Article 2(4)? or Changing Norms Governing the Use of Force by States," *American Journal of International Law* 64, no. 5 (1970): 812.

[42] Randelzhofer, "Article 51," 668; Schwebel, "Aggression, Intervention and Self-Defense in Modern International Law," 532.

[43] Most notably, the United States' insistence that its "quarantine" of Cuba during the 1952 missile crisis was empowered by regional treaty arrangement, not the Charter. For broader legal implications, see Feder, "Reading the U.N. Charter Connotatively," 422–24; Schachter, *In Defense*, 134–35. For emblematic legal commentary on the event itself, see Myres S. McDougal, "The Soviet-Cuban Quarantine and Self-Defense," *American Journal of International Law* 57 (1963); William T. Mallison, "Limited Naval Blockade or Quarantine-Interdiction: National and Collective Defense Claims Valid Under International Law," *George Washington Law Review* 31 (1962). This is not to say states have been fully unwilling to expand *any* definition; consider for instance the United States' 1986 bombing of sites in Libya for counterterrorism purposes, citing Article 51.

[44] Schachter, "In Defense of International Rules on the Use of Force"; *Nicaragua*; International Court of Justice, *Armed Activities on the Territory of the Congo (Democratic Republic of the Congo v. Uganda), Judgment*, ICJ Reports 168 (2005); International Court of Justice, *Oil Platforms (Islamic*

a singular definition, though it did provide regular judgment on responses to an accumulation of events (such as its resolutions on the Israeli security wall).[45] All these cases about the nature of lawful response suggest that any unified definition of an armed attack will remain elusive, but that more circumstance-specific scholarship can help provide meaningful analogies to understanding states' rights in the case of cyberattacks.[46] In the cyberattack context, the *Tallinn Manual* leaves mostly open the question of what actions constitute a use of force, but not an armed attack.[47] Even more developed, state-centric doctrine, such as the US DOD's, leave this matter open to significant measure of interpretation.[48]

Thus a reformulation is called for: questioning not whether a cyberattack meets a certain definition of an armed attack, but rather what are the key justifications a state would marshal to support a forceful response to a cyberattack under Article 51 and its subsequent interpretation? Four criteria, each presented in turn, draw together key lessons of case law and precedent to provide a basis for evaluating whether a cyberattack might be an armed attack: if the event was (1) discrete and (2) of sufficient "scale and effects," (3) it was strongly attributable, and (4) it was intended.

Scale and Effects

To be a cyberattack by this study's definition, an incident must already have some significance; likewise, to be a use of force under Article 2(4), the last chapter outlined even higher requirements. The ICJ in *Nicaragua* made clear its intention was to "distinguish the most grave forms of the use of force (those

---

Republic of Iran v. United States of America), Judgment, ICJ Reports 161 (2003) (hereafter, *Oil Platforms*).

[45] International Court of Justice, *Legal Consequences of the Construction of a Wall in the Occupied Palestinian Territory, Advisory Opinion*, ICJ Reports 136 (2004), 14, at 101–04, paras 1–95.
[46] Silver, "Computer Network Attack as a Use of Force under Article 2(4) of the United Nations Charter," 84, writing that "the basic conclusion appears to be that force is like pornography: the law will recognize certain forms of CNA as force when it sees them. The present state of legal development does not permit laying down any hard and fast rules as to when that will be. It does, however, permit one to make some predictions about the circumstances in which State use of CNA may be likely to be held to constitute force under Article 2(4)."
[47] *Tallinn 1.0*, 48.
[48] *Operational Law Handbook* (Charlottesville, VA: The Judge Advocate General's Legal Center and School, 2017): "Determining when a CO [cyber operation] amounts to a use of force or an armed attack has been the topic of academic and expert debate since the growth of the cyber domain."

constituting an armed attack) from other less grave forms."[49] Even some of the basic criteria of the use of force that found consensus among scholars is elusive in this case. The prior chapter noted, for instance, general agreement that "harm to persons or physical damage to property" would constitute a use of force, however, *Tallinn* experts split on whether the harm itself was a "condition precedent" to designation as an armed attack, or whether "the extent of ensuing effects" are more salient.[50] Though the facts and circumstances of any new cyberattack incident may well present novelties, it is important to be able to identify which events might have sufficient scale and effects, as the ICJ deemed them.[51] This section briefly covers two key criteria: how to identify it from a *de minimis* incursions, and second, whether an accumulation of smaller events might qualify.

Illegal But de minimis Events. The ICJ has been consistent in making clear that illegal use of force that is nonetheless *de minimis* in its effect would not invoke a right of self-defense. The hallmark case on this point (and many others) was *Nicaragua*, the judgment of which drew an oft-cited distinction between an armed attack and "a mere frontier incident."[52] This distinction was highly controversial among commentators, namely for either narrowing the concept of self-defense, or eroding the utility of the *jus ad bellum* regime in the face of an uptick in low-intensity conflict.[53] Nonetheless, there is an intuitive if not universally recognized distinction between full-scale invasion and an errant bullet over a border, a small-scale skirmish, or a destructive act only inconveniencing commerce in a contested area. For this reason, the UN General Assembly's 1974 *Definition of Aggression*—itself of contested legal status—did nonetheless include a *de minimis* clause excluding cases where "the events concerned or their consequences are not of sufficient gravity."[54] Those events would at the very least impose strict proportionality requirements on the response, perhaps to the point of precluding it outright.[55] There is no need to adopt one position or the other here, since a

[49] *Nicaragua*, para 191.
[50] *Tallinn 2.0*, 342.
[51] *Nicaragua*, para 195.
[52] Ibid.
[53] See Dinstein, *War, Aggression and Self-Defence*, 195; John Lawrence Hargrove, "The *Nicaragua* Judgment and the Future of the Law of Force and Self-Defense," *American Journal of International Law* 81, no. 1 (1987): 139; Michael Reisman, "Allocating Competences to use Coercion in the post Cold-War World, Practices Conditions, and Prospects," in *Law and Force in the New International Order*, ed. Lori F. Damrosch and David J. Scheffer (Boulder, CO: Westview Press, 1991), 40.
[54] United Nations General Assembly, *Definition of Aggression (A/RES/3314 [XXIX])*, Article 2.
[55] Brownlie, for instance, concludes the former and accepts no categorical limitation on the activation of the right, only on the scale of recourse. Brownlie, *International Law and the Use of Force by States*, 366.

response even if authorized would be so miniscule to be of little international consequence. As Gervais and others note, "not every use of force warrants the exercise of the right of unilateral self-defense . . . to know whether a cyberattack meets the threshold of 'armed attack' requires knowing where the *de minimis* threshold lies. However, this is a vague and fact-specific rule."[56]

So what criteria differentiate edge cases, particularly for those that do qualify as a use of force? In the case of cyberattacks, three seem immediately relevant. First, would be if a victim is capable of immediate or rapid recovery and reconstitution with minimal expenditure of resources.[57] Second, if the targeted infrastructure's functioning remains uninterrupted—in other words, a failed attempt. Third, if the attacker was successful at disrupting information infrastructure, and disabled critical infrastructure dependent upon it, but to no substantial civilian or military harm. One can envision an attempted cyberattack on recognizable military assets, or an attempted nationwide Estonia-style attack, but with little to no effect due to rapid remediation. Such an event may constitute a use of force but, arguably, not an armed attack.[58]

Accumulation of Events. The second issue is whether or not an accumulation of events, rather than a discrete and more severe single event, could invoke lawful self-defense. American officials, for instance, have at various times claimed that the Comprehensive National Cybersecurity Initiative constituted a declaration of intent to "fight back" against cyber operations from abroad based on an accumulation of (mostly espionage) events.[59]

The law on this question is unsettled. Schachter argues for a time limitation on events that are considered "discrete" for the purposes of response, but wisely does not propose a specific time frame.[60] That is likely the soundest, if least specific approach. Feder adds that the United Nations Security Council

---

[56] Michael Gervais, "Cyber Attacks and the Laws of War," *Berkeley Journal of International Law* 30, no. 2 (2012): 542.
[57] *Tallinn 1.0*, 52.
[58] Initially this appears to be a perverse set of conclusions, as it would seem to almost dissuade states from investing sufficiently in their own cyber-defense, lest they find themselves with fewer rights than those with less remediation capability. Upon further analysis it does, however, make some logical sense: those able to seamlessly recover from even a major cyber incident have less excuse to demand of international law for otherwise lawful defensive behavior and remedy than those suffering immense harm.
[59] Markoff, Sanger, and Shanker, "In Digital Combat, U.S. Finds No Easy Deterrent." This notion of an "accumulation of intolerable espionage" is of course prima facie well below the threshold most legal commentators would regard as "use of force," let alone "armed attack."
[60] Schachter, "In Defense of International Rules on the Use of Force," 132.

generally rejected the premise of a "pinprick" theory of armed attack.[61] Gray, however, argues it has "not gone so far," and that instead the ICJ's judgment in *Nicaragua* seems to leave open the possibility for lawful response to an accumulation of events.[62] The accumulation of events theory holds that "a state is permitted to equate the accumulation of these smaller attacks to an 'armed attack,' thus justifying a forcible response in self-defence."[63] Henderson writes that while this theory is "controversial from many perspectives, Israel's invasion into the Gaza Strip in 2008–2009 is an example of this theory in action."[64] In other cases such as *Cameroon/Nigeria, Oil Platforms,* and *Congo,* as Gray notes, the ICJ has left this potential open without precluding the notion.[65] There seems to be no definitive conclusion as to whether an accumulation of events could, as a general matter of law, invoke rights of self-defense, only that the notion is not categorically unjustifiable.[66] Indeed, the accumulation of events approach also raises concerns about the temporal nature of an armed attack under Article 51—namely, the injustice of forcing victims to wait too long to repel, particularly since (as we have seen) in-kind and instantaneous responses may be ill-suited to an effective reprisals to cyberattacks.

So what might "accumulation of events" in the cyber context activate rights against an armed attack in its current context? It is simple to envisage a cyberattack whose effects were slow and continuous; for instance, imagine a fact pattern involving not one, but several pieces of malware placed across a state's digital infrastructure, programmed to activate sequentially over a period of days or weeks, increasing friction in and ultimately creating cascade effects in the critical infrastructure systems reliant on it. Such insidious sabotage, if cascading to a point of substantial damage, would make for a significant test case in the case law, and force more concrete opinion on the matter. It is premature to consider its position within international law, and would arguably be a riper fact pattern to adjudicate the premise than the

---

[61] Feder, "Reading the U.N. Charter Connotatively." Feder focuses here on the 1982 Israeli incursion into Lebanon in response to the Palestinian Liberation Organization's frontier attacks on Israeli towns, and Lebanon's inability to restrain those attacks.

[62] Gray, *International Law and the Use of Force*, 155–56. Gray cites para. 231 as key evidence.

[63] Christian Henderson, "Non-State Actors and the Use of Force," in *Non-State Actors in International Law*, ed. Math Noortmann, Reinisch, August and Ryngaert, Cedric (London: Hart Publishing, 2015), 8.

[64] Ibid.

[65] Gray, *International Law and the Use of Force*, 156.

[66] Henderson observes that "there has been little discernable acceptance of this theory by states, and while the ICJ has, perhaps unwittingly, given a certain nod to it, the UNSC has seemingly rejected it. It, as such, remains an element of the law that is unclear." Henderson, "Non-State Actors and the Use of Force," 8. See also *Oil Platforms*, para 64.

1982 Israel–Lebanon case. Accepting the controversy on the status of law, all that is possible at this phase is to accept that a discrete cyberattack event would less controversially invoke rights of self-defensive force than an accumulation of cyberattack events.

Military Effect. A cyberattack with impact on military preparedness or deployment would almost certainly qualify as an armed attack. This is not a hard requirement, but likely a dispositive condition for edge cases in which it is relevant.[67] Earlier sections have touched on the notion that a cyberattack that spectacularly derails a military's ability to equip, deploy, and exercise command and control is an obviously hostile act—and more likely than actions against other government targets to meet the armed attack threshold.[68] In the *Oil Platforms*, in which the United States claimed rights to shell oil platforms in self-defense following an attack on a US-flagged vessel and a mine strike by one of its warships its judgment against the United States, the ICJ drew an important distinction between the legal effect of a single attack on a merchant vessel and a similar event targeting a more identifiably military vessel.[69] This argument is further supported—and made more relevant to cyberattacks—by the contents of the UN General Assembly's 1974 *Definition of Aggression*. As a general statement of customary law, it is notable that it demonstrably lowers this threshold when military targets are concerned, specifically citing as aggression an incursion "by the armed force of a State on the land, sea or air forces, or marine and air fleets of another State" without reference to the "significant effects" requirement found elsewhere.[70] Article 3(d) also suggests two valuable corollaries in engaging threshold cases: first, that acts against military assets need not be geographically limited to the borders of the victim state, and second, that acts against military assets, more starkly than other cross-border hostilities, must be interpreted

---

[67] Military effect is not necessarily a required precondition for evaluating whether a state my lawfully employ its right to self-defense, for the scale and effects of a cyberattack predominately harming the civilian government and private sector networks may be just as deleterious as a cyberattack that solely targets DOD networks. Perhaps for this reason the 2015 Cyber Strategy the Defense Department expressly signaled its commitment to protecting not only DOD networks from cyberattacks, but also civilian government and private sector networks: military preparedness or deployment "in addition to DOD's own networks, a cyberattack on the critical infrastructure and key resources on which DOD relies for its operations could impact the U.S. military's ability to operate in a contingency." US Department of Defense, *The Department of Defense Cyber Strategy*, 10. In addition, the Defense Department articulated its right to "use cyber operations to disrupt an adversary's command and control networks, military-related critical infrastructure, and weapons capabilities" during "heightened tensions or outright hostilities." Ibid., 14.
[68] Gorman and Barnes, "Cyber Combat: Act of War."
[69] See Gray, *International Law and the Use of Force*, 145 and note 32.
[70] United Nations General Assembly, *Definition of Aggression (A/RES/3314 [XXIX])*, Article 3(d).

as aggressive acts of exceptional illegality. The flexibility is necessary because today, large militaries hold assets permanently stationed globally and are subject to attack while outside their home state's borders. Likewise, the definition reflects the juridical reality that attacks against military targets serve an ostensible purpose of skewing a present or future armed conflict. As such, targeting clearly military assets is one of the more clear-cut characterizations of an armed attack.

Applying this notion to cyberattacks does run some risk of overinclusion, providing states seeking a broad remit to use force as an opportunity to justify that action on the margins of the law. To keep with a restrictive view of Article 51 and insulate the rationale from customary abuse, the parameters of what defines a "military asset" in the digital age require greater clarity. Some simplified cyberattack cases fall easily within this clause in the *Definition*. For instance, using digital means to weaken command and control of ballistic missile arsenal, particularly a nuclear arsenal, falls well within this definition, as these arsenals fall under the exclusive purview of militaries. In cases of obviously military (e.g., flagged, sole-purpose) equipment, cyberattacks on them are almost certain to fall under the Article 3(d) definition, and the ICJ's approach in *Oil Platforms*.

Article 3(d)'s decoupling of military infrastructure from the borders of a victim state is helpful but susceptible to abuse. For instance, prima facie, a cyberattack on a maritime navigational beacon (or satellite) essential to a fleet's deployment into a theatre of imminent conflict would seem to meet this definition of armed attack. This characterization would hold if that beacon were within a state's territorial waters and equally if it were positioned well beyond the victim's borders. Moreover, if a state incited, commissioned, or orchestrated the attack, it would bear responsibility for an armed attack.

A cyberattack must have the effect of damaging a military's ability to equip, deploy, and exercise command and control—not simply to organize and train—to meet this threshold. Not all digital infrastructure that is "important" to a military seems consistent with the spirit of Article 3(d). A cyberattack against servers used by the Royal Navy would to some appear as an attack against the UK's marine fleet, but not if those servers were simply used to process payroll across the Ministry of Defense. Those with a preference to see their rights of self-defense invoked could argue, for instance, that the infrastructure is ultimately part of the "overarching apparatus" of a military, and that without pay, soldiers will sew unrest, so the event was an armed attack against military preparedness. Even before questions of proportionality, the fact remains that while the assets may be military in ownership, a cyberattack may not constitute an action against military *capabilities* in any direct way.

Conversely, similar skepticism could be applied to the aforementioned case of that navigational beacon, or more accurately, the networked infrastructure that serves it.[71] A cyberattack rendering that infrastructure inoperable is certainly of military concern. That infrastructure, however, may not be military on its surface at all. It is exceptionally likely that beacon, like the vast majority of modern militaries' unclassified logistics systems, leverages shared information infrastructure. Knowing which infrastructure—for instance, a Maltese internet service provider providing that beacon's connectivity among thousands of its other contracts—could permit an attacker to precisely target that military asset. In this case, the "attack" would indeed be against a military and could impact the military's ability to deploy. Is self-defense therefore lawful?

It hardly seems that one logically follows from the other, and thus, that the event meets the threshold of an armed attack. Here, the argument that any event targeting marginally "military" information infrastructure is an armed attack, especially in the likely case that infrastructure was shared by the military and civilians, seems particularly reminiscent of the United States' unsuccessful arguments in *Oil Platforms*.[72] Crucially, the Court held that the attacks on US-owned or flagged vessels, "even taken cumulatively . . . do not seem to the Court to constitute an armed attack on the United States of the kind that the Court [in *Nicaragua*] qualified as a 'most grave' form of the use of force."[73] Surely, a US vessel's collision with an Iranian-laid mine that figured into the case was by no means minor, but as the next section will explore, the ICJ was (controversially) unable to find aggression *directed at the state exercising self-defense*. The relevant conclusion for analogy is that not all attacks on state-claimed property with military relevance constitute attacks on its military. A cyberattack disrupting a military is likely to cross this threshold, but in doing so it must have strategic effects greater than a number of technical inconveniences.

---

[71] Brandon Davenport and Rich Ganske, "'Recalculating Route,'" *War on the Rocks*, March 11, 2019.
[72] *Oil Platforms*, ICJ Pleadings, US *Rejoinder*, Section 5.
[73] *Oil Platforms*, ICJ Reports, (2003), para. 64.

Attribution

Even when a cyberattack has the prior features of an armed attack, without confidence (and publicly presentable evidence) of the aggressor, the would be difficult for the remedial *jus ad bellum* to operate. Chapter 1 accounted for many of the ways in which attribution is both a potential challenge, but also less fundamentally so than when it was confronted by many observers in the early internet age. Likewise, Chapter 3's analysis about how the ambiguity of who sits "behind the keyboard" is not dispositive for certain key security dynamics to operate. For the purposes of identifying an armed attack, there are both issues to overcome to meet the expectations of law and custom, but also limits to what a functioning remedial regime can require of states. For identifying armed attacks, three key criteria are key: *geopolitical accuracy, timeliness,* and *public disclosure.*

Geopolitical Accuracy. The attribution problem rapidly takes on a political dimension and from an analytical and international legal standpoint complicates, but is not sufficient to derail, a disciplined analysis of the topic altogether.[74] As prior sections have engaged with, attribution for a cyberattack is not purely a technical matter, any more than attribution for a missile launch is strictly a function of altitude and exhaust trail. This overreliance on technical circumstances is one of the key shortcomings of much of the early literature on the topic.[75] Technical circumstances are, after all, only one aspect of the case states can build against an attacker in responding with force.

The technological specifics of a cyberattack may be unusual, but the underlying challenges parallel others dealt with by modern militaries. A few parallels elucidate the matter. In the early days of long-range ballistic missiles and until advanced satellite and radar coverage was achieved over a range of launch sites, locating the origin of such a missile was a strategic uncertainty and profound liability.[76] Moreover, the increasing practice of basing missiles beyond national borders in crude measures of allied deterrence further complicated the matter. In this case, technical developments helped narrow attribution questions to, at the very least, a rough geography. But it is important to recall that a missile's trajectory hardly proves the identity of who gave orders to launch it. It was not inconceivable during the Cold War that the misfiring of an automatic trigger, or a military commander acting without

[74] Rid, *Cyber War Will Not Take Place*, Chapter 7.
[75] Libicki, *Cyberdeterrence and Cyberwar*, 41–52.
[76] Bundy, *Danger and Survival: Choices about the Bomb in the First Fifty Years*, 325–26.

orders but under internal rules of engagement, might launch (or test) absent a notification. Likewise, such a launch could quite realistically have been met with a denial, or pleas for time to investigate, from political leaders. In a more modern example, in 2007 the Chinese People's Liberation Army (PLA) conducted a test of an anti-satellite (ASAT) weapon. The test was met with great surprise and alarm in the West, but perhaps equal surprise within China's own civilian government, which met accusations of joining a "space arms race" first with confusion, then telling silence, before days later issuing a statement defending the test.[77] Despite perceptions of this highly escalatory move, most evidence suggests the PLA's unilateral decision to move forward with such a move, in spite of its political consequences and without the full knowledge of civilian political leadership. All this bears a striking resemblance to the human-interface challenge of cyberattack attribution: even with a breakthrough to identify the "launch site" of sorts, perfect attribution to identify the individual and orders under which the actor executed the program are imperfect.

The argument here is not that attribution is irrelevant, only that it is far more context-dependent than many commentators on cybersecurity give credit.[78] In some cases, a use of force is directly attributable to an armed force directly controlled by a state. In other cases, however, that relationship is less clear, as modern weaponry, tactics, and methods of covert support force "certitude" over the aggressor to mere "deductive culpability." In such cases—which today represent a significant number of potential armed attacks—technical evidence is rarely the determinant of perceived legality. The regulative regime clearly considers geopolitical context—in other words, the rational likelihood and perceived incentives of an attack—with at least as much gravity as the protestations of the involved parties. Otherwise, the 2001-era Taliban would have to be taken at its word that it had no incentive to participate in Al-Qaida's activities (or repeat what many American

---

[77] Brendan Nicholson, "World Fury at Satellite Destruction," *The Age*, January 20, 2007; *BBC News*, "Concern Over China's Missile Test," January 19, 2007; *BBC News*, "China Confirms Satellite Downed," January 23, 2007.

[78] Michael Schmitt, "'Below the Threshold' Cyber Operations: The Countermeasures Response Option and International Law," *Virginia Journal of International Law* 54, no. 3 (2014): 713. "It must be cautioned that geography is irrelevant to the issue of attribution. Non-State actors may, and likely often will, launch a cyber operation from outside territory controlled by the State to which the conduct is attributable. A paradigmatic example would involve non-State actors in one State under the direction and control of another State assimilating computers located in multiple States into a botnet and using the botnet to target the injured State. The determinative issue is the level of direction and control, not the location of the activities."

commentators regard as the Court's mistake in *Nicaragua*, accepting that country's claims of the necessity of attacking its neighbors at face value).[79]

Within the broader context of national security decision-making, and indeed the international security environment, cyberattacks do not simply materialize from an unknowable ether without motive or direction. They have and will continue in most instances to reflect already simmering geopolitical conflicts, rendering the kind of geopolitical attribution necessary to supplement (but not justify) a self-defensive attack possible, even absent unequivocal evidence of attribution.

Timeliness. As earlier chapters explained, one of the more significant realizations of the last several years has been both the reality and potential stability benefits of the dilation of the decision-making timeline for major cyber incidents.[80] Graham argued, emblematically of that period in scholarship, that "unfortunately, in cyberspace, there will likely not be sufficient time to consider peaceful resolution of the matter, fully understand the nature of the attack or the intended results, or to mobilize international peacekeeping forces."[81] Yet operators' prior clamoring for war-and-peace decisions to be delegated and automated has not come to pass.[82] It is likely no coincidence that as noted, attribution has in that time also made breakthroughs for some states, and thus strategically significant. Because the ability to fashion a *considered* response is possible, the time to construct one is now seemingly more acceptable.

With cyberattacks, it may be the case that activating the remedial *jus ad bellum* would require a combination of lucky breaks and unusual circumstances—or, as one State Department official put it, a willingness to "lash out blindly" at an attacker only remotely presumed.[83] The situation is in fact not so dire. Cybersecurity decision-making no longer takes place in a vacuum of technical operations distinct from national security policy.[84]

---

[79] For such arguments, see *American Journal of International Law*, 81 (1987), especially Franck, "Some Observations on the ICJ's Procedural and Substantive Innovations"; D'Amato, "Trashing Customary International Law"; Hargrove, "The Nicaragua Judgment and the Future of the Law of Force and Self-defense"; Moore, "The *Nicaragua* Case and the Deterioration of World Order."

[80] See Healey, Chapter 5, note 80.

[81] Todd H. Graham, "Armed Attack in Cyberspace: Deterring Asymmetric Warfare with an Asymmetric Definition," *Air Force Law Review* 64, no. 65 (2009): 98.

[82] See, e.g., US Senate Armed Services, *Nominations Before the Senate Armed Services Committee*, Second, April 15, 2010.

[83] Michele Markoff, "National And Global Strategies For Managing Cyberspace And Security" (paper presented at the Conference of the Atlantic Council: International Engagement On Cyber: Establishing Norms And Improved Security, Washington, DC, March 30, 2011).

[84] US Department of Defense, "Department of Defense Law of War Manual," 2016: "A State's right to take necessary and proportionate action in self-defense in response to an armed attack originating

Rather, the United States, United Kingdom, Russia, Australia, and others have integrated their senior-most cybersecurity policymaker into the apparatus of national security decision-making.[85] The practical result is that cybersecurity incidents are placed within the broader context of political, military, and diplomatic conditions and sensitive intelligence insights in which states invest exponentially more. With this context in mind, while the potential perennially exists for an unannounced, unanticipated attack from a previously unknown actor, those states most likely to invoke a right of self-defense are well aware of the threat profile of likely adversaries and would therefore monitor cyberattack capabilities and preparations just like any other national security threat.[86]

If it comes to pass as custom, it would bring the timeline in which states might investigate, claim, and then exercise their rights of self-defense in line with kinetic actions—and with similar guardrails. Attribution that should be uncertain but is made with suspicious speed of an unlikely actor should raise skepticism of political motive. Similarly, attribution that stretches on over years (or possibly many months) would weaken claims that circumstances had left no alternative. This is a policy question, based on broader precedent, that governments will have to manage—the more significant conclusion is that the key parameters they will have in making such a decision are no longer definitionally unique for cyberattacks.

Public Disclosure. Finally, for a state to activate the remedial *jus ad bellum* and prepare a forceful response, it has been customary to provide public evidence of the attack. Designed to prevent the sorts of deceptions used to launch wars under false pretense, this requirement is important to the maintenance of the remedial regime, even if it is not perfectly functional. In the

---

through cyberspace applies whether the attack is attributed to another State or to a non-State actor." Further, "decisions about whether to invoke a State's inherent right of self-defense would be made at the national level because they involve the State's rights and responsibilities under international law. For example, in the United States, such decisions would generally be made by the President."

[85] As of this writing those roles are, respectively: the Director of the Cabinet Office of Cybersecurity and Information Assurance (United Kingdom); Deputy Secretary of the National Security Council (Russia); and the Deputy National Security Advisor (Australia). With regard to United States Government's leadership on this front, in 2018 then national security advisor John Bolton "decided to phase out" the special assistant to the Obama-appointed president and cybersecurity coordinator position. The Biden administration restored and expanded these functions with the creation of a Deputy National Security Advisor for Cybersecurity and Emerging Technology. Brian Barrett, "White House Cuts Critical Cybersecurity Role as Threats Loom," *Wired*, May 15, 2018; Ayesha Rascoe, "Biden Adds Homeland Security, Cyber Heft to White House Team," *NPR News*, 2021.

[86] See Cassell Bryan-Low, "British Spy Chief Breaks Agency's History of Silence," *Wall Street Journal*, October 29, 2010.

case of cyberattacks, there are practical challenges. As Waxman notes, "even if forensic processes can trace a cyberattack to its source, States may be unable to publicize that information in a timely and convincing way, especially when those States are likely to have strong incentive not to discuss the technical details of informational security breaches or reveal their own capabilities to intruders."[87] This may indeed be true of many cyber incidents and is indeed supported by the long history of secrecy surrounding such incidents. Like attribution and timeliness, however, here too the circumstances may bend in favor of a functional remedial regime and given the ephemerality of many cyberattack tools. Waxman's observation may be less salient for the sorts of significant national security events under discussion here are far more likely to be worthy of the loss of the technical access used to obtain the evidence. On numerous occasions and breaking with earlier precedent, states have begun to release details of other countries' operations as part of international campaigns of delegitimization (covered in greater in Chapter 8).[88]

Intent

Finally, it seems essential that for a victim state to launch a lawful response, it must be able to articulate a coherent narrative of intent (*mens rea* in the criminal context) for specific harm by the aggressor (though this is not settled doctrine). As the *Oil Platforms* case demonstrates, an armed attack necessitates that the aggressor has the requisite intent to attack.[89] According to Wilmshurst, the ICJ references "this requirement when it inquired into the question of whether the U.S. was able to prove [with] certainty that Iran's

---

[87] Matthew C. Waxman, "Cyber Attacks as 'Force' Under UN Charter Article 2(4)," *International Law Studies* 87, no. 43 (2011): 51.

[88] See, e.g., "Seven Iranians Working for Islamic Revolutionary Guard Corps-Affiliated Entities Charged for Conducting Coordinated Campaign of Cyber Attacks Against U.S. Financial Sector," 2016; "North Korean Regime-Backed Programmer Charged With Conspiracy to Conduct Multiple Cyber Attacks and Intrusions," 2018; "Chinese Military Personnel Charged with Computer Fraud, Economic Espionage and Wire Fraud for Hacking into Credit Reporting Agency Equifax," 2020.

[89] As Wilmshurst points out regarding the *Oil Platforms* case, however, "to the extent that this [case] may be read as suggesting that military attacks on a state or its vessels do not trigger a right of self-defence as long as the attacks are not aimed specifically at the particular state or its vessels but rather are carried out indiscriminately, this part of the ICJ's ruling in *Oil Platforms* has been criticised as not supported by international law." Elizabeth Wilmshurst, "The Chatham House Principles of International Law on the Use of Force by States in Self-Defense," *International and Comparative Law Quarterly* 55, no. 4 (2006); *Oil Platforms*, para 64.

actions were 'specifically aimed' at the U.S. or that Iran had 'the specific intention' of harming US vessels."[90]

This notion is particularly important in the case of cyberattacks for the same reason that the ICJ (controversially) noted a need to ascertain the "circumstances and motivations" of an attack to distinguish it from a frontier incident.[91] The United States and Russia have consistently referred in public statements to the need to reduce misperception that could lead to escalation in cyberspace. In June 2013, the two parties concluded years-long negotiations to establish a series of crisis communications and de-escalation protocols for cybersecurity issues—using systems initially put in place for nuclear de-escalation.[92] While their operation and efficacy have been varied according to some accounts, these moves highlight the possibility that states' gross negligence could result in the appearance of a smaller-scale cyberattack emanating from its borders.[93] Such activity might provide pretext for conflict between a particularly unstable dyad, even if the event was entirely outside either government's control.

Comparison to Present Law. States guilty of gross negligence, or generalized force toward unspecific adversaries, are far less likely to find themselves on the receiving end of lawfully permissible defensive force than those intending specific harm. Cases at the intersection of force and indiscretion abound, but perhaps the most helpful is the already described *Iranian Oil Platforms* case. Judges in that case held that Iran's undersea mines, despite detonation on a US warship, were insufficiently "targeted" against US interests as to classify as an armed attack.[94] Specifically, the Court noted that Iran was simultaneously at war with the United States and Iraq. Moreover, it noted the nature of mining was not directed at any one single target or category of target (i.e., military vessels) but rather as a general deterrent to navigation. As such, the Court determined there were insufficient grounds to accept the United States' claims of rights of self-defense. This stance predictably ignited a strong rejoinder from the United States and scrutiny from the academic community and left unclear how generalized aggression was

---

[90] Wilsmhurst, "The Chatham House Principles of International Law on the Use of Force by States in Self-Defense," 6.
[91] Schachter, "In Defense of International Rules on the Use of Force," para 231.
[92] The White House, "U.S.–Russian Cooperation on Information and Communications Technology Security," June 17, 2013.
[93] William M. Arkin, Ken Dilanian, and Cynthia McFadden, "What Obama Said to Putin on the Red Phone About the Election Hack," *NBC News*, December 19, 2016.
[94] *Oil Platforms*, para 151–61.

not granted substantial and unjustifiable under the ICJ's standard.[95] Before engaging with that controversy, however, the Court did produce the straightforward conclusion that an event legitimating armed response must possess clear and specific intentionality to harm the responding state.

Judging Cyberattack Intent. Cyberattacks bear some resemblance to instruments as diverse as conventional weapons, land and naval mines, and biological weapons in the challenges they pose to ascertaining the attackers' intent. In successful cyberattacks, the initial targeting would be a delicate matter, requiring reconnaissance and intelligence gathering, often outside of the digital space. In some cyberattack examples, the target follows closely enough that intent is simple to ascertain. For instance, a kinetic cyberattack that physically disrupts critical information infrastructure could clearly reflect intent if the outage was targeted—for instance, disabling a military base's external network connections. The same would be true in the Estonia attacks, which targeted few if any networks outside the nation; likewise, if a cyberattack were to use carefully constructed tools that limited their effectiveness to certain national targets or geography. In all such cases, the difficulty in assigning culpability is not one of intent, but attribution.

The authors of the *Tallinn Manual* "took the view that intention is irrelevant in qualifying an operation as an armed attack and that only the scale and effects matter."[96] There is reason for skepticism here, as other cyberattack tools provide far less obvious signs of intent, resembling in some instances the complications posed by sea and land mines, and in another, by biological weapons. For instance, targeting shared information infrastructure serving a broad swathe of internet users (e.g., aspects of the Domain Name System, or Tier 1 backbone ISPs that serve government *and* private sector clients), would appear far more consistent with Iran's mining operation in *Oil Platforms*—disruptive, but difficult to ascertain specific targeting. In these cases, a state's objective may be large-scale disruption or simply obfuscation of a more targeted outage. Due to these networks' interconnection, disabling functionality in the victim state could require disrupting infrastructure in another, thousands of miles away; to the victims, however, there would be no clear delineation between "target" and "collateral damage." While typically

---

[95] This latter criticism was the crux of the rebuttal offered by the State Department Legal Adviser subsequent to the decision. See William H. Taft IV, "Self-Defense and the *Oil Platforms* Decision," *Yale Journal of International Law* 29 (2004): 294. Gray, however, finds this argument unconvincing given the clear existing illegality of such acts Gray, *International Law and the Use of Force*, 146.

[96] *Tallinn 1.0*, 57.

less effective, and almost certainly less compliant with the *jus in bello* (as the next chapter will address), these latter types of tools could be particularly attractive to an aggressor state seeking to frustrate the regulative regime on force. It happens that these are also the tools and techniques that are most easily acquired on the open market, as they exploit widely known vulnerabilities often through unsophisticated methods.

Similarly, the intent of a cyberattack that made use of a highly prolific virus to disable large swathes of pervasive infrastructure—rather than, for instance, by disabling the infrastructure by flooding it with traffic—would be subject to more straightforward scrutiny.[97] Indeed, in that case, multiple nations in ongoing hostilities with an attacker might claim an attack against them, which if the interpretation of *Oil Platforms* were to hold, would potentially stymie the case brought by anyone. Here emerge the parallels between certain types of cyberattacks and biological weapons—categorized under today's parlance as a WMD. Biological weapons are designated as such in part because their intent is obscured by the inability to exercise meaningful discrimination in targets. For the purposes of determining an armed attack, it is worth noting the development of such a special category in weaponry, in part to address this challenge of how such high-collateral weapons, could rightly and actionably demonstrate a discernable intent.

The Present Limits of the *Jus ad Bellum*

This section examined how existing international law and precedent could inform the legality of an act of self-defense to a cyberattack. The international law on the topic is unsettled and offers no simple formulae for determining compliance with Article 51, though many of its elements strongly suggest cyberattacks would be eligible to activate the remedial *jus ad bellum*.[98]

Ambiguities in the law make the practical consequences even muddier. Absent context, it is difficult to provide any detailed template of what specific responses the law might empower. Absent custom, the operation of the

---

[97] From a technical standpoint, the distinction here is between a virus like Stuxnet, which was reportedly designed to only have effect only on obscure hardware known to be in use at Iranian nuclear facilities, and a virus like Conficker, which infects and spreads to nearly any Windows machine to which it is introduced.

[98] Christopher M. Sanders, "The Battlefield of Tomorrow, Today: Can a Cyberattack Ever Rise to an 'Act of War?'," *Utah Law Review* 2, no. 6 (2018): 510.

remedial *jus ad bellum* is uncertain. Herein lie the limits of present-day customary law to guide restraint in cyberspace.

This stumbling block is not just one for academic commentators; it is, in fact, the basis for an important historical schism in formal government negotiations on the matter. Despite previous successful outcomes producing reports on the application of international law to cyberattacks and related activities, the 2017 GGE failed to reach consensus on precisely these remedial grounds. Experts "could not find common ground over the rights of states to respond to internationally wrongful acts committed through the use of ICTs," and more broadly, "the applicability of international humanitarian law in cyberspace."[99] In particular, the close of the 2017 GGE session revealed deeply divergent preferences and strategies to achieve them. To generalize, a Western group sought to affirm a strong right of self-defense, while other parties such as Russia and China were decidedly uncertain; they implicitly opposed but at a minimum were not willing to embrace it.[100] On this basis, several commentators declared the 2017 GGE as a "failure" in asking whether "international law in cyberspace is doomed," or at least whether there was cause for "pessimism over the future development of cyber norms."[101] While the pessimism proved to be somewhat premature, given the production of a 2021 GGE report that elaborated on some of these norms, later sections will explore why the breadth of the current project might limit its role as a basis for affirmative prohibitions.[102] The additional, UN-sponsored Open-Ended Working Group that emerged as an alternative to the Russian-led cybercrime treaty negotiations has similar status—and limitations.[103]

Even amongst its champions, regulative restraint appears stifled, with key US officials struggling to find evidence any restraint might be practically

---

[99] Samuele De Tomas Colatin, "A Surprising Turn of Events: UN Creates Two Working Groups on Cyberspace," (Tallinn, Estonia: NATO Cooperative Cyber Defence Centre of Excellence, 2018)
[100] "Explanation of Position at the Conclusion of the 2016–2017 UN Group of Governmental Experts (GGE) on Developments in the Field of Information and Telecommunications in the Context of International Security," 2017; Andrey Krutskikh, "Statement By Mr. Andrey Krutskikh, Special Representative of the President of the Russian Federation for International Cooperation in the Field of Information Security on 'Other disarmament measures and international security' Cluster of the 73rd Session of the UNGA" (Russian Ministry of Foreign Affairs, 2018).
[101] Arun Sukumar, "The UN GGE Failed. Is International Law in Cyberspace Doomed As Well?," *Lawfare*, 2017; Alex Grigsby, "The Year in Review: The Death of the UN GGE Process?," *Net Politics*, December 21, 2017; "A Surprising Turn of Events."
[102] *GGE 2021*.
[103] Though the Open-Ended Working Group contains many lines of effort, its most authoritative document is its first final report. See United Nations Open-Ended Working Group on Information and Communication Technologies, *Report of the Open-Ended Working Group on Security of and in the Use of Information and Communications Technologies 2021–2025* (Geneva: UNIDIR, 2021).

observed among its adversaries "out of a sense that it was legally compelled, not out of a sense of policy prudence or moral obligation."[104] This is not strictly a matter of formal negotiations "put[ing] the cart before the horse by calling for an affirmation of legal principles without detailing them or understanding their consequences" for policy; it is a more profound referendum on the utility of *jus ad bellum* in the context of cyberattacks—even if only captures one moment in time.[105]

6.3 Structural Remediation

States have yet to develop these norms at a level of detail that would give shape to the unformed aspects of applied international law, and formal mechanisms for seeking that elaboration have now diverged—perhaps irreconcilably. At a minimum, neither appears to be proceeding on a timeline needed to produce an effective consensus around the specifics of the remedial regime against cyberattacks, and with it, functional regulative restraint.

So where to from here? One approach would be, as with the *Tallinn Manual*, to develop an ambitious but representationally narrower "coalition of near-consensus" seeking to provide bright-line rules reflective of one interpretation of law but intended to shape it among those already inclined to receive its guidance. The OEWG may evolve into such a grouping, however until its work is better elaborated, it is too soon to tell. Another approach would be to accept some commentators' fatalism, to wait until sufficient state practice emerges over time, seek to locate complementary *opinio juris* after the fact and then locate a rule of customary international law. Certainly, this would reflect longstanding traditions of the field. Neither, however, are satisfying to a project seeking durable restraint. The former has little suasion among nonparticipants who happen to be the key pairs in the world's unstable dyads (Russia, China, Iran, Pakistan [or India], even Japan or South Korea). The latter is unsatisfying to those who see restraining cyberattacks as an urgent and growing international security need, as Chapter 1 outlined.

But this recalls Part II's commentary on rationalist restraint; here again, we have a plausible force of restraint—this time regulative—stifled by state

---

[104] Paul C. Ney Jr., "DOD General Counsel Remarks at U.S. Cyber Command Legal Conference," news release, March 2; Krutskikh, "Statement By Mr. Andrey Krutskikh, Special Representative of the President of the Russian Federation for International Cooperation."
[105] Sukamar, "The UN GGE Failed."

uncertainty and lack of consensus over how a key aspect of how the regime would function in practice. Here again, we have seen competition play out but then stall. It cannot be that states will simply go their own ways on interpretation of the remedial *jus ad bellum*; by definition they will, quite literally, come into conflict. States know this, and as a result, are engaged in a competitive process of *structural remediation*—the topic of this final section.

Locating the Competitive Dynamic

States are competing on different levels to fill the informational lacunae that cyberattacks create in international security. One is the project to expound on the application of positive international law, which is documented in the preceding sections. Formal (which is to say reflecting some expression of state policy) and straightforward in its competitive dynamic was the GGE, attempting and at times failing to find consensus on interpretations of customary international law.[106] With that formal competition stalled, bifurcated, or both (depending on perspective) other projects become of interest. Less formally, the *Tallinn Manuals* offer another avenue for competition over the application of law and what it permits, though international representation was by the authors' own admission somewhat narrow. Curiously, *Tallinn* has no peer document on the "other side" of the debate. This is a competition that would seem, at first glance, not very competitive at all.

Is it simply the case that countries with differing views of international law are not on the playing field at all, leaving the Western perspective to establish de facto preeminence with their tightly argued legal conclusions? Or might it be that this level of formal legal elaboration is, in fact, secondary—and to the other side, perhaps even irrelevant—to the establishment of custom that will animate the *jus ad bellum*?

Recent history preliminarily suggests there is indeed a novel competitive dynamic, deemed here "structural remediation," also at play. Structural remediation is a kind of operational preparation of the environment (OPE) for the legal battlefield. It is a competitive process taking place outside the debates over law but deserving of particular attention because of its potentially

---

[106] The GGE is of course yet one level of informality removed from government-to-government treaty negotiations that would provide the most official means of architecting international law, but as the first section of this chapter outlined, it is the closest to formal elaboration of law in present operation.

dispositive role in shaping the future contours of the law's role—specifically, remedial *jus ad bellum* in the context of cyberattacks. It is a customary process that begins with signaling but has now progressed to shaping: boundary-testing to habituate the other to its preferred reading of the law, but entirely removed from and at times contradictory to the state's avowed position in more formal fora.[107]

Three Strategies of Structural Remediation

Three key cyber powers—the United States, Russia, and China—offer emblematic, illuminating, and contrasting approaches to vindicate their preferred outcomes structuring the remedial *jus ad bellum* of cyberattacks. While no brief summary could do justice to all the nuances and competing details of their evolving strategies, the fact that these three powers are in simultaneous legal dialogue and operational conflict reveals telling details about the structural remediation project. All take as their starting point their formal efforts to influence the multilateral elaboration of international law already described, but quickly diverge in the means to achieve their preferred customary outcomes.

United States: Invitation. For Washington, the goal of normalizing lawful armed reprisal to cyberattacks is served in recent years by a strategy of (somewhat perversely) *inviting* threshold events to provoke reaction, blurring the line between preemptive and preventive self-defense. The US strategy can be understood as having two overlapping elements: first, a signaling period of overt contributions and statements of international legal interpretation, and later, an operational period that aims to create a stronger, if somewhat blurred, customary record of outcomes.

---

[107] As mentioned in Chapter 2, the process described here is certainly one of cultivating norms, but only cotangent to the political effort broadly described as "cyber norms process." While they stem from the same general notion—that patterns of peaceful behavior in cyberspace must be cultivated in the international community—the "cyber norms" efforts to date have mostly focused on narrow constructs and novel assertions: e.g., the United States' objection to cyber-enabled state theft of intellectual property, or that early warning obligations once reserved for nuclear and ballistic missile launches should bind in mutual interest the US–Russia cybersecurity relationship. Structural remediation describes an outcome more fundamental; competition over whether cornerstones of the contemporary legal order in international security are applicable. Thus, structural remediation is not simply another competition for a new norm; it is the competition to assert game-changing conditions of law to repel or invite the practice.

The signaling element has its doctrinal origins in some of its earliest cybersecurity strategies from the White House and DOD—covered in previous chapters—which spoke of the full applicability of international law including the *jus ad bellum* and "inherent rights of self-defense" activated by certain cyberattacks.[108] US officials sought to create a broader basis for these claims by including cyberattack response in several aforementioned bilateral defense statements, communiqués, and other interpretations of security treaty law.[109] The result was a clear basis for formal negotiations of a growing consensus, albeit with the United States at its hub, of policies extending the remedial *jus ad bellum* to cyberattacks. If activated, these policies would combine international treaties with custom to create a stronger case for that legal position. In this respect, this appears to have been a strategy waiting for—if not quite inviting—a use case.

The second element of the US strategy, operationalizing, is an extension, an acceleration, and an escalation of the prior approach. Fixed in the Trump administration's decision to enshrine in doctrine a policy to "defend forward," it is testing whether the international legal environment will sustain more robust acts of self-defense against legally dubious uses of force, as well as creating a customary record of reaction that would make more substantial response less jarring.[110]

Some commentators observe this transition to be a rejection of prior policies, in line with the US administration's rhetoric of the era. There may, however, be less change here than meets the eye. Fischerlekker and Harknett are widely credited with articulating "defend forward"—a willingness to disrupt or halt malicious cyber activity at its source, including activity that falls below the level of armed conflict, at its source—and advancing it

---

[108] See Brennan, *Remarks at the Launch of the U.S. International Strategy for Cyberspace*; The White House, *National Cyber Strategy of the United States of America*; US Department of Defense, *Summary of the 2018 Department of Defense Cyber Strategy* (Washington, DC, 2018); US Department of State, *Department of State International Cyberspace Policy Strategy*, Section 402.

[109] Australia Department of Foreign Affairs and Trade, *AUSMIN 2011: Transcript of Joint Press Conference with Defence Minister Stephen Smith, U.S. Secretary of State Hillary Clinton and U.S. Secretary of Defense Leon Panetta (15 September)*; Government of the United Kingdom, *National Security Strategy and Strategic Defence and Security Review 2015: A Secure and Prosperous United Kingdom*, 24; Government of the United Kingdom, *National Security Strategy and Strategic Defence and Security Review 2015: Third Annual Report*; Government of Japan, *Information Security Strategy for Protecting the Nation*; Cho, "Ha Tae Kyoung Interview on the Growing Cyber-Terrorism Threat from North Korea and the South's Response"; Government of Finland, *Finland's Cyber Security Strategy 2019*: The Security Committee, 2019; Government of France, *French National Cyber Security Strategy*: European Union Agency for Cybersecurity, 2015; Government of New Zealand, *New Zealand Strategic Defense Policy Statement*.

[110] US Department of Defense, *Summary of the 2018 Department of Defense Cyber Strategy*.

within the US military.[111] They offer a more nuanced perspective, making a compelling case consistent with the structural remediation concept; that defend forward is a strategy advancing national objectives including in it the contours of law despite the failure of formal negotiations (or in their words, "explicit bargaining").[112] The doctrine's actual evolution bears this out. Willingness to defend forward, as coined in the 2018 Defense Cyber Strategy, a subset of a broader concept of persistent engagement articulated in US Cyber Command's (USCYBERCOM's) 2018 strategic vision document, was met with fanfare for its novelty.[113] It was, however, foretold in part by the first USCYBERCOM commander's insistence that self-defense required that the United States engage in "active defense" at "network speed."[114] USCYBERCOM head General Nakasone pinned the origins of this evolution to 2013, a "strategic inflection point" in which his command's focus on supporting physical military campaigns and "maintain[ing] capacity to respond to an 'attack of significant consequence' against our critical infrastructure," evolved in light of "surprisingly capable adversaries now operat[ing] continuously against critical infrastructure, government networks, defense industries" and other strategic assets.[115] Doctrinally, a straight line connects this pivot to current practice even if, politically, more recent US administrations have seen particular value in broadcasting their intention to impose such "swift *and transparent* consequences."[116]

If the goal of the structural remediation process is to achieve vindication in the elaboration of customary international law, the risk in this second element of US strategy is of overextension. In expressing a willingness to defend

[111] Michael P. Fischerkeller and Richard J. Harknett, "Persistent Engagement and Tacit Bargaining: A Path Toward Constructing Norms in Cyberspace," *Lawfare*, November 9, 2018; Paul C. Ney Jr., *DOD General Counsel Remarks at U.S. Cyber Command Legal Conference* (Department of Defense, 2020).

[112] Harknett and Fischerkeller add, "to note the limited results of explicit bargaining is not to discourage negotiation efforts in pursuit of formal agreements on responsible behavior in the strategic space of armed conflict" ("Persistent Engagement and Tacit Bargaining").

[113] US Department of Defense, *Summary of the 2018 Department of Defense Cyber Strategy*. Specifically, from USCYBERCOM: "This approach will complement the efforts of other agencies to preserve our interests and protect our values. We measure success by our ability to increase options for decision makers and by the reduction of adversary aggression." US Cyber Command, "Achieve and Maintain Cyberspace Superiority: Command Vision for US Cyber Command," 2018.

[114] US Senate Armed Services, *Nominations Before the Senate Armed Services Committee*.

[115] Paul M. Nakasone, "A Cyber Force for Persistent Operations," *Joint Forces Quarterly* 92, no. 1 (2019). This notion of operating continuously is contested, as have other DOD statements attempting to characterize the regularity (and severity) of attempts against military and other networks. In prior years, senior DOD officials suggested the Pentagon was under digital "attack . . . millions of times per day"—though upon review, those remarks were clarified to indicate not attacks, but scans of its networks. See, for example Lynn, "Defending a New Domain."

[116] The White House, *National Cyber Strategy of the United States of America*, 21, emphasis added.

forward the United States could weaken the significance of its formal and stated position of a lawful recourse to force in response to a cyberattack, unless cases of subforce retorsion are known to be such.[117] It is too soon to evaluate the effectiveness of this strategy on the security environment, let alone on the formal negotiations that might use these episodes as a customary basis.[118] A second concern for the structural remediation project is how this strategy "necessitates non-consensual operations into the territory of other States" on a spectrum of perceived severity, including "monitoring the operation of cyber infrastructure, gathering intelligence by such means as exfiltration, prepositioning capabilities, and conducting operations that might cause effects in those countries."[119] Thus, as a strategy to shape outcomes in international law, Schmitt is pointing out the contradictions that may jeopardize the overall project. The "invitation strategy" of structural remediation trades patience for a more developed customary record, even if that record is not predictably at the "time and place of our choosing" that earlier US officials preferred.[120]

Russia: Negation. For Moscow, a goal of *negating* adversaries' lawful reprisal means is served by demonstrations and boundary-testing, creating a customary record of apparent inaction that delegitimizes calls to activate the remedial *jus ad bellum*. Generally, this strategy whittles down the circumstances under which adversaries *do* exercise rights of self-defense as a means to publicly negate their claims such actions *should* do so.

As a doctrinal matter, Russian policy and strategy has long recognized coercive, disruptive, and destructive activities as existing on a gradient spectrum with far less fidelity to the rigid dividing lines articulated in the *jus ad bellum* and advanced by for example the DOD. This structural deterrence strategy has a longer timeline than its present American counterpart; the key known examples that define it are spread over more than a decade. Among them, the most immediately relevant are the presumed cyberattacks on

---

[117] US Department of Defense, *Summary of the 2018 Department of Defense Cyber Strategy*.
[118] That said, the question that this strategy also raises is whether rights of limited preemption accompany the *ad bellum* assertions implicit in the doctrine. This may be a ripe subject for further scholarship as the historical record becomes fuller.
[119] Michael Schmitt, "The Defense Department's Measured Take on International Law in Cyberspace," *Just* Security, March 11, 2020: "It remains to be seen, for instance, how the Department will deal with issues such as the possible existence of a rule of due diligence vis-à-vis cyber operations from or through a State's territory or the numerous law of armed conflict issues surrounding the concept of cyber 'attack.'"
[120] "Statement by the President on Actions in Response to Russian Malicious Cyber Activity and Harassment," 2016.

CONSTRUCTING SELF-DEFENSE   233

Estonia in 2007,[121] the Ukrainian power grid in 2015[122] and 2016,[123] Georgia in 2019.[124] All these represented events that from the preceding analysis, were plausible candidates to meet the use of force and potentially armed attack standard; victims invoking the remedial *jus ad bellum* even rhetorically would have been reasonable. Estonia did just that, though its attempts to invoke collective rights of self-defense were of course mostly rebuffed by the alliance—countenanced after the fact by NATO's doctrinal shift over the dozen years that followed, but not yet by action. Georgia had no such alliance to draw upon, and seemingly no political will to seek Security Council assistance nor (unsurprisingly) to pursue an armed response in self-defense. Here, then, are two incidents, intended as demonstrations, in which Moscow's action can be understood to be not just signaling for deterrence purposes (as Chapters 3 and 4 explored), but also seeking to establish a customary record of inaction to justify their preferred outcome in law—and, in turn, to negate the effects of potential regulative restraint.

Russia's other actions suggest a pattern of expanding the "grey zone" of the remedial *jus ad bellum*—particularly when its scale and effects are debatable. The NotPetya incident targeted global shipping, causing billions of dollars in damage and delays in shipments some might regard as critical to readiness, but with a corporate entity as the direct target rather than a military.[125] The disruption of Swedish media in 2016 plausibly threatened political independence, but only tangentially, and were met with no visible response.[126] Attacks on the government of Montenegro websites in 2017 were one step more direct in threatening governance, but they were met with protest, not assertions of rights to self-defense.[127] Most spectacularly, the brazen attempts

---

[121] As Jason Healey noted in 2017, "Ten years ago, [Russia] put everyone on notice that it was willing to behave badly in cyberspace." Emily Tamkin, "10 Years After the Landmark Attack on Estonia, Is the World Better Prepared for Cyber Threats?," *Foreign Policy*, April 27, 2017.

[122] E-ISAC and SANS Institute, "TLP: White Analysis of the Cyber Attack on the Ukrainian Power Grid Defense Use Case" (Washington, DC, 2016).

[123] Dragos Inc., "Crashoverride: Analyzing the Threat to Electric Grid Operations" (Hanover, MD, 2017); Andy Greenberg, "How an Entire Nation Became Russia's Test Lab for Cyberwar," *Wired*, June 20, 2017.

[124] Dominic Raab, "UK Condemns Russia's GRU Over Georgia Cyber-Attacks," February 20, 2020; David and Santora Sanger, Marc, "U.S. and Allies Blame Russia for Cyberattack on Republic of Georgia," *New York Times*, February 21, 2020; Polish Ministry of Foreign Affairs, "Statement of the Polish MFA on Cyberattacks Against Georgia," February 2, 2020.

[125] Greenberg, "The Untold Story of NotPetya, the Most Devastating Cyberattack in History."

[126] Anthony Culbertson, "Major Cyber Attacks on 'False Propaganda' Swedish Media," *Newsweek*, March 21, 2016.

[127] Government of Montenegro, "Web Portal of Government of Montenegro and Several Other Web Sites Were Under Enhanced Cyberattacks," February 17, 2017.

to interfere in the US election in 2016 were several events, over an extended period of time, that clearly threatened political independence and were invasive (some hallmarks of uses of force). However, their lack of military effect and contested immediacy and directness would have frustrated attempts to assert rights of self-defense. All of these actions seem calculated to achieve not just near-term foreign policy goals against adversaries, or medium-term signaling effects for deterrence, but long-term in effects negating other states' ability to claim rights of self-defense. By selecting acts that fail to meet some of the tests, this strategy erodes other states' ability to invoke the remedial *jus ad bellum* more broadly, whittling its application down to only the most artificial of fact patterns.

China: Deflection. For Beijing, lack of apparent conviction over the outcome of the legal debate—or, perhaps more precisely, a desire to have it all—leads to a preference for ambiguity. This allows China to pursue moderated versions of both strategies while taking preferred outcomes (namely self-defense for borderline economic acts) off the table. China's strategy selectively borrows elements of the prior two, introducing a new element of intentional deflection that necessarily stalls further formal elaboration of the law.

From the US strategy of invitation, the Chinese strategy borrows some measure of signaling with a thin-skinned desire to frequently contest perceived slights that the Chinese government might want to reserve its defensive rights under the remedial *jus ad bellum*. While making bellicose statements about its preparations for cyber conflict as early as 2004, Beijing has when cornered on particular cases reasserted how "the Chinese government, military and relevant personnel never engage in cybertheft of trade secrets" and "firmly oppose and combat cyberattacks of any kind."[128] Experts note the extent to which China's strategies have emerged in "response to the changing cyber warfare approaches and practices of other countries, especially those of the US and Russia."[129]

---

[128] In 2004, China's National Defense "Strategy included language about making full preparations of battle environments: "The PLA takes as its objective to win local wars under the conditions of informationalization and gives priority to developing weaponry and equipment, to building joint operational capabilities, and to making full preparations in the battlefields." *China's National Defense in 2004*, Beijing, 2004. Anna Fifield, "China Rebuffs U.S. Charges of Cyberespionage Over Equifax Hack," *Washington Post*, February 11, 2020.

[129] Jinghua Lyu, "What Are China's Cyber Capabilities and Intentions?" (Washington, DC: Carnegie Endowment for International Peace, 2019), describing China's military strategy (2015), which states the state's objectives for developing cyber capabilities are "cyberspace situation awareness, cyber defense, support for the country's endeavors in cyberspace, and participation in international cyber cooperation." The strategy frames these objectives within the aims of "stemming

Simultaneously, its embrace of the Russian "negation" approach incorporates the grey zone adventurism that permits a narrowing of acceptable scenarios in which others might invoke the rights of self-defense. In particular, China seems fixated on not negating rights of self-defense for perceived attacks of a principally economic character. This may seem puzzling, given the clear legal consensus outlined above that excludes most economic coercion from the use of force standard and quite clearly from the armed attack standard of the remedial *jus ad bellum*. One explanation may lie in those early but aborted attempts by the United States to articulate an "accumulation of events" theory for numerous acts of espionage constituting illegal uses of force, even justifying self-defense. Another perhaps simpler explanation is that Beijing simply has not made up its mind on the preferred contours of law, and instead is focusing its structural remediation on ensuring its areas of orthogonal focus remain squarely permissible.

The combination is not without its risks. Perceptions of intentional deflection and hypocrisy would harm Beijing's ability to sway others to its preferred configurations of custom and law. If the strategy is too slow to evolve, China risks the playing field being overtaken by countries more evangelical about firmer convictions. Finally, this could also be construed as a missed opportunity for Beijing to visibly lead on the world stage as we enter an era of great power competition.

At present, insufficient public documentary evidence of contemporary Chinese cyber strategy and operations precludes a definitive conclusion on motive, but the net effects are traceable. This strategy deflects consensus and attempts to refocus on issues ancillary to the fundamental legal debate, muddying the waters and precluding a compelling customary record from grounding further elaborations of law.

So whose vision of remediation succeeds? With some of these strategies debuting only recently, and with limited public evidence, it is too soon to predict which of these strategies will overtake the others, if at all. With the strengths and weaknesses of each outlined, what is visible today are the fault lines that emerge in their interaction. These three strategies are among the most interesting due to their distinctions, but also because three Security Council members, among the world's most powerful states, espouse them. For the present-day observer, this dynamic will continue, in parallel with

major cyber crises, ensuring national network and information security, and maintaining national security and social stability."

and influenced by the structural deterrence project outlined in Chapter 4. If structural deterrence was trying to influence rationalist calculations by neoliberal means, structural remediation is trying to influence neoliberal regimes through rationalist habituation. The outcome of both are linked, and likely inseparable.

Conclusions

This chapter concluded the inquiry that the last began: whether the *jus ad bellum* was well-positioned to serve as a meaningful restraint to cyberattacks. Like the last chapter, it found considerable grounds that international law would recognize and provide some tools to oppose their use in the international system, it also identified crucial grey areas where law and practice provided few guarantees for states seeking the reassurance of a remedial regime. It also identified that states are rapidly rushing to fill that gap, pursuing a range of projects to structure the remedial landscape to realize their preferred outcome. Those strategies are showcasing governments' willingness to push boundaries and rapidly develop the customary environment. They do so, however, at considerable risk of emboldening their opponents or manufacturing outcomes other than those they prefer. The bifurcation of the multilateral negotiating process on precisely this issue of self-defense suggests this fissure will feature significantly into the evolution of the debate. It is too soon to tell the likely victor of these projects, and without any indication there, that these strategies are just as likely to stoke more cyberattacks and associated activity as they are to constrain it. Those seeking durable sources of restraint may, for now, have to look elsewhere.

PART IV
HUMANITARIAN PROTECTIONS

7
Humanitarian Protections

When the US president sits in the White House Situation Room to review options for combating terrorist threats, it is safe to assume that a chemical weapons strike is not presented as an option. Biological agents are not presented as opportunities to gain battlefield advantage, nor are blinding lasers proposed as ambush-thwarting add-ons to armed convoys in Iraq. Similarly, options that include mass leveling of towns sympathetic to Bashar Al-Assad or the bombing of dams to wash out advancing regime fighters, are not offered in Syria. For all the firepower associated with the largest, best-funded, most advanced military in world history, an observer unfamiliar with the laws of war might be puzzled by the United States' apparent restraint. Some of those options would not be militarily advisable, perhaps expending too many resources for a limited objective, or less effective in achieving it than other tools. Yet other tools, well-suited to a particular security objective, are nonetheless left off the table. Why?

One set of explanations was addressed in Part II: the expected retribution potentially in store for countries making such choices. Another was partially explored in Part III: how certain general prohibitions within international law, those actions rising to the level of a use of force and armed attack, violate legal agreements to which the country has committed—and, importantly, permit acts of self-defense. But a third, overlapping logic of restraint is also at play here: countries and their leaders maintain constitutive notions, for instance of being law-abiding or humanitarian, that differentiate their actions from others—or more often, their forbearers. This is the explicit motivation for Part IV of this study: how such a constitutive logic of restraint could hold back cyberattack decisions through strictures formal and informal, present and potential.

Part IV begins where the last chapter left off, continuing an inquiry into the international law governing force, but this time with a distinct canon of law: the *jus in bello* governing behavior after the outbreak of hostilities. Unlike the approach taken in Chapter 5, a broad textual analysis of cyberattacks *within* the *jus in bello* is of limited value, since our purpose is to find what might restrain cyberattacks, not regularize them, and condition militaries for their use. Here, the *jus in bello* serves a narrower but no less crucial purpose: to inform whether or not cyberattacks as defined in this study, might be *inherently* unlawful under its broad diktats and thus, as a practical matter for countries with humanitarian concerns, unusable. This would be a powerful disincentive if it can be justified in part because the motivations behind adherence to the *jus in bello* are significant: among them, a constitutive logic of restraint grounded in various concepts of civility and shared humanity. To engage effectively with the law in this narrower context, this part reframes its mode of analysis from regulative adherence to a more explicitly normative mutual constitution. Chapter 7 begins this inquiry.

These shared notions of humanity have also given rise to prohibitions more familiar to those outside of international law: a series of specific and formal bans on certain "means and methods" of warfare that raise unusual humanitarian concerns—chemical weapons, biological weapons, and land mines, to name a few.[1] Cyberattacks do not fall directly under any of those particular categories, but do they have salient features in common, and in turn, raise similar questions about their usability? Such resonance would offer two intriguing possibilities: first, cyberattack use may become a dividing line between groups of states giving basis for some kind of prohibitive norm; and second, the consensus dismissing informal or formal restraints on cyberattacks may be premature. Indeed, should cyberattacks inherently violate its provisions, history suggests some level of state restraint could form against their use, causing cyberattacks to suffer a similar fate to those other prohibited weapons. Chapter 8 carries that analysis forward.

Combined, these two chapters will probe regulative regimes for constitutive logics that could be applicable—even portable—to restraining cyberattacks. Humanitarian protection is the thread that binds these regimes together and, perhaps, provides clues to the defining characteristics and prospects of such a regime focused on cyberattacks.

---

[1] See Kim Coleman, *A History of Chemical Warfare* (New York: Palgrave Macmillan, 2005); Joshua Lederberg, *Biological Weapons: Limiting the Threat* (Cambridge, MA: MIT Press, 1999); Maxwell A. Cameron, Brian W. Tomlin, and Robert J. Lawson, eds., *To Walk without Fear: The Global Movement to Ban Landmines* (Oxford: Oxford University Press, 1998).

Outline of Argument

This final part of the study argues that where rationalist and regulative logics of restraint have revealed themselves to be unlikely sources of durable restraint, a constitutive logic draws together many of the missing pieces and may offer the best prospects.

Chapter 7 begins by framing the kind of humanitarian protections that emerge from and give shape to this logic of restraint—those governing the conduct of warfare. Though the range of such protections is vast, two areas are of particular interest: rules governing lawful means and methods, and "exceptional prohibitions" on extremely problematic weaponry.[2] With respect to the former, the substantial scholarly work on how the *jus in bello* regulates "lawful" cyber operations provides an opportunity for a distinct and focused inquiry: on what basis cyberattacks as defined herein may themselves be inherently *unlawful*. It discovers several key provisions of the *jus in bello* that in the abstract, fundamentally problematize the permissibility of large-scale cyberattacks. At a minimum, it suggests skepticism as to the usability of the tool, and perhaps a stronger basis for restraint. This result also provides a prism through which to understand one paradox of the present moment: a doctrine of normalization among Western states that has not been met by frequent and overt practice. It argues that there is a crucial missing piece to determining the impact of these conclusions: the basis that a customary (or even codified) prohibitive norm against cyberattacks might emerge.

Chapter 8 argues that properly scoped, this logic provides ample basis for a certain kind of prohibitive norm, if not a formal regime keeping a check on that restraint. It begins by asking the question of why, in light of the foregoing, conventional wisdom has dismissed the sort prohibitions on cyberattacks that exist for chemical or biological weapons. The chapter then draws together the arguments of those preceding it to confirm that while "usability" has been the defining competition among states for the last two decades, a deeper look into the logics of states' cyberattack policies reveals a parallel process called "structural prohibition," is also underway. That competitive process is unique among the others in that laid against state doctrine, it might provide a means to escape the present impasse. It then examines cyberattacks

---

[2] Of less interest to this study, though notable for the attention they have received by scholars, are the permissible modalities of use—the primary focus in, for instance, *Tallinn 2.0*.

in the context of exceptional prohibitions against certain means of warfare, arguing that cyberattacks share some key salient features with other exceptionally prohibited weapons, rendering cyberattacks preliminary candidates for similar treatment on the basis of law. It then argues that technological, economic, and political developments in recent years motivate a fresh evaluation of this question of specific prohibition of cyberattacks. Drawing on the rich literature of norm formation and novel weaponry and using the very frameworks that in much earlier analyses yielded dim prospects, it finds in new evidence the emergence of a tightly constructed prohibitive norm. The result, it argues, is the strongest potential for cyberattack restraint: a novel, narrowly focused humanitarian norm against cyberattacks—appealing equally and sequentially to states' constitutive, regulative, and rationalist logics of restraint.

7.1 Approaching Humanitarian Protections

This section provides a primer on the *jus in bello*—the humanitarian regulation of hostilities—that later sections will consider in the context of cyberattacks. It begins by recognizing the rich normative history of the concepts; then offers an account of the present law's key contemporary sources; distinguishes between specific and general rules of conduct; and outlines the obligations states and their militaries have to comply with both. The chapter's later sections will then consider whether and how cyberattacks violate these general protections.

Constitutive Origins and History

The origins of international law governing conduct in warfare are deep and longstanding, reflecting the establishment and evolution of custom that predates by centuries the Geneva, Hague, and other conventions associated with the modern law. By most accounts, one key concept—the distinction between combatants and civilian populations—extends to the earliest records of organized warfare, and even its positive incarnation in proto-international law far predates the Westphalian state system. The Greeks and Romans observed principles of order and restraint in their armed hostilities through a series of "unwritten conventions," amounting to "socially constructed and socially maintained rules of war" that were in turn reflected in epic accounts of great battles and reinforced by that same mythology.[3] Those same traditions—variously justified as matters of divine decree, honor, chivalry, or "humanity"—all contained some element distinguishing noncombatants or protected classes, informing more theologically grounded guidance recognized (if not always practiced) by European soldiery for centuries. At their core, these traditions emerged from constitutive notions, where restraint served a range of functions bound up in identity, observed as imperfect custom.

Eventually, these customs gave way to regulation. Among the earliest codifications was the 989 A.D. *Peace of God* declared between the Archbishop of Aquitania and warring nobility, which laid out clear protected classes from warfare that included women, children, church property, and rudimentary forms of neutral noncombatants and commerce.[4] Raymond of Peñafort's 1234 *Summa de casibus poenitentiae*, intended as a guide for confessors, was oft-cited after its publication and made clear requirements of, inter alia, a distinction between "offenders and the innocent."[5] In the Middle Ages, rules of engagement and chivalry were used to discipline armies and regularize the conduct of hostilities, drawing in turn on rigorous social distinctions between the armed *nobilis* and the "unarmed, vulgar heard of common humanity," in what became a rudimentary form of distinction.[6] In the seventeenth century, practice and certain limited treaties also sought to protect innocents caught in armed struggle, permitting the release of women and certain children free of ransom.[7] Similar concepts can also be found in Gustavus Adolphus's 1621 Articles of War drawn up for soldiers departing to fight Russia in the Baltics.[8]

These notions have had restraining effect not just on individual combatants, but on the conduct of states generally since their earliest interactions; from

---

[3] Robert C. Stacey, "The Age of Chivalry," in *The Laws of War: Constraints on Warfare in the Western World*, ed. Michael Howard, George J. Andreopoulos, and Mark R. Schulman (New Haven, CT: Yale University Press, 1994), 13, 17.

[4] R. G. D. Laffan, ed. *Select Documents of European History, 800–1482* (New York: Henry Holt, 1929), 94. as cited in Henrik Syse and Endre Begby Gregory M. Reichberg, ed. *The Ethics of War: Classic and Contemporary Readings* (Oxford: Blackwell Publishing, 2006), 94–95.

[5] Laffan, *Select Documents of European History, 800–1482*, 133.

[6] Stacey, "The Age of Chivalry," 29. See also Maurice Keen, ed. *Chivalry* (New Haven, CT: Yale University Press, 1984); Maurice Keen, *The Law of War in the Late Middle Ages* (New York: Routledge & Kegan Paul, 1965).

[7] Ingrid Detter, *The Law of War*, 2nd ed. (Cambridge: Cambridge University Press, 2000), 152.

[8] Adam Roberts and Richard Guelff, *Documents on the Laws of War*, 3rd ed. (Oxford: Oxford University Press, 2000), 3.

early modern Europe on, the *jus in bello* came to represent "a powerful combination of natural and divine law, ecclesiastical precepts, military law, common custom, and self-interest," imbued with "enduring consistency."[9] By the end of the seventeenth century—well before most recognized international law had taken shape—England, Switzerland, Sweden, and Germany had developed codes of conduct for their armed forces, which at a high level sought to protect civilians from marauding and other misdeeds. Following the transition from the limited wars of nobles and kings to the "wars of nations" synonymous with eighteenth- and nineteenth-century Europe, a "passion for codification" emerged. Adam Roberts describes this passion as starting with the 1856 Paris Declaration on Maritime Law and leading to the 1868 Saint Petersburg Declaration's famous statement "that the only legitimate object which states should endeavor to accomplish during war is to weaken the military forces of the enemy."[10] An ocean away, the first comprehensive and modern attempt to distill these traditions as guidelines for soldiers was ventured by the American lawyer Lieber, and codified by American President Lincoln to guide the conduct of his troops during the Civil War.[11] The Lieber Code was later adopted as the basis for similar guidelines by over a half-dozen powers in the period 1870–1893.[12] It was no coincidence that the Red Cross, devoted to the alleviation of suffering in war, was founded in 1870.[13]

Today, we the bedrock of the *jus in bello* the 1899 and 1907 Hague conferences that gave international relations its most famous examples of positive law seeking to restraining the manner in which warfare is conducted. The Conventions they produced remain among the most widely recognized and durable aspects of the positive law of war and a longstanding if partial

---

[9] Geoffrey Parker, "Early Modern Europe," in *The Laws of War: Constraints on Warfare in the Western World*, ed. Michael Howard, George J. Andreopoulos, and Mark R. Schulman (New Haven, CT: Yale University Press, 1994), 42.

[10] Adam Roberts, "Land Warfare: From Hague to Nuremberg," in *The Law of War: Constraints on Warfare in the Western World*, ed. Michael Howard, George J. Andreopoulos, and Mark R. Schulman (New Haven, CT: Yale University Press, 1994), 119.

[11] Instructions for the Government of Armies of the United States in the Field, General Orders, No. 100, April 24, 1863. See also Richard R. Baxter, "The First Modern Codification of the Law of Armed Conflict," *International Review of the Red Cross* 29 (1963).

[12] These included Prussia in 1870, the Netherlands in 1871, France in 1877, Russia in 1877 and 1904, Serbia in 1878, Argentina in 1881, Great Britain in 1883 and 1904, and Spain in 1893. See Thomas Erskine Holland, *The Laws of War on Land (written and unwritten)* (Oxford: Clarendon Press, 1908), 71–73.

[13] David P. Forsythe, *The Humanitarians: The International Committee of the Red Cross* (Cambridge: Cambridge University Press, 2005).

tradition of seeking restraints thereupon.[14] Today, they serve as the basis for the modern understanding of distinction as applied both to states, in the form of "neutral rights and obligations," and the more familiar version applied to "non-combatant" individuals.

Sources and Applications of Law

When governments and their militaries speak of restraint in war, they often reference these underlying constitutive notions of humanity and mercy, but more commonly position their actions with respect to positive international law: the *jus in bello*, also known as "international humanitarian law" (IHL), or the "law of armed conflict" (LOAC).[15]

These are the treaty commitments that represent the positive international humanitarian law, which fall into two general categories.

Exceptional Prohibitions. The first are laws prohibiting certain means and methods of warfare—typically types of weaponry—and tend to be specific and prohibitive. While later sections will return to these prohibitions, it is worth noting that they typically engage most explicitly with new technologies in warfare: innovations that for reasons discussed later, grant them a particular status of humanitarian incompatibility and attendant "unusability." As a formal matter, such agreements include the Chemical Weapons Convention, the Biological Weapons Convention, the Ottawa Treaty banning anti-personnel land mines, as well as more esoteric documents such as the Cluster Munitions Convention and Protocols Additional to the Convention on Certain Conventional Weapons covering blinding lasers, injurious fragments not detectable by X-ray, and more.[16] While no agreements

---

[14] A 1993 report by the UN Secretary-General to the Security Council reaffirmed this notion, citing only four documents that comprise "the part of conventional international humanitarian law which has beyond doubt become part of customary international law: this 1907 Hague Convention IV, the four 1949 Geneva Conventions, the 1948 Genocide Convention and the 1945 Charter of the International Military Tribunal at Nuremberg. See United Nations Secretary-General, "Report of the Secretary-General Pursuant to Paragraph 2 of Security Council Resolution 808 (1993)" (New York: United Nations, 1993).

[15] While textual nuances exist in various scholars' application of these phrases, here, they are used to generally describe this canon of law and used equivalently.

[16] Convention on the Prohibition of the Use, Stockpiling, Production and Transfer of Anti-Personnel Mines and on their Destruction (March 1); Convention on the Prohibition of the Development, Production, Stockpiling, and Use of Chemical Weapons and on Their Destruction; Convention on Cluster Munitions (August 1); Chemical Weapons Convention; Protocol on Blinding Laser Weapons (Protocol IV to the 1980 Convention on Certain Conventional Weapons) (October 13);

govern cyberattacks directly, later sections examine the commonalities between the means and methods subject to exceptional prohibition, their distinctions from their lawful counterparts, and the salient features they share with cyberattacks.

General Regulations. The second set of regulations govern all other nonprohibited means and methods. As more general articulations applicable across a wider range of conduct, they are consistently reflecting, reinforced by, and elaborated upon by custom—perhaps more so than the specific prohibitions mentioned above. Like those specific regulations, however, they are also expressions of principle that are designed to create a "civilized," "humanitarian," or at least "orderly" conduct of hostilities. Oxymoron though it may be, they have not just shaped the vocabulary of international security and law, but bled into the popular consciousness as well. That the Geneva Conventions (typically referring to the 1949 Geneva Conventions on the Protection of Victims of War and their Additional Protocols) are a source of general awareness reflects their hallowed customary status. Also central to the *jus in bello*'s general regulations, and central for this analysis, are the Hague Conventions of 1899 and 1907 and the aforementioned Geneva Conventions' 1977 Additional Protocols—all of which have since had various provisions incorporated directly into military manuals and doctrine.[17] Combined, they lay out a comprehensive set of expectations for everything from the conduct of soldiers to targeting, weapons selection, and the treatment of third parties.

Overarching Principles

The "right of belligerents to adopt means of injuring the enemy is not unlimited," the Hague Convention (IV) with Respect to the Laws and Customs

---

Convention on Prohibitions or Restrictions on the Use of Certain Conventional Weapons Which May Be Deemed to Be Excessively Injurious or to Have Indiscriminate Effects (and Protocols) (as Amended on 21 December 2001) (December 10).

[17] Protocol Additional to the Geneva Conventions of 12 August 1949, and relating to the Protection of Victims of International Armed Conflicts (Protocol I) (June 8). 1125 U.N.T.S. 3 (hereafter, "AP1"); Convention (II) with Respect to the Laws and Customs of War on Land and its annex: Regulations concerning the Laws and Customs of War on Land. The Hague, July 29, 1899 (July 29); Hague Regulations: Convention (IV) Respecting the Laws and Customs of War on Land and its annex: Regulations concerning the Laws and Customs of War on Land (October 18).

of War on Land famously proclaimed.[18] Embedded within that exhortation, and given expression by the documents of the modern LOAC, are certain basic principles animating the *jus in bello*: its bedrocks of distinction and proportionality, as well as concepts of military necessity, minimizing unnecessary suffering, and chivalry.

Distinction (also referred to as discrimination) is a deeply rooted principle of the *jus in bello* and as the brief introduction showed, has been a force in the conduct of states since their earliest interactions. While the following section will engage with the principle and key terms in greater depth, at its core it requires that during armed conflict states distinguish between combatants and military objectives, and civilians and civilian objects. Together the Hague and Geneva Conventions inform our contemporary understanding of distinction and how it applies to both the rights and obligations of states and different classes of individuals, as well as to any objects that may carry protected status. Additional Protocol I Article 48 enshrines this notion clearly, stating "parties to the conflict shall at all times distinguish between the civilian population and combatants and between civilian objects and military objectives and accordingly shall direct their operations only against military objectives."[19] Article 51(4) states that "indiscriminate attacks are prohibited."[20] Indiscriminate attacks can take the form of attacks that are not targeted at a specific military objective (e.g., carpet bombing).[21] Another form of an indiscriminate attack is using a combat method or means that is incapable of being focused against a specific military objective.[22] In addition, methods that produce harm to military objectives and civilians or civilian objects without distinction are prohibited.[23] While these are separate approaches to this requirement, they may overlap in practice—such as the problems created by "dropping munitions, guided or not, in a residential area without regard to whether there are combatants or military objectives in the area simply because there 'might be' adversary forces."[24] To that end,

---

[18] Hague Convention (IV) Respecting the Laws and Customs of War on Land, Art. 22: "The Hague Regulations do not as such specify that a distinction must be made between civilians and combatants, but Article 25, which prohibits 'the attack or bombardment, by whatever means, of towns, villages, dwellings, or buildings which are undefended,' is based on this principle"; International Committee of the Red Cross, "Customary International Humanitarian Law: Rule 1. The Principle of Distinction between Civilians and Combatants."

[19] *API*, Art. 48.

[20] Ibid., Art. 51(5)(a)(b).

[21] Ibid., Art. 51 para 4(a)

[22] Ibid., Art. 51 para 4(b)

[23] Ibid., Art. 51 para 4(c)

[24] As applied by a military manual with intent to guide cases like these, see *Air Force Operations and the Law*, 3rd ed. (US Air Force, Judge Advocate General's School, 2014), 271.

opposing parties in armed conflict must adhere to a two-part framework for distinguishing between such legal classes of persons and objects. The *DOD Law of War Manual* explains the two sets of duties for distinction as necessarily: "(1) discriminating in conducting attacks against the enemy; and (2) distinguishing a party's own persons and objects."[25]

The principle of proportionality demands taking precautionary actions to minimize collateral damage in armed conflict, and occupies much of Section 7.4. This notion of proportionality is distinct from its *ad bellum* counterpart.[26] It concerns not the response to another party's actions, but the relationship in a belligerent's own decision-making between military gain and the humanitarian consequences of a particular course of action. In essence, the analysis for proportionality entails evaluating the projected gains of a military operation alongside the forecasted harmful consequences to the civilian population.[27] For these reasons, proportionality is likened to being a "fulcrum" for balancing the other *jus in bello* principles of military necessity and unnecessary suffering.[28] Speaking to their customary significance, though the United States has not ratified Additional Protocols I and II (though is a signatory), and thus it is not under its domestic laws bound by them, this and other concepts are consistently referred to and underlie analysis in the country's military manuals.[29]

The third principle of military necessity aims to minimize violence to be the requisite amount necessary to defeat enemy forces. One of the earliest codifications of this concept appeared in the Lieber Code in 1863.[30] Article 14 of the Lieber Code codified military necessity and delineated that it "consists in the necessity of those measures which are indispensable for securing the ends of the war, and which are lawful according to the modern

---

[25] "Department of Defense Law of War Manual," 62.

[26] The terminological overlap between *ad bellum* and *in bello* concepts has created a stumbling block in the elaboration of the laws of war, and cyber operations in particular. See, for example, *Tallinn* Rules 13, 30, and 38 and accompanying commentary. *Tallinn 1.0*, 50.

[27] *AP1*, Art. 51; *AP1*; Art. 57(2)(iii). In application, this principle "does not establish a separate standard, but serves as a means for determining whether a nation, military commander, or others responsible for planning, deciding upon, or executing a military operation have acted with wanton disregard for the civilian population." *Air Force Operations and the Law*, 18.

[28] *Air Force Operations and the Law*, 18.

[29] Ibid., 12: "The United States has not ratified a number of international agreements. Notable examples include Additional Protocols I and II, the 1982 UN Convention on the Law of the Sea, the 1997 Ottawa Treaty banning anti-personnel mines, and the 2008 Oslo Treaty on cluster munitions. As a result, United States' allies and coalition partners may be operating under different laws relating to armed conflict."

[30] Francis Lieber, "Instructions for the Government of Armies of the United States in the Field," United States War Department, (Washington: Government Printing Office, 1898).

law and usages of war."[31] Article 23 of the Annex to Hague Convention IV expressly mentions the necessities of war and prohibits states from destroying or seizing enemy property, "unless such destruction or seizure be imperatively demanded by the necessities of war."[32] Thus, military necessity does not authorize any and all forms of military action and possible destruction.[33] The US Air Force's *Operations and the Law* manual states that "under no circumstances may military necessity authorize actions specifically prohibited by the law of armed conflict, such as the murder of prisoners of war or the taking of hostages."[34] To help oversee the proper application of this principle, the Rendulic Rule offers some temporal guidance.[35] Under the Rendulic Rule, military necessity is determined according to the information known at that specific point in time, not according to information received after the fact.

The fourth principle is the limitation of unnecessary suffering. This concept serves to minimize incidents of exceptionally grave humanitarian impact, even in the context of war.[36] Additional Protocol I Article 35 states: "It is prohibited to employ weapons, projectiles and material and methods of warfare of a nature to cause superfluous injury or unnecessary suffering."[37] While some critics hold a somewhat pessimistic view of the law of war's robustness, one would be remiss to discount the progressive efforts to improve upon the edifices of the law of war to reduce unnecessary suffering.[38] To this point, Roberts and Guelff concede that the laws of armed conflict helped precipitate the acceptance of certain norms to inhibit unnecessary suffering to certain classes of persons like children, and to certain locations such as hospitals and cultural property sites.[39]

---

[31] Ibid.
[32] Annex to 1907 Hague (IV), Article 23(g).
[33] *Air Force Operations and the Law*, 13.
[34] Ibid.
[35] "Department of Defense Law of War Manual," 57. "Military necessity does not justify actions that are prohibited by the law of war" (ibid., 53).
[36] Convention II with Respect to the Laws and Customs of War on Land and Its Annex: Regulations Concerning the Laws and Customs of War on Land. The Hague, July 29, 1899. Article 23 of the Annex forbids the use of "arms, projectiles or material calculated to cause unnecessary suffering."
[37] *AP 1*, Art. 35; *AP1*, Art. 51: "The civilian population and individual civilians shall enjoy general protection against dangers arising from military operations. To give effect to this protection, the following rules, which are additional to other applicable rules of international law, shall be observed in all circumstances."
[38] Roberts, *Documents on the Laws of War*, 31.
[39] Ibid. For example, "that prisoners of war are to have their lives spared and to be treated humanely; that a state may be entitled to be neutral *vis-à-vis* an armed conflict involving other states . . . that certain places (e.g. hospitals) are not legitimate targets in warfare; [and] that persons not

Lastly, the principle of chivalry (also referred to as honor) refers to fairness in the battle environment and the proper amount of mutual respect to opponent forces.[40] Its framing is controversial but some of its underlying requirements enjoy greater recognition. For instance, perfidy and perfidious acts such as misusing a flag of truce will be subsequently explored in this chapter. Perfidy, as defined in Additional Protocol I, Article 37(1) refers to "acts inviting the confidence of an adversary to lead him to believe that he is entitled to, or is obliged to accord, protection under the rules of international law applicable in armed conflict, with intent to betray that confidence."[41] Committing perfidious acts in the *jus in bello*—like using false flags and insignia for protection is also prohibited under the Lieber Code.[42] While the term "perfidy" is sometimes substituted for "treachery," as seen in the 1874 Brussels Declaration, and Hague IV regulations, this study will exclusively use the term perfidy.[43] At a basic level, perfidy is about leveraging protections under LOAC under a false pretense in order to gain an advantage (i.e., engaging in unchivalrous, or dishonorable conduct).[44] According to the United Kingdom's *Joint Service Manual of LOAC*, the prohibition of perfidy is necessary "to prevent the abuse, and the consequent undermining, of the protection afforded by the law of armed conflict."[45] Further, this examination will focus on both concepts of perfidy—conduct that is prohibited and forms of deception under AP I that may or may not be prohibited as a ruse of war.[46]

Distinction and proportionality are the most critical of these four overarching principles when analyzing whether or not cyberattacks are inherently violations of the *jus in bello* will occupy the balance of this chapter. Certain clauses seeking to limit unnecessary suffering will have relevance both here and especially in the chapter that follows.

---

taking an active part in a conflict (e.g. children) should be spared from the consequences as much as possible."

[40] *Air Force Operations and the Law*, 19.
[41] *AP1*, Art. 37.
[42] Lieber Code. Article 117: "It is justly considered an act of bad faith, of infamy or fiendishness, to deceive the enemy by flags of protection. Such act of bad faith may be good cause for refusing to respect such flag."
[43] *Project of an International Declaration Concerning the Laws and Customs of War*, Article 13(b); "Department of Defense Law of War Manual," 319.
[44] *AP1*, Art. 37.
[45] UK Ministry of Defence, *JSP 383: The Joint Service Manual of the Law of Armed Conflict* (London, 2004), 60.
[46] "Department of Defense Law of War Manual," 319; Norwegian Defence Command and Staff College, *Norway Manual of the Law of Armed Conflict* (Merkur-Trykk AS: The Chief of Defence, 2018), 197.

Obligations of States to Comply

Treaty commitments and the customary law they represent create not just general obligations of conformity, but also specific positive requirements relative to the advent of new and potentially problematic technologies in war.

Prior chapters have established how the cyberattacks under examination in this work are definitionally uses of force, potentially armed attacks, and thus straightforwardly initiate hostilities between belligerents if they did not already exist, inherently invoking the *jus in bello*.[47] Many regard the threshold for activation of IHL as even lower—for instance to any activities seeking injury to another party, or other activities that might enhance one military's capabilities at the expense of the other—but in light of the foregoing these are weaker grounds to recognize the applicability of the law. Some, however, have questioned whether "use of force" in the *jus ad bellum* is indeed synonymous with "a resort to armed force" or "hostilities" between two or more states, typifying international armed conflict under the *jus in bello*.[48] While the debate itself is ancillary to the key questions here, this study concurs with Roscini's view that cyberattacks "amount to a 'resort to armed force' when they entail the direct use of cyber means or methods of warfare in support of a belligerent to the detriment of another," and have the effects described in Section 1.3.[49]

New technologies are no less regulated within the *jus in bello* than longstanding ones, cyberattacks included. In fact, Roberts and Guelff go so far as to ground the entire Geneva and Hague conventions—and in turn much of modern IHL—on "the result not so much of blithe optimism, as of a real fear of *new weaponry* and of total war."[50] As matter of explicit applicability, the Martens Clause, first appearing in the preamble to the 1899 Hague

---

[47] See, e.g., Schmitt, "Cyber Operations and the Jus in Bello."

[48] That the subject of this study is interstate conflict is not to detract from the rich contemporary literature on intranational or internal conflicts has emerged within the *jus in bello*. See, for example, cases associated with the International Criminal Tribunal for the Prosecution of Persons Responsible for Serious Violations of International Humanitarian Law Committed in the Territory of the Former Yugoslavia Since 1991 (hereafter ICTY). The conclusions here are notionally portable to internal strife, consistent with one of most ICTY's most significant conclusions. In the *Tadić* case, noting "what is inhumane, and consequently proscribed, in international wars, cannot but be inhumane and inadmissible in civil strife"—albeit in "general essence" more than textual specifics. ICTY, *Prosecutor v. Duško Tadić, Decision on the Defence Motion for Interlocutory Appeal on Jurisdiction*, ICTY-94-1, paras 119, 126 (1995).

[49] Roscini, *Cyber Operations and the Use of Force in International Law*, 136.

[50] Roberts, "Land Warfare," 120 (emphasis added).

Convention II with Respect to the Laws and Customs of War on Land, is of seminal importance asserting these principles of law over new evolutions in technology: "In cases not included in the Regulations adopted by them, populations and belligerents remain under the protection and empire of the principles of international law, as they result from the usages established between civilized nations, from the laws of humanity and the requirements of the public conscience."[51] Article 1(2) of the 1977 Additional Protocol I to the 1949 Geneva Conventions (Additional Protocol I, or API) recalls and sharpens this concept: "In cases not covered . . . civilians and combatants remain under the protection and authority of the principles of international law derived from established custom, from the principles of humanity, and from the dictates of public conscience."[52]

The general applicability of these provisions to all instruments of conflict, not just those invented at the time of treaty signature, has since been firmly established by the International Committee of the Red Cross (ICRC), the UNGA, and most compellingly the ICJ.[53] In its *Nuclear Weapons Advisory Opinion*, the ICJ noted that the Hague and Geneva Conventions at the foundation of the law of armed conflict "[apply] to all forms of warfare and to all kinds of weapons, those of the past, those of the present, and those of the future" despite inevitable differences among them.[54] All these reasons support the ICRC's conclusion that "means and methods of warfare" leveraging cyber operations generally, including cyberattacks, "are subject to IHL just as any new weapon or delivery system has been so far when used in an armed conflict by or on behalf of a party to such a conflict"—in short, even if not "expressly prohibited or regulated by existing treaties . . . limits exist."[55] Rule

---

[51] Convention (II) with Respect to the Laws and Customs of War on Land. Its foundational role is affirmed in *Nuclear Weapons Advisory Opinion*, para 78. See also *Tallinn 2.0*, 378.

[52] *API*, Article I, para 2. Applicability is generally acknowledged but not entirely uncontested. One might claim that the United Kingdom's reservation that "the rules introduced by the Protocol apply exclusively to conventional weapons without prejudice to . . . other types of weapons" would in the UK's view limit applicability to cyberattacks. Such a perspective is, however, countertextual; the UK clearly intends to focus this reservation on nuclear weapons, as the United States did with its similar intervention.

[53] *API*, Article 36: "In the study, development, acquisition or adoption of a new weapon, means or method of warfare, a High Contracting Party is under an obligation to determine whether its employment would, in some or all circumstances, be prohibited by this Protocol or by any other rule of international law applicable to the High Contracting Party."

[54] *Nuclear Weapons Advisory Opinion*, para 86.

[55] International Committee of the Red Cross, "International Humanitarian Law and the Challenges of Contemporary Armed Conflicts" (Geneva: October 31, 2011), 36–37; International Committee of the Red Cross, "International Humanitarian Law and the Challenges of Contemporary Armed Conflicts" (Geneva: October 2015), 40.

80 of *Tallinn 2.0* seeks to reaffirm and establish this principle specific to cyber operations.[56]

To give discipline to this affirmation, Article 36 of the 1977 Geneva Protocol I creates, with cyberattacks as a novel instrument of warfare with uncertain international status, a positive obligation to ascertain compliance:[57] "In the study, development, acquisition or adoption of a new weapon, means or method of warfare, a High Contracting Party is under an obligation to determine whether its employment would, in some or all circumstances, be prohibited by this Protocol or by any other rule of international law applicable to the High Contract Party."[58]

Of course conducting weapons reviews for cyber capabilities is a matter for national militaries, and the associated complexities are only exacerbated by certain state-specific traditions and transparency limitations—notable but outside the scope of this study.[59] Rather, having firmly established the necessity to comply with the general provisions of the *jus in bello*, the sections that follow consider whether or not cyberattacks raise fundamental issues that would rightly prompt hesitation on the part of any county bound to the principles therein.

7.2 Indiscriminateness

As the ICJ made clear in the *Nuclear Weapons Advisory Opinion*, the first of the "cardinal principles contained in the texts constituting the fabric of international humanitarian law . . . is aimed at the protection of civilian

---

[56] *Tallinn 2.0*, 375. Its commentary does explicitly—if dubiously through a more contemporary lens—disclaim the 2007 events in Estonia as ineligible for this requirement, on the assertion those activities did not rise to the level of an armed conflict. Russia's actions against Georgia and Ukraine, however, would be eligible given the broader context of ongoing kinetic hostilities amounting to an armed conflict.

[57] Duncan Blake and Joseph S. Imburgia, "Bloodless Weapons: The Need to Conduct Legal Reviews of Certain Capabilities and the Implications of Defining Them as Weapons," *Air Force Law Review* 66 (2010).

[58] *Additional Protocol I (1977)*, Article 36. Arguably, the customs that have emerged from these bureaucratized weapons reviews and the international negotiation regarding their scope, content, and transparency, also serves a certain constitutive function—creating a "club" of states further signaling their general recognition of the *jus in bello*.

[59] Gary D. Brown and Andrew O. Metcalf, "Easier Said Than Done: Legal Reviews of Cyber Weapons," *Journal of National Security Law & Policy* 7 (2014). This study does not propose specific means by which militaries should conduct so-called Article 36 weapons reviews; however, the analysis to follow may well inform some of the key considerations factored into that undertaking.

populations and civilian objects."[60] This section considers the many contours of this contested notion, identifying whether cyberattacks might, regardless of context, run afoul of the following overarching protections.

Generally, Additional Protocol I Article 51 establishes that "indiscriminate attacks are prohibited," defining such attack as those which "are not directed at a specific military objective," "employ a method of means of combat which cannot be directed at a specific military objective," or "employ a means or method of combat the effects of which cannot be limited as required by this Protocol."[61] This leads to two potential grounds upon which cyberattacks might inherently violate distinction: first, if incapable by design of meeting requirements to distinguish, or second, if they necessarily injure specially "protected classes" of civilians and civilian objects.

Inability to Distinguish

The principle of distinction in armed conflict "requires a party to the conflict to only target other parties to the conflict—a party may not target a civilian or civilian object."[62] To that end, Additional Protocol I Articles 50–54 seek to reduce unnecessary suffering to the civilian population and individual persons.[63] Article 50 defines civilians as persons who are not members of the armed forces and defines the civilian population as all persons who are civilians.[64] Article 51 instructs that such persons "shall not be the object of attack" and that "acts or threats of violence the primary purpose of which is to spread terror among the civilian population are prohibited."[65] Article 52 articulates the general protection of civilian objects and, though less relevant to our purposes here, Article 53 decrees the protection of cultural objects and "historic monuments, works of art or places of worship which constitute the cultural or spiritual heritage of people."[66]

The most relevant input for these purposes is "civilian objects," which are essentially any objects that are not military objects.[67] Military objects are

---

[60] *Nuclear Weapons Advisory Opinion*, para 78.
[61] *API*, Art. 51 para 4(a)(b)(c).
[62] Peter Pascucci, "Distinction and Proportionality in Cyber War: Virtual Problems with a Real Solution," *Minnesota Journal of International Law* (2017): 430.
[63] *API*, Art. 50–54.
[64] Ibid., Art. 50.
[65] Ibid., Art. 51(2).
[66] Ibid., Art. 52; Art. 53(a)(b)(c).
[67] Ibid., Art. 52(1). Pascucci, "Distinction and Proportionality in Cyber War," 430.

defined in Article 52(2) as "those objects which by their nature, location, purpose or use make an effective contribution to military action and whose total or partial destruction, capture, or neutralization, in the circumstances ruling at the time, offers a definite military advantage."[68] Focusing on civilian objects, Article 52(1) decrees that "civilian objects shall not be the object of attack or of reprisals."[69]

Article 52(1)'s definitional understanding of "attacks" is informed by Article 49 of Additional Protocol I, which defines attacks as "acts of violence against the adversary, whether in offence or in defence."[70] Article 49 applies to "all attacks in whatever territory conducted."[71] The term "acts of violence" from Article 49(1) does not only apply to kinetic harm.[72] Rather, as the *Tallinn* experts held, the effects of the action determine if it constitutes "acts of violence" under Article 49(1).[73]

Can data itself be an object in armed conflict? On this question, Schmitt notes the majority of *Tallinn* experts "took the position that the law had not advanced that far and that pre-existing law could not be definitively interpreted to encompass data within the meaning of 'objects.'"[74] Under Article 52(1)'s distinction of military objectives, the key question to explore is: What is the relationship between civilian and military objects specifically? Granted, as Geiß and Lahmann concede, theoretically "a civilian object in the 'physical world' could also fall within the definition contained in Article 52(2) of Additional Protocol I. . . . however, most civilian objects in the real world simply have no significant military potential and therefore will never be used in a militarily conducive way."[75] On this nexus between civilian and

---

[68] *AP1*, Art. 51(2).

[69] Ibid., Art. 52; Art. 53(a)(b)(c).

[70] Ibid., Art. 51(2): "The provisions of this Section apply to any land, air or sea warfare which may affect the civilian population, individual civilians or civilian objects on land. They further apply to all attacks from the sea or from the air against objectives on land but do not otherwise affect the rules of international law applicable in armed conflict at sea or in the air." The *Tallinn Manual* notes that "by this widely accepted definition, [under AP1, Art. 49] it is the use of violence against a target that distinguishes attacks from other military operations. Non-violent operations, such as psychological cyber operations or cyber espionage, do not qualify as attacks." *Tallinn 1.0*, 106.

[71] Ibid., Art. 49(2).

[72] Pascucci, "Distinction and Proportionality in Cyber War," 443, 444.

[73] *Tallinn 1.0*, 106: "'Acts of violence' should not be understood as limited to activities that release kinetic force. This is well settled in the law of armed conflict. In this regard, note that chemical, biological, or radiological attacks do not usually have a kinetic effect on their designated target, but it is universally agreed that they constitute attacks as a matter of law.""

[74] Michael Schmitt, "The Notion of 'Objects' During Cyber Operations: A Riposte in Defence of Interpretive and Applicative Precision," *Israel Law Review* 48, no. 1 (2015): 81.

[75] Robin Geiß and Henning Lahmann, "Cyber Warfare: Applying the Principle of Distinction in an Interconnected Space," *Israel Law Review* 45 (2012): 389.

military objects in cyberspace, Pascucci opines that "increased reliance on civilian and commercial facilities and equipment blurs the distinction between civilian objects and military objectives, and thus the initial determination of lawfulness."[76]

For instance, when applied to cyberattacks, both military and civilian facilities—and the equipment housed within—rely upon a common cyber infrastructure to transmit data. On one hand, it is possible that under Article 54 data could constitute an object of "indispensable to the survival of the civilian population." On the other hand, the legal analysis is murkier since under international law, data has not been traditionally held as an object.[77] The majority in *Tallinn Manual* did not view data as being part of the traditional conceptualization of an object under the law of armed conflict as "data is intangible and therefore neither falls within the 'ordinary meaning' of the term object nor comports with the explanation of it offered in the ICRC Additional Protocols Commentary."[78] Other scholars have critiqued this understanding and called for a reinterpretation of an object under Article 52(2) based on emerging forms of state conflict in cyberspace.[79] Schmitt counters persuasively that classifying data as an object "provides no meaningful clarity to the identification of permissible military targets. This is because if data is an object and qualifies as a military objective, it may be attacked. If it is not an object, then such qualification is meaningless since the prohibition does not apply; it may be targeted provided a loss of functionality does not ensue."[80] It is therefore not terribly helpful to the study at hand.

Cyberattacks as Inherently Indiscriminate

Are cyberattacks capable of discriminating between military objectives and civilian objects? As a preliminary matter, the technological composition of cyberspace militates against applying a bright line rule for the *jus in bello* principle of distinction. As Geiβ and Lahmann point out, "the application of the accepted legal definition of military objectives in the interconnected

---

[76] Pascucci, "Distinction and Proportionality in Cyber War," 430.
[77] *API*, Art. 54; Pascucci, "Distinction and Proportionality in Cyber War," 420; *Tallinn 2.0*, 437.
[78] Schmitt, "The Notion of 'Objects' During Cyber Operations," 86.
[79] Ibid., 94–95.
[80] Ibid., 101: "From the perspective of those planning, approving, executing or commenting on an attack, labelling data as an object provides no greater clarity than saying it is not data."

cyber domain will render basically every cyber installation a legitimate military objective. In cyberspace, every component of the cyber infrastructure is a dual-use object."[81] On the matter of dual-use objects—an object that qualifies both under the definition of military objective contained in Article 52(2) of Additional Protocol I and as an object commonly used for civilian purposes—civilian telecommunications infrastructure, crucially relied upon by governments as well, are an emblematic example.[82] The interconnectedness and dependency of civilian and military cyber systems and infrastructure counteracts the argument that cyberattacks are capable of discriminating against military objectives and civilian objects in armed conflict. As evidence of this challenge, Jensen writes that:

> [Because] government communications [are] routinely traveling over civilian communication lines, there will be many civilian lines of communication that will carry targetable electronic traffic intermixed with civilian traffic. Those specific military communications are still targetable, but the networks and lines would not be. However, because of the nature of electronic communications, it is very difficult to target a single communication once it is in transit.[83]

Given these operational targeting challenges, as well as the complex, interconnected nature of cyberspace, it may be reasonable to find many cyberattacks inherently indiscriminate and, as we shall see, challenged under unidentifiability grounds.

Unidentifiability

For militaries to have any hope of observing distinction on the battlefield in real time, there must be rapid means to distinguish combatants and their matériel from civilian counterparts. The obligations of identification support this function, but as they were designed for a different era of warfare, they raise notable questions for cyberattacks. To comply with the *jus in bello*, perhaps the

---

[81] Geiß and Lahmann, "Cyber Warfare," 383.
[82] Stockton Center for the Study of International Law, "The Conduct of Hostilities and International Humanitarian Law: Challenges of 21st Century Warfare," *International Law Studies* 93 (2017): 328. See also Eric Talbot Jensen, "Cyber Warfare and Precautions Against the Effects of Attacks," *Texas Law Review* 88, no. 7 (2010): 1542.
[83] Jensen, "Cyber Warfare and Precautions Against the Effects of Attacks," 1545.

most specific obligation of a combatant for the purposes of distinction is self-identification, or declaration—in other words, making clear the individual is not a civilian. Much of the functioning of the law of war, particularly land war, is contingent upon this basic requirement. Its history and present-day status attest to its near-universal recognition. The Annex to the Hague Convention IV (1907) offers the clearest articulation of combatant obligations still in general operation today: that a state's belligerents must "have a fixed distinctive emblem," must "carry arms openly," and must "conduct their operations in accordance with the laws and customs of war."[84] The requirement can be summarized as a declaration, but it reflects a concept already common in this study: attribution. The notion that the agents of belligerence must themselves be attributed is almost universally respected among regular forces today, with requirements (perhaps less broadly observed) extending that obligation "to militia and volunteer corps," the irregular forces of the era.[85] These norms are now codified in Additional Protocol I's Article 44, obliging combatants to "distinguish themselves from the civilian population," and in Articles 37, 38, and 39, prohibiting the abuse of national, civilian, or other "distinguishing emblems."[86]

If such markings are a prerequisite for a permissible belligerent, a state's cyberattackers surely must face the same requirement. Doing so is, however, practically challenging. The badges on a cyberattacker's uniform, when said soldier is behind a machine several thousand miles away, offers little to other combatants. In fact, the characteristics of the individual executing the attack are from a humanitarian standpoint instrumental to the law having its intended effect, since it is unlikely that immediate harm would come to a person mistaken to be the operator of a cyberattack.[87] A rough analogy is possible, since a pilot is not only clad in uniform, but the aircraft she flies also has affixed to it certain emblems

---

[84] *1907 Hague (IV)*, Annex, Article 1.
[85] Ibid., Annex, Preamble.
[86] *AP1*, Art. 44, 37–39. As the *Tallinn 2.0* experts noted, this rule is further elaborated in the ICRC review of customary IHL, Rule 106: Jean-Marie Henckaerts and Louise Doswald-Beck, *International Committee of the Red Cross, Customary International Law*, vol. 1: Rules (Cambridge: Cambridge University Press, 2009).
[87] Exceptions exist, of course; the US assassination of Junaid Hussein and, outside the context of armed conflict, US criminal indictments and sanctions against cyber operators from North Korea and China. Presently, such actions are atypical. See "Junaid Hussain, ISIS Recruiter, Reported Killed in Airstrike;" US Department of Justice, "North Korean Regime-Backed Programmer Charged With Conspiracy to Conduct Multiple Cyber Attacks and Intrusions," news release, September 6, 2018; US Department of Justice, "Chinese Military Personnel Charged with Computer Fraud, Economic Espionage and Wire Fraud for Hacking into Credit Reporting Agency Equifax," news release, February 10, 2020.

distinguishing it from a civilian aircraft. The line between belligerent agent and instrumentality is, however, not perfectly clear. Pilots and planes carry emblems, as do intercontinental ballistic missiles; but artillery shells do not. As a particular matter, there is no such thing as a noncombatant artillery shell. There is no civilian object against which to distinguish. This further explains why unmanned instrumentalities, like drones and ballistic missiles, tend to carry such emblems. This argument is stronger than the supposition that only those belligerent instrumentalities carrying human persons must display emblems (to distinguish civilians therein).

Rather than focus on identification of the individual, the law seemingly demands identification of the instrumentality itself—a missile or, in the case of a cyberattack, the computer of origin or data stream that constitutes the delivery means. Since computers, networks, and the human processes upon which they rely might be subject to collateral damage of retribution, the law is clear that *something* recognizable to the victim must distinguish a cyberattacker at the time of execution.

The current practice certainly suggests that cyberattacks have difficulty complying with the requirement. The *Tallinn 2.0* experts came to no satisfying, practicable conclusion on the matter. As of this writing, no acts approximating cyberattacks have been publicly known to carry the kind of identification clearly required by international law and custom.[88] The present condition is one in which states have chosen to hide behind the realities of the technology and undertake those actions more covertly—perhaps in part recognizing the failure to comply with these strictures. At issue is whether in so doing they are acting in accordance with the most reasonable or practical interpretation of this rule as it applies to cyberattacks, or whether they actually reinforce the case that the act itself may be legally impermissible.

It is not, as a general matter, impossible for cyberattackers to distinguish themselves or their matériel accordingly; it is simply inconvenient to do so, and both technologically simple and militarily useful to do otherwise. Conversely, cyberattacks are not in all instrumentalities, in all technological scenarios, anonymous operations. Though much ink has been spilled decrying the permanent anonymity of the cyberattacker, and the impossibility of assigning that individual to any one state, this is a period-specific

---

[88] *Tallinn 2.0*, 405–06.

prognosis.[89] Methods of obfuscation will continue to be available, just as covert commandos and apparent merchant vessels laden with explosives remain available to conventional militaries. Not atypically, the question of compliance with the law has some inverse relationship to efficacy, surprise, and deniability. The most relevant legal question is whether the obfuscation that is common today is a derogation of either the affirmative obligation to identify, or the negative one against perfidy.[90]

At least under present conditions, cyberattacks bring the risks of perfidy front and center by certain aspects of the underlying technology they exploit. At a high level, the fact that internet traffic is traditionally routed irrespective of national borders, on the most efficient route between origin and destination, creates a kind of emblem (or more of a passport) in the form of its routing history, but an arbitrary one. Beyond the issues of violating neutral territory which will be discussed shortly, this phenomenon is widely known, and any state taking precautionary measures described below would be aware of this reality. As a result, the attacker is left with three choices. One is to accept the convenient ambiguity and permit the signals to create the appearance of wrongful origin—an act of mislabeling that appears on its face perfidious—a violation of Additional Protocol I's Article 39 on Emblems of Nationality.[91] A second would be to ensure that signals "hop," or transverse, multiple geographies to temporarily obfuscate their true origin, a common tactic among cyber operators. This approach is only somewhat less apparently perfidious, and potentially more escalatory, so unappealing at best. The third option would be to engage in the kind of precautions that would label the attack by nation of origin, but to do so would create significant and potential means by which the inbound signal could be identified, filtered, and here its effects neutralized, limiting attack efficacy.

One objection to this argument is that Article 39's reference to "flags and military emblems" limits the scope of its effect. But in the case of cyberattacks and for the reasons above, such technical signatures are indeed the only plausible means of satisfying the Article 44's obligations, which themselves are not

---

[89] US House of Representatives, Subcommittee on Technology and Innovation, Committee on Science and Technology, *Untangling Attribution: Moving to Accountability in Cyberspace (Testimony of Robert Knake)*, 2010.

[90] Affirmations of the prohibition on perfidy include Article 16 of the Lieber Code; Article 37 of the 1977 *Geneva Protocol*; Article 17 of the 1954 *Hague Convention for the Protection of Cultural Property*; and Protocol II of the 1980 *U.N. Convention on Prohibitions or Restrictions on the Use of Certain Chemical Weapons*.

[91] *API*, Art. 39.

limited to flags—only that combatants "distinguish themselves." A second objection might be that "ruses of war" designed to "mislead an adversary or induce him to act recklessly" are clear and delineated exceptions.[92] This is true, but importantly within Additional Protocol I, conditioned on the ruse "infring[ing] no rule of international law" and not relying upon confusion about protected status.[93] Enriching data with the traces of third-nation origin is not akin to "camouflage, decoys, or mock operations," to the extent they are relied upon as de facto identifiers by operators, in which case they would strike at the heart of the means by which a defender would recognize whether engagement was permissible.[94]

Noting this concern, a few commentators have implied a solution of ensuring every "packet" of data be authoritatively identified with a "national marker."[95] That solution is attractive but challenging.[96] This study will not dwell on the technical design of a regime that would suffice, particularly given the numerous and changing vectors for executing a cyberattack. Regardless, the difficulty of solution does not obviate the clarity of requirement, and the simplicity of dodging it does not from a legal (or customary) standpoint excuse attackers for making such a choice. The potential for a violation of law, perhaps for reasons endemic to the internet's technological architecture, is significant. When protection of innocents demands identification of belligerents, states make certain concessions of covertness. Cyberattacks are not legally questionable because they are so often anonymous. Rather, interstate actors carrying them out are legally suspect in leveraging technology to obfuscate their responsibility. So long as this practice of de-identification remains custom, cyberattacks will as a matter of law carry the stigma associated with violating this basic provision of the *jus in bello*.

---

[92] 1907 Hague (IV), Annex, Chapter 2, Article 24; *AP1*, Art. 37(2).
[93] *AP1*, Art. 37(2).
[94] Ibid.
[95] See, e.g., John Savage and Melissa Hathaway, "Stewardship of Cyberspace: Duties for Internet Service Providers," in *Cyber Dialogue: What is Stewardship in Cyberspace?* (Toronto: University of Toronto, Munk School of Global Affairs, 2011), (draft); John Savage and Les Bloom, "On Cyber Peace" (Washington, DC: The Atlantic Council, 2011).
[96] It may also be self-defeating. If a network signature were to identify military origin and likely the country thereof, as befits distinct emblems, doing so may well compromise the efficacy of the attack itself. It may be tantamount not to wearing a patch on a battlefield, but to revealing the location of combatants awaiting a surprise attack. The practical (i.e., political) opposition to complying with this norm is likely to be profound.

Neutrality

While the law of neutrality extends beyond the *jus in bello*, the practical reality of cyberattacks contemporaneously implicating third parties and their intended targets requires brief consideration here.

States not participating in a declared armed conflict, as well as states without any direct standing to be implicated in hostilities, are noncombatant entities said to be "neutral" to it—a condition that carries with it certain rights and duties.[97] As a phenomenon in international relations, neutrality is a concept as old as the notion of interstate war, as any state not party to a conflict was, by definition, neutral. Modern neutrality was particularly influential in maritime practice, providing a means to prevent a belligerent from interfering with vital interstate trade.[98] The constituent ideas of this principle are straightforward enough: namely, that there is collective benefit in keeping armed disputes limited to belligerents, and that the codification of certain rights guaranteed to those outside conflict would in turn help limit undue spread of war.

Over the last three centuries, these ideas crystallized into more specific customs. Those customs were, in turn, sufficiently common as to form the basis of positive legal obligations viewed for over a century as reflecting customary international law. After the first codification in the 1899 Hague Convention II, the 1907 Hague Convention V on *Respecting the Rights and Duties of Neutral Powers and Parties in the Case of War on Land* remains the foundational, systematic articulation of these rights and duties.[99]

The first obligation of neutrality falls to belligerents; they must treat "the territory of neutral powers" as "inviolable," and not to transit their territory in the movement "of troops or convoys of either munitions of war or supplies."[100] Two aspects of present-day cyberattacks might violate neutral territory by analogy: first, an attackers' data transiting of third-country

---

[97] Detter, *The Law of War*, 171.
[98] Roberts, *Documents on the Laws of War*, 85–87. Terminologically, Roberts notes that the terms "neutral," "non-belligerent," and "other states not Parties to the conflict" are effectively synonymous, with the same laws applying to all; the only distinction may come in the marginal case of a party that seeks to favor one party above another, while still acting short of participation in the conflict itself. Ibid., 86.
[99] Hague Convention (V) Respecting the Rights and Duties of Neutral Powers and Persons in Case of War on Land. Additional mention of neutral obligations can be found in the Geneva Conventions as well, specifically 1949 Geneva (IV), Article 11.
[100] 1907 Hague (V), Article 1. Further affirmed by the ICJ as customary international law in *Nuclear Weapons Advisory Opinion*, para. 88–89.

networks en route to the target network, and second, the use of a neutral states' "network resources" (i.e., machines) to carry out an attack.

Whether or not an attacker violates sovereign neutrality rests on whether a country's digital networks are more closely analogized to its territory, its territorial waters, or its radio airspace.[101] Does a packet of data transiting fiber-optic cables residing within one state's borders for a matter of milliseconds constitute an incursion on its face? That claim seems far-fetched—especially when the technical basis for how such signals are transmitted are by default border-agnostic—and thus either of the latter two comparisons is appealing. States have revocable obligations to permit "innocent passage" through its territorial waters. But that passage seems hardly innocent when the data in question is instrumental in a cyberattack. Likewise, states are under no international legal obligations to carry even "innocent" data traffic across their borders in the way they are maritime traffic; they do so for matters of efficiency.[102] Therefore, reviewing the letter of the law in the specific *jus in bello* context, the analogy to a state's radio airspace seems most apt. Notably, Hague V explicitly and presciently clarifies, states are "not called upon to forbid or restrict the use on behalf of the belligerents of *telegraph or telephone cables* or of *wireless telegraphy apparatus* belonging to it *or to companies* or private individuals."[103] Today's network cables and switches fall well within that same definition. The data used in a cyberattack is, fundamentally, a series of signals on telecommunications cables, sometimes sent wirelessly, and over infrastructure belonging in most cases to private companies. Straightforwardly, this analogy holds.

However, given the *jus in bello*'s broader intent of the maintenance of limited conflict, there is reason to reconsider whether the letter of the law matches its spirit. The basis for the protection afforded to neutral states is a desire to exclude them from unwarranted injury from a conflict in which they have no precipitating role. The prohibition on troops transiting neutral territory serves not as a mere ritual to inconvenience belligerents; its basis lies in protecting those on sovereign territory from shouldering the burden of those assets or injury for which they bear no responsibility.

---

[101] The latter refers to airspace not conventionally controlled (as it is with the passage of air traffic), but which a country could without violating international law limit third-party transmissions through. In this respect, radio airspace differs from territorial waters, another potential analogy, since there is no international-legal guarantee of innocent passage through radio airspace.

[102] There is great debate, for instance, as to whether or not the US president needs the domestic authority to unilaterally deny passage to foreign data for national security reasons. See Declan Mccullagh, "Renewed Push to Give Obama an Internet 'Kill Switch,'" *CBSNews*, January 24, 2011.

[103] 1907 Hague (V), Section 5, Article 8. Emphasis added.

Extending the analogy, it is more than plausible that a cyberattack, in transiting a neutral party's network, could result in undue harm to that neutral state. It is true that any network-based attack would transit third parties to reach its destination by virtue of the internet's basic operation. However, because of that same architecture, the attack would appear to be "emanating" from the neutral state's territory. If a victim state chooses to respond by striking the source of inbound fire, absent better intelligence about the source, it may well target networks in the neutral third state. This would be precisely the kind of delimitation of territory that the principle of distinction necessarily creates, and so much of the law of war seeks to reinforce.[104]

Consider also if an attacker were to co-opt infrastructure residing within a state's borders, for instance, by building malware on an infected machine in a neutral state before infecting the target computer. Doing so would not just run afoul of both the *jus in bello* premise of neutral distinction (by inviting counterattack), but also Hague's clear prohibition on belligerents "erect[ing] on the territory of a neutral power a wireless telegraphy station or other apparatus for the purpose of communicating with belligerent forces."[105] Even more obviously prohibited would be recruiting from a third state so-called patriotic hackers of the sort purportedly a part of the Russian campaign against Georgia. For the same principle of not drawing others unduly into conflict, Hague explicitly prohibits the formation of "corps of combatants" and "recruiting agencies . . . to assist the belligerents."[106] The conclusions of *Nicaragua* also recall this point, in the context of the ICJ's holding that the United States' arming of insurgents in Nicaragua constituted wrongful intervention.[107]

More general provisions and more recent commentary on the matter further support the general view of cyberattack transit violating the right of neutral parties; however, some state doctrine has bristled against this concept. Hague V Article 2 forbids belligerents from moving movement of troops *or munitions of war* across the territory of neutral states.[108] Most *Tallinn* experts saw a clear analogy to be drawn between how transmissions of a cyberattack must be broken down into packets as they transverse territory (literally, infrastructure located thereupon) to reach their destination and have effect.[109]

[104] Detter, *The Law of War*, 168.
[105] 1907 Hague (V), Article 3.
[106] Ibid., Art. 4.
[107] *Nicaragua*. 1986; see also *Air Force Operations and the Law*, 13.
[108] 1907 Hague (V), Art. 2.
[109] *Tallinn 2.0*, 554–55, 57.

Particularly with the concerns of perfidy and potential for violation of the spirit of neutral protections intended to keep innocent states out of war, this seems a more justifiable position, frustrating though it is to some militaries. It is not uncontested, however; a minority of *Tallinn 2.0* experts found it unduly burdensome.[110] The DOD acknowledges the legal implications of the transmission of "cyber weapons" via infrastructure that is owned, or located in a neutral territory, however, it is still unsettled on how "overflight rights" extend to cyberspace, if at all.[111] Its most recent cyberspace operating manual briefly acknowledges the issue of minimizing risks to neutral parties in conducting cyberspace operations. Specifically, it holds that "achieving a commander's objectives can be significantly complicated by specific elements of cyberspace being used by enemies, adversaries, allies, neutral parties, and other USG departments and agencies, all at the same time. Therefore, synchronization and deconfliction of [Commanding Officer] access is critical to successful operations of all types."[112] A final rejoinder might claim again that transiting a neutral state's networks, as many do, is a low-impact but essential

---

[110] Ibid., 555. While it is unsettled how "overflight rights" extend to cyberspace, the DOD has at least acknowledged the legal implications of the transmission of "cyber weapons" via infrastructure that is owned, or located in a neutral territory. US Department of Defense, *Department of Defense Cyberspace Policy Report: A Report to Congress Pursuant to the National Defense Authorization Act for Fiscal Year 2011, Section 934*, 2011. 8. The *Tallinn* experts also weighed in on the matter and were divided as to whether Article 2 of Hague Convention V prohibited the transmission of weapons by cyber means, or if an exception to this existed under Article 8 of Hague Convention V. *Tallinn 1.0*, 252; 1907 Hague (V).

[111] US Department of Defense, *Department of Defense Cyberspace Policy Report: A Report to Congress Pursuant to the National Defense Authorization Act for Fiscal Year 2011, Section 934*; Joshua E. Kastenberg, "Non-Intervention and Neutrality in Cyberspace: An Emerging Principle in the National Practice of International Law," *Air Force Law Review* 64, no. 43 (2009): 44–45; "U.S. policy since 1983 provides that the United States will exercise and assert its navigation and overflight rights and freedoms on a worldwide basis"; US Department of Defense, "U.S. Department of Defense Inspector General, Agency Financial Report for FY2018," 2017. Bothe writes that "overflight and stopover require permission. A neutral state may place conditions and restrictions on overflight." Michael Bothe, *The Handbook of International Humanitarian Law* (Oxford: Oxford University Press, 2013), 577. With regard to overflight permission requirements, Article 31 of AP1 reads: "Except by prior agreement, medical aircraft shall not fly over or land in the territory of a neutral or other State not a Party to the conflict. However, with such an agreement, they shall be respected throughout their flight and also for the duration of any calls in the territory. Nevertheless, they shall obey any summons to land or to alight on water, as appropriate." AP1, Art. 31(1). Lastly, for guidance on situations wherein a medical aircraft flies over the territory of a neutral party "in the absence of an agreement or in deviation from the terms of an agreement'," Rule 182 of the San Remo Manual on International Law Applicable to Armed Conflicts at Sea, directs the aircraft to "make every effort to give notice and to identify itself. Once the aircraft is recognized as a medical aircraft by the neutral State, it shall not be attacked but may be required to land for inspection. Once it has been inspected, and if it is determined in fact to be a medical aircraft, it shall be allowed to resume its flight." *San Remo Manual on International Law Applicable to Armed Conflicts at Sea* (June 12), Rule 182.

[112] "Joint Publication 3–12: Cyberspace Operations," I-5. JP 3-13 also advises Joint Force Commanders to "continuously seek to minimize risks to the joint force, as well as to friendly and neutral nations, societies, and economies, caused by use of cyberspace." Ibid., IV-20.

act of tactical subterfuge, a ruse of warfare long held to be both necessary and permitted in armed conflict.[113] It may be tactically advantageous, but the permission of rouses must be read in conjunction with broader affirmative obligations on identification of combatants just discussed. In the absence of this counterweight, the legality of the ruse is highly suspect.

The conclusion here is that in some configurations and to remain consistent with the law, absent clear identification and routing, many cyberattacks will certainly violate the guarantees to neutral third parties. The conclusion does not render cyberattacks unusable but does suggest a clear state interest in their circumscription, regulation, or proscription. Thus, in the interest of their own self-defense, such perceived violations might provide states a first basis to question the permissibility of the practice itself and certainly an opportunity, if not obligation, to prevent it.[114]

7.3 Injury to Protected Classes

In addition to general protections to civilian populations and objects, the *jus in bello* accords particular protections to certain would-be targets, adding further complexity to whether cyberattacks are capable or incapable of "distinguishing between civilian and military targets" as required by international law.[115] This section considers the objections that might be raised to cyberattacks on these specific grounds—including medical personnel; objects indispensable to the civilian population; installations holding back dangerous forces; and provisions for the civil defense. It will evaluate in turn whether the sorts of precautionary measures required in Article 57 may be plausible, and ultimately, their inherent legality as a category.

Medical Personnel and Duties

The protection of civilian medical personnel as an exceptionally protected class is fundamental to the *jus ad bellum* and international custom.[116]

---

[113] 1907 Hague (IV), Annex, Chapter 2, Article 24; *AP1*, Art. 37(2).
[114] See *Tallinn 2.0*, 558–59 (Rule 152).
[115] *Nuclear Weapons Advisory Opinion*, para. 78.
[116] Separately, military medical units have long been subject to protected treatment; these are however less relevant to the present analysis. See *AP1*, Art. 12.

Examining the status of civilian medical facilities first—under Article 13, such facilities are protected—as well as civilian hospitals in combat areas. On this matter, the Additional Protocol I is unequivocal: "civilian medical personnel shall be respected and protected" and the "protection to which civilian medical units are entitled *shall not cease* unless they are used to commit, outside their humanitarian function, acts harmful to the enemy."[117] Additional Protocol I even creates a positive obligation of assistance for the military, a rare provision in the context of the document, to provide "all available help ... to civilian medical personnel in an area where civilian medical services are disrupted by reason of combat activity," and further to ensure "access to any place where their services are essential."[118] This distinction, if not obligation, is firmly established as custom among states.[119] The question turns to whether cyberattacks raise particular concerns on this basis.

As recently as twenty years ago, the argument that cyberattacks substantially interfered with medical personnel in the performance of their duties would have been thin. While aspirations of widespread electronic medical records and telemedicine abounded in the early days of the internet, they often collided with realities of decidedly analog medical systems and minimal interoperability.[120] Gradually in the early 2010s, however, a combination of enhanced connectivity, increasing financial pressures on Western medical systems for efficiency, and the capability of certain medical devices to have internet-connected interfaces created a more sizable dependence of the civilian healthcare sector on functioning critical information infrastructure. Crucially during this period, large national health systems also transitioned to more centralized databases that were, in turn, dependent on internet connectivity.[121] Ransomware incidents in 2017 and 2022 on the

---

[117] Ibid., Art. 15(1); Art. 12. emphasis added.

[118] Ibid., Art. 15(2), (4).

[119] Norway's manual on the law of war, to choose one example, holds such an affirmative obligation. See Norwegian Defence Command and Staff College, *Norway Manual of the Law of Armed Conflict*, 82.

[120] In 2013 nearly three of every four physicians reported using Electronic Health Records and "with this increase in adoption, the medical community is now beginning to appreciate both the promise and perils of 'going electronic.' There is no question that computerization has made patients' records more available and legible. With respect to completeness, however, there are now complaints that the record is too complete: electronic notes are deemed by many clinicians as being full of extraneous details and obscuring important aspects of a patient's condition." James J. Cimino, "Improving the Electronic Health Record: Getting What We Wished For," *JAMA* 309, no. 10 (2013): 991.

[121] In 2018 the UK NHS attributed the reason for its data breach, involving the loss of privacy of 150,000 patients in England, due to a coding error. "Those affected had requested that their confidential health information only be used to help provide them with care. But it appears that there was a problem with the software used by GPs to record objections to the same data being used for research

UK National Health System (NHS) played out such case on a small scale, affecting dozens of trusts, hundreds of thousands of computer systems, and causing outages in the systems used to dispatch ambulances, book appointments, and issue emergency prescriptions.[122] This trend increased and took on new urgency during the COVID-19 crisis, when for reasons of prophylactic social distancing, telemedicine (e.g., mobile phone-based video visits with practitioners) finally entered into mainstream care, at least in developed countries.[123]

By targeting critical information infrastructure, cyberattacks can be expected to have three potential effects on civilian medicine, if that infrastructure is shared: on access to care (by interfering with telemedicine), on the administration of ongoing care (by interfering with access to records), and on the efficacy of treatment (by limiting the utility of internet-connected medical devices). As other sections have made clear, the unpredictability of secondary cyberattack effects makes this risk knowable to the attacker, but not necessarily manageable. Of course, when the victim country does not share the digital health trends outlined above, this concern is far less significant. Likewise, if countries rely on truly separate information infrastructure to serve their medical needs (no present examples of which are known, but could plausibly be the case in the future), this risk is further attenuated.[124]

---

and auditing purposes." *BBC News*, "NHS Data Breach Affects 150,000 Patients in England," July 2, 2018. The United States is an outlier here based on its private healthcare system, which as a function of its atomization causes it to lags behind in civilian access to electronic medical records in the private sector (less so, for instance, for the federally administered Veterans Affairs healthcare system, the nation's largest).

[122] Roger Collier, "NHS Ransomware Attack Spreads Worldwide," *Canadian Medical Association Journal* 189, no. 22 (2017); BBC News, "NHS 111 Software Outage Confirmed as Cyber-Attack," August 6, 2022.

[123] Judd E. Hollander and Brendan G. Carr, "Virtually Perfect? Telemedicine for COVID-19," *New England Journal of Medicine* (2020). Already, 50 US health care systems including some of the nation's largest have such systems, the use of which increased substantially during the crisis.

[124] Within a representative set of nationalized healthcare services, none appear to currently rely on distinct, non-internet connected networks for core functionalities. See, e.g., Australia: Australian Digital Health Agency, "My Health Record System Security," *My Health Record* (2018). Austria: Tosh Sheshabalaya, "Healthcare Information Technology in Austria and Switzerland," *Health Management* 5, no. 2 (2010). South Korea: Young Moon Chae, "Going Abroad of Korean Health Information Systems," *Healthcare Informatics Research* 20, no. 3 (2014). France: Merav Griguer and Jean Baptiste Thienot, "France Launches Healthcare Big Data," *Bird & Bird*, July 2017 and Bernard Nordlinger, Cédric Villani, and Daniela Rus, *Healthcare and Artificial Intelligence* (Berlin: Springer Nature, 2020). Switzerland: Carlo De Pietro and Igor Francetic, "E-Health in Switzerland: The Laborious Adoption of the Federal Law on Electronic Health Records (EHR) and Health Information Exchange (HIE) Networks," *Health Policy* 122, no. 2 (2018); Peter J. Meier-Abt et al., "The Swiss Approach to Precision Medicine," *Swiss Medical Weekly*, February 1, 2018; Thomas H. Payne et al., "Status of Health Information Exchange: A Comparison of Six Countries," *Journal of Global Health* 9, no. 2 (2019).

That said, those two moderating scenarios are artificial and against trends; if a cyberattack is to have the desired military effect, the victim state would by definition have some level of digital dependency. While digitalization lags in the health sector may indeed exist relative to military dependence thereupon (as in the United States in the early 2000s) these circumstances seem an exception to a linear trajectory, rather than a rule. Presuming that trends in digital health continue, the potential for cyberattacks to interfere with protected medical personnel and treatment is significant, and barring exceptional care, creates significant cause for concern as to their lawfulness.

Objects Indispensable

A no less significant issue is whether cyberattacks would inherently damage "objects indispensable to the civilian population"—namely food and water.[125] Additional Protocol I's Article 54 focuses its attention on material needs of human survival: "foodstuffs," "crops," "livestock," and "drinking water."[126] Should cyberattacks materially interfere with the food security of a civilian population, there may be additional basis of concern.

The scope of the prohibition is important as the manner in which populations are fed and supplied with water changes. Article 54's admonitions are at once a caveated, narrowing applicability to attacks on these objects *for the specific purpose* of denying them for their sustenance value to civilian population," but also a stringent one, prohibiting attacks on these objects "whatever the motive."[127] In an historical era where the targets of such an attack were crop fields, this was a more straightforward consideration. At that time, bombing wheat fields could have only a few purposes: to expose or destroy military installations there within, to deny food intended explicitly for

---

UK: Saira Ghafur et al., "The Challenges of Cybersecurity in Health Care: the UK National Health Service as a Case Study," *The Lancet Digital Health* 1, no. 1 (2019); "Health and Social Care Network (HSCN)," *NHS Digital*.

[125] *AP1*, Art. 54. GGE 2021 (para 45) provides an expanded—and too expansive for these purposes—list of "critical infrastructure that provides essential services to the public" that includes water and sanitation, but also education and electoral processes. *GGE 2021*, 13 (para 45). Such a broad definition points to the kind of narrowing that later chapters suggest may be required for the "cyber norms" project to draw upon the full strength of existing international law on its way to forming any kind of durable prohibitive norm against cyberattacks.
[126] *AP1*, Art. 54(2).
[127] Ibid. emphasis added.

the military (as 54(3) exempts from protection), or to (impermissibly) deny foodstuffs to a civilian population.[128]

In light of the complex interconnectedness and digital mediation of food supply chains, this Article's relevant scope becomes more complex. Article 54 section 3(b) arguably favors a more expansive reading in the modern light in removing from exemption "actions against these objects . . . which may be expected to leave the civilian population with such inadequate food or water as to cause its starvation or force its movement."[129] Of course, the emblematic case of bombing fields or even core facilities for food distribution are clear, but could there also a cyberattack equivalent? The architecture of today's water treatment systems, as well as the fragility of the modern-day food supply chain provides important insights.

Among the many facilities that leverage remote monitoring and control systems today are the water treatment facilities of numerous industrialized nations. As a technical matter, countless reports have documented the exploitability of these systems' vulnerabilities.[130] Reported incidents in the United States and Israel have demonstrated hacking attacks in the wild, attempting and in some cases succeeding at locking out authorities from the controls managing the water supply.[131] Some of these have had decidedly geopolitical flavor, such as a reported 2016 incident of Syrian-linked hackers attacking an American water district's systems.[132] The US Department of Homeland Security council charged with reviewing vulnerabilities identified

---

[128] *API*, Art. 54. The Art. 54 commentary on objects that are indispensable to the survival of the civilian population, includes a discussion of "scorched earth" strategies, noting that there are restrictions placed on an occupying power in withdrawing from an occupied territory. Scorched earth policies exercised by an Occupying Power withdrawing from occupied territory were judged legitimate if required by imperative military necessity. Article 54 does not change that situation except as regards objects indispensable to the survival of the civilian population. In other words, an occupation army which is withdrawing may, if military operations render it absolutely necessary, carry out destructions (bridges, railways, roads, airports, ports etc.) with a view to preventing or slowing down the advance of enemy troops, but may not destroy indispensable objects such as supplies of foodstuffs, crops ripe for harvesting, drinking water reservoirs and water distribution systems or remove livestock." *API* Commentary 1987 ICRC, para. 2121.

[129] *API*, Art. 54(3)(b).

[130] See, e.g., Joel Brenner, "Keeping America Safe: Toward More Secure Networks for Critical Sectors." Massachusetts Institute of Technology, 2017; US National Infrastructure Advisory Council, "Water Sector Resilience: Final Report & Recommendations" (Washington, DC: Department of Homeland Security, 2016); Idaho National Laboratory, "Protecting Drinking Water from Cyber Threats" (Washington, DC: Department of Energy, 2016).

[131] Christina Thompson and Katie Caviness, "Cyber Attack Targets ONWASA; Company Refusing to Pay Ransom," *WCTI News*, 2018; *Yediot Ahronot*, "Suspected of a Cyber Attack on a Series of Water Facilities in Israel," April 26, 2020.

[132] Ari Mahairas and Peter J. Beshar, "A Perfect Target for Cybercriminals," *New York Times* (Opinion), November 19, 2018.

in its report that "tight interdependencies," including on a range of properly functioning digital systems, "create high consequences of water service degradation and loss."[133] In particular, alongside severe weather, that same report lists "cyber dependency" as a "high-priority risk" and cites "attacks involving process control and monitoring systems" as "no longer hypothetical."[134] Indeed, amidst mounting tensions on the India–China border, ten distinct organizations associated with the Indian electricity sector found their control systems targeted with malware—a classic cyberattack precursor.[135] Likewise, in May 2022, Iranian attackers reportedly targeted water flow and wastewater treatment for two districts in Israel, but were thwarted by Israeli defenses.[136]

What distinguishes these cases from the inquiry here is the notion of inherence: Can a state planning a cyberattack expect one of the logical consequences to be creating supply-disrupting or tainting incidents? Official reports and commentary are largely silent on the sort of detail that would provide insights, potentially in part because the owners and operators of that infrastructure may not be eager to reveal the possibility, or may not know themselves. Most of the scenarios presented in homeland security studies tend to focus on dedicated actors intentionally infiltrating a system and manipulating controls, rather than accidentally causing such an event by, for instance, freezing out access. That said, security experts note that

> water utilities increasingly use industrial control systems to continuously control treatment processes and delivery, remotely monitor operations, and control the pressure and flows in pipelines. These automated systems allow small teams of operators to efficiently and remotely manage complex physical processes using digital controls. Growing reliance on industrial control systems over the last decade has resulted in increased connectivity.[137]

While one would hope that such systems would not be dependent on remote internet access for their operations, and that if shared information infrastructure were knocked offline there would be a guaranteed fail-safe,

---

[133] US National Infrastructure Advisory Council, "Water Sector Resilience," 18.
[134] Ibid., 24.
[135] David Sanger and Emily Schmall, "China Appears to Warn India: Push Too Hard and the Lights Could Go Out," *New York Times*, February 28, 2021.
[136] Joby Warrick and Ellen Nakashima, "Foreign Intelligence Officials Say Attempted Cyberattack on Israeli Water Utilities Linked to Iran," *Washington Post*, May 8, 2020.
[137] US National Infrastructure Advisory Council, "Water Sector Resilience," 23.

studies such as the above do not create the impression such fail-safes are uniformly in place. Nor do they indicate that such remote monitoring and control systems operate independently of shared information infrastructure, such as commercial ISPs. This telling omission suggests that significant outage scenarios, lasting periods of weeks, may well imperil the control and thus availability of the water supply at a regional level. It is also hinted in the 2021 GGE's list of interconnected infrastructure—beginning with energy and continuing to water and more.[138] In short, it may be that without shared information infrastructure, the owner-operators of these systems would not be able to perform their work and, in turn, unable to provide potable water. Likewise, scenarios that involve cyberattack tools spreading unintendedly from targeted to nontargeted SCADA systems are plausible and spotlight this concern. While it is too soon to definitively assign this legality risk to cyberattacks, this is a crucial vector to monitor for risk and compliance, given the growing global potential and Additional Protocol I's clear attention to this humanitarian risk.

The recent history of other key "objects indispensable," foodstuffs and livestock, may provide more readily demonstrable cause for concern. Indeed, much of today's food supply chain activities depend upon software and technology for such basic tasks such as account inventory, fleet management, the automation of warehouse operations, cloud data storage, and communications.[139] It also relies on this same digital infrastructure to ensure compliance with the Food and Drug Administration's and Food Safety Modernization Act.[140]

Here again, the COVID-19 crisis raised—and may portend continuation of—conditions problematic for mounting a lawful cyberattack. At the retail level, in numerous dense urban areas, the closure of retail food facilities where individuals previously tested positive for COVID left residents—particularly those within vulnerable populations—with few options for basic

---

[138] *GGE 2021*, 12–13 (para 45). See also "*Report of the Open-Ended Working Group*," 2021, 7 (para 10).

[139] Navickas Valentinas and Gruzauskas Valentas, "Big Data Concept in the Food Supply Chain: Small Markets Case," *Scientific Annals of Economics and Business* 63, no. 1 (2016): 20."

[140] Mary Shacklett, "How Technology Is Transforming the Food Supply Chain," *Food Logistics Magazine*, July 14, 2017; "U.S. retailers, wholesalers and distributors use technology to maintain documents from every supplier to verify their supply chain's compliance with the Food and Drug Administration's (FDA) Food Safety Modernization Act (FSMA). These documents can be facility registrations, foreign supplier verifications, food safety plans, food defense plans, or sanitary transportation records, depending on the supplier—but it all adds up to many documents that must be actively maintained."

foodstuffs. Particularly when compounded by a lack of mobility, the effect was an extreme reliance for some on digitally mediated food provision—either by social service support or even smartphone-based commercial delivery services.[141] A cyberattack disrupting such a service, or even more basically, the shared web hosting infrastructure upon which multiple services rely, could plausibly imperil the food security of a city or section thereof.

At the distribution level, just-in-time delivery patterns combined with market concentration in key sectors exacerbated localized shortages of particular foodstuffs—though not food availability writ large.[142] At the production level, outages at just a few crucial facilities in the United States (here caused by COVID diagnoses and close working quarters), resulted in radical swings in availability of core staples like beef and chicken, despite millions of pounds in available livestock.[143] The world's largest poultry producer, Tyson Foods, issued a warning that even due to that peacetime disruption "the food supply chain is breaking."[144] Days later, its farmers would euthanize millions of birds, unable to process them for meat due to shut down plants.[145]

As a temporary condition, these episodes are glimpses into scenarios far more plausible in war than in the referenced peacetime. For this reason, let alone if they represent the acceleration of current trends, particularly in dense urban areas, it argues for careful attention to this novel concern in cyberattack planning. *Tallinn* Rule 81 confirms this broad reading and forward-looking approach, irrespective of the intent of an attack—even if its commentary that "the Internet (or other communications networks) does not . . . qualify as indispensable" is in light of the above considerations, at best premature, and perhaps ultimately self-defeating.[146] It is too soon in this technological transformation to know with certainty whether cyberattacks

---

[141] "Record demand for online grocery shopping amid the COVID-19 pandemic has sent the apps for grocery pickup and delivery services up the charts. Walmart Grocery, as a result, has now hit an all-time high in downloads—grabbing the No. 1 ranking position across all Shopping apps in the U.S. on April 5, 2020, and surpassing Amazon by 20%. . . . The Walmart Grocery application retained that No. 1 position for at least two days, the firm said, citing data from both the Google Play store and the Apple App Store, combined." Sarah Perez, "Walmart Grocery App Sees Record Downloads Amid COVID-19, Surpasses Amazon by 20%," *TechCrunch*, April 9, 2020.

[142] Ron Knox, "Monopolies in Meat: Endangering Workers, Farmers, and Consumers," *The American Prospect*, May 4, 2020.

[143] Michael Corkery and David Yaffe-Bellany, "U.S. Food Supply Chain Is Strained as Virus Spreads," *New York Times*, April 13, 2020.

[144] Laura Reiley, "In One Month, the Meat Industry's Supply Chain Broke," *Washington Post*, April 28, 2020.

[145] Catherine Hauser, "Nearly 2 Million Chickens Killed as Poultry Workers Are Sidelined," *New York Times*, April 28, 2020.

[146] *Tallinn 1.0*, 225, 27.

would automatically, or in the majority of cases, imperil this particular "indispensable object"—however, it is far more plausible in light of technological developments, suggesting significant future potential for inherent violation.

Containing Dangerous Forces

If the previous category were objects and installations whose *functioning* is essential to civilian well-being, those which stand to create catastrophes for civilian well-being in the event of their *damage or destruction* are also and separately protected.[147] These "works and installations containing dangerous forces" are distinguished by the fact that attacks upon them would cause not slow suffering akin to hunger, but a more immediate injury through "release"—such as a breaking dam, or active cooling of a nuclear plant.[148] These severe humanitarian consequences are notably overriding in the original text, "even where these objects are military objectives."[149] There are two potential avenues for consideration here, one under a narrower reading of these provisions, one more expansive. The first asks whether cyberattacks are inherently prone to causing the precise humanitarian risks herein. The second is whether critical information infrastructure is "containing" other "dangerous forces" that might be recognized as covered under Article 56.

To the more literal matter of whether cyberattacks run the risk of causing nuclear meltdowns and burst dams, the evidence is limited and, for these purposes, less likely than other scenarios covered in the chapter. Recalling that the cyberattacks under discussion are broad-based attacks on shared information infrastructure, though the consequences would be graver, the risks here are paradoxically lower than with water treatment or the food supply, due largely to regulated resiliency. Comparative documentation is

---

[147] There has been additional commentary on the significance of this clause forbidding such installations from being the "object of an *attack*," with the contested nature of attack potentially exempting cyber operations from such requirements. See, e.g., Schmitt, "Cyber Operations and the Jus in Bello," 91–93. "Since the plain text of Article 49 appears to require a violent act for qualification as an attack, by a strict textual interpretation, non-kinetic operations, i.e., operations which themselves do not comprise physical force, would be excluded." However as Schmitt concludes, and this study concurs, the doctrine of kinetic equivalence is again properly rejected here, as "it is not the violence of the act that constitutes the condition precedent to limiting the occurrence of an attack, but the violence of the ensuing result." Ibid., 94.
[148] *API*, Art. 56(1), (2)(a–b).
[149] Ibid., Art. 56(1).

scant, but evidence suggests that leaving nuclear facilities and dams without external connectivity or even destroying the shared digital infrastructure upon which they might rely for data retrieval is unlikely to cripple their operations.[150] Such systems, under the regulatory requirements guiding the systems safety, would be designed to revert in such cases back to a safe "failure mode" designed to put their "dangerous forces" into a stable state. While imperfect, this contemplated, engineered, and audited general failover dynamic suggests that mere loss of connectivity, even if prolonged, cannot be *expected* to create the humanitarian catastrophe against which Article 56 seeks to protect.

This assessment, however, has several caveats. First, it is dependent on regulatory compliance, and even in highly regulated sectors such as aviation, episodes of industry capture or overreliance on self-certification raise important questions about even stringent safety regulations.[151] Second, it is country-specific; not all countries harnessing nuclear power will have the same regulatory requirement. However, the limited number of companies producing nuclear facilities, and the desire to standardize design for regulatory conformity where possible, may mitigate this concern somewhat.[152] The 2021 GGE nudges countries toward ensuring such resilience considerations, but without meaningful specificity or regulatory effect.[153] Third, it applies only to cyberattacks disrupting shared infrastructure but not to those destroying the machines, or entire power supply, to those facilities, as the latter might be more likely to cause malfunctions catastrophic to safety.[154] Though states taking the precautionary measures outlined in Article 57, which will be discussed shortly, would need to bear these conditions in mind, the evidence does not prima facie put cyberattacks in automatic violation of Article

---

[150] "Regulatory Guide 5.71: Cyber Security Programs for Nuclear Facilities" (Washington, DC, 2010). See, e.g., C.3.1.4 (p.17) regarding requirements to document infrastructure interdependencies. See also Federal Energy Regulatory Commission (Division of Dam Safety and Inspections), "FERC Security Program for Hydropower Projects Revision 3A" (2016), Sec. 9, 37–45.

[151] See, e.g., the case of the Boeing 737 MAX. Tommaso Sgobba, "B-737 MAX and the Crash of the Regulatory System," *Journal of Space Safety Engineering* 6, no. 4 (2019).

[152] The United States is the world's largest producer of nuclear power, accounting for more than 30 percent of worldwide nuclear generation of electricity. Presently, of the 440 nuclear reactors in operation across 30 countries, the US holds the highest number of operable nuclear reactors at 93, followed by France at 56, China at 55 Russia at 37, and Japan at 33. World Nuclear Association, "Nuclear Power in the World Today," November 2023.

[153] *GGE 2021*, 13.

[154] Examples include some rarer cyberattack vectors, such as test cases demonstrating the capability to physically ignite electrical transformers, or the otherwise-excluded case of an electromagnetic pulse. Chris Waltman, "Aurora: Homeland Security's Secret Project to Change How We Think About Cybersecurity (DHS FOIA Response)," *Muckrock*, November 14, 2016.

56. *Tallinn 1.0*'s Rule 80 accords with this conclusion, requiring only "particular care" during even direct attacks *against* such works and installations and those in their facility.[155]

A second and more dynamic reading of Article 56 would suggest that dams and nuclear installations were intended as emblematic examples of dangerous forces being held back of infrastructure; cyberattacks may imperil others, and as a result, create tantamount risks. Textual fidelity demands fixing such events to the release of dangerous *emissions* rather than general large-scale destructive risk (e.g., loss of air traffic control). Even with that addition, some examples of similar magnitude are salient today. Numerous countries rely upon near-offshore liquid natural gas (LNG) and related high-pressure facilities, compressed natural gas (CNG) transport ships, and the navigation, docking, and pressurization systems upon which both rely. Another, notable for its absence in the text, would be large-scale chemical production facilities working with noxious gases or other volatile chemicals. A third, perhaps less relevant due to its noninstantaneous effects, would be biological research facilities known to be experimenting with contagious pathogens. The heterogeneity of these installations makes categorical assignment of risk difficult. Generally, the degree to which such facilities lack the kind of fail-over conditions regulatorily mandated in US nuclear and hydropower facilities, the greater potential that broad-based cyberattacks might prompt the release of such a dangerous force. These are emerging conditions with some amount of technological path dependency; as such, they invite ongoing attention by both legal scholars and militaries.

Civil Defense

A final protected class particularly worthy of consideration here are provisions for the civil defense, a category significant enough to merit an entire Chapter (IV) of the Additional Protocol I. Article 61 defines civil defense as "the performance of some or all" of fifteen enumerated duties "intended to protect the civilian population against the dangers, and to help it to recover from the immediate effects, of hostilities or disasters and also to provide the conditions necessary for its survival."[156] It applies to both to "organizations"

---

[155] *Tallinn 1.0*, 223.
[156] *API*, Art. 61(a).

assigned by party to the conflict and "devoted exclusively to such tasks" as well as to "civilians who, although not members of [such organizations,] respond to an appeal from the competent authorities."[157] Among those fifteen enumerated tasks, several merit special consideration for militaries considering cyberattacks: warning and evacuation, rescue and medical services, detection and marking of danger areas, and repair of indispensable public utilities.[158] What binds all these cases and distinguishes them from less relevant clauses (such as decontamination measures or emergency disposal of the dead) is the extent to which modern-day civil defense mechanisms are increasingly built upon internet-connected devices—particularly smartphones—for officials and civilians in the field.

Warning and Evacuation. Measures to warn populations of impending threats, alert them to changes, and even direct their evacuation are increasingly centered around internet-connected mobile phones. A false alarm case illustrates the expectation of how such alerts would be used in the context of hostilities. In the early hours of January 12, 2018, hundreds of thousands of residents of the US state of Hawaii were sent an emergency alert reading "BALLISTIC MISSILE THREAT INBOUND TO HAWAII. SEEK IMMEDIATE SHELTER. THIS IS NOT A DRILL."[159] Only thirty-eight minutes later was the message, sent in error during routine testing procedures, withdrawn. This sort of notification was pushed to mobile phones, most of which permit such emergency communications to override regular phone settings and deliver visible and audible alerts. Apple's technical documentation for its iPhone notes, for instance, that "by default, Government Alerts are turned on for your device," including "alerts issued by your country or region's government; alerts involving imminent threats to safety or life; and alerts for extreme weather conditions."[160] Google's Android operating system has similar provisions.[161] Combined, the two represent an almost total market share of global smartphone operating systems outside China in 2019.[162] Even in countries with less advanced mobile broadband, governments—for over a decade—have been able to leverage a precursor

---

[157] Ibid., Art. 61(b), 62(2).
[158] Ibid., Art. 61(a)(i–ii,v,vi,xii).
[159] Adam Nagourney, David Sanger, and Johanna Barr, "Hawaii Panics After Alert About Incoming Missile Is Sent in Error," *New York Times*, January 13, 2018.
[160] Apple Inc., "About Emergency and Government Alerts on iPhone and Apple Watch," August 14, 2019.
[161] Google, "Public Alerts FAQs," 2020.
[162] International Data Corporation, "Worldwide Smartphone Shipment OS Market Share Forecast," 2020.

technology, SMS (text message), to deliver such messages, providing a level of redundancy designed to reach those without smartphones.[163]

These smartphone-based, internet-connected warning systems are new paradigms in civil defense that will only increase; as such, they demand consideration for military planning going forward. By targeting shared information infrastructure, particularly if mobile data or cellular networks are implicated, the consequences for disrupting civil defense are clear and knowable.

Rescue, Medical, and Marking Services. For similar reasons, the reliance on smartphones for the coordination and execution of civilian rescue and medical operations suggests cyberattacks may run afoul of clearly afforded protections. Increasing civilian reliance on telemedicine in some localities has already been discussed. In the emergency response context, the use of mobile phones to permit victims to call for rescue, or for rescuers to find them even beneath tons of rubble, is a notable feature of such operations.[164] Mobile phones, in concert with GPS signals and geographic information system (GIS) data, have been used by search and rescue teams in a range of natural disasters since the early 2000s.[165] Detection and marking of danger areas, outlined in Article 61(a)(viii), is similarly imperiled, since any modern-day version in a developed economy would leverage map data delivered by shared information infrastructure and is not, at present, cached (stored resident) on most phones that would permit functionality without persistent connectivity. As a net result, modern civil preparedness from the standpoint of both victim and authority increasingly depends on a range of infrastructures; the disruption of which is predictable in many cyberattack scenarios—especially those accompanying active military hostilities, as witnessed in part during Russia's 2022 invasion of the Ukraine.[166]

---

[163] Marius Cioca, Lucian-Ionel Cioca, and Sabin-Corneliu Buraga, "SMS Disaster Alert System Programming" (paper presented at the 2008 2nd IEEE International Conference on Digital Ecosystems and Technologies, 2008); Anas Aloudat and Katina Michael, "The Application of Location Based Services in National Emergency Warning Systems: SMS, Cell Broadcast Services and Beyond," in *Recent Advances in National Security Technology and Research: Proceedings of the 2010 National Security Science and Innovation Conference*, ed. P. Mendis and A. Yates (Canberra: Australian Security Research Centre, 2011).

[164] See, e.g., *BBC News*, "Philippines Landslide Victims 'Sent Texts from Underneath Rubble,'" September 21, 2018; Nathan Hodge, "Texts, Tweets Saving Haitians From the Rubble," *Wired*, January 21, 2018.

[165] Navigation and Timing National Executive Committee US Space-Based Positioning, "Public Safety & Disaster Relief" (Washington, DC: Department of Commerce, 2019).

[166] Notably, however, a cyberattack disrupting the function of the Global Positioning Satellite (GPS) system or its downlinks may disrupt GPS-coordinated civil rescue as a secondary effect, but

Notably from a global standpoint, military planners also cannot rely on a linear relationship between a country's level of digitization in a given geography and the reliance of emergency response and civil defense on critical information infrastructure. While it may seem intuitive that the more wired a nation is the more vulnerable it would be to this threat, that may not reliably be the case—there may, instead, be a more dangerous middle stage of development. The reason is that some of the most wired and best-resourced countries have begun to operate certain emergency services on dedicated systems to minimize the risk of disruption or interference.[167] Other countries, however, continue to rely on commercial mobile phone-based solutions because of their lower cost, relative to dedicated systems independent of shared information infrastructure. Thus, countries with significant mobile phone and mobile internet penetration rates, some civil defense capacity, but only moderate to low incomes and government expenditures may be the most likely to have their civil defense apparatus disrupted by a cyberattack, to grave civilian effect.[168]

Repair of Indispensable Public Utility. Finally, an area of less immediate concern but significant for future consideration is dependence upon shared information infrastructure for testing, repair, and ongoing operation of public utilities. Electricity is an emblematic case, as many utilities transition to a "smart grid" model that features both dynamic monitoring and power flow control, both of which are internet-mediated.[169] The restoration of power after a conflict would, in such cases, potentially require a range of

---

given the military utility, it would not qualify. Such a militarily significant dual-use target would not be accorded these sorts of protections. On relevant activities in the context of Russia's invasion of Ukraine, see Microsoft Digital Security Unit, "An Overview of Russia's Cyberattack Activity in Ukraine," (Redmond, WA: Microsoft Corporation, 2022), 8.

[167] See, for two differing models in the same country, the US National Communications System (since disbanded and rechartered); and the FirstNet First Responder Network.
[168] At least 10 countries "are deploying or have launched" public service-LTE (PS-LTE) networks and 9 countries "plan or are trialling PS-LTE networks" as of 2018. The countries that have deployed or that are deploying First-Net-like emergency response or civil defense networks include the United States, Australia, the United Kingdom, China, Kenya, Qatar, Spain, the UAE, Angola, and Canada. Global Mobile Suppliers Association (GMSA), "Public Safety LTE Networks: State of the Market and Device Ecosystem" (Farnham, UK: GSA, 2018).
[169] For instance a 2020 study by the European Commission found close to 225 million smart meters for electricity and 51 million for gas—representing 77 percent and 44 percent of consumers, respectively—will be rolled out in the EU by 2024. European Commission, "Benchmarking Smart Metering Deployment in the EU-28" (Brussels: Directorate-General for Energy, 2020). In the United States, around 111 million smart meters have been installed on the grid, representing about 69 percent of total meter installations. US Energy Information Admnistration, "EIA FAQs" (Washington, DC: EIA, 2022). See also US Department of Energy, "Smart Grid System Report: 2018 Report to Congress" (Washington, DC: Department of Energy, 2018).

systems which may be potentially disabled in a broad-based cyberattack. The same may be true for commercial technicians—no less protected than government agents in their capacity repairing a utility grid—who may rely on wireless connectivity and the data services riding atop it to diagnose, log, and monitor repairs to a grid. The *Tallinn* experts came to a similar conclusion on the affirmative duty held by the occupying power to "ensure the continuance of computer operations [e.g., SCADA systems] that are essential to the survival of the civilian population of the occupied territory" like water purification treatment centers, waste processing facilities, electrical grids.[170] To the extent that disabling critical information infrastructure limits the ability of such crews to restore electric power, cyberattacks have inherent risk of violating this protection.

One rejoinder to all these arguments might be, to the extent that the infrastructure upon which civil defense depends is dual-use, that infrastructure itself cannot constitute "organization" or "personnel" for civil defense. This objection does not hold, however, in cases where one accepts that such infrastructure is in the context of its usage matériel of civil defense, defined as "equipment, supplies, and transports" used for the civil defense purpose.[171] No plausible reading of the text, absent rejection of any dynamic reading of Additional Protocol I (in turn contrary to ICJ holdings), would exclude information infrastructure from equipment. A more plausible objection would challenge whether such broadly dual-use infrastructure can be eligible for protections under civil defense clauses. After all, blue triangles painted on the shells of servers do little good in halting digital attacks thereupon.[172] The complexity of how states should comply with the identification clause of Article 66 is not, however, sufficient to deny the protection. Unlike the affirmative obligations to protect asserted in earlier articles of the Chapter, Article 66 states that governments "shall endeavor" to identify civil defense objects with a distinctive emblem.[173] Technological evolution may indeed create the necessity for states to adopt new innovations to "make it possible to recognize . . . matériel upon which the international distinctive sign" is displayed.[174] Similar to new innovations that might avoid perfidy in

---

[170] *Tallinn 1.0*, 242.
[171] *AP1*, Art. 61(b–d).
[172] The distinctive emblem of civil defense is an "equilateral blue triangle on an orange ground." Ibid., Art. 66(4).
[173] Ibid., Art. 66(1).
[174] Ibid., Art. 66(2).

cyberattacks, this question would be an interesting subject for further inquiry. Nonetheless, for these purposes, it is clear that neither of these caveats limit the very real protections accorded to civil defense—and the very real inherent and knowable risks that cyberattacks create to it.

Conclusions on Civil Defense. Chapter VI of Additional Protocol I does not simply protect civil defense from being intentionally targeted but requires they shall be "respected and protected," and even more affirmatively "entitled to perform their duties."[175] This is a broad charge that weighs heavily in favor of protection even amidst legitimate military objectives. It is also buttressed by general clauses protecting even "complementary activities necessary to carry out any of the tasks" enumerated in Article 61, "including but not limited to planning and organization."[176] While military planners of days past did not contemplate knocking out corporate messaging platforms as grounds for a violation of the *jus in bello*, even this must be given its due consideration.

In light of the evolution of technology, cyberattacks inherently will confront real legal hazards, given the significant and knowable risks to a range of specially protected classes under the *jus ad bellum*—from medical facilities to the food and water supply, along with several forms of civil defense. Cyberattacks inescapably invite this significant scrutiny and, as the next section will explore and without exceptional due diligence, may not therefore be reliably lawful weapons of war.

7.4 Disproportionality

Even the right to injure combatants is not unlimited under the *jus in bello*. Protections falling under the concept of proportionality offer both new strictures and a means of evaluating some previously considered. After introducing the concept in the context of cyberattacks, this section considers three approaches to considering proportionality to, in turn, assess whether or not cyberattacks run the risk of being inherently disproportionate.

---

[175] Ibid., Art. 62(1).
[176] Ibid., Art. 61(a)(xv).

General Requirement of Proportionality

The ICJ summarized this requirement in the *Nuclear Weapons Advisory Opinion*: "It is prohibited to cause unnecessary suffering to combatants."[177] Of course, armed hostilities inherently involve suffering, and though the requirements of proportionality are difficult to concretize, it does not excuse militaries from recognizing them. Additional Protocol I provides an illustrative concept of how an action might be inherently disproportionate, as a subset of its prohibition on indiscriminate killing: "an attack which may be expected to cause incidental of civilian life, injury to civilians, damage to civilian objects, or a combination thereof, *which would be excessive in relation to the concrete and direct military advantage anticipated*."[178] This requirement is operationalized by precautionary requirements found later in the text.[179] Yet the ICJ, in recalling these provisions, does not speak of humanitarian suffering strictly in relationship to military gains. This difference reflects a lively debate in the scholarship about how to evaluate proportionality within the *jus in bello*: whether suffering is to be considered against an abstract standard of inhumanity; whether it simply requires selection of the "least bad tool" when feasible; or whether it is a balancing test.[180]

Although there is little question that the requirements of proportionality apply to cyberattack use, the next sections will show how not all have equal utility for this project of evaluating the necessity of restraint.[181] Cassese notes

---

[177] *Nuclear Weapons Advisory Opinion*, para 78.
[178] *AP1*, Art. 51(5)(b). Emphasis added.
[179] Ibid., Art. 57(2)(a).
[180] These three categories roughly track the obligations of AP1's Chapter IV, Article 57 on Precautions in Attack. Ibid., Art. 57(2)(a)(i–iii), (b). The duty to take "constant care" and precautions in mounting operations is covered under Article 57(2), which instructs that parties: "(i) do everything feasible to verify that the objectives to be attacked are neither civilians nor civilian objects and are not subject to special protection but are military objectives within the meaning of paragraph 2 of Article 52 and that it is not prohibited by the provisions of this Protocol to attack them; (ii) take all feasible precautions in the choice of means and methods of attack with a view to avoiding, and in any event to minimizing, incidental loss of civilian life, injury to civilians and damage to civilian objects; (iii) refrain from deciding to launch any attack which may be expected to cause incidental loss of civilian life, injury to civilians, damage to civilian objects, or a combination thereof, which would be excessive in relation to the concrete and direct military advantage anticipated." See Solis, *The Law of Armed Conflict*, 293. Also note that the nuances of the standard here that differ AP1's use of "all reasonable" precautions, relative to other sources' use of "feasible" or "all feasible," was briefly noted by *Tallinn* experts who recognized the former as "a little less far-reaching" than the later, a view validated by the ICRC's commentary on the provision. *AP1*, Art. 57(4); *Tallinn 1.0*, 163; Claude Pilloud et al., *Commentary on the additional protocols: of 8 June 1977 to the Geneva Conventions of 12 August 1949* (Leiden: Martinus Nijhoff Publishers, 1987), para. 2203.
[181] Presuming these events amount to attacks under international humanitarian law, which follows from the above. See Harold Hongju Koh, "International Law in Cyberspace," *Harvard International Law Journal* 54, no. December (2012): 595–96; *Tallinn 1.0*, 159.

the practical challenge: some key principles of proportionality are "rather vague and contain many loopholes," and that its value may really lie in identifying "the most glaring cases."[182] The next section evaluates which of these approaches offers the best combination of relevance to a study of restraint and durability in light of a proportionality analysis's practical limitations.

Evaluating Cyberattack Proportionality

The first approach—cyberattacks were to offend common sensibilities—can be dispensed of quickly at the present moment. In public consciousness, cyberattacks have not had a moment like the one captured by the novelist John Hersey in *Hiroshima*, crystallizing public fears about unique horrors.[183] Much of the press reaction to cyber operations, for instance, is marked more by intrigue than revulsion. Perhaps as a function of years of secrecy, serious and skeptical media consideration of cyberattacks' humanitarian consequences is more difficult to pinpoint than with other emerging weapons technologies. While Chapter 8 will examine the presence and sincerity of state calls for their limitation, it is also clear that no authorities such as the ICJ have had occasion to relegate cyberattacks to any particularly offensive humanitarian category, to date.

The second approach captured in Additional Protocol, examining whether a tool is the "least bad available option," has less support in the literature despite its intuitive appeal. The value of this frame is the emphasis it places on *unnecessary* suffering, recognizing the practical realities of commanders who may have a range of options at their disposal for a mission, but limited ability to conduct detailed analyses of every attack's foreseeable humanitarian possibilities. This is, arguably, where the majority of *Tallinn 1.0* experts arrived in articulating Rule 56, that when a "choice is possible between several military objectives" with similar advantage, states should select the one "expected to cause the last danger to civilian lives and civilian objects."[184] For the purposes of preemptively determining usability, however, it is analytically limited. While this chapter has outlined a number of grounds upon which

---

[182] Cassese, *International Law*, 419.
[183] John Hersey, *Hiroshima* (New York: Knopf, 1946). While scholarly consensus among historians is mixed on the effects of Hersey's novel on the nuclear abolition movement, Tannenwald notes that the book likely "contributed to a growing sense of dread and revulsion regarding atomic weaponry increasingly felt by Americans." Tannenwald, *Nuclear Taboo*, 92.
[184] *Tallinn 1.0*, 170–71.

cyberattacks raise significant concerns for the *jus in bello*, the question in this frame revolves around an abstract alternative. Absent knowledge of the other means that might achieve the objective, little more can be gained.

The third approach—a balance between knowable humanitarian risks and "definite military advantage"—is then the most satisfying, if still the most analytically fraught. Here, three questions inform whether cyberattacks may be inherently disproportionate: First, are cyberattacks of any military value; second, do cyberattacks inherently cause legally relevant "suffering"; and third, does the evaluation thereof lead to the kind of "glaring case" to which Cassese refers? The answer to the first was provided in Chapter 1; potential military gains are real and well-documented. The second has been the subject of this chapter; indeed, even in the abstract, cyberattacks inherently raise significant and unaddressed concerns for the suffering of civilian populations and protected classes. The operative question, then, returns to the fulcrum at the center of this balancing test.

How to reach a conclusion in such an analysis is fundamentally contested, but most debates fix on how cognizable the humanitarian effects are in the context of feasible battlefield decision-making. Emblematically, the *Tallinn* experts were not in agreement about how collateral damage in the context of cyberattacks should factor into proportionality analysis. Only a minority of experts, for instance, maintained the strict perspective: when, for instance engaging in a cyber operation against a ship at sea, "the attacker must perform those precautionary measures that are both technically possible and militarily feasible"—such as mapping out all the cyber infrastructure of which the ship is a part.[185] This minority view comports with the ICRC's position on the matter, and in light of this chapter's overall analysis, seems more defensible than the alternative—though many practitioners would have grounds to vehemently disagree. So whose knowledge is the right barometer of such an evaluation?

For advising combatants on their obligations, as is the subject of the *Tallinn* manuals, the question can be put to dozens of factors and analogies. The International Criminal Tribunal for the Former Yugoslavia evaluated the issue of how to determine whether an attack was proportionate in the *Galić* judgment. There, the Trial Chamber held that "it is necessary to examine whether a reasonably well-informed person in the circumstances of the actual perpetrator, making reasonable use of the information available

---

[185] Ibid., 163.

to him or her, could have expected excessive civilian casualties to result from the attack."[186] For these narrower purposes, however, there is a more straightforward cognizable approach: accepting the real and now well understood probability of humanitarian concerns creates a positive knowledge requirement which is not mutable by sizable gain in cases where the weapon's violations are inherent to it.

The predicate for this approach occupied the prior sections: incompatibility with general obligations to discriminate and narrower protections against certain classes. Its purpose is to operationalize those considerations under a practical framework. Its logic emerges from the same origins of the project of international humanitarian law itself: first, that states should be under a growing, not diminishing, obligation to assess collateral effects as technology to make such assessments improves. The *Tallinn* expert majority's argument against a network-wide, attack-by-attack review of consequences, preferring instead a consideration for the campaign overall, creates perverse incentives counter to the spirit and letter of IHL. Technology to conduct such analysis, at speed and considering even the substantial variables, is plausible today and continually increasing. To excuse it on the basis of a commander's limited ability to digest that data, or the military's lack of investment in those tools, is to equally excuse a commander's inability to read coordinates or order missiles with known faulty guidance. Nowhere does the *jus in bello* intend or express to give preference to an unguided weapon over a guided one. These requirements call for narrower cyber operations, not the encouragement of commander Luddism that would invite use of broader tools on the premise the consequences were not understood.

These collateral consequences are knowable and the categories of law they violate are numerous; as such, the prospects for a reliably proportionate—and thus lawful—cyberattack are, at a minimum, limited. For states to comply with their obligations under Article 57 of Additional Protocol I, they must engage in precautionary measures. To do so satisfactorily, they have to consider the range of general and specific preclusions laid out in law and humanitarian consequences cognizable in the event of that tool's use and the targets to which it is directed. Under the weight of the analyses of these prior sections, comfortably lawful scenarios to launch the kind of cyberattack described in this study are difficult to locate.

---

[186] ICTY, *Prosecutor v. Stanislav Galić*, Trial Chamber Judgment, para 58 (2003).

One counterargument is that Article 51(5)(b) of Additional Protocol I speaks only of "loss of life," "damage," and "injury," and thus exempts both nonkinetic effects and the secondary impacts of disablement. This is uncompelling. Kinetic equivalence has been previously argued; Geiß, Lahmann, Roscini, and the *Tallinn* experts all argue compellingly for the consideration of those secondary effects.[187] US (and other states') doctrine also supports this approach.[188] Another rejoinder, that cyberattacks are instead better understood as a collection of minor nonkinetic digital actions that only by virtue of interconnectedness cause humanitarian consequences of note, was in principle thoroughly rejected by the International Criminal Tribunal for the Former Yugoslavia (ICTY).[189] That conclusion hinged on a series of "grey area" effects "between indisputable legality and lawfulness," an ambiguity that cyberattacks would not likely not enjoy.

Conclusions

As the International Review of the Red Cross celebrated its 125th anniversary in 1995—almost twenty years after the conclusion of Additional Protocol I— its review made no mention of cybersecurity, the internet, or their impending impact on war.[190] Scholarship in the next decade by pioneers such as Schmitt and Dinstein began to highlight issues fitting cyber operations within the *jus in bello*, but in the years since, scholarly focus has tracked practitioner imperative: to determine the rules that cyber operations generally would need to abide by to comport with international legal obligations.

This chapter provided an opportunity to take a step back and conduct a fresh assessment of whether cyberattacks may be plausible lawful instruments of war—recognizing that, so-defined, there is no appropriate context but war in which to situate them. It identified significant reasons that

---

[187] Geiß and Lahmann, "Cyber Warfare," 395–98; Roscini, *Cyber Operations and the Use of Force in International Law*, 221; *Tallinn 1.0*, 169.

[188] US Navy, *Commander's Handbook on The Law of Naval Operations*, NWP 1-14M ed. (Washington, DC: Department of Defense, 2007), 8–17: "In employing non-kinetic means of [Computer Network Operations] against a military objective, factors involved in weighing anticipated incidental injury/death to protected persons can include, depending on the target, indirect effects (for example, the anticipated incidental injury/death that may occur from disrupting an electricity generating plant that supplies power to a military headquarters and to a hospital)."

[189] ICTY, *Prosecutor v. Kupreškić, Kupreškić, Kupreškić, Josipovic, Papic and Santic*, Trial Chamber, Judgment, para. 526 (2000).

[190] Jacques Meurant, "The 125th Anniversary of the International Review of the Red Cross—A Faithful Record," *International Review of the Red Cross* 306 (1995).

states, when compelled by a constitutive logic of restraint, might pause before choosing such a path. Cyberattacks create significant challenges for the *jus in bello*'s general requirements of discrimination between military and civilian objects; to identify their origins; and to avoid drawing neutral third parties into conflict. It considered narrower requirements as well, such as those protecting medical personnel and duties, indispensable objects, and certain aspects of civil defense, their potential for significant, unpredictable, collateral effect raise deep usability concerns. Even when weighing these humanitarian risks against the potential definite military objectives, the balance of the cyberattacks described herein appears to tilt away from proportionality and thus lawfulness.

As with the *jus ad bellum*, the question is now, to what restraining effect? One answer is evident in the scholarship: that military planners have sought to develop the parameters of more tailored cyber operations, with narrower effects, to help meet these requirements. This is where efforts like the *Tallinn Manuals* aim to have their most significant influence shaping state behavior—just as the authors of the *San Remo Manual* did for conflicts at sea.[191] It may well be that those volumes sit side-by-side on desks at the Pentagon and in Whitehall; official documents on operational decision-making are not generally available, so scholars are left relying on public remarks by legal advisors and occasional utterances by political and military leadership.[192]

If this is the case, though, and this important scholarship is having its intended effect, a paradox remains: Why have states been so historically reluctant to mention cyber operations, let alone describe their cyber operations their decision-making, in public? Why, to date, is Israel the only country to have affirmatively acknowledged a narrow offensive cyber operation, let alone a cyberattack?[193] This reluctance suggests something deeper at play than the "slow, cumbersome interagency process" that some military commentators regard as holding "hostage" greater operational freedom in cyberspace.[194] It suggests, instead, that the problem may not be that legal consideration is plodding, but rather, that planners do not like the answers they are receiving.

---

[191] *Tallinn 1.0*, 1.
[192] Ney, *DOD General Counsel Remarks at U.S. Cyber Command Legal Conference*.
[193] USCYBERCOM's reported January 2019 operation against the Russian Internet Research Agency may have crossed this threshold; however, neither the NSA nor Pentagon commented on the matter, and given the lack of operational specifics provided or evidence ascertainable beyond unnamed public statements by American officials, it is too early to formally recognize this example.
[194] James E. McGhee, "Liberating Cyber Offense," *Strategic Studies Quarterly* 10, no. 4 (2016): 59.

Historically in other contexts, patent incompatibility with the *jus in bello* has been a prerequisite for a weapon becoming unusable. This criterion is a necessary, but not sufficient condition of reliable restraint. The *jus in bello* does not have the same remedial procedures as the *jus ad bellum*. Instead, one might consider the remedial *jus in bello* to be the formation and maintenance of international norms restricting certain means and methods of warfare. Punishment for transgressions comes not from a legal regime internal to one treaty, but from overlapping influences of international opprobrium, military intervention, and in the most extreme cases, individual domestic or international criminal responsibility.[195] Combined, these are powerful forces of restraint on state behavior.

If the guidance military planners are receiving from their legal and diplomatic teams reflects even some of the conclusions reached in this chapter, leaders' restraint and public hesitation may have another explanation: their concern that the line between lawful cyber operations and likely impermissible cyberattacks is thinner than otherwise assumed. The relevance of these humanitarian considerations is only growing in light of the significant technological evolutions in recent years. It is too soon to test this hypothesis, but not too soon to recognize that the cumulative effect of the *jus in bello* may well be creating hesitation on the part of powers contemplating cyberattacks. If so, this hesitation has within it the kernel of restraint, if a durable norm of nonuse could emerge. It may even be that recognizing both the potential limitations and contestability of the law here, states have already taken up such efforts. This concept—and in turn, the potential for cyberattack-specific prohibitions—are the subject of the study's final chapter.

---

[195] "Grave breaches" are defined variously by the four Geneva Conventions of 1949 and Additional Protocols of 1977: *Geneva Convention for the Amelioration of the Condition of Wounded, Sick and Shipwrecked Members of Armed Forces at Sea (Second Geneva Convention)* (August 12), Article 50, Article 51; *Geneva Convention Relative to the Treatment of Prisoners of War (Third Geneva Convention)* (August 12), Article 130; *1949 Geneva (IV)*, Article 147; *Additional Protocol I (1977)*, Articles 11, 85.

8
Constructing a Prohibition

The last chapter revealed one of the enduring challenges for states concerned with both fidelity to international law and developing military capabilities in cyberspace: that room to maneuver within both may be rather limited. That said, what is to prevent a state from pursuing such actions in its own self-interest and later claiming ignorance or differing interpretation of general customary international law? Exploring this trust deficit is central to understanding whether the constitutive logic of restraint is not just analytically appealing but practically promising in the use of cyberattacks. It may also shed light on one of the central paradoxes of present-day cyberattacks: that states are ostentatiously organizing, training, and equipping to have those capabilities, but they are exceptionally quiet about their decisions to conduct cyber operations of any kind, and most acutely about those with broad disruptive potential.

According to former President Barack Obama, cyberspace "norms of responsible, just, and peaceful conduct among states . . . have begun to take hold."[1] Might a prohibition of cyberattacks—or some limitation of them—be the norms of which he spoke?[2] This final chapter considers the potential for and competition over a specific, prohibitive norm against cyberattacks built atop *jus in bello* incompatibility outlined in Chapter 7. It takes as a reference point the significant restraint states have observed with respect to other "notorious" tools such as biological weapons, as well as those less formally but just as functionally banned by taboo such as nuclear first use.[3] If states have been willing to observe restraint in these cases, were they doing

---

[1] The White House, *The United States' International Strategy for Cyberspace*, Foreword.
[2] Norms are shared expectations about acceptable behavior. Their effects on state behavior, identity, and interests animates an entire subfield of international relations, called Constructivism. See, foundationally within this school, Wendt, *Social Theory of International Politics*; Kratochwil, *Rules, Norms, and Decisions*; Ruggie, "What Makes the World Hang Together?"; Peter Katzenstein, ed. *The Culture of National Security: Norms and Identity in World Politics* (New York: Columbia University Press, 1996).
[3] To be clear, nuclear weapons are subject to a particular form of prohibitive norm as described here—one whose taboo is fixed around *first use*, but affords for other limitations on their spread, development, and stockpiling.

so on constitutive grounds, and what were the salient commonalities in those cases?

Outline of Argument

This final chapter evaluates, as a matter of substance and process, whether constitutive restraint might be possible through the development of a prohibitive norm. The chapter argues four points. First, there is already a competitive dynamic of *structural prohibition* underway to define whether a humanitarian regime governing cyberattacks could function. Second, this dynamic is unique in the potential for underlying alignment between key competing powers. Third, this dynamic may accommodate a narrow, prohibitive norm specific to cyberattacks built atop underlying agreement about the need to limit this weaponry. Finally, to the extent normative developments can be prefigured, insights from other prohibitions of emerging technology weapons suggest a strong case for how such a norm may gain a foothold in the international system. Cognizant evidence is not available to meaningfully examine whether such a norm has *already* taken hold within state planning decisions, but as new sources and episodes emerge, they may help observers gauge the progress toward—or diversion away from—a "cyberattack taboo," formal or otherwise.

Section 8.1 first scrutinizes the practical significance of the prior chapters' conclusions, connecting the pursuit of cyber norms and the rejection of "cyber arms control" to argue for a third and underexplored avenue: prohibitive norms. Section 8.2 then situates and identifies the competitive dynamic at play over cyberattacks usability as a constitutive matter—one that is not at the maturity of arguing over the contents and operation of an exceptional prohibition, but a more primitive competition for the appropriate venues in which to call for such a prohibition in the first place. Structural prohibition, it argues, is unique among those dynamics observed in other sections for the compatibility of aims and commensurability of approaches. It points to evidence that the nearly two-decade-long Russian attempt to create a new arms control framework specific to cyberattacks (strenuously opposed by the United States as unworkable and insincere) actually shares some intellectual alignment with Western powers' consensus about and adherence to the applicability of the *jus in bello* in their cyber operations. The Chinese government's flirtation with both positions, as well, suggests further possibility for a narrow consensus. Thus, of all the structural dynamics at play, structural prohibition seems not only the most well-aligned, but also potentially the most durable when viewed through the evidence of historical limitations on novel weaponry. In short, for states looking to limit or at least bring to heel the use of cyberattacks, this approach may well be the most promising.

The sections that follow consider the potential for the emergence and cascade of such a norm by applying the comparative lessons of prior exceptional prohibitions. After presenting concepts of norm formation generally, Section 8.3 argues that a series of key features define other successful prohibitions and considers how what is known about cyberattacks—particularly their coherence with other norms—could support emergence of a specific prohibition in their case.

Section 8.4 then argues for the key criteria that would favor such a norm reaching a tipping point of meaningful state awareness, and ultimately, a cascade of broad adoption. It concludes by considering how robust this alignment might be and how it might be achieved, as well as what gaps remain in assessing the pathway for such a norm.

Alongside the primary analysis, the sections that follow aim to support a broad and forward-looking research agenda into the prohibition of cyberattacks. For studies similarly situated, it provides one way to evaluate the potential for such a prohibition based on other novel phenomena in international security. For those seeking to track shifts in attitudes toward cyberattacks, it offers a rough methodology to conduct ongoing evaluation of a prohibitive norm as circumstances change. Finally, for those conducting a "genealogy" of whatever prohibitions might come to be, it may offer some early and potential sources thereof, capable of retrospective tracing based on presently unavailable documentary evidence.[4]

8.1 Moving Beyond Cyber Arms Control

The analysis of the preceding chapter might lead one to assume that given the potential for such extreme violation of law, that a deep literature arguing for and illuminating pathways to prohibit cyberattacks would exist. It does not.

---

[4] For more on studying the genealogy of a prohibitive norm, see Price, *Chemical Weapons Taboo*, 18–43, 174–76.

This paucity of research may reflect two assumptions, intertwined and further bound by the status quo of stated policy. The first is the well-documented and myriad challenges in architecting formal arms control regimes around cyberattacks—some of which hold true today, others may be overtaken by technological evolution.[5] A second is that certain powerful states' avowed opposition to what they regard as formal arms control measures gave the undue impression that any policy outcome built atop research on restraining cyberattacks might be dead on arrival. Thus, reflecting a legitimate desire for research in international relations to engage with useful problems in the world of policy, matters of a potential prohibition appears to have fallen to the bottom of an already packed research agenda.

For scholars engaging with states' near-term policy agendas, the cyber norms agenda introduced in Section 2.4 has been a readier point of departure—but for these purposes, an ultimately unsatisfying one. Despite its name, this agenda may be too scattershot in its current form to serve as a coherent basis for prohibition. For example, mutual prohibitions on cyber operations have—instructively—been narrow, such as the 2016 Obama–Xi agreement on state-sponsored intellectual property theft for commercial gain.[6] Others, such as prosecuting cybercrime laws and accepting responsibility for malicious technical activity emanating from within national borders, are worthy of mention as well.[7] The most recent UN GGE, which completed its work in 2021, affirmed a number of such norms as diverse as attribution considerations; mutual assistance; responsible vulnerability disclosure; and the humanitarian effects on restricted internet access.[8] Such peacetime norms are worthy of careful study for their genealogy and scrutiny for their durability. While the result may be a template to help inform some aspects of restraint in cyberspace generally, as an immediate matter, it speaks more to the toolkit of economic coercion and cooperation, or intelligence activities, than the restraint of the means and methods of war.

---

[5] See, e.g., Nye, "Deterrence and Dissuasion in Cyberspace," 61; Maness and Valeriano, *Cyber War versus Cyber Realities*, 226; Christopher A Ford, "The Trouble with Cyber Arms Control," *The New Atlantis* (2010): 52–53.

[6] See US Congressional Research Service. "U.S.–China Cyber Agreement" (Washington, DC: US Congress, 2015).

[7] These are, for instance, areas of notable continuity between US cyberspace doctrine under Presidents Obama and Trump. See The White House, *The United States' International Strategy for Cyberspace*, 9–10; The White House, *National Cyber Strategy of the United States of America*, 20–21.

[8] GGE 2021.

Perhaps more relevant are efforts to establish confidence-building measures (CBMs), as a means to unmenacingly concretize shared goals of avoiding unnecessary conflict or undue escalation.[9] These efforts are notable in their own right and worthy of further exploration of how the mechanisms of low-trust negotiation and national security institutions combine and evolve to address new issues, in this case, procedures developed to communicate about missile launches repurposed to cyber incidents.[10] Punctuated though they have been by the progressive nadirs in US–Russia relations, it is no accident that these discussions emerged bilaterally between the two nations even as other dialogues withered, given their shared arms control history, rather than from dyads with less of a history and developed vocabulary of CBMs. The expansion of these ideas to multilateral contexts such as later GGEs gives some hope for the use of these narrow best practices. Despite these halting dynamics, this work may have within it the germ of a prohibitive norm, primarily as an example of underlying alignment of interest leading to two powerful states building a security norm on cyber issues. The next section develops this idea further. That said, the cyber CBM project should not be overladen; cyberattack restraint does not necessarily follow from failsafe communications channels and notification protocols. These projects within the cyber norms agenda are valuable in their own right, but in present form, mostly adjacent to the matter of cyberattack restraint. The limited nature of the GGE's 2021 consensus suggests as much.[11]

The question then returns to regimes of control, and with the fit between existing arms control paradigms and cyberattacks quite poor, the pathways for further study seem quite limited. Or are they? There may be a third way: to reconcile the process of promulgating norms with the subject-matter of arms control, recognizing the latter is just an advanced point on a spectrum of constitutive norm-building. Using this frame, the sections that follow seek to challenge the conventional wisdom in several ways, shedding light on

---

[9] Michele Markoff, "Prepared Keynote Remarks of Michele Markoff: An Overview of the Identification of Norms in the GGE Delivered at the International Security Cyber Issues Workshop Series Workshop on 'The Future of Norms to Preserve and Enhance International Cyber Stability'" (Geneva: United Nations Institute for Disarmament Research, 2016). While these efforts have been semantically part of the cyber norms agenda, they are analytically distinct in their focus on the dividing line between peace and war, as well as for the political-military institutional apparatus built to support them.

[10] See "U.S.–Russian Cooperation on Information and Communications Technology Security," 2013; US Department of State. "U.S.–Russia Bilateral Presidential Commission: 2013 Joint Annual Report" (Washington, DC: Department of State, 2013).

[11] GGE 2021.

influential forces that have been overlooked or prematurely dismissed. The difference is one of framing: while much of the literature preemptively (and perhaps appropriately) dismissed cyber arms control as a valuable pursuit, the question here is more primitive. Instead of asking how such a regime would be built, it recognizes that preordination is not the pathway by which prohibitive norms emerge. Instead, it considers whether the conditions that tend to lead to such a norm are present and/or manifesting themselves. The first set of questions pertains to the alignment of state interests. Exploring these reveals more overlap than previously acknowledged: in light of the competition, states are already engaged in constructing this space, hinting that there may be potential for robust restraint without relying on the mechanisms of formal arms control. The next set of questions then concern how realistic a prohibitive norm against cyberattacks might be, informed by two kinds of adjacencies to other prohibited novel weapons: the qualities of cyberattacks, as well as the circumstances—social, political, and ethical—surrounding their use.

8.2 Structural Prohibition

To states whose notions of humanitarian conduct are bound squarely within the regulative construct of the *jus in bello*, cyberattacks raise inherent concerns, but leave many unanswered questions—particularly those of enforcement. Without knowing the price of derogation, or even other competitor states' willingness to recognize it, a fundamental lacuna exists, just as with deterrence and self-defense. Yet recognizing the role states have in constructing normative regimes from the outside, a new perspective emerges: a competition, deemed "structural prohibition," over where and how to restrict the use of cyberattacks. This section frames, then finds evidence for that competition, which suggests some notable potential for long-term alignment.

Locating the Competitive Dynamic

The principal argument between states is not over how cyber operations should be used; rather, the key debate is over how they ought to be limited. This is perhaps a counterintuitive framing, but this section argues that it is the proper one with which to understand the competition playing out between key actors, most notably the United States and Russia.[12] True, much has been made of the fundamental clash between those two states over their approach to cyberspace operations. Outside the immediate context of Russian expansionism and international reaction thereto, there has been longstanding US resistance to equally longstanding Russian calls for arms control-like limitations and new institutions to manage them.[13] Because it has been nearly two decades since those foundational positions were written, this merits another look.

The competition over where and how to establish a prohibition was for years among the most significant for both states' institutional, diplomatic, and ultimately military approaches to cyberattacks. In the absence of US opposition, it was conceivable that Russia have succeeded in finding new regimes under which to limit development, deployment, and use in ways favorable to its designs. There is some irony that as a natural consequence of the US position, mainstreaming cyberattacks within the *jus in bello* is to make the case for its regulation. This was an easily obscured fact early in the US positions on cyber issues, such as at the first two UN GGEs, since applicability of existing law was a position to be read *contra* Russian assertion both otherwise and for a differently restrictive regime. When the alternative is a cyber-SALT (Strategic Arms Limitation Treaty) or cyber-CTBT (Comprehensive Test Ban Treaty), calling to apply existing laws of war is conservative by comparison.

But might there be a better mechanism? As the prior chapter outlined, like many explicitly proscribed means and methods of war, cyberattacks raise myriad concerns within the *jus in bello*, even to extremity, quite plausibly rendering them unusable to some states motivated by the logic. Yet again, incompatibility with existing law is necessary but not sufficient for a cyberattack taboo to take hold. Even among international law's most ardent defenders, it is "fundamentally misguided to attribute to [it] an exclusive role in controlling state behavior."[14] Restraint in warfare is far from a strictly legal matter,

---

[12] This perspective is, of course, artificially two-dimensional; in reality numerous other states have played roles in the dynamic of this debate, and countless other consequential debates have animated discourse between other states. That said, for the purposes of understanding the dynamic as it relates to questions of arms control, disarmament, and the formation of prohibitive norms, the United States and Russia do represent the two powers with both the most agenda-setting power in the relevant forums detailed herein, as well as those with the longest history of establishing detailed public positions on those issues.

[13] Kanuck, "Sovereign Discourse on Cyber Conflict under International Law Symposium," 12. See also U.N. Doc. A/59/116 (June 23, 2004), 11.

[14] Gray, *International Law and the Use of Force*, 4.

and even strong legal analysis forms an incomplete picture of whether a prohibitive norm might take hold. Countless scholars commenting on the *jus in bello*, for instance, note at some point the endless pattern of advancement in military technology followed by outcry and moral disdain. Yet only a small number of weapons that cause legal or ethical anxiety end up earning the category of unusable. After all, in most cases, such outcry is quickly followed by regularization—not prohibition. The harshest critics of the *jus in bello* regard its provisions as either ethically bankrupt for baldly reflecting power relations or dysfunctional for only limiting military instruments of minor impact. How then, one might ask, can it serve as the basis for a norm against cyberattacks?

Though each year of the last fifteen brought new challenges in this competition, on the whole, Russia has achieved little progress in a new and formal institution or governing instrument for cyber arms control.[15] The most recent of many episodes—the vote Russia successfully led to open deliberations of a new global cybercrime treaty—stoked fears such a move was a major victory for this strategy.[16] While such a treaty raises other significant risks, for instance to free expression and normalization of election interference, there is little present evidence to suggest such negotiations will bring any new arms control–like pressures to bear.

For its part, US efforts to resist the formalization of an arms control approach may well be viewed as successful, at least insofar as its litmus test in whether or not cyber operations were broadly placed beneath arms control–like frameworks. Doctrine established in the earliest days of cyberattack capabilities has remained largely consistent; institutional positions and alliances formed to resist authority of the UN system from having primacy in internet matters appear successful. The result is that cyber operations face no novel arms-control-like strictures in the international community. The problem with this reading of the last fifteen years' developments, however, is that it focuses exclusively on institutional positioning without reference to growing consensus on the framing of these issues. While assiduously resisting arms control, the United States was advancing an agenda to meaningfully control cyber arms—simply through the means of existing international law.

---

[15] Kello, *The Virtual Weapon and International Order*, 127.
[16] Peters, "Russia and China Are Trying to Set the U.N.'s Rules on Cybercrime."

The evidence from nearly all the significant forums of intergovernmental deliberation on matters of international security point to agendas seeking various forms of restraint, but in unaligned ways. It is this competition—to determine how to manage the humanitarian risks that cyberattacks create and establish disincentives for their inappropriate use—that characterizes structural prohibition.

Prospects for Compatibility

Relative to other structural projects, however, what sets the *competitive* aspect of this dynamic apart might be its superficiality. That is not to say that the outcome of which venues host states' debates over restricting use of new weaponry is not significant; rather, what it conceals is underlying commensurability not found in its deterrent and regulative counterparts. It also suggests that its dynamics may be more amenable to change by external circumstances, such as a change in leadership or a state's views on the urgency of the cause or vulnerability to a threat.

The argument for the underlying commensurability of certain key nations' strategies of structural prohibition is simple: at their core, both strategies seek the regulation and more precisely, restriction of cyberattack capabilities. Under the full sweep of the nearly two decades that regulation in this space has been contemplated, the overall trajectory toward restriction has been notable. Through successive interactions and negotiations, several key states have found a rough consensus on two important matters: first, that cyberattacks and activities like them should not be unrestricted, and second, that existing international law represents one vehicle to do so. It was hardly preordained. An alternate path might have drifted toward complete lack of restraint through mutual rejection of control. Early in the history of its annual *Information Security* resolutions and in the run-up to GGEs, Russian experts openly questioned any applicability of existing international law.[17] This position included, by inference, the *jus in bello*—despite the clear and overwhelming legal and customary evidence to the contrary.[18] Likewise, the United States might have joined Russia in reserving some exceptional status

---

[17] See, e.g., A. A. Streltsov. "Application of International Humanitarian Law to Armed Conflicts in Cyberspace" (Moscow: Information Security Institute of Lomonosov Moscow State University, 2016).

[18] See Section 7.1.

for cyber capabilities—a more plausible policy at a time when its capabilities were potentially preeminent—and rejected any restrictions as premature as a means to sidestep calls for arms control. Yet the former did not hold long, and the latter never came to be.

Instead, the United States' assertion of existing international law's applicability, and the United States' diplomatic efforts to drive consensus on that point in four successful GGEs, pointed exclusively in the direction of some measure of control.[19] If a constitutive logic of restraint is not already in operation, the evolution in discourse has certainly established a firm basis for it to do so. This is what makes this potential source of restraint for cyberattacks so powerful: states are arguing over venues and scope, but not a question fundamental to the operation of the logic.

An important preemptive critique is worth addressing that between Russia and the United States, the two parties are not equally subject to the humanitarian, constitutive logic of restraint. This "insincere conformity" critique lies at the core of US mistrust of Russian motivations in seeking any sorts of controls on cyber operations: the United States would make good on such obligations, but Russia would not.[20] Within a short time horizon, there is of course ample reason to question Russia's concern for constitutive notions of humanitarianism or even fidelity to any rules-based system of international security.[21] Vladimir Putin's adventuring and general disregard for the strictures of international law (and much else) dim any near-term hopes for Russian engagement.

Yet the sorts of prohibitive norms under discussion in this section, and certainly any formal arrangements that may evolve out of them, are not in their full expression contingent on universal recognition. Other players may indeed, especially when doing so in concert with one another, be more globally significant to a cyberattack taboo's evolution. Nor does a constitutive

---

[19] *GGE 2010*; Secretary-General United Nations, "Developments in the Field of Information and Telecommunications in the Context of International Security, delivered to the General Assembly" (New York: UN, 2013); Secretary-General United Nations, "Developments in the Field of Information and Telecommunications in the Context of International Security, delivered to the General Assembly" (New York: UN, 2015); *GGE 2021*.

[20] On insincere conformity and the limitations of the critique, see Martha Finnemore and Duncan B. Hollis, "Constructing Norms for Global Cybersecurity," *American Journal of International Law* 110, no. 3 (2016): 443. On present-day examples of this mistrust in other international security contexts, see US Department of State, "Executive Summary of Findings on Adherence to and Compliance with Arms Control, Nonproliferation, and Disarmament Agreements and Comments" (Washington, DC, 2020).

[21] Michael Schmitt, "Grey Zones in the International Law of Cyberspace," *Yale Journal of International Law Online* 42, no. 2 (2017): 3; Buchanan, *The Hacker and the State*, 289.

logic of restraint only operate as a primary force; longer-term reputational harm manifesting itself in other matters of foreign policy may ultimately motivate reconsideration of a country's actions far after the fact. It is within this frame that some of the most challenging, formal, and verifiable disarmament agreements were reached even at the peak of the Cold War. Progress on them, too, has been uneven and at times reversing course. What matters for a consideration of a prohibitive norm's development are not the contours of the political moment, but the aggregate effects of myriad forces over decades. For this reason, whether the occupant of the Kremlin can be trusted *today* to observe an emerging norm is far less significant than whether the logic of the norm is sound, and whether even in their superficial utterances, they orient the direction of discourse toward control. Another leader might find taking up these causes advantageous, necessary, or both.

Responsiveness to Change

One outgrowth of this commensurability is the potential for state policy to evolve on the basis of changing circumstances, while still keeping an orientation toward the overall objective of regulation. Structural prohibition is more accommodating to perceived changes in interest than its deterrence or regulative counterparts because it does not dictate other fundamental questions of a state's power projection—for example, the ability to use or activate a conventional military. One current US policy preference for applying existing *lex generalis* over development of a new regime may well change if US self-perception of supremacy in cyber operations dramatically shifts. This would, importantly, not require any change to the United States' aggregate military capacity or power projection. US leaders could pursue a different strategy within this competitive dynamic. Since the relative distribution of cyber power may well shift more rapidly than traditional militaries, this is significant for visualizing how and on what timeline restraint may take place.

There is, of course, a gulf between an alignment of underlying motivations (to bring some measure of regulation to this novel weaponry) and knowing the shape of those regulations—and yet another between that and general agreement thereupon. The next two sections consider how this general alignment would be narrowed to be operationalized, and what the outcome for the restraint project is as a result.

Opportunity to Narrow

An explicit focus on a concrete, prohibitive cyberattack norm may be one example of the narrowing necessary for this alignment of motivation to result in compatible state strategies. At present, the central significant point of divergence within states' competitive dynamic is where regulation should be decided. The other key divergence is "how much," which as prior chapters outlined, have focused significantly on concerns that controls would extend into matters of content deemed "destabilizing information attacks," and thus, be overinclusive from a US perspective. So long as the scope of discussions on limiting cyber activities is as broad as cyber operations writ large, or even "disruptive cyber activities" broadly defined, both questions will provide a source of contention and limited analytical progress. Yet restraint of cyberattacks—defined by their disruption of shared critical information infrastructure—are not synonymous with curtailing all cyber operations, or even all disruptive activities. In other contexts, both the United States and Russia—as well as China and India—have devoted considerable energy to expressing concern for critical infrastructure and its subversion by cyberattacks.[22] Expanding this consensus, the 2021 GGE directed specific concern to cyber-enabled disruption of critical infrastructures that provide "services to the public."[23] It also expressed the need for states to further elaborate their critical infrastructure—a nod to the extent to which digital systems and their interdependence demand an expansion of traditional definitions—and specifically advocated for a form of protected class among Computer Emergency Response Teams (CERTs), a sort of national digital first responder.[24] Deepening this perspective, a few countries have called at the leader level for the prohibition of such subversion.[25] Some influential

---

[22] Russia: Russian Federation, *Convention on International Information Security (Concept)* (Moscow, 2011), Art. 5(14). United States: Jeh Johnson, "Statement by Secretary Jeh Johnson on the Designation of Election Infrastructure as a Critical Infrastructure Subsector" (Washington, DC: Department of Homeland Security, 2017). China: Cyberspace Administration of China, "Critical Information Infrastructure Security Protection Regulations," ed. Information Office of the State Council of the People's Republic of China (2017). India: India's National Cyber Security Coordinator, Lt. Gen. (Dr) Rajesh Pant announced in March 2020 that the Government of India is developing a new cybersecurity policy to "address the cyber threat and synergies between various stakeholders": *The Economic Times of India*, "Government Likely to Announce New Cyber Security Policy in Three Months," March 11, 2020.
[23] *GGE 2021*, 7 (para. 10), 12 (paras 42–45).
[24] Ibid., 9 (para 27), 16 (paras 65–68).
[25] "Joint Fact Sheet: The United States-Republic of Korea Alliance: Shared Values, New Frontiers," 2015.

scholars have taken this observation one step further and called for a proactive "duty to warn," the spirit of which was expressed in the lead US GGE expert's statement following the close of the 2016–2017 GGE meeting.[26]

Later sections will explore just how valuable these adjacencies might be, but as a preliminary matter, the potential to narrow the debate through a focus on critical infrastructure as a priority for a shared goal of regulation is notable. Doing so would not require trust, which has been lacking on a US–Russia bilateral basis for some time and unlikely to recover rapidly.[27] In fact, it may thrive on the lack of trust, as recrimination is itself an attempt to shift discourse toward restriction, if not prohibition, of a particular action. To be sure, this commensurability merely sets up the potential for further regulation; it does not in and of itself portend the emergence of a prohibition. That said, it is a necessary precondition for one, and on that basis alone, suggests the need to examine more deeply the potential for such a norm to take hold. Having established the potential for alignment with a narrowing of the competitive dynamic, the balance of this chapter will consider the plausibility of such a norm.

8.3 Understanding Prohibitive Norms

The international competition over cyberattacks' usability reflects underlying commensurability—leading, perhaps ultimately, to alignment. If narrowed, could there be space to evolve competition over the modalities of restriction into any kind of real prohibition on cyberattacks? The mere existence of a prohibition publicly observed by some states might weigh heavily on the consideration of others, even if it was of contested scope and had spotty adoption. The correct focus at this point is not on what institutional form restrictions could take—prior sections explained why that frame has been divisive and self-defeating. Thankfully, it is also premature. A rich literature in international relations has formed around seeking to explain

---

[26] See Michele Markoff, "Explanation of Position at the Conclusion of the 2016–2017 UN Group of Governmental Experts (GGE) on Developments in the Field of Information and Telecommunications in the Context of International Security," news release, 2017. See also Eneken Tikk, "Ten Rules for Cyber Security," *Survival* 53, no. 3 (2011): 126–27; Oren Gross, "Cyber Responsibility to Protect: Legal Obligations of States Directly Affected by Cyber-Incidents," *Cornell International Law Journal*, no. 3 (2015): 504.

[27] For example, see Nicole Perlroth and David Sanger, "Cyberattacks Put Russian Fingers on the Switch at Power Plants, U.S. Says," *New York Times*, March 16, 2018.

phenomena like the one which the last chapter concluded: why states observe fundamentally normative restraints—taboos—that sometimes lead to more formal prohibitions.

Evidence is not yet available to prove whether such a taboo is taking hold within state decision-making processes, however, prior chapters suggest there are the substantive, discursive, and institutional bases for one to emerge. The next two sections evaluate such a norm. This section explains the concept and methodology, then addresses some important critiques, before conducting a preliminary comparative analysis between the formative characteristics of a possible cyberattack norm and other novel weapons of war today subject to various forms of prohibition. The next section will then consider the prospects that such a norm might see conditions favorable to its adoption and general spread (the so-called tipping point and cascade) in the way those other successful prohibitions have.

Understanding Exceptional Prohibitions

The last chapter outlined how, as a matter of law, cyberattacks may inherently run afoul of the *jus in bello*, but it further recognized some of the limitations to such an abstract analysis having practical effects. That *lex generalis* is of course subject to far more interpretation than, for instance, the *lex specialis* that has emerged around land mines or chemical weapons. Additional Protocol I implies the need to create such a bridge from general principles to specific obligations in Article 51: the reality that certain "method or means of combat... *cannot* be directed at a specific military objective, [and/or] be limited as required."[28] Indeed, they have, and Cassese notes that "specific bans on specific weapons have proved more useful" than modern attempts to further elaborate general principles.[29] This is partly because of the extreme nature of their deviation from the *lex generalis* of the *jus in bello* outlined in the last chapter, in turn validating the enduring relevance of those very principles in law.[30] Yet extremity of violation argued in commentary does lead directly to

[28] *AP1*, Art. 51(4)(b–c).
[29] Cassese, *International Law*, 411.
[30] Bartels, for instance, notes that the *jus in bello* "has to be considered as the *lex specialis* during times of armed conflict, and thus takes precedence over the realm of the rules that (mainly) pertain to *post bellum* situations." Rogier Bartels, "From Jus In Bello to Jus Post Bellum: When do Non-International Armed Conflicts End?," in *Jus Post Bellum: Mapping the Normative Foundations*, ed. Carsten Stahn et al. (Oxford: Oxford University Press, 2014), 298. See also Robert Jervis, "Arms Control, Stability, and Causes of War," *Political Science Quarterly* 108, no. 2 (1993): 244–45.

new strictures on warfare; here, analysis of law begs to be put in a more holistic context that accounts for this change. For instance, the former speaks to the process of institutionalizing a norm, and the latter to building recognition for the basis of a norm in the first place. Some states may recognize violations of the *jus in bello* as carrying particular status by virtue of being a *legal* norm, but other factors surely determine state deliberations.[31] How might they come together to motivate restraint, and before that, to change the way states regard certain actions within warfare?

Built atop the observation that exceptional prohibitions do not simply present themselves, a rich literature has traced the processes by which they form.[32] Specific work tracing particular prohibitions itself draws on foundational work, helping give structure to these inputs—which, in turn, assists synthesis and adoption of insights from a range of fields: behavioral economics, political science, sociology, and evolutionary biology.[33] Most notably, Finnemore and Sikkink's "norm life cycle" offers a process accounting for not just change, but the actors and mechanisms by which states are induced to recognize and identify with a new norm, in turn shaping behavior and the formation of subsequent norms.[34] Their work also provides a means to conduct rigorous (if retrospective) empirical investigations of state restraint.

Of course a present-day study of cyberattacks, over fifteen years into their emergence, cannot possess the historical sweep of Tannenwald on nuclear weapons or of Price on chemical weapons.[35] That said, Tannenwald's *The Nuclear Taboo* is perhaps most notable for surfacing how policymakers early in the nuclear era were compelled to give those weapons exceptional status, and in turn, exercise an uneasy restraint. It is that kernel of a prohibition—and the processes that might support it—that the sections that follow aim to

---

[31] For more engagement with the status of legal norms relative to others, see Martha Finnemore, "Are Legal Norms Distinctive?," *NYU Journal of International Law and Policy* 32 (1999).

[32] Specific to the evolution of exceptional prohibitions on weaponry, emblematic examples include Tannenwald, *Nuclear Taboo*; Richard M. Price, "Reversing the Gun Sights: Transnational Civil Society Targets Land Mines," *International Organization* 52, no. 3 (1998); Price, *Chemical Weapons Taboo*; Ethan Nadelmann, "Global Prohibition Regimes: The Evolution of Norms in International Society," *International Organization* 44 (1990).

[33] On norm formation generally, see Martha Finnemore and Kathryn Sikkink, "International Norm Dynamics and Political Change," *International Organization* 52, no. 4 (1998); Thomas Risse-Kappen et al., *The Power of Human Rights: International Norms and Domestic Change*, vol. 66 (Cambridge: Cambridge University Press, 1999); Ann Florini, "The Evolution of International Norms," *International Studies Quarterly* 40 (1996); Jeffrey W. Legro, "The Transformation of Policy Ideas," *American Journal of Political Science* (2000).

[34] Finnemore and Sikkink, "International Norm Dynamics and Political Change."

[35] Tannenwald, *Nuclear Taboo*; Price, "Reversing the Gun Sights."

interrogate; not seeking to document it, but instead, locating the forces that would shape such views in the years to come.

Critiques of the Frame

The development and operation of such a norm also does not depend on full restraint or categorical nonuse. Take, for example, the nuclear taboo or the chemical weapons ban. Both technologies have been used, and each instance arguably strengthened opprobrium on the user and the norm against their nonuse, particularly for chemical weapons. Thus, as Kratochwil and Ruggie note, "the violation of a norm does not mean it no longer exists or that it ceases to have an impact on social behavior; what matters is how the violation is interpreted by others and what subsequent practices serve to rehabilitate or undercut the norm."[36] When they are used, "communicative dynamics" of rationale, justification, pleas for understanding, and admissions of guilt that emerge can "tell us far more about how robust a regime is than overt behavior alone."[37]

Nor do normative prohibitions restricting weaponry solely have value for powerful states that already possess them; Price carefully and convincingly discredits the "realist expectation," advanced by Van Crevald and others "that effective prohibitions are attended only for useless weapons."[38] Evidence of how the taboos against chemical weapons, biological weapons, land mines, and nuclear weapons evolved is not overwhelmingly attributable to inefficacy or to a desire to impose a prohibition to sidestep their use by weaker powers. Studies like Price's on chemical weapons and land mines and Tannenwald's on the nuclear taboo effectively undercut the argument that the operation of these norms is explainable strictly as a function of power-based interests or function only to restrain asymmetric tools.[39]

The final common criticism of the formation and value of a norm built atop the laws of war is that it would limit the wrong objects and "[refrain]

---

[36] Friedrich Kratochwil and John Gerard Ruggie, "International Organization: A State of the Art on the Art of the State," *International Organization* 40, no. 4 (1986).

[37] Ibid., 768.

[38] Richard Price, "A Genealogy of the Chemical Weapons Taboo," *International Organization* 49, no. 1 (1995): 88. In contrast to Martin Van Crevald, *Technology and War: From 2000 B.C. to the Present*, 2nd ed. (New York: Touchstone, 1991), 177.

[39] Price, "Reversing the Gun Sights"; Price, *Chemical Weapons Taboo*; Tannenwald, *Nuclear Taboo*; Price, "Norms and Deterrence."

from imposing restraints on the most dangerous forms of armed violence" precisely because those laws reflecting primarily the interests of powerful states that led their development.[40] Yet one does not follow from the other, if one accepts a remotely incremental (and thus, pragmatic) approach to the project of limiting suffering. The emergence of a cyberattack taboo would not, this study contends, be a distraction in the broader project of eliminating human suffering; rather, it would an increasingly important means to serve it. It is hard to argue that the nuclear taboo does not hold at bay a dangerous form of violence, and so, too, with chemical weapons. Thus, the demonstrated ability of such norms to meaningfully limit states' recourse to otherwise effective weapons illustrates the practical, and by many measures ethical importance of the enterprise.

Content and Process

Finnemore and Hollis have drawn attention to the need for more considered approaches not just to the content of what they call "cybersecurity norms," but the process by which they form—since the former is in no small part shaped by the latter.[41] This is no less true for norms that have laws buttressing them—as, in the case of the *jus in bello*, the one under examination here does.[42] The two sections that follow offer a preliminary contribution to this project by considering the existence and relative strength of possible contributors to the success of a prohibitive cyberattack norm built atop the *jus in bello*.

Locating the foundation of a cyberattack prohibition begins with the history of other prohibitive norms on emerging technologies, scanning for similarities in both the content and trajectories of the norm. This is the methodology that the following sections adopt: seeking first some initial hypotheses about the salient features uniting successful prohibitive norms, and second, for the features of cyberattacks that they share with other proscribed tools.[43] Of course, each of these features could sustain its own article-length

---

[40] Cassese, *International Law*, 399.
[41] Finnemore and Hollis, "Constructing Norms for Global Cybersecurity."
[42] Ibid., 442.
[43] This methodology draws on prior work by Mazanec, though likely due to narrower subject matter or the passage of time, shares few of its conclusions. Brian M. Mazanec, *The Evolution of Cyber War: International Norms for Emerging-Technology Weapons* (Lincoln: University of Nebraska Press, 2015), 141–60.

study, and as such, they are also offered in the spirit of supporting further research when documentary evidence and a historical record permits. Similarly, such an early inquiry into the formation of a prohibitive norm against cyberattacks is naturally limited in engaging with many debates in the constructivist scholarship, for instance how congruence plays out at the local level in reference to regional and cultural differences.[44] Nonetheless, it aims to provide some structure to a further pursuit of those ideas.

8.4 Cyberattack Norm Construction

This section focuses on the process that might inform a cyberattack norm in its early stages of development—so-called norm emergence, in which several features tend to inform success.[45] While no brief summary could do justice to the complexity and combinations that lead to all prohibitive regimes, the next sections connect the process of norm formation to the specifics of cyberattacks. Carrying forward the last chapter's analysis as one potential avenue, it begins by considering the coherence of a prohibitive cyberattack norm with the *jus in bello*, a natural place onto which it could be grafted. It then considers how states' present development, deployment, and use of cyberattacks may shape the norm formation process. Finally, it looks at how the dual phenomena of public awareness of the issue, and of the norms surrounding it, may play a role.

Coherence and Grafting

Among factors in a norm's emergence, first and perhaps most significant of all is whether a norm is coherent with others already recognized by states, and whether it can therefore be grafted onto an existing set of views. This coherence and grafting process helps shape the discourse and partially informs the success of a norm's emergence.[46] For instance, among a great many other points of coherence, chemical weapons resonated with longstanding

---

[44] See, e.g., Amitav Acharya, "How Ideas Spread: Whose Norms Matter? Norm localization and institutional change in Asian regionalism," *International Organization* 58, no. 2 (2004).

[45] This study does not attempt to examine the factors that would lead to the third phase, so-called internalization, which would be premature and of limited value absent known contours of an emerged and cascading prohibitive norm.

[46] Finnemore and Sikkink, "International Norm Dynamics and Political Change," 905–06.

revulsion to the use of poisons and were able to be grafted onto the *jus in bello*'s concepts of discrimination and limitations on undue suffering.[47]

Coherence with other prohibitive norms would be a powerful motivator for one concerning cyberattacks; though none apply directly, looking deeper at those weapons' salient characteristics offers some insights. Understanding why, for instance, chemical weapons or cluster munitions took on a reputation for being at the extreme end of *jus in bello* violations provides the means to understand whether cyberattacks might be similarly situated on that spectrum. Six characteristics, at varying levels, are common among several proscribed weapons—overlaying the prior *jus in bello* analyses chapter to help understand what qualities might consistently shape the discourse in separating the "extreme" from the "merely bad." Among the more concrete of these characteristics, all relate to a lack of control: over victims; over the timing of effects; over the geography of a conflict; or of the environmental consequences. All are functions, to varying degrees, of the kind of inherent lack of distinction described in the last chapter. Less measurable but still significant factors, at least for other prohibitions, include a sense that they are weapons only the weak would condescend to use; and that the tool is one against which no plausible defense exists. These factors relate more to concerns of unnecessary suffering and chivalry. Of course, none of these factors operates on its own, and no weapon possesses all of them; nonetheless, they offer some insights into *how* a prohibitive norm against cyberattacks might cohere with others—in a frame distinct from violations of law.

Control. Emblematically, biological weapons, land mines, and (to a large degree) cluster munitions are set apart from other weaponry on account of an inherent inability to observe distinction. In the case of land mines and cluster munitions, the fact that exploding fragments tend to not only injure noncombatants, but also children, was by many accounts material to the legal and ethical opprobrium leveled against them.[48] Chapter 7 pointed to the ways in which the secondary effects of cyberattacks may well be not reliably controllable, and thus create significant potential for collateral harm. The nature of this harm may vary, of course. That cyberattacks' unintentional victims would not principally be children or other innocents weighs in this

---

[47] Price, *Chemical Weapons Taboo*, 18–30.
[48] Price, "Reversing the Gun Sights," 618; Théo Boutruche et al., "The Title and Preamble of the Convention," in *The Convention on Cluster Munitions: A Commentary* (Oxford: Oxford University Press, 2010), 78; Alexander Breitegger, *Cluster Munitions and International Law* (New York: Routledge, 2012), 131.

respect against these tools taking on a status like chemical weapons or cluster munitions—although for the reasons outlined in Section 7.3, effects on medical services may cause the elderly or infirmed to suffer particular effects.

That possibility notwithstanding, the analogy to biological weapons is instructive. There, the inherent lack of control emanates from the transmission of the agent to *any* human sharing the same biology, not just combatants. With cyberattacks, some systems would include malware self-propagating and disrupting any machine eligible to receive the virus.[49] This is not a hypothetical concern; some of the most sophisticated pieces of malware have appeared on what appear to be unrelated machines, and some of the most common strains of malware propagate widely and quickly.[50] AI technologies render this kind of mutation-on-the-fly and cross-platform spread more likely, speedier, and almost certainly harder to control in the years to come.[51]

Duration. With the potential to explode after the cessation of hostilities, land mines and cluster munitions, and to a less reliable extent biological weapons, are exceptional as well for extending the duration of damage longer than militarily necessary. Cyberattacks run a weak but nonzero risk of this feature in two scenarios. A cyberattack designed in part to sow fear and create civil unrest in the victim state may well exhibit its effects over a period of time—infecting critical information infrastructure all at once, but only activating sequentially, causing increasing damage. Designing such malware with a "kill switch" that could be activated at the end of hostilities to render the tool inert would also be to provide the victim a template to defend against it all at once. While not impossible to develop, countries seeking to maximize the impact of their attack may not include such a feature (plausibly in violation of customary international law). In an alternate scenario, disrupted infrastructure might host dependencies that are not known until well after the initial action has taken place. For instance, it may be that a piece of infrastructure facilitates the communication of seldom-used Internet of Things (IoT) devices that in aggregate, are important to managing safety audits of

---

[49] Greenberg chronicles the saga of NotPetya's progress in indiscriminately harming systems, and that even when a "vaccine" to this malware was developed by Serper, "it was too late for all but a small fraction of the plague's victims to make use of it. NotPetya's $10 billion worth of damage was largely, irreversibly, underway. The angel of death had already made its rounds." Greenberg, *Sandworm*, 209.

[50] Stamatis Karnouskos, "Stuxnet Worm Impact on Industrial Cyber-Physical System Security" (paper presented at the IECON 2011–37th Annual Conference of the IEEE Industrial Electronics Society, 2011).

[51] For examples of the challenges associated with defending against these kinds of mutations—even when machine learning systems are used in the defensive context—see, e.g., Shackelford, "From Nuclear War to Net War."

industrial or energy facilities. Here again, the result may be the extension of a cyberattack's effects well beyond the period of formal hostilities. While one or both of these designs would raise significant humanitarian concerns shared with other prohibited weapons, they are not inherent to the weaponry; thus, the effect on an emerging norm is plausible but likely weak.

Geography. Biological weapons, nuclear first-use, and cluster munitions all share an inability to control the geography within which effects are felt—raising concerns of distinction and neutrality documented previously. Biological weapons, in the form of a virulent engineered disease, have the potential for widespread transmission outside the country and even continent of first delivery. The same would be true, differently and at sufficient megatonnage, of a nuclear strike, as winds take radioactive plumes across borders. Both of these characteristics set these weapons apart, and relative to others, help position them at the extremity of the *jus in bello*. Cyberattacks possess this quality to an even greater degree, though with less direct consequences. The reliance of numerous systems on shared infrastructure that typically resides outside their immediate geography—perhaps in another town, state, or even country—creates a likelihood of effect outside the immediate theater of operations. This may, of course, be by design. Akin to destroying a petroleum reserve, an attacker may find it advantageous to focus on an undefended resource far-afield if it creates the potential for battlefield advantage in-theater. That said, the concern here is not with anticipated primary effects in distinct geography, but secondary effects geographies not party to the conflict. This is a nontrivial issue that cyberattacks invoke, particularly to the extent concentration in the market for shared digital services (such as remote computing and storage) creates vulnerabilities across geographies with single points of failure.[52] To the extent that the damage and disruption of the attack is significant—this lack of geographic containment may be a strong basis of support for a prohibitive norm.

Environment. Nuclear weapons, chemical weapons, and to a different degree antipersonnel land mines and cluster munitions all raise the potential for "environmental degradation," a factor that features into accounts

---

[52] For example, for Amazon Web Services (AWS), one of the world's top cloud computing platforms, claims "there are tens of thousands of APN [Amazon Partner Networks] Partners across the globe. More than 90% of Fortune 100 companies and the majority of Fortune 500 companies utilize APN Partner solutions and services." Amazon Web Services, Inc., "What Is the AWS Partner Network? Helping Companies Build Successful AWS-based Business Practices and Solutions."

of norms circumscribing each.[53] Protections along these lines have been controversial; the Additional Protocol I's Articles 35(3) and 55(1) prohibit "widespread, long-lasting, or severe" damage to the environment—terms that Roberts and Guelff note are "so broad and vague as to place few limits on actual activities."[54] This is no less true of the concept's use in the Convention on Environmental Modification Techniques (ENMOD Convention), which focuses on using damaging environmental tactics *as a method* (rather than byproduct) of war.[55] Leaving aside the latter, it is true the ambiguity of the former obscures obvious common threads even among specifically prohibited means. The extent to which they may affect the environment is quite different: for example, through radiation, tainting ground water; or making terrain unnavigable. Certainly, the destruction of land or rendering buildings unsafe is no distinguishing factor. Neither would be the weapons' capacity to injure flora or fauna at the time of attack. If this characteristic is distinctive and shared among these weapons, a new framing of environmental degradation is needed.

What might tie these exceptionally prohibited weapons together instead is less directly the environmental effects in the sense of undue harm to nature, but a direct matter: the requirement to create long-lasting exclusion areas or hot/warm zones preventing the civilian access to (and thus exploitation of the resources of) affected areas.[56] In this respect, the contribution of awareness of environmental effects to the formation of a norm is closely tied to both geographic and temporal extension of conflict just described. What sets it apart from those two conditions is the notion that resources otherwise exploitable for peaceful purposes would no longer be available to civilians, even in peacetime.

Extending this concept to cyberattacks, one must first accept the concept—as the US Department of Defense has stated repeatedly in doctrine—that "although it is a man-made domain, cyberspace is now as relevant a domain . . .

---

[53] See, for example, the way in which the antiwar movement seized upon this (among other) factors in promotion of a nuclear taboo. Nina Tannenwald, "Stigmatizing the Bomb: Origins of the Nuclear Taboo," *International Security* 29, no. 4 (2005): 22.

[54] *AP1*, Art. 35(4), 55(1).

[55] *AP1*, Art. 35(4), 55(1); Convention on the Prohibition of Military or Any Other Hostile Use of Environmental Modification Techniques (May 18, 1977). 1108 U.N.T.S. 151; Roberts, *Documents on the Laws of War*, 408.

[56] Definitions and examples of managing such zones for chemical weapons can be found in Organization for the Prevention of Chemical Weapons (OPCW), "Practical Guide for Medical Management of Chemical Warfare Casualties" (The Hague: OPCW International Cooperation and Assistance Division, Assistance and Protection Branch, 2016).

as the naturally occurring domains of land, sea, air, and space."[57] Because it is man-made, it relies on infrastructure to exist—but importantly here—for its continued human exploitation. On that basis, effective cyberattacks both threaten the existence of that portion of the domain, and more directly, its exploitability for productive human endeavors. For instance: the Shamoon malware used in the Saudi Aramco attack, repurposed instead for a broader cyberattack against several information infrastructures, might yield precisely such an effect. In countries with limited connectivity or digital economies, this concern would be near-irrelevant. But for those with exceptional levels of dependency, it might be the equivalent of creating a massive exclusion zone, rendering that segment of the cyberspace environment unusable, and thus, unexploitable. The coherence is therefore plausible, though the contested nature of the underlying terms renders this force less considerable than others presented herein.

Condescension. Successful military innovations, by their nature, seek to shift the balance of a conflict in their user's favor, and exceptional ones might empower weaker states with asymmetrical power over otherwise stronger ones. The stigmatization discourse of a novel technology is, of course, inseparable from power dynamics, and here in particular the relegation of a technology to a tool of asymmetry can lead more powerful states to seek controls upon it. For instance, Sigal notes this feature in the emerging discourse of antipersonnel land mines, and Price convincingly traces shifts in support for the prohibition on chemical weapons to their redefinition, over the years and through the historical experience of conflicts in which they were used, from a "weapon of the strong" to a "weapon of the weak."[58] Of course, the opposite of this effect is also true; sought-after weapons that confer legitimacy (as noted later) may confer on the weapon higher attractiveness, and in turn, frustrate a prohibitive norm.

In this respect, cyberattacks fall at the intersection of both. For much of their early history, sophisticated cyber operations were kept strictly under wraps, in spite or perhaps because of the ease of their transmission.[59] Cyberattack capabilities' secrecy and novelty gave way to some journalists

---

[57] US Department of Defense, "Quadrennial Defense Review" (Washington, DC: Department of Defense, 2010), 37. See also US Department of Defense, *Department of Defense Strategy for Operating in Cyberspace*, 5–6.
[58] Leon V. Sigal, *Negotiating Minefields: The Landmines Ban in American Politics* (New York: Routledge, 2013), 10; Price, *Chemical Weapons Taboo*, 162.
[59] Adam Janofsky, "Gen. Michael Hayden: Over-Classification of Cyber Threats Puts Businesses at Risk," *Wall Street Journal*, October 31, 2018.

deeming them "the perfect weapon," semantically boosting the reputation these weapons have for being the sole provenance of a varsity league of states.[60] The last several years, however, may provide reasons to reconsider that status—and states' incentive to change it. Just as it served powerful state interests to advance the chemical weapons taboo, the development of cyberattack capabilities by nonsuperpowers with aspirations to disrupt status quo security dynamics—such as Iran and North Korea—may occasion a shift in the discourse. In this respect, the contribution of this factor to a cyberattack prohibition generally is mixed. Sophisticated cyberattack capabilities have been accorded a certain status, but their intrinsic qualities (particularly imprecision) could facilitate a rapid delegitimization.

Defenselessness. If a new innovation creates the "horror of a weapon against which there [is] no defense," this dynamic can help stimulate calls for prohibition. The notion that a particular tool cannot be defended against, once firmly established in the discourse, has some history of motivating states to pursue control.[61] For nuclear weapons, (the early but ineffective measures to constrain) strategic bombing, and biological weapons, these features factored into how and at what pace norms against them formed. This condition is usually temporary: Price details how this was both one salient factor for the revulsion against asphyxiating gas that helped animate early efforts for the ban on chemical weapons—and but also how "as soldiers became more familiar with the use of gas and defenses against it, many of the initial inhibitions ebbed," for a time.[62] That said, if the period of defenselessness is prolonged (as with nuclear weapons); permanent (as with biological weapons); or states are collectively beset by the concern (as with both), there may be more fertile ground for actors to enter this fact into discourse, use it to speed a norm's formation, and create interest in observing it. Whether advantage will perennially lie with the attacker; whether market failures will prevent the emergence of resilient digital economies; and whether nationwide cyber-defense is even possible are all significant and live topics in policy and scholarship.[63] In the narrowest sense, it is of course indisputable that every cyber vulnerability has

---

[60] Sanger, *The Perfect Weapon*.
[61] Mazanec, *Evolution of Cyber War*, 151.
[62] Price, *Chemical Weapons Taboo*, 64, 66.
[63] On the interplay between balancing offense and defense strategies in cyberspace, see Buchanan, *Cybersecurity Dilemma*. On market structure and cybersecurity incentives see Homeland Security and Governmental Affairs, *Hearing to Establish a Bug Bounty Pilot Program Within the Department of Homeland Security, and For Other Purposes*, 115th Congress, February 26, 2018. On the limited efficacy of even national cyber-defense initiatives, see Mark Warner, "2018 National Security Agency Law Day Speech" (Washington, DC: Lawfare, 2018): "There are no rules of the road in cyberspace,

a means to defend against it, even if that means is to use another variety of machine or rewrite its code. Effective cyber operations traditionally exploit bugs in software that are, in turn, patched in successive updates. Offensive tools can be used to defensive benefit.[64] This distinction turns instead on the notion of aggregate risk: whether the sheer size of the vulnerable surface area and the density of interconnectivity renders a reliable defense implausible. To borrow from Baldwin, it is a collective sense of dread that the zero-day will always get through.[65]

At present, even (or perhaps especially) governments in the most advanced economies seem fraught with this anxiety, consistently chartering and rechartering Reports and Commissions trying to signal a lack of preparation.[66] As over fifteen years of policy and intelligence community reports make clear, this is not a new development, nor has the sense of vulnerability materially waned. The US 2008 Annual Threat Assessment of the Intelligence Community warned that cyber threats to our information infrastructure are increasingly "being targeted for exploitation and potentially for disruption or destruction . . . over the past year, cyber exploitation activity has grown more sophisticated, more targeted, and more serious." In 2018, then-Director of National Intelligence Dan Coats warned, "it was in the months prior to September 2001 when, according to then-CIA Director George Tenet, the system was blinking red. And here we are nearly two decades later, and I'm here to say the warning lights are blinking red again. Today, the digital infrastructure that serves this country is literally under attack."[67] At a certain point, with the passage of sufficient time and expenditure of tens of billions of dollars by the federal government alone, queries whether overcoming this fatalism is possible—and the sense of defenselessness—may become permanent. Absent tectonic change, it may be insurmountable, and other countries'

---

which leaves us open to an accidental conflict. And the absence of an overt response to prior cyberattacks leaves the public and other nations with the impression that those activities are acceptable."

[64] Buchanan, Cybersecurity Dilemma, 47, 72.
[65] Baldwin's "A Fear for the Future" speech made famous the line "the bomber will always get through," a rallying cry among those in the interwar period seeking a robust (if ill-fated) prohibition on strategic bombing. Government of the United Kingdom, *Proceedings of the House of Commons*, London: His Majesty's Government, 1932, 632.
[66] Emblematic US examples from the last several years include the February 2016 Cybersecurity National Action Plan (CNAP), the December 2016 Commission on Enhancing National Cybersecurity, and the 2020 Cyber Solarium Commission.
[67] J. Michael McConnell, "Annual Threat Assessment of the Intelligence Community for the Senate Armed Services Committee" (Washington, DC: US Senate, 2008); Coats, "Transcript: Dan Coats Warns The Lights Are 'Blinking Red' On Russian Cyberattacks"; Jim Garamone, "Cyber Tops List of Threats to U.S., Director of National Intelligence Says," *DOD News (official)*, February 13, 2018.

Table 8.1 Summary of Potential for Discourse Coherence between Cyberattacks and other Exceptionally Prohibited Weapons

	Strong	Weak	Negative
Control	✓✓		
Duration		✓	
Geography	✓✓		
Environment		✓	
Condescension			☒
Defenselessness	✓✓		

perceptions may share similar alignment: China, for instance, with its repeated public claims of victimhood and vulnerability to cyberattacks.[68] The result, which Table 8.1 summarizes, suggests a strong potential for this sense of defenselessness to shape the development of a prohibitive norm against cyberattacks.

Development, Deployment, and Use

Separate from the characteristics of the tools themselves, the status of their development, extent of deployment, and frequency of use help shape the emergence of prohibitive norms. This section considers how cyberattacks fit relative to their habituation within military planning; whether their capabilities have been consistently demonstrated as to be widely known; and the extent to which they have proliferated to a range of states within the international system.

Preemptive Establishment. The establishment of a prohibition *before* a particular means or method of warfare has been habituated into multiple militaries' standard operations and states' coercive playbooks can play an important role in the viability of that norm.[69] This was clearly the case for

---

[68] Lyu, "What Are China's Cyber Capabilities and Intentions?"
[69] The seminal US National Research Council report on cyberattack issues suggested the need for this research agenda as far back as 2009, but few took up the charge. See "Technology, Policy, Law, and Ethics Regarding U.S. Acquisition and Use of Cyberattack Capabilities," 10–15: "An agreement might also involve restrictions on the use of cyberattack weapons. For example, signatories might

all militaries, for instance, in one category of weapons plausible though never deployed at scale: blinding lasers.[70] Likewise in the case of only one military's initial possession of the capability, as with the evolution of the nuclear taboo.[71]

While cyber operations are increasingly a feature of states' military apparatus, cyberattacks of the sort driving this analysis have not become regular features in international disputes in or outside of wartime. This is, of course, subject to change, and a range of previously cited doctrine makes clear that major military powers currently anticipate some level of cyber challenge during any upcoming campaign—making it even more notable that none (save for, at a small scale, Russia) have habituated nor signaled intent to engage in broad-based cyberattacks. On its own, this situation has the potential to strongly favor a norm's development, since advocating for it is not to demand a substantial shift in current state practice.

This present lack of regular practice may leave a window for a prohibitive norm to take hold, but it also surfaces a significant barrier that will recur throughout this analysis: that as with the preparation of the *Tallinn Manual*, semantic overlap in the world "cyberattack" itself may hinder a norm's formation and advancement in the life cycle. In pursuit of other cyber norms, governments occasionally borrow the phrase to make a point about emphasis: for instance, US officials have on multiple occasions referred to Chinese theft of intellectual property as an attack.[72] Ministries within the same government have even come to define cyberattacks differently, ranging from any exploitation, to bona fide disruption, to the sort of national security incidents described here.[73] Finding resonant phraseology will be key to

---

agree to refrain from striking at national financial systems or power grids, much as nations might avoid targeting hospitals in a kinetic attack, or to refrain from using lasers intended to blind soldiers."

[70] *Protocol on Blinding Laser Weapons*.
[71] Tannenwald, *Nuclear Taboo*, 365.
[72] US Attorney General William Barr said at a press conference to announce the charges against four Chinese hackers for hacking Equifax: "This kind of attack on American industry is of a piece with other Chinese illegal acquisitions of sensitive personal data." Brian Barrett, "How Four Chinese Hackers Allegedly Took Down Equifax," *Wired*, May 24, 2020.
[73] In the April 2013 Congressional hearing, the US Director of National Intelligence defined a cyberattack as "a non-kinetic offensive operation intended to create physical effects or to manipulate, disrupt, or delete data." Armed Services Committee, United States Senate, *Hearing on the Worldwide Threats to the National Security of the U.S.*, April 18, 2013, 10. Yet the FBI, part of the same Intelligence Community that the ODNI oversees, interchangeably uses the term cyber attacks and cyber intrusions on its Cyber Crime webpage: "The FBI is the lead federal agency for investigating *cyber attacks by criminals, overseas adversaries, and terrorists*.... Our nation's critical infrastructure, including both private and public sector networks, are targeted by adversaries. American companies are targeted for trade secrets ... and universities for their cutting-edge research.... Just as the

a norm benefiting from this "preemptive" status—in order to overcome the critique that because cyber *operations* have become routinized in advanced military practice, that hopes for restraining a particular category of their use are futile.

Demonstrated Capability. Certainty of the tool's destructive capability can strengthen a potential prohibition by preventing divergence of perspectives on whether a proscription is of value. Historians recount little debate over nuclear weapons' capabilities following the Hiroshima and Nagasaki blasts.[74] That said, there is a counterpoint to this criterion: policymakers' lack of exposure to the battlefield realities of some new technologies (in Price's observation, the history of gas warfare) can help amplify their revulsion if a "taboo issue[s] from a fear of the unknown."[75]

Cyberattacks likely fall into this latter category, aided by the substantial amount of popular and policy-focused literature trying to direct attention to the underresourced vulnerability. To date, Estonia represents the closest to a demonstrated incident, though that event was more of a small-scale harbinger of disruptive potential plausible to much greater effect in more countries, one or two decades later. The closest historical analogy might therefore not be 1945 for nuclear weapons, but rather the early years of the twentieth century for strategic bombing—when capability and corresponding dread were known, but the first major demonstrations had not yet taken place, let alone been habituated into most war planning.[76] The aforementioned sense of general vulnerability, combined with this lack of demonstration amplifying such a fear of the unknown, may strengthen such a norm's traction in the present moment.

Changes in this status quo of the unknown would be particularly significant. A repeat of the Estonia attack, on a small but wired nation, also with temporary duration and with a relatively rapid recovery, may have a negative effect on a prohibitive norm by both removing some of fear of the unknown

---

FBI transformed itself to better address the terrorist threat after the 9/11 attacks, it is undertaking a similar transformation to address the pervasive and evolving *cyber threat*." US Federal Bureau of Investigation, "What We Investigate: Cyber Crime" (Washington, DC: Department of Justice, 2020), emphasis added.

[74] Perhaps there could have been more. After all, the firebombing of Tokyo claimed more lives in aggregate—a point that Tannenwald deftly uses to illustrate how nuclear weapons began to take on a distinct exceptional status. Tannenwald, *Nuclear Taboo*, 79–80.
[75] Price, *Chemical Weapons Taboo*, 80.
[76] Lee B. Kennett, *A History of Strategic Bombing* (New York: Scribner, 1983), 59; Mazanec, *Evolution of Cyber War*, 81.

while obscuring broader disruptive and destructive potential if such tools were directed elsewhere and for longer. Conversely, several demonstrations of major power, yielding significant disruption and many of the collateral effects outlined in the prior chapter, might be a strong force accelerating the norm—distinct, even, from that state's reaction.

This effect is, however, plausibly contested, and a minor paradox of norm specificity and unknown effect may persist until a tipping point is reached. For instance, Cassese, in part, regards the success of "specific bans" as tied significantly to their specificity and concreteness.[77] As noted, some scholars have likewise questioned whether the rapid pace of technological change might create challenges in fixing precise rules to them, creating an unworkable rigidity.[78] Rather than preclude the formation of such a norm, however, these factors instead argue for the construction and definition set considered herein: fixed on certain enduring technological qualities of internet-based communications, but not individual technical tools; a significant reference to their targets and effects, but sidestepping artificial doctrines of equivalence. For those seeking concrete parallels, the "general purpose criterion" that undergirds Chemical Weapons Convention is not "not based on the objective characteristics of the materials but on the intent behind the use of chemicals."[79] Allowing for some dynamism in the norm under evaluation is methodologically essential to considering how the content of a norm might actually be shaped by the process it undergoes.[80]

Proliferation. Proliferation is a dynamic condition and thus a particularly challenging force to track in terms of directional contribution to the development of prohibitions. Comparing cases suggests that zero proliferation eases the creation of a prohibitive norm (blinding lasers); delays in proliferation may extend the time for preemptive establishment and thus support a norm's development (nuclear weapons); and rapid proliferation and low barriers to entry might demonstrate a neutral effect by pitting the negative effect of fatalism against the positive effect of shared vulnerability (as, imperfectly, with chemical weapons).

Cyberattack capabilities fall closest to the rapid proliferation-low barrier condition, but with caveats. These capabilities are not universally available,

---

[77] Cassese, *International Law*, 411.
[78] Kenneth W. Abbott et al., "The Concept of Legalization," *International Organization* 54, no. 3 (2000): 412–14; Finnemore and Hollis, "Constructing Norms for Global Cybersecurity," 467.
[79] Price, *Chemical Weapons Taboo*, 157.
[80] Finnemore and Hollis, "Constructing Norms for Global Cybersecurity," 438.

but not unlike nuclear weapons, they are within reach of dedicated states and have barriers that decline as proliferation increases. The case of North Korea's nuclear and cyber capabilities come to mind in the respect of the former. The outflow of US or Israeli military talent to the private sector, occasionally resulting in private-sector actors selling military-grade cyber tools to other actors, suggest the latter.[81] While cyberattacks have not yet had a singular A. Q. Khan-like figure, there appears to be some competition for that status among those providing states with hacking tools.[82] In recent years, the pace of proliferation might also be dramatically increased by the development of large language models (LLMs) such as OpenAI's ChatGPT, which have proven to be as capable digesting and producing computer code as natural language.[83] The time to produce computer custom code, including code identifying or exploiting software vulnerabilities, is likely to diminish by orders of magnitude in the coming years—even if the capabilities remain basic and not on par with the most sophisticated cyberattack actors.[84] The consequence here is that the opportune window before wide proliferation has taken hold may be short and disappearing. While proliferation must be considered dynamically in concert with other factors above, as Table 8.2 shows, its present status appears to weigh negatively on a proscription.

Awareness and Imperative

In the norm life-cycle model, a large number of candidate norms emerge, but only a small number have the traction to reach a tipping point and achieve cascade, let alone internationalization.[85] In addition to the factors just described, one crucial differentiator is the ability of that norm to become widely known, as well as the advocates for it to create an imperative based,

---

[81] Importantly, documented proliferation in these cases has been of tools useful for cyberattacks but put to surveillance (not attack) purposes. Chris Bing and Joel Schectman, "Project Raven: Inside the UAE's Secret Hacking Team of American Mercenaries," *Reuters*, January 30, 2019; Joseph Menn and Jack Stubbs, "FBI Probes Use of Israeli Firm's Spyware in Personal and Government Hacks—Sources," *Reuters*, January 30, 2020.

[82] See Gordon Corera, *Shopping for Bombs: Nuclear Proliferation, Global Insecurity, and the Rise and Fall of the AQ Khan Network* (Oxford: Oxford University Press, 2009).

[83] Castelvecchi, "Are ChatGPT and AlphaCode Going to Replace Programmers?"

[84] Groll, "ChatGPT Shows Promise of Using AI to Write Malware."

[85] Finnemore and Sikkink, "International Norm Dynamics and Political Change," 906. See also Florini, "The Evolution of International Norms."

Table 8.2 Summary of Potential for Development, Deployment, and Use Factors in the Formation of a Cyberattack Prohibition Norm (present-day)

	Strong	Weak	Negative
Preemptive Establishment	✓✓		
Demonstrated Capability		✓	
Proliferation			☒

in part, on first-hand knowledge of the consequences of failure. These two complete the prospects for norm formation, before turning to the potential to reach cascade.

Documentation and Dissemination. The ability of prohibitions to gain broad suasion is straightforwardly linked to awareness of their causes. The ability of those causes to publicize their message is linked, in turn, to their ability to document and share the concerns underlying their argumentation. In the creation of content, the global news media, and in particular its imagery of the weaponry's consequences, played a powerful role in building the transnational movement against antipersonnel land mines.[86] In its dissemination, what might be called the "grafting of fame" in norm formation played a role in that ban as well, as global media celebrities leveraged their roles in popular culture to disseminate imagery from advocates.[87] Today, real-time media both intermediated (broadcast) and disintermediated (social media), hold the potential to amplify the reach of such messages many times over.

At a high level, coverage of cyberattacks benefits from their very medium: the same reasons that their effects are rapid also permit rapid dissemination of evidence about them. Recent years have also observed numerous global press outlets creating positions covering cybersecurity

---

[86] Price, "Reversing the Gun Sights."
[87] See Andrew F. Cooper and Louise Frechette, *Celebrity Diplomacy* (New York: Routledge, 2015). Particularly in the field of international development, this phenomenon is not without substantial detractors; see, e.g., Heribert Dieter and Rajiv Kumar, "The Downside of Celebrity Diplomacy: The Neglected Complexity of Development," *Global Governance* 14, no. 3 (2008).

issues, with incumbents possessing the technical expertise to demystify cybersecurity incidents as they take place.[88] Nontraditional publications such as cybersecurity blogs also have also steadily increased their audiences, providing another means for careful scrutiny of events and dissemination of details about them.[89] The result is a global media apparatus that is likely far better positioned to document and describe preparations for or an instance of a cyberattack.

Coverage may be significant, but its resonance with the public is not automatic. One persistent challenge that media and norm entrepreneurs will have in documenting cyberattacks is the technically invisible nature of their primary effects. Exacerbating this issue was limiting public awareness of and even action on issues of cybersecurity generally; and thus, civil society actors have pushed for new programs to enhance and make more accessible the visualization of cybersecurity issues.[90] It is also not yet clear that organizations within civil society would organize around (or have organized) to advance a position decrying the consequences of a cyberattack. Such communities could play an important role using social media to actively disseminate and direct official attention to cyberattack concerns.

Celebrity endorsement may be an important avenue for dissemination, as shown by Angelina Jolie and Princess Diana's advocacy around the issue of land mines. In the context of cyberattacks, Former Estonian President Toomas Hendrik Ilves may well be the closest that exists to a present-day celebrity (albeit of diplomatic fame) advocating for measures leading to such a norm.[91] Microsoft president Brad Smith, with his proposals for a regulation of cyberattacks under a dedicated Digital Geneva Convention, may be another.[92] Neither command the following that Angelina Jolie or Princess Diana had on the issue of land mines, but as later sections will discuss, their

---

[88] See, e.g., SANS Institute, "Top Cyber Security Journalist Award Winners" (Rockville, MD: SANS, 2018).

[89] For instance, the popular cybersecurity and information security blog *ZDNet* attracts 36.7 million unique global visitors and 5.6 million unique US visitors on a monthly basis. ZDNet, "Advertise with ZDNet and TechRepublic." *KrebsOnSecurity* boasts "850,000 to 1.5 million pageviews a month and approximately 700,000–1 million unique visitors monthly." Brian Krebs, "KrebsonSecurity: Advertising," KrebsonSecurity.

[90] Eli Sugarman and Heath Wickline, "The Sorry State of Cybersecurity Imagery" (Menlo Park, CA: The William & Flora Hewlett Foundation, 2019).

[91] *ERR.ee*, "Former President Ilves Stresses Need for United Body to Fight Cyber Warfare," 30 May 2018.

[92] Brad Smith, "The Need for a Digital Geneva Convention" (Redmond, WA: Microsoft Corporation, February 14, 2017).

role as entrepreneurs may presage greater potential for such a norm than immediately apparent.[93]

Recognition of Prior Failure. Counterintuitively, the failure of a prior related norm to restrain behavior—particularly when its humanitarian effects were visible—is a common theme in successful prohibitions.[94] The utter failure, for instance, of the then-emerging prohibition against gas warfare in World War I provided an opportunity for reconsideration and reformulation in the interregnum, with newfound adherence by most parties in World War II a substantial source of momentum for the chemical weapons norm going forward.[95] The premise here is that the failure of a prior norm might help focus attention on the need for a differently or more carefully constructed prohibition to respond to a humanitarian catastrophe that is now metastasizing unchecked.

Cyberattacks present a few possibilities for just such a prior failure. The first was mentioned in this chapter's first section; the range of cyber norms projects that while significant on its own terms, would need to be both narrowed and sharpened to hold operational prospects for motivating restraint from cyberattacks. It remains too soon to tell whether, in retrospect, this broad norms project might represent a primordial distillation of what becomes a prohibitive norm (for example by suggesting particular protections for critical information infrastructure), or a project requiring a wholesale reboot to achieve such a significant effect.[96]

A significant cyberattack against the United States or one of its allies in this peacetime norm project may prompt a reevaluation of proactive "norm priorities" by the US government or those observing and seeking to influence it. A second has to do with its positions on international law. In cases not as clear-cut as the failure of the gas warfare norm, the *jus in bello* provides a kind of functional catch-all for this criterion and may be instructive here. While the United States and others have long held that the existing international

---

[93] Tracy McVeigh, "Angelina Jolie Joins Diana's Crusade to Ban Landmines," *The Guardian*, October 19, 2002.

[94] During the interwar period and into World War II, a crucial factor in the continued obloquy against CW was the existence at the highest political levels of decision makers who sought to uphold the international prohibition against the use of CW out of humanitarian concern, even if it meant giving up a military advantage. The moral obloquy that has come to be associated with CW since 1925 has coalesced around these practices, which instantiated the international prohibitionary norm against CW as embodied in the Geneva Protocol. Price, "A Genealogy of the Chemical Weapons Taboo," 94–95.

[95] The nontrivial exception during World War II being Japan in its campaign against China.

[96] See, e.g., *GGE 2021*, 12–13.

law is adequate to properly regulate cyber operations, several instances of use might signal a general breakdown of restraint explicitly calling that position into question. As Section 8.2 outlined, the competitive dynamic of structural prohibition would accommodate such a shift. Either may provide an opportunity for the kind of rapid reconfiguration, amplified by changes in perceived state interest, that could significantly propel a prohibitive norm toward its tipping point.

Summary of Findings

Table 8.3 provides an overview of this section's findings; namely, that while headwinds exist, several of the most significant unifying factors of successful prohibitive norms are observable in the case of cyberattacks. Most crucially and confirmed by the prior chapter, a norm prohibiting cyberattacks would have significant coherence with those against tools like chemical weapons and land mines. It would also benefit from the present moment in which though the tools to conduct them exist, their use has not been internalized into military practice. Finally, the ability of journalists and civil society to document a cyberattack and instantaneously disseminate its consequences suggest the timeline to emergence and tipping point could be compressed, if some further conditions enabling broad awareness are met. Further weak forces supporting a norm include partial demonstrated capability combined with fear of the known, as well as a plausible case for the failure of adjacent norms to prompt the consideration of a new one. The status of proliferation, however, may complicate the path for such a norm to emerge and gain traction, namely because the time in which most states do not possess such capabilities is fleeting, and low and declining barriers to entry will only exacerbate that concern—perhaps up to the point at which extreme proliferation triggers a sense of collective dread. Nonetheless, using the imperfect guide of comparison, present review suggests a prohibitive norm against cyberattacks would have significant potential to gain traction toward the tipping point of key state adoption as a cause.

8.5 Cyberattack Norm Evolution

In his brief consideration of a prohibitive cyberattack norm, Nye observes that presently, "the world is largely at the first stage" of the norm life

Table 8.3 Summary of Potential Contributions to the Formation of a Cyberattack Prohibition Norm (present-day)

	Strong	Weak	Negative
Coherence and Grafting (See details in Fig. 8.1)	✓✓		
Preemptive Establishment	✓✓		
Demonstrated Capability		✓	
Proliferation			☒
Prior Norm Failure		✓	
Documentation and Dissemination		✓	

cycle—emergence and entrepreneurship—or "perhaps entering the second," reaching tipping points and ultimately cascades.[97] While the present status is a matter of perspective (and likely too soon to assess, given the documentary record), outlining the conditions of the second stage can help investigations present and future. Carrying forward the project of assessing potential pathways to norm formation, this section considers—briefly, given it is intended as a preliminary survey—some of the key factors that might support a norm moving toward a tipping point and ultimately cascade of general recognition.

Unconventional Status

The stigmatization of particular weapons, distinguishing them from their "conventional" counterparts—both technically and, just as significantly, semantically—can play a significant role in successful norm formation. It is common knowledge today that chemical weapons, biological weapons, and nuclear weapons all fall under the weapons of mass destruction (WMD) banner that has in turn been central to the most consequential use of force decisions this century. Many regard the separation of these tools from the mainstream as important to the emergence and durability of prohibitive norms against each. This was, of course, the result of an extensive process of diligent norm entrepreneurship, framing, and burden-shifting.[98] While such

---

[97] Nye, "Deterrence and Dissuasion in Cyberspace," 62.
[98] Tannenwald, *Nuclear Taboo*, 102–5; Price, *Chemical Weapons Taboo*, 143–5.

processes are not yet readily traceable for cyberattacks, it remains clear that building recognition that certain weapons deserve special status can play a role in sharpening the norm as it emerges, building adherence, and ultimately helping it reach cascade.

Some debate has been devoted to whether or not cyberattacks deserve to be included in the traditional WMD category, with scholars such as Hatch finding merits and Carr dismissing the idea lest it water down existing prohibitions.[99] This debate is ongoing, but so long as cyber operations retain distinctive processes operationally, that particular argument may not be the most instructive. Rather, the focus lies in whether states continue to keep these actions and their development, deployment, and (most importantly) decisions about their use separate from conventional armed services.

Cyberattacks hold potential for such a designation, perhaps a begrudging consequence of the distinct, cautious approach certain states have taken to separate the practice of cyber operations from traditional military actions. The exceptional secrecy and denial that have accompanied even cyber operations not rising to the level of cyberattacks have created a distinct category for them in the procedural playbook of at least the United States.[100] There is admitted tension between this fact and certain states' apparent desire to "mainstream" into the military establishment the training and equipping of cyber-focused components of the armed forces. After all, the idea of a military elevating a component responsible solely for a sort of operation that might in many instances reach unconventional status seems perverse. Yet there are important operational and planning reasons for doing so, and it is further notable that in the most elaborate example of this elevation—the United States—US Cyber Command has reached Subordinate Unified Command status, not a full military branch (as Space Force has, for instance).[101] The presence of even a sizable and organized military apparatus responsible for appropriately managing such tools is by no means a barrier

---

[99] Benjamin B. Hatch, "Defining a Class of Cyber Weapons as WMD: An Examination of the Merits," *Journal of Strategic Security* 11, no. 1 (2018); Jeffrey Carr, "The Misunderstood Acronym: Why Cyber Weapons Aren't WMD," *Bulletin of the Atomic Scientists* 69, no. 5 (2013).

[100] See, e.g., The White House, "Fact Sheet on Presidential Policy Directive 20" (Washington, DC, 2013).

[101] US Department of Defense, "The Evolution of Cyber: Newest Subordinate Unified Command is Nation's Joint Cyber Force" (Washington, DC, 2022); The White House, "Space Force Announcement by Vice President Mike Pence (August 9, 2018)" (Washington, DC: Government Printing Office, 2018).

to this weaponry (or a subset thereof) reaching unconventional status, as the history of chemical weapons in the US army bears out.[102]

Diversity of Entrepreneurs

Beyond the mere existence of norm entrepreneurs, important prohibitions were driven by a *combination* of government actors advancing their cause, civil society actors building popular and transnational support, international organizations institutionally enrolling the norm into governance regimes, and ultimately even private-sector actors agitating for adherence.[103] A cyberattack prohibition may benefit from several influences—though early indications suggest that individual and industry entrepreneurship, supported by state "norm leaders" and energized by adjacently engaged NGOs, show more promise than the leadership of international organizations.

Individual Entrepreneurs. Individual-level entrepreneurs exerting the personal advocacy effects may be slowly emerging.[104] Present-day case studies to follow include the aforementioned examples of Microsoft executive Brad Smith and former Estonian President Ilves. These cases should be read in comparison to the most notable abandoned attempt at this project from the former Secretary-General of the International Telecommunications Union. That official, Hamadoun Touré, on numerous occasions sought to place a prohibition question on agendas for state dialogue and research programs within that system.[105] His personal attempts showed limited success. Despite Russian-sponsored resolutions with a clear aim at "cyber-disarmament"

---

[102] US Department of Defense, "DoD Recovered Chemical Warfare Material (RCWM) Program: History of United States' Involvement in Chemical Warfarm" (Washington, DC, 2019); US Centers for Disease Control and Prevention, "History of U.S. Chemical Weapons Elimination" (Washington, DC: Government Printing Office, 2014).

[103] See, e.g., Price, "Reversing the Gun Sights"; Richard Price, "International Norms and the Mines Taboo: Pulls Toward Compliance," *Canadian Foreign Policy Journal* 5, no. 3 (1998): 118. Note that some contest the idea that "transnational civil society" is even a coherent grouping, particularly to the extent it purports to represent a source of democratic legitimacy for a norm. See Kenneth Anderson, "The Ottawa Convention Banning Landmines, the Role of International Non-Governmental Organizations and the Idea of International Civil Society," *European Journal of International Law* 11, no. 1 (2000).

[104] On the role of individual entrepreneurs, see Finnemore and Sikkink, "International Norm Dynamics and Political Change," 895; Stacie E. Goddard, "Brokering Change: Networks and Entrepreneurs in International Politics," *International Theory* 1, no. 2 (2009).

[105] *Agence France-Presse*, "U.N. Chief Calls for Treaty to Prevent Cyber War," January 30, 2010. Touré's efforts are also evident in the efforts of UN programs like UNIDIR on the issue.

appearing on the agenda for over a decade, neither was the ITU able to take on the role of servicing bureaucracy for such a norm (see below), nor were there indications that discourse at the UN generally shifted as a result. This fact suggests that that the influence of international organization leadership is a function of, but also limited by, their bureaucratic ability to force otherwise recalcitrant states to entertain dialogue on the issue. While only one data point, this history may bode poorly for technologically (rather than international security)-focused international organizations' leadership as entrepreneurs of such a norm.

Firms. By contrast, the participation of key industry players—particularly in the case of dual-use technologies—may be a far more interesting and notable dynamic for comparative purposes play. In the case of chemical weapons, for instance, the Chemical Manufacturers Association (CMA) played a significant supporting role in the development of the Chemical Weapons Convention (CWC); by contrast, the pharmaceutical industry "contributed to the weakening of the proposed inspection regime," sowing doubt among potential adherent states as to the protocol's efficacy.[106]

Some cybersecurity efforts aforementioned are notable for their enrollment of two constituencies that may play an outsize role in the emergence of a prohibitive norm: industry and the human rights community. The Microsoft Cybersecurity Tech Accord (the latter-day Digital Geneva Conventions called for by its president) commits its signatories to "oppose cyberattacks on innocent citizens and enterprises from anywhere," including a commitment to "not help governments" do so.[107] The French-sponsored Paris Call was launched by French President Emmanuel Macron in 2019, perhaps not coincidentally just one day after the observed centennial of the end of World War I, and reflects an intentionally multistakeholder effort with both public and private-sector participation.[108]

What this collection of potential norm entrepreneurs has in diversity of composition and focus, it presently lacks in specificity and a community dedicated to strict prohibition. None are at present focused on an explicit cyberattack prohibition—though the Cybersecurity Tech Accord comes close

---

[106] Karen Winzoski, "Unwarranted Influence?: The Impact of the Biotech-Pharmaceutical Industry on U.S. Policy on the BWC Verification Protocol," *The Nonproliferation Review* 14, no. 3 (2007): 475.
[107] Cybersecurity Tech Accord, "The Cyber Tech Accord: Over 100 Companies Committed to Protecting Cyberspace."
[108] Government of France, "Cybersecurity: Paris Call of 12 November 2018 for Trust and Security in Cyberspace" (Paris, 2019).

in seeking to ban attacks on private information infrastructure. This lack of a "disarmament" or "abolition" community is notable, and while potentially weakening to such a norm's prospects of reaching a tipping point, is perhaps more indicative of the early stage at which such a norm finds itself. The engagement of industry in related efforts suggests sufficient overlap that a carefully constructed prohibitive norm might be a natural extension of their advocacy agendas.

Nongovernmental Organizations. These prospects are enhanced to some extent by the enrollment of human rights groups, who might be the most natural entities to translate general norms agendas into a concrete disarmament frame. As the prior section on coherence and grafting suggested, a potentially important bridge that could be built between cyber-focused norm entrepreneurs in this space and organizations championing human rights (and/or internet access as a manifestation of free expression). The effects here may be synergistic, mainstreaming advocacy on a cyberattack prohibition into the well-established discourse and mechanisms of human rights practice, while giving human rights norm entrepreneurs an opportunity to prove the continual evolution and relevance of their issues. Looking ahead, a growing focus on elaborating international law's requirements for lethal autonomous weapons systems (LAWS), known pejoratively as "killer robots," has also created a small civil society movement on prohibition of artificial intelligence (AI) weaponry.[109] While the issues have for most of the last decade been distinct technological phenomena, there may be ultimate adjacency in the two agendas, particularly if those seeking a ban on LAWS recognize interim value in a narrow cyberattack prohibition as a relevant precedent upon which to rest a more future-looking LAWS norm.[110] The role of this constituency as a potential norm entrepreneur, given that their coherence and grafting strategies may be closely aligned, merits continued attention.

Government Entrepreneurs. Several governments stand out as potential norm leaders in this space. The government of Estonia has achieved

---

[109] See Edward Moore Geist, "It's Already Too Late to Stop the AI Arms Race—We Must Manage It Instead," *Bulletin of the Atomic Scientists* 72, no. 5 (2016); Frank Sauer, "Stopping 'Killer Robots': Why Now is the Time to Ban Autonomous Weapons Systems," *Arms Control Today* 46, no. 8 (2016); Mark Gubrud, "Stopping Killer Robots," *Bulletin of the Atomic Scientists* 70, no. 1 (2014).

[110] The two might overlap insofar as a LAWS could be designed to engage in a cyberattack, and/or a sophisticated future cyberattack could be aimed at intentionally disrupting the operation of safety-critical AI systems. This is becoming increasingly plausible with the rapid progress in advanced machine learning-driven systems—a topic further explored briefly in the conclusion. With respect to norm formation however, to date, the two constituencies do not appear to have explicitly sought that alignment.

exceptional notoriety relative to size for its dogged pursuit of awareness of its 2007 incident and the international security questions that it raised. The government of the Netherlands has played a significant role in supporting both development of "non-binding norms of behavior by states," and more evidently, "well-functioning international legal order that provides a measure of predictability, *stability and conflict prevention.*"[111] The UK government also was the inaugural sponsor and active participant in a series of gatherings aimed explicitly at norm cultivation, informally referred to as the London Conference, and at which then-US Vice President Joe Biden noted that "we all face the threat that our critical infrastructure will be compromised by a cyberattack," and that his government intended to confront it by "building a global consensus around universal values and shared norms" to achieve "shared prosperity as well as security."[112] The Paris Call reflects similar intent.[113] All speak to, at various levels, national security norms, and in some instances, bringing cyberattacks or their tools under the stricter control of international law.

International Organizations. The United Nations has emerged as the preeminent international organization engaging with cyberattack prohibitions—and though its bureaucratic engagement may be significant (see below), to date it does not show immediate promise as a key entrepreneur. The organizers of the GGEs discussed in prior chapters, would be a natural vehicle for advancement of a prohibitive norm. These institutions sit in the UN First Committee (on Disarmament and International Security) and are administered by the United Nations Institute for Disarmament Research (UNIDIR).[114] The GGEs, in dutiful response to the mandate given to them by the General Assembly and participants there within, have focused exclusively on voluntary norms of behavior and taken a broad scope that has included a range of security issues including applicability of international law and confidence-building measures.[115] It suggests two relevant features for

---

[111] Government of the Kingdom of the Netherlands, "Letter of 5 July 2019 from the Minister of Foreign Affairs to the President of the House of Representatives on the International Legal Order in Cyberspace" (The Hague, 2019).

[112] The White House, "Remarks by the Vice President at the London Conference on Cyberspace" (Washington, DC, 2011).

[113] Government of France, "Cybersecurity: Paris Call of 12 November 2018."

[114] United Nations Institute for Disarmament Research (UNIDIR), "The United Nations, Cyberspace and International Peace and Security" (Geneva: United Nations, 2017).

[115] *GGE 2010*; *GGE 2012*; *GGE 2015*; *GGE 2021*. For emblematic commentary on GGE scope, see NATO Cooperative Cyber Defence Centre of Excellence, "2015 UN GGE Report: Major Players Recommending Norms of Behaviour, Highlighting Aspects of International Law" (Tallinn, Estonia, 2016).

norm entrepreneurship in the UN system: first, that efforts may follow rather than lead powerful state alignment on international security norms relating to cybersecurity, but second, that they may play a role identifying candidate norm areas. In brief, the GGEs, and the Open-Ended Working Group (OEWG), may support norm entrepreneurs' establishment and prioritization of an agenda, but are unlikely to serve directly as such an entrepreneur grouping.

International and Domestic Legitimacy

Should a norm provide an opportunity for governments to earn international legitimacy—especially if it can then transfer domestic legitimacy among a population—there will be further incentive to participate.[116] In this construction, adherence to a prohibition is partly a search for esteem; the quest for leaders to "want others to think well of them, and they want to want to think well of themselves."[117] The international politics of prohibition are also never far from home. As Moravcsik documented with the development of human rights norms generally, domestic concerns importantly inform the incentives of actors on the international stage, and in turn, credible activities are locked in through international commitments.[118] If alignment and even feedback can be found between the effect of an international prohibition and the domestic regimes (and actors) supporting it, prospects appear to improve.

As of now international legitimacy incentives for acquiring cyberattack capabilities might weigh against mild value in joining with a norm prohibiting them, netting out to—at best—a weak force in favor of a prohibition.

This argument seeks to reconcile multiple dimensions of incentive. On acquisition, the dynamic proliferation condition raised above comes into play. With low proliferation, such as nuclear weapons, states may seek the proscribed weapon as a means to ballast domestic legitimacy, international status, and/or increase their international coercive power.[119] At greater

---

[116] Finnemore and Sikkink, "International Norm Dynamics and Political Change," 903.
[117] James D. Fearon, "Signaling Foreign Policy Interests: Tying Hands Versus Sinking Costs," *Journal of Conflict Resolution* 41, no. 1 (1997).
[118] Andrew Moravcsik, "The Origins of Human Rights Regimes: Democratic Delegation in Postwar Europe," *International Organization* 54, no. 2 (2000): 220.
[119] Scott D. Sagan, "Why Do States Build Nuclear Weapons? Three Models in Search of a Bomb," *International Security* 21, no. 3 (1997). Kapstein, however, raises an important critique of the domestic

proliferation levels, however, joining an emerging prohibition by rejecting acquisition or use may confer even more compelling status.

Some cyberattack-like incidents suggest their orchestrators were also playing in part to a domestic constituency. For instance, the affront created by the film *The Interview* was one acute within North Korean self-perception and domestic politics, rather than significant to its international standing, thus suggesting that attack was as much about domestic legitimacy as message-sending to its adversaries.[120] The Iranian attempts on US commercial banks are a more marginal case—with potential domestic motivations appearing to confront those Western powers whose sanctions were causing domestic hardship as much as attempted contestation of those pressures. Neither of these events necessarily suggest that cyberattacks are accorded any particular, outsize significance in the domestic legitimacy they confer, yet such a motivation cannot be ruled out—particularly to the extent a regime's domestic dynamics depend on the ability to asymmetrically coerce a larger power.

Simultaneously, cyberattacks may presently occupy an unusual, intermediate position on the continuum of conferred advantage. With their destructive capabilities partly appreciated but not fully known, there is some potential prestige in their acquisition. The limited ability to demonstrate capabilities will continue to challenge the precision of foreign or domestic perception of capability for prestige purposes.[121] The result is that legitimacy conferred by acquisition represents a comparatively weak force against a prohibitive norm.

In opposition, however, the incentives to join any regime or movement toward prohibition are presently weak as well. Domestically, the existence of a strong domestic constituency calling for abolition or the ability for partisan political gain by opposing a government's active use of cyberattacks could serve such a function—following the trajectory of, for example, human rights norms.[122] Internationally, the establishment by a grouping of states of

---

legitimacy argument, specifically its ability to account for the dynamics that lead to empowered substate actors realizing their ambitions in national policy. Ethan B. Kapstein, "Is Realism Dead? The Domestic Sources of International Politics," *International Organization* 49, no. 4 (1995).

[120] For more on this dynamic, see Martin, *Under the Loving Care of the Fatherly Leader*.
[121] See Section 3.2.
[122] Risse-Kappen et al., *The Power of Human Rights*, 66. It is premature to evaluate how, for instance, a cyberattack prohibition might specifically appeal to the domestic processes they identify: instrumental adaptation/strategic bargaining; raising moral consciousness; and institutionalization/habituation.

this norm as an expectation for current or new members could create such a motivation—the OECD's Internet Policymaking Principles, for matters of digital regulation, being an analogue in the economic context.[123] Likewise, preemptive statements by a significant military alliance such as NATO would give NATO aspirants an incentive to join or lead on such a prohibition in their own policy. These are areas to watch. At present, the combined force and evidence is scant—suggesting the power of legitimacy as key to a prohibition reaching a tipping point or cascade.

Regulation and Bureaucracy

The existence of an international organization or other organized bureaucracy eligible to receive and nurture the institutional aspects of a prohibitive norm, also known as "organizational platform," can be significant.[124] As Finnemore and Hollis point out, it is also important to the norm's overall context and legitimacy.[125] The international arms control and disarmament bureaucracy at the United Nations and elsewhere can enhance prospects, if aligned. It does so most directly by both slowly increasing regulatory pressure on the use of weapons within armed conflict (including as a form of institutional survival and/or competition).[126] It also does so indirectly by providing a number of organizational platforms and networks on and within which to spread a prohibitive norm. Chemical and biological weapons benefitted, in their varied histories, from these phenomena from the first Hague and Geneva Conventions through to the Organisation for the Prevention of Chemical Weapons.[127]

Here, and perhaps in spite of the United States and its allies' stated policy views, considerable potential to support a prohibitive norm exists. Dejection

---

[123] Organisation for Economic Cooperation and Development, "Principles for Internet Policymaking" (Paris: OECD, 2014).
[124] Finnemore and Sikkink, "International Norm Dynamics and Political Change," 869–901.
[125] Finnemore and Hollis, "Constructing Norms for Global Cybersecurity," 427.
[126] Barbour and Wright note, "bureaucratic culture increases employees' belief in the programs they administer, their commitment to the survival and growth of their agencies, and the tendency to rely on rules and procedures rather than goals. Agencies work actively for their political survival. They attempt to establish strong support outside the agency, to avoid direct competition with other agencies, and to jealously guard their own policy jurisdictions." Christine Barbour and Gerald C. Wright, *Keeping the Republic: Power and Citizenship in American Politics*, Sixth Edition ed. (Washington, DC: CQ Press, 2014), 356.
[127] Price, *Chemical Weapons Taboo*, 155.

over the failure of the 2017 GGE and the slow elaboration of the 2021 edition may indeed be premature when recognizing the bigger picture: that the principal discussion for the elaboration of international security norms for cybersecurity is the United Nations' disarmament apparatus. To recall, GGE processes are managed by UNIDIR.[128] The newer and more widely attended OEWG, running on a parallel track to the GGEs is also situated within the UN's First Committee.[129] Even private efforts that might be considered alternatives to the United Nations-led process, such as the *Tallinn Manual* process, are fundamentally about activating the profession of bureaucrats and lawyers to bring regulation to bear over the use of these tools. All of this is not to suggest that prohibitive regulation is a foregone conclusion, only that a norm approaching tipping point would have an unusually well-acquainted arms control and legal bureaucracies in a position to receive it. Moreover, taking in the sweep of ten or fifteen years, it is becoming increasingly clear that these bureaucracies and their state supporters are having the effect—observed in the formation of other prohibitive norms such as the applicability of international humanitarian law—of creating (albeit soft) forms of increasing regulatory pressure on the use of these tools. Combined, these appear to favor such a norm reaching a tipping point.

Summary of Findings

This early survey yields some notable, if preliminary, conclusions about what will likely factor into the success or failure of an early prohibitive norm against cyberattacks. States' unconventional approaches to managing cyberattack capabilities and activities give momentum to their treatment as unconventional weapons. A large and diverse collection of norm entrepreneurs may well take on a prohibition and have any number of global platforms upon which to do so—however those actors are largely disunified. A notable addition and stronger force, however, may emerge from industry, which is both significant for its early leadership in advancing such a prohibition and

---

[128] UNIDIR, "The United Nations, Cyberspace and International Peace and Security."
[129] In 2018 the General Assembly established via resolution 73/27, an OEWG, including all UN members, to security in the information and communications technologies from 2019–2021 United Nations General Assembly, "Developments in the Field of Information and Telecommunications in the Context of International Security" (New York: UN, 2018).

Table 8.4 Summary of Potential Contributions to the Maturation of a Cyberattack Prohibition Norm

	Strong	Weak	Negative
Unconventional Status	✓✓		
Diversity of Entrepreneurs		✓	
Industry Congruence	✓✓		
Domestic and International Legitimacy		✓	
Regulation and Bureaucracy	✓✓		

relevant due to the dual-use nature of these tools. Domestic and international legitimacy is an unclear force, where incentives to acquire and adopt a norm are clearly at odds, though acquisition incentives seem weaker than the potential draw of institutional affiliations capable of selecting for supporters of such a norm. Much more significant is the presence, fluency, and activation of the international arms control bureaucracy, the cumulative efforts of which do appear to be drawing some preliminary lines around cyberattacks and may be well positioned to both advocate for and administer institutional aspects of a norm, were it to reach a tipping point. As factors observed in previously successful prohibitive norms, they suggest the potential contours of the pathway a cyberattack prohibition might have to reach a tipping point—and which will almost certainly shape it along the way. Table 8.4 summarizes these observations.

Conclusions

Arguments of law may not be enough to hold back even the most significant humanitarian threats; to do so, they must be animated by a process that creates shared expectations of restraint. This chapter outlined that some key states are surprisingly aligned on the need to do so, but in seeking to fill the gaps in international security, they have diverged in their institutional approaches. But there is less to this divergence than meets the eye. This chapter has illustrated one possible and particularly strong candidate for a prohibitive norm against cyberattacks: one built, in part, upon inherent challenges raised by the *jus in bello*, and made possible due to the present competition over *structural prohibition*.

Structural prohibition, as a multidimensional process, begins to provide a richer view of how the law functions, expanding it beyond legal terms and integrating the institutional and normative dynamics material to understanding the ultimate impact on restraint. As with other structural dynamics described in this study, it is also activated by problems of limited information about the functioning of a restraining regime. As international relations scholars have noted, it also stands apart from analysis of the law itself to explain how norms both reflect and come to embody it in guiding state behavior.[130]

---

[130] Finnemore and Hollis, "Constructing Norms for Global Cybersecurity," 478.

Conclusion

Bridging Analyses

Maness and Valeriano contend that "cyber threats are toothless because taboos prevent the display of cyber force in the first place"—suggesting, in essence, that a specific prohibitive norm has taken hold.[1] The paucity of case studies could provide such a false sense of security; on the whole, evidence that such restraint has actively held back attacks otherwise contemplated is unproven. So how might future scholars uncover whether such restraint is taking hold?

Part II of this study considered the argument that deterrence could be responsible but concluded that it was both unlikely to be a driving feature of restraint and that convergence of state positions was unlikely. Part III considered whether the *jus ad bellum* could be behind such restraint, but again observed that it would have difficulty operating as intended, even if consensus existed about its relevance. Neither of these forces can, under this analysis, be presently dispositive to such restraint. Thus, Part IV considered whether the *jus in bello* should serve as a basis for prohibition. It found significant basis for it doing so. The stumbling block here is not the operation of the logic of restraint. Rather, it is merely misapplied focus and perceived incongruity: that a dominant "cyber norms agenda" appeared at first glance to be preoccupied with other matters, and that seeking prohibition was impossible absent an "arms control" frame. These presumptions held back analysis, but need not going forward, particularly as changes in technology and state practice have rendered some prior assumptions obsolete. Instead, engaging with the question of norms enriched by the perspective of other prohibitions, the value of cyberattacks' *jus in bello* challenges becomes highly salient: as a strong source of coherence and basis onto which a prohibitive norm could be grafted.

History provides some preliminary analogies that argue for paying closer attention to a prohibitive norm. For its emergence, a diverse series of norm entrepreneurs uniting public and private sector suggest potential

---

[1] Maness and Valeriano, *Cyber War versus Cyber Realities*, 61.

for dedicated advocacy, particularly before states have integrated into their operations or even fully recognized the military potential of such tools. If it were to emerge, such a prohibitive norm may also encounter more favorable odds owing to the unconventional status states have granted it to date; strong congruence with industry positions; and situation within an existing bureaucracy.

It is clear that for the purposes of restraining cyberattacks, the constitutive whole may be greater than the sum of its rationalist and regulative parts. There may not be the evidence to *trace* an *existing* norm proscribing cyberattacks, but there may well be the basis for one to take shape. The potential for a cyberattack prohibition is coming into focus, as is its ability to appeal to all three logics of restraint. By creating mutual restraint without requiring demonstrations of power, it satisfies rationalist conditions. By permitting compliance with the letter and spirit of the *jus ad bellum*, it appeals to regulative obligations. And by operating through processes of identity and discourse, it leverages the strength of the constitutive logic to shape long-term behavior despite short-term disagreement.

Future Directions

This analysis of a cyberattack norm's process is necessarily incomplete as its history has not yet been written. In the years that follow, and as both cases and technology mature, additional work will be possible to understand the incentives, methods of persuasion, and processes of socialization that those pursing such a norm—or one like it—will undertake. Those studies will hopefully take even further the lessons of prior prohibitions and the methodologies of those studying them, including among the varying and ripe directions for future research outlined in the pages that follow.

Alternative Adjacencies. There are a range of other norms with which a cyberattack prohibition may find some coherence and onto which entrepreneurs might graft it. For further studies with slightly different orientations to this, two others may serve as equally fitting starting points for a similarly fashioned norm.

First are guarantees of certain fundamental freedoms in peacetime, specifically those concerning expression. Significant work has been done, for instance, to expand the contours of guaranteed rights of freedom of expression (such as those found, inter alia, in Article 19 the Universal Declaration of

Human Rights) to internet access itself.[2] This rights matter has become particularly salient as complete internet shutdowns have entered the playbook of autocrats seeking to ballast their imperiled regime—former Egyptian President Mubarak most famous among them.[3] Cyberattacks' likely effect of denying swathes of the population access to the internet may serve as a complicating factor for their enduring permissibility. It is particularly notable that given its composition, the 2021 GGE is explicit connecting state conduct in this space to the "promotion, protection and enjoyment of human rights on the Internet . . . including the freedom of expression"—even if caveated with the traditional limitations required to gain consensus in a UN forum.[4]

The second are the emerging, but far less universal, norms providing exceptional status for critical infrastructure itself. As noted previously, the United States, South Korea, China, Russia, and several other countries have proposed exceptional measures for duties of care regarding the treatment of such infrastructures in peacetime and otherwise. It may be that in the absence of the success placing this norm in the context of hostilities, that entrepreneurs reframe it entirely and pursue it as an extension of such obligations to protect. While the underlying bases appear at this moment to be weaker, nonetheless, this may be an area to watch going forward.

Opportunities for Process Bundling. Commentators have lamented that the "cyber norms agenda" has been laden with "process fatigue," with too many commissions, groupings, and accords to produce any singular or governing instrument.[5] This may simply be part of any norm formation in emerging fields, and as the prior chapters argued, suggests many lacking the substantive or procedural advantages of a narrow prohibitive norm might simply

---

[2] As a matter of international human rights law, see Frank La Rue, "Report of the Special Rapporteur on the Promotion and Protection of the Right to Freedom of Opinion and Expression" (Geneva: United Nations Human Rights Council, 2011). As a matter of domestic and foreign policy, see Steven Feldstein, "Why Internet Access Is a Human Right," *Foreign Affairs*, June 1, 2017. As a matter of applied philosophy, see Merten Reglitz, "The Human Right to Free Internet Access," *Journal of Applied Philosophy* 37, no. 2 (2020).

[3] In response to the civil unrest and protest demonstrations in Egypt in 2011 Mubarak's regime ordered "the withdrawal of more than 3,500 Border Gateway Protocol routes by Egyptian service providers, shutting down approximately 88 percent of the country's internet access, according to networking firm BGPMon." Spencer Ackerman, "Egypt's Internet Shutdown Can't Stop Mass Protests," *Wired*, May 26, 2011. This practice, through various technical means, has become more common since; the watchdog group Access Now found at least 187 instances of internet shutdowns across 35 countries in 2022. Access Now, "Weapons of Control, Shields of Impunity: Internet Shutdowns in 2022" (New York: Access Now, 2022).

[4] *GGE 2021*, 11, Norm 13 (e).

[5] Finnemore and Hollis, "Constructing Norms for Global Cybersecurity," 46: "We remain in a period of 'infinite meetings,' with nearly every day witnessing an international conference or gathering dedicated to cybersecurity and norms to govern it."

fall by the wayside. However, for states seeking to accelerate the process toward more concrete norms, the present situation raises interesting questions about how states, industry, and civil society, negotiate "process bundling" to align agendas in fields of emerging technology. The multistakeholder nature of internet governance may offer lessons, and complexities to navigate, on this front.

Cultures of Cybersecurity. Clearly "the reality of modern cybersecurity belies any single cultural system," leading to an instinct to generalize in how actors might engage with certain cybersecurity issues.[6] While not inherently problematic, given that issues such as management of certain technical internet functions are truly technical in nature, such an "islands of normativity" approach does run a risk of essentialization. A forward research agenda may confront this question head-on, for instance through comparative studies of how the international cybersecurity concerns are embedded within and are shaped by national, regional, and other contexts, ultimately sculpting state perceptions and response.

Changes in Perception of the Security Environment. The prior discussion of structural prohibition's capacity to accommodate change may be even more significant in the years to come. Consider the United States' long-standing resistance to treaty-based instruments in cyberspace. While possibly a function of a broader trend away from treaty instruments altogether, more plausible is a stated desire to reserve for itself some measure of operational flexibility, room to maneuver in military terms, while policies are still under development.[7] Assumptions underlying the latter position would be straightforward enough; that US capabilities were significant and ideally not hemmed in by novel obligations (beyond those around which they were already designed, such as the LOAC), and that vulnerabilities of adversaries to those capabilities exceeded the vulnerabilities the United States had to their capabilities under such a regime. The forward-looking question is whether this calculation will long endure. US digital dependency is presently higher than several of its key potential adversaries—including major powers—and that gap may well grow larger. Likewise, the uniqueness of US capabilities could decline in coming years. If the result of that calculation is that predictability of stifling some adversaries' use of this asymmetric tool outweighs

---

[6] Ibid., 472.
[7] On the debate over the status of treaties, see "Agora: The End of Treaties?" For a recent example of US doctrinal preference, see US Department of Defense, *Summary of the 2018 Department of Defense Cyber Strategy.*

potential advantages, one might observe the United States shifting its norm entrepreneurship toward a prohibitive cyberattack norm.

Persistent Engagement and Agreed Competition. The United States' development and reported early implementation of a "persistent engagement" strategy and its "agreed competition" corollary also emerged late in the development of this work—too late to engage with any evidence of, or peer-reviewed scholarship reflecting on it. Future scholarship might consider whether this policy is a temporary deviation of unilateral policy fashioned around domestic constituencies—enabling operational efficiencies and more public boasts of activity—or something with more enduring and global significance. The latter is entirely possible, and at one extreme, could accept cyberattacks as part of an agreed competition or "grey zone" of regular subwar conflict.[8] But might near-term flexibility lead to long-term straightjacketing? Expanding the grey zone may well perversely encourage more attacks with lower expectations of retribution, as former US Undersecretary of Defense James Miller points out, while also depriving them of the opportunity to relegate it to unconventional status and stigmatize its users, as this chapter argued.[9] For states with significant vulnerability, the potential for self-sabotage might be obscured by the near-term appeal of winning the day.[10]

AI and the Pace of Change. As noted throughout, advanced machine learning tools and techniques—often shorthanded as artificial intelligence (AI)—represent another potential epochal change in assumptions underlying cybersecurity in international affairs. Just as the last fifteen years have afforded reconsideration of questions like the timing, proliferation, and attribution of cyberattacks, the ability of emerging capabilities such as openly available Large Language Models (LLMs) to analyze and generate functional computer code at unprecedented speed may shift offense/defense dynamic as well as the ability of countries to develop and release at scale certain offensive cyber tools.[11] Future research will need to consider, for instance, how ability of these tools to emulate the style or tools of publicly available code from one country's offensive cyber program might be emulated to scale by another, or nested many times within other styles, potentially frustrating current

---

[8] Fischerkeller and Harknett, "Persistent Engagement and Tacit Bargaining."
[9] James Miller and Neil Pollard, "Persistent Engagement, Agreed Competition and Deterrence in Cyberspace," *Lawfare*, April 30, 2019.
[10] Ibid.
[11] Groll, "ChatGPT Shows Promise of Using AI to Write Malware."

attribution techniques. More broadly, to the extent such AI models become central to the operation of commercial software, government workflows, or other economically significant activities, there may be a need to consider whether these AI models themselves could constitute critical information infrastructure. In this respect, AI represents both a new capability, and a new vector, for cyberattacks explored in this study.

War Crimes and Crimes Against Humanity. As this book was headed to print, an effort led by the Oxford Institute for Ethics, Law, and Armed Conflict (ELAC) during the COVID-19 pandemic sought to build scholarly consensus against cyber operations targeting the health sector, contending that "cyber operations against medical facilities will amount to international crimes, if they fulfil the specific elements of these crimes, including war crimes and crimes against humanity."[12] As a prospective matter, weighing culpability—and plausibility—for violations of the proposed norm is premature. However, if humanitarian protections are to keep up with changes in technology, they will need to reckon with questions of whether and when cyberattack actions might merit this kind of response by the international community. In fact, to realize its ambition, it is arguable that an effective and mature prohibitive norm would need explicit reference to these tools, helping to fill the remedial gap that renders the *jus in bello* inadequate as a sole source of restraint.

Concluding Thoughts

Estonia was no anomaly; it was a rehearsal. Fifteen years have passed since we glimpsed into the future of what cyberattacks, unrestrained in the international system, might one day deliver. Knowing what we know, are we confident that the next fifteen should be on a similar path?

"The United States opposes arms control in cyberspace." It was perhaps the only received wisdom handed down by my State Department elders in the early 2000s, a time when precious little was settled policy on cybersecurity. It seemed to make sense: you cannot control what you cannot count; just try counting "cyber warheads."

---

[12] Law & Armed Conflict (ELAC) Oxford Institute for Ethics, "The Oxford Statement on the International Law Protections Against Cyber Operations Targeting the Health Care Sector."

Predating even the attacks on Estonia, this conviction was the prism through which much of US cyber foreign policy could be understood. I remain unconvinced by the near-term potential for formal "cyber arms control"—certainly in the sense of SALT and START. But equal skepticism is warranted on whether any policy, conceived in the doctrinal exhaust fumes of the Cold War, colored by the unilateralism of a few formative coincidences in American foreign policy and economic development, should endure the developments of another two decades. Policy choices have consequences, and one of those—not just for the United States, but for much of the field's scholarship—was the brushing aside of prohibition of any sort, "arms-controlled" or otherwise. Here again, the rationale seemed just as plausible: cyber tools were spreading to nearly anyone with a computer; attribution was impossible for the purposes of response; life-and-death decisions would be needed at network speed; US vulnerabilities were no greater than Russia's.

As each of those petals now falls off the rose, the opportunity reemerges to contemplate options. As US cyber policy crystallized, it inadvertently ruled out some of the most powerful forces of restraint—the specific body of norms regulating tools so heinous, their mere use was predicate for intervention.

There is no guarantee that pursuit of a prohibition on cyberattacks will be successful—far from it. But it is even less clear that developed states can succeed in a world that regularizes disruption of shared critical information infrastructure. If such insurance is sought, deterrence must be informed by explicitness and action. International law needs not just elaboration, but animation. Neither will serve the needs of the public on their own. The basis upon which both can take place is a recognition of a special, terrible status for cyberattacks—a shared expectation to forgo such activity. The sort of status that leads to formal prohibition and, over the sweep of history, to restraint.

Deemphasizing prohibitive norms was a mistake, but not a self-fulfilling prophecy. The process of developing that sort of a prohibition will likely occupy many volumes in the years to come. Technology, state practice, and humanitarianism have evolved. Scholarship has as well. Will policy? That is a challenge to which some of us may now, more confidently, choose to turn.

Bibliography

Abbott, Kenneth W., Robert O. Keohane, Andrew Moravcsik, Anne-Marie Slaughter, and Duncan Snidal. "The Concept of Legalization." *International Organization* 54, no. 3 (2000): 401–19.

Abu-Ghazaleh, Nael, Dmitry Ponomarev, and Dmitry Evtyushkin. "How the Spectre and Meltdown Hacks Really Worked." *IEEE Spectrum* (February 2019). https://spectrum.ieee.org/how-the-spectre-and-meltdown-hacks-really-worked

Access Now. "Weapons of Control, Shields of Impunity: Internet Shutdowns in 2022." New York: Access Now, 2022.

Acharya, Amitav. "How Ideas Spread: Whose Norms Matter? Norm Localization and Institutional Change in Asian Regionalism." *International Organization* 58, no. 2 (2004): 239–75.

Acharya, Amrit P., and Arabinda Acharya. "Cyberterrorism and Biotechnology When ISIS Meets CRISPR." *Foreign Affairs* (June 1, 2017).

Ackerman, Spencer. "Egypt's Internet Shutdown Can't Stop Mass Protests." *Wired*, May 26, 2011.

Adamitis, Danny, David Maynor, and Kendall McKay. "It's Alive: Threat Actors Cobble Together Open-Source Pieces Into Monstrous Frankenstein Campaign." San Jose, CA: Cisco Talos, 2019.

Adee, Sally. "The Hunt for the Kill Switch." *IEEE Spectrum* (May 1, 2008). https://spectrum.ieee.org/the-hunt-for-the-kill-switch

Adler, Emanuel. "The Spread of Security Communities: Communities of Practice, Self-Restraint, and NATO's Post—Cold War Transformation." *European Journal of International Relations* 14, no. 2 (June 2008): 195–230.

Administrative Office of the US Courts. "Courts Deliver Justice Virtually Amid Coronavirus Outbreak." News release, April 8, 2020. https://www.uscourts.gov/news/2020/04/08/courts-deliver-justice-virtually-amid-coronavirus-outbreak

Afanasyev, A. L., and V. A. Khryapin. "Conceptual Principles of Strategic Deterrence." *Military Thought* 14, no. 1 (March 2005).

Agence France-Presse. "Growing Threat from Cyber Attacks: US General." April 7, 2009.

Agence France-Presse. "U.N. Chief Calls for Treaty to Prevent Cyber War." January 30, 2010.

Ago, Robert. "Addendum—Eighth Report on State Responsibility by Mr. Roberto Ago, Special Rapporteur—the Internationally Wrongful Act of the State, Source of International Responsibility (Part 1)." *Yearbook of the International Law Commission* II(1) (1980): 14–86.

"Agora: The End of Treaties?" *AJIL Unbound* 108 (March 2014–July 2015): 30–78.

Agreement on Cooperation in Ensuring International Information Security between the Member States of the Shanghai Cooperation Organisation. Yekaterinbourg: Shanghai Cooperation Organisation, June 16, 2009.

Air Force Operations and the Law. 3rd ed. Montgomery, AL: US Air Force, Judge Advocate General's School, 2014.

Alberts, Davis, and Richard Hayes. *Power to the Edge: Command . . . Control . . . in the Information Age.* Washington, DC: DOD Command and Control Research Program, 2005.

Albright, Madeleine K. *The Mighty & The Almighty: Reflections on America, God, and World Affairs.* New York: Harper Collins, 2006.

Alexander, David. "Pentagon to Treat Cyberspace as 'Operational Domain.'" *Reuters,* July 14, 2011. https://www.reuters.com/article/idUSTRE76D5FA/

Alger, John. "Introduction to Information Warfare." In *Information Warfare: Chaos on the Electronic Superhighway,* edited by Winn Schwartau. New York: Thunder's Mouth Press, 1994.

Allison, Graham. *Destined for War: Can America and China Escape Thucydides's Trap?* New York: Houghton Mifflin Harcourt, 2017.

Allison, Graham, and Philip Zelikow. *Essence of Decision: Explaining the Cuban Missile Crisis.* 2nd ed. New York: Pearson, 1999 [1971].

Aloudat, Anas, and Katina Michael. "The Application of Location Based Services in National Emergency Warning Systems: SMS, Cell Broadcast Services and Beyond." In *Recent Advances in National Security Technology and Research: Proceedings of the 2010 National Security Science and Innovation Conference,* edited by P. Mendis and A. Yates, 21–49. Canberra: Australian Security Research Centre, 2011.

Amaro, Silvia, and Hadley Gamble. "Cyberattacks Are the Single Greatest Threat to Global Stability, German Defense Minister Says." CNBC.com, February 17, 2018. https://www.cnbc.com/2018/02/17/munich-security-conference-german-defense-minister-on-global-stability.html.

Amazon Web Services, Inc. "What Is the AWS Partner Network? Helping Companies Build Successful AWS-Based Business Practices and Solutions." https://aws.amazon.com/partners/#:~:text=The%20AWS%20Partner%20Network%20(APN,%2C%20technical%2C%20and%20marketing%20support.

An, Anne. "Chinese Cybercriminals Develop Lucrative Hacking Services." San Jose, CA: McAfee Labs, 2018.

Anderson, Kenneth. "The Ottawa Convention Banning Landmines, the Role of International Non-Governmental Organizations and the Idea of International Civil Society." *European Journal of International Law* 11, no. 1 (2000): 91–120.

Anderson, Ross. *Security Engineering: A Guide to Building Dependable Distributed Systems.* 2nd ed. Indianapolis: Wiley & Sons, 2008.

Andress, Jason, and Steve Winterfeld. *Cyber Warfare: Techniques, Tactics, and Tools for Security Practitioners.* Oxford: Syngress, 2011.

Annan, Kofi. "Address of the Secretary-General to the General Assembly (23 September)." New York: United Nations, 2003.

Apple Inc. "About Emergency and Government Alerts on iPhone and Apple Watch." August 14, 2019. https://support.apple.com/en-us/HT202743.

Arkin, William M., Ken Dilanian, and Cynthia McFadden. "What Obama Said to Putin on the Red Phone About the Election Hack." *NBC News,* December 19, 2016.

Arquilla, John, and David Ronfeldt. "Emergence and Influence of the Zapatista Social Netwar." In *Networks and Netwars,* edited by John Arquilla and David Ronfeldt, 171–200. Santa Monica, CA: RAND Corporation, 2001.

Arquilla, John, and David Ronfeldt. *Networks and Netwars: The Future of Terror, Crime, and Militancy.* Santa Monica, CA: RAND Corporation, 2001.

BIBLIOGRAPHY 345

Assante, Michael J. "Confirmation of a Coordinated Attack on the Ukrainian Power Grid." Rockville, MD: SANS Institute, 2016.

Association of Southeast Asian Nations (ASEAN) Regional Forum. "Statement by the Ministers of Foreign Affairs of the ASEAN Regional Forum Participating States on Cooperation in Ensuring International Information Security." Bandar Seri Begawan, Brunei: ASEAN, September 12, 2010. https://aseanregionalforum.asean.org/wp-content/uploads/2020/09/ADOPTED_ARF-Statement-on-Cooperation-in-the-Field-of-Security-of-and-in-the-Use-of-ICTs-in-the-Context-of-International-Security.pdf

Australia Department of Foreign Affairs and Trade. "AUSMIN 2011: Transcript of Joint Press Conference with Defence Minister Stephen Smith, U.S. Secretary of State Hillary Clinton and U.S. Secretary of Defense Leon Panetta (15 September)." Canberra: Government of Australia, 2011.

Australian Digital Health Agency. "My Health Record System Security." *My Health Record*, March 22, 2018.

Baezner, Marie. "Study on the Use of Reserve Forces in Military Cybersecurity: A Comparative Study of Selected Countries." Zurich: Center for Security Studies, ETH Zurich, 2020.

Baker, Stewart A., and Charles J. Dunlap Jr. "What Is the Role of Lawyers in Cyberwarfare?" *American Bar Association Journal* (2012). https://www.abajournal.com/magazine/article/what_is_the_role_of_lawyers_in_cyberwarfare

Bamford, Jason. "NSA Snooping Was Only the Beginning. Meet the Spy Chief Leading Us Into Cyberwar." *Wired*, June 12, 2013.

Barbour, Christine, and Gerald C. Wright. *Keeping the Republic: Power and Citizenship in American Politics*. 6th ed. Washington, DC: CQ Press, 2014.

Barlow, John Perry. "A Cyberspace Independence Declaration." *Electronic Frontier Foundation*, February 8, 1996. http://w2.eff.org/Censorship/Internet_censorship_bills/barlow_0296.declaration.

Barnes, Julian E. "Cyber-Attack on Defense Department Computers Raises Concerns." *Los Angeles Times*, November 28, 2008.

Barrett, Brian. "How Four Chinese Hackers Allegedly Took Down Equifax." *Wired*, May 24, 2020.

Barrett, Brian. "The Mysterious Return of Years-Old APT1 Malware." *Wired*, October 18, 2018.

Barrett, Brian. "White House Cuts Critical Cybersecurity Role as Threats Loom." *Wired*, May 15, 2018.

Bartels, Rogier. "From Jus In Bello to Jus Post Bellum: When do Non-International Armed Conflicts End?" In *Jus Post Bellum: Mapping the Normative Foundations*, edited by Carsten Stahn, Jennifer S. Easterday, and Jens Iverson, 297–314. Oxford: Oxford University Press, 2014.

Baxter, Richard R. "Multilateral Treaties as Evidence of Customary International Law." *British Yearbook of International Law* 41 (1965): 275–300.

Baxter, Richard R. "The First Modern Codification of the Law of Armed Conflict." *International Review of the Red Cross* 29 (1963).

Baylis, John, Steve Smith, and Patricia Owens, eds. *The Globalization of World Politics*. 6th ed. New York: Oxford University Press, 2014.

BBC News. "China Confirms Satellite Downed." January 23, 2007.

BBC News. "'China Hackers' Attack NY Times." January 31, 2013.

BBC News. "Concern Over China's Missile Test." January 19, 2007.

BBC News. "Estonia Hit by 'Moscow Cyber War.'" May 17, 2007.
BBC News. "Interview with Prime Minister Gordon Brown: 'We must not be victims.'" June 25, 2009.
BBC News. "New 'Cyber Attacks' hit S Korea." July 9, 2009.
BBC News. "NHS 111 Software Outage Confirmed as Cyber-Attack." August 6, 2022.
BBC News. "NHS Data Breach Affects 150,000 Patients in England." July 2, 2018.
BBC News. "Philippines Landslide Victims 'Sent Texts from Underneath Rubble.'" September 21, 2018.
BBC News. "Ransomware Cyberattack Threat Escalating—Europol." May 14, 2017.
BBC News. "South Korea Blames North for Bank and TV Cyber-Attacks." April 10, 2013.
BBC News. "UK Government Defends PM's Use of Zoom." April 1, 2020.
BBC News. "US Cyber War Defences 'Very Thin', Pentagon Warns." March 16, 2011.
Becker, Elizabeth. "Pentagon Sets Up New Center for Waging Cyberwarfare." *New York Times*, October 8, 1999: A16.
Benner, Katie, and Kate Conger. "U.S. Accuses 4 Russians of Hacking Infrastructure, Including Nuclear Plant." *New York Times*, March 24, 2022.
Bergman, Ronen, and Mark Mazzetti. "The Battle for the World's Most Powerful Cyberweapon." *New York Times Magazine*, January 28, 2022.
Betz, David J., and Tim Stevens. "Chapter Two: Cyberspace and Sovereignty." *Adelphi Series* 51, no. 424 (July 2011): 55–74.
Betz, David J., and Timothy C. Stevens, eds. *Cyberspace and the State: Towards a Strategy for Cyberpower (Adelphi series)*. London: Routledge, 2012.
Biddle, Stephen. *Military Power: Explaining Victory and Defeat in Modern Battle*. Princeton, NJ: Princeton University Press, 2004.
Bing, Chris, and Joel Schectman. "Project Raven: Inside the UAE's Secret Hacking Team of American Mercenaries." *Reuters*, January 30, 2019. https://www.reuters.com/article/idUSKCN1PO1CV/
Black, Max. *Models and Metaphors*. Ithaca, NY: Cornell University Press, 1962.
Black, Max. "More About Metaphor." In *Metaphor and Thought*, edited by Andrew Ortony. Cambridge: Cambridge University Press, 1979.
Blair, Dennis C. "Annual Threat Assessment of the US Intelligence Community for the Senate Select Committee on Intelligence." Washington, DC: Congressional Record, US Government Printing Office, 2010.
Blake, Duncan, and Joseph S. Imburgia. "Bloodless Weapons: The Need to Conduct Legal Reviews of Certain Capabilities and the Implications of Defining Them as Weapons." *Air Force Law Review* 66 (2010): 157–207.
Blank, Laurie R. "International Law and Cyber Threats from Non-State Actors." *International Law Studies* 89 (2013): 416–17.
Blinder, Alan, and Nicole Perlroth. "A Cyberattack Hobbles Atlanta, and Security Experts Shudder." *New York Times*, March 27, 2018.
Borg, Scott. "The Cyber Defense Revolution: A Synthesis (Presentation of the U.S. Cyber Consequences Unit)." Tallinn, Estonia: NATO CCD-COE, 2009.
Borghard, Erica D. "What Do the Trump Administration's Changes to PPD-20 Mean for U.S. Offensive Cyber Operations?" New York: Council on Foreign Relations, 2018.
Borghard, Erica D., and Shawn W. Lonergan. "The Logic of Coercion in Cyberspace." *Security Studies* 26, no. 3 (2017): 452–81.
Bothe, Michael. *The Handbook of International Humanitarian Law*. Oxford: Oxford University Press, 2013.

Boutruche, Théo, Stuart Casey-Maslen, Andrew Clapham, Thomas Nash, Markus Reiterer, and Dedan Smyth. "The Title and Preamble of the Convention." In *The Convention on Cluster Munitions: A Commentary*, 37–94. Oxford: Oxford University Press, 2010.

Bowett, D. W. *Self-Defence in International Law*. New York: Praeger, 1958.

Bradley, Jennifer. "Increasing Uncertainty: The Dangers of Relying on Conventional Forces for Nuclear Deterrence." *Air & Space Power Journal* 29, no. 4 (2015): 72–83.

Breitegger, Alexander. *Cluster Munitions and International Law*. New York: Routledge, 2012.

Brennan, John O. "Remarks at the Launch of the U.S. International Strategy for Cyberspace." Washington, DC: The White House, 2011.

Brenner, Joel. *America the Vulnerable: Inside the New Threat Matrix of Digital Espionage, Crime, and Warfare*. New York: Penguin, 2011.

Brenner, Joel. *Glass Houses: Privacy, Secrecy, and Cyber Insecurity in a Transparent World*. Reprint ed. New York: Penguin, 2013.

Brenner, Joel. "Keeping America Safe: Toward More Secure Networks for Critical Sectors." MIT Internet Policy Research Initiative. Cambridge, MA: Massachusetts Institute of Technology, 2017.

Brenner, Susan W. *Cybercrime and the Law: Challenges, Issues, and Outcomes*. Boston: Northeastern University Press, 2012.

Brodie, Bernard. *Strategy in the Missile Age*. Princeton, NJ: Princeton University Press, 1959.

Bromiley, Matt. "Hard Pass: Declining APT34's Invite to Join Their Professional Network." *Mandiant Threat Research*. July 18, 2019. https://www.mandiant.com/resources/blog/hard-pass-declining-apt34-invite-to-join-their-professional-network

Brown, Deborah. "Cybercrime is Dangerous, But a New UN Treaty Could Be Worse for Rights." *Human Rights Watch*, August 13, 2021.

Brown, Gary D., and Andrew O. Metcalf. "Easier Said Than Done: Legal Reviews of Cyber Weapons." *Journal of National Security Law & Policy* 7 (2014): 115–39.

Brownlie, Ian. *International Law and the Use of Force by States*. Oxford: Oxford University Press, 1963.

Bryan-Low, Cassell. "British Spy Chief Breaks Agency's History of Silence." *Wall Street Journal*, October 29, 2010.

Bucala, Paul, and Caitlin S. Pendleton. "Iranian Cyber Strategy: A View from the Iranian Military." *Critical Threats*, November 24, 2015. https://www.criticalthreats.org/analysis/iranian-cyber-strategy-a-view-from-the-iranian-military

Buchanan, Ben. *The Cybersecurity Dilemma: Hacking, Trust, and Fear Between Nations*. Oxford: Oxford University Press, 2016.

Buchanan, Ben. *The Hacker and the State*. Cambridge, MA: Harvard University Press, 2020.

Bulckaert, Ninon. "How France Successfully Countered Russian Interference During the Presidential Election." *Euractiv*, July 17, 2018.

Bundy, McGeorge. *Danger and Survival: Choices about the Bomb in the First Fifty Years*. New York: Random House, 1988.

Burenok, V. M., and O. B. Achasov. "Non-Nuclear Deterrence." *Military Thought* 17, no. 1 (2008).

Burns, Alexander. "Clinton Weighs in on Google-China Clash." *Politico*, January 14, 2010.

Burt, Tim. "New Action to Disrupt World's Largest Online Criminal Network." Microsoft blog. Redmond, WA: Microsoft Corporation, March 10, 2020. https://blogs.microsoft.com/on-the-issues/2020/03/10/necurs-botnet-cyber-crime-disrupt/.

Buzan, Barry, Ole Waever, and Jaap de Wilde, eds. *Security: A New Framework for Analysis.* Boulder, CO: Lynne Rienner Publishers, 1998.

Cameron, David. *Securing Britain in an Age of Uncertainty: The Strategic Defence and Security Review.* London: The Stationary Office, Her Majesty's Government, 2010.

Cameron, Maxwell A., Brian W. Tomlin, and Robert J. Lawson, eds. *To Walk without Fear: The Global Movement to Ban Landmines.* Oxford: Oxford University Press, 1998.

Carafano, James Jay. "Fighting on the Cyber Battlefield: Weak States and Nonstate Actors Pose Threats." *Washington Examiner,* November 8, 2013. https://www.washingtonexaminer.com/fighting-on-the-cyber-battlefield-weak-states-and-nonstate-actors-pose-threats

Carlin, John P., and Garraett M. Graff. *Dawn of the Code War: America's Battle Against Russia, China, and the Rising Global Cyber Threat.* New York: Hachette, 2018.

Carr, Jeffrey. "The Misunderstood Acronym: Why Cyber Weapons Aren't WMD." *Bulletin of the Atomic Scientists* 69, no. 5 (2013): 32–37.

Cassese, Antonio. *International Law.* 2nd ed. Oxford: Oxford University Press, 2005.

Castelvecchi, Davide. "Are ChatGPT and AlphaCode Going to Replace Programmers?" *Nature,* December 8, 2022.

Chae, Young Moon. "Going Abroad of Korean Health Information Systems." *Healthcare Informatics Research* 20, no. 3 (July 2014): 161–62.

Charney, Scott, Erin English, Aaron Kleiner, Nemanja Malisevic, Angela McKay, Jan Neutze, and Paul Nicholas. "From Articulation to Implementation: Enabling progress on cybersecurity norms." Redmond, WA: Microsoft Corporation, 2016.

Chayes, Abram, and Antonia Handler Chayes. *The New Sovereignty Compliance with International Regulatory Agreements.* Cambridge, MA: Harvard University Press, 2009.

Chekinov, S. G., and S. A. Bogdanov. "Strategic Deterrence and Russia's National Security Today." Voennaya Mysl *(Military Thought)* 21, no. 3 (March 2012): 11–20.

"China's National Defense in 2004." Information Office of the State Council of the People's Republic of China. Beijing, 2004.

Cho, Jong Ik. "Ha Tae Kyoung Interview on the Growing Cyber-Terrorism Threat from North Korea and the South's Response." *NK Vision,* May 15, 2013.

Chosun Ilbo. "N. Korea 'Confident' in Cyber Warfare Capabilities." April 8, 2013.

Church, William. "Information Operations Violates Protocol I." 1999. https://security.ase.md/publ/en/puben06.html

Cimino, James J. "Improving the Electronic Health Record: Getting What We Wished For." *JAMA* 309, no. 10 (March 13, 2013): 991–92.

Cimpanu, Catalin. "A Decade of Hacking: The Most Notable Cyber-Security Events of the 2010s." *ZDNet,* December 11, 2019. https://www.zdnet.com/article/a-decade-of-hacking-the-most-notable-cyber-security-events-of-the-2010s/

Cioca, Marius, Lucian-Ionel Cioca, and Sabin-Corneliu Buraga. "SMS Disaster Alert System Programming." Paper presented at the 2008 2nd IEEE International Conference on Digital Ecosystems and Technologies, 26–29 February 2008. https://ieeexplore.ieee.org/document/4635212

Clark, David D., and Susan Landau. "Untangling Attribution." In *Proceedings of a Workshop on Deterring Cyberattacks,* edited by Herbert Lin, 25–40. Washington, DC: National Academies Press, 2010.

Clarke, Richard A. "Vulnerability—What are Al Qaeda's Capabilities?" *Frontline,* March 18, 2003.

Clarke, Richard A., and Robert K. Knake. *Cyber War: The Next Threat to National Security and What to Do About It.* New York: HarperCollins, 2010.

Clinton, Hillary. "Remarks on Internet Freedom." Washington, DC: Department of State, 2010.
Coats, Daniel R. "Transcript: Dan Coats Warns The Lights Are 'Blinking Red' On Russian Cyberattacks." Washington, DC: Hudson Institute, July 13, 2018.
Colatin, Samuele De Tomas. "A Surprising Turn of Events: UN Creates Two Working Groups on Cyberspace." (Tallinn, Estonia: NATO Cooperative Cyber Defence Centre of Excellence, 2018) https://ccdcoe.org/incyder-articles/a-surprising-turn-of-events-un-creates-two-working-groups-on-cyberspace/
Coleman, Kim. *A History of Chemical Warfare*. New York: Palgrave Macmillan, 2005.
Collier, Roger. "NHS Ransomware Attack Spreads Worldwide." *Canadian Medical Association Journal* 189, no. 22 (2017): E786–87.
Commission on Cybersecurity for the 44th Presidency. "Securing Cyberspace for the 44th Presidency." Washington, DC: Center for Strategic and International Studies, 2008.
"Commission Statement and Guidance on Public Company Cybersecurity Disclosures." In *17 CFR Parts 229 and 249*. Washington, DC: The Securities and Exchange Commission, 2018.
"Constitution of the International Telecommunications Union." In *Constitution and Convention of the International Telecommunications Union*. S. Treaty Doc. No. 104-34, 21, 2010.
Convention on Cluster Munitions. Dublin: May 30, 2008. UNTS No. 47713
Convention on the Prohibition of Military or Any Other Hostile Use of Environmental Modification Techniques. New York: December 10, 1976. UNTS No. 17119
Convention on the Prohibition of the Development, Production, Stockpiling, and Use of Chemical Weapons and on Their Destruction. Geneva: September 3, 1992. UNTS No. 33757.
Convention on the Prohibition of the Use, Stockpiling, Production and Transfer of Anti-Personnel Mines and on their Destruction. Oslo: September 18, 1997. UNTS No. 35597.
Convention on Prohibitions or Restrictions on the Use of Certain Conventional Weapons Which May Be Deemed to Be Excessively Injurious or to Have Indiscriminate Effects (and Protocols) (as Amended on 21 December 2001). Geneva: December 10, 1980. UNTS No. 22495
Convention (II) with Respect to the Laws and Customs of War on Land and Its Annex: Regulations Concerning the Laws and Customs of War on Land. The Hague: July 29, 1899.
Cooper, Andrew F., and Louise Frechette. *Celebrity Diplomacy*. New York: Routledge, 2015.
Corera, Gordon. *Shopping for Bombs: Nuclear Proliferation, Global Insecurity, and the Rise and Fall of the AQ Khan Network*. Oxford: Oxford University Press, 2009.
Corkery, Michael, and David Yaffe-Bellany. "U.S. Food Supply Chain Is Strained as Virus Spreads." *New York Times*, April 13, 2020.
Corn, Gary P., and Robert Taylor. "Sovereignty in the Age of Cyber." *AJIL Unbound* 111 (August 22, 2017): 207–12.
Corrin, Amber. "Cyber Executive Order Close, Napolitano says." *Federal Computer Weekly*, September 28, 2012.
Council of Europe. "Convention on Cybercrime." Strasbourg: Council of Europe, 2004.
Council of Europe. "Details of Treaty No.185." Accessed November 2, 2023. https://www.coe.int/en/web/conventions/full-list/-/conventions/treaty/185.

Council of the European Union. "Cyber-Attacks: Council Is Now Able to Impose Sanctions. European Council." News release, May 17, 2019. https://www.consilium.europa.eu/en/press/press-releases/2019/05/17/cyber-attacks-council-is-now-able-to-impose-sanctions/

Council on Foreign Relations. "Cyber Operations Tracker." Accessed November 6, 2023. https://www.cfr.org/interactive/cyber-operations.

Cross, Tom. "New Changes to Wassenaar Arrangement Export Controls Will Benefit Cybersecurity." *Forbes*, January 16, 2018.

Culbertson, Anthony. "Major Cyber Attacks on 'False Propaganda' Swedish Media," *Newsweek*. March 21, 2016. https://www.newsweek.com/major-cyber-attacks-false-propaganda-swedish-media-438881

Cybersecurity and Infrastructure Security Agency. "Mozilla Patches Critical Vulnerability." News release, January 10, 2020. https://www.cisa.gov/news-events/alerts/2020/01/08/mozilla-patches-critical-vulnerability

Cybersecurity Tech Accord. "The Cyber Tech Accord: Over 100 Companies Committed to Protecting Cyberspace." Accessed November 6, 2023. https://cybertechaccord.org/accord/.

Cyberspace Administration of China. "Critical Information Infrastructure Security Protection Regulations." Information Office of the State Council of the People's Republic of China, 2017.

D'Amato, Anthony. "International Law, Cybernetics, and Cyberspace." In *Computer Network Attack and International Law*, edited by Michael Schmitt and Brian O'Donnell, 59–72. Newport, RI: Naval War College, 2002.

Daniel, Michael. "Heartbleed: Understanding When We Disclose Cyber Vulnerabilities." Washington, DC: The White House, 2014.

Davenport, Brandon, and Ganske, Rich. "'Recalculating Route': A Realistic Risk Assessment For GPS." *War on the Rocks*, March 11, 2019. https://warontherocks.com/2019/03/recalculating-route-a-realistic-risk-assessment-for-gps/

Davis, Joshua. "Hackers Take Down the Most Wired Country in Europe." *Wired*, August 21, 2007.

Davis, Lance, and Stanley Engerman. *Naval Blockades in Peace and War*. New York: Cambridge University Press, 2006.

De Aréchaga, E. Jiménez. "International Law in the Past Third of a Century." *Recueil des Cours de l'Academie de Droit International (RCADI)* 159, no. 1 (1978). doi: 10.1163/1875-8096_pplrdc_A9789028603592_01

De Freytas-Tamura, Kimiko. "Junaid Hussain, ISIS Recruiter, Reported Killed in Airstrike." *New York Times*, August 27, 2015, A3.

De Pietro, Carlo, and Igor Francetic. "E-health in Switzerland: The Laborious Adoption of the Federal Law on Electronic Health Records (EHR) and Health Information Exchange (HIE) Networks." *Health Policy* 122, no. 2 (February 1, 2018): 69–74.

Dell SecureWorks. "LYCEUM Takes Center Stage in Middle East Campaign." August 27, 2019. https://www.secureworks.com/blog/lyceum-takes-center-stage-in-middle-east-campaign#

Denning, Dorothy. *Information Warfare and Security*. Reading, MA: Addison-Wesley, 1999.

Denning, Dorothy, and B. J. Strawser. "Moral Cyber Weapons." In *The Ethics of Information Warfare*, edited by Luciano Floridi and Mariarosaria Taddeo, 85–103. Cham, Switzerland: Springer, 2014.

Department of Foreign Affairs and Trade, Australia. *AUSMIN 2011: Transcript of joint press conference with Defence Minister Stephen Smith, US Secretary of State Hillary Clinton and US Secretary of Defense Leon Panetta (15 September)*. Canberra 2011.
Detter, Ingrid. *The Law of War*. 2nd ed. Cambridge: Cambridge University Press, 2000.
Dieter, Heribert, and Rajiv Kumar. "The Downside of Celebrity Diplomacy: The Neglected Complexity of Development." *Global Governance* 14, no. 3 (2008): 259–64.
Dinstein, Yoram. "Computer Network Attacks and Self-Defense." In *Computer Network Attack and International Law*, edited by Michael Schmitt and Brian O'Donnell, 99–120. Newport, RI: Naval War College, 2002.
Dinstein, Yoram. *The Conduct of Hostilities under the Law of International Armed Conflict*. Cambridge: Cambridge University Press, 2004.
Dinstein, Yoram. "International Law as a Primitive Legal System." *NYU Journal of International Law and Policy* 19, no. 1 (1986–1987): 1–32.
Dinstein, Yoram. *War, Aggression and Self-Defence*. 4th ed. Cambridge: Cambridge University Press, 2005.
Dipert, Randall R. "The Ethics of Cyberwarfare." *Journal of Military Ethics* 9, no. 4 (2010): 384–410.
Donilon, Thomas E., and Samuel J. Palmisano. "Commission on Enhancing National Cybersecurity." Washington, DC: National Institute of Standards and Technology, 2016.
Donilon, Tom. "Remarks By Tom Donilon, National Security Advisor to the President: 'The United States and the Asia-Pacific in 2013.'" The White House. Washington, DC, 2013.
Dragos Inc. "Crashoverride: Analyzing the Threat to Electric Grid Operations." Hanover, MD: Dragos Inc., 2017.
Dunham, Ken, and Jim Melnick. *Malicious Bots: An Inside Look Into the Cyber-Criminal Underground of the Internet*. Boca Raton, FL: CRC Press, 2008.
Dunlap, Charles J. Jr. "Meeting the Challenge of Cyberterrorism." In *Computer Network Attack and International Law*, edited by Michael Schmitt and Brian O'Donnell, 59–72. Newport, RI: Naval War College, 2002.
E-ISAC and SANS Institute. "TLP: White Analysis of the Cyber Attack on the Ukrainian Power Grid Defense Use Case." Washington, DC, 2016.
Edelman, R. David. "Cyberattacks in International Relations." D.Phil. diss., University of Oxford, 2009.
Edelman, R. David. "NATO's Cyber Decade?" In *NATO: From Regional to Global Security Provider*, edited by Yonah Alexander and Richard Prosen, 23–32. New York: Lexington Books, 2015.
Education Week. "Map: Coronavirus and School Closures." April 17, 2020.
Efrony, Dan, and Yuval Shany. "A Rule Book on the Shelf? Tallinn Manual 2.0 on Cyberoperations and Subsequent State Practice." *American Journal of International Law* 112, no. 4 (2018): 583–657.
Eglof, Florian. "Cybersecurirty and the Age of Privateering." In *Understanding Cyber Conflict: 14 Analogies*, edited by George Perkovich and Ariel E. Levite. Washington, DC: Georgetown University Press, 2017. https://carnegieendowment.org/2017/10/16/cybersecurity-and-age-of-privateering-pub-73418
Eisenhower, Dwight D. "Farewell Address by President Dwight D. Eisenhower, January 17, 1961" (Washington, DC: National Archives and Records Administration, 1961). https://www.archives.gov/milestone-documents/president-dwight-d-eisenhowers-farewell-address#transcript

"Emerging Cyber Threat Reports, 2011." Atlanta: Georgia Tech Information Security Center, 2011.

ERR.ee. "Former President Ilves Stresses Need for United Body to Fight Cyber Warfare." May 30, 2018. https://news.err.ee/835758/former-president-ilves-stresses-need-for-united-body-to-fight-cyber-warfare

European Commission. "Benchmarking Smart Metering Deployment in the EU-28." Brussels: Directorate-General for Energy, 2020.

European Union. "Cybersecurity Strategy of the European Union: An Open, Safe, and Secure Cyberspace." Brussels: EU, 2013.

Evron, Gadi. "Battling Botnets and Online Mobs: Estonia's Defense Efforts During the Internet Wars." *Georgetown Journal of International Affairs* 9, no. 1 (2008): 121–26.

Falk, Richard. "The Decline of Normative Restraint in International Relations." *Yale Journal of International Law*, no. 2 (1984): 263–70.

Fallon, Michael. "Defence Secretary's speech at Cyber 2017 Chatham House Conference." London: Ministry of Defence, Her Majesty's Government, 2017.

Farwell, James P., and Rafal Rohozinski. "The New Reality of Cyber War." *Survival* 54, no. 4 (2012): 107–20.

Farwell, James P., and Rafal Rohozinski. "Stuxnet and the Future of Cyber War." *Survival* 53, no. 1 (February1, 2011): 23–40.

Fearon, James D. "Signaling Foreign Policy Interests: Tying Hands Versus Sinking Costs." *Journal of Conflict Resolution* 41, no. 1 (1997): 68–90.

Feder, Norman M. "Reading the U.N. Charter Connotatively: Toward a New Definition of Armed Attack." *NYU Journal of International Law and Policy* 19 (1986–7): 395–432.

Federal Energy Regulatory Commission (Division of Dam Safety and Inspections). "FERC Security Program for Hydropower Projects Revision 3A." Washington, DC, 2016.

Federal Republic of Germany. "Cyber Security Strategy for Germany." Federal Ministry of the Interior. Berlin, 2011.

Feldstein, Steven. "Why Internet Access Is a Human Right." *Foreign Affairs* (June 1, 2017). https://carnegieendowment.org/2017/06/01/why-internet-access-is-human-right-pub-70151

Fettweis, Christopher J. "Pessimism and Nostalgia in the Second Nuclear Age." *Strategic Studies Quarterly* 13, no. 1 (April 1, 2019): 12–41.

Fifield, Anna. "China Rebuffs U.S. Charges of Cyberespionage Over Equifax Hack." *Washington Post,* February 11, 2020. https://www.washingtonpost.com/world/asia_pacific/china-rebuffs-american-charges-of-cyber-espionage-over-equifax-hack/2020/02/11/b95fd932-4ca2-11ea-967b-e074d302c7d4_story.html#

Finnemore, Martha. "Are Legal Norms Distinctive?" *NYU Journal of International Law and Policy* 32 (1999): 699–705.

Finnemore, Martha. "Cultivating International Cyber Norms." In *America's Cyber Future: Security and Prosperity in the Information Age*, edited by Kristin and Travis Sharp Lord, 87–121. Washington, DC: Center for New American Security, 2012.

Finnemore, Martha. *National Interests in International Society.* Ithaca, NY: Cornell University Press, 1996.

Finnemore, Martha, and Duncan B. Hollis. "Constructing Norms for Global Cybersecurity." *American Journal of International Law* 110, no. 3 (2016): 425–79.

Finnemore, Martha, and Kathryn Sikkink. "International Norm Dynamics and Political Change." *International Organization* 52, no. 4 (1998): 887–917.

Fischerkeller, Michael P., and Richard J. Harknett. "Persistent Engagement and Tacit Bargaining: A Path Toward Constructing Norms in Cyberspace." *Lawfare*, November 9, 2018. https://www.lawfareblog.com/persistent-engagement-and-tacit-bargaining-path-toward-constructing-norms-cyberspace.

Fleck, Dieter. "Searching for International Rules Applicable to Cyber Warfare—A Critical First Assessment of the New Tallinn Manual." *Journal of Conflict and Security Law* 18, no. 2 (2013): 331–51.

Florini, Ann. "The Evolution of International Norms." *International Studies Quarterly* 40 (1996): 363–89.

Follath, Erich, and Holger Stark. "The Story of 'Operation Orchard': How Israel Destroyed Syria's Al Kibar Nuclear Reactor." *Spiegel Online International*, November 2, 2009. https://www.spiegel.de/international/world/the-story-of-operation-orchard-how-isr ael-destroyed-syria-s-al-kibar-nuclear-reactor-a-658663.html

Fonseca, Felicia. "Vandalism in Arizona Shows the Internet's Vulnerability." *Associated Press*, February 26, 2015. https://apnews.com/general-news-27601adeb3144ec7b7a42 95fdb399e46

Ford, Christopher A. "The Trouble with Cyber Arms Control." *The New Atlantis*, Fall 2010.

Forsyth, James Wood. "Nuclear Weapons and Political Behavior." *Strategic Studies Quarterly* 11, no. 3 (2017): 115–28.

Forsythe, David P. *The Humanitarians: The International Committee of the Red Cross*. Cambridge: Cambridge University Press, 2005.

Franck, Thomas M. *Recourse to Force: State Action Against Threats and Armed Attacks*. Cambridge: Cambridge University Press, 2002.

Franck, Thomas M. "Who Killed Article 2(4)? or Changing Norms Governing the Use of Force by States." *American Journal of International Law* 64, no. 5 (1970): 809–37.

Fraunces, Michael. "The International Law of Blockade: New Guiding Principles in Contemporary State Practice." *Yale Law Journal* 101 (1999): 893–918.

Frederick, Howard H. "Cuban-American Radio Wars: Ideology in International Telecommunications." *Foreign Affairs* 15, no 2 (1986): 294–96.

Freedman, Lawrence. *Deterrence*. Cambridge: Polity, 2004.

Freedman, Lawrence. *The Evolution of Nuclear Strategy*. New York: St. Martin's Press, 1981.

Freedman, Lawrence, ed. *Strategic Coercion: Concepts and Cases*. Oxford: Oxford University Press, 1998.

Fritz, Audrey. "China's Evolving Conception of Civil-Military Collaboration." In *China Innovation Policy Series*. Washington, DC: Center for Strategic and International Studies, 2019.

Froehlich, Fritz E., and Allen Kent. *Froehlich/Kent Encyclopedia of Telecommunications*. Vol. 15. New York: Marcel Dekker, 1997.

Fukuyama, Francis. "The End of History?" *The National Interest*, no. 16 (1989): 3–18.

Fulghum, David. "Israel Used Electronic Attack in Air Strike Against Syrian Mystery Target." *Aviation Week*, October 8, 2007.

Gallagher, Ryan. "Google China Prototype Links Searches to Phone Numbers." *The Intercept*, September 14, 2018. https://theintercept.com/2018/09/14/google-china-prototype-links-searches-to-phone-numbers/

Garamone, Jim. "Cyber Tops List of Threats to U.S., Director of National Intelligence Says." *DOD News (official)*, February 13, 2018. https://www.defense.gov/News/News-Stories/Article/Article/1440838/cyber-tops-list-of-threats-to-us-director-of-natio nal-intelligence-says/#:~:text="From%20U.S.%20businesses%2C%20to%20the,achieve%20strategic%20and%20malign%20objectives.

Garey, Julie. *The US Role in NATO's Survival After the Cold War*. London: Palgrave Macmillan, 2020.

Gartzke, Erik, and Jon Lindsay. "Cross-Domain Deterrence, From Practice to Theory." In *Cross-Domain Deterrence: Strategy in an Era of Complexity*, edited by Erik Gartzke and Jon Lindsay, 1–26. Oxford: Oxford University Press, 2019.

Gartzke, Erik, Jon Lindsay, and Michael Nacht. "Cross-Domain Deterrence: Strategy in an Era of Complexity." Paper presented at the International Studies Association Annual Meeting, Toronto, 2014.

Gartzke, Erik, and Jon R. Lindsay, eds. *Cross-Domain Deterrence*. Oxford: Oxford University Press, 2019.

Geiß, Robin, and Henning Lahmann. "Cyber Warfare: Applying the Principle of Distinction in an Interconnected Space." *Israel Law Review* 45, no. 3 (2012): 381–99.

Geist, Edward Moore. "It's Already Too Late to Stop the AI Arms Race—We Must Manage It Instead." *Bulletin of the Atomic Scientists* 72, no. 5 (2016): 318–21.

Geist, Michael. "Cyberlaw 2.0." *Boston College Law Review* 44 (2003): 323–58.

Geller, Eric. "Trump Scraps Obama Rules on Cyberattacks, Giving Military Freer Hand." *Politico*, August 16, 2018.

Geneva Convention for the Amelioration of the Condition of Wounded, Sick and Shipwrecked Members of Armed Forces at Sea (Second Geneva Convention). Geneva: August 12, 1949.

Geneva Convention (IV) Relative to the Protection of Civilian Persons in Time of War. Geneva: August 12, 1949

Geneva Convention Relative to the Treatment of Prisoners of War (Third Geneva Convention). Geneva: August 12, 1949.

George, Alexander, and Richard Smoke. *Deterrence in American Foreign Policy: Theory and Practice*. New York: Columbia University Press, 1974.

Gervais, Michael. "Cyber Attacks and the Laws of War." *Berkeley Journal of International Law* 30, no. 2 (2012): 525–79.

Ghafur, Saira, Emilia Grass, Nick R. Jennings, and Ara Darzi. "The Challenges of Cybersecurity in Health Care: The UK National Health Service as a Case Study." *The Lancet Digital Health* 1, no. 1 (May 1, 2019): e10–e12.

Global Mobile Suppliers Association (GMSA). "Public Safety LTE Networks: State of the Market and Device Ecosystem." Farnham, UK: GSA, 2018.

Goddard, Stacie E. "Brokering Change: Networks and Entrepreneurs in International Politics." *International Theory* 1, no. 2 (2009): 249–81.

Goldman, Adam. "Takeaways from the Times's Investigation Into Hackers for Hire." *New York Times*, March 21, 2019. https://www.nytimes.com/2019/03/21/us/politics/nso-darkmatter-government-spies.html

Goldman, Emily O., and John Arquilla, eds. *Cyber Analogies*. Monterey, CA: Naval Postgraduate School, 2014.

Goldsmith, Jack. "Against Cyberanarchy." *University of Chicago Law Review* 65 (1998): 1199–250.

Goldsmith, Jack, and Tim Wu. *Who Control the Internet? Illusions of a Borderless World*. Oxford: Oxford University Press, 2006.

Goodman, Will. "Cyber Deterrence: Tougher in Theory than in Practice?" *Strategic Studies Quarterly* Fall (2010): 102–35.

Goodwin, Jacob. "FERC Seeks to Close Any Cyber-Security 'Gaps' at Nuclear Plants." *Government Security News*, March 25, 2009.

Google. "1.5 billion users and counting. Thank you." @Gmail: Twitter, October 26, 2018.

Google. "A New Approach to China." *Google Official Blog*, January 12, 2010. https://googleblog.blogspot.com/2010/01/new-approach-to-china.html

Google. "Public Alerts FAQs." 2020. Accessed November 6, 2023. https://support.google.com/publicalerts.

Gordon, Edward. "Article 2(4) in Historical Context." *Yale Journal of International Law* 10 (1985): 271–78.

Gorman, Siobahn, and Julian E. Barnes. "Cyber Combat: Act of War." *Wall Street Journal*, May 30, 2011.

Government of Australia. "The Australian Cyber Security Centre Threat Report 2015." Canberra: Australian Signals Directorate, 2015.

Government of Australia. "Cyber Security Strategy." Canberra: Department of the Attorney General, 2009.

Government of Australia. "E-Security Review." Canberra, 2008.

Government of Canada. "Canada's Cyber Security Strategy: For a Stronger and More Prosperous Canada." Ottawa: Public Safety Canada, 2010.

Government of Finland. "Finland's Cyber Security Strategy." Helsinki: Secretariat of the Security and Defence Committee, 2013.

Government of Finland. "Finland's Cyber Security Strategy 2019." Helsinki: The Security Committee, 2019.

Government of France. "Cybersecurity: Paris Call of 12 November 2018 for Trust and Security in Cyberspace." Paris: France Diplomatie, 2019.

Government of France. "Déclaration de Madame Florence Parly, ministre des armées, sur la stratégie cyber des armées." Paris: Ministre des Armées, 2019.

Government of France. "France Defence and National Security Strategic Review." Paris: Ministre des Armées, 2017.

Government of France. "French National Cyber Security Strategy." Paris: European Union Agency for Cybersecurity, 2015.

Government of France. "Information Systems Defence and Security: France's Strategy." Athens: Agence Nationale de la Sécurité des Systèmes d'Information, 2011.

Government of Germany. *German National Cyber Security Strategy*. Athens: European Union Agency for Cybersecurity, 2016.

Government of Israel. "Decision No. 3611 of the 32nd Government: Promoting National Cyber Capabilities." Jerusalem, 2011.

Government of Japan. *Common Standards for Information Security Measures for Government Agencies and Related Agencies (FY2018)*. Tokyo: National Center of Incident Readiness and Strategy, 2018.

Government of Japan. "Information Security Strategy for Protecting the Nation." Tokyo: Information Security Policy Council, 2010.

Government of Montenegro. "Web Portal of Government of Montenegro and Several Other Web Sites Were Under Enhanced Cyberattacks." News release, February 17, 2017. https://www.gov.me/en/article/169508--web-portal-of-government-of-montenegro-and-several-other-web-sites-were-under-enhanced-cyberattacks

Government of New Zealand. "New Zealand Strategic Defense Policy Statement." Wellington, 2018.

Government of New Zealand. "New Zealand's Cyber Security Strategy." Wellington: Innovation & Employment, Ministry of Business, 2011.
Government of Norway. "Cyber Security Strategy for Norway." Oslo: Reform and Church Affairs; Ministry of Government Administration, 2012.
Government of Poland. "Cyberspace Protection Policy of the Republic of Poland." Warsaw: Internal Security Agency, Ministry of Administration and Digitisation, 2013.
Government of Switzerland. "National Strategy for the Protection of Switzerland Against Cyber Risks." Bern: Civil Protection and Sport; Federal Department of Defence, 2012.
Government of the Kingdom of the Netherlands. "Letter of 5 July 2019 from the Minister of Foreign Affairs to the President of the House of Representatives on the International Legal Order in Cyberspace." The Hague: Ministry of Foreign Affairs, 2019.
Government of the Kingdom of the Netherlands. "National Cyber Security Strategy 2: From Awareness to Capability." The Hague: National Coordinator for Security and Counterterrorism, 2013.
Government of Turkey. "National Cyber Security Strategy and 2013–2014 Action Plan." Ankara: Maritime Affairs and Communications, Ministry of Transport, 2013.
Government of the United Kingdom. "The National Cyber Security Strategy 2016 to 2021." London: Her Majesty's Government, 2017.
Government of the United Kingdom. "National Security Strategy and Strategic Defence and Security Review 2015: A Secure and Prosperous United Kingdom." London: Her Majesty's Government, 2015.
Government of the United Kingdom. "National Security Strategy and Strategic Defence and Security Review 2015: Third Annual Report." London: Her Majesty's Government, 2019.
Government of the United Kingdom. "Proceedings of the House of Commons." House of Commons, 525–641. London: His Majesty's Government, 1932.
Graham, Bradley. "Military Grappling with Guidelines for Cyberwar." *Washington Post*, November 8, 1999, A1.
Graham, Todd H. "Armed Attack in Cyberspace: Deterring Asymmetric Warfare with an Asymmetric Definition." *Air Force Law Review* 64, no. 65 (2009): 65–102.
Gray, Christine D. "The Charter Limitations on the Use of Force: Theory and Practice." In *The United Nations Security Council and War*, edited by Vaughn Lowe, Adam Roberts, Jennifer Welsh and Dominik Zaum, 86–98. Oxford: Oxford University Press, 2010.
Gray, Christine D. *International Law and the Use of Force*. 3rd ed. Oxford: Oxford University Press, 2008.
Gray, Colin. *The Future of Strategy*. Cambridge: Polity, 2015.
Greenberg, Andy. "How an Entire Nation Became Russia's Test Lab for Cyberwar." *Wired*, June 20, 2017.
Greenberg, Andy. "Inside Olympic Destroyer: The Most Deceptive Hack in History." *Wired*, October 17, 2019.
Greenberg, Andy. "A Notorious Iranian Hacking Crew Is Targeting Industrial Control Systems." *Wired*, November 20, 2019.
Greenberg, Andy. *Sandworm: A New Era of Cyberwar and the Hunt for the Kremlin's Most Dangerous Hackers*. New York: Doubleday, 2019.
Greenberg, Andy. "The Untold Story of NotPetya, the Most Devastating Cyberattack in History." *Wired*, August 22, 2018.
Grigsby, Alex. "The End of Cyber Norms." *Survival* 59, no. 6 (November 12, 2017): 109–22.

Grigsby, Alex. "The Year in Review: The Death of the UN GGE Process?" *Net Politics*, December 21, 2017.

Griguer, Merav, and Jean Baptiste Thienot. "France Launches Healthcare Big Data." *Bird & Bird*, July 2017.

Groll, Elias. "ChatGPT Shows Promise of Using AI to Write Malware." *CyberScoop*, December 6, 2022. https://cyberscoop.com/chatgpt-ai-malware/

Groll, Elias. "NSA Official Suggests North Korea Was Culprit in Bangladesh Bank Heist." *Foreign Policy*, March 21, 2017.

Gross, Oren. "Cyber Responsibility to Protect: Legal Obligations of States Directly Affected by Cyber-Incidents." *Cornell International Law Journal*, no. 3 (2015): 481–512.

Group of 8 (G8). "Deauville Declaration: Internet (Final Declaration of the G8 Leaders at the Deauville Summit)." Deauville, France, 2011.

Grove, Gregory D., Seymour Goodman, and Stephen Lukasik. "Cyber-Attacks and International Law." *Survival* 42, no. 3 (2000): 89–103.

Gubrud, Mark. "Stopping Killer Robots." *Bulletin of the Atomic Scientists* 70, no. 1 (2014): 32–42.

Hague Convention (IV) Respecting the Laws and Customs of War on Land. The Hague: October 18, 1907.

Hague Convention (V) Respecting the Rights and Duties of Neutral Powers and Persons in Case of War on Land. The Hague: October 18, 1907.

Hague Regulations: Convention (IV) Respecting the Laws and Customs of War on Land and its annex: Regulations concerning the Laws and Customs of War on Land. The Hague: October 18, 1907.

Hague, William. *Foreign Secretary's Closing Remarks at the London Conference on Cyberspace*. Foreign & Commonwealth Office. London: The Stationary Office, Her Majesty's Government, 2011.

Hammond, Philip. "Chancellor Speech: Launching the National Cyber Security Strategy." London: Cabinet Office of Cybersecurity, 2016.

Hargrove, John Lawrence. "The *Nicaragua* Judgment and the Future of the Law of Force and Self-Defense." *American Journal of International Law* 81, no. 1 (January 1987): 135–43.

Harrell, Peter. "The Right Way to Sanction Cyber Threats." *The National Interest*, October 1, 2015.

Harris, Shane. *@War: The Rise of the Military-Internet Complex*. New York: Mariner Books, 2014.

Harvey, Nick. *Armed Forces Minister—Responding to Cyber War*. UK Ministry of Defence. London: The Stationary Office, Her Majesty's Government, 2011.

Hatch, Benjamin B. "Defining a Class of Cyber Weapons as WMD: An Examination of the Merits." *Journal of Strategic Security* 11, no. 1 (2018): 43–61.

Hathaway, Oona, and Rebecca Croontof. "The Law of Cyber-Attack." *California Law Review*, no. 817 (2012): 817–86.

Hauser, Catherine. "Nearly 2 Million Chickens Killed as Poultry Workers Are Sidelined." *New York Times*, April 28, 2020.

Healey, Jason. "Claiming the Lost Cyber Heritage." *Strategic Studies Quarterly* 6, no. 3 (2012): 11–19.

Healey, Jason. *A Fierce Domain: Conflict in Cyberspace, 1986 to 2012*. Washington, DC: Cyber Conflict Studies Association, 2013.

Healey, Jason, John C. Mallery, Klara Tothova Jordan, and Nathaniel V. Youd. "Confidence-Building Measures in Cyberspace: A Multistakeholder Approach for Stability and Security." Washington, DC: Atlantic Council, Brent Scowcroft Center on International Security, 2014.

National Health Service of the United Kingtom. "Health and Social Care Network (HSCN)." *NHS Digital*. https://digital.nhs.uk/services/health-and-social-care-network

Heller, Nathan. "Estonia, The Digital Republic." *The New Yorker*, December 11, 2017. https://www.newyorker.com/magazine/2017/12/18/estonia-the-digital-republic

Henckaerts, Jean-Marie, and Louise Doswald-Beck. *International Committee of the Red Cross, Customary International Law*. Vol. 1: Rules. Cambridge: Cambridge University Press, 2009.

Henderson, Christian. "Non-State Actors and the Use of Force." In *Non-State Actors in International Law*, edited by Math Noortmann, Reinisch, August and Ryngaert, Cedric 77–96. London: Hart Publishing, 2015.

Hersey, John. *Hiroshima*. New York: Knopf, 1946.

Hesse, Mary B. *Models and Analogies in Science*. London: Sheed & Ward, 1963.

Higgins, Rosalyn. *The Development of International Law through the Political Organs of the United Nations*. Oxford: Oxford University Press, 1963.

Hill, Richard. "WCIT: Failure or Success, Impasse or Way Forward?" *International Journal of Law and Information Technology* 21, no. 3 (2013): 313–28.

Hobbes, Thomas. *Leviathan (with selected variants from the Latin edition of 1668)*. Edited by Edwin Curley Indianapolis: Hackett, 1994 [1668].

Hodge, Nathan. "Texts, Tweets Saving Haitians From the Rubble." *Wired*, January 21, 2018.

Hollander, Judd E., and Brendan G. Carr. "Virtually Perfect? Telemedicine for COVID-19." *New England Journal of Medicine* (2020): 1679–81.

Huth, Paul, and Bruce Russett. "General Deterrence Between Enduring Rivals: Testing Three Competing Models." *American Political Science Review* 87, no. 1 (1993): 61–73.

Idaho National Laboratory. "Protecting Drinking Water from Cyber Threats." Washington, DC: Department of Energy, 2016.

International Data Corporation. "Worldwide Smartphone Shipment OS Market Share Forecast." 2020.

Ikenberry, G. John. "Institutions, Strategic Restraint, and the Persistence of American Postwar Order." *International Security* 23, no. 3 (1998–1999): 43–78.

International Cable Protection Committee. "Subsea Landslide is Likely Cause of SE Asian Communications Failure." News release, March 21, 2007. https://www.iscpc.org/documents/?id=9

International Committee of the Red Cross. "Customary International Humanitarian Law: Rule 1. The Principle of Distinction between Civilians and Combatants." https://ihl-databases.icrc.org/en/customary-ihl/v1/rule1

International Committee of the Red Cross. "International Humanitarian Law and the Challenges of Contemporary Armed Conflicts." (Geneva: October 31, 2011).

International Committee of the Red Cross. "International Humanitarian Law and the Challenges of Contemporary Armed Conflicts." (Geneva: October 2015).

International Court of Justice, *Armed Activities on the Territory of the Congo (Democratic Republic of the Congo v. Uganda), Judgment*. ICJ Reports 168 (2005).

International Court of Justice, *Legal Consequences of the Construction of a Wall in the Occupied Palestinian Territory, Advisory Opinion*. ICJ Reports 136 (2004).

International Court of Justice, *Legality of the Threat or Use of Nuclear Weapons, Advisory Opinion*. ICJ Reports 226 (1996).
International Court of Justice, *Military and Paramilitary Activities in and against Nicaragua (Nicaragua v. United States of America), Merits, Judgment*. ICJ Reports 14 (1986).
International Court of Justice, *Oil Platforms (Islamic Republic of Iran v. United States of America), Judgment*. ICJ Reports 161 (2003).
International Criminal Tribunal for the Former Yugoslavia, *Prosecutor v. Duško Tadić, Decision on the Defence Motion for Interlocutory Appeal on Jurisdiction*, October 2, 1995.
International Criminal Tribunal for the Former Yugoslavia, *Prosecutor v. Kupreškić, Kupreškić, Kupreškić, Josipovic, Papic and Santic*, Trial Chamber, Judgment January 14, 2000.
International Criminal Tribunal for the Former Yugoslavia, *Prosecutor v. Stanislav Galić*, Trial Chamber Judgment, December 5, 2003.
International Institute of Strategic Studies. "Cyber Capabilities and National Power: A Net Assessment." London: IISS, 2021.
International Law Commission. *Report of the International Law Commission to the General Assembly*. Geneva: ILC, 1980.
International Telecommunications Union. "ICT Indicators Database 2010." Geneva: ITU, 2010.
International Telecommunications Union. "Two-Thirds of the World's Population Uses the Internet, But 2.7 Billion People Remain Offline." Geneva: United Nations, 2022.
Internet Governance Forum. "Chair's Summary, Connecting Continents for Enhanced Multistakeholder Internet Governance." Paris: IGF, 2014.
Internet Governance Forum. "WS #304 Responsible Behaviour in Cyberspace." Paper presented at the Internet Governance Forum, Paris, November 12–14, 2018.
Israeli Defense Force (IDF). "We thwarted an attempted Hamas cyber offensive against Israeli targets. Following our successful cyber defensive operation, we targeted a building where the Hamas cyber operatives work. HamasCyberHQ.exe has been removed," @IDF: Twitter, May 5, 2019.
Jacobs, Andrew, and Miguel Helft. "Google, Citing Attack, Threatens to Exit China." *New York Times*, January 12, 2010: A1. https://www.nytimes.com/2010/01/13/world/asia/13beijing.html
Janofsky, Adam. "Gen. Michael Hayden: Over-Classification of Cyber Threats Puts Businesses at Risk." *Wall Street Journal*, October 31, 2018. https://www.wsj.com/articles/gen-michael-hayden-overclassification-of-cyber-threats-puts-businesses-at-risk-1541018014.
Jensen, Eric Talbot. "Cyber Sovereignty: The Way Ahead." *Texas International Law Journal* 50, no. 2 (2015): 275–304.
Jensen, Eric Talbot. "Cyber Warfare and Precautions Against the Effects of Attacks." *Texas Law Review* 88, no. 7 (2010): 1533–70.
Jervis, Robert. "Arms Control, Stability, and Causes of War." *Political Science Quarterly* 108, no. 2 (Summer 1993): 239–53.
Jervis, Robert. "Deterrence Theory Reconsidered." *World Politics* 39 (1979): 289–324.
Jervis, Robert. *Perception and Misperception in International Politics*. Princeton, NJ: Princeton University Press, 1976.

Johnson, Jeh. "Statement by Secretary Jeh Johnson on the Designation of Election Infrastructure as a Critical Infrastructure Subsector." Washington, DC: Department of Homeland Security, January 6, 2017. https://www.dhs.gov/news/2017/01/06/statement-secretary-johnson-designation-election-infrastructure-critical

Joyner, Christopher C., and Catherine Lotrionte. "Information Warfare as International Coercion: Elements of a Legal Framework." *European Journal of International Law* 12, no. 5 (2001): 825–65.

Kanuck, Sean. "Sovereign Discourse on Cyber Conflict under International Law Symposium: Law at the Intersection of National Security, Privacy, and Technology: II. Cybersecurity and Network Operations." *Texas Law Review*, no. 7 (2009): 1571–98.

Kaplan, Fred. *Dark Territory: The Secret History of Cyber War.* New York: Simon & Schuster, 2017.

Kapstein, Ethan B. "Is Realism Dead? The Domestic Sources of International Politics." *International Organization* 49, no. 4 (1995): 751–74.

Karnouskos, Stamatis. "Stuxnet Worm Impact on Industrial Cyber-Physical System Security." Paper presented at the IECON 2011–37th Annual Conference of the IEEE Industrial Electronics Society, November 7–10, 2011.

Karrar, Tahani. "Third Undersea Cable Reportedly Cut Between Sri Lanka, Suez." *Dow Jones Newswire*, February 1, 2008. https://www.wired.com/2008/01/fiber-optic-cab/

Kaspersky Lab. *Kaspersky Lab Identifies Operation "Red October," an Advanced Cyber-Espionage Campaign Targeting Diplomatic and Government Institutions Worldwide.* Moscow: Kaspersky Lab, 2013.

Kastenberg, Joshua E. "Non-Intervention and Neutrality in Cyberspace: An Emerging Principle in the National Practice of International Law." *Air Force Law Review* 64, no. 43 (July 1, 2009): 43–64.

Katzenstein, Peter, ed. *The Culture of National Security: Norms and Identity in World Politics.* New York: Columbia University Press, 1996.

Keen, Maurice, ed. *Chivalry.* New Haven, CT: Yale University Press, 1984.

Keen, Maurice. *The law of war in the late Middle Ages.* New York: Routledge & Kegan Paul, 1965.

Kello, Lucas. *The Virtual Weapon and International Order.* New Haven, CT: Yale University Press, 2017.

Kelsen, Hans. *General Theory of International Law and State.* Cambridge, MA: Harvard University Press, 1945.

Kennedy, Paul. *The Parliament of Man: The Past, Present, and Future of the United Nations.* New York: Random House, 2006.

Kennedy, Robert F., and Arthur Meier Schlesinger. *Thirteen Days: A Memoir of the Cuban Missile Crisis.* New York: Norton, 1999.

Kennett, Lee B. *A History of Strategic Bombing.* New York: Scribner, 1983.

Kenyon, Henry. "Work Commences on $1B NSA 'Spy' Center." *Defense Systems*, January 7, 2011.

Keohane, Robert O. *After Hegemony: Cooperation and Discord in the World Political Economy.* Princeton, NJ: Princeton University Press, 1984.

Keohane, Robert O., and Joseph S. Nye Jr. "Power and Interdependence." *Survival* 15, no. 4 (July 1, 1973): 158–65.

Kerr, Donald M. "Remarks by the Principal Deputy Director of National Intelligence at the Association for Intelligence Officers (AFIO) Annual Intelligence Symposium." McLean, VA: AFIO, 2008.

Kerry, John. "An Open and Secure Internet: We Must Have Both." Washington, DC: Department of State, 2015.

Kessler, Oliver, and Wouter Werner. "Expertise, Uncertainty, and International Law: A Study of the Tallinn Manual on Cyberwarfare." *Leiden Journal of International Law* 26, no. 4 (2013): 793–810.

Khalilzad, Zalmay, and John P. White, eds. *Strategic Appraisal: The Changing Role of Information in Warfare*. Santa Monica, CA: RAND Corporation, 1999.

Kheel, Rebecca. "GOP Senators Urge UN Security Council Action on North Korea." *The Hill*, May 16, 2017.

Khong, Yuen Foong. *Analogies at War: Korea, Munich, Dien Bien Phu, and the Vietnam Decisions of 1965*. Princeton, NJ: Princeton University Press, 1992.

Kilovaty, Ido. "Rethinking the Prohibition on the Use of Force in the Light of Economic Cyber Warfare: Towards a Broader Scope of Article 2(4) of the UN Charter." *Journal of Law & Cyber Warfare* 4, no. 3 (2015): 210–44.

Kingsbury, Alex. "In Georgia, a Parallel War Rages Online." *U.S. News & World Report*, August 13, 2008.

Kiras, James. "Irregular Warfare." In *Understanding Modern Warfare*, edited by David Jordan, 225–91. Cambridge: Cambridge University Press, 2008.

Kirkpatrick, David D. "Signs of Russian Meddling in Brexit Referendum." *New York Times*, November 15, 2017.

Kissinger, Henry. *Diplomacy*. New York: Simon & Schuster, 1994.

Klimberg, Alexander. *The Darkening Web: The War for Cyberspace*. New York: Penguin, 2017.

Knox, Ron. "Monopolies in Meat: Endangering Workers, Farmers, and Consumers." *The American Prospect*, May 4, 2020.

Koh, Harold Hongju. "International Law in Cyberspace." *Harvard International Law Journal* 54 (December, 2012): 1–12.

Koh, Harold Hongju. "Remarks as Prepared for Delivery to the USCYBERCOM Inter-Agency Legal Conference." Paper presented at the USCYBERCOM Inter-Agency Legal Conference, Fort Meade, Maryland, September 18, 2012.

Komov, Sergei, ed. *International Information Security: The Diplomacy of Peace*. Moscow: Russian Federation Official Publications, 2009.

Komov, Sergei. "Russian Federation Military Policy in the Area of International Information Security: Regional Aspect." In *International Information Security: The Diplomacy of Peace*, edited by Sergei Komov, 34–44. Moscow: Russian Federation Official Publications, 2007.

Kramer, Franklin D., Stuart H. Starr, and Larry K. Wentz, eds. *Cyberpower and National Security*. Washington, DC: Potomac Books, Inc., 2009.

Kratochwil, Friedrich V. *Rules, Norms, and Decisions*. Cambridge: Cambridge University Press, 1989.

Kratochwil, Friedrich, and John Gerard Ruggie. "International Organization: A State of the Art on the Art of the State." *International Organization* 40, no. 4 (1986): 753–75.

Krebs, Brian. "KrebsonSecurity: Advertising." KrebsonSecurity.

Kroenig, Matthew. "The History of Proliferation Optimism: Does It Have a Future?" *Journal of Strategic Studies* 38, no. 1–2 (January 2, 2015): 98–125.

Krutskikh, Andrey. "Advancement of Russian Initiative to Ensure International Information Security (Chronicles of the Decade)." In *International Information

Security: The Diplomacy of Peace, edited by Sergei Komov, 116–41. Moscow: Russian Federation Official Publications, 2009.

Krutskikh, Andrey. "Information Challenges to Security (1999)." In *International Information Security: The Diplomacy of Peace*, edited by Sergei Komov. Moscow: Russian Federation Official Publications, 2009.

Krutskikh, Andrey. "Statement By Mr. Andrey Krutskikh, Special Representative of the President of the Russian Federation for International Cooperation in the Field of Information Security on 'Other disarmament measures and international security' Cluster of the 73rd Session of the UNGA." Permanent Mision of the Russian Federation to the United Nations: Russian Ministry of Foreign Affairs, 2018.

Kuehl, Daniel T. "China and Cybersecurity." Paper presented at the National Security Seminar, Heritage Foundation, Washington, DC, April 28, 2010.Lacey, Elena. "The Biggest DDoS for Hire Site Goes Down." *Wired*, April 28, 2018.

Laffan, R. G. D., ed. *Select Documents of European History, 800–1482*. New York: Henry Holt, 1929.

Lahmann, Henning. *Unilateral Remedies to Cyber Operations: Self-Defence, Countermeasures, Necessity, and the Question of Attribution*. Cambridge: Cambridge University Press, 2020.

Landler, Mark, and Ana Swanson. "About That Much Vaunted U.S.-U.K. Trade Deal? Maybe Not Now." *New York Times*, March 2, 2020.

La Rue, Frank. "Report of the Special Rapporteur on the Promotion and Protection of the Right to Freedom of Opinion and Expression." Geneva: United Nations Human Rights Council, 2011.

Lebow, Richard Ned, and Janice Gross Stein. "Rational Deterrence Theory: I Think, Therefore I Deter." *World Politics* 41, no. 2 (January 1989): 208–24.

Lederberg, Joshua. *Biological Weapons: Limiting the Threat*. Cambridge, MA: MIT Press, 1999.

Legro, Jeffrey W. "The Transformation of Policy Ideas." *American Journal of Political Science* (2000): 419–32.

"Letter Dated 23 September 1998 from the Permanent Representative of the Russian Federation to the United Nations Addressed to the Secretary-General." New York: United Nations, 1998.

Lewis, James A. *Assessing the Risks of Cyber Terrorism, Cyber War and Other Cyber Threats*. Washington, DC: Center for Strategic and International Studies, 2002.

Lewis, James A. "Cognitive Effect and State Conflict in Cyberspace." Washington, DC: Center for Strategic and International Studies, 2018.

Lewis, James A, ed. *Cyber Security: Turning National Solutions into International Cooperation*. Washington, DC: Center for Strategic and International Studies, 2003.

Lewis, James A. "A Cybersecurity Agenda for the 45th President." Washington, DC: Center for Strategic and International Studies, 2017.

Lewis, James A. "The Cyber War Has Not Begun." Washington, DC: Center for Strategic and International Studies, 2010.

Lewis, James Andrew. "Advanced Experiences in Cybersecurity Policies and Practices: An Overview of Estonia, Israel, South Korea, and the United States." Washington, DC: Inter-American Development Bank, 2016.

Libicki, Marin C. *Cyberdeterrence and Cyberwar*. Santa Monica, CA: RAND Corporation, 2009.

Libicki, Marin C. *Cyberspace in Peace & War*. Annapolis, MD: Naval Institute Press, 2016.

Libicki, Marin C. "Information War, Information Peace." *Journal of International Affairs* 51, no. 2 (1998): 411–28.

Lieber, Francis. "Instructions for the Government of Armies of the United States in the Field." United States War Department. (Washington, DC: Government Printing Office, 1898).

Lim Min, Zhang. "Singapore Budget 2020: $1b Over Next 3 Years to Shore Up Cyber and Data Security Capabilities." *The Straits Times*, February 18, 2020.

Lin, Herbert. "Attribution of Malicious Cyber Incidents : From Soup to Nuts." *Journal of International Affairs* 70, no. 1 (2016): 75–137.

Lin, Herbert S. "Cyber Conflict and International Humanitarian Law." *International Review of the Red Cross* 94, no. 886 (June 2013): 515–31.

Lin, Herbert S. "Offensive Cyber Operations and the Use of Force Cybersecurity Symposium: National Leadership, Individual Responsibility." *Journal of National Security Law & Policy* 4, no. 1 (2010 2010): 63–86.

Lin, Herbert S. "Reflections on the New Department of Defense Cyber Strategy: What It Says, What It Doesn't Say." *Georgetown Journal of International Affairs* 17, no. 3 (2016): 5–13.

Lobosco, Katie. "When Will You Get Your Stimulus Cash, and How?" *CNN*, April 2, 2020. https://www.cnn.com/2020/04/01/politics/stimulus-money-distribution-individuals/index.html

Long, Tony. "Sept. 26, 1983: The Man Who Saved the World by Doing . . . Nothing." *Wired*, September 26, 2007.

Lord, Kristin, and Travis Sharp, eds. *America's Cyber Future: Security and Prosperity in the Information Age*. Washington, DC: Center for New American Security, 2011.

Lowe, Vaughn, Adam Roberts, Jennifer Welsh, and Dominik Zaum, eds. *The United Nations Security Council and War*. Oxford: Oxford University Press, 2010.

Lucas, George R. "Permissible Preventive Cyberwar: Restricting Cyber Conflict to Justified Military Targets," in *The Ethics of Information Warfare*, edited by Luciano Floridi and Mariarosaria Taddeo (New York: Springer, 2014), 73–83.

Lynch, Colum, and Jack Detsch. "The Virtual Transition." *Foreign Policy*, December 8, 2020.

Lynn, William J. III. "Defending a New Domain: The Pentagon's Cyberstrategy." *Foreign Affairs* September/October (2010): 97–108.

Lyu, Jinghua. "What Are China's Cyber Capabilities and Intentions?" Washington, DC: Carnegie Endowment for International Peace, 2019.

Maayan, Gilad. "Five Years Later, Heartbleed Vulnerability Still Unpatched." *MalwareBytes*, September 16, 2019. https://www.malwarebytes.com/blog/news/2019/09/everything-you-need-to-know-about-the-heartbleed-vulnerability

Mahairas, Ari, and Peter J. Beshar. "A Perfect Target for Cybercriminals." *New York Times* (Opinion), November 19, 2018.

Mallison, William T. "Limited Naval Blockade or Quarantine-Interdiction: National and Collective Defense Claims Valid Under International Law." *George Washington Law Review* 31 (1962): 335–98.

Maness, Ryan C., and Brandon Valeriano. *Cyber War versus Cyber Realities: Cyber Conflict in the International System*. Oxford: Oxford University Press, 2015.

Mann, Simon. "Cyber War Added to ANZUS Pact." *Sydney Morning Herald*, September 16, 2011.

Markoff, John. "A Silent Attack, But Not a Subtle One." *New York Times*, September 26, 2010.

Markoff, John, and Mark Lander. "Digital Fears Emerge After Data Siege in Estonia." *New York Times*, May 29, 2007.

Markoff, John, David Sanger, and Thom Shanker. "In Digital Combat, U.S. Finds No Easy Deterrent." *New York Times*, January 25, 2010, A1.

Markoff, John, and Thom Shanker. "Halted '03 Iraq Plan Illustrates U.S. Fear of Cyberwar Risk." *New York Times*, August 1, 2009, A1.

Markoff, John. "Military Breaks the Rules of Military Engagement." *New York Times*, October 17, 1999, L5.

Markoff, Michele. "Advancing Norms of Responsible State Behavior in Cyberspace." *DIPNOTE: US Department of State Official Blog*. Washington, DC: US Department of State, July 9, 2015.

Markoff, Michele. "Explanation of Position at the Conclusion of the 2016–2017 UN Group of Governmental Experts (GGE) on Developments in the Field of Information and Telecommunications in the Context of International Security." Washington, DC: US Department of State, June 23, 2017. https://2017-2021.state.gov/explanation-of-position-at-the-conclusion-of-the-2016-2017-un-group-of-governmental-experts-gge-on-developments-in-the-field-of-information-and-telecommunications-in-the-context-of-international-sec/

Markoff, Michele. "National and Global Strategies for Managing Cyberspace and Security." Paper presented at the Conference of the Atlantic Council: International Engagement On Cyber: Establishing Norms And Improved Security, Washington, DC, March 30, 2011.

Markoff, Michele. "Prepared Keynote Remarks of Michele Markoff: An Overview of the Identification of Norms in the GGE Delivered at the International Security Cyber Issues Workshop Series Workshop on 'The Future of Norms to Preserve and Enhance International Cyber Stability.'" US Department of State. Geneva: United Nations Institute for Disarmament Research, 2016.

Marks, Joseph. "That Muscular Response Strategy May Sow Confusion and Risk Escalation." *NextGov*, September 5, 2018. https://www.defenseone.com/threats/2018/09/dhs-secretary-urges-hit-back-harder-response-cyber-strikes/151036/

Martin, Bradley K. *Under the Loving Care of the Fatherly Leader: North Korea and the Kim Dynasty*. New York: St. Martin's Griffin, 2004.

Maurer, Tim. "Cyber Norm Emergence at the United Nations." *An Analysis of the UN's Activities Regarding Cyber-Security*. Cambridge, MA: Belfer Center for Science and International Affairs, 2011.

Maurer, Tim. "Why the Russian Government Turns a Blind Eye to Cybercriminals." *Slate*, February 2, 2018. https://carnegieendowment.org/2018/02/02/why-russian-government-turns-blind-eye-to-cybercriminals-pub-75499

Maxwell, Stephen. *Rationality in Deterrence*. Adelphi Papers, Vol. 50. London: International Institute of Strategic Studies, 1968.

Mazanec, Brian M. *The Evolution of Cyber War: International Norms for Emerging-Technology Weapons*. Lincoln: University of Nebraska Press, 2015.

McAfee Labs. *Global Energy Cyberattacks: "Night Dragon."* San Jose, CA: McAfee Labs, 2011.

McAfee Labs. *Protecting Your Critical Assets: Lessons Learned from "Operation Aurora."* San Jose, CA: McAfee Labs, 2010.

McAfee Labs and Good Harbor Consulting. "Virtual Criminology Report 2009." San Jose, CA: McAfee Labs, 2009.

McConnell, J. Michael. "Annual Threat Assessment of the Intelligence Community for the Senate Armed Services Committee." Washington, DC: US Senate, 2008.

McConnell, John M. "The Cyber War Threat Has Been Grossly Exaggerated." Paper presented at the Intelligence Squared Debate, Washington, DC, June 8, 2010.

Mccullagh, Declan. "Renewed Push to Give Obama an Internet 'Kill Switch.'" *CBSNews* January 24, 2011. https://www.cbsnews.com/news/renewed-push-to-give-obama-an-internet-kill-switch/.

McDougal, Myres S. "The Soviet-Cuban Quarantine and Self-Defense." *American Journal of International Law* 57 (1963): 597–604.

McDougal, Trevor. "Establishing Russia's Responsibility for Cyber-Crime Based on Its Hacker Culture." *International Law and Management Review* 11 (2015): 55–80.

McGhee, James E. "Liberating Cyber Offense." *Strategic Studies Quarterly* 10, no. 4 (2016): 46–63.

McMillan, Robert. "Siemens: Stuxnet Worm Hit Industrial Systems." *Computerworld*, September 14, 2010.

McVeigh, Tracy. "Angelina Jolie Joins Diana's Crusade to Ban landmines." *The Guardian*, October 19, 2002.

Mearsheimer, John J. *Conventional Deterrence*. Ithaca, NY: Cornell University Press, 1983.

Meier-Abt, Peter J., Adrien K. Lawrence, Liselotte Selter, Effy Vayena, and Torsten Schwede. "The Swiss Approach to Precision Medicine." *Swiss Medical Weekly*, February 1, 2018.

Melzer, Nils. "Cyberwarfare and International Law." Geneva: United Nations Institute for Disarmament Research, 2011.

Menn, Joseph, and Jack Stubbs. "FBI Probes Use of Israeli Firm's Spyware in Personal and Government Hacks—Sources." *Reuters*, January 30, 2020. https://www.reuters.com/article/idUSKBN1ZT38A/

Meron, Theodor. "The Continuing Role of Custom in the Formation of International Humanitarian Law." *American Journal of International Law* 90, no. 2 (1996): 238–49.

Meurant, Jacques. "The 125th Anniversary of the International Review of the Red Cross—A Faithful Record." *International Review of the Red Cross* 306 (June 30, 1995): 447–68.

Meyers, Adam. "Meet The Threat Actors: List of APTs and Adversary Groups." *CrowdStrike Blog*, February 24, 2019. https://www.crowdstrike.com/blog/meet-the-adversaries/

Microsoft Digital Security Unit. "An Overview of Russia's Cyberattack Activity in Ukraine." Redmond, WA: Microsoft Corporation, 2022.

Miller, James, and Neil Pollard. "Persistent Engagement, Agreed Competition and Deterrence in Cyberspace." *Lawfare*, April 30, 2019. https://www.lawfareblog.com/persistent-engagement-agreed-competition-and-deterrence-cyberspace.

Miller, Matthew, Jon Brickey, and Gregory Conti. "Why Your Intuition About Cyber Warfare is Probably Wrong." *Small Wars Journal* (November 29, 2012). https://smallwarsjournal.com/jrnl/art/why-your-intuition-about-cyber-warfare-is-probably-wrong

Miller, Steven E. "Cyber Threats, Nuclear Analogies? Divergent Trajectories in Adapting to New Dual-Use Technologies." In *Understanding Cyber Conflict: 14 Analogies*, edited by George Perkovich; Ariel E. Levite. Washington, DC: Georgetown University Press, 2017. https://carnegieendowment.org/2017/10/16/cyber-threats-nuclear-analogies-divergent-trajectories-in-adapting-to-new-dual-use-technologies-pub-73413

Milner, Helen V. "The Enduring Legacy of Robert Gilpin: How He Predicted Today's Great Power Rivalry." *Foreign Affairs,* August 15, 2018. https://www.foreignaffairs.com/united-states/enduring-legacy-robert-gilpin

Moravcsik, Andrew. "The Origins of Human Rights Regimes: Democratic Delegation in Postwar Europe." *International Organization* 54, no. 2 (2000): 217–52.

Morgan, Patrick. *Deterrence: A Conceptual Analysis.* Thousand Oaks, CA: SAGE Publications, 1997.

Morgan, Patrick. *Deterrence Now.* Cambridge: Cambridge University Press, 2003.

Morgenthau, Hans J. *Politics Among Nations: The Struggle for Power and Peace.* 5th ed. New York: Knopf, 1973.

Morrow, James D. "International Law and the Common Knowledge Requirements of Cross-Domain Deterrence." In *Cross-Domain Deterrence: Strategy in an Era of Complexity,* 188–205. New York: Oxford University Press, 2019.

Mozur, Paul, Jonah M. Kessel, and Melissa Chan. "Made in China, Exported to the World: The Surveillance State." *New York Times,* April 24, 2019. https://www.nytimes.com/2019/04/24/technology/ecuador-surveillance-cameras-police-government.html

Mueller, John. *Retreat from Doomsday: The Obsolescence of Major War.* New York: Basic Books, 1989.

Mueller, Robert S. III. *Report on the Investigation into Russian Interference in the 2016 Presidential Election.* Washington, DC: Department of Justice, 2019.

Mutual Defense Treaty Between the United States and the Republic of Korea, October 1, 1953. TIAS 3097, 5 UST 23602376
https://www.usfk.mil/Portals/105/Documents/SOFA/H_Mutual%20Defense%20Treaty_1953.pdf

Myre, Greg. "Tech Companies Take a Leading Role In Warning Of Foreign Cyber Threats." *National Public Radio: All Things Considered,* January 23, 2020.

Nadelmann, Ethan. "Global Prohibition Regimes: The Evolution of Norms in International Society." *International Organization* 44 (1990): 479–524.

Nagourney, Adam, David Sanger, and Johanna Barr. "Hawaii Panics After Alert About Incoming Missile Is Sent in Error." *New York Times,* January 13, 2018.

Nakashima, Ellen. "The NSA Has Linked the WannaCry computer Worm to North Korea." *Washington Post,* June 14, 2017.

Nakashima, Ellen. "Pentagon Launches First Cyber Operation to Deter Russian Interference in Midterm Elections." *Washington Post,* October 23, 2018.

Nakashima, Ellen. "Russia Has Developed a Cyberweapon That Can Disrupt Power Grids, According to New Research." *Washington Post,* November 6, 2017.

Nakashima, Ellen. "U.N. Votes to Advance Russian-Led Resolution on a Cybercrime Treaty." *Washington Post,* November 19, 2019.

Nakashima, Ellen. "The U.S. Is Urging a No Vote on a Russian-Led U.N. Resolution Calling for a Global Cybercrime Treaty." *Washington Post,* November 16, 2019.

Nakashima, Ellen. "White House Authorizes 'Offensive Cyber Operations' to Deter Foreign Adversaries." *Washington Post,* September 20, 2018.

Nakasone, Paul M. "A Cyber Force for Persistent Operations." *Joint Forces Quarterly* 92, no. 1 (2019): 10–14.

Napolitano, Janet. *Appointment of New Deputy Under Secretary for Cybersecurity.* Washington, DC: Department of Homeland Security, 2013.

Napolitano, Janet. *Remarks at the Launch of the U.S. International Strategy for Cyberspace.* Washington, DC: The White House, 2011.

National Cyber Security Centre. "The Cyber Threat to UK Business." Government Communications Headquarters (GCHQ), 2017–2018. https://www.ncsc.gov.uk/files/ncsc_nca_report.pdf

NATO. "Bucharest Summit Declaration." News release, April 3, 2008. https://www.nato.int/cps/en/natolive/official_texts_8443.htm

NATO Cooperative Cyber Defence Centre of Excellence. "2015 UN GGE Report: Major Players Recommending Norms of Behaviour, Highlighting Aspects of International Law." Tallinn, Estonia: 2016.

Neustadt, Richard E., and Ernest R. May. *Thinking in Time: The Uses of History for Decision-Makers*. New York: Free Press, 1986.

Newman, Lily Hay. "Cut Undersea Cable Plunges Yemen Into Days-Long Internet Outage." *Wired*, January 13, 2020.

Newman, Lily Hay. "North Korea Is Recycling Mac Malware. That's Not the Worst Part." *Wired*, February 25, 2020.

Ney, Paul C. Jr. "DOD General Counsel Remarks at U.S. Cyber Command Legal Conference." Washington, DC: Department of Defense, 2020.

Nicholson, Brendan. "World Fury at Satellite Destruction." *The Age*, January 20, 2007.

Nordlinger, Bernard, Cédric Villani, and Daniela Rus. *Healthcare and Artificial Intelligence*. Berlin: Springer Nature, 2020.

North Atlantic Treaty. April 4, 1949. 63 Stat. 2241, 34 U.N.T.S. 243.

North Atlantic Treaty Organization. *Active Engagement, Modern Defence: Strategic Concept for the Defence and Security of the Members of the North Atlantic Treaty Organization*. Lisbon: NATO, 2010.

North Atlantic Treaty Organization. "Cyber Defense: Background & History." Last updated September 14, 2023. http://www.nato.int/cps/en/SID-CC11FE39-6C487843/natolive/topics_78170.htm.

North Atlantic Treaty Organization. *Lisbon Summit Declaration Issued by the Heads of State and Government Participating in the Meeting of the North Atlantic Council in Lisbon*. Lisbon: NATO, 2010.

North Atlantic Treaty Organization. "Press Conference by NATO Secretary General Anders Fogh Rasmussen Following the NATO Defence Ministers Meeting on 4 June 2013." News release, June 4, 2013. https://www.nato.int/cps/en/natolive/opinions_101151.htm

North Atlantic Treaty Organization. "Wales Summit Declaration." Brussels: NATO, 2014.

Norwegian Defence Command and Staff College. "Norway Manual of the Law of Armed Conflict." Norwegian Ministry of Defence. Merkur-Trykk AS: The Chief of Defence, 2018.

"Nuclear Power in the USA." London: World Nuclear Association, December 2023. https://world-nuclear.org/information-library/country-profiles/countries-t-z/usa-nuclear-power.aspx

Nuclear Threat Initiative. "Nuclear Disarmament—NATO." Washington, DC, 2019.

Nye, Joseph. "Deterrence and Dissuasion in Cyberspace." *International Security* 41, no. 3 (Winter 2016–2017): 44–71.

Nye, Joseph. *The Future of Power*. New York: PublicAffairs, 2011.

Nye, Joseph S. *Nuclear Ethics*. New York: Simon & Schuster, 1988.

Obama, Barack. "Statement by the President on Actions in Response to Russian Malicious Cyber Activity and Harassment." News release, December 29, 2016. https://obamawhitehouse.archives.gov/the-press-office/2016/12/29/statement-president-actions-respo nse-russian-malicious-cyber-activity#:~:text=These%20actions%20follow%20repeated%20private,be%20alarmed%20by%20Russia%27s%20actions.

O'Dwyer, Gerard. "Finland's Top National Security Risk? Cyber." *Fifth Domain*, March 26, 2018.

Oh, Adelaide, Daria Osipova, Ryan Ramseyer, and Nick Stathas. "The Roles of Companies in Cybersecurity: A Case for Private Sector Involvement in Cyberspace Governance." Cambridge, MA: MIT, 2019.

O'Neill, Patrick Howell. "Germany Launches New Cybersecurity Research Agency Modeled After DARPA." *Cyberscoop*, August 30, 2018. https://cyberscoop.com/germany-cybersecurity-research-agency-modeled-after-darpa/

Operational Law Handbook. Charlottesville, VA: The Judge Advocate General's Legal Center and School, 2017.

Oppenheim, L. *International Law, A Treatise*. Vol. 2, London: Longmans, Green and Co., 1912.

Organisation for Economic Cooperation and Development. "Principles for Internet Policymaking." Paris: OECD, 2014.

Organisation for the Prevention of Chemical Weapons (OPCW). "Practical Guide for Medical Management of Chemical Warfare Casualties." The Hague: OPCW International Cooperation and Assistance Division, Assistance and Protection Branch, 2016.

Organization for Security and Co-Operation in Europe (OSCE). "Remarks of the Coordinator for Cyber Issues, U.S. Department of State." Paper presented at the OSCE Conference on a Comprehensive Approach to Cyber Security: Exploring the Future OSCE Rule, Vienna, May 9–10, 2011.

Oxford Institute for Ethics, Law & Armed Conflict (ELAC). "The Oxford Statement on the International Law Protections Against Cyber Operations Targeting the Health Care Sector." https://www.elac.ox.ac.uk/the-oxford-process/the-statements-overview/the-oxford-statement-on-cyber-operations-targeting-the-health-care-sector/

Pagliery, Jose. "The Inside Story of the Biggest Hack in History." *CNN*, August 5, 2015.

Painter, Christopher. "G20: Growing International Consensus on Stability in Cyberspace." *DIPNOTE: US Department of State Official Blog*. Washington, DC: US Department of State, 2015.

Palo Alto Networks. "How to Break the Cyber Attack Lifecycle." Santa Clara, CA, 2020.

Panarin, Igor. "Supremacy in Cyberspace: Obama's 'Star Wars'?" *RT*, January 11, 2012.

Panetta, Leon. *Remarks on Defending the Nation from Cyber Attack (11 October)*. Washington, DC: Department of Defense, 2012.

Pape, Robert A. Jr. "Coercion and Military Strategy: Why Denial Works and Punishment Doesn't." *Journal of Strategic Studies* 15, no. 4 (1992): 423–75.

Parker, Geoffrey. "Early Modern Europe." In *The Laws of War: Constraints on Warfare in the Western World*, edited by Michael Howard, George J. Andreopoulos and Mark R. Schulman, 40–58. New Haven, CT: Yale University Press, 1994.

Pascucci, Peter. "Distinction and Proportionality in Cyber War: Virtual Problems with a Real Solution." *Minnesota Journal of International Law 257* (2017): 419–60.

Patil, Swapnil. "Government Sector in Central Asia Targeted with New HAWKBALL Backdoor Delivered via Microsoft Office Vulnerabilities." *Trellix Insights*. June 6, 2019. https://kcm.trellix.com/corporate/index?page=content&id=KB92958&locale=en_US

Payne, Thomas H., Christian Lovis, Charles Gutteridge, Claudia Pagliari, Shivam Natarajan, Cui Yong, and Lue-Ping Zhao. "Status of Health Information Exchange: A

Comparison of Six Countries." *Journal of Global Health* 9, no. 2 (2019). doi:10.7189/jogh.09.020427.
PBS NewsHour. "How Estonia Built a Digital First Government." April 29, 2018. https://www.pbs.org/newshour/show/how-estonia-built-a-digital-first-society
Perez, Sarah. "Walmart Grocery App Sees Record Downloads Amid COVID-19, Surpasses Amazon by 20%." *TechCrunch*, April 9, 2020. https://techcrunch.com/2020/04/09/walmart-grocery-app-sees-record-downloads-amid-covid-19-surpasses-amazon-by-20/
Perkovich, George, and Ariel E. Levite, eds. *Understanding Cyber Conflict: 14 Analogies*. Washington, DC: Georgetown University Press, 2017.
Perlroth, Nicole. "In Cyberattack on Saudi Firm, U.S. Sees Iran Firing Back." *New York Times*, October 23, 2012, A1.
Perlroth, Nicole, and David Sanger. "Cyberattacks Put Russian Fingers on the Switch at Power Plants, U.S. Says." *New York Times*, March 16, 2018, A1.
Perlroth, Nicole and Shane Scott. "In Baltimore and Beyond, a Stolen N.S.A. Tool Wreaks Havoc." *New York Times*, May 25, 2019, A1.
Perritt, Henry H. Jr. "Cyberspace and State Sovereignty." *Journal of International Legal Studies* 3 (1997): 155–204.
Peter G. Peterson Foundation. "U.S. Defense Spending Compared to Other Countries." New York: Peter G. Peterson Foundation, 2020.
Peters, Allison. "Russia and China Are Trying to Set the U.N.'s Rules on Cybercrime." *Foreign Policy*, September 16, 2019.
Peters, Robert, Justin Anderson, and Harrison Menke. "Deterrence in the 21st Century: Integrating Nuclear and Conventional Force." *Strategic Studies Quarterly* 12, no. 4 (2018): 15–43.
Pilloud, Claude, Yves Sandoz, Christophe Swinarski, and Bruno Zimmermann. *Commentary on the additional protocols: of 8 June 1977 to the Geneva Conventions of 12 August 1949*. Leiden: Martinus Nijhoff Publishers, 1987.
Pinker, Steven. *The Better Angels of Our Nature: Why Violence Has Declined*. New York: Penguin, 2011.
Plano, Jack, Lawrence Ziring, and Roy Olton. *International Relations: A Political Dictionary*. Santa Barbara, CA: ABC-CLIO, 1995.
Polish Ministry of Foreign Affairs. "Statement of the Polish MFA on cyberattacks against Georgia." News release, February 2, 2020. https://www.gov.pl/web/diplomacy/statement-of-the-polish-mfa-on-cyberattacks-against-georgia
Powell, Robert. "Nuclear Deterrence and the Strategy of Limited Retaliation." *American Political Science Review* 83, no. 2 (1989): 503–19.
Powell, Robert. *Nuclear Deterrence Theory: The Search for Credibility*. Cambridge: Cambridge University Press, 1990.
Price, Richard. "A Genealogy of the Chemical Weapons Taboo." *International Organization* 49, no. 1 (1995): 73–103.
Price, Richard. "International Norms and the Mines Taboo: Pulls Toward Compliance." *Canadian Foreign Policy Journal* 5, no. 3 (1998): 105–23.
Price, Richard M. *The Chemical Weapons Taboo*. Ithaca, NY: Cornell University Press, 1997.
Price, Richard M. "Reversing the Gun Sights: Transnational Civil Society Targets Land Mines." *International Organization* 52, no. 3 (1998): 613–44.

Price, Richard, and Nina Tannenwald. "Norms and Deterrence: The Nuclear and Chemical Weapons Taboos." In *The Culture of National Security*, edited by Peter Katzenstein. New York: Columbia University Press, 1996.

Project of an International Declaration Concerning the Laws and Customs of War. (Brussels, 27 August 1874). https://web.ics.purdue.edu/~wggray/Teaching/His300/Handouts/Brussels-1874.html

Protocol Additional to the Geneva Conventions of 12 August 1949, and Relating to the Protection of Victims of International Armed Conflicts (Protocol I). June 8, 1977.

Protocol on Blinding Laser Weapons (Protocol IV to the 1980 Convention on Certain Conventional Weapons). October 13, 1995.

Questor, George. *Deterrence Before Hiroshima*. New York: John Wiley, 1966.

Questor, George. *The Future of Nuclear Deterrence*. Lexington, MA: Lexington Books, 1986.

Raab, Dominic. "UK Condemns Russia's GRU Over Georgia Cyber-Attacks." News release, February 20, 2020. https://www.gov.uk/government/news/uk-condemns-russias-gru-over-georgia-cyber-attacks

Radio Free Europe. "After BRICS, Putin Hosts Shanghai Cooperation Organization Summit in Ufa." July 10, 2015.

Radziwill, Yaroslav. *Cyber-Attacks and the Exploitable Imperfections of International Law*. Leiden: Brill Nijhoff, 2015.

Randelzhofer, Albrecht. "Article 2(4)." In *The Charter of the United Nations: A Commentary*, edited by Bruno Simma, 106–28. Munich: C. H. Beck, 1995.

Randelzhofer, Albrecht. "Article 51." In *The Charter of the United Nations: A Commentary*, edited by Bruno Simma. Munich: C. H. Beck, 1995.

Rascoe, Ayesha. "Biden Adds Homeland Security, Cyber Heft to White House Team." *NPR News*, 2021.

Rattray, Greg. *Strategic Warfare in Cyberspace*. Cambridge, MA: MIT Press, 2001.

Reardon, Marguerite. "Vandals Blamed for Phone and Internet Outage." *CNet News*, April 10, 2009. https://www.cnet.com/tech/mobile/vandals-blamed-for-phone-and-internet-outage/

Reglitz, Merten. "The Human Right to Free Internet Access." *Journal of Applied Philosophy* 37, no. 2 (May 1, 2020): 314–31.

"Regulatory Guide 5.71: Cyber Security Programs for Nuclear Facilities." Washington, DC: US Nuclear Regulatory Commission, 2010.

Reich, Pauline C., and Eduardo Gelbstein. *Law, Policy, and Technology: Cyberterrorism, Information Warfare, and Internet Immobilization*. Hershey, PA: IGI Global, 2012.

Reichberg, Gregory M., Henrik Syse, and Endre Begby, eds. *The Ethics of War: Classic and Contemporary Readings*. Oxford: Blackwell Publishing, 2006.

Reiley, Laura. "In One Month, the Meat Industry's Supply Chain Broke." *Washington Post*, April 28, 2020.

Reisman, Michael. "Allocating Competences to use Coercion in the post Cold-War World, Practices Conditions, and Prospects." In *Law and Force in the New International Order*, edited by Lori F. Damrosch and David J. Scheffer, 26–49. Boulder, CO: Westview Press, 1991.

Reiss, Mitchell. *Bridled Ambition: Why Countries Constrain Their Nuclear Capabilities*. Washington, DC: Woodrow Wilson Center Press, 1995.

Report of the Select Committee on Intelligence, the U.S. Senate on Russian Active Measures Campaigns and Interference in the 2016 Election. Washington, DC: Government Printing Office, 2019.

Republic of Austria. "Austrian Cyber Security Strategy." Vienna: Federal Chancellery, 2013.

Rid, Thomas. "Cyber War Will Not Take Place." *Journal of Strategic Studies* 35, no. 1 (2012): 5–32.

Rid, Thomas. *Cyber War Will Not Take Place.* London: C Hurst & Co. Publishers, Ltd., 2013.

Rid, Thomas. "Deterrence Beyond the State: The Israeli Experience." *Comparative Security Policy* 33, no. 1 (2012): 124–47.

Rid, Thomas, and Ben Buchanan. "Attributing Cyber Attacks." *Journal of Strategic Studies* 38, no. 1–2 (January 2, 2015): 4–37.

Riley, Chris. "Interview with Toomas Hendrik Ilves: Cyber attacks, NATO—and Angry Birds." *NATO Review Magazine*, June 13, 2013.

Risse-Kappen, Thomas, Thomas Risse, Stephen C. Ropp, and Kathryn Sikkink. *The Power of Human Rights: International norms and domestic change.* Vol. 66. Cambridge: Cambridge University Press, 1999.

Roberts, Adam. "Land Warfare: From Hague to Nuremberg." In *The Law of War: Constraints on Warfare in the Western World*, edited by Michael Howard, George J. Andreopoulos and Mark R. Schulman, 116–39. New Haven, CT: Yale University Press, 1994.

Roberts, Adam, and Richard Guelff. *Documents on the Laws of War.* 3rd ed. Oxford: Oxford University Press, 2000.

Rodgers, Bethany, and Taylor Stevens. "Utah Legislature Calls Historic Special Session to Address Coronavirus Impacts." *Salt Lake Tribune*, April 13, 2020.

Rogin, Josh. "The White House's Use of Zoom for Meetings Raises China-Related Security Concerns." *Washington Post*, March 3, 2021.

Romanosky, Sasha, and Benjamin Boudreaux. "Private Sector Attribution of Cyber Incidents: Benefits and Risks to the U.S. Government." Santa Monica, CA: RAND Corporation, 2019.

Roscini, Marco. *Cyber Operations and the Use of Force in International Law.* Oxford: Oxford University Press, 2014.

Roscini, Marco. "Threats of Armed Force and Contemporary International Law." *Netherlands Law Review* 54 (2007): 229–77.

Roscini, Marco. "World Wide Warfare—Jus Ad Bellum and the Use of Cyber Force." *Max Planck Yearbook of United Nations Law* 14 (2010): 85–130.

Rosenzweig, Paul, Steve Bucci, and David Inserra. "A Congressional Guide: Seven Steps to U.S. Security, Prosperity, and Freedom in Cyberspace." Washington, DC: The Heritage Foundation, 2013.

Rowe, Neil C. "Towards Reversible Cyberattacks." In *Leading Issues in Information Warfare and Security Research*, edited by Julie Ryan, 150–64. Reading, UK: Academic Conferences Limited, 2011.

Rublee, Maria Rost. *Nonproliferation Norms: Why States Choose Nuclear Restraint.* Athens: University of Georgia Press, 2009.

Rudesill, Dakota S. "Trump's Secret Order on Pulling the Cyber Trigger." *Lawfare*, August 29, 2018. https://www.lawfaremedia.org/article/trumps-secret-order-pulling-cyber-trigger

Ruggie, John Gerard. "What Makes the World Hang Together? Neo-utilitarianism and the Social Constructivist Challenge." *International Organization* 52, no. 4 (1998): 855–85.

Russian Federation. "Conceptual Views on the Activities of the Armed Forces of the Russian federation in the Information Space." Moscow, 2000.

Russian Federation. "Convention on International Information Security (Concept)." Moscow: Ministry of Foreign Affairs, 2011.

Russian Federation, People's Republic of China, Tajikistan, and Uzbekistan. "Letter to the Secretary-General on a Draft International Code of Conduct for Information Security." New York: United Nations, September 12, 2011.

Ryan, Daniel J., and Julie C. H. Ryan. "Protecting the National Information Infrastruture Against InfoWar." In *Information Warfare: Chaos on the Electronic Superhighway*, edited by Winn Schwartau. New York: Thunder's Mouth Press, 1994.

Sagan, Scott D. "Why Do States Build Nuclear Weapons? Three Models in Search of a Bomb." *International Security* 21, no. 3 (1997): 54–86.

Sanders, Christopher M. "The Battlefield of Tomorrow, Today: Can a Cyberattack Ever Rise to an 'Act of War?'" *Utah Law Review* 2, no. 6 (May 2018): 503–22.

Sanger, David. *The Perfect Weapon: War, Sabotage, and Fear in the Cyber Age*. New York: Crown, 2018.

Sanger, David, and William Broad. "Trump Inherits a Secret Cyberwar Against North Korean Missiles." *New York Times*, March 4, 2017, A1.

Sanger, David E., and Catie Edmondson. "Russia Targeted Election Systems in All 50 States, Report Finds." *New York Times*, July 25, 2019.

Sanger, David, Nicole Perlroth, and David D. Kirkpatrick. "The World Once Laughed at North Korean Cyberpower. No More." *New York Times*, October 15, 2017.

Sanger, David, Jim Rutenberg, and Eric Lipton. "Tracing Guccifer 2.0's Many Tentacles in the 2016 Election." *New York Times*, July 15, 2018.

Sanger, David, and Marc Santora. "U.S. and Allies Blame Russia for Cyberattack on Republic of Georgia." *New York Times*, February 21, 2020.

Sanger, David, and Emily Schmall. "China Appears to Warn India: Push Too Hard and the Lights Could Go Out." *New York Times*, February 28, 2021.

San Remo Manual on International Law Applicable to Armed Conflicts at Sea. June 12, 1994. (Livorno, Italy: International Lawyers and Naval Experts Convened by the International Institute of Humanitarian Law, 1994). https://ihl-databases.icrc.org/assets/treaties/560-IHL-89-EN.pdf

SANS Institute. "Analysis of the Cyber Attack on the Ukrainian Power Grid." Rockville, MD: SANS Institute & Electricity Information Sharing & Analysis Center (E-ISAC), 2016.

SANS Institute. "Top Cyber Security Journalist Award Winners." Rockville, MD: SANS, 2018.

Sauer, Frank. "Stopping 'Killer Robots': Why Now is the Time to Ban Autonomous Weapons Systems." *Arms Control Today* 46, no. 8 (2016): 8–13.

Sauer, Tom. "A Second Nuclear Revolution: From Nuclear Primacy to Post-Existential Deterrence." *Journal of Strategic Studies* 32, no. 5 (October 1, 2009): 745–67.

Savage, John, and Les Bloom. "On Cyber Peace." Washington, DC: The Atlantic Council, 2011.

Savage, John, and Melissa Hathaway. "Stewardship of Cyberspace: Duties for Internet Service Providers." Draft. In *Cyber Dialogue: What is Stewardship in Cyberspace?* University of Toronto, Munk School of Global Affairs: University of Toronto, 2011.

Schachter, Oscar. "In Defense of International Rules on the Use of Force." *University of Chicago Law Review* 53 (Winter 1986): 113–46.

Schachter, Oscar. "The Right of States to Use Armed Force." *Michigan Law Review* 82, no. 5/6 (April-May 1984): 1620–46.

Schelling, Thomas C. *Arms and Influence*. New Haven, CT: Yale University Press, 1966.

Schelling, Thomas C. *The Strategy of Conflict*. Cambridge, MA: Harvard University Press, 1960.

Schmitt, Michael. "'Below the Threshold' Cyber Operations: The Countermeasures Response Option and International Law." *Virginia Journal of International Law* 54, no. 3 (2014): 697–732.

Schmitt, Michael. "Classification of Cyber Conflict." *International Law Studies* 89 (2013): 245–48.

Schmitt, Michael. "Computer Network Attack and the Use of Force in International Law: Thoughts on a Normative Framework." *Columbia Journal of Transnational Law* 37 (1999): 885–937.

Schmitt, Michael. "Cyber Operations and the Jus in Bello: Key Issues." *Naval War College International Law Studies* (March 2011): 89–110.

Schmitt, Michael. "The Defense Department's Measured Take on International Law in Cyberspace." *Just Security*, March 11, 2020. https://www.justsecurity.org/69119/the-defense-departments-measured-take-on-international-law-in-cyberspace/

Schmitt, Michael. "Grey Zones in the International Law of Cyberspace." *Yale Journal of International Law Online* 42, no. 2 (October 18, 2017): 1–21.

Schmitt, Michael. "The Law of Cyber Warfare: Quo Vadis?" *Stanford Law and Policy Review* 25 (2014): 269–99.

Schmitt, Michael. "The Notion of 'Objects' during Cyber Operations: A Riposte in Defence of Interpretive and Applicative Precision." *Israel Law Review* 48, no. 1 (2015): 81–109.

Schmitt, Michael, ed. *Tallinn Manual 2.0 on the International Law Applicable to Cyber Operations: Prepared by the International Group of Experts at the Invitation of the NATO Cooperative Cyber Defense Centre of Excellence*. 2nd ed. Cambridge: Cambridge University Press, 2017.

Schmitt, Michael, ed. *Tallinn Manual on the International Law Applicable to Cyber Warfare: Prepared by the International Group of Experts at the Invitation of the NATO Cooperative Cyber Defence Centre of Excellence*. Cambridge: Cambridge University Press, 2013.

Schmitt, Michael, and Brian O'Donnell, eds. *Computer Network Attack and International Law*. Newport, RI: Naval War College, 2002.

Schmitt, Michael, and Liis Vihul. "The Nature of International Law Cyber Norms." *NATO Cooperative Cyber Defence Centre of Excellence Tallinn Papers*, no. 5 (December 1, 2014): 1–31.

Schmitt, Michael N., and Liis Vihul. "Respect for Sovereignty in Cyberspace." *Texas Law Review* 95 (2016): 1639–70.

Schmitt, Michael, and Andru E. Wall. "The International Law of Unconventional Statecraft." *Harvard National Security Journal* 5 (June 18, 2015): 349–76.

Schneider, Jacquelyn. "Deterrence In and Through Cyberspace." In *Cross-Domain Deterrence*, edited by Jon R. Lindsay and Erik Gartzke, 95–120. Oxford: Oxford University Press, 2019.

Schroeder, Matthew. "Stop Panicking About the Stingers." *Foreign Policy* (July 28, 2010). https://foreignpolicy.com/2010/07/28/stop-panicking-about-the-stingers/

Schwartz, Ari, and Robert Knake. "The Government's Role in Vulnerability Disclosure." Cambridge, MA: Harvard Kennedy School, 2016.

Schwarzenberger, Georg. "The Fundamental Principles of International Law." *Recueil des Cours de l'Academie de Droit International (RCADI)* 87 (1955): 191–386.

Schwebel, Stephen. "Aggression, Intervention and Self-Defense in Modern International Law." In *Justice in International Law: Selected Writings of Judge Stephen M. Schwebel*, edited by Stephen Schwebel, 530–92. Cambridge: Cambridge University Press, 1994.

SecDev Group. "Tracking GhostNet: Investigating a Cyber Espionage Network." *Information Warfare Monitor*, March 29, 2009.

Security Treaty Between the United States, Australia, and New Zealand (ANZUS). San Francisco: September 1, 1951. UNTS No. 1736.

Segal, Adam. *The Hacked World Order: How Nations Fight, Trade, Maneuver, and Manipulate in the Digital Age*. Reprint ed. New York: PublicAffairs, 2017.

Segall, Anna. "Economic Sanctions: Legal and Policy Constraints." *International Review of the Red Cross*, no. 836 (1999): 763–84.

Sen, Ashish Kumar. "U.S. Sen. Mark Warner and Adm. Michael Rogers make the case for cyber security." Paper presented at the Atlantic Council's Annual Forum, Washington, DC, December 14, 2018.

Sengupta, Kim. "'We Are Constantly One Step Behind': Finland Worries About Cyber Warfare in Shadow of Russia." *The Independent*, October 1, 2018.

Sgobba, Tommaso. "B-737 MAX and the Crash of the Regulatory System." *Journal of Space Safety Engineering* 6, no. 4 (2019): 299–303.

Shackelford, Scott J. "From Nuclear War to Net War: Analogizing Cyber Attacks in International Law." *Berkeley Journal of International Law* 27 (2009): 192–252.

Shacklett, Mary. "How Technology Is Transforming the Food Supply Chain." *Food Logistics Magazine*, July 14, 2017. https://www.foodlogistics.com/software-technol ogy/article/12344804/how-technology-is-transforming-the-food-supply-chain

Shaer, Matthew. "North Korean Hackers Blamed for Sweeping Cyber Attack on US Networks." *Christian Science Monitor*, July 8, 2009.

Shalal, Andrea and Alina Shelyukh, "Obama Seeks $14 Billion to Boost U.S. Cybersecurity Defenses." *Reuters*, February 2, 2015. https://www.reuters.com/article/us-usa-budget-cybersecurity/obama-seeks-14-billion-to-boost-u-s-cybersecurity-defenses-idUSKB N0L61WQ20150202/

Shanghai Cooperation Organisation. *Agreement between the Governments of the Member States of the Shanghai Cooperation Organisation on Cooperation in the Field of International Information Security*. Yekaterinbourg: Shanghai Cooperation Organisation, June 16, 2009.

Sharp, Walter Gary. *The Use of Force in CyberSpace*. Falls Church, VA: Aegis Research Corporation, 1999.

Sheshabalaya, Tosh. "Healthcare Information Technology in Austria and Switzerland." *Health Management* 5, no. 2 (2010). https://healthmanagement.org/c/intervention/ issuearticle/healthcare-information-technology-in-austria-and-switzerland

Shoorbajee, Zaid. "Chinese Hackers Tried to Spy on U.S. Think Tanks to Steal Military Strategy Documents, CrowdStrike Says." *CyberScoop*, December 21, 2017. https://cyb erscoop.com/chinese-hackers-tried-to-spy-on-u-s-think-tanks-to-steal-military-strat egy-documents/

Sigal, Leon V. *Negotiating Minefields: The Landmines Ban in American Politics*. New York: Routledge, 2013.

Silver, Daniel B. "Computer Network Attack as a Use of Force under Article 2(4) of the United Nations Charter." In *Computer Network Attack and International Law*, edited by Michael Schmitt and Brian O'Donnell, 73–98. Newport, RI: Naval War College, 2002.

Singel, Ryan. "Pakistan's Accidental YouTube Re-Routing Exposes Trust Flaw in Net." *Wired*, February 26, 2008.

Smeets, Max. "A Matter of Time: On the Transitory Nature of Cyberweapons." *Journal of Strategic Studies* 41, no. 1–2 (February 16, 2018): 6–32.

Smith, Brad. "The need for a Digital Geneva Convention." News release, February 14, 2017. Microsoft Corporation. https://blogs.microsoft.com/on-the-issues/2017/02/14/need-digital-geneva-convention/

Smith, Steven. "Minister for Defence–Australia-United States Ministerial Consultations (AUSMIN)." News release, (Canberra, Austrlian Ministry of Defence, September 16, 2011). https://parlinfo.aph.gov.au/parlInfo/search/display/display.w3p;query=Id:%22media/pressrel/1416907%22

Snyder, Glynn. *Deterrence and Defense: Towards a Theory of National Security*. Princeton, NJ: Princeton University Press, 1961.

Solis, Gary D. "Cyber Warfare." *Military Law Review* 219 (2014): 26–27.

Solis, Gary D. *The Law of Armed Conflict: International Humanitarian Law in War*. Cambridge: Cambridge University Press, 2016.

Song, Sang-ho. "Military eyes 'proactive cyberactivities'." *Korea Herald*, October 8, 2014. http://www.koreaherald.com/view.php?ud=20141008001223

Sridharan, Vasudevan. "Russia Setting up Cyber Warfare Unit Under Military." *International Business Times*, August 20, 2013.

Stacey, Robert C. "The Age of Chivalry." In *The Laws of War: Constraints on Warfare in the Western World*, edited by Michael Howard, George J. Andreopoulos and Mark R. Schulman, 27–39. New Haven, CT: Yale University Press, 1994.

Starks, Tom. "Albania Is the First Known Country to Sever Diplomatic Ties Over a Cyberattack." *The Cybersecurity 202*, September 8, 2022.

"Statement by H. E. Mr. Rodrigo Malmierca Díaz, Permanent Representative of Cuba to the United Nations," UN 29th Session, May 1, 2007.

Steele, Brent J. *Restraint in International Politics*. Cambridge: Cambridge University Press, 2019.

Stein, George J. "Information Warfare." *Airpower Journal* 9, no. 1 (1995): 30–55.

Stevens, Timothy C. "A Cyberwar of Ideas? Deterrence and Norms in Cyberspace." *Contemporary Security Policy* 33, no. 1 (April 2012): 148–70.

Stewart, Emily. "Hackers Have Been Holding the City of Baltimore's Computers Hostage for 2 Weeks." *Vox News*, May 21, 2019.

Stewart, Phil. "Old Worm Won't Die After 2008 Attack on Military." *Reuters*, June 16, 2011. https://www.reuters.com/article/idUSTRE75F5TB/

Stockton Center for the Study of International Law. "The Conduct of Hostilities and International Humanitarian Law: Challenges of 21st Century Warfare." *International Law Studies* 93 (2017):" 322–88.

Stolberg, Sheryl Gay. "House Democrats Back Changing Rules to Allow Remote Voting During Pandemic." *New York Times*, April 16, 2020. https://www.nytimes.com/2020/04/16/us/politics/house-coronavirus-remote-voting.html

Stone, Julius. *Aggression and World Order: A Critique of United Nations Theories of Aggression*. Clark, NJ: The Lawbook Exchange, Ltd., 1958.

Streltsov, Anatoly A. "International Information Security: Description and Legal Aspects." In *International Information Security: The Diplomacy of Peace*, edited by Sergei Komov, 45–57. Moscow: Russian Federation Official Publications, 2008.

Streltsov, A. A. *Application of International Humanitarian Law to Armed Conflicts in Cyberspace*. Moscow: Information Security Institute of Lomonosov Moscow State University, 2016.

Stürchler, Nikolas. *The Threat of Force in International Law*. Cambridge: Cambridge University Press, 2007.

Sugarman, Eli, and Heath Wickline. "The Sorry State of Cybersecurity Imagery." Menlo Park, CA: The William & Flora Hewlett Foundation, 2019.

Sukumar, Arun. "The UN GGE Failed. Is International Law in Cyberspace Doomed As Well?" *Lawfare*, July 4, 2017. https://www.lawfareblog.com/un-gge-failed-internatio nal-law-cyberspace-doomed-well.

Svensson, Peter. "Finger-Thin Undersea Cables Tie World Together." *The Associated Press*, January 31, 2008.

Sydney Morning Herald. "Estonia Urges Firm EU, NATO Response to New Form of Warfare: Cyber Attacks." May 16, 2007.

Symantec Corporation. "Here Comes the CNCI, and the Era of Proactive IT Security." Symantec News Forum, 2008.

Taft, William H. IV. "Self-Defense and the *Oil Platforms* Decision." *Yale Journal of International Law* 29 (2004): 295–306.

Talbot, David. "Russia's Cyber Security Plans: As Washington Airs Plans for a New 'Cyber Command,' A Top Russian Official Discusses the Threat of Cyberweapons." *MIT Technology Review*, April 16, 2010.

Tamkin, Emily. "10 Years After the Landmark Attack on Estonia, Is the World Better Prepared for Cyber Threats?" *Foreign Policy*, April 27, 2017.

Tannenwald, Nina. "Stigmatizing the Bomb: Origins of the Nuclear Taboo." *International Security* 29, no. 4 (2005): 5–49.

Tannenwald, Nina. *The Nuclear Taboo: The United States and the Non-Use of Nuclear Weapons Since 1945*. Cambridge: Cambridge University Press, 2007.

Technological Capabilities Panel, Science Advisory Committee, United States. "Meeting the Threat of Surprise Attack." The White House, 1955.

Testart, Cecilia, Philipp Richter, Alistair King, Alberto Dainotti, and David Clark. *Profiling BGP Serial Hijackers: Capturing Persistent Misbehavior in the Global Routing Table*. Proceedings of the Internet Measurement Conference. Amsterdam: Association for Computing Machinery, 2019.

The Economic Times of India. "Government Likely to Announce New Cyber Security Policy in Three Months." March 11, 2020. https://economictimes.indiatimes.com/ news/defence/government-likely-to-announce-new-cyber-security-policy-in-three-months/articleshow/74580639.cms

Thompson, Christina, and Katie Caviness. "Cyber Attack Targets ONWASA; Company Refusing to Pay Ransom." *WCTI News*, October 15, 2018. https://wcti12.com/news/ local-crime/cyber-attack-targets-onwasa-company-refusing-to-pay-ransom.

Thompson, Iain. "Russia 'Hired Botnets' for Estonia Cyber-War: Russian Authorities Accused of Collusion with Botnet Owners." Computing.co.uk, May 31, 2007. https:// www.itnews.com.au/news/russia-hired-botnets-for-estonia-cyber-war-82600

Tikk, Eneken, ed. *Frameworks for International Cyber Security: Legal and Policy Instruments*. Vol. 1. Tallinn, Estonia: NATO Cooperative Cyber Defence Centre of Excellence, 2010.

Tikk, Eneken. "Ten Rules for Cyber Security." *Survival* 53, no. 3 (July 1, 2011): 119–32.

Tikk, Eneken, and Kadri Kaska. "Legal Cooperation to Investigate Cyber Incidents: Estonian Case Study and Lessons." In *Proceedings of the 9th European Conference on Information Warfare and Security, Thessaloniki, Greece, 1–2 July 2010*, 288–94. Reading, UK: Academic Publishing Limited.

Tikk, Eneken, Kadri Kaska, and Liis Vihul. *International Cyber Incidents: Legal Considerations*. Edited by Eneken Tikk Vol. 1, Tallinn, Estonia: NATO Cooperative Cyber Defence-Centre of Excellence, 2010.

Tikk-Ringas, Eneken. "International Cyber Norms Dialogue as an Exercise of Normative Power." *Georgetown Journal of International Affairs* 17, no. 3 (2016): 47–59.

Tiku, Natasha. "A Top Google Exec Pushed the Company to Commit to Human Rights. Then Google Pushed Him Out, He Says." *Washington Post*, January 2, 2020.

Tiyagi, Amit Kumar, and G. Aghila. "A Wide Scale Survey on Botnet." *International Journal of Computer Applications* 34, no. 9 (2011): 9–22.

Tor, Uri. "'Cumulative Deterrence' as a New Paradigm for Cyber Deterrence." *Journal of Strategic Studies* 40, no. 1–2 (February 2017): 92–117.

Treaty of Mutual Cooperation and Security Between Japan and the United States of America. August 19, 1960. UNTS No. 5321.

Trend Micro. "Russian Underground 101." Cupertino, CA: Trend Micro, 2012.

Tsagourias, Nicholas. "Cyber Attacks, Self-Defence and the Problem of Attribution." *Journal of Conflict & Security Law* 17 (2012): 229–44.

Tubbs, David, Perry G. Luzwick, and Walter Gary Sharp. "Technology and Law: The Evolution of Digital Warfare." In *Computer Network Attack and International Law*, edited by Michael Schmitt and Brian O'Donnell, 7–20. Newport, RI: Naval War College, 2002.

UK Cabinet Office. *Keeping the UK Safe in Cyberspace*. London: The Stationary Office, Her Majesty's Government, 2013.

UK Centre for the Protection of National Infrastructure. "Process Control and SCADA Security." London: CPNI, 2008.

UK Ministry of Defence. "JSP 383: The Joint Service Manual of the Law of Armed Conflict." London, 2004.

United Nations. "Charter of the United Nations." October 24, 1945.

United Nations. "Statute of the International Court of Justice." 1946.

United Nations. "Vienna Convention on the Law of Treaties." 1969.

United Nations General Assembly. "Declaration on the Enhancement of the Effectiveness of the Principle of Refraining from the Threat or Use of Force in International Relations." New York, 1987.

United Nations General Assembly. *Definition of Aggression (A/RES/3314 [XXIX])*. 1974.

United Nations General Assembly. "Developments in the Field of Information and Telecommunications in the Context of International Security." New York, 2011.

United Nations General Assembly. "Developments in the Field of Information and Telecommunications in the Context of International Security." New York, 2018.

United Nations General Assembly. "Developments in the Field of Information and Telecommunications in the Context of International Security." New York, 2002.

United Nations General Assembly. *Universal Declaration of Human Rights*. (A/RES/217[III]). New York, December 10, 1948.

United Nations General Assembly (Third Committee). "Countering the Use of Information and Communications Technologies for Criminal Purposes." New York, 2019.

United Nations Group of Governmental Experts (2008–9). *Report Group of Governmental Experts on Developments in the Field of Information and Telecommunications in the Context of International Security (2008–9)*. Geneva: United Nations Institute for Disarmament Research, 2010.

United Nations Group of Governmental Experts (2011–12). *Report of the Group of Governmental Experts on Developments in the Field of Information and Telecommunications in the Context of International Security (2011–12)*. Geneva: United Nations Institute for Disarmament Research, 2013.

United Nations Group of Governmental Experts (2014–15). *Report of the Group of Governmental Experts on Developments in the Field of Information and Telecommunications in the Context of International Security*. Geneva: United Nations Institute for Disarmament Research, 2015.

United Nations Group of Governmental Experts (2019–21). *Report of the Group of Governmental Experts on Developments in the Field of Information and Telecommunications in the Context of International Security*. Geneva: United Nations Institute for Disarmament Research, 2021.

United Nations Institute for Disarmament Research. "The United Nations, Cyberspace and International Peace and Security." Geneva: UNIDIR, 2017.

United Nations Open-Ended Working Group on Information and Communication Technologies. *Report of the Open-Ended Working Group on Security of and in the Use of Information and Communications Technologies 2021–2025*. Geneva: UNIDIR, 2021.

United Nations Secretary-General. "Developments in the Field of Information and Telecommunications in the Context of International Security, Delivered to the General Assembly." June 24, 2013.

United Nations Secretary-General. "Developments in the Field of Information and Telecommunications in the Context of International Security, Delivered to the General Assembly." July 22, 2015.

United Nations Secretary-General. "Developments in the Field of Information and Telecommunications in the Context of International Security: Report of the Secretary-General." New York, 2011.

United Nations Secretary-General. "Report of the Secretary-General Pursuant to Paragraph 2 of Security Council Resolution 808 (1993)." New York, 1993.

United States of America v. Park Jin Hyok (Criminal Complaint). Washington, DC: Department of Justice, 2018.

US Air Force. "Air Force Doctrine Document 2-11: Cyberspace Operations." Washington, DC: LeMay Center for Doctrine Development and Education, 2008.

US Attorney's Office (Southern District of New York). "Manhattan U.S. Attorney Announces Charges Against Seven Iranians for Conducting Coordinated Campaign Of Cyber Attacks Against U.S. Financial Sector On Behalf Of Islamic Revolutionary Guard Corps-Sponsored Entities." Washington, DC: Department of Justice, 2016.

US Centers for Disease Control and Prevention. "History of U.S. Chemical Weapons Elimination." Washington, DC: Government Printing Office, 2014.

US Central Intelligence Agency. *Soviet Motivations for the Use of Chemical Weapons in Afghanistan and Southeast Asia: An Intelligence Assessment, CIA Historical Review Program Released As Sanitized 1999*. McLean, VA: Directorate of Intelligence, 1983.

US Congress, Homeland Security and Governmental Affairs. *Hearing to Establish a Bug Bounty Pilot Program Within the Department of Homeland Security, and For Other Purposes*, 115th Congress, February 26, 2018.

US Congressional Research Service. "Computer Attack and Cyber Terrorism: Vulnerabilities and Policy Issues for Congress." Washington, DC: US Congress, 2003.

US Congressional Research Service. "Creating a National Framework for Cybersecurity: An Analysis of Issues and Options." Washington, DC: US Congress, 2005.

US Congressional Research Service. "Iranian Offensive Cyber Attack Capabilities." Washington, DC: US Congress, 2020.

US Congressional Research Service. "U.S.–China Cyber Agreement." Washington, DC: US Congress, 2015.

US Cyber Command. "Achieve and Maintain Cyberspace Superiority: Command Vision for US Cyber Command." Washington, DC: Department of Defense, 2018.

US Cyberspace Solarium Commission. *U.S. Cyberspace Solarium Commission Report.* Washington, DC, 2020.

US Department of Defense. "The Department of Defense Cyber Strategy." Washington, DC, 2015.

US Department of Defense. "Department of Defense Cyberspace Policy Report: A Report to Congress Pursuant to the National Defense Authorization Act for Fiscal Year 2011, Section 934." Washington, DC, 2011.

US Department of Defense. "Department of Defense Law of War Manual." Washington, DC, 2016.

US Department of Defense. "Department of Defense Strategy for Operating in Cyberspace." Washington, DC, 2011.

US Department of Defense. "DOD Announces Start of Exercise Ulchi Freedom Guardian." Washington, DC, August 18, 2017. https://www.defense.gov/News/News-Stories/Article/Article/1282738/dod-announces-start-of-exercise-ulchi-freedom-guardian/#:~:text=South%20Korea%20and%20U.S.%20Combined,31%2C%20defense%20officials%20announced%20today.

US Department of Defense. "DOD Has Enduring Role in Election Defense." News release, February 10, 2020. https://www.defense.gov/News/News-Stories/Article/Article/2078716/dod-has-enduring-role-in-election-defense/.

US Department of Defense. "DoD Recovered Chemical Warfare Material (RCWM) Program: History of United States' Involvement in Chemical Warfarm." Safety & Occupational Health Network and Information Exchange (DENIX) DOD Environment, 2019.

US Department of Defense. "The Evolution of Cyber: Newest Subordinate Unified Command is Nation's Joint Cyber Force." News release, December 19, 2022. https://www.cybercom.mil/Media/News/Article/3250075/the-evolution-of-cyber-newest-subordinate-unified-command-is-nations-joint-cybe/.

US Department of Defense. "Joint Publication 3-12: Cyberspace Operations." Washington, DC: Joint Chiefs of Staff, 2018.

US Department of Defense. "Quadrennial Defense Review." Washington, DC, 2010.

US Department of Defense. "Summary of the 2018 Department of Defense Cyber Strategy." Washington, DC, 2018.

US Department of Defense. "Summary of the Department of Defense Cyber Strategy." Washington, DC, 2018.

US Department of Defense. "U.S. Department of Defense Inspector General, Agency Financial Report for FY2018." Washington, DC, 2017.

US Department of Energy. "Smart Grid System Report: 2018 Report to Congress." Washington, DC, 2018.

US Department of Homeland Security. "Alert (TA18-074A) Russian Government Cyber Activity Targeting Energy and Other Critical Infrastructure Sectors." Washington, DC, 2018.

US Department of Homeland Security. *Alert: Increasing Threat to Industrial Control Systems*. Industrial Control Systems Cyber Emergency Response Team Washington, DC, 2012.

US Department of Justice. "Chinese Military Personnel Charged with Computer Fraud, Economic Espionage and Wire Fraud for Hacking into Credit Reporting Agency Equifax." News release, February 10, 2020. https://www.justice.gov/opa/pr/chinese-military-personnel-charged-computer-fraud-economic-espionage-and-wire-fraud-hacking

US Department of Justice. "Nine Iranians Charged with Conducting Massive Cyber Theft Campaign On Behalf Of The Islamic Revolutionary Guard Corps." News release, March 23, 2018. https://www.justice.gov/opa/pr/nine-iranians-charged-conducting-massive-cyber-theft-campaign-behalf-islamic-revolutionary

US Department of Justice. "North Korean Regime-Backed Programmer Charged With Conspiracy to Conduct Multiple Cyber Attacks and Intrusions." News release, September 6, 2018. https://www.justice.gov/opa/pr/north-korean-regime-backed-programmer-charged-conspiracy-conduct-multiple-cyber-attacks-and

US Department of Justice. "Seven Iranians Working for Islamic Revolutionary Guard Corps-Affiliated Entities Charged for Conducting Coordinated Campaign of Cyber Attacks Against U.S. Financial Sector." News release, March 24, 2016. https://www.justice.gov/opa/pr/seven-iranians-working-islamic-revolutionary-guard-corps-affiliated-entities-charged

US Department of Justice. "Two Chinese Hackers Associated with the Ministry of State Security Charged with Global Computer Intrusion Campaigns Targeting Intellectual Property and Confidential Business Information." News release, December 20, 2018. https://www.justice.gov/opa/pr/two-chinese-hackers-associated-ministry-state-security-charged-global-computer-intrusion

US Department of Justice. "Two Chinese Nationals Charged with Laundering Over $100 Million in Cryptocurrency from Exchange Hack." News release, March 2, 2020. https://www.justice.gov/opa/pr/two-chinese-nationals-charged-laundering-over-100-million-cryptocurrency-exchange-hack

US Department of Justice. "U.S. Charges Five Chinese Military Hackers for Cyber Espionage Against U.S. Corporations and a Labor Organization for Commercial Advantage." News release, May 19, 2014. https://www.justice.gov/opa/pr/us-charges-five-chinese-military-hackers-cyber-espionage-against-us-corporations-and-labor

US Department of State. "Department of State International Cyberspace Policy Strategy." March 2016. https://2009-2017.state.gov/documents/organization/255732.pdf

US Department of State. "Executive Summary of Findings on Adherence to and Compliance with Arms Control, Nonproliferation, and Disarmament Agreements and Comments." Washington, DC, June 2020. https://www.state.gov/wp-content/uploads/2020/06/2020-Adherence-to-and-Compliance-with-Arms-Control-Nonproliferation-and-Disarmament-Agreements-and-Commitments-Compliance-Report-1.pdf

US Department of State. "Joint Statement on Australia-U.S. Ministerial Consultations (AUSMIN) 2021." News release, September 16, 2021. https://www.state.gov/joint-statement-on-australia-u-s-ministerial-consultations-ausmin-2021/.

US Department of State. "Press Briefing with Deputy Assistant Secretary Robert Strayer." News release, October 15, 2019. https://2017-2021.state.gov/telephonic-press-briefing-with-deputy-assistant-secretary-robert-strayer-cyber-and-international-affairs-and-information-policy-bureau-of-economic-and-business-affairs/index.html.

US Department of State. "Recommendations to the President on Deterring Adversaries and Better Protecting the American People from Cyber Threats." Office of the Coordinator for Cyber Issues, May 31, 2018. https://www.state.gov/wp-content/uploads/2019/04/Recommendations-to-the-President-on-Deterring-Adversaries-and-Better-Protecting-the-American-People-From-Cyber-Threats.pdf

US Department of State. "The Third U.S.–France Cyber Dialogue." News release, January 22, 2020. https://2017-2021.state.gov/the-third-u-s-france-cyber-dialogue/

US Department of State. "U.S.–Russia Bilateral Presidential Commission: 2013 Joint Annual Report." Washington, DC: Department of State.

US Energy Information Admnistration. "EIA FAQs." 2022. https://www.eia.gov/tools/faqs/

US Federal Bureau of Investigation. "What We Investigate: Cyber Crime." US Department of Justice. https://www.fbi.gov/investigate/cyber

US Government Accounting Office. *Computer Security: Hackers Penetrate DOD Computer Systems*. Washington, DC: GAO, 1991.

US House Armed Services Committee, Subcommittee on Terrorism, Unconventional Threats, and Capabilities Subcommittee. "Statement for the Record by Lieutenant General Keith Alexander Commander Joint Functional Component Command for Network Warfare." May 5, 2009.

US House of Representatives Committee on Armed Services, Subcommittee on Intelligence, Emerging Threats and Capabilities. *Information Technology and Cyber Operations: Modernization and Policy Issues to Support the Future Force*. March 14, 2013.

US House of Representatives, Subcommittee on Technology and Innovation, Committee on Science and Technology. *Untangling Attribution: Moving to Accountability in Cyberspace (Testimony of Robert Knake)*. July 15, 2010.

US Joint Chiefs of Staff. *JP1-02: Department of Defense Dictionary of Military and Associated Terms*. Washington, DC: Department of Defense, 2001.

US Joint Chiefs of Staff. *National Military Strategy*. Washington, DC: Department of Defense, 2008.

US National Infrastructure Advisory Council. "Water Sector Resilience: Final Report & Recommendations." Washington, DC: Department of Homeland Security, 2016.

US National Research Council. "Technology, Policy, Law, and Ethics Regarding U.S. Acquisition and Use of Cyberattack Capabilities." Washington, DC, 2009.

US Navy. *Commander's Handbook on The Law of Naval Operations*. NWP 1-14M ed. Washington, DC: Department of Defense, 2007.

US Office of the Director of National Intelligence. "Background to 'Assessing Russian Activities and Intentions in Recent US Elections': The Analytic Process and Cyber Incident Attribution." Washington, DC, 2017.

US Office of Technology Assessment. "Information Security and Privacy in Network Environments." Washington, DC: Government Printing Office, 1994.

US Office of the Director of National Intelligence. "Five Eyes Intelligence Oversight and Review Council (FIORC)." https://www.dni.gov/index.php/ncsc-how-we-work/217-about/organization/icig-pages/2660-icig-fiorcUS Senate Armed Services Committee. "Cyber Deterrence Statement by Dr. Craig Fields Chairman, Defense

Science Board and Dr. Jim Miller Member, Defense Science Board Former Under Secretary of Defense (Policy) before the Armed Services Committee, United States Senate." March 2, 2017.

US Senate Armed Services Committee. "Hearing to Consider the Nomination of Hon. Leon E. Panetta to be Secretary of Defense." June 9, 2011.

US Senate Committee on Armed Services. Hearing to Consider the Nomination of Lt. Gen. Keith B. Alexander to Commander, U.S. CYBERCOMMAND. April 15, 2010.

US Senate Armed Services Committee. "Nominations Before the Senate Armed Services Committee, Second." April 15, 2010.

US Senate Select Committee on Intelligence. "Statement for the Record on the Worldwide Threat Assessment of the US Intelligence Community." January 29, 2014.

US Senate Select Committee on Intelligence. "Statement for the Record on the Worldwide Threat Assessment of the US Intelligence Community." February 13, 2018.

US Senate Select Committee on Intelligence. "Statement for the Record on the Worldwide Threat Assessment of the US Intelligence Community." January 29, 2019.

US Space-Based Positioning, Navigation and Timing National Executive Committee. "Public Safety & Disaster Relief." Washington, DC: Department of Commerce, 2019.

Valentinas, Navickas, and Gruzauskas Valentas. "Big Data Concept in the Food Supply Chain: Small Markets Case." *Scientific Annals of Economics and Business* 63, no. 1 (December 17, 2016): 15–28.

Valentino-DeVries, Jennifer, and Danny Yadron. "Cataloging the World's Cyberforces." *Wall Street Journal*, October 11, 2015. https://www.wsj.com/articles/cataloging-the-worlds-cyberforces-1444610710

Van Crevald, Martin. *Technology and War: From 2000 B.C. to the Present*. 2nd ed. New York: Touchstone, 1991.

Van Evera, Stephen. *Guide to Methods for Students of Political Science*. Ithaca, NY: Cornell University Press, 1997.

Vavra, Shannon. "'China Chopper' Web Shell Makes a Comeback in Lebanon, Other Asian Countries." *CyberScoop*, August 27, 2019. https://cyberscoop.com/china-chopper-talos-apt10-apt40/

Volz, Dustin. "Trump, Seeking to Relax Rules on U.S. Cyberattacks, Reverses Obama Directive." *Wall Street Journal*, August 15, 2018.

Volz, Dustin. "U.S. Lacks Key Abilities to Avert Cyberattacks, Commission Says." *Wall Street Journal*, March 10, 2020.

Volz, Dustin. "White House Expands Use of Cyber Weapons but Stays Secretive on Policies." *Wall Street Journal*, December 30, 2019.

Von Clausewitz, Carl. *On War*. Translated by Howard Michael and Paret Peter. reprint ed. Princeton, NJ: Princeton University Press, 2008 [1832].

Walker, George K. "Information Warfare and Neutrality." *Vanderbilt Journal of Transnational Law* 33, no. 5 (November 2000): 1079–202.

Waltman, Chris. "Aurora: Homeland Security's Secret Project to Change How We Think About Cybersecurity (DHS FOIA Response)." *Muckrock*, November 14, 2016. https://www.muckrock.com/news/archives/2016/nov/14/aurora-generator-test-homeland-security/.

Waltz, Kenneth N. *Theory of International Politics*. Reprint ed. New York: Waveland, 2010 [1979].

Walzer, Michael. *Just and Unjust Wars*. 4th ed. New York: Basic Books, 1977.

Wardrop, Murray. "William Hague: 'Britain Faces Growing Cyberspace Arms Race.'" *The Telegraph*, October 18, 2011.
Warner, Mark. "2018 National Security Agency Law Day Speech." Washington, DC: Lawfare, 2018.
Warren, Tom. "A Major New Intel Processor Flaw Could Defeat Encryption and DRM Protections." *The Verge*, March 6, 2020.
Warrick, Joby, and Ellen Nakashima. "Foreign Intelligence Officials Say Attempted Cyberattack on Israeli Water Utilities Linked to Iran." *Washington Post*, May 8, 2020.
"Wassenaar Arrangement on Export Controls for Conventional Arms and Dual-Use Goods and Technologies." (The Hague: December 19, 1995). https://www.wassenaar.org/app/uploads/2021/12/Public-Docs-Vol-I-Founding-Documents.pdf
Waxman, Matthew C. "Cyber-Attacks and the Use of Force: Back to the Future of Article 2(4)." *Yale Journal of International Law* 36 (2011): 421–58.
Waxman, Matthew C. "Cyber Attacks as 'Force' Under UN Charter Article 2(4)." *International Law Studies* 87, no. 43 (2011): 43–57.
Weber, Amalie M. "The Council of Europe's Convention on Cybercrime." *Berkeley Technology Law Journal* 18, no. 1 (2003): 425–46.
Weiss, Andrew. "Russia the World's Outlaw State." In *Aspen Ideas*. Washington, DC: Aspen Institute, 2018.
Wendt, Alexander. *Social Theory of International Politics*. Cambridge: Cambridge University Press, 1999.
Westbrook, Tom. "Severed Cable Sends Tonga 'Back to Beginning of the Internet.'" *Reuters*, January 24, 2019. https://www.reuters.com/article/us-tonga-internet/severed-cable-sends-tonga-back-to-beginning-of-the-internet-idUSKCN1PI0A8/?edition-redirect=ca
The White House. "Administration Presents President Trump's Fiscal Year 2020 Budget Request." March 11, 2019. https://trumpwhitehouse.archives.gov/briefings-statements/administration-presents-president-trumps-fiscal-year-2020-budget-request/
The White House. Executive Order 13694. 2016.
The White House. Executive Order 13757. 2015.
The White House. "Fact Sheet on Presidential Policy Directive 20." News release, 2013. https://irp.fas.org/offdocs/ppd/ppd-20-fs.pdf
The White House. "Fact Sheet: Biden-Harris Administration Delivers on Strengthening America's Cybersecurity." News release, October 11, 2022. https://www.whitehouse.gov/briefing-room/statements-releases/2022/10/11/fact-sheet-biden-harris-administration-delivers-on-strengthening-americas-cybersecurity/.
The White House. "Fact Sheet: The 2016 G-20 Summit in Hangzhou, China." News release, September 5, 2016. https://obamawhitehouse.archives.gov/the-press-office/2016/09/05/fact-sheet-2016-g-20-summit-hangzhou-china.
The White House. "Fact Sheet: The 2022 NATO Summit in Madrid." News release, June 29, 2022. https://www.whitehouse.gov/briefing-room/statements-releases/2022/06/29/fact-sheet-the-2022-nato-summit-in-madrid/.
The White House. "Fact Sheet: U.S.-United Kingdom Cybersecurity Cooperation." News release, January 16, 2015. https://obamawhitehouse.archives.gov/the-press-office/2015/01/16/fact-sheet-us-united-kingdom-cybersecurity-cooperation.
The White House. "Joint Fact Sheet: The United States-Republic of Korea Alliance: Shared Values, New Frontiers." News release, October 16, 2015. https://obamawhitehouse.archives.gov/the-press-office/2015/10/16/joint-fact-sheet-united-states-republic-korea-alliance-shared-values-new

The White House. "Joint Fact Sheet: U.S. and UK Cooperation on Cyberspace." News release, May 25, 2011. http://www.whitehouse.gov/the-press-office/2011/05/25/joint-fact-sheet-us-and-uk-cooperation-cyberspace.

The White House. "Joint Statement on the Visit to the United Kingdom of the Honorable Joseph R. Biden, Jr., President of the United States of America at the Invitation of the Rt. Hon. Boris Johnson, M.P., the Prime Minister of the United Kingdom of Great Britain and Northern Ireland." News release, June 10, 2021. https://www.whitehouse.gov/briefing-room/statements-releases/2021/06/10/joint-statement-on-the-visit-to-the-united-kingdom-of-the-honorable-joseph-r-biden-jr-president-of-the-united-states-of-america-at-the-invitation-of-the-rt-hon-boris-johnson-m-p-the-prime-min/.

The White House. "National Cyber Strategy of the United States of America." September 21, 2018. https://trumpwhitehouse.archives.gov/wp-content/uploads/2018/09/National-Cyber-Strategy.pdf

The White House. "National Security Presidential Memoranda [NSPMs] Donald J. Trump Administration." (Washington, DC: Government Printing Office 2017). https://irp.fas.org/offdocs/nspm/index.html

The White House. *The National Strategy to Secure Cyberspace*. Washington, DC: US Government Printing Office, 2009.

The White House. "Remarks by the President at the National Cybersecurity Communications Integration Center." January 13, 2015. https://obamawhitehouse.archives.gov/the-press-office/2015/01/13/remarks-president-national-cybersecurity-communications-integration-cent

The White House. "Remarks by the Vice President at the London Conference on Cyberspace." November 1, 2011. https://obamawhitehouse.archives.gov/the-press-office/2011/11/01/vps-remarks-london-cyberspace-conference

The White House. "Space Force Announcement by Vice President Mike Pence (August 9, 2018)." https://trumpwhitehouse.archives.gov/briefings-statements/remarks-vice-president-pence-future-u-s-military-space/

The White House. "The United States, Joined by Allies and Partners, Attributes Malicious Cyber Activity and Irresponsible State Behavior to the People's Republic of China." News release, July 19, 2021. https://www.whitehouse.gov/briefing-room/statements-releases/2021/07/19/the-united-states-joined-by-allies-and-partners-attributes-malicious-cyber-activity-and-irresponsible-state-behavior-to-the-peoples-republic-of-china/.

The White House. *The United States' International Strategy for Cyberspace*. Washington, DC: US Government Printing Office, 2011.

The White House. *U.S.–ROK Leaders' Joint Statement (May 21, 2021)*. Washington, DC: Government Printing Office, 2021.

The White House. "U.S.–Russian Cooperation on Information and Communications Technology Security." News release, June 17, 2013. https://obamawhitehouse.archives.gov/the-press-office/2013/06/17/fact-sheet-us-russian-cooperation-information-and-communications-technol

White House Council of Economic Advisors. "The Cost of Malicious Cyber Activity to the U.S. Economy." Washington, DC: Executive Office of the US President, 2018.

Williams, Westin. "Russia Launches Anti-Satellite Weapon: A New Warfront in Space?" *Christian Science Monitor*, December 22, 2016.

Wilmshurst, Elizabeth. "The Chatham House Principles of International Law on the Use of Force by States in Self-Defense." *International and Comparative Law Quarterly* 55, no. 4 (October 2006): 963–72.

Winzoski, Karen. "Unwarranted Influence?: The Impact of the Biotech-Pharmaceutical Industry on U.S. Policy on the BWC Verification Protocol." *The Nonproliferation Review* 14, no. 3 (November 2007): 475–98.

Wirtz, James J. "How Does Nuclear Deterrence Differ from Conventional Deterrence?" *Strategic Studies Quarterly* 12, no. 4 (2018): 58–75.

Wong, Yuna Huh, John Yurchak, Robert W. Button, Aaron B. Frank, Burgess Laird, Osonde A. Osoba, Randall Steeb, Benjamin N. Harris, and Sebastian Joon Bae. "Deterrence in the Age of Thinking Machines." Santa Monica, CA: RAND Corporation, 2020.

Wood, Michael. "International Law: Lecture 3." In *Hersch Lauterpacht Memorial Lectures*. Cambridge: Cambridge University Press, 2006. https://www.lcil.cam.ac.uk/press/eve nts/2006/11/lauterpacht-lectures-2006-united-nations-security-council-and-intern ational-law-sir-michael-wood

Woodcock, Andrew. "Coronavirus: UK's First Digital Cabinet Meeting Takes Place as Three Ministers Self-Isolate." *The Independent*, March 31, 2020.

World Federation of Scientists Permanent Monitoring Panel on Information Security. *Toward a Universal Order of Cyberspace: Managing Threats from Cybercrime to Cyberwar*. Edited by Henning Wegener. Erice, Italy: World Federation of Scientists, 2003.

World Nuclear Association. "Nuclear Power in the World Today." November 2023. https://world-nuclear.org/information-library/current-and-future-generation/nucl ear-power-in-the-world-today.aspx

Wright, Bruce A. "Remarks Before the Defense Colloquium on Information Operations." Quoted in William Church, "Information Operations Violates Protocol I," 1999. https://security.ase.md/publ/en/puben06.html

Wu, Tim. "Cyberspace Sovereignty—The Internet and the International System." *Harvard Journal of Law and Technology* 10 (1996): 647–66.

Wu, Xu. *Chinese Cyber Nationalism*. New York: Lexington Books, 2007.

"Wyden Questions DNI Director Blair About Cyber Terrorism Threats." In *Senate Intelligence Committee Hearing*, 2009, https://www.wyden.senate.gov/news/videos/ watch/wyden-questions-dni-director-blair-about-cyber-terrorism-threats.

Xinhua News Agency. "U.S. Cyber Strategy Dangerous: Chinese Experts." *China Daily USA*, 2011.

Yediot Ahronot, "Suspected of a Cyber Attack on a Series of Water Facilities in Israel." April 26, 2020.

ZDNet. "Advertise with ZDNet and TechRepublic." https://www.zdnet.com/advertise/.

Zeidanloo, Hossein Rouhani, Farhoud Hosseinpour, and Farhood Farid Etemad. "New Approach for Detection of IRC and P2P Botnets." *International Journal of Computer and Electrical Engineering* 2, no. 6 (2010): 1029–38.

Zetter, Kim. *Countdown to Zero Day: Stuxnet and the Launch of the World's First Digital Weapon*. New York: Broadway Books, 2014.

Zetter, Kim. "Experts Are Still Divided on Whether North Korea Is Behind Sony Attack." *Wired*, December 23, 2014.

Zetter, Kim. "Google Hack Attack Was Ultra Sophisticated, New Details Show." *Wired*, January 14, 2010.

Zetter, Kim. "Inside the Cunning, Unprecedented Hack of Ukraine's Power Grid." *Wired*, March 3, 2016.

Zetter, Kim. "Microsoft Seizes ZeuS Servers in Anti-Botnet Rampage." *Wired*, March 26, 2012.

Zissis, Carin. "Backgrounder: China's Anti-Satellite Test." New York: Council on Foreign Relations, 2007.

Zittrain, Jonathan. *The Future of the Internet—and How to Stop It*. New Haven, CT: Yale University Press, 2008.

Index

For the benefit of digital users, indexed terms that span two pages (e.g., 52–53) may, on occasion, appear on only one of those pages.

advanced persistent threats (APTs), 46–47
Afghanistan
   anti-aircraft weapons in, 57 n.12
   restraint in, 59–60, 60 n.18
   Taliban, 219–20
aggression, 148, 149 n.82, 208–9, 215–16, 217, 223–24
agreed competition, 339
Albania, cyberattacks on, 35, 188
Al-Qaida, 41, 219–20
Al-Shabab, 41
alternative adjacencies, 336–37
analogical reasoning, 63–66
anti-satellite (ASAT) weapons tests, 23, 218–19
ANZUS Treaty, 32 n.90, 137–38, 140, 143–44
APT 33 (hacker group), 25
armed attack
   cyberattacks as, 75, 134 n.17, 173–74, 177–78
   military force and, 174–75
   self-defence, requirement for, 209–11
      overview, 201–2, 207–9
      attribution and, 218, 219–20
      intent, 222–24, 225
      scale and effects of cyberattacks and, 212–17
artificial intelligence (AI)
   generally, 28–29, 339–40
   deterrence and, 123–24
   Large Language Models (LLMs), 317–18, 339–40
   machine learning, 123–24
   structural prohibition and, 317–18, 327, 327 n.110
assumptions regarding cyberattacks, historical
   generally, 7, 40

attribution, 47–51
   companies, role of, 42–47
   cyberwar as independent concept, 51–52
   state-based actors, focus on, 40–42
attribution
   assumptions regarding cyberattacks, 47–51
   deterrence and, 100–1
   elimination, by, 100–1
   ICBMs and, 101–2
   identity, by, 100
   monopoly, by, 100, 101
   self-defence and
      generally, 218
      armed attack, 218, 219–20
      geopolitical accuracy, 218–20
      public disclosure, 221–22
      timeliness, 220–21
AUSMIN Summit (2011), 137–38
Australia
   ANZUS Treaty and, 32 n.90, 137–38, 140, 143–44
   Cyber Security Centre, 15
   documents on cyber policy, 67
   mutual defense treaties and, 162
   self-defence and, 220–21, 221 n.85
   structural deterrence and, 137–38, 140, 142–44, 147–48, 150

Bank of Bangladesh, 28–29
Belarus, structural deterrence and, 147–48
biological weapons
   IHL generally, 239, 240, 241–42
   judging intent, 224–25
   structural prohibition and, 289–90, 304, 307–9, 312–13, 322–23, 331

Biological Weapons Convention (1972), 245–46
blinding lasers, 245–46, 314–15, 317
blockades, 130–31, 131 n.8, 131 n.9
Border Gateway Protocol (BGP), 22 n.43, 337 n.3
botnets, 43–44, 110, 204–5, 219 n.78
Bowman Avenue Dam, hacking of, 24–25
Brazil, Shanghai Cooperation Organisation and, 151
Browns Ferry Nuclear Facility, hacking of, 24–25
Brussels Declaration (1874), 250
Budapest Convention on Cybercrime (2001), 146–47, 159–60

Canada, government definition of cyberattack, 33–34
celebrity endorsement, 320–21
chemical weapons
  deterrence and, 101 n.37
  IHL generally, 239, 240
  restraint and, 59–60, 60 n.18, 67–68
  structural prohibition and, 302–5, 306–8, 309–10, 311–13, 326, 331
Chemical Weapons Convention (CWC) (1992), 245–46, 317, 326
China
  anti-satellite weapons tests in, 23, 218–19
  "civil-military fusion" in, 43–44
  conception of cyberspace, 191
  duty of care regarding infrastructure and, 337
  early histories of cyberattacks and, 76
  economic sanctions and, 132 n.11
  intellectual property, theft of, 315–16
  leakage of offensive cyber tools in, 121–22
  National Defense Strategy, 234 n.128
  People's Liberation Army, 218–19
  self-defence and, 226, 227
  structural deterrence and, 133–34, 144, 147, 148, 149–50,
  structural prohibition and, 290–91, 300–1, 313–14
  structural remediation and, 6, 228–29
China Chopper (malicious code), 115 n.73

chivalry, 250
civil defense, injury to
  generally, 281
  overview, 276–77
  repair of indispensable public utilities, 279–81
  rescue, medical, and marking services, 278–79
  warning and evacuation, 276–78
civilian objects
  distinction and, 247–48
  indiscriminateness and, 253–57, 258–59
"civil-military fusion," 43–44
cluster munitions, 67–68, 245–46, 307–10
Cluster Munitions Convention (2008), 245–46
collateral damage
  IHL generally, 248, 259, 284
  self-defence and, 224–25
collective self-defence, 206, 209–10
companies
  attributors, as, 45–46
  cybersecurity firms, 46–47
  defenders of government systems, as, 43–44
  providers of materiel, as, 42–43
  victims of cyberattacks, as, 44–45
compellence, 95 n.18
Computer Emergency Response Teams (CERTs), 300–1
computer network exploitation (CNE), defined, 27 n.73
computer network operations (CNO), defined, 30 n.82
Conficker virus, 225 n.97
confidence-building measures (CBMs), 293
constructivist logic, 58, 59–60, 62, 63
Convention on Certain Conventional Weapons (1983), 245–46
Convention on Environmental Modification Techniques (ENMOD Convention) (1977), 309–10
Council of Europe Cybercrime Convention. *See* Budapest Convention on Cybercrime)
COVID-19 pandemic, 183–84, 183 n.84, 183 n.85, 188–89, 267–68, 272–73

crimes against humanity, 340
critical infrastructure
　dams, hacking of, 24–25, 274–75, 276
　duty of care regarding, 337
　electricity facilities, hacking of, 179, 197, 279–80
　financial infrastructure, hacking of, 36, 44–45, 83, 330
　hacking of, 24–26
　manufacturers, hacking of, 180–81
　protected classes, injury to, 269–74
　scale and effects of cyberattacks, 213, 214–15
　structural prohibition and, 300–1
　structural remediation and, 230–31
　water facilities, hacking of, 179–80
cross-domain deterrence, 132–33
Cuba
　blockades and, 130–31
　influence operations and, 37–38
　protest of radio transmissions into, 37–38, 38 n.114
　Radio Martí, 37–38
　structural deterrence and, 147–48
Cuban Missile Crisis (1962), 130–31, 210 n.43
cyberattacks. *see also specific topic or country*
　generally, 19
　armed attack, as, 75, 134 n.17, 173–74, 177–78
　assumptions regarding (*see* assumptions regarding cyberattacks)
　companies, role of, 42–47
　context, 19–26
　deterrent, effectiveness as (*see* deterrence)
　espionage distinguished, 36–37
　exploitation distinguished, 36–37
　formal definition of, 27–34
　frequency of, 53 n.2
　influence operations distinguished, 37–39
　inherently indiscriminate, as, 256–57
　jus ad bellum and, 209–27
　kinetic elements of, 22–23, 172–73, 224, 255, 255 n.73, 286
　nonkinetic cyberattacks, 22–23, 30, 286
　other cybersecurity incidents distinguished, 36–40
　political independence, as threat to, 195–97
　proportionality, evaluation of, 283–86
　risk from, 3
　self-defence, scale and effects of cyberattacks and
　　generally, 211–12
　　accumulation of events, 213–15, 213 n.59
　　armed attack requirement, 212–17
　　illegal but de minimis effects, 212–13
　　military effects, 215–17, 215 n.67
　self-defence against (*see* self-defence)
　sovereignty, as threat to, 185–87
　territorial integrity, as threat to, 185–95
　timeline of, 34–36
　ubiquity of digital systems and, 19–26
　unconventional status of, 323–25
　use of force, as (*see* use of force)
　vulnerability of digital systems and, 19–26
cybercrime, 146–47, 159–60, 161 n.10, 226
cyber-defense budgets, 15–16
cyber norms, 77–78, 229 n.107, 289–90, 289 n.2, 292
Cybersecurity Center for Defense Center of Excellence (CCD-COE), 76
Cybersecurity Tech Accord. *see* Digital Geneva Conventions, proposal for
cyberspace
　global, as, 193–95
　infrastructure as sovereign, 193–95
　national territory, as, 191–93
　physical infrastructure and, 190
　post-Westphalian, as, 190–91
　sovereignty and, 189–91, 193–95
　UN Charter, applicability of, 140–41
cyber-terrorism, early concept of, 18 n.29, 40–41
cyberwar as independent phenomenon, 51–52

dams, hacking of, 24–25, 274–75, 276
dangerous forces, containing, 274–76
DCLeaks, 41–42
Declaration of the Independence of Cyberspace, 190–91

Declaration on Friendly Relations (1970), 169–70
Declaration on the Non-Use of Force (1987), 169–70, 209–10
defending forward, 77–78, 123–24, 133, 230–32
Definition of Aggression (1974), 169–70, 172, 212–13, 215–16
deterrence
  generally, 17, 84, 87–89, 90
  alternative deterrence frames, 121–24
    in-kind deterrence, 123–24
    self-deterrence, 121–23
  artificial intelligence (AI) and, 123–24
  attribution
    generally, 100
    elimination, by, 100–1,
    identity, by, 100
    monopoly, by, 100, 101
  chemical weapons and, 101 n.37
  coercion and, 94–95
  compellence, 95 n.18
  deterrent influence, 90 n.2
  dissuasion, 90 n.2
  effectiveness of cyberattacks as deterrent
    generally, 88, 102–3, 125, 335
    cyberattack capabilities and, 117t
    deployment network and, 104–5, 109–11, 111t
    development environment and, 104–9, 109t
    disaggregation of cyberattack capabilities, 103–14
    execution tools and, 104–5, 111–14, 113t
    implications of, 116–18
    malware and, 105–9, 112–13
    specificity paradox and, 114–15
  entanglement, by, 96 n.23
  general deterrence, 95–97
  historical background, 91–92
  immediate deterrence, 97–102, 129
  in-kind deterrence, 130
  international relations theory and, 92
  meaningful deterrence of cyberattacks, 88, 125
  moving beyond, 125–26
  narrowing of concept, 94–98

  nuclear weapons and, 91–92, 93, 93 n.11, 99, 125, 210
  questions regarding, 89
  realism and, 92
  recognition and
    generally, 100
    effect recognition, 99
    instrument recognition, 99
  structural deterrence (see structural deterrence)
  timescale of, 95–98
  uncertainty regarding retaliation and, 126
Digital Geneva Conventions, proposal for, 320–21, 326–27
digital "kill-switches," 25–26, 308–9
distinction, 247–48, 250
distributed denial-of-service (DDoS) attacks, 36, 104, 111 n.64
doxxing, 38–39, 39 n.119
Draft Code of Conduct. see Shanghai Cooperation Organisation (SCO)
drone strikes, 41
dual-use technologies, 20–21, 175–78

economic sanctions, 131–32, 204–5
effect recognition, 99
Egypt
  internet shutdown in, 337 n.3
  nuclear weapons and, 55–56
electricity facilities, hacking of, 179, 197, 279–80
electro-magnetic pulse, 189 n.102, 275 n.154
Electronic Health Records, 267 n.120
elimination attribution, 100–1,
emblems, 257–59, 260–61, 261 n.96, 280–81
ENMOD Convention (1977), 309–10
entanglement, deterrence by, 96 n.23
espionage, 27–28, 36–37, 42–43, 51, 70–71, 213, 235
Estonia
  cyberattacks on, 11–14, 28–29, 35, 41–42, 110, 160, 188, 232–33, 233 n.121, 316, 340
  NATO and, 142–43, 232–33
  structural prohibition and, 327–28

ethical concerns, 18–19
European Union General Data Privacy Regulation (GDPR), 192–93
exceptional prohibitions, 240, 241, 245–46, 302–4

fiber optic cables, 20–23, 22 n.46, 263. *see also* undersea cables
First Committee on Disarmament and International Security, United Nations, 328–29, 331–32
First Gulf War, 91–92
Fourth of July cyber incident (ROK/US), 36
France
 blockades and, 130–31
 cyber-defense budget in, 15–16
 human rights law and, 135 n.24
 structural deterrence and, 141–42
Friendly Relations Act (1970), 174–75
future directions
 generally, 84
 agreed competition, 339
 alternative adjacencies, 336–37
 artificial intelligence (AI) and, 339–40
 crimes against humanity, 340
 cybersecurity cultures, 338
 persistent engagement, 339
 process bundling, 337–38
 security environment, changes in perception of, 338–39
 war crimes, 340

gas pipelines, 24–25
Geneva Conventions (1949)
 generally, 67–68
 Additional Protocols (*see* Additional Protocols to Geneva Conventions (1977))
 biological weapons and, 331
 chemical weapons and, 331
 distinction and, 247–48
 general regulations, 246
 historical background, 242–43, 245 n.14
 obligations of states to comply, 251–53
Geneva Conventions, Additional Protocols to (1977)
 generally, 67–68
 chivalry and, 250
 distinction and, 247–48
 environmental damage and, 309–10
 exceptional prohibitions, 302–3
 general regulations, 246
 IHL generally, 286
 inability to distinguish and, 255 n.70
 indiscriminateness and
  generally, 254
  cyberattacks as inherently indiscriminate, 256–57
  inability to distinguish, 254–56
  neutrality, 265 n.110, 265 n.111
  unidentifiability, 257–58, 260–61
 obligations of states to comply, 251–53, 252 n.52, 252 n.53, 253 n.58
 perfidy and, 250
 precautionary measures, 266, 282 n.180
 proportionality and, 248, 282, 283–84, 285–86
 protected classes, injury to
  generally, 266
  civil defense, 276–77, 278, 280–81
  critical infrastructure, 269–70, 269 n.125, 270 n.128
  dangerous forces, containing, 274, 275–76
  indispensable objects, 269–70, 269 n.125, 270 n.128
  medical personnel, 266–67
  unnecessary suffering, minimization of, 249
Genocide Convention (1948), 245 n.14
Georgia
 cyberattacks on, 26, 232–33, 264
 military asymmetry and, 51–52
Germany
 defining cyberattacks in, 33–34
 military codes of conduct in, 243–44
 nuclear weapons and, 55–56
GGEs. *see* Groups of Governmental Experts (GGEs)
Global Positioning System (GPS), 278, 278–79 n.166
gravity, concept of, 136, 171–72, 188, 212–13, 219–20

Groups of Governmental Experts (GGEs)
  cyberattacks and, 20–21, 33, 66–67
  cyber norms, 292–93
  self-defence and, 226, 228, 228 n.106
  structural deterrence and, 142–43, 145–46, 147–48
  structural prohibition and, 295, 300–1, 328–29, 331–32
  use of force and, 164, 164 n.18, 166–67, 170–71
G20, 66–67
Guardians of the Peace, 41–42
Guccifer 2.0, 41–42
Gulf War, 91–92

hackers-for-hire, 28–29, 41–42
Hague Convention (1899)
  generally, 67–68
  biological weapons and, 331
  chemical weapons and, 331
  distinction and, 247–48
  general regulations, 246
  historical background, 242–43, 244–45, 245 n.14
  IHL generally, 246–47, 247 n.18
  indiscriminateness and, 262
  Martens Clause, 251–52
  obligations of states to comply, 251–53
Hague Convention (1907)
  generally, 67–68
  distinction and, 247–48
  general regulations, 246
  historical background, 242–43, 244–45, 245 n.14
  indiscriminateness and, 257–58, 262–63, 264–66
  military necessity and, 248–49
  obligations of states to comply, 251–53
  perfidy and, 250
Hatch Nuclear Power Plant, 24–25
humanitarian intervention, 195 n.125, 203
human rights law, 135–36, 135 n.24

ICJ. *see* International Court of Justice (ICJ)
identity attribution, 100
IHL. *see* international humanitarian law (IHL)

India
  cyberattacks on, 270–71
  deterrence and, 91–92
  self-defence and, 227
  structural prohibition and, 300–1
indiscriminateness
  generally, 253–54
  cyberincidents in, 256–57
  inability to distinguish and, 254–56, 255 n.70
  national markers and, 261, 261 n.96
  neutrality and, 262–66
  unidentifiability and, 257–61
indispensable objects, injury to, 269–74
influence operations, 37–39
information advantage, 69 n.32
information warfare, 68–69, 69 n.32
infrastructure. *see* critical infrastructure
injury to protected classes. *see* protected classes, injury to
innocent passage, 263, 263 n.101
instrument recognition, 99
intellectual property, theft of, 315–16
intent, self-defence and
  generally, 222–23
  judging cyberattack intent, 224–25
  present law compared, 223–24
intercontinental ballistic missiles (ICBMs), attribution and, 101–2
International Committee of the Red Cross (ICRC), 243–44, 252–53, 256, 284, 286
International Court of Justice (ICJ)
  cases
    Cameroon/Nigeria case, 213–14
    Congo case, 213–14
    Nicaragua case, 169–70, 172, 177–78, 195–96, 207–8, 209–10, 211–14, 219–20, 264
    Nuclear Weapons case, 172–73, 252–54, 282
    Oil Platforms case, 213–14, 215–16, 217, 222–25, 222 n.89
International Covenant on Civil and Political Rights (ICCPR), 135 n.24
International Criminal Tribunal for the Former Yugoslavia (ICTY)
  Galić case, 284–85
  Tadić case, 251 n.48, 255 n.73

INDEX 393

international humanitarian law (IHL)
  generally, 17, 84, 239–40, 242, 286–88
  applications of law, 245–46
  chivalry, 250
  collateral damage and, 248, 259, 284
  discrimination (*see* distinction)
  distinction, 247–48, 250
    generally, 253–54
    cyberattacks as inherently indiscriminate, 256–57
    inability to distinguish and, 254–56, 255 n.70
    national markers and, 261, 261 n.96
    neutrality and, 262–66
    unidentifiability and, 257–61
  exceptional prohibitions, 240, 241, 245–46
  general regulations, 246
  historical background, 242–45
  indiscriminateness (*see* distinction)
  malware and, 264
  military codes of conduct, 243–44
  military necessity, 248–49
  obligations of states to comply, 251–53
  overarching principles, 246–50
  perfidy, 250, 260
  prohibited means and methods (of warfare), 240, 241, 245–46
  proportionality (within IHL)
    generally, 281
    balancing humanitarian risks and military advantage, 284
    evaluation of cyberattack proportionality, 283–86
    general requirement of, 282–83
    least bad available option, 283–84
    offending common sensibilities, 283
    overarching principle, as, 248, 250
  protected classes, injury to
    generally, 266
    civil defense (*see* civil defense, injury to)
    critical infrastructure, 269–74
    dangerous forces, containing, 274–76
    indispensable objects, 269–74
    medical personnel, 266–69
  restraint and, 239–40, 241
  sources of law, 245–46
  structural prohibition (*see* structural prohibition)

unnecessary suffering, minimization of, 249
International Military Tribunal (Nuremberg), 245 n.14
International Telecommunications Union (ITU), 160, 325–26
internet architecture, 176, 177, 189–90, 261
Internet Governance Forum, 66–67
Internet of Things (IoT), 308–9
Internet Policymaking Principles (OECD), 330–31
The Interview (film), 44–45, 330
Iran
  critical infrastructure, hacking by, 25
  cyberattacks by, 36, 44–45, 83, 188, 330
  cyberattacks on, 35
  early histories of cyberattacks and, 76
  economic sanctions and, 131–32
  military asymmetry and, 51–52
  self-defence and, 223–24, 227
  structural prohibition and, 311–12
Iraq
  deterrence and, 91–92
  self-defence and, 223–24
Iraq War. *see* Second Gulf War
irregular forces, 257–58
ISIS/ISIL, 41
Israel
  blockades and, 130–31
  cyberattacks on, 270–71
  cyber-defense budget in, 15–16
  deterrence and, 91–92, 97 n.31
  military asymmetry and, 51–52
  Operation Orchard, 30
  proliferation and, 317–18
  self-defence and, 214 n.61, 214–15
  Syria, cyberattacks on, 30

Japan
  government definition of cyberattacks, 33–34
  mutual defense treaties and, 162
  nuclear weapons and, 55–56
jus ad bellum
  generally, 6, 84
  civil defense, protection of, 281
  cyberattacks and, 209–27
  limits of, 225–27

jus ad bellum (cont.)
   logics of restraint and, 58–59
   medical personnel, protection of, 266–67
   proportionality in, 212–13, 216–17
   remedial *jus ad bellum*, 201, 202, 203
   self-defence and, 208–9
   structural remediation and, 227–36
   UN Charter Art. 2(4) and, 166–67
   use of force (*see* use of force)
jus cogens, prohibition on use of force as, 167–68, 184–85
jus in bello. *see* international humanitarian law (IHL)

Kazakhstan
   cyberspace, on, 191
   structural deterrence and, 149–50
Kellogg-Briand Pact, 56
"killer robots," 327, 327 n.110
"kill-switches," 25–26, 308–9
kinetic elements of cyberattacks, 22–23, 172–73, 224, 255, 255 n.73, 286
Kosovo, cyberattacks in NATO action in contemplated, 13, 73

land mines
   generally, 67–68
   IHL generally, 240, 245–46
   judging intent, 225
   Ottawa Treaty (1997), 245–46
   structural prohibition and, 302–3, 304, 307–10, 311, 319, 320–21, 322
law of armed conflict (LOAC). *see* international humanitarian law (IHL)
Lebanon, self-defence and, 214 n.61, 214–15
legal literature on cyberattacks, 73–75
lethal autonomous weapons systems (LAWS), 327, 327 n.110
lex specialis, 136, 139, 159–60, 161–62
Libya, nuclear weapons and, 55–56
Lieber Code, 243–44, 248–49, 250, 250 n.42
LOAC. *see* international humanitarian law (IHL)
logics of restraint, 57–61
London Conference on Cyberspace (2011), 66–67, 327–28

London Declaration Concerning the Laws of Naval War (1909), 131 n.9

malware
   generally, 35, 49
   deterrence and, 105–7, 108–9, 112–13
   IHL generally, 264
   malicious code, 106–9
   structural prohibition and, 308–9
Martens Clause, 251–52
Means and methods (of warfare), limitations, 17, 240, 245–46, 252–53, 288
medical personnel, injury to, 266–69
military asymmetry, 51–52
military codes of conduct, 243–44
military force
   structural deterrence and, 128–29, 131–32, 134, 137–38, 144–45, 148, 153
   use of force, requirement for, 174–75
military necessity, 248–49
monopoly, attribution by, 100, 101
Montenegro, cyberattacks on, 233–34

national markers, 261, 261 n.96
NATO. *see* North Atlantic Treaty Organization (NATO)
necessity, 248–49
neoliberalism
   restraint and, 58–59
   structural deterrence and, 151
neorealism, 92
neutrality
   indiscriminateness and, 262–66
   norm construction and, 309
New Zealand
   ANZUS Treaty and, 32 n.90, 137–38, 140, 143–44
   mutual defense treaties and, 162
   structural deterrence and, 137–38, 140, 143–44
Nicaragua. *see* International Court of Justice (ICJ)
noninterference principle, 147, 191–92, 196
nonstate actors, 17–18, 40–42, 41–42 n.127
normative logic, 58, 59–60
North Atlantic Treaty Organization (NATO)
   Cybersecurity Center for Defense Center of Excellence (CCD-COE), 76

cyber strategy, 31–32, 32 n.91
Estonia cyberattack and, 12–13
Lisbon Summit Declaration (2010), 141–42
mutual defense treaty, as, 162
New Strategic Concept (2010), 31–32, 140–42
North Atlantic Council, 140–41
structural deterrence and, 140–43
structural prohibition and, 330–31
use of force, on, 167–68
Wales Summit Declaration (2014), 140–41
North Korea
cyberattacks by, 28–29, 36, 44–45, 48–49, 330
cyberattacks on, 35
malicious code in, 108–9
military asymmetry and, 51–52
proliferation and, 317–18
structural prohibition and, 311–12
structural remediation and, 6
NotPetya event, 34–35, 233–34, 308 n.49
nuclear power
Browns Ferry Nuclear Facility, 24–25
hacking of power plants, 24–25
Hatch Nuclear Power Plant, 24–25
international utilization of, 275 n.152
nuclear taboo, 303–5
nuclear weapons
deterrence and, 91–92, 93, 93 n.11, 99, 125, 210
false alarms, 277–78
restraint and, 55–56
structural deterrence and, 129
structural prohibition and, 304, 309–10, 312–13, 316, 317–18, 323–24, 329–30

oil pipelines, 24–25
operational preparation of environment (OPE), 228–29
Organisation for Economic Cooperation and Development (OECD), 330–31
Organization for Security and Cooperation in Europe (OSCE), 142–43

Organisation for the Prevention of Chemical Weapons (OPCW), 331
organized crime, 28–29, 41–42
Ottawa Convention (1997), 245–46, 248 n.29

Pakistan
deterrence and, 91–92
self-defence and, 227
YouTube, disruption of, 21–22
Paris Call for Trust and Security in Cyberspace (2019), 326, 327–28
Paris Declaration Respecting Maritime Law (1856), 131 n.9, 243–44
perfidy, 250, 260
persistent engagement, 339
Phoenix, wire cuts in, 22–23
political independence, cyberattacks as threat to, 195–97
privateering, 65–66
process bundling, 337–38
proportionality in *jus ad bellum*, 212–13, 216–17
proportionality in *jus in bello*
generally, 281
balancing humanitarian risks and military advantage, 284
evaluation of cyberattack proportionality, 283–86
general requirement of, 282–83
least bad available option, 283–84
offending common sensibilities, 283
overarching principle, as, 248, 250
protected classes, injury to
generally, 266
civil defense (*see* civil defense, injury to)
critical infrastructure, 269–74
dangerous forces, containing, 274–76
indispensable objects, 269–74
medical personnel, 266–69

Quemoy–Matsu Crisis (1958), 93 n.11

Radio Martí, 37–38
rational choice theory, 91–92
rationalist logic, 58, 62, 63
realism
deterrence and, 92
practical force, as, 93

realism (cont.)
  stability distinguished, 93
  structural deterrence and, 151
recognition, deterrence and
  generally, 100
  effect recognition, 99
  instrument recognition, 99
regulative logic, 58–59, 62, 63
Rendulic Rule, 248–49
restraint
  generally, 53–54
  analogical reasoning and, 63–66
  analytical framework, 54–55
  chemical weapons and, 59–60, 60 n.18, 67–68
  critiques of
    improbability, based on, 79
    inadequacy, based on, 81–83
    inadvisability, based on, 79–80
    inhumanity, based on, 83–84
    operation, based on, 80–81
  defining, 55–57
  evaluation of, 63
  IHL generally, 239–40, 241
  imperative of, 2–4, 15
  international law, in, 56
  international relations theory, in, 64–65
  logics of
    generally, 57–58, 60–61
    normative-constitutive, 58, 59–60, 62, 63
    rationalist, 58, 62, 63
    regulative, 58–59, 62, 63
  necessity of, 4
  nuclear weapons and, 55–56
  potential developments, 7, 14
  practice, in, 61–62
  purposes of studying, 6–7
  reluctance regarding, 3
  scholarly literature, in, 56
  structural prohibition and, 336
  study of, 4, 5
  use of force and, 335
risk from cyberattacks, 3
rogue actors, 28–29, 41–42
Rome (Ancient), humanitarian law and, 242–43

Russia
  anti-satellite weapons tests in, 23
  blockades and, 130–31
  Budapest Convention on Cybercrime and, 146–47
  critical infrastructure, hacking by, 24–25
  cybercrime, on, 159–60, 161 n.10, 226
  cyber norms and, 229 n.107
  cyberspace, conception of, 191–92, 194–95
  development environment in, 106
  documents on cyber policy, 67
  doxxing by, 38–39, 39 n.119
  duty of care regarding infrastructure and, 337
  early histories of cyberattacks and, 76
  elections, interference in, 28 n.75, 37–39, 40, 41–42, 233–34
  Estonia, cyberattacks on, 11–12, 41–42, 232–33
  Georgia, cyberattacks on, 26, 232–33, 264
  GRU, 39 n.119
  hackers in, 111 n.64
  influence operations and, 37–39
  information security and, 145, 146–47, 340
  military asymmetry and, 51–52
  self-defence and, 220–21, 221 n.85, 223, 226, 227
  South Korea, cyberattacks on, 49
  structural deterrence and, 133–34, 144–50, 153
  structural prohibition and, 290–91, 294–95, 296, 297–98, 300–1, 315
  structural remediation and, 6, 228–29, 232–35
  Ukraine, cyberattacks on, 30, 35, 232–33
  Ukraine, invasion of, 278

Saint Petersburg Declaration (1868), 243–44
San Francisco Conference (1945), 169–70, 184–85, 200
San Remo Manual, 131 n.9, 265 n.111, 287
Saudi Aramco incident, 35, 44–45, 45 n.140, 83, 310–11

INDEX

Second Gulf War
  cyberattacks in contemplated, 13, 73
  pre-emption and, 91 n.3
  restraint in, 59–60
security environment, changes in perception of, 338–39
self-defence
  generally, 200–1, 236
  armed attack requirement, 209–11
    overview, 201–2, 207–9
    attribution and, 218, 219–20
    intent, 222–24, 225
    scale and effects of cyberattacks and, 212–17
  attribution and
    generally, 218
    armed attack, 218, 219–20
    geopolitical accuracy, 218–20
    public disclosure, 221–22
    timeliness, 220–21
  collateral damage and, 224–25
  collective self-defence, 206, 209–10
  controversy regarding, 202–3
  framing of law, 202–3
  intent and
    generally, 222–23
    judging cyberattack intent, 224–25
    present law compared, 223–24
  jus ad bellum and, 208–9
  limitations of, 225–27
  scale and effects of cyberattacks and
    generally, 211–12
    accumulation of events, 213–15, 213 n.59
    armed attack requirement, 212–17
    illegal but de minimis effects, 212–13
    military effects, 215–17, 215 n.67
  structural remediation (*see* structural remediation)
  UN Charter and
    generally, 166–68
    Article 39, 202, 204–5
    Article 51, 202, 206–9
    contested scope of, 206–9
    economic sanctions, 204–5
    provisional measures, 204–5
    self-defense, inherent right of, 206
self-determination, 195 n.125
self-deterrence, 121–23
severity of effect, 31–32, 33, 179, 180–81
Shamoon incident, 35, 41–42, 45 n.140, 310–11
Shanghai Cooperation Organisation (SCO), 147, 149–50, 151, 160–61, 163–64, 191, 194–95
Silicon Valley, wire cuts in, 22–23
smart meters, 180–81, 279 n.169
Somalia, fiber optic cables and, 22–23
Sony Pictures incident, 28–29, 41–42, 44–45, 48–49
South Korea
  cyberattacks on, 36, 49
  mutual defense treaties and, 162
  structural deterrence and, 140, 143–44
  Winter Olympics (2018), 49
sovereignty
  cyberattacks as threat to, 185–87
  cyberspace and, 189–91, 193–95
specificity paradox, 114–15
state-based actors, focus on, 17–18, 40–42
state responsibility, 77, 195 n.124
Strategic Arms Limitation Treaty (SALT), 341
Strategic Arms Reduction Treaty (START), 341
structural competition, introduced, 5–6
structural deterrence
  generally, 6, 84, 89, 127–28, 152–53
  comparison of approaches, 150–52
  conditions for
    direct assessment of threat not possible, 129–30
    in-kind deterrence not possible, 130
    state-ending capability not present, 129
  definition of
    immediate deterrence compared, 129
    rational deterrence compared, 128–30
  evidence of, 133–34
  exclusive strategy, 144–50
  inclusive strategy, 134–44, 150
  military force and, 128–29, 131–32, 134, 137–38, 144–45, 148, 153
  necessity of, 89–90

398   INDEX

structural deterrence (cont.)
  novel and unregulated, cyberattacks as, 144–50
  nuclear weapons and, 129
  parallels to
    generally, 130, 133
    blockades, 130–31, 131 n.8, 131 n.9
    cross-domain deterrence, 132–33
    economic sanctions, 131–32
  realism and, 151
  threat of force and, 128–29
  unremarkable weapons, cyberattacks as, 134–44
structural prohibition
  generally, 6, 84, 241–42, 289–91, 294, 333–34
  argument, 290
  arms control, moving beyond, 291–94, 335
  artificial intelligence (AI) and, 317–18, 327, 327 n.110
  biological weapons and, 289–90, 304, 307–9, 312–13, 322–23, 331
  change, responsiveness to, 299
  chemical weapons and, 302–5, 306–8, 309–10, 311–13, 326, 331
  cluster munitions and, 307–10
  compatibility, prospects for, 297–99
  competitive dynamic, 294–97
  historical analogies, 335–36
  land mines and, 302–3, 304, 307–10, 311, 319, 320–21, 322
  malware and, 308–9
  narrowing, opportunity for, 300–1
  norm construction
    generally, 306, 322, 323t, 333t
    awareness, 318–22
    coherence, 306–14, 314t
    condescension, 311–12
    control, 307–8
    defenselessness, 312–14
    demonstrated capability, 316–17
    development, deployment, and use, 314–18, 319t
    dissemination, 319–21
    documentation, 319–21
    duration, 308–9
    environment, 309–11
    geography, 309
    grafting, 306–14
    imperative, 318–22
    preemptive establishment, 314–16
    proliferation, 317–18
    recognition of prior failure, 321–22
  norm evolution
    generally, 322–23, 332–33
    bureaucracy and, 331–32
    domestic legitimacy, 329–31
    entrepreneur diversity, 325–29
    firms, 326–27
    government entrepreneurs, 327–28
    individual entrepreneurs, 325–26
    international legitimacy, 329–31
    international organizations, 328–29
    nongovernmental organizations, 327
    regulation and, 331–32
    unconventional status, 323–25
  nuclear weapons and, 304, 309–10, 312–13, 316, 317–18, 323–24, 329–30
  prohibitive norms
    generally, 301–2
    content and process, 305–6
    critiques of frame, 304–5
    exceptional prohibitions, 302–4
  restraint and, 336
structural remediation
  generally, 6, 84, 158, 227–28, 236
  competitive dynamic, 228–29
  jus ad bellum and, 227–36
  operational preparation of environment (OPE), as, 228–29
  strategies of
    generally, 229
    comparison of, 235–36
    deflection, 234–35
    invitation, 229–32
    negation, 232–34, 235
Stuxnet virus, 34–35, 41–42, 107 n.53, 225 n.97
Supervisory Control and Data Acquisition (SCADA) systems, 23–25, 23 n.51, 271–72
Sweden
  cyber incidents in, 233–34
  human rights law and, 135 n.24
  military codes of conduct in, 243–44
  nuclear weapons and, 55–56

INDEX

Switzerland
  human rights law and, 135 n.24
  military codes of conduct in, 243–44
Syria
  cyber incidents in, 30
  deterrence and, 91–92
  hacking events by, 270–71
  military asymmetry and, 51–52

Taliban, 219–20
Tallinn Manuals
  IHL generally, 252–53, 253 n.56, 287
  indiscriminateness and, 255, 255 n.73, 256, 259, 264–66
  intent and, 224–25
  proportionality and, 283–85, 286
  protected classes, protection of, 273–74, 275–76, 279–80
  restraint and, 75, 80–81
  scale and effects of cyberattacks, on, 211–12
  self-defence and, 227, 228
  sovereignty and, 185–86, 193–94
  structural prohibition and, 315–16, 331–32
  use of force and, 160, 165, 174, 175, 178, 181, 210–11
technological dependence, 19 n.33
Ten Days of Rain cyber incident, 36
territorial integrity, cyberattacks as threat to, 185–95
terrorism, 18 n.29, 40–41
threat of force, structural deterrence and, 128–29
Thucydides trap, 57 n.12
timeline of cyberattacks, 34–36

Ukraine
  cyberattacks on, 30, 35, 41–42, 232–33
  Russian invasion of, 278
undersea cables, 20–23, 22 n.46, 263
unfriendly acts, 70–71, 89, 90, 163–64, 173–74
United Kingdom
  attribution and, 46–47
  blockades and, 130–31
  critical infrastructure, hacking of, 25–26
  cyberattacks on, 36
  cyber-defense budget in, 15–16
  documents on cyber policy, 67
  Joint Service Manual of LOAC, 250
  military codes of conduct in, 243–44
  National Health Service (NHS), 36, 139, 267–68, 267–68 n.121
  remote conduct of governmental business in, 183–84, 188
  self-defence and, 220–21, 221 n.85, 223–24
  Strategic Defence and Security Review (2010), 139
  structural deterrence and, 133–34, 139–40, 141–43, 147–48, 150
United Nations
  attempts to define cyberattacks by, 33
  Charter
    arms control, 205 n.19
    Art. 2(4) (*see* use of force)
    cyberspace, applicability to, 140–41, 147
    pacific settlement of disputes, 205 n.19
    provisional measures, 204–5
    self-defence and (*see* self-defence)
    travaux préparatoires, 169–70, 210
    use of force and (*see* use of force)
  Declaration on Friendly Relations (1970), 169–70
  Declaration on the Non-Use of Force (1987), 169–70, 209–10
  Definition of Aggression (1974), 169–70, 172, 212–13, 215–16
  First Committee on Disarmament and International Security, 328–29, 331–32
  Friendly Relations Act (1970), 174–75
  General Assembly, 66–67, 142–43, 160–61, 167–68, 191, 252–53
  Groups of Governmental Experts (GGEs) (*see* Groups of Governmental Experts (GGEs))
  Institute for Disarmament Research (UNIDIR), 328–29, 331–32
  Open-Ended Working Group (OEWG), 163–64, 226, 227, 328–29, 331–32
  San Francisco Conference (1945), 169–70, 184–85, 200
  Security Council, 167–68, 204–5, 210–11, 213–14, 214 n.66

United States
  Additional Protocols to Geneva
    Conventions and, 248, 248 n.29
  agreed competition and, 339
  ANZUS Treaty and, 32 n.90, 137–38,
    140, 143–44
  arms control in cyberspace, on, 340–41
  attribution and, 46–47, 48–49
  blockades and, 130–31
  Budapest Convention on Cybercrime
    and, 146–47
  Comprehensive National Cybersecurity
    Initiative, 213
  critical infrastructure, hacking of,
    24–25
  Cyber Command (USCYBERCOM),
    230–31, 231 n.113, 324–25
  cyber-defense budget in, 15–16
  cyber norms and, 77–78, 229 n.107
  cyberspace, conception of, 194–95
  Cyberspace Strategy (2015), 31
  Defense Department (DOD), 31, 33,
    148, 210–11, 215 n.67, 230, 310–11
  Defense Strategy for Operating in
    Cyberspace (DSOC), 148
  defining cyberattacks in, 33
  Democratic Congressional Campaign
    Committee (DCCC), 39 n.119
  Democratic National Committee
    (DNC) incident, 39 n.119
  Department of Defense Cyber Strategy
    (2018), 215 n.67, 230–31
  Department of Defense Law of War
    Manual, 220–21 n.84, 247–48
  deterrence and, 91–92, 93
  development environment in, 106
  documents on cyber policy, 67
  drone strikes by, 41
  duty of care regarding infrastructure
    and, 337
  economic sanctions and, 132 n.11
  Executive Order 13694, 43 n.130
  Executive Order 13757, 43 n.130
  Federal Bureau of Investigation (FBI),
    25, 48–49, 315–16 n.73
  fiber optic cables and, 22–23
  financial infrastructure, hacking of, 36,
    44–45, 83, 330
  Food and Drug Administration (FDA),
    272, 272 n.140
  Food Safety Modernization Act
    (FSMA), 272, 272 n.140
  Homeland Security Department (DHS),
    25, 270–71
  human rights law and, 135–36, 135 n.24
  in-kind deterrence and, 123–24
  International Strategy for Cyberspace,
    17–18, 134–37
  military asymmetry and, 51–52
  military codes of conduct in, 243–44
  mutual defense treaties and, 162
  National Cyber Strategy, 134–35, 135 n.20
  National Security Presidential
    Memorandum (NSPM), 13, 30 n.82
  Nicaraguan contras, arming of, 264
  Office of Net Assessment, 68–69
  persistent engagement and, 339
  Presidential Policy Directive 20 (PPD-
    20), 30 n.82
  proliferation and, 317–18
  remote conduct of governmental
    business in, 183–84
  Russian interference in elections, 28
    n.75, 37–39, 40, 41–42, 233–34
  self-defence and, 136–37, 215–16, 217,
    220–21, 221 n.85, 226–27
  Space Force, 324–25
  State Department, 77 n.66
  Strategy for Operating in Cyberspace
    (DoD), 135 n.19
  structural deterrence and, 133–37, 140,
    142–44, 147–48, 150, 153
  structural prohibition and, 290–91,
    294–95, 296, 297–98, 299, 300–1,
    331–32
  structural remediation and, 228–32
Universal Declaration of Human Rights,
  135 n.24, 194–95, 336–37
unnecessary suffering, minimization of,
  249
use of force
  generally, 17, 84, 157–58, 197–99
  cyberattacks as
    dams, on, 24–25, 274–75, 276
    directness and, 178–82
    dual-use technologies and, 175–78

effects, evaluation of, 172
electricity facilities, on, 179, 197, 279–80
immediacy and, 178–82
instrument, evaluation of, 172–73
invasiveness and, 178–82
lesser uses of force, 169–71
manufacturers, on, 180–81
measurability of effects and, 178–82
military force requirement, 174–75
political independence, as threat to, 195–97
presumptive legality and, 178–82, 198
sovereignty, as threat to, 185–87
target, evaluation of, 171
territorial integrity, as threat to, 185–95
UN Charter, under, 158–59, 168–69, 197, 198–99
water facilities, on, 179–80
jus cogens, prohibition as, 167–68, 184–85
opinio juris, as, 166–67
relevant law
  generally, 159
  additional sources, 162–66
  executive agreements, 163–64
  general germane sources, 162
  GGE commentary, 164, 164 n.18, 166–67, 170–71
  ICJ, 162–63, 167–68, 169–70
  Shanghai Cooperation Organisation, 163–64
  specific germane sources, 160–62
  specific peripheral sources, 159–60
  Tallinn Manuals, 165
  treaties, 163t
  unilateral statements, 164–65
restraint and, 335
scholarly literature, 67–68
self-defence (*see* self-defence)
structural remediation (*see* structural remediation)
UN Charter Art. 2(4) and
  generally, 56, 67–68, 162
  bedrock of *jus ad bellum,* as, 166–67
  cyberattacks generally, 158–59, 167–69, 197–99
  dual-use technologies and, 175–78
  lesser uses of force, 169–71
  military force requirement, 174–75
  political independence, as threat to, 195–97
  relevant language, 167–68, 184–85
  territorial integrity, as threat to, 185–95
  violations of purposes of, 182–84
United Nations Institute for Disarmament Research (UNIDIR), 328–29, 331–32
United Nations Open-Ended Working Group (OEWG), 163–64, 226, 227, 328–29, 331–32

Vienna Convention on the Law of Treaties (1969), 137
vulnerability equities processes (VEPs), 122–23

WannaCry incident, 28–29, 36, 139
war crimes, 340
water facilities, hacking of, 179–80
weapons of mass destruction (WMD), 323–24
Winter Olympics incident (2018), 49
World Summit on the Information Society, 191

"zero-day exploits," 42–43